W9-AUI-546

JOHN WAYNE: AMERICAN

THE FREE PRESS

New York London Toronto Sydney Tokyo Singapore

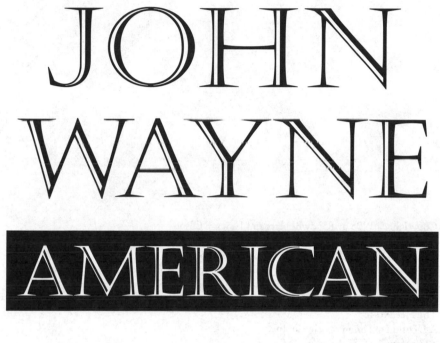

JOHN WAYNE

AMERICAN

RANDY ROBERTS · JAMES S. OLSON

The Free Press
A Division of Simon & Schuster Inc.
1230 Avenue of the Americas
New York, N.Y. 10020

Printed in the United States of America

printing number

8 9 10

Text design by Carla Bolte

Library of Congress Cataloguing-in-Publication Data

Roberts, Randy
  John Wayne: American / Randy Roberts, James S. Olson.
      p.   cm.
  Includes bibliographical references and index.
  ISBN 0–02–923837–4
  1. Wayne, John, 1907–1979. 2. Motion picture actors and actresses—
Unites States—Biography.   I. Olson, James Stuart.   II. Title.
PN2287.W454R63   1995
791.43'028'092—DC20   95–12536
  [B]   CIP

To Burl Noggle, with thanks
—RR

To my children: Susan, Karin, Heather, and Bradley
—JSO

Contents

A Note to the Reader

John Wayne: American began germinating in our minds ten years ago during a summer afternoon jog in the hot Texas sun. He seemed a biographer's dream. Wayne's career spanned fifty years of Hollywood history, from silents and serials, to B movies, to modern epics, and during the quarter-century between 1949 and 1973 he was the leading box-office star in motion pictures. He also became an icon that transcended Hollywood—a symbol of rugged pioneers in the Old West, the American soldier in World War II, and 100 percent Americanism in the Cold War. He trumpeted his right-wing beliefs (as they were then called) in many of his films and in hundreds of interviews. The fullness of his life and the bluntness of his opinions also made him wonderful biographical material. Not only did he star in over one hundred and fifty films, working for and playing opposite the leading names in the industry, he was never afraid to speak his mind, express unpopular opinions, and twit his political opponents. He was "the most important American of our time," according to culture critic Eric Bentley. "Richard Nixon and Ronald Reagan are only camp followers of Wayne, supporting players in the biggest Western of them all, wagons hitched to Wayne's star. In the age when the image is the principal thing, Wayne is the principal image. . . ."

Much to our surprise, we soon discovered that serious biographers had ignored Wayne. Why? Cultural snobbery explains some of the mystery. In recent decades, the doyens of high culture, ensconced in academic ivory towers and leading editorial offices, have lost influence to the purveyors of popular culture. In an act of self-preservation, they dismiss the leading lights of mass culture, denying their significance in American life. As Neal Gabler wrote in his recent biography of Walter Winchell, cultural elitists do so to "maintain their control over the past even as they have surrendered control over the present." Not surprisingly, they marginalized John Wayne, the brightest star in the pop culture firmament.

Part of the explanation is also political. As the cultural elite turned increasingly liberal, Wayne remained wedded to rock-ribbed, traditional values. He was no ideologue. He was a classical liberal, in a true Barry Goldwater sense, a mainstream American small-town conservative and a mainstream 1940s anti-Communist. Only as first Hollywood, then the country, moved to the left did he feel compelled to speak out. "The liberal imagination," film critic Andrew Sarris wrote in 1979, "steadfastly resists the idea of incorrigible evil, and the absolute vengeful morality it spawns in the persona of John Wayne." In person and in his films, John Wayne insisted that evil had to be punished, violently if necessary. Communism, he believed, was an incorrigible evil, socialism and liberalism mere fellow travelers, and he remained unrepentant about his convictions. Liberal critics could never give John Wayne his due because they could never see beyond his politics.

John Wayne may have irritated the cultural elite in America, but his popularity never dimmed in middle America. Even today, sixteen years after his death, he remains a constant in American popular culture. While critics and historians talk of Chaplin, Keaton, Stewart, Bogart, and Brando, fans continue to rent movies from John Wayne sections of video stores or watch John Wayne weeks of televised movies. Middle America grew up with him in the late 1920s and 1930s, went to war with him in the 1940s, matured with him in the 1950s, and kept the faith with him in the 1960s and 1970s. In an age when patriotism became suspect among liberals, he wrapped himself in the flag, expressing repeatedly a deep, heart-felt love of his country. He was *so* American, *so* like his country—big, bold, confident, powerful, loud, violent, and occasionally overbearing, but simultaneously forgiving, gentle, innocent, and naive, almost childlike. In his person and in the persona he so carefully constructed, middle America saw itself, its past, and its future. John Wayne was his country's alter ego.

The biography took us to archives from one side of America to another. We conducted seventy-five interviews and read more than three hundred unpublished oral histories. We poured over thousands of journal, magazine, and newspaper articles and books. Although we discuss his films in *John Wayne: American*—he was first and foremost an actor—this is not a critical examination of those movies. Although we discuss the development of John Wayne as a cultural icon, this is not a cultural study on John Wayne. It is a full biography, an attempt to describe his life and understand his popularity, to explain how he connected to so many Americans in such a visceral way and why his image has been so enduring.

Millions of people, from all corners of the world, feel familiar with John Wayne. A patron saint for conservatives, a misguided Neanderthal for liberals, the soul of the United States for non-Americans, John Wayne was and is something much more than just an actor. A few people, however, did know him very well, knew him as a man with all his strengths and faults. We thank all those who were willing to discuss with us their relationships with Duke. In almost every interview we were treated with unexpected courtesy, honesty, and friendliness. Our bibliography contains a list of the people we interviewed, but we would like here to single out a few of them.

Mary St. John was more than a personal secretary for John Wayne; she was his friend in the fullest and best meaning of the word. For nearly thirty years, she accompanied him on locations, handled his mail, tried to screen his visitors, and listened to him when he had a problem he wanted to discuss. Although like the "Don" in *Godfather* she eventually went into "semiretirement," she was there for Duke, until the end of his life, whenever he needed something special done. Mary took us inside John Wayne's private world. Our first interview with her lasted from 9 A.M.—she insisted on punctuality and we were punctual—to somewhere around 1 A.M. Subsequent interviews were a bit shorter—though never short—but always insightful. Mary's dead now. I hope she knew how much she meant to us.

Louis Johnson, Joe De Franco, Dan Ford, Maureen O'Hara, Nancy Marshall, and Harry Carey Jr. went way beyond the call of duty. They knew different sides of Duke—from business partner to brother to traveling companion to fellow actor. And they all knew him as a friend. "There is not a day goes by that I don't think of him. I miss him terribly," Joe De Franco told us, and we sensed that the other people we talked to feel the same. Their memories of Wayne attest to the strength and warmness of his character. Tim Lilley, editor of *The Big Trail*, was also extremely helpful, showing a generosity of spirit that Duke would have appreciated.

We wish to express our appreciation to the curators, archivists, and librarians at the Margaret Herrick Library of the Academy of Motion Picture Arts and Sciences, the Lilly Library of Indiana University, the Ransom Center of the University of Texas at Austin, Brigham Young University, Southern Methodist University, the University of Southern California, the University of California at Los Angeles, and Wesleyan University. Gerald MacCauley, our literary agent, helped us launch the project. Nicholas Pappas, John Payne, and Robert Shadle of Sam Houston State University read portions of the manuscript and deserve our thanks as well. Bruce Nichols, our editor at The Free Press, could not have been more helpful. He has been supportive, encouraging, and critical, all in ideal measures. Our wives, Suzy and Judy, have shown an uncommon tolerance given the fact that neither one was nor has become a John Wayne fan, in spite of our ceaseless efforts to convert them.

Randy Roberts and James S. Olson

Prologue

By 1959 John Wayne's politics were universally known. He was a Robert Taft and Barry Goldwater Republican and an outspoken anti-communist. He was prominent among the leaders of the attack against the Hollywood Left and had supported Joe McCarthy. But none of that mattered to Nikita Khrushchev when he visited the United States that September. The Soviet premier had been invited by President Dwight Eisenhower and promised a first-class tour. After stops in Washington, D.C., and New York City he had gone to Los Angeles and was bent on seeing Disneyland and meeting John Wayne. Although the Disneyland visit was thought to be too great a security risk, the government did arrange for him to meet Wayne. Duke received an invitation to attend a luncheon for Khrushchev at a Hollywood gathering hosted by Twentieth Century-Fox president Spyros P. Skouras and Eric Johnson, head of the Motion Picture Association of America. Although he was having problems filming *The Alamo* at the time, Wayne did not want to embarrass Eisenhower by turning down the invitation. Khrushchev was quietly greeting guests when he spied Duke. His face burst into a smile of recognition, and he asked to have a private conversation with Duke later in the evening.

Now, *that* was a meeting! Two opinionated men in their primes: John Wayne, America's leading cowboy star and anticommunist, and Nikita

Khrushchev, the world's most powerful communist. For years the Soviet premier had enjoyed pirated copies of John Wayne films, insisting that Russian film editors dub them for him. When the formalities were concluded, Khrushchev took Duke by the arm, walked him over to a bar, and mumbled a few sentences to his translator: "I am told that you like to drink and that you can hold your liquor." "That's right," Wayne replied. Khrushchev offered that he too was known to enjoy a drink or two. Wayne acknowledged that he had heard as much. For a few minutes they compared the virtues of Russian vodka and Mexican tequila, talk that worked up a considerable thirst. Then they began to match each other drink for drink—on and on, eventually leading to a true Cold War draw. Three months later a large wooden crate, boldly stamped with the Russian letters *CCCP* (USSR) and shipping instructions written in Russian, arrived at Duke's offices in Beverly Hills. Wayne's secretary was uncertain what to do with the box. "Hell, open it," Duke said when he arrived for work. "It's too damn big for a bomb." They needed a crowbar to pry the crate open; inside, cushioned in straw, were several cases of top-quality Russian vodka and a note: "Duke. Merry Christmas. Nikita." Wayne laughed from his gut and told his secretary to send Khrushchev a couple of cases of Sauza Conmemorativo tequila and sign it, "Nikita. Thanks. Duke."

By 1975, if his politics had not mellowed much, he was nonetheless not surprised when Emperor Hirohito of Japan requested a meeting with him. In Duke's World War II films he had killed hundreds of Japanese warriors, but that hardly mattered to Hirohito. In 1974 President Gerald Ford had invited Hirohito to visit the United States, and it had taken American and Japanese diplomats and security officials almost nine months to work out the details. The final itinerary was bound in two thick volumes, and it included visits to many of the country's historical sights. The Japanese emperor inspected the museums of New York and Washington, D.C.; he walked through the narrow streets of Williamsburg, Virginia, and Cape Cod, Massachusetts; he toured the attractions in Los Angeles and San Francisco, California, and Honolulu, Hawaii.

For Hirohito, Wayne too was a landmark. The emperor loved movies, and to him Duke's Westerns, with their strict moral code and showdowns between good and evil, had the same moral clarity as Akira Kurosawa's samurai films. Thus when he made his one-day stop in Los Angeles and Governor Jerry Brown and Mayor Tom Bradley asked him if there was anything he particularly wanted to see, Hirohito echoed Khrushchev: John Wayne and Disneyland. Duke was invited to a luncheon in Hirohito's honor on October 8, 1975, at the Music Hall in Los Angeles. More than five hundred other guests jammed the room, and Duke's table was so far from Hirohito's that he contemplated leaving. Hirohito was as upset by the seating arrangements as Wayne; he was not interested in the state and local officials who surrounded him. As the luncheon drew toward its end, the emperor asked to be escorted to the actor's table. Duke stood up when Hirohito arrived, his six-foot-four-inch frame towering a full twelve inches above the Japanese leader. Hirohito's eyes seemed to come alive as the two exchanged pleasantries. Duke pulled out one of his autograph cards and gave it to the emperor. "I was almost tempted to ask if he had seen any of my older war movies," he later told Pat Stacy, his secretary and companion. "Between them all, I must have killed off the entire Japanese army!"

There was something about the man that drew friend and foe like a magnet. He was oversize, powerful, and dramatic; part Daniel Boone, part Mike Fink, and all-American. He was the Ringo Kid and Sgt. John M. Stryker, Thomas Dunston and Capt. Kirby York, Pittsburgh Markham and Capt. Nathan Brittles, Sean Thornton and Hondo Lane, Ethan Edwards and Tom Doniphon, George Washington McLintock and Rooster Cogburn. Over the years he lost the smooth, fresh handsomeness of his youth. His hair fell out, his waist thickened, his face became lined and weathered. But the changes seemed to make him even more appealing. His face took on a chiseled, Mount Rushmore quality, as if it had been around forever. As much as any man of his century, he became a symbol of America.

John Wayne's life—wielding cavalry swords, slinging six-guns, firing Winchesters, storming enemy barricades, or burning the ears of liberal reporters— was a tour de force. He was by far the most popular actor in history. For twenty-five consecutive years, he ranked among the top ten box-office attractions, a record to which no one before or since has even come close. His impact on American society was even more profound than that of that other politically conservative (and active) B-movie star, Ronald Reagan. As Wayne lay on his deathbed in 1979, President Jimmy Carter detoured from a campaign stop in California and went to the UCLA Hospital. The two men exchanged small talk and wished each other well. When Wayne died a few weeks later, the president mourned his passing: "John Wayne was bigger than life. In an age of few heroes, he was the genuine article. But he was more than a hero; he was a symbol of many of the qualities that made America great." Like America, he was larger than life, overpowering, and idealistic, but also, in unique ways, innocent to the point of naiveté. "Wayne is," commented writer Paul Krassner in 1969, "one of the floats in the Macy's Thanksgiving Parade." His life spanned most of the twentieth century, coinciding perfectly with

America's spreading influence around the world. He became the superpower's superstar.

But of what are heroes made? John Wayne was just an actor. He never really battled Indians in the Old West or dispatched desperadoes with a six-gun or slaughtered Japanese soldiers with abandon. He spent most of his life in Glendale, Los Angeles, Encino, and Newport Beach. He never served in the military. So what is it about him that evokes such powerful, enduring feelings? Why were medals struck, and airports and schools named, for this actor? Why today, some sixteen years after his death, do many video stores maintain separate sections for his films? Why does his portrait still adorn the walls of truck stops, gas stations, pool halls, sports bars, saloons, garages, gun shops, auction barns, hunting camps, tool sheds, rifle clubs, and auto parts stores—wherever men tend to gather? Why do channel surfers still come across his old movies every night?

In a country delirious with the ideas of freedom and democracy but worried about the alienation of cities and the tyranny of bureaucracies, John Wayne personified individual liberty. He was a provocative, outspoken, but nonideological conservative who only reluctantly entered the political fray in 1949 when that fray was impossible to ignore any longer. As a child his father told him: "Never insult anybody unintentionally." And Wayne did not. His political insults were always delivered with thoughtful, intentional passion. When he attacked American liberals, socialists, and communists—groups he tended to see as interchangeable—he meant his words to provoke actions. He criticized politicians who were not "willing to take the responsibility of leadership instead of checking polls and listening to the few that screamed." He said what was on his mind and did not concern himself with the consequences. For millions of moviegoers John Wayne was what they wanted to believe Americans once were and perhaps still are. "It is every person's dream," commented Maureen O'Hara as Duke lay close to death, "that the United States will be like John Wayne and always like him."

Loyal to alcohol, steak, cigarettes, and, most of all, friends, he was not a dutiful husband. He left three wives and refused to marry the last woman in his life. His was a man's world in which partners were taken for granted and energies were focused on work and a circle of close male friends. For Wayne life was intensely personal. He held certain things as sacred. One was friendship, another was his country: Both were inviolate.

It was that hardened implacability, that determined inflexibility, that marked Wayne's best film roles and actual life. Even his critics could not escape the appeal. Abbie Hoffman said in 1969 that he "liked Wayne's wholeness, his style. As for his politics, well—I suppose even cavemen felt a little admiration for the dinosaurs that were trying to gobble them up." Wayne may have seemed like a dinosaur to some in the 1960s, but his values were American bedrock, and they have survived Wayne and Hoffman alike. John Wayne is better remembered for what he did on screen than what he said: He restored order. Sometimes his methods were harsh, occasionally his manner was gruff, but the result was always the same. He affirmed that there was a rough justice at work, and that if good was not always rewarded, evil was always punished.

But if his appeal remains unquestionable, why have critics and historians refused to grant Wayne his deserved spot in the pantheon of Hollywood greats? Why did the New York and Los Angeles critics turn on him, starting in the 1960s, blasting almost all his films except *True Grit*? Why have Westerns been pronounced dead at least once in every decade since the 1930s despite Wayne's (and after him, Clint Eastwood's) continual proof to the contrary? Why has Wayne never been given as much credit as an actor as he deserved?

During the 1960s and 1970s, when the antiwar movement, the women's movement, politicians, cultural critics, and a wide range of other groups and individuals assaulted traditional ideals of masculinity, individualism, and patriotism, John Wayne kept the faith. That faith, and the image it spawned, continues to have a powerful, almost intoxicating effect on popular culture in the United States and around the world. Nobody is immune, not presidents or premiers or princes or emperors, not Khrushchev or Hirohito or Carter, not paupers or peasants. As America rose in the world during the twentieth century, John Wayne came along for the ride, becoming his country's most recognizable symbol. It will take much more than a shift in the balance of power for Wayne's symbol to fade. John Wayne's Americanness is as deeply etched as was his face.

1

God, Lincoln, and the Golden Gate

It was happening again. Another slight. Another slight in a string of slights that stretched back to the time before he was John Wayne, even before he was Marion Mitchell Morrison—the name he was finally given at age five—back probably to his mother's unforgiving impatience with his father, which had transferred unerringly to him. "How children dance to the unlived lives of their parents," poet Rainer Maria Rilke once observed. John Wayne always danced to his mother, Molly's, unrealized dreams.

She made sure the dance was painful, holding tight the strings of his emotions and jerking them sharply whenever she wanted to keep him in line. He was his mother's son, so like her in his ambition and drive, his stubbornness and toughness. Unlike his father, Wayne fulfilled his mother's dreams of success, and she never forgave him for it. She refused to acknowledge his accomplishments or praise his achievements, rejecting his attempts to demonstrate his love. In Molly's eyes even his spectacular success was only a prelude to his ultimate failure. Until it came—as she was certain it would—she would continue to remind Duke, as he was later called, that he was nothing special.

The latest slight involved his most recent display of love. Each year he sent his mother and her second husband, Sidney Preen, on a spectacular vacation. Wherever they wanted to go and however long they wanted to stay, it was his treat. He was a dutiful son. He always remembered her birthday, invited her

MoTher - Molly

to family gatherings, and inquired about her welfare. The people in Long Beach, California, where the Preens lived, knew her and her famous son and were aware of the attention he paid her. In 1962 Wayne sent Sidney and Molly Preen on an around-the-world, all-expenses-paid vacation that took them to every major tourist attraction on the planet. They flew first class, traveled on luxury ships, rented big cars, ate in the finest restaurants, watched the most popular shows, and shopped in the best stores. Duke wanted his mother to have a good time, and he laid out thousands of dollars to ensure the success of the trip.

When the Preens returned to Long Beach, Wayne greeted them and asked if they had enjoyed themselves. Sidney Preen, who may already have been thinking about next year's vacation, thanked him profusely, talking about their wonderful experiences. But Molly, true to form, could only complain: how long the flights had been, how tired she had become, how poor the service was, how the trip had not turned out to be what she had expected, and how it would have been better if Wayne had done this or that. Duke was visibly disappointed. He had spent a lifetime trying to please his mother, and she had spent the same lifetime making him feel inadequate to the task. Mary St. John, Wayne's longtime private secretary, went up to Molly when Duke left the room and said, "Don't you think you could be a little nicer to him sometimes?" Molly curtly replied, "I don't give a damn about him."[1]

Molly never did give a damn. She first demonstrated that in Iowa, half a century before and half a continent away. A few days before Christmas in 1912, after a long train ride with his father from Keokuk to their home in Earlham, young Marion Morrison met his new little brother for the first time. Molly had named the baby Robert Emmett after her own father, Robert Emmett Brown. "Bobby" had come into the world a few days earlier on December 18, and Molly was still in bed holding him. All the way from Keokuk, Clyde Morrison had been telling his five-year-old son about the baby and when they arrived at the house on Ohio Street, beside the railroad tracks, Marion bounded into the bedroom, rubbed his shoes on the carpet, and inadvertently touched the metal headboard of the bed, touching off a spark or two of static electricity and irritating his mother. Like a flash of lightning in the night, the sparks illuminated the new emotional landscape of Duke's life.[2]

When Molly told him that his new brother had been named Robert after Grandpa Brown, Marion was confused. *He* was Marion Robert Morrison, and he knew that he had been named after both of his grandfathers—Marion

Mitchell Morrison and Robert Emmett Brown. She had even taken to calling him "Bobby." But now Molly told him that they were going to change his name, giving the name Robert to his little brother. From now on, they told him, his new name would be Marion Mitchell Morrison, the same name as his paternal grandfather, and the new baby would bear the name of Robert Emmett. Baby brother would now be "Bobby." His name had been stolen. The change was neither inadvertent nor coincidental. For Molly the new baby was going to be special, and she wanted him to have her father's name. For almost sixty years Molly would shower attention on Bobby, worrying about him constantly, trying to meet his every need, and giving him undivided support. There would not be much left for anyone else, and almost none for her older son. Molly did not like Marion, and he, even in his childhood, knew it. She no doubt harbored some guilt about those feelings and perhaps even loved him, but in a strange, disinterested manner. Her chilly disdain was the great mystery of his life—unfathomable, inexplicable, and undeserved. He spent many decades trying to please her, but Molly would not be pleased.[3]

Not surprisingly he grew up wondering what was wrong with him, what his mother did not like about him, seeking outside his own psyche and family the approval, security, and self-confidence that should have been his birthright. Molly was a capricious woman. Her moods were unpredictable, her anger petty and vicious. Marion grew up fearing and resenting this anger, and he developed a deep intolerance for pettiness. All his life he was attracted sexually to women but avoided emotional intimacy. He was always somewhat afraid of them, of their inability to hide their feelings, and of their need to talk about their pain. Even before he became John Wayne, the people closest to him were men, not women, and they were friends, not family. He preferred the company of men who accepted loyalty as a cardinal virtue, guarded their innermost feelings carefully, and kept their word.

In the 1950s John Wayne remarked to a Hollywood reporter that he was "just a Scotch-Irish little boy." In the ancient past, the Morrison clan had originated on the island of Lewis, in the Outer Hebrides, off the coast of Scotland. They moved to Northern Ireland—Ulster—with the great migration during the seventeenth century, when tens of thousands of Scots Presbyterians, at the invitation of the English, crossed the Irish Sea and crushed the Roman Catholic peasants who occupied the land. Over the next century they became known as the Scotch-Irish, and that part of the world has been embroiled in a life-and-death struggle ever since. In the serious and sometimes fatal political world of Northern Ireland, where John Wayne's Scotch-Irish ancestors had their beginnings, trust and loyalty were supreme virtues, more important than money, religion, or even family. Promises, and a man's word, were kept because unkept promises meant imprisonment or death.[4] Unkept promises drove his great-great-grandfather—Robert Morrison—to America. Robert was born in County Antrim, Northern Ireland, in 1782, to John Morrison and Nancy de Scrogges. His father died when Robert was a *unre-* baby, but he passed on to the infant the tenacity of his ancestors. Lord Rose- *lated* bury, who owned a large tract of land in County Antrim, remarked in 1790 that the Scotch-Irish were "the toughest, the most dominant, the most irresistable race that exists in the universe at this moment." Robert Morrison embodied those qualities. Northern Ireland had been a bloody battleground for Catholics and Protestants since the early 1600s, but Morrison could not identify with either side. A Scotch-Irish Presbyterian who did not think highly of Catholics, he also despised the British government that made life so miserable for everyone. Even as a teenager he was politically active in the United Irishmen, an insurgent group opposed to British rule in Ulster. After being betrayed to the British by a "friend" in the United Irishmen and learning that a warrant had been issued for his arrest, Morrison knew he had only one option—to head across the Atlantic with hundreds of thousands of other Scotch-Irish and start over again in America.[5]

He arrived with his mother in New York in 1799. The Scotch-Irish immigrants were a restless lot, strong-willed and opinionated, blessed with and cursed by a dogged sense of right and wrong. In the seventeenth century they had left the lowlands of Scotland for Northern Ireland, and in the eighteenth century they moved again, this time to America. They were accustomed, even eager, to pull up stakes again and again and head west, where land was cheaper and more plentiful. Their migration across the continent took two directions. Most initially traveled west toward the Appalachians and then south, straggling over the course of several generations down the eastern foothills across the frontiers of Maryland, Virginia, North Carolina, South Carolina, Georgia, and the Florida Panhandle. By the early 1800s their descendants were scattering throughout Alabama and Mississippi, and by the 1820s into Louisiana and Texas. They conquered the local Indian tribes, cleared land, trafficked in African slaves, and became southerners. The other wave of Scotch-Irish settlers, however, avoided the South, crossing the Appalachians in Pennsylvania and gradually settling throughout Ohio, Kentucky, Illinois, Indiana, and Iowa. They became midwesterners.[6]

The two groups developed dramatically different cultures. Because of the presence of so many African-American slaves in the South, the Scotch-Irish there developed a strong sense of racial consciousness. When the Civil War devastated their way of life in the 1860s, the Scotch-Irish behaved like many other wealthy landowners, wallowing in a "lost cause" political separatism and developing both religious fundamentalism and a virulent racism. But the Scotch-Irish in the Midwest who won the Civil War gained a self-confidence that made for religious complacency and relative ethnic and racial harmony. It was that self-confidence, an inarrogant, healthy feeling, which became the centerpiece of midwestern values. Unfortunately for John Wayne, however, it would be possible to be raised in a midwestern culture of confidence and optimism but in a home full of insecurity and self-doubt.

Robert Morrison initially took the southern route of the Scotch Irish migration, settling briefly in Chester County, South Carolina, before moving out to northern Kentucky. When he heard of a large colony of Morrisons across the Ohio River near Cherry Creek in Adams County, Ohio, he moved again and spent the rest of his life there. Morrison's fifth child, James, born in 1811, grew up in Cherry Fork but then pushed west, living out his life in Monmouth, Warren County, Illinois.[7]

One of James's sons—Marion Mitchell Morrison—was just sixteen years old when the family reached Monmouth. He fought in the Union Army during the Civil War, returned to Monmouth after mustering out in 1865, and married Weltha Chase Parsons in 1869. Her family had its roots in seventeenth-century New England. Like the Morrisons they were faithful Presbyterians. Marion and Weltha Morrison lived in Monmouth, Illinois, for the next sixteen years. Then they were ready for their own odyssey, and they moved to Indianola, Iowa.[8]

Marion built a successful life for himself, his wife, Weltha, and his children, George, Guy, Clyde, and Pearl, in Indianola. He was charming and, like his father, politically gifted, able to make small talk with farmers, railroad workers, professors at the local Simpson College, and downtown merchants. After farming for a few years, Morrison launched a real estate business in 1890 and became prosperous, at least by Indianola standards. In 1899 he was elected county treasurer, a position of trust and responsibility. An inveterate joiner, he was a deacon in the Presbyterian Church and active in the local Masonic lodge. His wife played a prominent role in several women's clubs and auxiliaries.[9]

Their son Clyde Leonard Morrison, who was born on August 20, 1884, back in Monmouth, Illinois, had been only three years old when they arrived in Iowa. After leaving Indianola High School in 1898, Clyde enrolled in the Middle Academy, a preparatory school of Simpson College. He spent a se-mester playing football at Iowa State University in Ames, but then went back to Simpson College, registered as a freshman in 1901, and completed the in-troductory courses. As a sophomore Clyde enrolled in the local conservatory of music at Simpson. An unusually gifted student and passionate for both football and music, he was also handsome and sensitive, an artist and a jock—irresistible to many young women.[10]

In 1903 Clyde opted for the practical. He left Simpson College and en-tered the pharmacy program at the Highland Park College of Pharmacy (later part of Drake University) in Des Moines. Pharmacy in the early twentieth century, like medicine and dentistry, was leaving the barber shops and patent medicine wagons. The new generation of formally trained pharmacists viewed themselves as scientists and professionals, practitioners of a respected discipline. The curriculum at Highland Park was rigorous and demanding. Clyde graduated in 1905, passed the licensing examination, and received his professional credentials as a registered pharmacist.[11]

During his last summer at the college, Clyde met Mary Alberta Brown, a short, red-haired, green-eyed woman who worked as a telephone operator in Des Moines and attended the same Methodist church as he. Her parents called her May, but she was Molly to her friends. Her father, Robert Emmett Brown, had been born in Armstrong County, Pennsylvania, in 1849 to Scotch-Irish parents who moved west to Kansas when he was still a child. After mustering out of the army in 1868, Robert Brown settled in Lincoln, Nebraska, and went to work as a printer. He married a young woman of Irish descent. Margaret was born in County Cork in 1848 and came to the United States after the Civil War in the postfamine Irish migration. When she arrived in 1874, she was a spinster who had had no marriage prospects in Ireland. Maggie, as she was called, was a talented seamstress and clothing designer, a trade she continued to practice after their marriage in 1874. Mary Alberta, their third child, was born in Lincoln in 1885. Robert Brown was a Presbyterian and Maggie was a teetotaling Irish Catholic, but they raised their children as Protes-tants. They too moved in the early 1890s, settling in a small house on 1716 Hight Street in Des Moines, where Robert worked as a printer and Maggie ran a seamstress shop. Molly Brown grew up in a comfortable middle-class, urban world.[12]

Molly was energetic, outspoken, and opinionated. She smoked cigarettes in private and in public, long before it was fashionable for women to do so, and she did not give a damn who knew about it. But she was not a Bohemian; she appreciated the comforts of middle-class life. She dated college boys because she found them interesting and because she wanted to marry well. Clyde was twenty and Molly nineteen when they met. She fell in love with him because he was kind, handsome, and well educated. He would, she thought, be easy to live with and a good provider. They had not dated long and did not know each other very well, but Clyde was about to take a job at a pharmacy in Waterloo, Iowa, and they decided to get married. Rather than bother with a church wedding, they eloped, traveling to Knoxville, in Marion County, where Justice of the Peace I. H. Garritson married them on September 29, 1905. They made their first home in Waterloo.[13]

Married young and in haste, they had years to learn just how mismatched they were. John Wayne once remarked that his father and mother "were complete opposites." In Clyde's personality kindness mixed easily with dreamy optimism. Like Mark Twain's Colonel Sellers in *The Gilded Age*, he was forever waiting for fortune to find him, always expecting some windfall, always hoping to make it big but not knowing quite how to do it. He had no sense of money and was not inclined to save. He was patient and gentle, and he enjoyed an occasional drink, which usually rendered him more mellow and sweet. Conventional wisdom among those who knew him in Iowa was that if "Clyde Morrison only had four bits left in his pocket, he'd give one quarter to a friend, buy a beer for himself, and sit down and talk." All too often, as far as Molly was concerned, Clyde came home empty-handed. Adding to his domestic difficulties, Clyde attracted and was attracted to women. Women found it easy to talk to him about their problems. He was handsome, sincere, sensitive—and sexy. People noticed the earnest conversations he had with women in the store. Clyde did not cheat on Molly; his moral standards and sense of propriety would not permit it, but she became angry and jealous if he even looked twice at another woman in the drugstore.[14]

Molly was proud and impatient, quick to anger, and easily offended. There was an icy rigidity to her, and she had a difficult time accepting the weaknesses inherent in human nature. Her own mother had long complained that alcohol ruined Irishmen, and Molly had no respect for people who destroyed themselves and their families with drink. Clyde was not an alcoholic, and later in his life would hardly drink at all, but Molly refused to look past even a single beer bottle. She was deeply unhappy, a condition that best expressed itself in acts of meanness and inhospitality. She had a long memory, was unforgiving, and did not make friends easily. She pinched pennies and wanted to

build a family nest egg. Clyde's smile had won her heart, but his easygoing nature and difficulty making a decent living just as easily lost it. Alice Miller was
a little girl living across the street from the Morrisons when Marion was born.
She thought the baby was a "beautiful little boy," and she would sometimes
walk with Molly and push Marion in a carriage. "Molly Morrison was a stern
woman," Miller recalled decades later. "You had to be real careful around her.
She could fly off the handle when you least expected it." "Mrs. Morrison was ~Mom~
as tough as nails," a former resident of Winterset, Iowa, recalled. "But Mr.
~Dad~ Morrison was just the opposite, as soft and sweet as a marshmallow." Their
marriage was doomed from the start.[15]

The instability that stalked them for the rest of their time together appeared
early. They both wanted to leave Waterloo and get closer to their parents.
Molly was emotionally tied to her mother and father, as was Clyde to his family. Waterloo was more than 115 miles from Des Moines and 140 miles from
Indianola, and the journey was a long, hard two-day ride by wagon. Clyde
contacted the job placement office at Highland Park College, and both of
them were ecstatic when they found out that the M. E. Smith Drugstore in
Winterset, Iowa, was looking for a registered pharmacist. Winterset, the county seat of Madison County, was about 35 miles from Des Moines and only 20
miles from Indianola, perfect for both of them. They rented a small frame
house on South Second Street in Winterset and started a new life there.[16]

W interset was a perfect heartland emblem for John Wayne's cradle. The
Mesquakie Indians abandoned the area several years before the first
white settlers arrived in 1846. The state legislature designated Winterset as the
county seat of Madison County in 1849, and construction began on a courthouse the next year. The city was incorporated in 1857. By the early 1850s it
had become "town" to the surrounding farmers, who were raising corn, wheat,
flax, oats, barley, cattle, horses, and hogs. The population of Madison County
reached 7,339 in 1860, 17,224 in 1880, and 17,710 in 1900.[17]

By the time Molly and Clyde arrived in Winterset, the town's charming
character was well developed. Situated on rolling bluffs between two rivers,
Winterset looked like the prototype for Norman Rockwell paintings and
Andy Hardy movies. Its streets were straight and wide, its public square
guarded by a stately courthouse made from milky white Madison limestone.
Along West Jefferson and West Court Streets, the large Victorian homes recall
Hardy's hometown of Carvel, WASP America's best image of itself, "a world,"
commented Charles Champlin of Carvel, "not as it was but as it ought to

have been, with virtues intact, pieties unfeigned, commandments unbroken, good rewarded, evil foiled."[18]

Winterset joined its history to the nation's. The imposing courthouse was completed in 1876 and honored America's centennial birthday. One of its smaller parks announced the town's Civil War loyalties in the wording of a somber monument: "To the patriotic dead who fell during the Great Rebellion." But Winterset was also a bit like Molly herself: Both town and woman had ambitions that were never realized, and both seemed certain of a prosperity that never really materialized.

In the beginning, however, the Morrisons prospered in Winterset. Clyde had a decent job, they lived in a nice east side neighborhood, and Molly was soon pregnant with her first child. They drank fifteen-cent ice cream sodas at the Candy Kitchen on the south side of the square and attended Sunday evening band concerts down by Dabney's Lake. On Wednesday evenings church bells summoned them and the rest of the Protestants to Bible study sessions at the Baptist, Presbyterian, and Methodist churches. They attended the Chautauqua lectures at the pavilion just north of the Methodist Church and occasionally went out for dinner at the Farmers' Hotel. Clyde and Molly both liked to read, and they were frequent visitors to the public library, presided over by the dictatorial Miss Mary Cassiday, who, in the words of a former Winterset resident, "protected the reading room's decorum with the zeal of a convent nun loyal to vows of silence."[19]

Molly got good prenatal care from Dr. Jessie Smith, one of Iowa's few female physicians, and they formed a close relationship. On May 25, 1907, when she went into labor, Molly put out a call to Dr. Smith, and the baby came the next day. It was a torturous delivery, marked by a long labor and a huge, thirteen-pound baby that, in Molly's opinion, almost killed her. Marion Robert Morrison, the future John Wayne, had come into the world.[20]

For Madisonians patriotism was more than just a sentiment expressed on Civil War monuments. They loved their country with a reverence and passion that come only from blood sacrifice. In 1859 the population of Madison County totaled 7,071 people. Approximately 900 of them were young men between the ages of eighteen and thirty-five, and 710 of them had joined the Union Army. Of these 104 never came home, succumbing to disease, accidents, and Confederate bullets and bayonets. Another 106 were severely wounded or had spent years as Confederate prisoners-of-war. The Civil War lived on a long time in Winterset. Each spring a touring troupe performed *Uncle Tom's Cabin,* complete with Little Eva driving her ponies in a parade around the town square. For July 4—Independence Day—the most important holiday of the year, much bigger than Christmas, Thanksgiving, or Easter—town and city fathers planned the celebration months in advance. In the 1860s, 1870s, and 1880s, so many men marched as veterans in the Winterset July 4 parades—carrying the flag of the United States, the banner of the Grand Army of the Republic, and the ensigns of their individual army units—that there were hardly any younger men left among the spectators. Even in the early 1900s several hundred of them still marched in the parades, telling anyone who would listen where they had fought during the "War of the Southern Rebellion." At Winterset High School in the late 1800s and early 1900s, William Cooper, a wounded veteran of the Civil War and a spellbinding orator, appeared annually before an assembly of all the students on Lincoln's Birthday and gave his eyewitness account of Pickett's Charge at Gettysburg.[21]

Clyde's father had enlisted in Company B of the 83rd Illinois Infantry in February 1864; from there he transferred to Company E of the 61st Illinois Infantry. At the Battle of Pine Bluff, Tennessee, a few weeks after he put on the Union blue, Marion found himself in hand-to-hand combat with Confederate troops. He took saber wounds to the chest and neck and was hit by bullets in the nose and the top of his head. Morrison played dead for several hours, then lost consciousness for two days before crawling down to the Tennessee River, where a Union gunboat picked him up. He carried the bullet in his head, and suffered from the accompanying headaches, for the rest of his life.

Molly's father, Robert Brown, tried to enlist in the Union Army in 1865, but he was only fifteen years old. His turn at combat came two years later when he volunteered for the 18th Kansas Cavalry and spent two years fighting Cheyenne and Arapaho warriors along the Union Pacific Railroad line in Kansas and Colorado Territory. Both Clyde and Molly were raised on a steady diet of war and love-your-country stories. When their country called, men served.[22]

Madisonians were not just patriots; they were Republicans as well—dyed-in-the-wool Republicans who equated the Democratic party with disunion and treason. The Republican party first appeared in Madison County in 1856, the year John C. Fremont, its first candidate, ran for president. Four years later Democrats divided their votes among three candidates, giving Madison County to Abraham Lincoln and the Republicans. The county stayed Republican until the bottom of the Great Depression in 1932, when Franklin D. Roosevelt edged Herbert Hoover out by 260 votes. It quickly returned to the Grand Old Party, however. John Wayne came honestly by his Republican party credentials.[23]

Madisonians, without knowing the term, were WASPs. In fact, Madison County, Iowa, was one of the most white, Anglo-Saxon, Protestant regions of the country. Winterset was unconcerned about immigrants or blacks or Catholics or Indians. There were simply too few to fear or hate. The 1910 census listed 2,817 people in the city. Of that number only 57 were immigrants, and of them 26 were English, Anglo-Canadians, or Anglo-Irish, and 5 were Scotch or Scotch-Irish. Only 27 people in Winterset did not speak English as their native language, and most of them were Germans, Swedes, and Danes. The WASP roots were deep as a well. Only 429 of the 2,817 people in Winterset had even one immigrant parent.[24]

Everyone was Protestant—Presbyterian, United Brethren, Campbellite, Dutch Reformed, Baptist, Episcopalian, Methodist, Congregationalist, and Quaker. Most of the area's small Roman Catholic population lived in Lee Township, up in the northeast corner of the county. Dr. Jessie Smith, one of them, was both a devout Catholic and beloved in the community. Most of the Catholics were descendants of famine Irish immigrants who reached Iowa in the late 1850s. Only two black families lived there in 1910: Charlie Moore, a hardworking black, saw his children finish high school in Winterset, while "Nigger John," who lived in a shack just off the town square, muddled through life in a perpetual state of poverty and benign neglect.[25]

WASP values permeated every level of Winterset culture. Protestant individualism generated a particular vision of community. Society existed, they believed, to promote individual needs. Communal roots were unimportant; it was the needs of the moment, and the individual, that mattered. The United States, even more than Britain, was rootless and capitalist in that the American people were as mobile geographically as they were economically, ready to sever ties and move on to new opportunities, even if it meant leaving friends, family, and familiar places. To give themselves a temporary sense of community, they became joiners, forming clubs and associations. The people of Winterset and Madison County were moving out of the area almost as fast as, or sometimes faster than, they were moving in, always looking for new homes, new farms, new opportunities farther west. To compensate, in addition to the churches of Madison County, there were organizations—the Grand Army of the Republic, the Women's Relief Corps, the Country Club, the Chamber of Commerce, the Women's Club, Masonic Lodges, the Order of the Eastern Star, the Independent Order of Odd Fellows, the Crown Rebekah Lodge, the

Knights of Pythias, the Rathbone Sisters, the Modern Woodmen of America, the Knights of the Maccabees, the Woodmen of the World, the Woodman Circle, the Highland Nobles, the Knights and Ladies Security, the Whist Club, the Phi Kappa Thetas, the Bachelor Maids Club, the Birthday Club, the Indian Club, the Jolly Owls Club, and the Sewing Club. When new settlers arrived in Madison County, they came from communities with similar groups, and when they left to head west, they transported these organizations along with their plows and household goods.[26]

The Morrisons, like the rest of Winterset, worked hard and joined the requisite community groups. But the Morrisons were hardly the ideal American family. Though Clyde was happy enough working at the M. E. Smith Drugstore, he could not help but notice that the real money was in owning the business, not working for wages. The weekly pay never seemed to stretch far enough, especially with Clyde spending money and loaning it to friends. Molly could not pinch enough pennies, and she found herself shuffling payment of the bills from month to month and all too frequently having to call on their parents for help. She was terribly unhappy. Will C. Johnson, who ran a grocery store in Winterset and made deliveries to the Morrison home, was always wary of Molly. "When I took the groceries in the home," he remembered, "the baby was in the carriage asleep. I walked in quietly so as not to wake the baby." Years later Duke told one of his friends: "Mom was just not a happy woman. No matter what I did, or what Dad did, it was never enough."[27]

Clyde's father knew of his son's ambitions and put the word out to friends and family that his son wanted to "better himself." A Morrison cousin in Malcolm, Iowa, wrote back that there was an opening for a druggist in Brooklyn, a town about one hundred miles away. In the summer of 1909, with no real future in Winterset, Clyde pulled up stakes and moved to Brooklyn. It was another quiet, peaceful Iowa town. Located on the main line of the Chicago, Rock Island & Pacific Railroad, 105 miles west of Davenport, Brooklyn was the "city" for thousands of farmers. There were three pharmacies in Brooklyn, and Clyde got a job at Raimsburg Drug on Front Street. He rented a tiny house for Molly and the baby, but the family only lived there for a few months before moving across town to a more spacious home on the corner of Jackson and Des Moines Streets. By that time Clyde and Molly, though married for less than four years, had already lived in three separate homes. Worse yet, the job was no different from the old one. Clyde hated working for someone else. He wanted profits, not just a salary. He wanted his own business. When his mother died soon after he settled in Brooklyn, he started worrying about his father's loneliness and got homesick.[28]

When he learned that the Rexall Drug Store in Earlham was for sale, it seemed like a dream come true. Earlham was close to friends in Winterset and relatives in Indianola and Des Moines—or at least some of those relatives. With his wife dead, Marion Mitchell Morrison's Scotch-Irish blood was soon bubbling again, and he decided to move west to California, where he heard the opportunities in real estate were booming. Before he left he lent Clyde the money to make the down payment on the drugstore—just the business, not the property. Clyde signed the papers in December 1910, rented a house that backed onto a railroad track at 328 Ohio Street, brought Molly and the baby from Brooklyn, and opened the Rexall Store for business on Main Street. He and Molly felt at home again.[29]

But the store did not make money. Clyde was the victim of Iowa demographics and his own good nature. With Earlham's mainline location, town boosters had high hopes for the place. But Clyde's father was not the only Iowan to pull up stakes for California. A great exodus began, and the population of Madison County actually declined between 1900 and 1910. Although Earlham itself grew from 630 to 749 people during the decade, it was hardly enough to support the drugstore. Earlham's rural population base was shrinking. And Clyde as always was an easy touch for a hard luck story. John Wayne once said that "he [Clyde] couldn't pay his bills because he hated to press his customers to pay their bills." Creditors started showing up at the store and even at the house, demanding payment and embarrassing Molly. She hated Clyde's inability to make a decent living. On December 30, 1911, the Morrisons declared bankruptcy. C. C. Couch, who held the mortgage, foreclosed on the business. Clyde and Molly were broke and felt like deadbeats.[30]

After the Rexall went under, Clyde spent a few months working for the new proprietor, but that too came to an end in the spring, just when Molly learned she was pregnant with Bobby. There was no work for Clyde in Earlham, and Molly was sick and tired of moving. If she stayed in Earlham she would be able to have Dr. Jessie Smith deliver the baby. And Earlham was close to her parents in Des Moines. Clyde went looking for work and ended up at the other end of the state, in Keokuk, where he got a job as a clerk in a downtown store and rented a house at 11 South Ninth Street.

Neighbors were not surprised when Molly sent Marion to live with his father. From Marion's infancy father and son had been inseparable. When the baby was irritable and upset, Clyde could comfort and quiet him. Before bedtime, Clyde spent an hour or so reading to Marion. When the family moved to Earlham in 1910, Marion was already headstrong. Molly would send the four-year-old to the store, where he would spend the day playing with toy pistols or with his father's horse, Sadie, who was tied up in back. Maurice Zolotow interviewed a longtime resident of Earlham who told him: "That little boy often requested me to see if his daddy's horse was still tied back of the store." A patient man, Clyde enjoyed having his son around. Marion was his "Daddy's boy," and Molly grew jealous of their relationship. Late in the summer of 1912, when she was five months pregnant, she told Clyde to come and get the boy. He took Marion back to Keokuk and enrolled him on September 3 as a first-grader at the George Washington Elementary School.[31]

The Keokuk job was another dead end. Clyde was a clerk, not even a druggist; the idea of spending the rest of his life working for pennies was intolerable. There had to be a better way. Clyde had also developed heart trouble, complete with a nasty cough and shortness of breath, which three packs of Chesterfields a day did not help. A local physician suggested a drier climate; maybe California was the answer. In 1909 his father had purchased a home at 503 South Westlake Avenue in Los Angeles. Marion Mitchell Morrison dabbled in real estate and bragged about the weather. He also came up with the harebrained idea of Clyde and Molly taking up farming. Perhaps he was just a desperate father tired of seeing his son fail, or perhaps he was already suffering from the dementia that would eventually kill him. But both Clyde and Molly were city bred, and the nearest they had been to a farm was when they rode in their wagon between Winterset and Des Moines. Nevertheless, Marion heard that homesteaders were taking up land in Lancaster County, just outside the Los Angeles Basin. Maybe that would be a good place for his son's family to start over. Clyde agreed. The land Marion picked for his son, daughter-in-law, and grandsons was in the middle of the Mojave Desert. It would certainly be dry enough there.

A few weeks after Bobby was born in December 1912, they had all left Earlham and moved home to Des Moines, taking a back room in Molly's childhood house. They were broke and completely dependent on Robert and Maggie Brown. Clyde was almost twenty-nine years old, a college graduate, the father of two children, and living off the generosity of his in-laws. He worked odd jobs throughout 1913, waiting for his own father to complete the arrangements on the California homestead. Late in 1914 Marion Morrison wrote Clyde and Molly that the land still needed months of hard work, and that Clyde would have to move out there alone, unless she wanted to live in a tent with the boys. Molly declined, staying in Des Moines while Clyde headed west. The old man agreed to pay Clyde two dollars a day so he would have at least some money to send home. Molly had little to show for nearly nine years of marriage except the baby whom she adored, the unruly Marion whom she already resented, and a husband she no longer trusted or even liked. There was no home, no property, no savings account. She believed that she had married a bum, and it looked as if he was going to drag her far from home.

When Marion Mitchell Morrison had arrived in Los Angeles, California, late in 1909, everyone said the weather was perfect year round and the opportunities to make a living selling property were extraordinary. He found a job with Ryder, Munch, and Grants, a Los Angeles real estate firm, rented a house at 503 S. Westlake, and soon married Emma Johnson, a widow in his neighborhood.[32]

Marion convinced Clyde that he had a plan for the family. He would file a claim on cheap property in the Mojave Desert, invest his own capital in improving it, live on it for a while, secure title to the land, and then leave it to Clyde in his will. At sixty-nine years of age and in poor health, Marion might not be around much longer anyway, and in the meantime, Clyde, Molly, and the kids could live on it free. It seemed a perfect arrangement. They would have virtually no bills to pay, and the cash from their first crop of corn or wheat would get them off to a good start for the rest of their lives. Eighty acres was a sizable farm, in Iowa at least, and any farmer worth his salt could make a living from it. Clyde had not farmed in Iowa, except as a chore when he was a boy, but Marion was certain he could teach him if they lived, planted a crop, and harvested it together. Marion also bragged that the growing season in Southern California was almost 250 days a year, enough to bring in two crops. Respectable prosperity seemed certain.

When the Morrisons headed west in 1914, the region they entered had already assumed mythic dimensions in the national imagination. Late-nineteenth-century American popular culture had glorified the westward movement, making heroes out of the settlers and soldiers and villains out of the Indians. Kit Carson, Buffalo Bill Cody, and Jim Bridger were central characters in popular history and pulp novels, and Cody's "Wild West Show" toured the country in the 1880s. Most Americans believed that the frontier had made them unique, and that the reason for social and political stability in the United States had always been the abundance of land.

But the frontier, long revered as the cradle of individualism and self-reliance, no longer existed in the early 1900s, and many prominent Americans mourned its passing. Traditional values appeared to be vanishing as well, overwhelmed from below by hordes of immigrants and urban poor, and from above by the crass commercialism of corporate capitalists. Plutocrats and the proletariat—money and the mob—seemed to have the upper hand. Owen Wister, whose novel *The Virginian* (1902) would help create the modern myth of the West, worried that "this continent does not hold a nation any longer, but is merely a strip of land on which a crowd is struggling for money."

Owen Wister went west in 1885, not because he had to—he was from a well-educated, well-to-do family—but because he hoped to discover there an answer to the national crisis, a moral alternative to the commercial decadence and cultural malaise afflicting the East. During an extended stay in Wyoming before entering Harvard Law School, he managed a large cattle ranch and observed firsthand the range wars and Lincoln County violence of the late 1880s and early 1890s. He did not necessarily equate progress with the arrival of settlers, law, and order on the frontier, because newcomers often brought with them effete eastern values. What was to be revered out west, and what Wister immortalized in *The Virginian*, was the need for armed, virile men willing to break rules and ignore social conventions, to take the law into their own hands and resort to violence when necessary to protect decent people—civilization—from the menacing, debilitating effects of greedy capitalists, mindless mobs, and oppressive government officials.[33]

Wister, along with people like Frank Norris, Hamlin Garland, Jack London, and Stewart White, produced a genre of "red-blooded" fiction in the early 1900s to counter what they perceived to be the emasculating effects of commercialism, bureaucracy, urban squalor, and class conflict. The frontier no longer existed as a real place, but it could be perpetuated as a way of life, a symbolic world, through literature and education. The time was at hand for a revival of manly virtues—virility, toughness, courage, leadership, and determination. The literary mythology Wister and others invented helped entertain, and educate, a nation—highbrow readers as well as popular audiences—and spawned a set of values and expectations that shaped real-world discourse for the next two generations.

This cult of masculinity found new expression and continuing vitality in early silent films and in the novels of Zane Grey in the second and third decades of the twentieth century; movie serials, B Westerns, and Max Brand novels in the 1930s; war movies and feature Westerns in the 1940s; and television serials and Louis L'Amour novels in the 1950s and 1960s. By that time John Wayne's screen persona would become the ultimate symbol of "red-blooded" masculinity and the flashpoint in a cultural battle between liberals and conservatives for the heart of America.

Marion's vision for his son was part of that western mythology, and Clyde bought it whole. He had always had a hard time saying no to anybody, particularly his strong-willed father, and he had been discouraged by his run of bad luck. Besides, he had few alternatives. Maybe California was the answer. As usual, with his lack of business sense, he came to the game late. Clyde's dreams were always one step behind the times. By the early 1900s the best California farmland was taken. Huge volumes of public-domain land were still available in the arid deserts of the Far West. John Wesley Powell, who explored the "arid lands" in the early 1870s, said that four sections (about 2,500 acres) constituted a reasonable minimum size for a farmer-stockman. The Homestead Act's limit of 160 acres was simply not enough to make a living where water was so limited. To alleviate the problem Congress passed the Desert Land Act of 1877, which allowed settlers to acquire up to 640 acres of land for $1.25 an acre, if they worked to convert the land to agricultural purposes. But the only land available under the law was desert property incapable of producing an agricultural crop without irrigation. The federal government wanted to encourage settlement of sparsely populated areas and create incentives for their economic development. The Desert Land Act was followed up by the Carey Act of 1894 and the Newlands Act of 1902, which gave federal land to state governments to promote irrigation. The land that Marion found for Clyde, Molly, and the boys was desert property available for homesteading.[34]

Clyde joined his father in California late in 1913, and they spent a good part of 1914 working the land and trying to meet the minimum requirements to secure title and get it ready for the family. Marion had selected the southern half of the northeastern quarter of Section 34, Township 7N, north of Range 12, west of the San Bernardino Meridian—a total of 80 acres. If they managed to develop the property, they could later lay claim to the surrounding 560 acres. The property was located near the Southern Pacific Railroad tracks, about three miles south of Lancaster. Marion put nearly three thousand dollars of his own money into the land. One hundred yards from the railroad tracks they built a three-room frame house, approximately five hundred feet square, and topped it with a tin roof. John Wayne later described it as "a glorified shack." They constructed a small barn—only twelve by sixteen feet—just in case they might acquire a horse and cow, and built a small corral behind it. And they made a shelter for the twenty-horsepower Victor Horizontal gas engine and the Ingersoll-Rand air compressor that would run the water pump. They placed the outhouse about forty yards behind the house. Marion and Clyde both knew that Molly would hate the outhouse after living with indoor plumbing, but at least for the time being they had no choice.[35]

They contracted a drilling company to install a well. His father's health was slipping, so under Marion's supervision, Clyde dug ditches—three feet wide and eighteen inches deep—by hand all around the property and laid galvanized-iron pipe to deliver the water. He plowed ten acres, planted experimental plots of corn and wheat, and irrigated them. He and Marion then filed the necessary papers with the Los Angeles office of the Bureau of Land Management, testifying to their improvements on the property and asking for title.[36]

Ominously, the corn and wheat crops did poorly, even with the irrigation. Actually the well did not produce nearly enough water for the land. In his affidavit to the land office, Clyde attributed the poor yield to the fact that May had been too late in the season to plant corn or wheat, and that he had ended up cutting the crop early in September for fodder and feed. But he was convinced, as always, that everything would work out just fine, that the land had potential, that he could make a new life for his family, that his father's plans and money had not just been sunk into a pipe dream. Clyde wrote home at the end of 1914 that it was time for Molly and the boys to come west. "I'm sure he didn't give her any details in the letter," John Wayne later told Mary St. John. "If he had, there's no way she would have left Iowa."[37]

When she told her parents the plan, the looks on their faces were probably not very reassuring. In the first place, it seemed as if half of Iowa was already heading there. And Robert and Maggie liked their son-in-law—as a human being. But they shared Molly's frustration about Clyde's inability to settle down. And why way off to the Mojave Desert? The Browns had always been a close-knit family. The idea of being two thousand miles from their daughter and grandsons, and them living in a desert, was frightening. The Browns decided to sell their home in Des Moines and move with her to California.[38]

Molly and the two boys, along with Robert and Maggie Brown, boarded the train in Des Moines. The baby was only two years old in 1914, but Marion was seven. It was a great adventure for him. For Molly and her parents, however, adventure gave way to reality after they switched trains in Sacramento, California. The Southern Pacific line ran down through the San Joaquin Valley. As they headed south, the landscape changed. Gradually, almost imperceptibly, the trees thinned out and mountains gave way to grassy hills. The land became sandier. "Dust devils"—tiny, tornadolike wind bursts—skipped across the flatlands. This valley—resting between the coastal ranges and the Sierra

Nevadas—was one of nature's most powerful wind tunnels. As they chugged south, the winds blew more powerfully and the temperature rose. "When I got off the train in Lancaster, I couldn't believe my eyes," Molly told Mary St. John years later. "My father had the grimmest look on his face." It was not only as bad as they expected, it was worse—Clyde had chosen a no-man's land.[39]

He picked up his family in a wagon and headed toward their new home. Lancaster had the look of the Old West—a real frontier town—with five saloons, two large hotels, two banks, a real estate office, two cafés, and a dry goods store across the street from the station. A two-hundred-foot-long wooden trough for watering horses ran down Main Street. The Hannah Hotel had recently burned down, giving the downtown a somewhat depressing look, but the Lancaster Grammar School—a handsome two-story building—had just gone up on Cedar Avenue, and a new Baptist church had recently opened on Tenth Street and Herald. Only two streets were paved— Tenth Street and Antelope Avenue—but there were plans for more, and there were forty or so houses in town. There were no electric lines anywhere in sight. (Edison Electric would not come to Lancaster until 1914.)[40]

As they drove south toward the house, the wagon stirred up clouds of dust. The town abruptly ended a few blocks from the station, and there appeared to be nothing as far as the eye could see, all the way to the San Gabriel Mountains. The dirt road meandered around clumps of juniper bushes, sagebrush, and sandy soft spots, making for a twisting, bumpy ride. As they approached the Morrison property, the Browns did not see what Clyde had described as a house and barn. All they saw was a shack and a shed. "Guess you'd have to call it a miserable little shanty," Wayne later told Maurice Zolotow. "Didn't have gas nor electricty nor water. . . . Evenings we lit kerosene lamps to read by. Mother cooked on a woodburnin' stove. No telephone lines out our way, of course. . . . We were cut off from the world. . . . A stranger visitin' from Iowa wouldn't have believed he was in the twentieth century." There were no trees and no shrubs, not so much as a blade of grass—in fact, not a single green plant on the whole place, just sagebrush and sand. They must have known, in an instant, that Molly would despise the place. In fact their daughter was going to be absolutely, chronically miserable. Like the first generation of women to settle the Great Plains seventy years earlier, she would age before her time, growing wrinkled, sunburned, and bitter. Robert and Maggie must have been heartsick about their daughter's future and loath to leave her and go on to Los Angeles. They decided to stay in Lancaster, moving in with their daughter and son-in-law.[41]

Clyde Morrison was not the first farmer to cast his lot, and lose, on Section 34, Township 7N, Range 12W, S.B. Meridian. In 1884 Edward Carlson first claimed the land, but he soon lost hope and returned it to the Bureau of Land Management. During the next twenty-five years, fourteen other people tried their hand at making a living on the section, but they all gave up, some after a few months, others after several years.[42]

Jackrabbits and rattlesnakes made farming hazardous, physically and financially. The Antelope Valley teemed with rabbits. To control the pests, local farmers and ranchers sponsored "jackrabbit roundups." It was a sight unlike anything in Iowa—half blood sport, half picnic. Hundreds of well-dressed men and women stood outside the temporary corral, many of them from Los Angeles on a weekend outing, all gathered for the fun. The town fathers had constructed a ring of wire and light fencing several acres in size, and far away to the east, on the horizon of the Mojave Desert, great clouds of dust rose as hundreds of horseback riders and dogs approached at breakneck speed. As the clouds and horses drew closer, thousands of terror-stricken jackrabbits ran ahead of them, racing to escape the horde. Two temporary fences formed an increasingly narrower chute that fed the jackrabbits into the corral. The riders closed in a huge but steadily shrinking semicircle, driving the rabbits into the enclosure, where they milled about in a frenzy. Then dozens of farmers, anxious to get even with the varmints that so often destroyed their crops, systematically clubbed the animals to death. The bedlam was deafening, with the crowds outside the corral roaring their approval. The wholesale slaughter was followed by a huge beef barbecue and street dance in downtown Lancaster.[43]

The rattlesnakes were even worse. "And I don't just mean a few," John Wayne remembered in 1973. "Seems to me like there musta' been millions. The more you killed—the more they kept on comin'." Molly was afraid to walk too far from the house, and she kept the boys close at hand as well. There were just too many snakes. Clyde took young Marion on rattlesnake hunts. Years later Wayne could still remember having nightmares. "Shooting those snakes also gave me some sleepless nights—visions of thousands of slithering snakes coming after me. I used to wake up in a cold sweat in the middle of the night, but my dad, or my family, never knew it. I kept my fears to myself."[44]

Clyde was not lazy. He struggled to make a success of the farm, working long hours, seven days a week, but he did not know the first thing about farming. Clyde had been raised as a city boy. The rest of the farmers in Antelope Valley, California, at least those who survived, raised hay and alfalfa on their land. But not Clyde. The profits on corn and wheat were higher per acre than on hay and alfalfa, so he tried corn and wheat. But grain crops also demanded heavier volumes of water—which he did not have. Even though the experimental corn and wheat crops of 1914 had been a bust, he confidently pushed ahead. Clyde, Molly, and even little Marion worked from dawn to dusk in the spring of 1915 clearing sagebrush off the property, tilling the soil, and planting corn—lots of Iowa corn. They also put in a crop of black-eyed peas. After a couple of weeks, the plants sprouted, but within two days jackrabbits had eaten them all. Their entire crop and four months of heavy labor was gone. Wayne remembered it as a turning point in the marriage:

> We were in bad shape financially. . . . The biggest disappointment of all was when we planted black-eyed peas. We had five acres of greenery going, beautiful tender young shoots. We went away for a weekend and when we came back, they'd been completely eaten by rabbits. It was tough. Like any married couple, they were going through a rough time. But that broke them. They never made that adjustment where they could get together again.[45]

But even after that disastrous first year, Clyde's faith was undimmed. Molly must have been miserably unhappy; they were broke; the heat was oppressive, the house drafty, and the wind unceasing. She could not keep the house clean, at least not up to her standards. There always seemed to be a film of dust on the tablecloths, dishes, glasses, floor, shelves, and pillows. During the summer the heat inside the house hit 90 degrees, and it continued throughout the summer. Clyde and Marion had built the house Iowa-style, with relatively low ceilings. Even minimum comfort in the desert, however, required high ceilings to let the heat rise. Outside the temperature went as high as 118 degrees. They had known heat spells back in Iowa, but nothing like this. Molly also had to keep the stove on to cook and to heat water for washing and bathing, adding to the oppressiveness inside. And to get the water to cook and wash, Molly had to carry it in five-gallon buckets from the well some distance away.[46]

It did not take long before Molly started venting her wrath directly on Clyde and indirectly on little Marion, whom she could barely tolerate. She complained to her parents every day and just as frequently yelled and screamed at Clyde. Robert and Maggie Brown felt sorry for Molly but worried that their presence in the household was only complicating matters, making a bad situation worse. The Browns were also fed up with the desert. Life in Antelope Valley was just too different from the comforts of Des Moines. It was too hot, too dusty, and too crowded in the three-room house. They decided to move to Los Angeles and told Clyde that he should do the same.

Robert got a job as a proofreader at a print shop, Maggie found work as a seamstress, and they rented a house at 812 East Fourteenth Street. A few months later they moved to a somewhat larger home on Valencia Street.[47]

After that first crop failure in September 1914, Clyde and Molly enrolled young Marion as a second-grader in the Lancaster Grammar School. Sixty children attended. He soon earned the nickname "Skinny" because of the mare he rode to school every day. The animal had a metabolic disorder of some kind, which gave her the proverbial swayback exposed-rib-cage look. After school Marion rode the three or so miles back home, but since there were no other children nearby, he occupied his own time or did chores for his father.[48]

The poverty was bad enough, but Molly also had to deal with its social implications. She had grown up in a self-respecting, middle-class family known for its financial stability. The years in Iowa—despite the bad debts, bill collectors, and bankruptcy—seemed idyllic compared to life in the Mojave Desert. If it were not for both sets of parents, they would be destitute. Nor did Molly make friends in California, leaving her even more isolated. To get into town she had to hitch up the wagon and make the three-mile journey, but the trip was always disappointing since the prosperous ladies of Lancaster showed no interest in the poverty-stricken Morrisons. Her only interaction with polite society in Lancaster and Palmdale came when several local women accused the Morrisons of neglecting the mare that Marion rode to school each day. The animal was so skinny that they were convinced that the family was starving her. An examination by a veterinarian proved them wrong, but for Molly, the experience was still humiliating.[49]

Lancaster and Palmdale were not without prospects, even though the local economy was somewhat depressed. Between 1907 and 1912, the construction of the Los Angeles Aqueduct, bringing water from the Sierra Nevadas through Kern County to Los Angeles, had provided the city with hundreds of construction jobs. But completion of the canal brought an end to the infusion of government money, and all of Antelope Valley went through a painful period of adjustment. Most of that adjustment was over by the time the Morrisons arrived in 1914, and new construction plans were moving forward. A public library and new high school had just opened. Saturday-night street dances were weekly affairs. There was a Methodist Church on Date Avenue near Ninth Street, and its members were engaged in a campaign to fund construction of a new chapel. Lodge 437 of the Masonic Order opened in 1915, and the Woman's Independence Club rented out part of its building at the corner of Tenth Street and Cedar to a motion picture operator who opened a nickelodeon—a storefront movie theater.

There were more than twenty thousand nickelodeons operating around the country, catering to a working-class clientele, who would go to the small theaters and watch a vitascope project a film on a wall or screen. The movie industry also came to Lancaster in a more tangible way. Antelope Valley was only an hour by train from the growing number of film studios in Los Angeles, and the valley's desert landscape was perfect for Westerns, which were nickelodeon staples. Film production companies arrived at the railroad station every week to make movies, and film stars roared over the San Gabriel mountains and down into the valley in their Stutz Bearcats, Crosley tourers, luxury Locomobiles, Cadillacs, and Houpt-Rockwell tourers. At night the film crews met in the Lancaster Grammar School on Cedar Avenue and reviewed the day's shooting. Townsfolk gathered outside the building to peer through the windows.[50]

Most of the Western films of the time employed the basic themes of Zane Grey's *Riders of the Purple Sage* (1912), which sold an astonishing one million hardcover copies and was followed up with annual bestsellers until 1925. Taking up where Owen Wister and *The Virginian* left off, Grey created a mythical West in which strong men see to justice. But while Wister made sure the heroes were well-bred, well-to-do men capable of governing a society, the hero of *Riders of the Purple Sage* is Lassiter, a mysterious gunman without a past who rescues the heroine, Jane Withersteen, from the clutches of a greedy Mormon land baron and a mob of rustlers. Withersteen, if she is going to survive in a red-blooded world, must learn to accept, even revere, the legitimate violence existing in "true men." Lassiter is a hero capable of any amount of violence and cruelty to protect the innocent; he is perfectly comfortable with the demands of revenge and retribution. In him the cowboy-gunslinger became the new icon of Western literature.[51]

When the good people of Lancaster and Palmdale peeped through the windows of the schoolhouse to view the rushes, they saw formula Westerns. The Edison Company had made a Western—*Cripple Creek Barroom*—in 1898, but the first real Western movie was Edwin S. Porter's *The Great Train Robbery* (1903), from which G. M. "Bronco Billy" Anderson emerged as the first Western star. Dozens of other Westerns followed, all of them melodramas, such as *In the Badlands*, *Boots and Saddles*, *Stampede*, *On the Border*, and *Pine Ridge Feud*. D. W. Griffith turned his talents to Westerns in 1911, making *The Last Drop of Water* and *Fighting Blood*. William S. Hart soon succeeded Bronco Billy as the premier Western star in the 1910s. The formula was clear-cut and morally unambiguous: Heroic cowboy-gunslingers save women and children from hostile Indians, acquisitive land barons, lecherous villains, and greedy capitalists. The Western film would eventually make young Marion Morrison one of the most famous men in the world.[52]

But in 1915 Molly was sick of the heat, the wind, the dust, and the smelly outhouse. She badgered Clyde to do something—anything—to get them away from what was fast becoming a domestic catastrophe. More than once she threatened divorce. John Wayne remembered a warning she gave to Clyde: "One of these days, mark my words, I'm just going to pack and go back to Des Moines." As usual Clyde saw a sliver of hope. In September 1915, he came up with what he thought was the answer to their problems. Another piece of land—the 320-acre tract in Section 26, Township 11 North—was available, and Clyde decided to lay claim to it. If he could get those 320 acres and then purchase or inherit from his father the 640 acres they were already living on, the family would own nearly one thousand acres of land.[53]

Molly would have none of it. The marriage, already weak by the time they arrived in California, was approaching the breaking point. Their arguments increased in frequency and intensity. She shouted and screamed at him every night, demanding that Clyde relieve her of her misery. Clyde refused to shout back, tried to calm her down, and gave the children the distinct impression that their mother was unreasonable, that the problems in the marriage rested with her, not him. Eight-year-old Marion would lie in bed at night and cover his ears with a pillow to muffle the shrill sounds of his mother's complaints, wondering what was wrong, why she was so upset, and why she hated his dad. Early in 1916 Molly had had enough. She gave Clyde an ultimatum—either move across the San Gabriel Mountains and get a job, or get a lawyer, because she was going to file for divorce.[54]

Her demands came as no surprise to Clyde. By the end of 1915 they were not only out of luck but out of money. Clyde did not have the funds to make the necessary improvements to the larger plot, and he could not sell the existing property because he had not lived on it long enough to satisfy the federal title requirements. Nor was his father in any position to help. Marion was fast becoming senile and suffering from tuberculosis, and early in 1915 he became so mentally incompetent and physically incontinent that his wife, Emma, could no longer take care of him. Clyde committed him to the Thornycraft Sanitarium in Glendale for three weeks, but they soon had him transferred across town to Patton Veterans Hospital.[55]

Clyde, along with Molly and the boys, visited his father a few times at the sanitarium and the VA hospital. They took the railroad through the San Gabriel Mountains and then rode a taxi out to the hospital. The taxi took them through downtown Glendale and then north to the Verdugo foothills. The visits only intensified Molly's unhappiness with the farm. Compared to Lancaster, Glendale seemed like paradise. The city sat up against the foothills, where the temperature averaged about seventy degrees. Even in the summers, when the heat was most intense, the evening breezes from the Pacific Ocean cooled the late afternoons and nights. Many of the streets were paved, and automobiles were everywhere. It was a beautiful community full of Protestant churches, Masonic lodges, schools, houses, apartments, drugstores, parks, theaters, electricity, and, best of all, plumbing. It was like Des Moines, only with mountains and a better climate. The Morrisons had read about the beauties of Glendale in the *Palmdale Post* and *Antelope Valley Press*: "Good roads, prosperous appearance of the homes, the hospitable residents and the thriving towns." But it was the visits to Marion Morrison's hospital that convinced Molly that she wanted to relocate there. The old man's illness and death later that year removed one more barrier to moving out of the desert. John Wayne described the decision quite simply: "Mother convinced [Clyde] after many bitter discussions that almost broke up the marriage, that he was not fit for agriculture."[56]

After his father's funeral, Clyde began taking the Southern Pacific train into Los Angeles to look for work. He stayed with the in-laws on Valencia Avenue and studied the classified ads in the *Los Angeles Times* and the *Los Angeles Evening Herald*. But 1915 Los Angeles was a busy place, a city in the midst of an unprecedented boom. Clyde Morrison knew that they could not live any longer in Lancaster, but he was still a small-town person, and Los Angeles was just too big and chaotic. Molly had really liked Glendale when they came in for the hospital visits, and he was anxious to try to please her. So he looked there as well, searching the classifieds of the *Glendale Evening News*. The Glendale Pharmacy on West Broadway was looking for a registered pharmacist, and Clyde charmed them, as he always did, in the interview. They offered him the job, and he went to work early in 1916. Molly liked the small house at 421 South Isabel, and the Morrisons rented it. They abandoned the farm in Lancaster, sold off what little equipment they had, and came over the mountains on the Southern Pacific Railroad to start, once again, a new life together.[57]

2

"He's Just Been Playing Himself All These Years"

It was a common sight in the neighborhood: Clyde was out in the front yard playing football with his oldest son, Marion. Back in Iowa, Clyde had been a talented athlete at Simpson College, playing tackle on the football team and winning All-State honors. He was just a little over five feet ten, 185 pounds, with a well-muscled body. Marion was tall but thin in 1918, his eleven-year-old body no match for his father's yet, but they were not in any real contest anyway. Clyde patiently taught the boy how to throw, kick, run, block, and tackle. Frank Hoyt, one of Marion's close boyhood friends, often played with them. He even remembered one magical day when the Morrisons took him along to the beach in Southern California. Clyde was decked out in a striped, one-piece bathing suit, while Molly was in one of those Victorian women's bathing dresses—black, full length, long-sleeved. The boys had a glorious time. Standing along the edge of the beach, Clyde had them run pass patterns into the surf, throwing them the ball just before the waves crashed into them. He showed them how to bodysurf. "The only problem with the whole day," Hoyt remembered, "was Mrs. Morrison. You could never tell how she would feel. She complained all day about the long drive from Glendale and the sand getting in their car and clothes." But the front-yard father-son football was everyday; the beach was an occasional luxury.[1]

When the Morrisons left the Mojave in 1916, they could hardly be civil to, let alone love, each other. But life in Glendale was pleasant enough to post-pone disaster for another ten years. The streets were paved and well-lighted, and the homes and apartments enjoyed electricity, indoor water, and telephone hookups. Hundreds of new fire hydrants protected the frame and stucco houses. The city was surrounded by thousands of square miles of vineyards and orange, apricot, and lemon groves. To locals Glendale was known as "Jewel City."[2]

Like the rest of the American Southwest, Glendale had been Mexican territory until 1848. José María Berdugo, a young soldier in the Spanish army stationed at the San Gabriel Mission east of Los Angeles, first explored the area of what is today Glendale in the early 1770s. When he took his first look at the San Fernando Valley, Berdugo was overwhelmed by its beauty, describing it as "the gate of Heaven." When his enlistment was over, he managed to secure from the king of Spain a land grant there of more than 32,000 acres. He named it the San Rafael Rancho. The land stayed with the family for nearly a century before Anglo settlers got title to it. After the end of the Mexican War in 1848, the United States assumed sovereignty over the Southwest. The Treaty of Guadalupe-Hidalgo guaranteed all Hispanic residents American citizenship, freedom of religion, and protection of their land titles. But those guarantees proved to be little protection later, when millions of Anglo pioneers settled in the West.[3]

Because of the large-scale immigration during the first years of the Gold Rush, the Mexican inhabitants of California, who were known as *Californios*, were soon outnumbered by 65,000. When the gold rush played out, tens of thousands of Anglo immigrants squatted on *Californio* land. To resolve the question of title, the state legislature passed the Land Act of 1851, creating a Board of Land Commissioners to hear and mediate conflicting claims. The board was hopelessly biased: The commissioners were all Anglos, the hearings were conducted in English, and the burden of proof rested on the *Californio* owners, not the Anglo squatters. By 1860 the board had turned more than four million acres of Spanish land over to the squatters. When the board decided in favor of the *Californio* owners, the squatters often resorted to the federal court system, where cases took an average of seventeen years to resolve. During the litigation the squatters were allowed to remain on the land. The San Rafael Rancho was just one small piece in that historical puzzle. The Berdugos lost it piecemeal—through lawsuits and sale—in the late nineteenth century, and early in the twentieth century, San Rafael Rancho was swallowed up by the great California land boom.[4]

By 1900 Southern California was in the midst of an unprecedented economic and demographic expansion, much of it engineered by Harry Chandler. In 1892 he had married the daughter of Harrison Gray Otis, owner of the *Los Angeles Times*. Over the years, Chandler built the *Times* into the most powerful newspaper on the West Coast. He also created a vast real estate empire in the Imperial Valley, deep in Southern California near the Mexican border, and in the San Fernando Valley north of Los Angeles. Using the *Times* to spread the word about his economic crusade, Chandler convinced Southern California voters in 1903 and 1907 to pass large bond issues to bring water out of the Sierra Nevadas to the San Fernando Valley. As these plans were being developed, Chandler secretly bought up large ranches in the area. Eventually, he controlled more than sixty million acres, which he carved up into real estate subdivisions. To bring new settlers to Southern California, Chandler used the *Times* for a promotional advertising, distributing tens of thousands of copies during the winter months in the Midwest.[5]

Midwesterners responded to the propaganda and headed for California by the millions. The population of Los Angeles was only 50,000 in 1890, but it doubled to 102,000 in 1900. It more than tripled to 319,000 in 1910 and nearly doubled again to 577,000 in 1920. In 1930 Los Angeles counted more than 1,238,000 residents. Rich in land, Chandler and the other founding fathers of modern Los Angeles wanted everybody driving a car and living in a single-family suburban house. That type of growth maximized profits on land sales, and there was no premium on space anyway. They did not want city tenements and apartment houses. Southern California obediently exploded in every direction.[6]

Nestled between the Verdugo foothills to the north and the Hollywood hills to the south, Glendale was at the eastern end of the San Fernando Valley, near the center of the boom. At the turn of the century only three hundred people lived in Glendale, but local boosters asserted it had real economic possibilities, primarily because it was so close to Los Angeles—only ten miles northeast of downtown city center. The Glendale Improvement Association, composed primarily of real estate interests, successfully campaigned for an interurban commuter railroad, and by 1904 the Pacific Electric Railway Company was making thirty-three round-trips to Los Angeles every day. The daily fare was seven cents, and the trip—beginning at Sixth and Main, going past Echo Park, and then crossing the Los Angeles River—took only twenty minutes. Glendale quickly became a commuter suburb.[7]

Real estate agents began selling 50- by 125-foot lots in the city for $250 to

$600, requiring a 25 percent down payment followed by eighteen monthly payments. The cheapest lots sold for $10 down and twenty-four monthly payments of $10. Affordable land prices, good weather, and the easy commute to Los Angeles transformed Glendale, swelling its population from 300 in 1900 to 2,746 in 1910. When the Morrisons arrived there in 1916, the population had tripled to nearly 9,000 people, and when Clyde and Molly split in 1926, Glendale had a population of more than 53,000. Town boosters bragged that Glendale was the fastest-growing city in the country, and because of its resources, they dubbed it "Playground of the World."[8]

They were also proud of its wholesomeness and progressive spirit. Glendale was a "dry" city in the early 1900s, and its chapter of the Women's Christian Temperance Union (WCTU) led the fight for Prohibition in California. To avoid the problems of urban machines controlled by powerful bosses and large corporations—so common in the Northeast and Midwest—Glendale adopted a city-manager system of government complete with modern tax assessment methods, public utility regulation, annual city budgets, and centralized, audited purchasing. Progressive Republican values shaped Glendale's political culture as they had much of that of Los Angeles, and both cities prided themselves on their ability to maximize economic growth while preserving good government.[9]

The city also had a distinctly midwestern flavor to it, which limited the culture shock for families like the Morrisons. In 1910, 735 families lived in Glendale, overwhelmingly white Anglo-Saxon Protestants who had been born in the Midwest and Northeast. Only eighty-nine of the heads of those families were foreign-born, and half of them were English and Canadian. The largest minority group was Japanese, with sixteen families; and the second largest was Hispanic, with twelve families. Only a handful of people were from the southern states. More than 90 percent of the families came from New England and the Midwest. Only 6 percent were even second-generation Californians. On its face and in its faces, Glendale was not much different from Winterset.[10]

Midwesterners, so used to transient societies in which kinship ties were weak or nonexistent, equated community life with community organization. Like Winterset, Glendale had its collection of Protestant churches—Methodist, Baptist, Presbyterian, and Episcopalian—as well as a small Roman Catholic congregation. A full slate of fraternal lodges arrived with the Midwestern migration, including the Masons, Eastern Star, Elks, Knights Templars, Rebekah Lodges, Oddfellows, Knights of Pythias, Good Templars, and Modern Woodmen. Also as in Winterset, patriotism ran strong. Civil War veterans had their Grand Army of the Republic building at South Glendale Avenue, and their wives attended the Women's Relief Corps. The Daughters of the American Revolution (DAR) met every week to promote love of country. The Sons of Veterans was an auxiliary of the Grand Army of the Republic. There was also an organized group of Spanish War Veterans, and after World War I Glendale had chapters of the American Legion and the Red Cross as well.[11]

When the Morrisons arrived in Glendale in the fall of 1916, they felt as if they had returned home. They moved into a house at 421 S. Isabel, and Clyde had a good job as a druggist at the Glendale Pharmacy on West Broadway. He sold everything from medicine to ice cream and, as he had done in Earlham and Winterset, gave away free advice. Soon he was again being called "Doc" and was a popular figure in the store. Marion was enrolled in the fourth grade at the Sixth Street Elementary School, and the family joined the First Methodist Church, which was in the middle of a construction campaign to finish the new chapel at Wilson Avenue and Kenwood Street. Clyde joined the Unity Chapter of the Royal Arch Masons, and Molly stayed home taking care of Bobby. The Morrisons had all the appearances of an ideal family.[12]

Young Marion even managed to get rid of his name, which he had always hated. Kids teased him, saying he had a girl's name, and the abuse frequently led to fights. He also came to despise the way Molly screeched it out when she was mad at him. Back in Lancaster, his friends had nicknamed him "Skinny," but Marion was no fonder of that name, thinking it implied either weakness or unattractiveness. He began insisting that his friends just call him "Morrison" until 1918, when a group of local firemen provided him with the nickname that would last for life. The family had a pet dog—a huge Airedale—named "Duke," and the animal dutifully followed Marion to school every day. When they passed Fire Department Station No. 1 at 315 East Broadway, the dog would stay behind, sleeping there until the eleven-year-old boy came from school. The firemen began referring to Marion as "Little Duke," or just "Duke," and he liked the sound of it. "Until I got the dog's name," Wayne laughed in 1973, "everyone used to call me Marion." From then on, one of the first things out of his mouth when he introduced himself to people would be, "Just call me Duke."[13]

The Morrisons' domestic tranquillity was short-lived. Few dysfunctional families solve their basic problems merely by relocating, and the Morrisons were no exception. Clyde had a job, but he never brought home enough money to go around, never enough to pay the bills. And he drank too much. Liquor dulled some of the pain, making Molly's outbursts and his own failures easier to live with. Molly came to despise Clyde, sober or drunk. He also made too many friends and helped too many of them when they ran short of cash. With married life all but intolerable, Clyde spent too much of his time in pool halls and bars. The family was also on the move, changing houses frequently. In 1917 they rented another house, at 315 South Geneva Street, but the stay was only temporary. By the end of the year they were living at 443 West Colorado. They bought a house of their own at 404 North Isabel in 1918 but lost it before the year was out; the owners of the Glendale Pharmacy let the Morrisons move into a tiny apartment above the drugstore. Clyde and Molly managed to buy another house in 1920. It was a nice six-room dwelling at 313 Garfield Avenue, the finest they had ever had, but Clyde defaulted on the payments in 1921. They then rented another place at 815 South Garfield.[14]

Even more humiliating than the constant moves, at least for Molly, was the frequency with which they had to use Duke's money for household expenses. In the summer of 1918, Duke went to work in the orchards, picking apricots and oranges. He also got a paper route delivering the *Los Angeles Examiner* on his bicycle, a job that required him to get up at 4:30 A.M. seven days a week and ride through his neighborhood in the dark. On Sunday mornings, when the papers were too heavy to carry, Clyde would get up, too, and drive the boy along the paper route in the Nash. That fall, when he became an eighth grader at the Wilson Intermediate School, Duke continued to work, obtaining an after-school job making deliveries for the Glendale Pharmacy. On Saturdays he often passed out handbills for downtown Glendale businesses. More often than not, Molly had to ask her son to help her buy groceries and pay utility bills. "You won't believe this," Molly told Mary St. John in the 1960s, "but sometimes I had to take Duke's paper route money to pay bills." Mary brought the subject up to Duke a few days later, and he was nonchalant about it. "Hell," he told her, "times were hard then. I didn't mind if my folks needed some of my money. Dad would've given me the shirt off his back." But whatever shred of respect or affection Molly had for her husband died during those first years in Glendale.[15]

Duke shared none of his mother's resentments. In fact, the one constant in life was Clyde. Frank Hoyt also delivered drugs for the Glendale Pharmacy and papers for the *Los Angeles Examiner*. He remembered rushing downtown from Wilson Intermediate after school to the pharmacy, where Clyde would greet both boys with a smile and an ice-cold Coke. In the evenings and on Sunday afternoons, Clyde played football and baseball with the boys, umpiring games, keeping score, and settling arguments. Hoyt recalled Clyde as "a great guy—strong, friendly, and gentle. Sometimes Mr. Morrison would even drive me around on Sunday mornings to get my papers delivered. I envied the relationship Duke had with his father. They spent a lot of time together and really enjoyed each other."16

Molly was another story. Her feelings for Duke were directly related to her growing dislike for Clyde. Duke was tentative and hesitant around her, never sure how she was feeling or how she was going to react. Hoyt remembered times when she would storm into the pharmacy to give Clyde a "dressing down, embarassing Duke and Doc in front of everybody." She insisted that Duke take little Bobby along whenever he left the house to play with his friends. "When we were ten, Bobby was only five," Hoyt recalled, "and when we were fifteen Bobby was only ten. He was always too little. And if Bobby was ever unhappy or crying, she immediately blamed Duke for it. You could tell Duke often hated having to bring Bobby along, but he kept his mouth shut. He was not about to cross his mother." Not surprisingly Duke was reluctant to bring friends home or even to play in the yard unless Clyde was there. "She would get mad for no apparent reason," Hoyt remembered.17

Under the best of circumstances, adolescence is difficult, but rather than wallow in unhappiness, Duke began to reveal the drive and resources that would power his career. Between the part-time jobs and community activities, and later high school, Duke became the busiest teenager in Glendale. Molly wanted him out earning money, and Clyde wanted him busy enough to stay out of trouble. Clyde also wanted his boy involved in respectable, middle-class pursuits that would put him in touch with important people and their children. But most important, the boy himself wanted mainly to be out of the house. As long as he was working or going to meetings, he was insulated from his mother's wrath. In those formal settings he was also free of his little brother. Years later Duke remarked that the "biggest trial of my young life was shepherding my little brother around. Wherever I went, Bob had to follow." But not, thankfully, to the Boy Scouts or YMCA. Those groups had age limits. Gradually Duke discovered something in these gatherings that had been suppressed at home: He was smart, talented, and popular.18

As a city of recently uprooted midwestern farm families who found urban life at once delightful and unsettling, Glendale was an ideal setting for the Boy

Scouts and the YMCA. The unprecedented growth during the first three decades of the twentieth century created the need for a formal way to instill stable and traditional values. The Boy Scouts and YMCA, both organized in Great Britain in the nineteenth century as training institutions for the youth who would later populate the clubs of the aristocratic "ruling class" of the British Empire, had become in the United States ideal institutions for middle-class men to express patriotism, individualism, and voluntarism. Boy Scouting had been especially popular in the Midwest, and it was an organization Clyde Morrison supported wholeheartedly. In 1919, when he was twelve years old, Duke joined Troop Four of the Boy Scouts and started attending YMCA activities. He was a serious Boy Scout, still active in the troop four years later. He went on the campouts and summer camps, learned to tie knots, recited the Scout Oath and Scout Law, completed the skills requirements, earned the merit badges, conducted the service projects, and advanced through the ranks of Tenderfoot, Second Class, and First Class. Perhaps the only surprise on the future John Wayne's résumé is that he did not make Eagle Scout. He was part of the Boy Scouts "Bicycle Battalion," a bike drill and military group that went on extended trips and engaged in competitive races. On March 9, 1920, Duke received his first newspaper notice. The *Glendale Evening News* reported that "Marion Morrison got the thumb of his left hand caught between the chain and sprocket wheel of his bicycle last Saturday while tuning it up for practice on the boys speedway at the corner of Hawthorne and Central Avenue. He hoped to enter the races. The flesh was badly lacerated and the joint spread somewhat, necessitating the care of a surgeon."[19]

The Young Men's Christian Association (YMCA) first came to Glendale in 1919 and Duke joined immediately. Although the YMCA's program was less formal than that of the Boy Scouts, it nevertheless provided some structure and an outlet. The YMCA's focus was athletic; it sponsored basketball and baseball teams, took the boys on weekend trips and more extended camping during the summer and spring breaks, and gave them opportunities for swimming and boating. The YMCA sponsors would drive the boys down to Long Beach, put them on a boat, and sail them across the twenty-mile channel to Catalina Island. On those trips Duke acquired a love for the sea that lasted throughout his life.[20]

As if these organizations were not enough, the Masonic Lodges in Glendale established a De Molay chapter in the summer of 1922. The De Molay fraternity was founded in 1919 in Kansas City, Missouri, by Frank S. Land, a Freemason concerned about encouraging the "development of good citizenship and character among youth." At the time the United States was caught up in its first Red Scare, one that has been overshadowed by Joe McCarthy and the early Cold War; but at the time, in the wake of Lenin's astonishing ascent to the helm of one of the largest and most powerful nations on earth, the first was terrifying. Many Americans worried about the erosion of their values. Each De Molay chapter had to be sponsored by a Masonic Lodge, and only boys whose fathers were Masons could join. De Molay emphasized what it called the seven "jewels" in the "Crown of Youth": filial love, reverence for sacred things, courtesy, comradeship, fidelity, cleanliness, and patriotism. From its inception De Molay was overtly anticommunist. It sponsored service projects, vocational guidance, speech contests, and teenage safety instruction for boys. When the local Masons started a De Molay chapter in Glendale in 1922, Clyde made sure that Duke was inducted and that he attended the weekly meetings at the Masonic Temple. From the time he was fourteen, Duke consumed a steady diet of anticommunist rhetoric at those meetings, rhetoric that hardened into convictions. In California the midwestern Scotch-Irish Morrison values were thus transformed into all-American values by the Boy Scouts, the YMCA, and De Molay.[21]

By the time he was fourteen years old, Duke was spending 95 percent of his waking moments away from home. He would get up before dawn and ride his bicycle to the corner of Broadway and South Maryland to roll and tie the newspapers. The route took him up and down several miles of Glendale streets before he headed home for breakfast. After a full day in school, he then headed for the Glendale Pharmacy to make deliveries. He went to Boy Scout meetings on Tuesday nights, YMCA on Wednesday nights, and De Molay on Thursday nights. Every other weekend there was some Boy Scout campout or YMCA excursion on the calendar. On those weekends when he was not out with the scouts or the YMCA, he was usually working at the pharmacy, distributing handbills, or doing odd jobs.

There were other ways of getting out of the house as well, of escaping into a fantasy land where life seemed simpler, issues clearer-cut, people easier to figure out. Glendale has, and has had for the last eighty years, one of the finest public libraries in the country. Duke was bright; he could read before he went to school. And he loved to read: "I became a confirmed reader when I was growing up in Glendale," he told a reporter in 1972. "I've loved reading all my life." He would check books out to bring them home, but he also spent hours reading in the solitude of the library, losing himself and his troubles in romantic adventure novels like *Ivanhoe*, *The Last of the Mohicans*, and *Robin-*

son Crusoe. Biography intrigued him—the stories of heroic men, George Washington, Abraham Lincoln, John Paul Jones, Kit Carson, Buffalo Bill Cody, George Rogers Clark, and Jim Bridger, men who triumphed over long odds and made a place for themselves in the world and in history. He also became an avid reader of Zane Grey's Western novels.[22]

There was also the magic of movies which attracted his attention as he got older. Inside the theaters Duke watched mythical heroes act out morality plays, with good triumphing over evil, and patriotism, competition, and individualism prevailing in every encounter. Glendale was a great place to watch movies. The Glendale Theater was built on West Fourth Street in 1910, and four years later Jensen's Palace Grand Theater, complete with "opera chairs, [an] asbestos and iron-lined projection room, and a motion picture machine," went up at 319 South Brand. The new Glendale Theater was constructed at 124 South Grand in 1920, and Duke went as often as he could. "My folks always let me go to the movies every Saturday," he recalled years later. "We were really motion-picture goers. In those days, it was the most inexpensive entertainment in the country; movies cost about ten cents and the Saturday afternoon show was a nickel."[23]

Many times during junior high and high school, he escaped to the cool, dark theaters, alone, to watch and dream. "Movies fascinated me," he told an interviewer in 1969. "I went on average, four or five times a week. I used to mimic Douglas Fairbanks. I admired his duelling, stunts, fearlessness and impish grin." The Western was just coming of age. William S. Hart dominated the Western film landscape in the teens and early twenties, rescuing Westerns from the bland mediocrity that had engulfed the genre. He brought to the screen—as an actor, director, and writer—the rugged authenticity of what Americans believed the real West had been like. In *Hell's Hinges* (1916), a classic Western, Tracey (William S. Hart) rides into the town of Hell's Hinges, which has been taken over by a brutal saloon gang. His guns blazing, he restores order so that decent men and women can get on with the work of building lives for their families.

At the same time that William S. Hart was bringing realism to the screen, Tom Mix created a different cowboy hero. Between 1911 and 1917, Tom Mix made seventy-one one- and two-reel Westerns for producer William Selig and gained a following in the South and West. Mix signed with Fox in 1917 and eventually made more than three hundred more films. He eclipsed Hart as the nation's favorite Western star. His clothes were crisp, clean, and freshly pressed. The neckerchief, tied tight and high around his neck, looked decorative, not functional, and his trousers, with the dry cleaner's crease often visible, were tucked into shiny, new boots. His long-sleeved Western shirt sported pearl buttons. The costume was topped off with Mix's gigantic signature cowboy hats. If William S. Hart resembled a real cowboy working cattle in the dusty, dirty Old West, Mix seemed right off a dude ranch. But America loved him.

Other producers and directors turned to Westerns as well. Triangle and Artcraft Studios promoted Douglas Fairbanks Sr. as a Western hero in their movies. In 1923 John Cruze made *The Covered Wagon*, the first epic Western, and a year later John Ford's *The Iron Horse* established him as one of Hollywood's greatest directors. Sitting in those Glendale theaters, Duke also watched the fictional exploits of actors like Hoot Gibson, Dustin Farnum, Rudolph Valentino, and Harry Carey Sr. When Clyde was working for Jensen's Drug Store, the owners let the boy in free whenever he wanted to go to the Palace Grand Theater. He would also ride his bike for miles along the San Fernando Road distributing handbills for the Palace Grand and Glendale Theaters. The pay was all he needed: free admission whenever he wanted to watch a film. When Rudolph Valentino and *The Four Horsemen of the Apocalypse* played the Glendale Theater in the summer of 1921, he watched the movie fourteen times during the week.[24]

But there was more to the movie business than just going to the theater. Filmmakers were shooting movies in Glendale constantly in the early 1900s. The Sierra Photoplays Studio was located at 315 West Chestnut and Kalem Studios was at 400 North Verdugo Road. Other studios in Los Angeles regularly brought their actors and cameras out to Glendale on the Pacific Electric Railway to shoot films in the Verdugo foothills. From the time he was nine years old, Duke spent hours, especially during the summers, at the Kalem Studio lot watching the camermen shoot the films. On lucky days the grips would let him be their gofer, giving him chores to do and then letting him eat a box lunch with them at noon. During World War I, film stars came out to Glendale and gave patriotic speeches urging Americans to buy war bonds. The kids often went over to a vacant lot on Louise Street to "play movies," creating their own dramas, operating a makeshift wooden camera, and pretending to be Douglas Fairbanks, Tom Mix, or Rudolph Valentino. In 1921, as one of his ongoing stunts to promote Glendale nationally, Leslie Brand, a local real estate developer, sponsored America's first "fly-in" lunch, in which prominent people, especially film stars, flew private planes into Glendale to dine. It was one of the biggest events of the year in Glendale and made the national newspapers as well as the theater newsreels.[25]

Duke frequently retreated into a fantasy world of books and movies, but he did not live there nor grow up an introvert. His feet were firmly planted on the ground, and he gradually discovered that success in the outside world compensated at least partially for emptiness and insecurity inside. He yearned to have his father's assets—an understanding nature and the ability to make friends—without Clyde's undeniable liability: an inability to succeed financially. Duke loved his father deeply and felt loved unconditionally by him. A childhood friend of Duke's remembered, "Even as a teenager, Duke was not afraid to greet his father with a hug and kiss. They were very close." He forgave Clyde his weaknesses, but he had no desire to become a carbon copy of his old man. He sought success and recognition, not a happy-go-lucky series of failures.[26]

He loved his mother in an abstract way; children are supposed to love their mothers, but she frightened him. Duke admired her toughness, honesty, and spunk, but he wanted none of Molly's bad-tempered capriciousness and irrational dislikes. It is overwhelmingly clear that Duke yearned for acceptance, and since it was not naturally forthcoming from Molly, the only way to get it was to earn it—to prove to his mother that he could do what Clyde had failed to do. Meanwhile, while Duke was doing all the right things in life, his brother Bobby was checking out, missing more and more school, getting poor grades, drinking, refusing to earn his own money—acting out a script that could have been written by Clyde. Nevertheless, in her convoluted way, Molly attached herself to Bobby, the boy most like the husband she despised, and ignored Duke, the son who worked so hard at being a "good boy."

Although Duke never satisfied Molly, most other people took to him easily. He impressed and attracted the people with whom he came in contact. When Duke entered Glendale Union High School as a freshman in 1921, he found an acceptance and popularity that had escaped him at home. Early-twentieth-century America enshrined good looks, casual gentility, intelligence, and athletic prowess, and Duke had more than his share of all four.

When he started high school, he was nearly six feet tall and weighed about 135 pounds. He was thin but no longer "skinny," with piercing blue eyes, a shock of dark hair he combed straight back, and, as schoolmate Ruth Conrad remembered, a smile that had "a funny little way of twisting his mouth up in one corner." Mildred Power used to "stand outside the fence on East Broadway, where they put up a makeshift netball basket and the gang used to practice shots. Duke was the tallest and most handsome thing you ever saw. I was in awe." Dorothy Hacker, another schoolgirl friend, recalled years later: "I don't think it's possible to realize from watching his movies how absolutely stunningly handsome he was then. His looks alone would stop traffic. He was about the handsomest young man that ever walked on two legs."[27]

Duke showed little interest in girls, however. More often than he could remember, Molly had accused Clyde of flirting with the women who came into the stores, so Duke did not want to flirt. He was uncomfortable around females. Undoubtedly irascibility had something to do with it; all his life he acted as if the safest thing to do was maintain some emotional distance from women, even the ones he liked. The popular high school girls wanted to date him—some prayed for dates with him—but as Dorothy Hacker remembered, "Believe it or not, he was very bashful with girls in high school. He was very popular, but as far as I know he didn't date in those days." Actually there were a few dates. He would occasionally drive a girl over to the Tam-o-Shanter Inn, a drive-in hamburger joint on Los Feliz Boulevard, and then go to a movie, but he preferred group dates or just going with a bunch of guys down to the La Monica Ballroom in Ocean Park to dance with young women they met there. Duke's relationships with schoolgirls were characterized by genuine politeness, impeccable manners, and a prudent caution.[28]

Students and teachers also remembered him as being very friendly, but careful and judicious with most people. After a steady diet of arguments, Duke could not stand conflict, arguing, or verbal battles. All his life he had watched Molly openly vent every frustration regardless of the circumstance, while Clyde stifled his feelings in a futile attempt to keep the peace. He had seen too many arguments started and too few resolved. Duke grew up suspicious of people who talked too much, who "aired their dirty laundry" when silence would have been more appropriate. And he could not abide bullies. Archie Neel, one of Duke's classmates in Glendale, remembered him as a "nice-looking, clean-cut, All-American boy. Everybody liked him. He always took care of the underdog. He either stopped fights or took over for the little guy." Ralph "Pexy" Eckles, a close friend, said that Duke "was never in trouble and was not looking for it." Norm Nelson played football with Duke at Glendale. "He was a great guy," Nelson recalled in 1979. "I thought a lot of him. He was one of the popular fellows, but not the least bit uppish. He was very friendly. . . . I never knew him to be mean or nasty with people."[29]

Actually Duke was a far more guarded, private person than anybody except his closest friends realized. As a teenager he developed a public persona—displayed in front of parents, adults, and casual acquaintances—that seemed conservative, serious, quiet, mature, reserved, and anxious to please. Bob Hatch, who served on the student council with Duke at Glendale, remembered him as "mature and conservative. He had a confidence and maturity that most of us didn't have. . . . He was a good leader." Beneath that well-behaved exterior, however, was a different person who revealed himself only to his closest, most trusted friends. This side was more of a typical teenager, spending nights drinking rotgut Prohibition liquor with friends and ending the occasion by driving them to their homes. He had a sense of humor that manifested itself in practical jokes, whether it was contaminating the chemistry lab with hydrogen sulfide or pelting streetcars with eggs and tomatoes. During the course of his life, the huge gap between his public and private personas gradually narrowed. Years later, when the John Wayne screen persona—the hell-raising, masculine individualist who was polite with but distant from women, socially liberal, and politically conservative—reached its fullest expression, close friends recognized it immediately as quintessentially Duke Morrison. After Duke's death in 1979, Archie Neel remarked that he "always acted natural, walked slow, talked slow. His motion picture career was like his life. . . . I don't think he's ever had to act—he's just been playing himself all these years."[30]

There was more to Duke than good looks and a pleasant disposition. From the time he was in grammar school he impressed teachers not just with the quality of his mind but with his work habits. At the graduation ceremonies at Wilson Intermediate School in 1921, teachers selected him to give the valedictory remarks, and he expounded on the evils of World War I. At Glendale Union High School, he was on the fast track, taking every college preparatory class offered, including algebra, geometry, trigonometry, calculus, chemistry, biology, physics, and Latin. Park Turril, who taught chemistry at Glendale, said Duke was "a fine student. He did fine work, understood write-ups and never complained. He got A's all the way through." He headed the school's debate team, won honors pins several years in a row, played an aggressive game of chess, was all but unbeatable at bridge and hearts because of an uncanny ability to count cards, and graduated with a four-year average of ninety-four, the salutatorian in a class of two hundred students.[31]

Finally, he excelled in football, at a time in the 1920s when Americans were first becoming captivated by the game. As a halfback at the University of Illinois, Harold "Red" Grange, the "Galloping Ghost," captured national attention in 1923, 1924, and 1925 and put college and professional football on the map. Glendale was caught up in the mania. When Duke tried to make the flyweight team as a freshman, he weighed too much, even after several weeks of drinking a diet beverage called "Pluto." As a sophomore he played on the Midgets, the lightweight team, but in the spring of 1923 he started

putting on some weight, getting up to 155 pounds, and in the fall he attracted regional attention as a left guard. Glendale played Long Beach for the state
championship in 1923, when Duke was a junior, losing by a score of 15 to 8,
but a sportswriter wrote that "Morrison was supposed to be opposite the best
prep guard in Southern California. If he was, Morrison has established the
right to that title, for he made that jackrabbit look like a fuzzy bunny." By the
opening of the 1924 season, when he was a senior, Duke had grown to nearly
six feet three inches and 175 pounds, with most of the weight gain in his
upper body. He was just as quick as before but much stronger. Glendale won
the state championship in 1924, and college recruiters took a close look at
Duke Morrison.[32]

All his life he enjoyed football, first as a player and then as a fan. But even
in high school it was probably more than just a game for him. Perhaps it was
another psychological strategy to prove himself, and not simply because of the
popularity that came from being a first-stringer on a state championship high
school team. In Glendale, Duke was smart and good-looking, but he also
knew that he came from the lower rungs of society, that his home life was a
mess, and that people talked about his father, his mother, and his family. Over
the years there had been too many public arguments, unpaid bills, eviction
notices, moves, and job changes. The Morrisons were not part of the "better
half." But most of Duke's friends in high school belonged to the elite of the
community. Their fathers had good jobs, and their families lived in the best
homes. Football was a great equalizer. The line of scrimmage was the most
democratic arena on earth, one of the few places where ability, and ability
alone, prevailed. Head to head, one on one, the best man prevailed, every
time. Years later, when a journalist asked him if football really prepared a boy
for life, Duke responded: "Do you know a better way to learn to respect
someone than to have him across the line of scrimmage from you? Do you
think the color of your skin or the amount of your father's property or your
social position helps you there?"[33]

Football, scholastics, good looks, and personality made Duke the most
popular student at Glendale Union High School. Students elected him vice
president of the freshman class and a member of the student council during
his sophomore year. But by the time he was a junior, Duke's home life was out
of control. He had outgrown the Boy Scouts and the YMCA. High school
was another escape, a new way of avoiding Molly and Bobby and earning
some respect, and he approached it like a job. During the 1923–24 school
year, Duke worked on the advertising staff for the yearbook, *Stylus*, selling

space to local businessmen. He was again elected to the student council, as junior representative; had small roles in two dramatic productions; worked on the stage crew that presented the monthly films, and served as a member of the Roll Room Council. Students elected him president of the senior class in 1924 and inducted him into the Boys "G" Club. He served as sports editor of the student newspaper and chaired the senior dance committee.[34]

Somehow he *also* managed to keep working several part-time jobs, using the family car before his parents got up to deliver the *Los Angeles Examiner* in the mornings, and after football practice making deliveries for Jensen's Drug Store. In addition, on afternoons and weekends, he got a job hauling large blocks of ice around town to businesses and homes for their coolers. Between the morning newspaper route, school classes, football practice, pharmacy and ice deliveries, school extracurricular activities, and studying at the library, he was able to avoid home, and that suited him just fine. At the age of seventeen he was a workaholic. He remained one the rest of his life. Outside home he found happiness, then and forever.

Early in his senior year, Clyde started making college plans for Duke. The family had a high regard for education, and Clyde told his son over and over again that the only way to make it in modern America was to get a degree. For a poor family in the early 1920s, however, college was a distant dream. The idea of higher education as a democratic birthright was a phenomenon of the post–World War II era, when the GI Bill sent millions of veterans to school. In 1924 and 1925, when Duke was considering college, there were no Pell Grants, student loans, or work-study programs. Universities were still the province of economic and social elites, with only a few "scholarship boys" allowed. Clyde wanted his son to be one of them, but as a backup he urged him to secure an appointment to one of the military academies. All those YMCA trips to Catalina Island, as well as summer surfing escapades in the Southern California beaches, had deepened his love of the sea, but his decision to try to get into the U.S. Naval Academy was only tangentially connected to the smell of sea breezes. He wanted to be a midshipman for the same reason generations of poor Irish peasant boys had decided to become Roman Catholic priests: It was the only way to get a formal education and escape the circumstances of their births. When the appointment did not come through, Duke was only modestly disappointed.[35]

Fortunately he had another option. President Rufus Bernhard von Klein-Smid of the University of Southern California in Los Angeles was intent on building the school's endowment, and he believed that fielding a nationally ranked football team was one way of doing it. KleinSmid successively hired Elmer C. Henderson and the legendary Howard Jones as head coaches, and both men were determined to build a powerhouse. Duke Morrison fitted into those plans. In the spring of 1925, a few months before high school graduation, USC offered him a football scholarship—which provided enough money to cover tuition and books—and he could work part-time to support himself. His years of hard work had been rewarded. He talked at some length with his father about majors and career choices. After spending ten years in Southern California, Clyde knew that the people who were making money were either selling real estate or handling the transactions through their title companies. A legal career was the ticket to success, and USC had just finished a new building for its law school. Duke Morrison decided to become a USC Trojan, a member of the "Thundering Herd."[36]

3

Scholarship Boy

When Lou Gehrig, the legendary first baseman for the New York Yankees, died of amyotrophic lateral sclerosis on June 2, 1941, America mourned. During the 1920s Gehrig had been a symbol of stability and propriety in a changing world. His record of playing in 2,130 consecutive games seemed unbreakable. Gehrig's life and slow, heroic death quickly became grist for the Hollywood mill. With the Yankee star only freshly buried, Hollywood paid homage to him in *The Pride of the Yankees* (1942). Gary Cooper was cast in the lead. It was a perfect role for the emotionally reserved, laconic Cooper. John Wayne loved the film. One scene was especially powerful and poignant, at least for Duke. Lou Gehrig, the son of German immigrants, was a "scholarship boy" who gained admission to Columbia University because of his brains and in spite of his working-class origins. Gehrig had a baseball scholarship to Columbia, but the grant did not cover all of his expenses, and he had to wait tables in one of the fraternity houses to make ends meet. In the film some of the rich boys in the frat house ridicule Gehrig's background in subtle ways, poking fun at his German accent and servant's clothes. When Wayne saw the scene, he thought of his own years waiting on tables and washing dishes at the Sigma Chi House on the campus of USC. He remembered the sense of shared brotherhood he had enjoyed there, but also the feeling that somehow he was not as good as the rest of them and would never really be part of the club. Baseball rescued Lou Gehrig from what would have been a lifelong struggle to get inside the closed door. Hollywood did the same for John Wayne.[1]

Duke Morrison went to USC on a football scholarship, but in those days there were few full rides. USC tuition was $130 a semester. The scholarship covered tuition and provided one meal a day on weekdays for the players on the regular squad. Eugene Clarke, who played football with Wayne at USC, remembered that "we sort of had to search around for our other meals and all of our meals on weekends. We were always pretty hungry by Monday morning." To make ends meet, Duke took a part-time job at the Sigma Chi house, busing tables and washing dishes. Then, as now, Sigma Chi was known as the fraternity of jocks, rich kids, and party boys, and Duke was accepted as a pledge. He was popular with most of his fraternity brothers, who respected his wit, intellect, and athletic ability. But every morning he served them breakfast, wearing a tight, high-collared white uniform. Most of them acted as if his servant's role and clothes made no difference, but Duke knew better. He was not on the social register. He was still a scholarship boy giving his friends their bacon and eggs in the morning and then washing their dishes.[2]

When Duke enrolled at USC in the fall of 1925, the school was forty-five years old and on the make. The Methodist Church founded USC in 1880, locating the campus west of the original town plaza on Olvera Street. The city of Los Angeles boomed around it, and by 1900 USC, though still at the same site, was downtown. When midwestern immigrants poured into Los Angeles during the first three decades of the twentieth century, USC grew along with the city. Its enrollment jumped from 329 students in 1903 to 4,600 in 1920. But the rapid growth was a mixed blessing. Because USC and the city of Los Angeles were so young and their growth so recent, the university had only limited resources. Alumni in general, let alone active alumni, were few in number, the endowment was under $1 million, and the resources of the Methodist Church did not stretch very far. If the university was to have any chance of achieving greatness, it needed to improve its resource base.[3]

Von KleinSmid became president of USC in 1921 and set out to do just that. Between 1921 and 1928 he gradually secularized the university, severing its connection to the Methodist Church. Pressed for cash themselves, the members of the Methodist Conference went along with his plans. Although he lost some financial support from the church, he compensated by courting real estate developers and oil producers in Southern California. Von Klein-Smid vastly improved the law school and school of international affairs, established a medical school, built graduate programs in arts and sciences, and developed outstanding programs in social work, architecture, business, and engineering. He cultivated friends in the best and highest places of Los Angeles society and business, giving USC an elitist WASP respectability. Woody Strode, a black athlete from UCLA who played professional football and went on to a film career, wrote that USC in the 1920s and 1930s "was the biggest, richest, most popular school . . . so for a kid to go there he had to have either parents with a lot of money or tremendous athletic ability."[4]

College football, beginning in the 1920s, proved to be a cash cow for schools like USC, a way of raising money, generating enthusiastic community support, and binding together students, faculty, and alumni—albeit on a much smaller scale than in the television era. Von KleinSmid was influenced by Knute Rockne at Notre Dame. Rockne took over as head football coach at Notre Dame in 1918, and by the 1920s he was the most famous coach in the country. He put Notre Dame on the cultural map of the United States, helping to complete the small Roman Catholic university's move from obscurity to fame. Knute Rockne and Notre Dame football epitomized the old frontier values of hard work, individual effort, teamwork, dedication, and success. Football also put Notre Dame in the black financially during the 1920s.[5]

Von KleinSmid planned to do for USC what Knute Rockne had done for Notre Dame. In 1919 Elmer C. Henderson had been named as head coach, and the next year the Trojans managed to get into the Pacific Coast Conference. In 1922 Henderson took them to the Rose Bowl, where they defeated Penn State and became the sports talk of the town. Two years later KleinSmid hired Howard Jones as head coach, and the team went undefeated. KleinSmid and Jones then hit on a brainstorm: Match USC up with Notre Dame and create the greatest rivalry in sports. They did. A USC–Notre Dame rivalry pitted East against West, Catholic against Protestant, wet against dry, and Democrat against Republican. It was a perfect match. The Fighting Irish came out to Los Angeles for the last game of the 1926 season, filling the Rose Bowl with more than 100,000 people and defeating USC 13 to 12. In 1927 Notre Dame and USC played before 114,000 people at Soldier Field in Chicago. The Trojans lost 7–6. By that time USC football was so popular that season tickets were practically impossible to come by. Loew's State Theater in Los Angeles ran some of the game films as second features. KleinSmid tripled the endowment between 1921 and 1927, and enrollment jumped from 4,600 to 9,000. USC was on its way to becoming a major university.[6]

Duke Morrison played a part, albeit a small one, in von KleinSmid's grand design for his university. During the summer of 1925 Duke went through another growth spurt, shooting up to six feet four inches and adding another twenty pounds. His shoulders broadened and chest expansion increased. When he showed up in August for the preseason workouts on the Trojan freshman team, he was taller than anyone else on the squad. Howard Jones immediately moved him from guard to tackle. It was a long time from early August to October 3, when the frosh played their first game. Freshmen college players have to unlearn bad high school habits, and Howard Jones worked those habits out of them with a vengeance. The two-a-day drills in August were brutal, especially after the Santa Ana winds started blowing desert air into the Los Angeles Basin, raising temperatures into the 90s for several weeks in a row and forcing the players to deal with dehydration as well as Jones's legendary temper. (Those were the days when it was considered an unmanly act to drink water during practice.) But the hard work paid off. The freshmen Trojans went undefeated in seven games, outscoring their opponents 261 to 20. Duke played enough to win a freshman letter and catch the eye of Jones, who was already making plans for the 1926 season.[7]

By temperament and design USC was a midwestern Protestant school. Students and faculty were overwhelmingly Protestant and Republican. Next to the campus, the Southern California Masons had constructed the huge Shrine Civic Auditorium. The Greek fraternities and sororities were the campus equivalents of the Masons, DeMolay, Eastern Star, Elks, and Moose. President von KleinSmid spent USC money on football and academics; there was not enough money left over to build dormitories on campus, so he encouraged the development of fraternities and sororities. Social events revolved around the Greek social calendar, as did the intramural sports program and extracurricular events. The vast majority of USC students commuted to school by automobile and were not accepted as pledges, which virtually froze them out of nonacademic campus activities. To attend school dances or play softball, students had to be Greeks.[8]

Duke had a good year academically and socially. He took the standard prelaw curriculum, won academic honors, became a leader of the freshman debate team, and pledged the most popular fraternity on campus. At USC in the 1920s, Sigma Chi was inhabited by rich, handsome young men and athletes. Duke took the fraternity, and its sense of brotherhood, quite seriously. Sigma Chi became the first real family he had ever had, an all-male community in which he did not have to worry about what a woman thought about him and was free to be himself, at least up to a point. For the first time in his life, he had a place to go at night where he felt comfortable and relaxed. And for the rest of his life, when Duke met someone who had been in the fraternity, he would give them the secret Sigma Chi handshake-grip.[9]

After the end of the football season, one of Duke's Sigma Chi brothers got him to agree to a blind date with Polly Ann Belzer, the older sister of Gretchen Belzer, who would soon be known to movie audiences as Loretta Young. Polly was a student at the Ramona Convent, an exclusive Catholic boarding school in Alhambra, out in the San Fernando Valley. This blind date led to another, with Carmen Saenz, one of Polly's school friends. Duke, Carmen, and several other couples went down to the Rendezvous Ballroom in Balboa, near present-day Newport Beach, and when they returned to the Saenz home, Duke met Carmen's younger sister Josephine and was immediately infatuated. They began seeing each other regularly. For Duke she was the perfect opposite of his mother. Molly was impatient, capricious, quick to anger, and viciously outspoken. Josie was beautiful, dignified, intelligent, and blessed with a sense of discipline and self-control. She measured her words carefully, attended Mass regularly, and moved comfortably in Los Angeles high society. She was the daughter of a prominent Southern California businessman. She was self-confident but at the same time seemed comfortable with the role assigned to her by Hispanic and Roman Catholic culture, in which men were accorded obedience and respect.[10]

The Saenz family were Hispanic bluebloods. Although the Spanish-speaking *Californios* had lost most of their land during the mass migration of Anglos in the nineteenth century, certain Hispanic families in Southern California were still widely recognized as Social Register types and enjoyed the respect of the Anglo elite. Such families as the Sepulvedas, Verdugos, and Figueroas maintained influence in Los Angeles, and when Dr. José Saenz and his family moved there on the eve of World War I, they fitted into upper-class culture. The Saenzes had immigrated to the United States from Spain in the early 1880s; José Saenz earned a medical degree but eventually branched out into business, establishing a chain of successful pharmacies in the Southwest. In 1921 several Caribbean and Latin American countries—including Haiti, Panama, Dominican Republic, and El Salvador—retained him as their consul for Los Angeles.[11]

Like so many upper-class Hispanics in the Southwest, the Saenzes described themselves as "Spanish Americans" rather than "Mexican Americans." Aware of the American prejudice against Mexicans, they distanced themselves from the *mestizo* progeny of Spaniards and Indians. Ever since the 1890s, when poor Mexican immigrants began arriving in the Southwest, the older Hispanic residents felt the need to distinguish themselves from the newcomers, and Anglo society acknowledged the perceived differences. They nurtured a sense of "pure" origins and hoped Anglos would continue to distinguish between them and the others. When José Saenz and his family arrived in Los Angeles, the local elite accepted them as social equals.[12]

The Saenzes were also devout Roman Catholics. In the Spanish colonial empire, the church was responsible for the moral and spiritual guidance of the people, but the Catholic clergy were under the political control of the Spanish crown. Highly dependent on the governing classes, the church became a conservative force closely identified with the interests of the elite. Far more so than the lower classes, upper-class Catholics in the Southwest attended Mass regularly, contributed financially to the church, gave their children parochial school educations, and sent boys into the priesthood. They accepted the importance of internal faith as well as external observances of piety. Priests were permanent fixtures in the Saenz home, eating dinner there regularly, accompanying the family on vacations and weekend trips, and offering counsel and support during family emergencies. The Saenz children attended parochial school.[13]

When Duke met Josie's parents, he knew enough about the pharmacy business to make polite conversation, but the family immediately had misgivings about the relationship. Part of the problem was the youngsters' age. Duke was a nineteen-year-old college student; she was only sixteen. The Saenzes worried about the difference. Each time Josie returned to the Ramona Convent after weekend trips home or vacations, they felt relieved, knowing Duke would not be able to see her there. José Saenz was also concerned about Duke's background. The *Social Register* was Saenz's bible, and he expected his daughters to marry equals—young men from the best Southern California families. Duke Morrison was not even from a "good" family. He was a scholarship boy from a poor family, and he washed dishes at the Sigma Chi house. Added to José's worries was the fact that the Morrison marriage was in distress and headed for divorce. To the Saenzes, bad marriages and divorces were among the most offensive moral issues, proof that the parties involved lacked breeding, self-discipline, spirituality, and religious commitment. From the moment Josie told her parents about Clyde and Molly, Duke was suspect in their eyes. And, of course, the religious issue loomed large for them. From their earliest years all three of the Saenz children heard repeatedly that God, the church, and the family expected them to marry other Catholics and raise their children within the faith. Duke was a Protestant, and not a very religious one at that. "In their opinion," Pilar Wayne later wrote, "he had no breeding, no money, and no prospects." Duke later told Mary St. John, "They were good people, but they never really accepted me. Being around them was like being around my mother. I was always ill at ease."[14]

Duke harbored prejudices of his own, biting animosities that shaped his behavior. The Saenzes were registered members of the *Los Angeles Blue Book* who danced at the Ambassador Club, dined at the Little Club and finest restaurants, attended consulate parties, and staged coming-out balls for their daughters. Even at home they were thoroughly conscious of etiquette—dressing for dinner and meticulously observing the niceties of polite conversation. And nothing social happened at the Saenz home without the presence of Roman Catholic priests, who were practically members of the family. When he was with Josie's family, Duke had to put on his proper face—the soft spoken, polite, deferential, hardworking successful-young-man image that had so endeared him to students and teachers back in Glendale and that he had thought for so long might please his parents, especially his mother, and help him get ahead in life. At the time that persona occupied a prominent place in Duke's makeup. As a USC prelaw student, he was preparing for a lifetime of interacting with people like Dr. José Saenz and decades of being on his best behavior, rubbing shoulders with the leaders of Los Angeles, preparing to become part of the WASP east-side establishment.

Yet, at a deeper level, he rejected the very establishment he yearned to join. There was an increasing tension between the "good boy" persona and the laughing, hard-drinking, hell-raiser at Sigma Chi who just wanted to be himself. The tension was magnified by an east-west split in the city itself. By the mid-1920s the real political and economic power center in Los Angeles was in the downtown area, in the San Fernando Valley, and out to the east in Glendale and Pasadena. The old money in Los Angeles was bound up in land and railroads; the power brokers were conservative Republican Protestants who read Harry Chandler's *Los Angeles Times*. They wanted to create Los Angeles in their own image and spent their lives bringing water in from the Owens Valley and the Colorado River and filling the Los Angeles Basin with automobiles, highways, and single-family homes.[15]

Over on the west side of town, however, another power center was just emerging, and it revolved around the film colony. The leaders of West Los Angeles, Beverly Hills, Santa Monica, and Hollywood were more likely to be liberal than conservative, Democratic than Republican, and Jewish and Catholic than Protestant. They considered the east-siders staid, straitlaced, and bigoted. The east-siders, for their part, saw Hollywood as a dark, greasy, radical, exotic place threatening to blacken their image of sunny California. The USC campus was just south of downtown, right on the border between the east and west sides of the city, between the old and the new money. When Wayne went to USC in the fall of 1925, he traveled the ten miles or so southwest out of Glendale to the frontier of a brave new world.

In the summer of 1926, Duke crossed that frontier. Seats at the USC home games were the hottest-selling ones in town, and Tom Mix, the famous star of so many Hollywood Westerns, wanted his own personal box at the Coliseum. He approached Howard Jones, the USC football coach, and Jones struck a bargain with him: If Mix would agree to put some USC football players on Fox Studio payrolls during the summer, he would see to it that the star had his own personal cluster of box seats. Mix agreed immediately, and in June 1926 Jones made sure that Duke Morrison, one of his most promising sophomores, got one of the summer jobs. Duke went to work for the Fox Studio on Western Avenue for thirty-five dollars a week.[16]

A decade and a half earlier there had been no Hollywood. Then came the Jewish producers—Adolph Zukor, William Fox, Louis B. Mayer, Samuel Goldwyn, Carl Laemmle, Harry Cohn, Joseph Schenck, and the Warner brothers—fleeing the restraints of Edison's film trust and their own origins. They were short—the overused joke in Hollywood was that you could swing a scythe five-and-a-half feet from the floor and not touch a hair on the head of one of them—and ambitious. Most had come to the United States from Eastern Europe, still spoke with thick accents, and worked in sales before turning to the infant film industry. Some had sold furs or clothing or gloves or ice cream; others had been junk dealers or peddlers or had operated vaudeville shows and amusement parks. In the film industry, and especially in Hollywood, they found respectability, money, and power.[17]

Between 1910 and 1927, the movie industry mushroomed in the United States. Major studios—Metro-Goldwyn-Mayer, Universal, Fox, RKO, and Paramount—began to produce full-length, high-budget motion pictures, appealing to a more affluent, middle-class audience than had the cheaper one reelers. By 1920 there were 20,000 theaters in the United States, and that number grew to 28,000 in 1929. In the cities, new theaters dubbed "palaces" seated from 1,000 to 2,000 people in luxurious splendor. Actors and actresses like Charlie Chaplin, Buster Keaton, Fatty Arbuckle, William S. Hart, Gloria Swanson, Mary Pickford, Greta Garbo, Rudolph Valentino, Clara Bow, Tom

Mix, Theda Bara, and Douglas Fairbanks became household figures, familiar to millions. The cultural impact of movies was enormous. Back in the late nineteenth century, with great waves of immigration, American culture had begun to divide along ethnic and regional lines. Mass entertainment no longer consisted of band concerts in the town park. Ethnic theaters, foreign-language newspapers, regional and ethnic dialects, and local legends and heroes had proliferated widely. But Hollywood reversed the trend. All over the country Americans attended the same movies, watched the same stars, laughed at the same gags, and listened to the same theater music. Vaudeville and the ethnic theaters rapidly declined, giving way to a new mass culture.[18]

Hollywood was also pushing the boundaries of moral acceptability, rejecting Victorian values and worshiping at the altar of individual freedom and expression. In the 1920s, Hollywood came to symbolize all that was wrong with modern America—the embodiment of materialism, uninhibited sexuality, divorce, and instability. Gossip columnists, radio soap operas, fan magazines, and the establishment press headlined the escapades of the stars. Clara Bow, "the It Girl," was the premier flapper of the 1920s, portraying a liberated woman who smoked, drank, caroused, and rejected the repressed Victorian code and manners. Theda Bara, "the Vamp," often issued publicity photos showing her as a pallid woman, peering out of heavily darkened eyes, with the skeleton of a man lying at her feet. Fatty Arbuckle's name was plastered on the front pages of newspapers around the country in 1921, when he allegedly raped and then killed Virginia Rappe with a champagne bottle. Arbuckle stood trial three times for the crime. During those trials it became clear that Virginia Rappe had a history of prostitution and had had five abortions between the ages of fourteen and sixteen. The first two juries could not reach a verdict, and the third acquitted Arbuckle, but by that time his career was ruined. Rudolph Valentino's purported sexual exploits titillated millions of American women.[19]

As a member of the popular USC football team, Duke got a chance to mix occasionally with movie stars. Clara Bow used to hold a party at her home on Bedford Drive for the Trojans each Saturday night after a home game. A few other actresses, such as Joan Crawford and Lina Basquette, were regulars. Duke attended the parties with teammate Lowry McCaslin. "We had a good time," said McCaslin. "But it wasn't *that* exciting." By "*that*" McCaslin was referring to the salacious rumors of *GraphicC*, a quasi-pornographic New York City tabloid, which claimed that Bow had had sex with the entire Trojan football team one Saturday evening in 1926, with Duke one of the young men waiting his turn, and afterward showered them with gold cigarette cases, gold cufflinks, and bootleg booze. Kenneth Anger's *Hollywood Babylon* (1975) further embellished the myth. There *was* plenty of drinking, loud music, and dancing, followed by sunrise swims in the pool, but Clara Bow's biographer denied the rumors: "Her escapades with the U.S.C. football team were not the stuff of legend."[20]

Duke saw through the rumors, but he was fascinated by the way Hollywood managed to stand apart from the existing establishment, by how culturally and personally free the stars had become. He did not like some of the stars' values, but he admired their freedom to behave as they pleased. During his freshman year at USC, he earned pocket money working as an extra. Pexy Eckles, a friend from Glendale and a USC classmate, remembered several jobs they got with MGM. Duke doubled for Francis X. Bushman in *Brown of Harvard*, and he portrayed a spear-carrying guard in *Bardelys the Magnificent*. "Duke and I enjoyed such work," Eckles recalled, "and were grateful for the pay, which was about eight or ten dollars a day—good money back then." Football films were popular in Hollywood. "Nearly all the studios were making them," Eckles went on, "and so were coming over to USC and using students as extras. Duke worked as a football player in several of them." MGM released *Brown of Harvard* and *Bardelys the Magnificent* in the spring of 1926, near the end of Duke's second semester at USC. Duke also worked that semester as an extra in MGM's *Annie Laurie*. Intrigued with the industry, he wangled a screen test at MGM. Iron Eyes Cody, an Indian actor, remembered meeting Wayne in the spring of 1926. "Well, I believe I worked with John Wayne longer than anybody. . . . John Wayne took some tests at MGM and didn't pass."[21]

Duke's real break came a few months later at the Fox Studio. William Fox had the reputation among his peers as the loudest and tallest mogul of them all. An immigrant from Hungary obsessed by success and respectability, he saw early that the film industry could satisfy both his financial and emotional desires. Although he continued to live in the East at Fox Hall, his mansion on Long Island, where he controlled his family and his financial affairs with gothic machinations, Fox built his studio in Hollywood on the corner of Sunset Boulevard and Western Avenue. There his tightfisted production men, Sol Wurtzel and Winfield Sheehan, made profitable movies. And there his gifted directors— John Ford, Howard Hawks, Raoul Walsh, William Wellman, Allan Dwan, and David Butler—made great films. Fox had talent, vision, and money.[22]

When Duke started working at Fox in the summer of 1926, he thought his main duties would be to serve as a trainer to Tom Mix and go on location with him to Colorado to film the *Great K & A Train Robbery*. At the beginning of the summer, "Tom Mix met us at his boxing ring," Duke remembered, "where he was working out. The room was plastered with his pictures. He told us he was gonna make a movie in Colorado and take us along to work out with him and do bits. We got pretty excited. The next day he got his box seats. The day after that I met him driving in the gate [at Fox Studio] and said, 'Good morning, Mr. Mix.' He looked right through me." Mix had talked about having a trainer and keeping himself in shape, even leaving the impression that Duke and some of the other players might get bit parts in the film. But when they got to Colorado, Duke never spoke to the star. He propped the film, and that was it. When Duke arrived back in Hollywood at the end of June 1926, the studio put him to work on a swing gang as a glorified furniture mover. He also moonlighted as an extra in First National's *The Dropkick*.[23]

Abandoned by Mix, Duke soon met a more valuable benefactor. One day John Ford saw Duke working on a set. Ford called out to him, "You one of Howard Jones's bright boys?" Duke said, "Yes," and Ford then said, "Let's see you get down in position." Duke had barely got into a three-point stance before Ford kicked out both of his hands and sent him sprawling in the dirt. Ford laughed and said, "And you call yourself a football player. I'll bet you couldn't even take me out." Duke said, "I'd like to try." In the next ten seconds, Duke ran at Ford, drove his leg into the director's chest, and sent him sprawling. The set was absolutely quiet. Everybody waited for the explosion of Ford's legendary wrath, for Duke to be banished forever from Hollywood. Instead Ford burst out laughing, taking an immediate liking to the young man who would not be intimidated. The encounter changed both of their lives.[24]

Duke lived in Glendale that summer, but not at home. When USC's spring semester ended in June 1926, he left the Sigma Chi house and headed back north to Glendale. There was no homecoming. Duke walked by the last house his family had lived in at 207 West Windsor; another family had already rented it. Molly and Clyde had legally separated on May 1, 1926, officially ending a relationship that had died years before. Both had hoped to keep the marriage together until the kids were grown, but neither of them could stand the misery anymore. They had probably waited too long already. Molly took Bobby, who was just finishing the eighth grade, and moved in with her folks in Los Angeles. Clyde moved to Beverly Hills. Duke had no place to go. Pexy Eckles invited Duke home, and Eckles's parents let him sleep in a room over their garage.[25]

Molly Morrison was forty-one years old in 1926. Her parents were almost eighty and not in the best of health. After more than a decade in California, she was no better off than when she was living with the Browns back in Des Moines in 1914. She had a high school diploma but no real work experience, except for her short term as a telephone operator before meeting Clyde. In a matter of just a few months, she had lost her favorite verbal targets, the two men on whom she had unleashed her frustrations for the previous fifteen years. Clyde and Duke were both out of her life, at least on a daily basis.

Clyde had left Glendale and rented a room near the Beverly Hills electrical supply store where he found a job. Getting work as a druggist was not as easy as it used to be. More pharmacists had graduated in recent years, and Clyde's résumé, with so many job and residence changes, scared off most prospective employers. Nor was his health good. The asthma or tuberculosis that had driven him from Iowa to California in 1914 had become a heart disease. He complained frequently of being short of breath and feeling weak. To maintain the facade of a possible reconciliation, Molly and Clyde were slow to file formal divorce papers. Divorce, which still carried a powerful social stigma, was legally complicated in the 1920s, although that stopped fewer and fewer couples. There was a minimum waiting period of one year before the law recognized any divorce as final. In 1880 there had been only one divorce for every twenty-one marriages in the United States; in 1900 one of every twelve marriages ended in divorce and in 1920 one in nine. Clergymen and social commentators decried the "decline in American morality," citing these statistics and urging Americans to reform their ways. Actually, the rise in divorce had little to do with morality and much to do with expanding economic opportunities for women, who were entering the workforce at a rapid rate. On February 13, 1929, Clyde and Molly at last filed the necessary papers.[26]

During the next year, while waiting for the divorce to become final, mutual friends introduced Clyde to Florence Buck, a twenty-nine-year-old divorcée who worked at Webb's Department Store in Glendale. Florence had a young daughter, Nancy. Florence appeared to be everything that Molly was not, and Clyde was enchanted with her. She had a pleasant, engaging personality and an easy smile, and she thought Clyde was the kindest, most understanding man she had ever met. Several weeks after Clyde's divorce became final in February 1930, they married. After kissing his new bride at the wedding ceremony, Clyde had turned to little Nancy, knelt, embraced her, and whispered into her ear, "I will always love you as my one and only daughter." Florence and Nancy moved in with Clyde in Beverly Hills.

For Clyde the difference between marriage to Florence instead of Molly was like that between night and day. He was happy at home and brought his drinking under control. After he remarried Clyde rarely had more than a small glass of wine for dinner. Because of the depression, finding and keeping work was hard, and in 1931 he lost his job at the electrical supply store. With commercial and residential construction at a standstill, his job as a retail salesman was expendable. Florence managed to get her old job back at Webb's, and the Morrisons returned to Glendale, renting a house at 227 North Cedar. After a few more months out of work, Clyde secured a retail sales job at a local paint store, but it did not last long. In 1932 they moved to Santa Barbara, where he tried his hand again at pharmacy. The business did not prosper, and they returned to Beverly Hills in 1935.[27]

In spite of the financial setbacks, Clyde was happy. Florence continued to consider him a kind and gentle man. She was a patient, upbeat woman who enjoyed people and treated him with devotion and respect. Each evening when he got home from work, the family enjoyed dinner together, and Clyde would sit on the couch next to Nancy and do crossword puzzles with her or read to her. Florence and Nancy brought out the best in him, the part Duke had always seen but his mother had forgotten. Without the need to escape from Molly's moods, Clyde became a success at home and at work, in spite of his heart problems. He managed a paint store in Beverly Hills and became a popular figure in the local business community, serving as president of the Beverly Hills Lions Club in 1936 and 1937.[28]

Duke would eventually come to love Florence as a stepmother and accept the divorce as good for both of his parents, but 1926 was a very complicated crossroads. His family dissolved, he worked full-time at Fox, and he met John Ford. Ever since he was a kid, Duke had loved the ocean, and on weekends during the summer of 1926, when he was not working at Fox, he frequently headed to the beaches south of Los Angeles. Duke and his friends would go in somebody's car or just hitchhike. Some days they would drive to Redondo Beach or Santa Monica; others, they headed southeast, sometimes sleeping overnight at a place called "Tin Can Beach," between Seal Beach and Huntington Beach. They loved to bodysurf, and the waves along much of the Southern California coast were ideal for it, curling and breaking relatively close to shore in four to five feet of water. But occasionally the waves were violent and unpredictable. One day, just a week before summer football workouts started at USC, Duke was showing off for some college coeds on the beach, and he caught a wave too late. Instead of gliding down its front, he was thrown around uncontrollably in the breaking foam and went crashing to the bottom, probably breaking his collarbone and separating his right shoulder. The next morning he could barely lift his arm.[29]

For interior linemen, shoulder injuries are catastrophic. When summer drills started a week later, Duke tried to use his right shoulder, but the pain was excruciating. Coach Howard Jones noticed right away that Duke was hesitating on the blocking dummies and even avoiding use of the injured right shoulder by contorting himself to use his left. According to Eugene Clarke: "All hell broke loose. Jones accused the Duke of being yellow, of being afraid to block, and demoted him to the scrubs." Trainers tried to fit Duke with a shoulder harness, but it was no use. Duke recalled that he worked out all year "with a harness on my shoulder, but, Jesus, how it hurt." The shoulder needed months to heal, and his sophomore year as a football player was ruined.[30]

The injury had other consequences. When Howard Jones dropped Duke from the regular team, he also lost training-table privileges—the one meal a day at which the team members ate their fill. "That was a disaster for the Duke," Clarke remembered. "Money was very tight for the Duke in those days." Clyde tried to help out, sending Duke five dollars a week whenever he could, but even that was not enough. Duke went to work nights at the telephone company for sixty cents an hour, plotting maps of existing telephone lines. He kept washing dishes, but over the course of the school year, he accumulated a good-sized debt for room, board, and dues at Sigma Chi. His fraternity brothers began pressuring him to clear the books, and he felt as he used to in Glendale when the landlords forced the Morrisons to move. The last thing he wanted was to live the way his parents had.[31]

When the spring term ended in 1927, Duke reached an unsettling conclusion about the world of money and power. As a student he had been prelaw, served as a member of the debate team, and planned an eventual career with one of the prestigious East Los Angeles law firms. But USC taught him more than the law; it taught him that he was a poor scholarship boy surrounded by money. Unlike so many of his fraternity brothers and friends, he lacked the contacts vital to a successful law career. As he remembered years later, even if he were brighter than his classmates and worked harder than they did, he would still end up working for them because their fathers and uncles ran the best firms. It would be just like life in Sigma Chi, where he served the meals and washed the dishes while his frat brothers laughed and ate. He would do the dirty work; they would become the partners. "If I keep on studying law, [he thought,] I'm gonna end up writing briefs in somebody's back room for people who aren't as smart as I am." He decided not to return to school.[32]

The decision displeased his father. Clyde urged him repeatedly to stay and get a degree, even if it meant playing football with a bum shoulder and working day and night. "Daddy really wanted Duke to stay in school," Nancy Morrison recalled. "The movie business seemed too risky, too fly-by-night." Making movies at Fox was good enough for a summer job, Clyde told his son, but careers had to be built in more reliable areas, such as real estate and the law. They talked at length about college and careers in the spring of 1927. Duke would often stop by the paint store and talk to Clyde about life at college. Clyde listened patiently but always delivered the same advice: Stay in school.[33]

Confused and depressed, Duke decided late in May to head for San Francisco to find a job. George O'Brien, an actor at Fox, gave him the names of some friends who would put him up and told him to look up his father, the police chief. After a few weeks jobless in the city, he launched into a foolish adventure. Duke stowed away on the SS *Malolo,* a steamship making the San Francisco–Honolulu journey. At first, he mingled with other passengers and slept in an unoccupied stateroom, but he could not get enough food. Famished, he turned himself over to the ship's captain on the morning of the fourth day at sea. They threw him in the brig for the rest of the round trip, and when the *Malolo* docked in San Francisco at the end of June, police officers handcuffed him and put him in jail. Fortunately the police chief convinced the Matson Navigation Company not to press charges, and he put Duke on a train bound for Los Angeles.[34]

As soon as Duke got back, he went to work at Fox to make some money, as he had the year before. He was broke, and his junior year was only two months away. He propped that summer for films directed by Raoul Walsh and John Ford. In August, just before football practice started, Duke sought out John Ford for advice. He felt comfortable in Hollywood. The mixture of Irish and Jewish accents, old money and new, hustle, greed, and optimism appealed to him. Hollywood was the place where money and futures were made, where background and breeding did not matter. Duke wanted to join; he wanted to follow. Ford told him he would find a place for him at Fox.

Though Duke wanted to stay with Ford, he was not ready yet to reject Clyde's advice. The boy and his father were just too close. Duke checked back into the Sigma Chi house, picked up the waiter outfit for morning breakfast duty, and got outfitted for football. But the always-imperious Howard Jones had already written him off. Duke was about to become an early victim of big-time college football. Anxious to give Duke's money to a new recruit, Jones wanted him off the team. Duke was only too happy to leave: "I was washing dishes for my board at the Sigma Chi house and working all summer to pay back the money I had borrowed to go to school," Duke recalled years later, "so when my shoulder didn't feel any better at the start of my junior year, I decided to drop out for a year and let it heal. I never got back." He did not have much choice. Without the football scholarship, he could not pay for his tuition or buy books.[35]

Although his own family no longer existed as a unit, Duke's family responsibilities continued. Molly soon discovered that with Clyde and Duke not around, Bobby was increasingly difficult to control. The boy had just turned fourteen when the Morrisons separated, and he was already exhibiting a troubled personality. Bobby inherited all of his father's charm but none of his mother's backbone. He was like Clyde in so many ways—ingratiating, kind, and pleasant—but he had no ambition. Bobby enjoyed talking, laughing, and drinking, killing time rather than using it. He was destined to become, as Mary St. John described him, the kind of man whose ambitions never got very far past the lifeguard towers in Long Beach, where he spent many summers getting a tan and flirting with women on the beach. Bobby was the kind of man who did not want a real job because it might ruin a really good tan.

Bobby started drinking and smoking when he was in junior high school, and although he was intelligent enough, his grades never showed it. He loved watching and playing sports, but they were not enough to keep him in school. After Molly moved to Los Angeles when he was a freshman, he started skipping classes more and more, heading for the water and sand at Long Beach or Balboa. Duke, on the other hand, was just the opposite—tough, demanding, honest, and hardworking. Molly was equally blind to Duke's virtues and Bobby's vices. Duke could never please her, and Bobby could never fail to.

When Bobby finally dropped out of high school altogether in 1927, Molly somehow held Duke responsible, telling him that it was his obligation to see that Bobby got back in school. Duke talked to his younger brother, but it was no use. Bobby had made his own adjustment to the family soap opera, and that was that. He was on his way to becoming, in the words of Mary St. John, "the most easygoing human being on earth." While Duke used hard work and accomplishments to earn respect, Bobby made apathy into an art form. Molly asked Duke to let Bobby live with him and to try to get him back in school. Duke agreed: "I was happy to have him there, loved him, and the only thing I expected of him were good grades. He didn't have to do any outside work, just get his grades." For his part Bobby was only too happy to get away from his mother and grandparents, and he moved into Duke's apartment in Beverly Hills. Duke got him back into high school, kept track of him for three years, and in 1930 Bobby graduated. He attended a junior college for a year and then entered the University of Southern California in 1931.[36]

Meanwhile, Duke's decision to leave USC did not endear him to the Saenzes family. Even when he was enrolled full-time and playing football for the most popular team in California, they had not thought much of him. Clyde and Molly's divorce had deepened their suspicions about Duke's "trashy" family. But his decision to leave USC for Hollywood confirmed their worst fears. Hollywood, as far as Dr. Saenz and his wife were concerned, was a den of iniquity inhabited by lowlifes who had no sense of class or breeding. It was an intemperate world where traditional moral values were either badly blurred or invisible. If Duke Morrison was going to enter that Babylon, they wanted to make sure that their daughter did not follow him into it. In the fall of 1927, they told Josie in the most direct way not to see him ever again.[37]

Duke's life would never be the same after 1927. Like his father, grandfather, great-grandfather, and great-great-grandfather, he looked west for opportunity. But he would not be traveling over long distances in a covered wagon or on a railroad. He went to Hollywood, it was irrelevant if your parents were divorced and your father unemployed. For a young man yearning to be himself, to be rid of the rules and expectations of polite society, to cast off the superficial persona that had helped him to survive a troubled youth, Hollywood was the place to be. Hollywood was the land of rebirth, the place where stars could invent themselves. Late in August 1927, Duke told Clyde he was dropping out of USC and going to work for John Ford at Fox. Clyde accepted what was a *fait accompli* and gave his son his blessing. Duke Morrison moved a step closer to being John Wayne.

4

Driven by a Ford

It is one of the great questions of Hollywood history why John Ford took an interest in odd-jobber Duke Morrison in the summers of 1926 and 1927. Perhaps it was the incongruity of the young football player, at least in comparison to the other Jones boys; if so, Morrison must have reminded Ford of his own youth. Morrison was tall, well built, and had the WASPish good looks of a leading man, but in high school and college he had been a debater, a chess player, and a diligent, accomplished student. He was always quick to please, though those efforts stopped short of obsequiousness. As Morrison worked on the different sets, Ford noticed that the youth quietly paid attention to everything that was going on around him. Slowly, almost imperceptibly, Ford began to test Duke, giving him a little responsibility here, another task there. When the cameras were not rolling, Ford challenged, belittled, and befriended him, testing the quality of the man as well as the intellect. Whatever sparked the approach, Morrison passed Ford's private tests. Like Ford, he was a football player adept at concealing his ideas behind a facade of anti-intellectualism.

John Ford fancied himself a primitive, and like every other person in the industry he dressed his part. Outfitted in a dirty shirt, grimy, baggy pants, and worn sneakers or boots, he barked orders, chewed on an Irish linen handkerchief or pipe, and dominated his world. Other leading directors in the 1920s and 1930s were fastidious about their dress, often parading about their sets in starched shirts and riding pants accented by an ascot, polished English boots, and a crop. They looked as if they were participating in a lifelong search for some particularly elusive fox. Ford looked like a day laborer standing on a street corner with a gang of other men waiting for a job. It was, of course, a pose, announcing that here was a man who had renounced all the posturing that Hollywood stood for and was . . . well, just another hardworking, five-thousand-dollars-a-week Irish stiff who was not afraid to get his hands dirty.[1]

John Ford claimed that his real name was Sean Aloysius O'Feeney; it wasn't. He was born John Martin Feeney on February 1, 1894, in Cape Elizabeth, Maine, the tenth child of Irish immigrants. His hardworking, dependable father earned a good living bootlegging alcohol and running an illegal saloon along Portland's waterfront. Making the natural transition from the liquor business to politics, he became a leader of the local Democratic machine and a patriotic American, once instructing his son, "When the flag passes, take off your cap." When John pointed out that he was not wearing a cap, his father shot back, "Then cross yourself, damnit!"[2]

Although Ford tended to romanticize the tough waterfront environment of his youth, he grew to manhood in fairly comfortable surroundings, his family only a step or two away from being "lace curtain" Irish. At Portland High School he was a standout fullback on the football team, an above-average student, and a renowned wit. But he was restless, and when he graduated from high school in 1914, he set out for California rather than take the more respectable college route.[3]

He had a brother in Hollywood who called himself Francis Ford and had made a mark in the movies. Concealment and wanderlust, it seemed, were part of a family tradition. Francis had married at sixteen, left Portland a year later to enlist in the Spanish-American War, and, when his father's political connections got him out of a cholera camp, lit off again to join a circus. Eventually he found his way to Hollywood, changed his name, and became an actor and director. By the summer of 1914 when John Feeney went looking for his long-lost brother, Francis Ford was making films at Carl Laemmle's Universal City. The brothers reunited; John adopted the name Ford and went to work for Francis, who was a relaxed, tolerant employer. While War War I consumed a generation of European men, John Ford worked alongside his brother and learned about moving pictures.[4]

Ford was a natural, a cinematic genius—and a deeply troubled man. By 1917 he was working with Harry Carey and making Western feature films for

Universal. Ford greatly admired the gentle, easygoing Carey, a man everyone seemed to like. For Ford, Carey was the embodiment of American manhood—democratic, dignified, quiet, dependable, and at ease with himself. Carey was the silent era's no-frills cowboy. He was not a dandy like Tom Mix or a matinee idol like Hoot Gibson or Bob Steele, but he had a powerful movie presence—a thin-lipped, plain-dressed sincerity. In an age of theatrical pyrotechnics and broad pantomime, Carey's style emphasized economy. In the late teens and 1920s, he was America's good bad man, the reluctant hero. In such films as *Straight Shooting* (1917), *The Phantom Riders* (1918), and *Desperate Trails* (1921), Ford and Carey capitalized on and refined Carey's screen image, one that would be transferred whole to John Wayne. "Duke," Ford later told a young John Wayne, "take a look over at Harry Carey and watch him work. Stand like he does, if you can, and play your roles so that people can look upon you as a friend."[5]

During the 1920s the careers of John Ford's two most important mentors declined. Francis Ford's interests were too thinly spread, and he lacked the single-mindedness to become either a great actor or a great director. He left Universal, failed to establish his own studio, and seemed to float aimlessly from one adventure to the next. By the late 1920s he had become one of the thousands of character actors looking for work in Hollywood. The industry also moved past Carey. He too left Universal, ending his four-year, twenty-five-film collaboration with John Ford. He bounced from one studio to another and was nearly broke by 1928. No longer a leading man, in the 1930s he carved out a new career for himself as a character actor in "poverty row" Westerns—low-budget films made by independent production companies that did not own any theater outlets.[6]

While his brother's and friend's careers languished, Ford's shot forward. Francis Ford, Harry Carey, John Ford—they all had the talent, but only John had the drive, the will, and the ruthless toughness to remain on top. He was a strange, complex, oddly balanced man, intensely loyal, often petty and just as often mean, and yet regularly generous. Fellow director Frank Capra called Ford "half-tyrant, half-revolutionary; half-saint, half-satan; half-possible, half-impossible; half-genius, half-blah; half-Irish, half-man—but all director and all American." He belittled and humiliated almost everyone with whom he ever worked, but he used the same troupe in picture after picture, and every member of the group loved him. He expressed a low opinion of the movie industry but was truly happy only on a set. His films often evince warm family values, but he seemed to take pleasure in humiliating his older brother Francis, had trouble living in peace with his wife, and alienated his only son. He was a lousy drunk, a distant father, a tyrannical employer, and a great devoted friend. In all these ways, he was just a bit more extreme than John Wayne would become. When Ford was dying of stomach cancer in 1973, Wayne bought space in *Variety* for a simple handwritten message: "Dear Coach, Thanks for a wonderful and eventful life. Duke."[7]

John Ford needed Hollywood. Uncomfortable in his own skin and with the world around him, he re-created himself and his world on his sets and in his films. Actors and actresses, stuntmen and cameramen, screenwriters and grips—they formed his surrogate family. On his sets Danny Borzage, a Ford regular, played "Bringing in the Sheaves," "Red River Valley," "Wild Colonial Boy," and the director's other favorite tunes on the accordion; Earl Grey tea was served every afternoon; there was a twenty-five-cent fine for anyone who talked shop at the communal lunches and dinners. Men treated women with respect, avoiding foul language and watching their manners. Ford himself sat at the head of the table and was the paterfamilias; older men called him "Pappy" and felt like kids when he was around. "If you were in Big Trouble, Ford'd be the first guy you'd go to—rape, murder, assault. But if you just wanted to gossip or talk about girls, you wouldn't tell it to him," recalled Harry Carey Jr. "He set it up that way, then was almost sorry he did. No, he wasn't a fitter-inner, sort of an outsider." He was even a little uncomfortable in the world he had created.[8]

He reveled in legends, creating them for himself and for America. "This is the West, sir. When the legend becomes fact, print the legend," remarked a character in one of his later films. All his life Ford manufactured and printed legends. He liked the image of himself as the gruff, Irish intruder who always spoke his mind. In fact he often had trouble articulating his feelings and was apt to withdraw for long periods of time into the bottle or silence. His films invoked an America where silent, hard, good bad men—men like Harry Carey and later John Wayne—maintained order but remained on the outside, apart from civilization.

Ford's need for Hollywood was so great, and his talent and vision so complete, that success came almost without effort. In 1921 he left Universal for Fox Film Corporation, at the time a minor studio that catered to working-class and rural audiences. But William Fox and Winfield Sheehan, his chief of production in Hollywood, were ambitious and smart. They recognized that Ford had talent and gave him wide latitude in script development, filming, and editing. For a few years Ford flirted with various working-class subjects, ranging from New York Jewish ghetto and rural New England life to Maine fishing towns and riverboat gambling. Then, in 1923 and 1924, he made *The Iron Horse*, the story of the building of the Union Pacific Railroad. It was an expensive film involving thousands of extras and location filming in the Sierra Nevadas. A series of blizzards stretched a four-week shoot to ten, and caused serious budget overruns. Fox considered canceling the expensive project, but when he and his executives saw the dailies he approved the added costs. The gamble paid off. Critics instantly recognized the film as a classic, and it was a huge commercial success, grossing more than two million dollars worldwide. John Ford never looked back.[9]

By the time Duke met him in 1926, Ford was one of the leading directors in Hollywood. For Duke it was a summer job, a chance to earn money to allow him to return to USC and pursue his plans to become a lawyer. But Ford fascinated him. The director seemed wired into everything and everyone around him; nothing escaped his notice—no nuance, no look, no movement. He was "a labored learned man," Duke later recalled. He "absorbed everything—mood, wine, lines, everything." He was an artist, with an artist's eye for scene and texture; an intellect, with an intellectual's concern for ideas. Duke noticed that Ford would argue with anyone about almost anything, playing devil's advocate just to learn what the other person knew. But if anyone had called him an artist or an intellectual, Ford would have told the person to get off the set. Duke had seen no one like him at USC or anywhere else. It was Ford who inspired Duke to begin to consider a life in the motion picture industry.[10]

Ford got Duke a thirty-five-dollar-a-week job as an assistant property man and a general go-getter, the same job his brother Francis had given *him* thirteen years before. Duke found a home on the older man's set. Because of the lack of unions and craft guilds in Hollywood during the 1920s, there were no hardened labor lines, and property men often earned extra money doubling as stunt men, extras in crowd scenes, or assistant gaffers, juicers, and grips. Between 1927 and 1929, Duke learned the industry from the bottom up. It was an education not offered at USC.[11]

Working as a property man, he learned how to dress a set so that it look authentic. It was the art of the little details—a well-placed photograph or book, a lit cigarette or a flowerpot—that transformed a set into a believable room. A property man had to be attuned to camera angles and the action of a scene. Duke had an eye for those details, and he liked propping, even considering a career as a prop man. It was good work; in the late 1920s, a skilled property man earned $120 or more a week. In fact, he never lost his eye for details. In later years he enjoyed buying presents for friends, especially women. He had a near-infallible judgment for clothing sizes and styles, and for what pieces of art or other objects would look best in his friends' homes. "Duke never, ever asked what size a woman was," his longtime personal secretary Mary St. John remembered. "He would meet the wife of some associate one time and a month or two later see some dress in a catalog and say, 'You know Mary, I think so-and-so would like this. Order a size seven.'"[12]

Not only did propping teach Duke to see a set as it would look on film, it exposed him to different directors. He propped for Raoul Walsh, Frank Borzage, and several of Fox's other leading directors. But he most enjoyed working for Ford, who treated him with the same mixture of disgust and respect that he treated everyone else in his troupe.

On the set of Ford's *Four Sons*, the story of a Bavarian mother who lost three of her four sons in World War I, Duke made the mistake of not paying close enough attention. In one of the film's crucial scenes, Margaret Mann, who played the mother, learned of the death of her third son. Ford set the scene on the porch of the family's home in the last autumn of the war, and to give a visual sense of the loss, he ordered Duke to use a fan to blow dead leaves across the front of the porch. Rehearsals went badly; from nine in the morning until well into the afternoon, Ford worked with his two leads. Duke spent the long day blowing leaves and then sweeping them during the breaks. He became bored and distracted. Shortly after four-thirty he once again blew the leaves across the porch and then began to sweep. "Cut!" he heard Ford bellow. No one had told Duke that the camera was rolling. "Shit, there I was. I just threw down my goddamn broom and started to walk off."

"Ford roared like a lion," Duke recalled years later, and told him to stop. Then he marched Duke around the set and got a Serbian actor to pin an Iron Cross on him. Ford told him: "Assume the position." Duke knelt down and the director kicked him like he had never been kicked before. That done, Ford cursed him for a few minutes, laughed, and went back to work.[13]

Duke was embarrassed, humiliated, and concerned for his job. But after his explosion, Ford laughed and forgave him. Although Ford was often mean and had a cruel sense of humor, he cared about the people with whom he worked, even assistant property men. Remembering Ford and the incident, Duke told biographer Maurice Zolotow, "He kept his distance from everybody—and yet he had a way of talking to you that made you feel he understood you and your problems. He was the first person who ever made me want to be a person— who gave me a vision of a fully rounded human being."[14]

John Ford provided the role model that Clyde Morrison, especially during the years of his marriage to Molly, never could. As far as Duke could see, Ford was in total control of his life. On a set he knew exactly what he wanted from each actor, actress, and technician; he gave orders and people responded instantly, without question. If he occasionally lashed out at someone who made a mistake, he was just as likely to be compassionate or humorous. Ford enjoyed practical jokes, most of which were fairly harmless. Duke remembered that in those days Ford would hand him a pipe and say, "Here's a new pipe. Try it." Only after four pipes did Duke realize that Ford was using him to break in his pipes. Duke took no offense and laughed at his own gullibility. Before long he called Ford "Pappy" or "Coach," and Ford filled both roles for him. "Duke Wayne was just a stick of wood when he came away from USC," director Allan Dwan commented. "Jack gave him character."[15]

Not only did Ford get Duke to help prop his films, he gave the handsome assistant bit parts and added responsibilities in his pictures. Duke appeared briefly in a crowd scene and as the silhouette of a condemned man in *Hangman's House* (1928), and as an Annapolis midshipman in *Salute* (1929), a film about the rivalry between two brothers played against the backdrop of the annual Army-Navy football game.[16]

After their 27–14 victory over Notre Dame, a Rose Bowl triumph, and an undefeated season, the USC Trojans were the darlings of the West Coast, and college football was popular throughout the country. Ford correctly assumed that a film about college football featuring members of the USC team would be a box-office draw. He had scheduled much of the shooting in the spring of 1929 at Annapolis, before the midshipmen left campus and before the end of USC's term. This made for a difficult task. Reformers had recently increased their criticism of the "professionalization" and "commercialization" of college football, and USC administrators were leery of involving the team with Hollywood.

Since Duke had attended USC and been on the football team, Ford gave him the assignment of recruiting the players and getting the administrative sanction. Duke first approached George von KleinSmid, one of his Sigma Chi brothers, who also happened to be the son of Rufus. George got Duke access to President von KleinSmid, and somehow, by making vague promises of a trip to the nation's capital and packaging the entire adventure in patriotic wrapping, Duke convinced him that the Annapolis trip would be a worthwhile cultural experience and that the players should be given their final exams a few weeks early. He then told the football players at Sigma Chi about the casting call.

Ford chose twenty-five players for the trip, most of them Duke's fraternity brothers, but a few non–Sigma Chi men won parts as well. One of the second group was Wardell Bond, a rugged lineman with big ears and thick lips whose "ugly" face interested Ford. Duke disliked Bond and tried to convince the director that he knew a "double ugly" Sigma Chi player who would be even better than Bond for a minor heavy part. Ford said he wanted Bond, and as a joke assigned Duke and Ward the same sleeping compartment on the train from Los Angeles to Annapolis. Sure enough, on the trip the the two became friends.

Bond was irrepressible—"all ego and gall," Duke noted years later. He was capable of any effrontery, giving offense without thinking and never bothering to consider the consequences. Most people who knew Bond disliked him; the rest loved him. Ford was immediately attracted to Bond's boldness. One night on the trip East, Bond needed a few dollars. Bypassing all intermediaries, he went straight to Ford, the source of all funds. Bond knocked on the director's stateroom door, entered before there was an answer, caught him shaving in the bathtub, and, seeing Ford's wallet on a dresser, took twenty dollars for a night on the town, mumbled a quick thanks, offered the director a chance to come along, and left before Ford could respond. Stars, producers, studio owners—no one treated John Ford like that, except Wardell Bond, who treated all people as though they had been placed on earth to serve him. Ford loved him for it. Perhaps Bond, more than any other man, made John Ford feel like one of the boys. "Ward is a son-of-a-bitch, but he's our son-of-a-bitch," he told Duke.

Since Duke was in charge of the football players, Bond was a constant problem. Money was always an issue. The players were hired at fifty dollars a week and expenses, but their definition of "expenses" invariably differed from that of Eddie O'Fearna, Ford's older brother who served as his purely ceremonial assistant director and very real paymaster. Notoriously cheap, O'Fearna skimmed on meal money. Most players grumbled but reasoned that there was nothing they could do about their small meals. Bond, on the other hand, simply ordered what he wanted, ate until he was full, and signed O'Fearna's name. O'Fearna held Duke responsible and threatened nearly daily to fire him.

Rather than getting Duke fired, Bond brought Duke closer to Ford. Ward and Duke became a pair in Ford's mind. Although Duke was reserved and kept a respectful distance from Ford, Ward's antics and outrageous boasts drew Duke into constant controversies. Ford was so delighted with Bond's unconventional behavior that Duke benefited by association. By the end of the trip East, the three had formed a friendship that would last until the end of their lives, a friendship that survived marriages, occasional fights, and career fluctuations.

They almost lost Bond two weeks into filming *Salute*. Soon after the cast and crew arrived in Annapolis, Ford took up with a local, redheaded groupie who wanted to become an actress. She shared his hotel room, and his bed, for several days. Oblivious to the fact that Ford was sleeping with the woman, Bond made one of his trademark passes—sneaking up behind her, sticking his tongue into her ear, and then, with the formalities over, introducing himself. She pirouetted quickly, French-kissed him on the spot, and jumped from Ford's bed to Bond's. In a lusty mood that night, Ford unsuccessfully tried to locate her, asking Wayne and several other crew members if they had seen the young woman. The next morning, when Duke saw her stumble out of Bond's hotel room, he burst in and confronted a smiling Bond: "Jesus Christ, Ward," Duke boomed. "Don't you know she's Ford's girl? The old man's gonna fire you." Bond did not give Ford a chance. Scared and chagrined, he packed his bags, hitchhiked into Baltimore, and boarded a westbound B & O train. A few hours later, when Ford learned why Bond had missed his scene, he told Wayne: "Get over to Western Union and wire that dumb, ugly sonofabitch to get his big ass back here." Bond got the wire in Pittsburgh. The next morning, he was back on the set—smiling.

Salute, Ford's second sound film, was a critical and financial success. Comparing it with other films about college football, *Variety* called it "the best picture of its kind to date," and it was Fox's top moneymaker in 1929. Ward Bond was singled out for his performance. "Bond will probably stick in pictures after this effort," commented the *Variety* reviewer. No reviewers noticed Duke's brief appearance, however, and he continued propping on Fox sets, occasionally receiving additional work as an extra or stunt man. It was while doing double duty on director James Tinling's *Words and Music* (1929) that "Duke Morrison" received his first screen credit.[17]

By 1929 Duke had given up any idea of returning to USC. Satisfied with his work in the film industry, his attachment and friendship with Ford deepened. There was little that he would not do for Ford, even risk his life. In the autumn of that year Ford was making *Men Without Women*, a naval film that involves a scene in which fourteen men are trapped in a disabled submarine. On a cold, bleak day Ford filmed the rescue scene. The day was perfect for cinematic effect—the "gunmetal-gray" overcast sky created ideal backlighting and a mood of foreboding—but the sea between Long Beach and Catalina Island was rough and dangerous. "The waves were about the size of houses,"

Duke recalled. The scene called for sailors to be shot out of torpedo tubes. To create that effect Ford had hired several professional skin divers to dive off the camera boat, swim underwater eight or ten feet, and surface amid a swirl of bubbles created by an air hose. Duke's job was to handle the air compressor and hose, which created the bubbles. After the cameras were set, the divers assessed the water conditions and told Ford it was too dangerous to dive. Duke saw what was happening. "Here comes the fleet with that black smoke comin' out of the destroyer, and the light just hitting everything right, and I knew. 'Jesus, what the hell.'" Ford called out, "Duke," and his assistant said, "Yessir!" and "Hit the god-damned water." He did the stunt work for all four rescues, no questions asked.[18]

Duke's only regret about the day was that he never got paid for the work. He had just lost several hundred dollars on the USC–Notre Dame game— Notre Dame won 13–12 at Soldiers Field in Chicago—and needed the extra money. He was "stiffed," however, by Eddie O'Fearna.[19]

Money had become more important to Duke. Thirty-five dollars a week, augmented by additional cash earned for stunt work or small roles, provided him with enough to survive during the late 1920s but not enough to marry into a family listed in the Los Angeles *Social Register.* He had continued to date Josephine Saenz. He tried to save, but his intentions were better than his effort. Throughout his life he remained loose with money, quick to reach for a check, and an easy touch for a friend or acquaintance who needed a loan. But if he was going to marry Josie, he needed a windfall.[20]

It came with hurricane suddenness and force in the late summer of 1929. Duke had just finished propping *Cheer Up and Smile,* a light Sidney Lanfield comedy starring Arthur Lake and Dixie Lee. He had a bit part in the film as a college student, and his hair was cut short in the fashion of the day. The walk-on was a lagniappe, a small but thoughtful gift from Ford, and Duke knew it. He was a property man, not an actor, and when the shooting finished he helped the other laborers dismantle the set and take the furniture back to the property warehouse. As he was unloading a truck full of furniture and other props, a one-eyed man watched as a bare-chested Duke carried an overstuffed chair into storage, noticing the former football player's wide shoulders and height. He watched Duke "juggle a solid Louis Quinze sofa as though it was made of feathers and pick up another chair with his free hand." One of the other helpers made Duke laugh, and the one-eyed man was intrigued by Duke's expression—"it was so warm and wholesome." He was pleased by what he saw and heard—"the fine physique of the boy, his casual strength, the grace of his movements, the easy accents of his voice." The one-eyed man was Raoul Walsh, one of Fox's leading directors. He told his casting director to make a screen test of the handsome property man.[21]

That same day casting director Eddie Grainger approached Duke: "Say, Duke, how'd you like to slip on a pair of buckskin pants and make a test— just for fun?" "Sure," Duke answered. A few weeks later, after his hair had grown out a bit, a preliminary test without sound was made. Walsh just wanted to see what the camera would pick up. After watching the rushes, he told Winnie Sheehan, "That's the man. Sign him up."[22]

The story of Duke's discovery reads like one of the great Hollywood legends, the kind that breeds fan magazine headlines: STAR SURFACES AT SCHWAB'S SODA FOUNTAIN, or STARDOM TAPS FURNITURE CARRIER. And it is true that Walsh noticed Duke moving furniture. But beneath the simple discovery is a complex story of great wealth, greater greed, political intrigue, and the fall of an industrial empire. Unknown to Duke Morrison, he was about to play a small part in a much larger drama—one that had everything to do with the movies but nothing to do with make-believe.

By 1929 the "talkies" had changed the economics of Hollywood and affected studios and stars alike. The process had begun in 1925 at Warner Bros., a small but ambitious studio that was attempting to compete with the majors. Although Warner's lacked the large theater chains of Loew's Metro-Goldwyn-Mayer (MGM) or Paramount, it had creative leadership and the financial backing of the Wall Street investment firm of Goldman, Sachs & Company and several leading eastern banks. In 1925 Warner's and Western Electric began jointly experimenting with sound, and in 1926 the two companies formed the Vitaphone Corporation to develop sound motion pictures. At that time Warner's was less interested in "talkies" than the idea of canned shorts and musical accompaniment for its silent films. Always money conscious, the brothers saw Vitaphone as a way to save on the fees they paid to live vaudeville acts and orchestras in their large movie theaters. In addition Vitaphone would allow Warner's to provide midsize theaters in smaller towns with a taste of the experience of the movie palace. On August 6, 1926, at Warner's Theatre in New York, Warner's and Western Electric presented the first offspring of its collaboration. The evening's entertainment consisted of eight "Vitaphone Preludes"—ranging from Will Hays, president of the Motion Picture Producers and Distributors Association, congratulating Warner's and Western Electric, to the New York Philharmonic playing the

Tannhäuser Overture, to Metropolitan opera tenor Giovanni Martinelli singing an aria from *I Pagliacci,* to a Roy Smeck comic skit—and the film *Don Juan,* which had a Vitaphone musical score. *New York Times* reporter Mordaunt Hall was so impressed by the result that he predicted: "It may be only a relatively short time before a talking photoplay is produced." Sound had arrived.[23]

If Warner's did not set out to make talkies, the success of *Don Juan* convinced the brothers to move in that direction. In 1927 Darryl F. Zanuck, Warner's leading producer, hired Al Jolson to star in the film adaptation of Samson Raphaelson's New York stage play *The Jazz Singer.* It was an odd choice for the first talkie. The sentimental story of the conflict between an Orthodox rabbi and his son, who enters show business, seemed distant from the concerns of most Americans. Indeed Protestant America was unlikely to relate to the crucial moment in the story when the son has to decide between singing "Kol Nidre" on Yom Kippur for his dying father or debuting in the big time. But Zanuck believed in the project, and on October 6, 1927, *The Jazz Singer* opened at the Warner's Theatre in New York. It used the Vitaphone process for its score, Jolson's songs, and two passages of dialogue. Before singing "Toot, Toot, Tootsie," Jolson crossed the barrier from silent film to talkies by crying, "Wait a minute. You ain't heard nothin' yet!" With those words he buried silent movies.[24]

Variety's headline announced TALKING PICTURE SENSATION. Mordaunt Hall of the *New York Times* wrote that on opening night he "almost forgot that the real Jolson was sitting in a box listening to his own songs, for it seemed as though in the darkness Mr. Jolson had crept behind the screen and was rendering the songs for his black and white image." More important than the reviews was the public's reaction. *The Jazz Singer* played before packed houses for extended engagements from New York to Los Angeles. Hit by the Warner's earthquake, the leaders of the other studios began converting their recently completed films to sound and wiring their theaters for talkies.[25]

William Fox moved more quickly than the other moguls. Several years before the premiere of *The Jazz Singer*, he had acquired the rights to a sound-on-film process begun by Lee De Forest's Phonofilm system. Refined by Theodore W. Case and Earl I. Sponable, Phonofilm became the basis for the Movietone process. Vitaphone depended on the synchronization of film with photograph records, a delicate process prone to breakdowns. The slightest break in the synchronization between record and film was certain to turn any comedy into a tragedy or vice versa. Movietone, however, used a photoelectric cell to record the sound track directly on the film. Direct recording of sound on film was a more reliable system than Vitaphone and eventually became the industry's standard. It also gave William Fox a technological advantage over the other moguls and a brief window of economic opportunity.[26]

Fox first began to use Movietone in his newsreels, but in 1927 he presented F. W. Murnau's *Sunrise* with a Movietone score. After the success of *The Jazz Singer*, Fox announced in 1928 that all his pictures for the following season would contain Movietone. It was an expensive process that entailed developing new equipment, building sound stages, wiring theaters, and hiring directors, writers, actors, dancers, singers, and technicians who understood the demands of dialogue and sound. Fox spent $15 million just hiring Broadway talent. But the potential payoff seemed worth the gamble. From 1926 to 1930 average weekly movie attendance shot up 45 percent; between 1927 and 1930 the industry's assets more than tripled. Studio leaders rushed to cash in on the talkie bonanza. During this period of industrial growth, Fox, financed by the Chicago investment house of Halsey, Stuart & Company, initiated a program of building and buying. His designs had monopolistic overtones. Not only did he begin construction on a national chain of five-thousand-seat movie palaces and a new studio in Hollywood, he went after other production, distribution, and exhibition corporations. He purchased a 45 percent interest in Gaumont, England's most important film company. Then, in February 1929, almost eighteen months after the death of Marcus Loew, Fox acquired the corporate officers' and the Loew family's stock—a total of 53 percent, for which he paid 25 percent above the market price—in Loew's, Inc., the parent company of MGM, which had extensive theater holdings, production facilities, and moviemaking talent. A man obsessed by success and the achievement of respectability, a giant in the movie industry who chose to live on an estate on Long Island rather than in the hills surrounding Hollywood, Fox was now the most powerful mogul of them all. The man with a crippled left arm, which he tried to hide by keeping his hand stuck in his pocket, now threatened to dominate the entire industry.[27]

Louis B. Mayer, the short, overweight vice president and general manager of MGM, was determined that he would not be a victim of Fox's empire building. The most political of the moguls, Mayer was active in the Republican party and a personal friend of the newly elected Herbert Hoover. Less than two weeks after Fox purchased the Loew's stock, Mayer attended Hoover's inauguration and warned the new president of the monopoly developing in Hollywood. Shortly afterward, the Justice Department began an investigation of the buyout. In the midst of the antitrust crisis, while Fox was en route to a golfing engagement, his chauffeur smashed into another automobile. The accident killed the chauffeur and badly injured Fox. His empire, barely a month old, began to crumble.[28]

Anticipating creditors at his door—he had not exactly paid for the fifty-million-dollar Loew's deal with his own money—Fox looked for a quick fix. He turned, again, to technology. Movietone had been a huge success; perhaps the formula could be repeated. In the summer of 1929 Paramount demonstrated its Magnafilm, a 56 mm-wide film that was projected onto an enlarged screen. Impressed by the big-screen effect, Fox had his technicians develop a 70 mm (the standard film in use was 35 mm) process dubbed Grandeur Pictures. A forerunner of Cinerama, Grandeur Pictures employed double-wide film as well as wide-angle lenses and a huge screen to give the illusion of depth. When it was previewed at the Gaiety Theatre in New York on September 18, 1929, the film writer for the *New York Times* praised it, remarking that the scenes of Niagara Falls were "the finest thing of its kind that has come to the screen. When the mere sight of rushing water and spray, together with flashes of foliage on the banks of the rapids, can make a blasé first-night audience applaud, it bespeaks much for this Grandeur photography." Fox predicted that the new technology would revolutionize the motion picture industry. Unfortunately he was wrong; nothing would ever have the impact of sound—not even color. As for the wide-screen and wider-filmed epics, history revealed a much greater willingness to suspend disbelief than insist on a vision approaching 180 degrees. Several experiments were tried, and 70 mm never disappeared, but the plot and the stars mattered more.[29]

In 1929 it remained to be seen whether Grandeur would have an impact on feature films. It was Raoul Walsh's assignment to find out. One of Fox's most highly regarded directors, Walsh specialized in action pictures. "To Raoul Walsh a tender love scene is burning down a whorehouse," Jack Warner once commented. Walsh had directed *In Old Arizona* (1929), Hollywood's first outdoor talkie, which was so successful that it convinced Fox executives to make nothing but sound films. It was on location shooting *In Old Arizona* that Walsh had lost an eye when a frightened jackrabbit crashed through his car's windshield, and he was recovering in Hollywood when Fox production chief Sheehan told him it was time to go back to work. The new project was a Western entitled *The Big Trail*. Sheehan wanted it shot outdoors using Movietone sound and Grandeur photography. A high-budget project, *The Big Trail* was supposed to help save Fox's empire.[30]

Walsh immediately began to cast the epic story of a wagon train's struggle along the overland trail between Missouri and Oregon. He had no difficulty casting most of the parts. Like other early sound directors, he searched for talent with stage experience. Marguerite Churchill—a product of New York's Professional Children's School, the Theatre Guild Drama School, and Broadway—had only recently arrived in Hollywood, but she had a trained voice and incandescent beauty. Walsh chose her for the female lead. The best secondary roles also went to proven stage actors: Ian Keith, an experienced Broadway and movie performer; Tyrone Power, Sr., grandson of a famous Irish actor and a former Broadway matinee idol whose booming voice could easily fill a good-size range; Tully Marshall, a West Coast stage actor; and El Brendel, a Broadway comedian famed for his Swedish dialect.

Casting male leads in Westerns during those early days of sound presented the greatest problems. Many of the silent stars lacked the voices or proper accents for talkies. Even the ones with good voices had trouble handling dialogue and were frequenting the schools that had mushroomed overnight along Melrose Avenue and Hollywood and Sunset advertising "Voice Training for All Talking Pictures." There were additional problems with New York actors. They had no experience riding horses and lacked the natural air of the Hollywood cowboy. The established stars Walsh wanted were not available. Tom Mix, Fox's major Western star, was working on another film. Gary Cooper, under contract to Samuel Goldwyn, was working nearly nonstop in 1929. (Ten films starring Gary Cooper were released in 1929 and 1930, including *The Virginian* and *Morocco*.) It was during his search for a man to play Breck Coleman that Walsh saw Duke Morrison moving furniture. Duke looked and sounded right. And he was available.[31]

Winnie Sheehan was not so sure, even after the first silent test. He wanted to do a screen test with sound. To deepen Duke's voice to get him ready for the second test, Walsh told him to "go up to Mulholland and yell your bloody lungs out and then get a paper and read the editorials out loud to get used to hearing your own voice and practice enunciation." Duke followed Walsh's orders and was ready for the second screen test, which involved him answering questions on tape. Ian Keith, Tyrone Power, and Marguerite Churchill helped with the test. Duke was told to assume that he was a scout about to lead a wagon train from Missouri to Oregon, and to answer questions from Keith and Churchill, two members of the party. Keith had read the script, knew his part, and was full of the right questions to ask. He fired one after another at Duke, who had not read the script, did not know his part, and knew very few answers. Embarrassed and angry, Duke tired of stumbling for answers, took the offensive, and began asking Keith questions: "Where are you from? Why are you going West? Can you handle a rifle?" The questions showed Duke at his best and satisfied Walsh.[32]

Still nervous about using an unknown actor in such an expensive project, Sheehan wanted to see how Duke handled dialogue. Walsh knew that in *The Big Trail* dialogue would be secondary to action and landscape scenes. "You don't need words to describe deserts and valleys and rivers. The camera will do that," he told Sheehan. But he nonetheless set up a third screen test. Dressed once again in a buckskin costume and a Stetson, Duke read several scenes, and although he made the usual beginner's mistakes of overdramatizing, Walsh was again satisfied. Still Sheehan hesitated, until Walsh told him: "You'll never get anyone better. He's the best we got. He's the only one we got."[33]

Sheehan agreed and turned to business matters. Duke Morrison, he proclaimed, was a bad name; it did not sound American enough. They kicked a few names back and forth but none satisfied Sheehan. Walsh, a Revolutionary War buff, finally suggested Anthony Wayne. No good. Walsh later told Zolotow that Sheehan believed Anthony Wayne sounded "too Italian," and Tony Wayne "like a girl's name." Someone suggested John Wayne. "Fine." Sheehan alone passed judgment. Without even being a party to the meeting, Duke Morrison had become John Wayne.[34]

Sheehan's next concern was the newly christened actor's salary. John Wayne might be the star of *The Big Trail,* but Sheehan wanted to pay him as if he were still Duke Morrison, property man. He generously suggested raising Duke's weekly salary from thirty-five to forty-five dollars a week. As Walsh told Zolotow, he was shocked. "Listen," he told Sheehan. "If it ever gets out that we're paying our leading man $45 a week and the supporting players like Tully Marshall are getting $500 we'll be the laughingstock of the industry." Walsh's argument pricked Sheehan's conscience: He bumped Duke's weekly salary up to fifty dollars, and after some more discussion, he agreed to go to seventy-five dollars—but not a penny more. John Wayne had just become the best deal in Hollywood.[35]

Duke resented his new name more than his low salary. To his oldest friends and his family he remained Marion Morrison; his newer friends called him Duke Morrison. It took him years to grow accustomed to the name "John Wayne," and he never answered to "John." "No," he said recalling the name change. "I've always been either Duke, Marion, or John Wayne. It's a name that goes well together and it's like one word—John Wayne. But if [people] say John, Christ, I don't look around. . . . And when they say Jack, boy, you know they don't know me."[36]

He accepted both the name change and the salary as part of the illusion and business of Hollywood. *The Big Trail* was his ticket to fame, bigger pay-days, and respectability within the industry, and he was determined to suc-ceed. As Walsh prepared to take his crew on location, Duke went into training. Walsh prescribed a regimen of lessons—riding, shooting, roping, and acting. Wayne learned to be a cowboy from cowboys turned stuntmen. Steve Clemente, a weapons expert, taught him to throw a knife; Jack Padgin, a cowboy from Montana who was one of Fox's leading stuntmen, showed him how to pull a gun, mount a horse, and ride as naturally as he breathed. West-ern skills came easily, and Duke enjoyed working with the stuntmen—as he would for the rest of his career.[37]

But acting lessons and acting instructors were another matter entirely. Walsh sent Wayne to Lumsden Hare, one of the voice "experts" Fox had hired to train their actors and actresses to handle dialogue in sound films. The transformation of silent-screen stars to talkies was traumatic. For years the *sine qua non* of Hollywood success was face and body. Profile, chest, arms, and legs were everything. Voice was unimportant, foreign accents, strong regional dialects, odd pitches—all were meaningless. Sound sent a wave of fear through the industry and added a new requirement to the success formula: face, body, and *voice*. One MGM actor recalled the arrival of sound: "It was the night of the *Titanic* all over again with women grabbing the wrong chil-dren and Louis B. [Mayer] singing 'Nearer My Got to Thee.'" Sound affected many careers. It was said that when Marion Davies, an MGM star who had a stuttering problem, saw *The Jazz Singer*, she turned to an MGM publicist and said, "M-m-mister Voight, I-I-I have a p-p-problem." She overcame hers. But John Gilbert, along with Valentino, one of the silent era's great lovers, failed fully to overcome his. His high-pitched voice lacked the romance of his soul-ful eyes.[38]

Like many of the other voice experts and dialogue coaches attracted to Hollywood by the sound gold rush, Lumsden Hare believed in the broad, classical style fashionable on the British and American stages during the nine-teenth century. He labored to turn Duke into a thespian. Hare's idea of West-ern dialogue, Duke later recalled, was "'Greeting, Great Bear, tell the Great White mountain hello for me,' all in great rounded vowels." In a short time Hare had Duke rolling his *r*'s, elongating his vowels, posturing, mincing the-atrically, gesturing grandly, and moving about like a bantam rooster. Duke felt like a poor man's Edwin Booth. It was a cruel and unusual punishment. He had been around Ford long enough to realize how poorly Hare's techniques would play in front of a camera and how foolish he would appear on screen. He wanted the part, but not *that* badly. After two weeks Duke told Hare, "This is foolish. I'm going to stop these lessons." Hare replied, "You're very wise, Mr. Wayne. You'll never be an actor." Duke then told Walsh, "If you want me to be that kind of actor, I can't cut the mustard." Walsh didn't want that kind of actor. The lessons stopped.[39]

While Walsh prepared to take his crew on location, Duke completed his crash course in acting. Duke followed John Ford's advice and made Harry Carey his standard. In 1968 Wayne told Harry Carey Jr.: "I watched your dad since I was a kid. I copied Harry Carey. That's where I learned to talk like I do; that's where I learned many of my mannerisms. Watching your father." Ignoring Hare's classical style, Duke practiced the broken cadence of Harry Carey. For Wayne the Harlem-born Carey epitomized the real West in his plain dress and his plain speech. His style was direct and unvarnished, a manner that was a product of the frontier rather than the Broadway stage. In *The Big Trail* and in later films, John Wayne labored to make Harry Carey's style his own.[40]

In the early spring of 1930, Walsh took his cast and crew to Yuma, Arizona, the first stop on a five-state, two-thousand-mile trip for location shootings. Before Walsh arrived, a team of Fox technicians had re-created along the banks of the Colorado River the town of Independence, Missouri, as it looked in the 1840s when it was the departure point for settlers headed for California and Oregon. Never before had such a large set been built on location. There were more than forty aged and weathered buildings with interior sets: a blacksmith shop, blackened by soot, with a veteran forge; a trading post filled with piles of furs and skins; a hospital; a hotel; and a tent camp. Corrals held seventeen hundred head of stock, and nearly two hundred covered wagons were equipped as they would have been in the 1840s. When John Wayne and the other actors got off the train in Yuma, they were taxied to a West none had ever seen.[41]

"Discipline on the trails of the pioneers was strict," Raoul Walsh wrote in the pressbook for *The Big Trail*. "In the making of *The Big Trail*, I knew what many members of my staff only half realized—that the company would have to undergo hardships comparable with those of the early pioneers. Before we entrained I warned them. Nobody dropped off."[42]

Brave words. But Walsh's Hollywood pioneers fell considerably short of the standards set by their ancestors. As Walsh later noted, *The Big Trail* should have been called *The Big Drunk*. During the first days in Yuma, discipline sagged in direct proportion to the amount of bootleg liquor that was consumed, and consumption was high. A New York screenwriter and several Broadway actors fell off the wagon the hardest. Walsh said that the New York talent "probably scattered more empty whiskey bottles over the Western plains than all of the pioneers." They drank late into the night; complained bitterly about, and occasionally missed, early calls; and appeared red-eyed and hung over on the set. They were unaccustomed to the heat of the West or the demands of the camera, ignorant about the need to film in the early mornings before the sun rose so high that it washed out shots, or the difference between stage acting and movie acting. Even worse, neither the actors nor the writer had much talent.[43]

Walsh anticipated problems with his inexperienced leading man. On the first day of shooting in Yuma, he told Duke to sit behind the camera and watch how the professional Broadway actors employed pauses and other tricks of the stage to give strength to their lines. After Duke spent a week watching Tyrone Power, Tully Marshall, and several other professionals drink and act, Walsh decided that they were his real problem and told Duke to quit his informal studies. Duke, Walsh later told Zolotow, "was speaking naturally and these New York tenderfeet were godawful. . . . They were a bunch of bums. Full of booze, they over-acted. . . . John was the only one who knew his lines and the rewrites." Although Duke had not yet employed what became his trademark, pause-filled vocal cadence, he was one of the first actors to avoid a stagy British style.[44]

Duke followed every order or suggestion Walsh made. Once again he was the star pupil and athlete—attentive, respectful, coachable. He did not drink, keep late hours, or make a pass at his leading lady. Marguerite Churchill, Walsh observed, "looked stunning in a sunbonnet, but young Wayne's full attention seemed to be concentrated on the part he was to play. If Lady Godiva had ridden across [the set] with her hair cut off, it was a safe bet he would not even have glanced at her."[45]

After twenty-six days in Yuma, Walsh took his nearly three-hundred-person crew to Sacramento to shoot a river scene. During the next four months, Walsh shot scenes in Jackson Hole, Wyoming; the Grand Teton Pass; St. George, Utah; Sequoia National Park; and Moisie, Montana. Walsh filmed the wagon train struggling in mud slides, crossing snow-covered mountain paths, being lowered down cliffs, and fording rivers. Wagons toppled, wheels broke, and extras and stuntmen fell into icy rivers. Cast and crew suffered from mosquito and blackfly attacks, desert sun, spring snows, and bad whiskey. Walsh denied requests from several of his leading actors to hire more female extras and struggled to keep to his grueling schedule. Through it all Walsh's New York actors bitched and drank. "They hated the retakes. They hated the movies. They hated the desert sun. They couldn't get used to sitting around and waiting for the next camera set-up," Walsh later recalled.[46]

The complaint about retakes was a legitimate one. Since most theaters were not equipped for Grandeur Pictures, Walsh had been instructed to shoot everything twice, once in 70 mm and once in standard 35 mm. After four months of filming, he had shot more than 1,300,000 feet of Grandeur and standard film. To further complicate Walsh's job, he had been ordered to make a German version of *The Big Trail* using German speaking leads. *Die Grosse Fahrt* was intended to appeal to Fox's recently expanded European audience. The result was retakes after retakes, and seemingly endless hours to drink and complain.[47]

When it was all over Walsh had a film that conformed to the accepted standards of an American epic—if only they could have guaranteed success. The story unfolds against a canvas of raging rivers, snowcapped mountains, parched deserts, deep canyons, and tall sequoias. The action sequences, Walsh's trademark, are spectacular. He devoted weeks to staging and shooting river crossings, buffalo stampedes, mud slides, and snowscapes. But his crowning achievement was a scene of pioneers using ropes to lower wagons, people, and animals over a cliff to the floor of a canyon. He located cameras at the top and bottom of the canyon and captured the drama of the scene. A knot slipped unexpectedly when the last wagon was being lowered, and it swayed, hung lopsided for a moment, then fell to the canyon floor, splintering apart surrounded by rocks and white water. Walsh claimed that he held his breath until he was sure that his cameras had caught the action and he knew that he had his clincher. It was an action scene that could not have been duplicated.[48]

The Big Trail also recounts the epic story of America's westward movement—the country's Manifest Destiny. It is a tale of struggle and hardship but, more important, of strength, determination, and the will to overcome all geographic and psychological barriers. John Wayne plays Breck Coleman, a young, innocent Natty Bumppo, a trailblazer adept at knife throwing, hunting, and other frontier skills. He is also something of an historian and moral philosopher. His nation's destiny is fixed in his genes. At one point a snow-blocked mountain pass causes some of the weaker settlers to think of turning back. Breck refuses to entertain negative thoughts, lecturing his wards:

> We can't turn back! We're blazing a trail that started in England. Not even the storms of the sea could turn back those first settlers. And they carried on further. They blazed it on through the wilderness of Kentucky. Famine, hunger, not even massacres could stop them! And now we've picked up the trail again. And nothing can stop us—not even the snows of winter, not the peaks of the highest mountains! We're building a nation! But we've got to suffer! No great trail was ever blazed without hardship. And you gotta fight! That's life! And when you stop fightin', that's death! What're you going to do? Lie down and die? Not in a thousand years! You're going on with me![49]

Forward the push of empire was the great American theme, particularly popular during the last two decades of the nineteenth century and the first three decades of the twentieth. It was the substance of Frederick Jackson Turner's seminal 1893 essay, "The Significance of the Frontier in American History," and Theodore Roosevelt's seven-volume *The Winning of the West*. It celebrated the settlement of the continent and created heroes out of Buffalo Bill Cody, Kit Carson, and George Armstrong Custer, as well as countless frontier guides, Indian fighters, and railroad builders. It had been swallowed whole by Hollywood's early producers and directors, including those whom Marion Morrison had watched making movies in Glendale in the second decade of the twentieth century, as well as the more famous men who made such silent and sound films as *The Covered Wagon* and *The Pony Express* (James Cruze, 1923 and 1925), *The Iron Horse* and *Three Bad Men* (John Ford, 1924 and 1926), *The Virginian* (Victor Fleming, 1929), and *Cimarron* (Cecil B. DeMille, 1931). It was hardly a surprise that Fox's desperation stab at a Movietone, 70 mm blockbuster should be an epic frontier flick.[50]

In *The Big Trail* the villains are all obstacles to expansion. Some are human. The slick southern gambler Bill Thorpe (Ian Keith) threatens the push westward as surely as real southern politicians blocked expansion during the 1840s and 1850s. The Mexican Lopez (Charles Stevens) creates problems just as Mexico did in the 1840s. And Indians are a constant threat. But the major obstructions are natural—rivers, plains, deserts, and mountains. In this celebration of Manifest Destiny, however, every problem is solved, every challenge met.

Intertwined within the larger national theme, of course, are the personal themes of revenge and love. Breck Coleman follows three trails: He leads the wagon train, pursues the murderers of his friend, and awkwardly courts a woman. He alternates between pathfinder, judge, jury, executioner, and best man. "I'm the law out here. And the law is justice," he announces. No one questions his opinion or fitness to do the job—any job. "Coleman, you're the breed of man who would follow a trail to the end," comments one of the leading characters. Breck does just that. He leads his settlers to Oregon, tracks down and kills the man who murdered his friend, and finally meets up with the woman he loves in a grove of Sequoias. As the lovers meet, embrace, and kiss, the camera pans up toward heaven and the closing credits.

For John Wayne, playing his first substantial role, the film's weak script was hardly his biggest problem. There are hints that he paid too much attention to Lumsden Hare; he speaks about "a grea-a-a-t valley" and engages in grandiloquent theatrics his later fans would have howled at. His expressions of surprise and anger have the pantomimed quality of acting in silent films, and he seems uncomfortable delivering dialogue. Throughout the film he smiles too much, almost as if he had been caught in the act of some petty mischief, a mannerism exaggerated in love scenes, and his voice is high and stilted. But hints of his more mature style occasionally flash through. The basic cadence of his voice is there, although it lacks control and timing. At times his smile is easy and natural, and his silent, snake-eyed stare is effective. The cadence, the smile, the stare—all would become stock John Wayne trademarks.

His greatest strength on film—and his greatest weakness for the role—was his looks. He had the unlined beauty and profile of a matinee idol, a handsomeness that was soft and gentle. His looks seemed made for a tuxedo, not buckskins, and his eyes were more tender than hard. Two generations later Jane Tompkins described the soft beauty of Duke's young face: "He has not yet gotten the cowboy face, the leathery wall of noncommunication written over by wrinkles, speaking pain and hardship and the refusal to give in to them, speaking the determination to tough it out against all odds, speaking the willingness to be cruel in return for cruelty, and letting you know, beyond all shadow of a doubt, who's boss." Tompkins saw something else in the youthful Wayne: "The other expression, the expression of the young John Wayne, is tender, and more than a little wistful; it is delicate and incredibly sensitive. Pure and sweet; shy, really, and demure." The contrast between the young and the old made her wonder: "Where is she, this young girl that used to inhabit John Wayne's body along with the Duke?" Tompkins is right. There was not even a hint of ruggedness in his features then, and he and Marguerite Churchill look as if they were about to be crowned king and queen of

Sigma Chi's frontier-night ball. Miriam Hughes, a writer for *Photoplay*, described Duke's "shy, boyish" appeal and gray eyes, commenting, "If he doesn't go Hollywood he'll be a big star someday. He's got the stuff it takes." The "stuff," she made clear, was his looks and charm—not his talent.[51]

The most troubling aspect of *The Big Trail* was not Duke's acting, the weak script, or even the drinking on and off the set. Walsh overcame all these, but he had no quick fix for William Fox's or the country's economic problems. The Great Crash of October 1929 had caught Fox overextended by some $91 million. Assuming that he could finance a monstrous short-term debt by floating more stocks and bonds, Fox had paid too much for Loew's stock. But such bull market optimism ended overnight, and he was forced to sell off holdings to prevent bankruptcy. In early November he sold his stock holdings in First National Pictures Corporation to Warner Bros., and he prepared to unload more stock. In late November the government finally filed suit against him in federal court for antitrust violations. Fox had been working for months to avoid the suit, and it could not have come at a worse time. Fox Film stock, which had been a robust 105 3/8 earlier in the year, slumped to 56 7/8 the day the suit was filed, and was down to 50 by the end of the following week. Scrambling to save his holdings, in early December Fox announced that he had voluntarily relinquished control of his various companies to a board of trustees. But his last-minute plan failed. While Louis Mayer smiled in Hollywood, Fox's empire came crashing down. By mid-April Fox, who less than a year earlier had been the most important man in movie production, distribution, and exhibition in America and Europe, was forced out of the film industry.[52]

Fox Film Company, reorganized under new management, calmly announced that it planned to continue development and expansion of the use of Grandeur. Continue! It had been developed, and many of Fox's theaters were supposed to have been equipped for it. But Grandeur was part of Fox's grander vision that had gone bust. By the time *The Big Trail* premiered at Grauman's Chinese Theater on October 24, 1930—the one-year anniversary of Black Thursday—only two theaters, nationwide, had made the expensive conversion to 70 mm Grandeur film.

Grauman's Chinese Theater was a monument to American excess. Sidney Grauman, a midwestern carnival barker and Alaskan gold rusher turned entrepreneur, built the lavish Egyptian Theater in 1922 and single-handedly created the gala movie premiere as an American institution. When Cecil B. De Mille's *The Ten Commandments* opened at the Egyptian in 1924, Grauman lined

Hollywood Boulevard with dozens of army searchlights, filling the sky with billions of volts of white light. The Hollywood press came out in force, as did superstars, moguls, and curious residents. Tens of thousands of fans, hungry for a glimpse of America's newest celebrities, thronged the sidewalks from Western Avenue to La Brea. Wire services picked up the premiere, and stories appeared in newspapers throughout the country.[53]

In 1927, after five years of staging successful premieres and hoping for more, Grauman constructed the Chinese Theater. He located the entrance 150 feet back from Hollywood Boulevard, providing enough space for crowds to line up fifty deep and ogle the stars. With its 90-foot-high green jade pagoda roof, coral piers, stone dragons, ornate obelisks, bronze gargoyles, and jeweled lamps, the Chinese Theater was luxuriously decadent, a perfect setting for the vamps, sheiks, swashbucklers, and Babylonian princesses of the 1920s movies.

The Big Trail premiere was another Sid Grauman extravaganza. It was also the biggest night of Duke's life. He was only twenty-three years old. William Fox and Sidney Grauman planned to highlight him that night—to introduce him to the world as Hollywood's next leading man—but Winfield Sheehan, tightfisted as ever, gave Duke only two guest passes to the premiere. Duke invited Clyde and Molly to declare a temporary truce and join him for the evening, to sit in the limousine ferrying him down Hollywood Boulevard, to walk with him through the crowds lining the entrance to Grauman's Chinese, and to sit with him through the movie. Clyde agreed. He was excited for his son. Molly was not so excited. She refused to go anywhere with Clyde and insisted that Duke give the guest passes to her so that she and Bobby could attend. Duke pleaded with her, but she refused to listen to his reasoning. She delivered an ultimatum: Either give her both passes or she would not attend.

Anxious to provide Duke a way out of the dilemma, Clyde told him to take Bobby and Molly to the premiere. After the weekend, Duke, Clyde, Florence, and Nancy could go out to dinner and then go see *The Big Trail* as a family. But for the first time in his life, Duke called his mother's bluff. Molly and Bobby stayed home on the evening of October 24, 1930. Duke proudly picked up Clyde and Florence at their home in Beverly Hills. It was the only time he ever saw his father in a tuxedo.

The premiere was nearly a great success. Sid Grauman pulled out all the stops. He assembled so many army searchlights that people all over the Los Angeles Basin could see the glow, almost as if a full moon were hovering just below the horizon. Spectators crowded Hollywood Boulevard and spilled over on to Sunset. Duke, Clyde, and Florence made their way through the crowds;

ushers seated them in a roped-off section of seats reserved for William Fox, Raoul Walsh, Winfield Sheehan, John Wayne, Marguerite Churchill, and their guests. California governor James Rolph attended the grand opening, hailing the vision of William Fox and the wonder of the Grandeur process, but at the critical moment he suffered an inexcusable loss of memory. After congratulating almost everyone connected to the film and the industry, Rolph said, "And now, ladies and gentlemen, let us sit back in our chairs and watch the most spectacular motion picture ever made in this country of ours—*The Big Parade*." With the mention of John Gilbert's silent classic, the house lights dimmed and the musical prelude to *The Big Trail* commenced.

Most early reviewers liked what they saw on the wide screen. *Film Daily* called it "stupendous" and predicted great success. The *New York Times* agreed that the film was "magnificent," adding that it was "a testimonial to the progress of motion picture work." *Variety*, however, questioned whether making a $2 million epic made sense in a nation mired in a year-long depression. The problem with *The Big Trail*, the reviewer observed, was that it was not a "holdover picture." With an undistinguished cast, it was little more than "a noisy *Covered Wagon*," an already-popular silent Western. Even worse, the reviewer noted, the cast's age suggested that only elderly people made the overland trip and the film's plot limped along from start to finish: "The recurrence of the same things, interrupted now and then by a 'big scene' such as a river or cliff crossing, or El Brendel's dragged-in comedy with his mother-in-law, or the simple romance and the silly melodrama, commences to weary, for it's all the same thing over and over again." Beyond scenery, the only thing the film offered was historical accuracy—a thin thread on which to hang an expensive epic.[54]

The *Variety* review raised serious concerns at Fox. Nothing could be done about the film's trite plot-continuity problems; it was and had to remain a standard good-guy bad-guy Western. And nothing could be done about the fact that at the time of the film's release only Hollywood's Grauman's Chinese and New York's Roxy were equipped to show Grandeur film. But something could be done about the picture's two unknown stars, both of whom received mixed reviews. Winnie Sheehan promptly dispatched Marguerite Churchill and John Wayne on national tours to increase their visibility and promote the film.

For Duke the tour was a humiliating nightmare. Accompanied by a Fox publicity man, he uncomfortably watched the rewriting of his life. He was billed as a cross between Frank Merriwell and Daniel Boone, a knife-throwing, frontier-loving, clean-living football hero with sex appeal. The fan magazines gushed. Writing for *Screen Play*, Dorothy Cummings observed, "If I were an artist or a sculptor, I would ask John Wayne to sit for me as the personification of the young pioneer. His body is long, rangy, controlled. It is as lazy as a house cat's when relaxed, like the leap of a panther in action." Miriam Hughes of *Photoplay* was captured by Duke's energy, virility, and shy, boyish charm. *Motion Picture* writer Elizabeth Goldbeck judged, "John is just as he looks. Simple and forthright, appreciative and loyal—a good boy with all the steadfastness that could be expected of a young pioneer, and much more humor."[55]

Sheehan's idea, Wayne later told Zolotow, was to send Duke east looking like a refugee from Buffalo Bill's Wild West Show. Dressed in a green shirt and yellow boots, and with hair that was almost shoulder length, he pleaded with his publicity man, "Don't make me do this. I'm going to be an embarrassed man. You don't put a red dress on an elephant. It makes me look like a loudmouth." Putting aside the Western pimp ensemble, Sheehan dictated a new costume. Dressed as if he were trying to walk the fence in the Indian wars, Duke wore a beaded Indian jacket, moccasins, and a Tom Mix ten-gallon hat. "They're going to laugh me right out of New York," Duke told his publicity man. "Nonsense, we know about publicity," came the reply.[56]

Duke was right. In New York City he became an instant joke. One New York daily printed a photograph of Wayne stepping off the Twentieth-Century Limited in full frontier dress and sporting a watch. "The old frontiersmen never had to worry about the right time," read the caption. A female reporter asked Duke, "Mr. Wayne, do you normally wear these clothes?" "What do *you* think, sister?" Duke answered. He was a sideshow, reduced to making a canned speech about being in *The Big Trail*, riding a horse in Central Park, and giving a knife-throwing exhibition.[57]

Even more galling to Duke was the fake bio of him that the studio had sent out. He was billed as a veteran of the Great War, a former Texas Ranger, and All-American football player. He tried to set the record straight. "I'm not a Texas Ranger or a doughboy. I don't know what the studio is trying to do with me," he told reporters, but the movie columnists chose to print the hype. The lies frustrated Wayne and made him gun-shy of publicity and reporters. But he endured the small humiliations—students laughing at him at Yale, reporters casting knowing glances at each other—and played the role of a small-time Buffalo Bill.[58]

The Big Trail, however, languished at the box office. The 35-mm version, which played across the country, lacked the epic quality of the Grandeur process. Expensive to make, the film came nowhere near recovering its costs. It stood as a monument to the vision, ambition, and greed of William Fox.

But in Hollywood, everything fosters myths. *The Big Trail* contributed to a general belief in the industry that the day of the big Western epic was over, that an increasingly urban public had become too sophisticated for horse operas, and that in rural America, where Westerns remained popular, the market was too small to sustain an expensive production.

In an industry where a star is only as good as his or her last picture, the careers of Marguerite Churchill and John Wayne were stopped dead. Winfield Sheehan had discovered Churchill on Broadway, signed her to a Hollywood contract, nourished her career, and predicted great success. He quickly promoted her to leading roles, casting her opposite Paul Muni in *The Valiant*, a film in which he won a Best Actor nomination. Fox's publicity department touted her as a talented ingenue— "gracious, aristocratic and refined"—who lived with her mother in Beverly Hills, was always perfectly groomed but thought little of clothes or shopping, and—though she missed the excitement of New York—believed California was "the most wonderful state in the Union." Then *The Big Trail* happened. The publicity campaign ended. In 1931 she played secondary roles in such B pictures as *Girls Demand Excitement*, *Charlie Chan Carries On*, and *Riders of the Purple Sage*. In 1932 she returned to New York and Broadway. The film roles she obtained in the 1930s tended to be in inexpensive murder and horror films. Her film career was effectively ended by the picture that marked John Wayne's debut.[59]

Duke's brief, bright career took a similar, albeit temporary, plunge. Still under contract with Fox, he made two films in 1931—the aforementioned *Girls Demand Excitement* and *Three Girls Lost*. In the first, a campus comedy, Wayne plays the ringleader of a gang of males who are attempting to oust all females from their college. The issue is decided by a basketball game—men against women, winner take all. Duke believed it was the silliest picture of his career. Although he made scores of bad films, his assessment of *Girls Demand Excitement* was sound. In one scene a psychology experiment measures the "emotional reaction" to kissing. In another, Virginia Cherrill, the female lead, crawls into bed with Wayne to discredit his political cause. Director Seymour Felix added to the film's plot problems. A musical dance stager, he choreographed each scene, moving actors and actresses about as if they were engaged in a ballet. One can almost hear him counting—"and one and two and three and four"—during the basketball game sequence. "It was just so goddamn ridiculous that I was hanging my head," Duke later recalled. Reviewers agreed. *Variety* quietly noted: "Theatres playing to a clientele of class will find nothing in it."[60]

Three Girls Lost was little better. The film miscast Wayne as an architect, opposite Loretta Young, in an urban drama. He plays a gentleman who in one scene passively stands silent and watches a gangster abduct his girl. Duke hated the scene, and he told director Sidney Lanfield that he should at least attempt to stop the abduction. "Duke, you're playing a gentleman," Lanfield responded. Wayne questioned his definition of a gentleman but played the part. *Variety* thought Duke showed promise but panned the film. The *New York Times* reviewer best summed up the movie: "It is all rather silly."[61]

In three leading roles Duke had failed to attract much critical attention. All three films lost money. Fox had signed Duke to a five-year contract with an option clause that had to be renewed every six months. After the failure of *Three Girls Lost* the studio leaders had seen enough and chose not to renew his contract. In one of America's and Hollywood's worst years, Duke was free to negotiate with other studios. Put another way, he was unemployed.

5

Poverty Row

Hard times. By 1931 the nation was moving into the second full year of the depression. Industries trimmed their budgets and sloughed off workers. Banks failed in record numbers. Men walked about town looking for work or selling apples for five cents each on street corners. In Washington the president of the United States agonized about trying even half measures to solve the country's problems and left millions of Americans with the inescapable impression that he simply did not give a damn. It took a while, but by mid-1931 the hard times and the oozing fear of the future had reached Hollywood.

Sound had prevented the depression from hitting Hollywood sooner. But as the novelty of talking pictures wore off, box office receipts registered the grim fact that the industry was not depression proof. Warner Bros., which had shown profits of $17 million in 1929 and $7 million in 1930, lost almost $8 million in 1931. RKO went from a $3 million surplus in 1930 to a $5.6 million deficit in 1931. During the same period, profits at Paramount fell from $18 million to $6 million, and Fox went from $9 million in the black to $3 million in the red. And if the present was bleak, greater darkness loomed on the horizon. As more and more Americans swelled the unemployment lines, movie attendance fell. The average weekly attendance in 1930 was 80 million; in 1932 it was down to 50 million. As people stopped going to the movies, actors, actresses, writers, and technicians became members of the great unemployed.[1]

John Wayne, fresh from a series of failures, was one of the many. Not only had Fox cast him adrift, John Ford had severed his personal relationship with Duke. Understanding Ford's motives for doing anything was a difficult calculus. A man of deep insecurities, and sensitive to slights real and imagined, something or other was always getting under his skin. Perhaps he was upset that Duke had left his small stock company to work for other directors. Perhaps he misinterpreted a remark or action by Duke. Perhaps he heard a rumor that set him on edge. Perhaps nothing at all happened and Ford was just being mean and contrary.

Whatever the reason, after Duke finished *The Big Trail*, Ford put an icy distance between himself and the actor. One day in 1930, Duke saw Ford on the Fox lot, where he was directing *Up the River*. Duke ambled over, said, "Hi, Coach," and watched the director breeze by him without a word of acknowledgment. Assuming that Ford had either not heard him or was too distracted to answer, Wayne thought no more about it. But a few days later the scene was repeated. Wayne said "Hi, Coach, hi," and Ford never looked at him. The next time Duke saw Ford, he made sure the director also saw him. He stood right in front of him and offered his greeting. Ford stared straight ahead as if he was looking through Duke and walked over to talk to someone else. "That's that—he won't talk to me," Duke remembered in an interview with Peter Bogdanovich. Instead of trying to discover what was bothering Ford, Wayne stopped saying hello, cutting his ties to Fox's leading director.[2]

Unlike many of his peers, Wayne was not unemployed for long. Harry Cohn, head of productions at Columbia Pictures, signed him to a standard five-year contract, which the studio could renew or terminate every six months. Located on the corner of Sunset Boulevard and Gower, in the heart of Poverty Row, Columbia Pictures was a studio apart—and it was in a better position than the other studios to battle the effects of the depression. From Columbia's inception in 1924, its leaders made it their mission to make films cheaply. They shot their films on tight budgets, demanded that their directors print only one take of a scene, kept their talent on short-term contracts, and made a policy of using holdouts and defectors from other studios as well as freelancers, has-beens, and never-quite-weres. People other studios discarded were the stock-in-trade of Columbia's casts. Furthermore, unlike MGM, Warner's, Fox, Paramount, and RKO, Columbia did not own a chain of theaters and thus did not have the added worry of the decline in weekly attendance. In the early years of the Great Depression, Columbia's major concerns were simple: continued frugality and profit from others' losses by upgrading its pictures.[3]

Harry Cohn was determined to make sure both those things happened, and he was not particularly concerned whom he destroyed in the process. By the early 1930s the handsomeness of Cohn's youth had begun to give way to a certain thickening around the waist, and baldness. But neither in his youth nor in his middle age was there anything soft or publicly sentimental about Harry Cohn. Around Hollywood he was known as a son-of-a-bitch's son-of-a-bitch. Frank Capra, Columbia's star director, nicknamed him "His Crudeness." Writer Ben Hecht dubbed him "White Fang." "In the general run of humanity," Capra noted, "people either give you a lift, or depress you; or bore you, or, as with most, leave you indifferent. But not Harry Cohn. Just his presence would make your hackles rise and your adrenals pump furiously. He annoyed and belittled—until he made you hate." Columnist Hedda Hopper agreed, commenting that Cohn was "the man you stood in line to hate."[4]

None of the other moguls inspired more stories and legends as Cohn. He hid his intelligence behind layers of coarseness, vulgarity, and anti-intellectualism. He declined an invitation to a ballet with the remark, "Watch those fags chase each other for three hours and not catch each other?" Prideful of his own lack of formal education, he belittled the Ivy Leaguers on his staff; in group meetings he often asked Dartmouth graduate Collier Young to pronounce some word he claimed not to understand and then announced, "Gentlemen, the only reason I have Collier Young here is to piss on him. Isn't that right, Collier?" "Yes, sir," came the standard reply.[5]

The put-downs and humiliations he dealt out like cards were simply by-products of the exercise of power, the one pursuit above all others that Cohn delighted and excelled in. His dark, penetrating eyes, broad shoulders, and foreboding smile struck fear into his employees. "Nobody could fail to be unnerved by such concentration of personal power," noted one person who watched Cohn work. "I don't get ulcers. I give 'em!" Cohn boasted. And anyone who worked for Cohn soon learned that the producer lived by his own oft-repeated version of the Golden Rule: He who has the gold makes the rules.[6]

By the spring of 1931, when Duke arrived at the studio, Columbia was poised to crash the gates of the majors. While the other studios lost money, Columbia reported substantial profits. In addition, the studio had Frank Capra under contract. That spring his *Dirigible* became the first Columbia film to play in Grauman's Chinese Theater. Two years later his *The Bitter Tea of General Yen* became the first Columbia picture to open at the Radio City Music Hall. Then, in 1935, Columbia won seven Oscars, five of which were for Capra's *It Happened One Night.*[7]

Duke seemed a perfect Cohn acquisition: He had starred in a major film for a major studio, had some name recognition, and came cheap. As soon as he signed a contract, Cohn put him to work in *Men Are Like That* (originally released as *Arizona*), a film directed by George Seitz, who had worked on Pearl White serials, dominated serial production in the 1920s, and earned a reputation as one of Columbia's fastest, most economical, and most productive directors. Wayne plays an army lieutenant, stationed in Arizona, whose former girlfriend is now the wife of his best friend and commander. In a series of improbable adventures, the woman attempts to lure the virtuous lieutenant into a compromising position, but honor, commitment to the army and another woman, and friendship overcome all temptations. A trite plot and unconvincing performances by Duke and Laura La Plante in the leading roles doomed the film to poor reviews.[8]

But they were the least of Wayne's worries. Rumors from the set had circulated that his containment of his own passions fell below West Point standards. A prop man told Cohn that Wayne was having an affair with a Columbia actress who had attracted the studio head's attention. Unhappy in his own marriage and accustomed to treating his lot as a bordello, Cohn exploded. "When you're at this studio, you keep your pants buttoned," he shouted at Wayne. The force and vulgarity of Cohn's attack threw Duke off balance, and he chose the wrong defense. He attempted politely to deny the rumor, waving the red flag of respectability in front of Cohn, who viewed any show of manners as a singular weakness. "He was a son-of-a-bitch," Duke later recalled, who did not respect manners. "I'd been brought up to respect older people and he talked to me like a sewer rat." At that time in his career, Duke did not know what the strongest men and women at Columbia had learned: If you fought Cohn, occasionally you could win. If you resorted to polite reasoning, you always lost. In his only meaningful conversation with Cohn, Duke lost—big.[9]

Duke was on Cohn's "shit list," and the studio head treated him as something best swept into the gutter. But not before he had a little sadistic fun at the young actor's expense. In *The Deceiver*, Duke's next film, Cohn let the actor know where he stood in the Columbia pecking order by casting him as a corpse, which appropriately enough had been mysteriously knifed in the back. No lines, no movement—just dead. His point made, Cohn assigned

Wayne to the studio's "B" division, where films were shot fast on fifty-thousand-dollar budgets. In *Range Feud*, *Texas Cyclone*, and *Two Fisted Law*, Duke played steadily less significant supporting roles in Buck Jones and Tim McCoy Westerns. Although *Range Feud* was a better than average Western and Duke was given a substantial part, in *Texas Cyclone* he played a juvenile role, and in *Two Fisted Law* his part was reduced to what Duke later called "sagebrush window dressing." Along with his demotion to Columbia's B division, it was a clear indication that his stay at the studio would be short. Harry Cohn knew how to nurse a grudge.[10]

Wayne's final film at Columbia was *Maker of Men*. If Cohn was scripting the downfall of John Wayne, the film was a humiliating farewell. Duke played Dusty, a worthless college football player willing to sell out his team for a few pieces of silver. During his career he played no single more objectionable role. It was the sort of part that later in his career he would never have played under any circumstances. But in 1931 he had no leverage. He was Harry Cohn's "property"—a word the producer used for scripts and actors—and he played the parts Harry Cohn assigned him. When shooting for *Maker of Men* ended and Wayne's contract came up for renewal, Cohn abruptly severed the relationship. In time Cohn forgot or forgave the incident that poisoned his relationship with Wayne and frequently tried to entice him back to Columbia. But Duke never forgot the incident or the string of humiliations. And he never forgave Harry Cohn: He said he would rather leave the industry than make a picture for that "son-of-a-bitch."[11]

Duke's revenge would take time, however. Only a major star could snub Harry Cohn, and for Duke that status was still some fifteen years in the future. Poverty was no revenge, and in early 1932 he was just another unemployed actor who had had a couple of good chances but had failed to make the grade. Bad timing, temperamental producers, poor scripts—they were all good excuses, but Hollywood was a town addicted to the bottom line and accepted no excuses. At Fox and at Columbia, John Wayne had starred in films that lost money or generated very little. By the accepted rules of the only game in town, he was a loser. The industry praised and rewarded success, conferring a godlike status on its biggest moneymakers. There was little sympathy for losers.

Duke's only option was to move further down Poverty Row. On the advice of George O'Brien, a friend from his Fox days, Duke had acquired an agent, Al Kingston of the Leo Morrison Agency. Morrison personally handled his firm's leading clients—Jean Harlow, Buster Keaton, Francis X. Bushman, and

Spencer Tracy. Kingston shepherded the firm's lesser talents and projects. And Duke was certainly a project. He was too tall, too handsome, and too full of raw talent to play anything but a leading man, yet he had failed too often. Kingston, however, liked Duke. In an industry of prima donnas and fakes, Duke worked hard to please and sought nothing more than work.[12]

The agent quickly earned his percentage, signing Wayne to a deal with Nat Levine, the short, cigar-smoking head of Mascot Pictures. Levine, a poor man's mogul, prowled Poverty Row like a king, making money on his pictures and losing much of it at the racetrack. He liked to cast animals in his films, so it was fitting that he was himself a one-trick pony. He knew how to do one thing well—produce inexpensive, action-packed serials that turned a nice buck, as decades later men and women like him would make profitable movies for video release, unknown, unremarked, and yet viable. Year after year during the late 1920s and early 1930s, unaffected by the coming of sound, changes in public tastes, or economic hard times, Levine performed his routine.[13]

Typical of other moguls, Levine had entered the film industry at the bottom. Dropping out of school after junior high, he started as an office boy in New York for Marcus Loew, and after a few years rose to the position of Loew's personal secretary. From there he traveled to Kansas City, where he obtained a job as sales manager for Margaret Winkler, a distribution outfit that handled the Felix the Cat cartoons. Over the next two years Levine learned the distribution business and acquired useful contacts throughout the country. In 1921, after almost a decade in the industry, he moved to Hollywood and inched cautiously into production.[14]

At first he only bought and marketed properties. He had a knack for anticipating what would sell, and a sense of pricing. It was almost as much fun as playing the horses. He would buy a picture that was entangled by a lien, pay off the creditors, and market it on a states' rights basis, often making 200 or 300 percent profit. States' rights distribution was a complicated process in which an independently produced film was sold to independent distribution companies dominating regional markets. From there it was only a small shuffle for Levine into independent production. After a modestly successful debut in 1926, with *The Sky Flyer*, a ten-chapter serial starring a Rin Tin Tin wanna-be named Silver Streak, Levine formed his own production company, Mascot Pictures, to provide serials which he sold to independent exchanges. Serials, called "chapter plays" in the 1920s and 1930s, were as much a part of the moviegoing experience as cartoons, shorts, and features, and they were particularly popular on matinee programs targeting children and juveniles. Each serial was divided into ten to fifteen parts. The first chapter ran three reels (about thirty minutes) to allow for plot and character development. All other chapters ran two reels (averaging eighteen to twenty minutes) and featured thrilling rescues, tragic deaths, and mysterious doings. The idea was to end each chapter but the last in the middle of a cliff-hanger scene to draw the viewer to the next week's matinee. For many kids serials were more important than features, and Nat Levine's chapter plays developed a large and loyal following. The difference between Levine's serials and those of Pathé and Universal, the other leading makers of serials, was action. If such a thing is possible, Pathé and Universal made thinking-men—or thinking-boy—serials that emphasized plot continuity and action. Levine's exhibited little concern for plot plausibility but gave his viewers action, action, and more action.[15]

Enos Edward "Yakima" Canutt, a hook-nosed, weatherbeaten, rawboned cowboy, was Levine's great acquisition. He had picked up the nickname "Yakima" during a distinguished rodeo career. From 1917 to 1924, he dominated the rodeo circuit, and in the off-season he earned additional money as an extra and a stunt man in Hollywood. By the mid-1920s Canutt concluded that there was more money to be made falling off horses on cue than staying on them for eight seconds. For $125 a week he performed stunts never seen before. Had he had more regular features—and, after the advent of sound, a less raspy high-pitched voice—he might have become a Western hero, but as a heavy and a stunt man he enjoyed steady work. By 1928, when Levine hired him to coordinate all of Mascot's stunt and second unit work, Canutt was already recognized as the best action man in the industry. More than any other person, he changed stunt work from an occupation for foolhardy men who would try anything for a price to a profession in which survival was an important factor.[16]

Canutt admired Levine, even the producer's tendency of issuing orders impossible to carry out. Levine was a genuine character who knew when to laugh as well as yell. Occasionally Levine would make an outrageous demand, and an actor or crew member would look at him and laugh, prompting the producer to laugh along. "He was a shrewd businessman who had a keen appreciation for what people were going through," Canutt remembered, and he got the most out of the people who worked for him.[17]

During the late 1920s and early 1930s, Mascot blossomed into a small but successful production company. Making two or three serials a year, and remaining within a strict thirty-thousand-dollar-per-serial budget, Levine turned a steady profit. He hired talented actors, directors, writers, stunt men, and technicians and got them to work long hours for little money. If Levine's eye for horses at the track bordered on the blind, his vision for filmmaking talent was crystal clear. He hired and gave considerable artistic freedom to men like Canutt, screenwriter Wyndham Gittens, and director Richard Thorpe. He avoided prima donnas and costly payrolls by employing hungry actors whose careers had not yet taken off or seemed on a downhill slide. He simply recognized talent and character, whether in such newcomers as Boris Karloff and Gene Autry or in such damaged goods as Harry Carey and John Wayne.

That ability allowed Levine to weather the stock market crash and the transition to talkies. While Universal's serial department delayed the move to sound, and Pathé abandoned serials after its purchase by Joseph P. Kennedy, Mascot entered the 1930s stronger than ever. In 1930 Levine went against the collective wisdom of the industry and hired an actor whom the leaders of the other studios had believed had been killed by sound: Rin Tin Tin. Rinty was one of the gods of the silent era. "This dog is the most sympathetic and human creature on the screen today," commented a reviewer in 1925. "Rin Tin Tin could do anything," said Darryl F. Zanuck, and he was in a good position to know since he earned his keep at Warner Bros. writing scripts for the dog. D. Ross Lederman, a gifted director who made all three of John Wayne's Columbia Westerns and had directed Rinty at Warner's, agreed:

> You probably think his trainer, Lee Duncan, always told him what to do. He may have in the beginning. I don't know. But when I worked with him we needed very few retakes and almost no extensive rehearsing. That dog knew just what was expected of him. He would watch Duncan for a signal, if movement was required. He couldn't tell time. But as for emoting, or playing a scene right, he didn't need any coaching. That's the unusual thing about that dog. He actually seemed to understand the story line well enough to bring off his role better than most of the other actors in the picture. I had more trouble with Tim McCoy and Buck Jones later at Columbia than I ever had with Rinty at Warners. He was one of the few truly professional actors we had in Hollywood at the time. He just went about his business.

And that business was as profitable as a gold mine. But after making several part-barking films in 1929, Warner's chose not to renew Rin Tin Tin's contract.[18]

Levine snatched Rinty from the cruel list of the unemployed and gave him another chance. *The Lone Defender* (1930), noted Jon Tuska in his wonderful history of Mascot pictures, was "the first all-talking, all-barking serial in canine or human history." Levine paid Rinty and Duncan a mere five thousand dollars, budgeted the film at forty thousand dollars, assigned Richard Thorpe to direct it, and profited greatly. He followed up his success the next year with *The Lightning Warrior* (1931), another action serial starring Rin Tin Tin. Quite old by this time, and better suited to emoting than action, Rinty left the more dangerous action sequences to his team of doubles—including a stuffed wolf used for scenes where the dog had to leap from high places—and concentrated on his famed limping routine and close-ups. In one scene he even wore a fake beard and leather booties as a disguise. The serial was another success. It was, unfortunately, Rinty's last. After proving that he was still box-office magic and validating Levine's faith in him, Rin Tin Tin died in the summer of 1932.[19]

Mascot was running smoothly when John Wayne joined the outfit in the beginning of 1932. In 1931 Levine had produced three films: *The Galloping Ghost*, featuring Red Grange; *The Vanishing Legion*, starring Harry Carey, fresh from his comeback success in *Trader Horn*; and *The Lightning Warrior*. Three serials, huge hits. Tight budgets, inventive scripts, constant action, and hardworking, imaginative talent had moved Levine to the forefront of the serial market. There was little likelihood that John Wayne would fail in a Nat Levine production, despite the "wisdom" of the industry.

Duke went back to work. He was now on Levine time, Hollywood's answer to Henry Ford's production line. No wasted motions, no added costs. Shooting began at sunrise and often continued long after sunset, occasionally with scenes lit by torches. "We worked so hard on those Mascot serials we didn't have time to think," Duke told an interviewer in 1978. "We would put twenty-five reels in the can in sixteen to twenty-three days of shooting—and that's nights too. A working day was from twelve to twenty hours. They didn't hire you for acting, they wanted endurance. You had to be able to last through it." To streamline production, Levine began to use two directors on each film, one for interior scenes, the other for exterior shooting. Discussing the work of codirectors Armand Schaefer and Benjamin Kline, Tuska commented, "While Schaefer was filming his interiors, Kline would be setting up and planning the next day's exterior shooting. When Kline was shooting, Schaefer would be overseeing set design, available space, props, and viewing both his rushes and Kline's from previous days' shooting so he could properly match his interior shots with Kline's exteriors." Working in this manner for six days a week, twelve hours a day, Levine's team ground out a five-hour, twenty-five-reel serial in three weeks. If an unexpected delay occurred, Levine jumped back on schedule by working seven days a week, eighteen hours a day.[20]

Levine sensed that Duke had a sincerity, an almost Boy Scout–like sense of decency, that would translate well to the serial format. "I was impressed with his honesty, his character," Levine recalled. "You could believe him. There was nothing phony about the guy, and that came through on the screen. As an actor, he wasn't the best and he wasn't the worst. He was okay. What helped him more than anything else was his naturalness—along the lines of Spencer Tracy."[21]

Levine immediately cast Duke as the hero of *Shadow of the Eagle*, which was in preproduction. Wayne played Craig McCoy, a stunt pilot determined to save a carnival and the woman he loved by unmasking and defeating a mysterious criminal known as the Eagle. *Shadow of the Eagle*, like many of Mascot's serials, capitalized on a current interest. Since Lindbergh's Atlantic crossing pilots had been on the public's mind. William Wellman's *Wings* (1927), Frank Capra's *Flight* (1929) and *Dirigible* (1931), Howard Hawks's *The Dawn Patrol* (1930), and Howard Hughes's *Hell's Angels* (1930) had all done well at the box office. *Shadow of the Eagle*, featuring John Wayne, who had the fresh, clean look of Charles Lindbergh, brought the craze for pilots to the matinee.[22]

In Hollywood terms Duke made *Shadow of the Eagle* for pennies. Levine had signed him to star in three serials for a total of fifteen hundred dollars. But Duke never complained. In 1932, the most heartless year of the Great Depression, when fifteen million workers were unemployed and jobs were as scarce as veterans' bonuses, five hundred dollars for less than a month's work was a small fortune. Nor did Duke complain about the long hours. He made sure he was on the set before shooting began and stayed there until the cameras were shut down for the night. On one seemingly endless day, director Ford Beebe managed 114 camera setups before midnight.

In fact, Duke's earnestness and willingness to please attracted the interest of his coworkers. Yakima Canutt and Bud Osborne, who played heavies and handled the film's stunt work, decided to test the young actor. Osborne had worked with Wayne before, and he introduced him to Canutt. Wayne almost gushed, carrying on about how pleased he was that Yakima was doubling for him and about how much he had heard of Yakima's rodeo career and stunt work. Later Osborne discreetly informed Duke that Yak was Levine's stool pigeon and to watch what he did or said around him. Glancing toward Canutt, Wayne noticed that he was standing off by himself jotting something in a little red notebook. After that Duke avoided Canutt as if he had the plague, moving quickly away from him whenever Yak attempted a conversation. The gag lingered for a week. Once during a break Osborne and another actor convinced Duke to have a quick drink with them. Duke took a swig, and as he was passing the bottle to Osborne he spied Yak looking at his watch and making a note. "That did it," Canutt remembered. Duke "blew his top and I made a hasty retreat."[23]

When told of the gag, Duke laughed as hard as anyone else, although he remained suspicious of Canutt for a few days. Gradually Duke's wariness turned to friendship. One night, shooting on location in the Antelope Valley wrapped up near midnight. The schedule called for it to begin again at four o'clock the next morning at a nearby quarry. Rather than drive the open-top roadster the studio had lent him back to Los Angeles for only an hour or two of sleep, Wayne decided to spend the night on the set. Canutt had reached the same conclusion and had built a fire to fight the chill. Wayne walked over, and the two shared a bottle of whiskey. "It doesn't take very long to spend all night here, does it?" Yak asked. Duke agreed. It was the first of many nights on location that they would spend together. During the next several decades, Canutt would make more films with Wayne than with any other actor.[24]

The long hours on location were no guarantee of success. Duke moved through *The Shadow of the Eagle* with a wooden stiffness. Perhaps too aware of the camera, he seemed overly conscious of his hands and his movements. He held his hands rigidly in front of him with his palms turned slightly upward as if he was preparing to catch a ball that someone had lobbed at him, and he walked in an awkward half stride.

A poor script added to Duke's physical problems. Serial dialogue served a purely utilitarian function; since its sole purpose was to explain what was going on and to set up the next stunt, it often tended to be little more than telegraphed directions. A typical scene begins with a discussion between a ventriloquist and his dummy. It's late and the dummy is ready to go to sleep:

VENTRILOQUIST: "We got to stay up until Craig and the rest of the bunch comes back from the factory."

DUMMY: "Ah, gee." [He hears the sound of an approaching automobile.] "That sounds like them now." [The two leave their tent and greet Craig (John Wayne) and the circus midget and strongman.]

CRAIG: "Everything worked out perfectly. Where's Mr. Gregory?"

VENTRILOQUIST: "Well, I haven't seen him. Wasn't he with you?"

CRAIG: "Well, that's strange. I thought he was ahead of us."

STRONGMAN: "Maybe we should go back and see what happened to him."
CRAIG: "No, you two fellows turn in. If he doesn't show up pretty quick, Henry (the midget) and I will go look for him."

The scene does its job perfectly. It informs the viewer that something has happened to Mr. Gregory, the circus owner, and that Craig, the serial's hero, will solve the mystery. But for an actor, such directional dialogue is difficult to deliver with any sense of realism, particularly when the standard rule was to shoot only one take. For the typical adolescents who watched serials, the issue was moot. Stunts, not dialogue, were the genre's raison d'être. But such wooden dialogue forced Duke to learn how to deliver bad lines. Later in his life he stressed the positive side commenting, "It was a great experience. It was helpful, and it made me realize how wonderful it is to work in an 'A' picture where you're given the chance to walk into a situation and react rather than tell the audience what's going to happen and tell them where you're going to go and then telling them that you're there and then telling them what you're going to do."[25]

Had *The Shadow of the Eagle* cost more money to make, it would have been a financial failure. Produced on a shoestring, it was still a box-office disappointment. Levine had cut costs on the picture, anticipating that John Wayne's minor celebrity status would carry the serial. But Levine's expectations were unreasonable. In 1932, and for several years after that, Duke's name was not enough to guarantee success, even for inexpensively made Poverty Row productions.[26]

After *The Shadow of the Eagle,* he played a secondary part as a boxer in Paramount's *Lady and Gent* before returning to Mascot for his second serial. *The Hurricane Express* continued Hollywood's infatuation with the railroad, an affair that stretched back to *The Great Train Robbery*, the first narrative film. Once again Wayne plays the serial's hero. The credits for *The Hurricane Express*, however, demonstrate his continued slide in the industry. Unlike *The Shadow of the Eagle,* in which he received top billing, he is listed third in the credits, a certain indication of his box-office troubles.

In *The Hurricane Express* Levine attempted to build a serial around the theme of progress. An opening montage features the evolution of transportation, cutting from rolling wagon wheels and walking men to planes and boats to trains. Progress is interpreted as a cliché of movement. "Onward the wheels of civilization roll—ever faster—and faster," notes the film's prologue. The theme of progress is underscored by the opening dialogue between father and son, played by J. Farrell MacDonald and John Wayne. Both men are devoted to transportation: The father is a railroad engineer and the son a pilot. The son remarks that trains are slow and out of date; the father calls planes "playthings." The banter is good natured, but this light rivalry ends when the father is killed in a train wreck masterminded by a villain known only as the Wrecker, a man who uses rubber mask disguises. From that point on, *The Hurricane Express* returns to the more familiar confines of the genre. Train wreck follows train wreck, innocent men are accused of terrible deeds, hopes are raised and dashed, and every episode ends in a cliff-hanger until the last rubber mask is pulled off the Wrecker. As the serial's hero, John Wayne is pounded by chairs, beaten with fists, and pelted by rocks; he has bullets shot at him and wrenches thrown at him; he confronts almost certain death on trains, planes, and automobiles. But in the end he solves the mystery of the Wrecker and wins the love of the heroine. The return of order and progress is reinforced when two of the falsely accused, a railway executive and an airline manager, decide to merge their trains and planes to form a transportation company.[27]

The conservative message of the triumph of order and progress was not always reflected in feature films during the early 1930s. As Andrew Bergman has argued in his study of depression Hollywood, the early 1930s witnessed the emergence of a cinema skeptical of the notion of progress and defiantly anarchic. Feature movies of the period were populated by gangsters and shysters, men on the make and women on the take, deadbeat cops and corrupt pillars of the community. In *Little Caesar* and *The Public Enemy*, Edward G. Robinson and James Cagney transformed gangsters into heroes. Even comedies sounded the same cynical note. W. C. Fields mocked rugged individualism and the cherished institution of the home, and the Marx Brothers created a world turned upside down and inside out with nations such as Klopstockia—where all men answer to the name George and all women, Angela—and Freedonia—whose prime minister, Rufus T. Firefly, sends one of his citizens off to battle with the comment: "While you're out there risking life and limb . . . we'll be in here thinking what a sucker you are." The popularity of Cagney, Robinson, and the Marx Brothers reflected the unrest and concerns of a troubled nation.[28]

Levine's Mascot serials share some of the characteristics of the more popular features. The villain in *The Shadow of the Eagle* is an executive of a large airplane manufacturing corporation; in *The Hurricane Express* he is an unscrupulous lawyer with a pencil-thin mustache. A healthy distrust of wealth, the general impression that police and government officials are more likely to complicate than to solve any problem, and a general populist air pervades both serials. Levine's heroes, however, affirm individualism and initiative. They restore order, they dispense justice, they ensure progress—they fit perfectly into the Western genre of Zane Grey and Max Brand.

The conservative values and populist attitudes of Poverty Row suited Duke. He liked the no-frills, democratic environment of Levine's company, where the cowboy stunt men were bigger stars than the leading men and where everyone was expected to work the same grueling schedule. Being a member of the cast, just one of the boys, was important to him, and he even took comfort in the small discomforts of life on a Mascot set: the bad lunches, the absent dinners, the late nights, the early calls. In such surroundings it was impossible to become a prima donna and difficult to take yourself too seriously.

Yakima Canutt recalled that Duke was "a regular kind of guy." Decades later he remembered with utter clarity one episode that captured the essence of John Wayne. It happened during the filming of *The Hurricane Express*. Early one morning between takes on location at a railroad site, Duke noticed a hobo cooking a stew. He ambled over and had a conversation and breakfast with the man. Duke "got the biggest kick out of it." He was impressed by the hobo's generosity and opinions. "You know," he repeatedly told Canutt, "that was damn good stew."[29]

In March 1933 Wayne completed his contract with Mascot. With the rest of the cast, he traveled to Yuma, Arizona, to work in the serial *The Three Musketeers*. He had been in Yuma before, and the memories were still painful. During the shooting of *The Big Trail* he had gotten sick, lost weight, missed work, and watched Raoul Walsh's unsuccessful attempt to curb the alcoholic excesses of his writers and actors. This time there were fewer cast and crew members and slightly less whiskey, but the problems were the same. Levine's supporters have observed that the producer "ran a tight ship"; in fact, he was cheap on a heroic scale and even in the best of times his parsimony ran toward obsession. Duke remembered one time when Levine saved a buck by convincing him to share a bedroom with two older actors. In Yuma he had a convenient excuse for trying to save money: The banks were closed. A day or two before the cast arrived, Franklin D. Roosevelt had been inaugurated and ordered a short bank holiday.[30]

Duke recalled that Levine had refused to spend money to send good stunt horses from Hollywood, and Yakima Canutt got "stuck with a two-and-a-half-dollar horse that had never seen lighting reflectors before." Everything from the reflectors to the bedsheets worn by the "Arabs" frightened the horse, and it balked repeatedly. In one scene in which Canutt was doubling for Duke, the horse balked, and Yakima had to beat it to make it move. As a crowd of interested spectators watched the scene, Duke yelled, "That ain't John Wayne beating that horse!" "Yeah, and this ain't John Wayne doin' this stunt, either," Canutt shot back.[31]

Intense heat compounded the financial problems. Ruth Hall, the female lead, worked without a double and fried under the desert sun. She developed sun blisters, and her face swelled so much that many of the later scenes had to be shot with her back to the camera. Shooting in the Mojave Desert near Yuma, the sun exacted a brutal schedule. Most of the filming took place in the early morning and the late afternoon, but even then the heat was severe. But Wayne seldom complained. "John Wayne was always on the set," Ruth Hall said. "You learned never to give in to the elements," Duke later observed.[32]

In *The Three Musketeers* Duke once again plays a pilot struggling to defend order. El Shaitan, a mysterious masked figure, is plotting an Arab uprising against the French Foreign Legion in North Africa. (In the early 1930s, Hollywood studios heads still staunchly defended the European empires). Arabs are seen in *The Three Musketeers* as the North African equivalent to American Indians, a people incapable of self-government. And anyone who inflamed anticolonial sentiments was exactly what the name El Shaitan implied—"the Devil." Had it not been for the Dumasian, D'Artagnan-like American pilot and three Musketeer-like legionnaires, the Arab uprising would have succeeded.

Duke's acting in *The Three Musketeers* shows a greater sense of confidence. His movements are more fluid and his delivery more relaxed, and although he received only fourth billing, his performance energizes the serial. *The Three Musketeers* is the first film in which he seems natural in his role as a savior. In the opening scene the legionnaires, outnumbered and outgunned by the Arabs, battle and die until only three remain. They, too, prepare for death when Wayne's biplane dips from the sky, its mounted machine gun firing fast, hot rounds, and saves them.

It was a scene Duke would repeat hundreds of times during the next fifty years. His attacks would be directed more often at Indians, Japanese, and communists than at Arabs, but the role of the American savior, the defender of the innocent and the protector of civilization, would come to define his career to such an extent that it became a cliché. The phrase "doing a John Wayne" entered the English language, denoting any act of bravery against seemingly hopeless odds. Even to suggest such an action would draw the response, "Who do you think you are, John Wayne?"

The persona would become the greatest source of Duke's appeal—and the reason so many Americans attacked him. Commenting (in the wake of the Vietnam War) on the scene in *The Three Musketeers,* film historian Jon Tuska observed, "This was not only to become John Wayne's persona for most Americans; sadly, it was the way a great many Third World people came to regard Americans, dropping fire and bombs from the sky." The persona was overdone, oversold, and oversize, but in the world of Hollywood, where nothing was too mawkish or too blatant, it struck a perfect note.[33]

Duke's confidence on screen was welcome. After a long slide from starring in a major picture to starring in a minor picture to playing backup roles in minor films to starring in a serial to receiving third or fourth billing in a serial, his career had bottomed out. Fortunately, Wayne's contract with Mascot Pictures was nonexclusive, and throughout 1932 Al Kingston continued to find work for his client. Finally, a bit role in *Lady and Gent* for Paramount led to a better deal with Warner Bros.

When Warner's absorbed First National in the late 1920s, it acquired an impressive silent film list that included Ken Maynard's well-produced Westerns. Sidney Rogell, a former First National executive, insisted that Maynard's films still had value, and he approached Warner's producer Leon Schlesinger with a novel plan. Although Maynard's career was moving downward in an alcoholic fog, and he had never been much of an actor, he was a great stunt rider who had once been the leading attraction in the Kit Carson Show and Ringling Brothers Circus. He could stand on a galloping horse, swing under a horse, perform trick roping. And his horse Tarzan was the best in the business. Rogell believed it was a shame to allow Maynard's First National work to waste away in storage. He had a simple plan: Recycle the best parts of the films. Schlesinger liked the idea, and he and Rogell convinced Jack Warner to make a series of low-budget Westerns including the Ken Maynard stunt sequences. Budgeted at twenty-eight thousand dollars each, the Westerns were designed for Warner's rural markets and as the bottom half of double features. All they needed were sound effects and another actor who looked something like Maynard for dialogue and close-ups.[34]

Duke had the same wiry build as Maynard and looked enough like him to pull off the trick. Rogell and Schlesinger hired him for $825 a picture on a six-picture contract. In the year between mid-1932 and mid-1933 he—and Duke, the "Devil Horse," who looked like Maynard's Tarzan—made *Ride*

Him Cowboy, The Big Stampede, Haunted Gold, The Telegraph Trail, Somewhere in Sonora, and *The Man from Monterey*. Four of the films are direct remakes of Maynard pictures, and the other two use footage from them. In each Duke played a character whose first name was always "John," and the films combined Maynard's stunts with light humor and romance. Standard material, but as the *Motion Picture Herald* commented about one of the films, "John Wayne's drawl and deliberate style of movement are fitted to effect a likeable picture." They were modest productions, and none of them attracted much attention at Warner's, a studio that viewed Westerns as a social disease. But they returned excellent profits and received enthusiastic reviews.[35]

The combination of Duke and Warner Bros. was a bit like "Home on the Range" sung by George Jessel. Warner's was Al Jolson's *Jazz Singer* and Edward G. Robinson's *Little Caesar*, James Cagney's *Public Enemy* and Warren William's *Shyster*, Dorothy Mackaill's *Lost Woman* and Ruby Keeler's *Big Break*. Warner's was fast talk, machine guns, city grit, and swims in the East River. Duke was a horsey frat boy. Yet, without trying to bring Wayne into the Warner's stable, the studio did use him in several 1933 films. He made a walk-on appearance in the big-budget *Central Airport*, spoke one line in *College Coach*, played a small but satisfying part as a prizefighter in *The Life of Jimmy Dolan*, and had a small role in *Baby Face*. In *Baby Face* Barbara Stanwyck's performance as an unscrupulous gold digger angered Will Hays, caused a controversy in the press, and helped lead to the acceptance of the Motion Picture Production Code. But Wayne's supporting role as one of Stanwyck's stepping-stones generated little notice, and by the end of 1933 Warner's concluded that Wayne did not fit its talent profile.[36]

Between Warner's and Mascot, Duke had kept working, and as Will Rogers had told him in 1930, if you were working you were better off than millions of Americans. He accepted what was offered, from the major studios to the cheap, low-budget independent productions of Poverty Row, from Warner's *Baby Face* to Showmen's Pictures' *His Private Secretary*, a light comedy in which Duke played a tipsy playboy. He took roles large and small, cashed the checks, and learned his craft. By the end of 1933 he had a career, something that was not at all certain when the year began. He also had a wife.[37]

6

"Suppose You Could Tell Her You Like Her Biscuits?"

66 Josephine Saenz to Wed John Wayne." A brief twelve-line announcement followed. It was not exactly the sort of publicity that stirs an actor's dreams. In late December 1932, when the *New York Times* announced the engagement of John Wayne and Josephine Saenz, Duke received second billing. What little interest there was in the event stemmed from the position of Josie's father. The headline had little to do with Wayne's status in Hollywood.[1]

Duke and Josie had dated for seven years. For at least half that time Josie's father had fought against the marriage, insisting that his daughter would not marry a marginally employed actor. But in 1933, as Duke's career began to inch upward, Dr. Saenz relented. Religion, however, still presented a problem. Duke was not a particularly devout Presbyterian, and he attended church irregularly at best, but he was not about to convert to Catholicism, which ruled out a church wedding before the altar. Loretta Young offered to help. Duke always called Loretta by her real name of Gretchen, and over the years they had developed a good friendship. It was Loretta's older sister Polly Ann whom he had dated before he met Josie, and Loretta had aided Duke at Warner's. As the female lead in *The Life of Jimmy Dolan,* she had lobbied to get Duke a small role. To help her friends, she suggested that they get married in the gardens of her mother and stepfather's Bel-Air estate.[2]

Josie insisted on a society rather than a Hollywood wedding. The social reporter for the *Los Angeles Times* labeled it "one of the most notable of the season's weddings" and headlined his story on the wedding: CONSUL SAENZ'S DAUGHTER BRIDE OF MARION MORRISON. The mention of Dr. Saenz and the use of Duke's real name distanced the affair from Hollywood. The June 24, 1933, late-afternoon ceremony emphasized style and tradition, not glitz and glamour. Monsignor Francis J. Conaty, who almost twenty years earlier had given Josie her first communion, performed the ceremony, while a hundred relatives and friends watched. A gown of heavy white duchesse satin covered Josie's thin body. Duke wore an ascot and evening tails. Henry Fonda attended. So did Grant Withers, Duke's friend and Young's former husband. But Loretta Young was the only Hollywood personality mentioned in the *Times* article. Wayne's best man and all eight ushers were Sigma Chi fraternity brothers, and the fact that Duke had attended USC and played football received more attention than did his film career.[3]

Viewed from a distance, the marriage was clearly a mistake. Duke had met Josie when he was a nineteen-year-old freshman at USC and she was a sixteen-year-old student at Romona Convent. They had fallen in love, an emotion that neither had experienced before. Over the next seven years the passion of the early months changed into respect and caring. Duke's mother came to believe that by the time of the marriage the "fire" had gone out of their relationship. Whether or not she knew it at the time, there is no doubt that Duke had changed more than Josie during their long unofficial engagement. He had dropped out of USC, given up his hopes of becoming a lawyer, and entered the intoxicating, mercurial motion picture business. He had been both a star and a failure, felt the promise of new contracts and the disappointment when they were not renewed, traveled across the country on publicity tours, and engaged in a few casual affairs with college coeds and small-time Poverty Row actresses. During the same years Josie had remained in her parents' fashionable Hancock Park home, insulated from all but the world of Los Angeles society and the Catholic Church. She had learned how to throw successful dinner parties and had strictly followed the tenets and rituals of her faith. She had become a very fine woman, but not one who fitted well into Duke's world.[4]

Wayne made an attempt, perhaps sincere but never very successful, to live in two worlds, one in which his name was Marion Morrison, the other in which he was John Wayne. He and Josie settled into a fashionable three-room Hancock Park apartment close to her parents' and became part of the Los Angeles social scene. Duke attended formal dinner parties and grew accustomed to eating his meals with priests. Before their first anniversary, Josie became pregnant, and Michael Anthony Morrison was born on November 23, 1934. During the next six years she had three other children—Mary Antonia (February 26, 1936), Patrick John (July 15, 1939), and Melinda Ann (December 3, 1940). Both Josie and Duke wanted the marriage to work. The problem was that the pull of Duke's other world—of Hollywood, films, and movie friends—was too strong. In time he came to resent Josie's proper world of society and church. It became his straitjacket, and he pulled and twisted when he wore it, making his discomfort known to everyone close to him.[5]

Women, and particularly women like Josie, played only small roles in the world he loved. Between 1933 and 1938 Duke spent most of his time making B Westerns and socializing with his friends. From April to September, he remembered, he "worked like hell," moving from location to location, spending twelve or fourteen or more hours a day on the sets, punching out quickie Westerns like sausages. Sometimes Josie would accompany him on location. Clyde and Florence Morrison were living in Santa Barbara then, and Duke and Josie would drop Michael off with them for a few days. Nancy Morrison remembered how much Clyde enjoyed having the baby around, especially taking him down to the beach to build sandcastles and dip his little feet in the surf. But most of the time, the out-of-the-way locations were not much fun for Josie. She stayed in dingy hotels while Duke worked from dawn to dusk. Most of the time, she stayed at home. Then from September to April, as the film industry moved into its seasonal slowdown, he worked less. He was, as he told Maurice Zolotow, free to do what he wanted, free to choose to spend time with Josie and his young children, free to choose to go "out hunting and doing the things that really keep you physically fit." But he seldom chose either Josie or fitness. Instead, as he recalled in the last decade of his life, "I wanted to be a big shot so I gave up that stuff."[6]

Being a big shot meant living his version of the Hollywood life. It was a man's world, centered around the single dominating figure of John Ford. Shortly before Duke's wedding Ford reappeared in his life as suddenly as he had left it. For more than three years after Ford had refused to speak to Duke in 1930, the two men had avoided each other. Ford continued at Fox, although he also directed an occasional picture for other studios, and Duke moved from Columbia to Mascot and Warner's. Then one day in the summer of 1934, Duke was in Christian's Hut, a bar on Catalina Island's Isthmus Harbor, with Ward Bond, "having a belt," when Ford's ten-year-old daughter,

Barbara, came up to him. "Daddy wants to see you," she said. "Whoa, wait a minute, Barbara, you got the wrong boy—must be Ward," Duke replied. "No, it's you, Duke," she insisted. Wayne still believed she was mistaken and told her to "run along, you know this is a bar."[7]

Shortly afterward Ford's wife, Mary, came into the bar and told Duke that her husband wanted to see him on his ketch, the *Araner*. It was a command performance that Duke could not refuse. When he climbed aboard the *Araner*, Ford was sitting at a table telling a story to five or six other guests. Ford paused for a moment, saying "Hi, Duke, sit down," and then continued his tale. Wayne sat quietly, listening. At dinner time Ford announced that his shore boat would take his guests back to Catalina. As Wayne was getting up, Ford turned to him and asked, "Duke, could you stay for dinner?"

"To this goddamn day I don't know why he didn't speak to me for [three] years," Duke later told Ford's grandson and biographer, Dan. It was in Ford's nature not to say and Duke's not to ask. Such matters, sensitive, fragile, perhaps even touching on the deep sadness that seemed so much a part of Ford's personality, were not discussed. Perhaps Ford, who viewed himself as a mentor and even surrogate father, resented Duke's decision to make *The Big Trail* with Raoul Walsh. Perhaps the old man was punishing Duke. Or it could simply have been Ford's legendary, unpredictable mean streak. Neither Duke nor Ford placed much stock in "shrinks," and neither were particularly given to confessionals. But once Ford had rebuilt his bridge to Duke, he made sure that he never again tore it down completely. One senses from their reminiscences and occasional letters that there was much left unsaid in their relationship.

What they did share were experiences. From 1934 until Ford went on active duty at the beginning of World War II, the two spent much of their free time together. When they were both working they would meet at the Hollywood Athletic Club on Wilcox Street, between Sunset and Hollywood Boulevards, and talk in the steam room or get together at night for a game of cards. "Whenever I had vacations or he had vacations we usually took 'em together," Duke said. Their vacations, some only a day or two, others that stretched into a month or more, varied from quiet and relaxing to loud and dangerous. Most often they entailed cruises aboard the *Araner*, the 110-foot yacht Ford had purchased in June 1934 and named after the Aran Islands off the coast of Galway. Most often their families were left at home. Many Sundays they drove down to the San Pedro pier just to have tea aboard the boat.[8]

The *Araner* was Ford's private retreat, and he gave it more love and attention than he gave his family. Explaining the role of the *Araner* in his financial life, Ford said that he made three films a year: one for the Internal Revenue Service, one to live on, and the other for the *Araner*. It was a magnificent yacht with two fireplaces, two bathrooms, a teakwood deckhouse, and comfortable beds. Aboard the ketch he escaped the telephones and producers and agents and scores of other people determined to interrupt his life. It was a small, controllable environment. Ford alone determined who sailed with him; he alone was in charge. Only friends, no business. Those aboard the *Araner* learned the unspoken rules set down by the complex, troubled director. Duke and other frequent guests knew that Ford preferred to sleep in the small cabin, that he liked to read without interruptions, that he might go for days without speaking.[9]

Duke spent more time on the *Araner* than any of Ford's other friends. To gether they took short cruises to Catalina and the Isthmus, or longer ones along the rugged, mountainous coast of Baja California to La Paz and sometimes sailing north into the gentle waters of the Gulf of California, then south to Mazatlán or Acapulco. Both men enjoyed solitude. On long voyages Ford would lug along "a cord of books," reading three for every one Duke read. When it was just the two of them, they would say hello to each other at breakfast and again at lunch, and after dinner they would play cards for a few hours. "We had a nice comfortable relationship that didn't depend on continuous or continual conversation, and we never had to explain [anything to] each other. On most of those trips Jack never drank," Wayne told Dan Ford.[10]

When other friends came along the tranquillity was less than total, and the alcohol flowed. In late December and early January, 1934–35, Ford, Duke, Ward Bond, Henry Fonda, and Dudley Nichols sailed from San Pedro, where the *Araner* was harbored, to La Paz and then to Mazatlán. During the day they fished for bonito, dorado, and marlin, and at night they drank tequila with beer chasers and told lies. George Goldrainer, the master of the *Araner*, described the trip in his logbook. The voyage to La Paz passed uneventfully, but a week out at sea, and no doubt influenced by too much alcohol, Ford claimed that he saw a "green slimy vicious" sea serpent. When Fonda challenged his story, Duke and Bond supported Ford's account. Then, Fonda insisted, he had seen a pink sea elephant.[11]

The next day they reached Mazatlán and went ashore. It was one of Duke's and Ford's favorite towns, a place they could go barefoot and unshaven, dressed in work khakis spotted with fish blood, to wander the streets, drink,

nett, Wingate Smith, and Gene Markey; and actors Johnny Weissmuller, Frank Morgan, and Preston Foster.

Ford was the heart of the group, which as a whole reflected his tastes and interests. Cooper had attended Annapolis, been shot down as a pilot in World War I, flown in the Kościuszko Flying Squadron in the Russo-Polish War, traveled the Near and Far East making films, and finally landed in Hollywood, where he became famous with his film *King Kong*. Garnett had attended MIT before becoming a navy pilot in World War I. Irish novelist, nationalist, and occasional Marxist O'Flaherty had written such classics as *Mr. Gilhooley*, *The Assassin*, and *The Informer*. Nichols was Ford's leading screenwriter, and along with O'Flaherty pushed the director politically toward the Left. Morgan made a career at MGM playing amiable, absentminded, and essentially harmless rogues, and is best remembered for playing the Wizard in *The Wizard of Oz*. Wurtzel and Markey worked with Ford at Fox, Smith was the director's brother-in-law and assistant, and at one time or another Wayne, Bond, and Foster acted in Ford's films.[16]

The group contained radicals, liberals, and conservatives; Irish Catholics, Jews, and WASPs; anti-Semites, racists, and fellow travelers. But each individual member tended to view himself as an outsider, and most, in fact, would *not* have been welcomed at the most elite country clubs in Los Angeles. Not that they wanted to break into LA society; Duke, in fact, was working hard to stay out of it. What they wanted most was to enjoy each other's company, to drink, swear, laugh, and relax. Sometime in 1933 or 1934 they decided as a joke to form their own highly exclusive club. Boasting "Jews but no dues," they elected black steam room attendant John "Buck" Buchanan as their president. In their charter they boldly announced that they had formed the club to "promulgate the cause of alcoholism," and they required all members and applicants to be "career-oriented" or "gutter-oriented" drunkards. Sadly, most of them qualified for membership.[17]

The members devoted lengthy discussions and considerable correspondence to deciding who should be accepted into the organization and who should be kicked out. "Rabbi" Harry Wurtzel lived under the constant threat of expulsion, and for a time he was booted out for attempting to seduce a black maid, a charge that he denied. Dudley Nichols, always more liberal and intellectual than most of the others (and less of a drinker), also had a checkered career in the club. In early 1937 his name was struck from the rolls because he had never been treated for "acute alcoholism"; however, the members said they would reconsider if Nichols would "establish a record" for heavy drinking. Nichols mounted an instant defense, claiming that while he was "not a gutter or ambulance drunkard" he had years of solid experience. True, he could not drink like director Emmett Flynn—who could?—or like Ward Bond—who had two good kidneys and a large frame to absorb the alcohol— but, like John Ford, he had "never opened a bottle without throwing the cork out the window." Finally he cautioned the members against the sin of snobbery. "There is no snobbery in the bottle, sir," he wrote. Nichols even got author Gene Fowler to write in his behalf. Supporting his friend as a true drunk, Fowler noted that Nichols had tied one on in November 1918, fallen into a manhole, convinced himself that "he had been laid," and sent bouquets to the manhole for weeks. Nichols promised that if he were readmitted he would not be modest or "silently proud," that henceforth he would be "a boaster, a braggart, a swaggering fellow!"[18]

Nichols was finally allowed to return, but only after Ward Bond was tossed out for being seen drunk at the Hollywood Athletic Club trying to kiss the manicurist on the back of the neck with a lighted cigar in his mouth. Bond's plea of extenuating circumstances—that the Troy baseball team had come in last in the Tri-State League—was dismissed by the harsh executive board.[19]

And so it continued. Members were scornfully exiled and then warmly reembraced. Sitting in the steam room they debated the relative merits and problems of California jails run by Irishmen and Irish gaols run by Englishmen. They belittled Nichols's liberal-radical politics as well as his sex life. They did exactly what they intended to do—drink, relax, and laugh.[20]

By the summer of 1937 the informal association evolved into the "Young Men's Purity Total Abstinence and Yachting Association." "Brother Buchanan (colored)" introduced a motion for the *Araner* to become the flagship of the new club. With only Ford voting against it, the motion was quickly approved, and Buchanan promised "to take his family and relatives with box lunches down to the boat to spend a day." The idea of a yacht club appealed to Ford and the others, and in the summer of 1938 they changed their name to the Emerald Bay Yachting Club and widely announced their intention of applying for admission into the prestigious Southern California Yachting Association. As a yachting club they purchased elaborate uniforms, posed for pictures, held outrageous parties, and, although it remained primarily a drinking association that spoofed all pretentious clubs, it attracted a following in Hollywood. Proclaiming itself "the yacht club for people who don't like yacht clubs," it held its first Saint Patrick's Day dinner at the Coconut Grove at the Ambassador Hotel, and although the club's members were asked not to return to the exclusive restaurant, the event, which continued elsewhere, remained a "hot ticket." By 1940 the Emerald Bay Yachting Club's membership rolls included such leading actors and directors as William Wellman, Howard Hawks, Henry Fonda, Victor Fleming, Dick Powell, James Cagney, Ronald Colman, and James Stewart.[21]

Dudley Nichols was right: "There is no snobbery in the bottle." Sailing with Ford and participating in the antics of the "Young Men's Purity Total Abstinence and Snooker Pool Association" (or Yacht Club) brought Duke into close association with some of the important personalities in Hollywood. Aboard the *Araner* and at the Hollywood Athletic Club, he drank and joked with Fonda and Colman, Wellman and Hawks. But when it was time for work, they left the rough democracy of the bottle and went in different directions. For most of the 1930s Duke was not part of the glamorous world of MGM, Paramount, or Twentieth Century-Fox. He inherited a different world, one that had been fostered by the depression, nurtured by frugal businessmen, and sustained by rural audiences. During much of the decade, Duke labored in the salt mines of the B Westerns, developing his craft and waiting for another chance.

B movies emerged informally in the beginning of the 1930s as a promotional idea to get Americans into the movie houses. As movie attendance sagged between 1930 and 1933, industry leaders and individual exhibitors scrambled for ways to solve the problem. Theater owners attempted to entice customers into their houses through various rebate schemes as well as giveaway programs. They staged such lottery games as Bank Night, Race Night, and Screeno, holding drawings and giving away money before the curtain rose on the feature presentation. They gave away free pottery, china, and other gifts with the price of admission. They discounted tickets and allowed two admissions for the price of one. Many of these practices were outlawed by the National Recovery Administration (NRA), but when the Supreme Court declared the NRA unconstitutional in 1935, theater owners once again resorted to lotteries and giveaways. They hoped that if they could pinch pennies long enough, if they could maximize profits from food and drink sales and weather the hard times, their audiences would return.[22]

No scheme or gimmick, however, had a greater impact on the industry than the double feature. In 1932 many independent theater owners began to offer their patrons more movie enjoyment for their money; in fact, measured by the number of films, twice as much enjoyment. At first the major studios and their theater chains resisted the double feature because it cut into the producer's percentage of the box-office revenue, but as the novelty spread and gained audience support, the majors accepted the innovation. By 1935 the practice was both standard and standardized. Each double feature consisted of two films, an A picture and a B picture, a top and a bottom half of a twin bill. Most A pictures were exhibited on a percentage basis; the more people who paid to see them, the more money they earned. Depending on the film, the percentage would range from 60/40—60 percent for the distributor, 40 percent for the exhibitor—to 90/10. B pictures, however, were rented for fixed rates. They never made a dime more than their rental fees—but they never made a dime less, either.[23]

The bottom line of B production was the profit margin. As long as producers could make movies for less than the guaranteed rental fees, they could make money. By the standards of the major studios, the money made in B pictures was chump change. Even when it was done right—that is, cheaply— a B film might only clear ten or fifteen thousand dollars. And, given the overhead of the majors, the investment in talent, equipment, sound stages, and back lots, it was difficult for them to make Bs cheaply. Although most of the majors used the production of Bs to groom actors and actresses, during the 1930s most gradually lost interest in B production and left those crumbs for the studios that specialized in the genre.[24]

Up and down Poverty Row, studios, some with no more facilities than rented office space, sprouted like mushrooms. Like a trailer park named Oak Woods Estates, they had grand names—Tiffany, Grand National, Sono Art–World Wide, Chesterfield, Liberty, Victory, Action, Mayfair, Invincible, Puritan, Ambassador-Conn, Majestic. Starting a business in the depths of the depression was at best a gamble, and most of the studios stayed around a year or two and then merged with another B company or folded. A few proved particularly adept at churning out assembly-line movies and stayed in business until changes in the industry and public tastes ended the standard double feature in the late-1940s and 1950s.

In 1934 *New York Times* film writer Lewis Jacobs described the world of the Bs. They were that "creature on the double bill the neighborhood movie is ashamed to advertise." Many B producers, he wrote, rented studio space by the day, shot on free locations when they could, hired cameramen who owned their own equipment, and offered liens on the films to raise money for negative and laboratory work. They hired "has-beens whose names were in marquees before the World War" and "second-rate" stars at "secret low-price arrangements." Occasionally they even hired a name actor for a day, shot as many scenes as possible, and afterward employed the back of an extra to stand in for the star. Casting for Westerns took place on the streets of Poverty Row, in the part of town known as Gower Gulch, where cowboys waited in Levi's, Stetsons, and boots for an extra's wage. Jacobs concluded that a producer would shoot a low rent Western on a shoestring budget, then advertise it as a "Mighty Epic of the West!!" During the 1930s, John Wayne worked for the two most successful of these "B-Hives."[25]

Shortly before he married Josie, Duke signed a deal with Trem Carr at Monogram Pictures to star in eight Westerns. Carr put veteran producer Paul Malvern in charge of the films and released them under Monogram's Lone Star Productions label, a name that was used only because of its associations with Texas and the West. Monogram's pedigree reached back to the mid-1920s. W. Ray Johnston founded Rayart Productions in 1924, changed the company's name to Syndicate Film Exchange in 1928, and changed it again to Monogram in 1931. Different names, same essential product, which one authority on the company characterized as largely "cheap, vulgar, inept, and ultimately forgettable." There were, of course, exceptions. Monogram's Bowery Boys, Charlie Chan, The Shadow, and Cisco Kid series attracted large followings, as did such comic strip series as Maggie and Jiggs, Snuffy Smith, and Joe Palooka. The company also owned a great ranch and had a stable of former silent Western stars that included Tex Ritter, Johnny Mack Brown, Ray "Crash" Corrigan, Buck Jones, Tim McCoy, Ken Maynard, Hoot Gibson, and Bob Steele.[26]

Monogram, like the other successful B studios, cut costs whenever possible. Producers used stock footage for fight, chase, battle, and natural disaster scenes, and they studied scripts searching for any scenes that might require retakes. They knew that they could save money on the small details. Todd McCarthy and Charles Flynn described the process: "A script called for the actor to light a cigarette in mid-scene? A fumble would call for a retake; the actor entered with the cigarette lit. In fact, as often as not, the scene would begin with our cigarette-puffing hero already in the room! (Why waste the time, and risk the retake, by having him open the door?)" Perhaps women were even more hampered by the B mentality of frugality. To save money on costumes and hairdressers, heroines in B Westerns often wore riding pants and hats. "Minimal" was the best word to describe the world of the B—minimal acting, minimal sets, minimal scripts, minimal costs, and minimal profits. It was a world, as the standard joke went, where sets shook when an actor slammed a door.[27]

The sum of all that minimalism was usually a flat product. Most Bs were unscored and weak on sound effects, which gave them a cheap, hollow feel.

Some performers overacted; others did not act at all, delivering lines as if they were reading cue cards badly. The only times the scripts were not wordy was during fight and chase scenes. Yet B movies found an audience. During the 1930s, when the major studios made very few A Westerns, B Westerns often played on single-feature programs in small towns in the South, Southwest, and West, regions where the independent exhibitors could not afford an A film from a major studio. Many were featured on Saturday night, or, as it was called in the 1930s and 1940s, "action night," when farmhands and cowboys would drift to town looking for a good movie, a good fight, and a good time. Steve Broidy, who worked for decades at Monogram, said that the owners of small-town, independent theaters would show a B Western on Saturday nights "because they were sure of a maximum gross that day, irrespective" of the quality of the movie. And profits were not their only concern. "The type of people that used to gravitate to these small towns . . . were once-a-week visitors to the theaters. They were farmhands and the poorer element, and they were more interested in an action picture . . . than in a bedroom farce or a comedy or a sophisticated picture such as Metro made." Tastes differed. "Not everybody likes to eat cake," Broidy commented. "Some people like bread, and even a certain number of people like stale bread rather than fresh bread."[28]

During the next few years those rural stale-bread eaters would form a large part of Duke's audience, but in 1933 when he began his first Monogram picture he had not yet carved out a niche in the industry. Although he had starred in a few Westerns, he had performed in more non-Westerns. He had played a pilot in three serials and a college athlete in several films; he was a boxer, an army officer, a bank employee, and a wealthy playboy. His best roles had been small parts, his worst ones leads. All that would change at Monogram. Trem Carr, the company's vice president in charge of production, slotted Duke into a single role: Western hero. For the next two years in sixteen Monogram pictures—each a five-reeler with a running time of less than an hour and budgeted at ten to twelve thousand dollars—Wayne would play essentially what were variations of the same role. He would ride into town alone, stumble across a community problem, be charged with some crime he did not commit, uncover and catch the guilty person, save the community, and win the heart of the heroine. They were one-kiss movies. Audiences learned that when the female lead kissed Duke the movie was over. Taken as a whole the films were cliché-ridden, formulaic—and quite successful. Duke recalled in 1978 that in the Monogram pictures, "My main duty was to ride, fight, keep my hat on, and at the end of shooting still have enough strength to kiss the girl and ride off on my horse or kiss my horse and ride off on the girl—whichever they wanted." But in the small towns, farms, and ranches of the South, West, and Southwest during the 1930s, John Wayne became a familiar face to millions of Americans.

There were problems with his first Monogram film. In *Riders of Destiny* Duke played Singin' Sandy Saunders, a cowboy who rides into town on a white horse, strumming a guitar, and singing in a rich baritone. Producer Paul Malvern and director Robert North Bradbury, the father of one of Wayne's Glendale and USC friends, had planned for Duke to make a series of Singin' Sandy movies, but the actor clearly looked uncomfortable in the scenes that called for him to strike up a song. All his life Wayne disliked the trappings of the Wild West–show cowboy. He knew that chaps decorated with silver conchos, pearl-buttoned shirts, fringed and beaded jackets, and fringed cuffed gloves were seldom if ever seen on a real cowboy. He felt the same way about singing cowboys; real cowboys simply did not ride the range picking guitars. In one scene, as Singin' Sandy walks toward an antagonist in preparation for a classic high-noon gunfight, he sings a ditty. Adding to his discomfort, he could not carry a tune and the songs had to be dubbed in by Bradbury's son Bill. The experience was enough to convince Duke and Malvern to abort the Singin' Sandy series.[29]

Years after the timely demise of Singin' Sandy, Gene Autry, the country's first important singing cowboy, remarked that Duke's Sandy was doomed from the start. "Two factors weighted against Wayne's rise as a Western singer, other than the obvious one of finding a leading lady who wouldn't crack up. To begin with, his songs had to be dubbed by someone else, and, in those days, the lip-synch was unreliable. But the clincher was the fact that when he appeared in public and his fans pleaded for a ballad or two, he had to decline."[30]

If the voice of Singin' Sandy did not suit Wayne, his character and action did. The film centers on the most powerful of Western issues—water. With the Dust Bowl in Oklahoma and a drought in the Midwest, "water" and "irrigation" were words that aroused passion in rural America. In the film James Kincaid dams the valley's only water supply in an effort to force ranchers to sell him their land. Singin' Sandy is a Secret Service agent sent undercover by Washington to investigate and solve the problem. Of course there are the usual complications. For a time both the ranchers and the heroine are uncertain of Sandy's loyalties, but in the end his actions return the water to "the boys" and the woman to him.

Riders of Destiny is a surprisingly good B Western. Although the script is poor and predictable, Bradbury movingly portrays the importance of water to the thirsty West. An early scene shows the arrival of a water wagon in town. Men and women rush to the wagon with buckets, children cry with delight, and a dog drinks the spilled water. But even more impressive is a montage toward the end of the film. A dynamite blast exposes an underground creek, and in successive shots Bradbury shows the water breaking through the parched ground, moving into the dry creek bed, and swelling into a river. Cattle, horses, ducks, and geese gather by the water while children and grown men submerge themselves. The scene has the visual quality of Pare Lorentz's *The River*, which was made almost four years later.

In the world of Bs montage and art were hardly selling points, just as bad scripts and acting were not necessarily weaknesses. In fact, the only mistakes that mattered were the ones that cost money. *Riders of Destiny* showed that Wayne was not a singing cowboy, but the film did demonstrate that he was a cowboy actor. He had an undeniable presence, a combination of strength, boyish charm, and innocence. Malvern noticed it. Wayne had not made a strong impression on the producer at their first meeting, but by the end of their first film together Malvern thought, "Here's a guy that is going to be all right." Not only did Duke make a good screen impression, his capacity for work was suited to the demands of the B picture industry. He learned his lines, took instructions well, and did not make demands. "Handled himself real well," Malvern commented. "And we had no problems with him."[31]

Malvern expected as much as Levine from his cast and crew. He filmed his five-reel Westerns in five or six days, three days if necessary. It was common for his directors to shoot fifty or sixty setups a day. Director Robert North Bradbury was a master of B picture economy. To save time and money, he would set up a cameraman in a position where he could film one scene, then move five or six feet and film another. He could get "three or four scenes with one set-up when normally you might get just one," Malvern remembered. And through the long days Wayne waited for his calls, delivered his lines, took his falls, and was back on the set ready to do it all again the next day.[32]

Malvern churned out John Wayne oaters with numbing regularity. *Riders of Destiny* was released on October 10, 1933. In the next twenty-one months it was followed by *Sagebrush Trail* (December 15, 1934), *The Lucky Texan* (January 22, 1934), *West of the Divide* (February 15, 1934), *Blue Steel* (May 10, 1934), *The Man from Utah* (May 15, 1934), *Randy Rides Alone* (June 15, 1934), *The Star Packer* (July 30, 1934), *The Trail Beyond* (October 22, 1934), *The Lawless Frontier* (November 22, 1934), *'Neath the Arizona Skies* (December 28, 1935), *Texas Terror* (February 1, 1935), *Rainbow Valley* (March 12,

1935), *The Desert Trail* (April 22, 1935), *The Dawn Rider* (June 20, 1935), and *Paradise Canyon* (July 20, 1935). Almost a film a month. Duke finished one eight-picture contract and then signed and completed another.[33]

All the pictures have the same general cast of five characters: the hero, a defender of the defenseless always played by Duke; the hero's best friend; the heroine; the "brain heavy," a constant schemer and planner of criminal deeds; and the "dog heavy," a kicker of dogs who does the brain heavy's dirty work. They differ only in how the common ingredients are mixed together. That was the only place where individual directors' and writers' imagination came into play. Robert North Bradbury commonly doubled as director and writer, and he developed ingenious variations of the classic plot. In *The Dawn Rider*, for example, the hero and his best friend are both in love with the same woman, whose brother happens to have killed the hero's father. Somehow the hero has to revenge his father's death, win the heart of the heroine, and keep his buddy's friendship. Problem? Not for Bradbury, who concluded the film by having the best friend save the hero's life by shooting the heroine's brother as that dog heavy is about to fire a bullet into the hero's back. To solve the sticky love triangle issue, Bradbury then has another heavy shoot the best friend, who dies apologizing for ever doubting the hero's friendship, concluding, "It's gettin' dark, John! . . . Tell Alice I won't be home for dinner."

If critics did not hail any of the films as masterpieces, they did acknowledge the success of John Wayne in the pictures and comment on his growing popularity. In the early films he attracted merely passing comments. Reviewers judged him "physically attractive" in *Sagebrush Trail* and "well enough" in *The Lucky Texan*, but even as early as in *The Lucky Texan* one reviewer mused: "Young Wayne is popular, has a following, and may well be capitalized on in the selling." By Duke's fourth or fifth Monogram Western there was complete agreement among trade reviewers about his screen appeal. The *Motion Picture Herald* review of *Blue Steel* noted: "Of Wayne's popularity there can be little question, and a certain quota of Western fans can be relied upon to respond to the call of the Wayne name on the theatre marquee." A half year and six films later the same paper reached a similar conclusion about *'Neath the Arizona Skies*: "This picture has in the lead the lively and young John Wayne, who has a substantial following. The selling, with a concentration on Wayne and a strong play for the youngsters, appears to call for nothing unusual." After a succession of studios and a string of failures, Duke finally found his first taste of success with Monogram Westerns.[34]

With the success came an image, immediately recognizable and etched in the stone of typecasting. His days as a whiny *Baby Face* banker were over. His new image was part Western hero, part attitude, and all "real man." Unlike most of the Western matinee idols of the 1920s, Duke did not play the well-dressed, clean-living, white-hatted dandy. Remembering the lessons John Ford had taught him about realism, he followed in the tradition of William S. Hart and Harry Carey, not Tom Mix or Hoot Gibson. His dress, manners, and speech veered toward the plain. He wore dusty denims and learned to say "ain't," but his actions defined him more than his dress and words. "I made up my mind," Wayne explained,

> that I was going to play a real man to the best of my ability. I felt many of the Western stars of the twenties and thirties were too goddamn perfect. They never drank nor smoked. They never wanted to go to bed with a beautiful girl. They never had a fight. A heavy might throw a chair at them, and they just looked surprised and didn't fight in this spirit. They were too goddamn sweet and pure to be dirty fighters. Well, I wanted to be a dirty fighter if that was the only way to fight back. If someone throws a chair at you, hell, you pick up a chair and belt him right back. I was trying to play a man who gets dirty, who sweats sometimes, who enjoys kissing a gal he likes, who gets angry, who fights clean whenever possible but will fight dirty if he has to. I made the Western hero a roughneck.[35]

The cowboy persona fitted Duke's evolving personality like a glove. Increasingly uncomfortable at home and more and more alienated from Josie's high-society, Roman Catholic world, he sought refuge with his buddies on the *Araner* or at the Hollywood Athletic Club. The decades of maintaining a false persona to please his mother and teachers and wife were coming to an end. He wanted to be himself, to be real, to put an end to all the posturing, whether as a phony cowboy dandy on screen or a proper husband in the *Social Register.* "In those days," Duke recalled in 1969, "I was always apologizing for something all the time I was home." Weary of apologies, of trying to be something he was not, he turned away from polite Los Angeles society. He also began to leave behind his wife and children, who still lived in that black-tie world.[36]

On screen Duke eschewed the ostentatious trappings of most silent movie Western stars. In the absence of dialogue, many silent films had adopted strong visual images—hyperactive movement, lavish costumes, and exaggerated facial expressions—to convey meaning. When "talkies" suddenly added dialogue to movies, most directors and actors still relied on the old physical mannerisms and costumes, destroying subtlety and art in favor of cartoonish, almost laughable scenes. When Duke invented himself on screen in the mid-1930s, he adopted the mannerisms of "real" cowboys. Ironically, he had never been around real cowboys, only seen them on screen and read about them in the novels of Zane Grey, whom he considered a "hell of a good Western writer." Novelists Owen Wister, Zane Grey, and Max Brand and artist Frederic Remington supplied his image of the real cowboy, not Tom Mix in his shiny boots and gigantic hats or Gene Autry in his pressed Western shirts or Bronco Billy in his ill-fitting neckerchiefs and bushy sheepskin chaps. George O'Brien, Tim McCoy, Nelson Eddy, William Boyd, Lash LaRue, and Johnny Mack Brown remained true to the dime-store costumes, performing in talkies the same as they had in silents. In darkened movie theaters as a teenager and young man, Duke had identified more with the rough, rugged Western cowboy than the fancy dude. Instead of being another cowboy dandy, Duke walked away from them, taking on the hard, tough aura of Lassiter and the Virginian, not Hopalong Cassidy. For millions of Americans familiar with the works of Wister, Brand, and Grey, John Wayne became the most realistic, the most believable, Western star.[37]

Duke's search for realism extended beyond costume and acting to stunt work. In eleven of his sixteen Monogram films he worked with Yakima Canutt, and together they developed new Western techniques. Working with Robert Bradbury, they began with the basic fight. In the 1920s and early 1930s, actors and stunt men swung at each other's shoulders and chests in fight scenes, actions that resembled scuffles between six-year-old boys. They looked as fake as a Tom Mix costume. Wayne and Canutt worked so often together that Bradbury allowed them to choreograph their own fights, and gradually they developed the "pass system." Instead of punching shoulders, they took haymaker swings at each other's jaw, missed by an inch or two, and finished with long follow-throughs. Filmed from behind one of the fighters, and with added sound effects, the near-misses looked like direct hits.[38]

It was not easy, but Duke's determination to play his role truly is visible in his many mistakes as well as his few successes. Although mistakes normally end on the cutting room floor in A films, they were often preserved in B pictures, where the custom of one take was almost an inflexible law. Two examples stand out. In *The Trail Beyond* the script called for a high-speed chase scene in which Duke leaps off his horse onto a wagon. It was a difficult transfer, but one he had been taught by Yak Canutt and had done before. Only this time he did not get his horse close enough to the wagon, caught his left foot in his stirrup, was stretched between the horse and wagon, and after struggling to adjust his body position fell to the ground hard, tumbling over three times before he stopped. He messed up another stunt in *'Neath the Arizona Skies*. It involved riding quickly down a steep hill toward a camera setup. Canutt was set to do the stunt, but the cameraman thought that he would pass so close to the camera that his face would be clearly visible. Duke said he would perform the stunt. "As he mounted," Canutt recalled, "I told him to bring the horse over the top of the hill on the run, but to be sure and check him just before he hit the bottom where the ground levelled off. . . . John came over the hill really carrying the mail and raced down the steep ground, never checking the horse. I held my breath as he hit the level ground, sensing the horse couldn't collect himself. He fell, turning a real hoolihan and John did a spectacular fall."[39]

In a B picture it was not unusual for an action star do some of his own stunt work, or to fail in some of the stunts. But Duke's reaction to both failures was out of the ordinary. In both instances, the cameras kept rolling as he picked himself up, climbed back onto his saddle, and finished the job. In *The Trail Beyond* he races after the wagon and completes the transfer; in *'Neath the Arizona Skies* he scrambles to his feet, leaps on his horse, and rides by the camera. What people watching the movies saw was a man hard at work, a man willing to get dirty or injured and determined to give his best. Under Canutt's guidance, Duke learned to transfer from a horse to another horse, a stagecoach, or a train. He mastered the art of leaping onto and falling off a horse. He spent hours handling guns, practicing quick draws and the added flourish of a twirl as he pulled his .45 out of its holster or put it back. By the end of his second Monogram contract, he demonstrated a confidence born of practice and experience. He had worked to develop a character that he could transfer from one role to the next, and by the mid-1930s he had succeeded.[40]

Once he had formed his character, he labored just as hard to protect it. Although Wayne performed most of his own stunts, Canutt doubled for him in the most dangerous and technical ones. By 1935, however, Canutt had started to go bald, a problem made even more obvious by its pattern. Yak's hair remained thick in the front and back and on both sides, but on the crown was an apple-size bald spot. Since he usually played a dog heavy, his baldness was securely hidden beneath a black hat, but in his few roles as the brain heavy—parts such as in *The Dawn Riders* that placed him indoors and hatless—his bald spot was capable of stealing a scene. It was also a problem in some of his stunt work. In one scene in *Paradise Canyon* the script called for Yak and Duke to grapple. "I was supposed to throw Wayne in a flip over my head,"

Canutt noted, so they had me double him and another stunt man double me. The action started and I crashed through a table, ending up sitting on the floor with my back to the camera." When Duke later previewed the film at a small theater, the scene attracted his complete attention. Everyone sitting in the audience would think that he had done the stunt, and that the bald spot—Yak's bald spot—was his. He "really chewed me out," Canutt said. "From then on, whenever I doubled for Wayne, he would say, 'Get the shoe blacking on that bald spot!'"[41]

His attitudes toward women also broke with the tradition of the Western hero. At a time when Joseph Ignatius Breen was using the power of the Catholic Church and the Motion Picture Production Code to crack down on sex in the movies, Duke's Westerns exhibited a relaxed attitude toward sexual relations. At the end of *Riders of Destiny*, Fay Denton is too embarrassed to talk because she is ashamed that she has misjudged Singin' Sandy. In a line that could only have been uttered in a B Western, Dad Denton asks Sandy to revive his daughter's spirit: "Suppose you could tell her you like her biscuits?" Sandy, with a smile of anticipation on his face, assures him: "I'm going to tell her more than that!" Such double entendres were employed again in *The Desert Trail*, when John Scott (Wayne) takes a particular interest in Juanita as they ride in a stagecoach together toward Rattlesnake Gulch. "Maybe I'll be able to see a lot of you while I'm there," he suggests as his eyes sweep across her body. Further on in the film, he makes an attractive shopkeeper climb a ladder to retrieve a nerve tonic, even though, as she tells him, "You don't need any." "No," he says, "but my horse does. He's all run down." Liking what he sees and for the good of his "horse," he then sends her up the ladder for a second bottle.

Wayne's roughneck hero also occasionally worked outside the law. To be sure, he was always on the side of justice and was even occasionally a marshal or a sheriff, but almost invariably some confusion led others to suspect him of criminal activity. This pattern became so common that audiences came to suspect it and jokes about it were written into the scripts. Early in *The Desert Trail*, just as John Scott is arriving in Poker City, a sheriff attempts to arrest him. "You can't put me in jail yet, I just got in town," he protests. Always forced to clear his name, the hero seeks justice the same way that he fights— by any means necessary. He joins the bandits to gather information, takes by gunpoint what is rightly his, and holds up stages to prevent real robberies.

In his Monogram Westerns, Duke became a hero for depression America. His is a West besieged by evil—ruthless merchants, monopolistic land and water agents, greedy bankers, and even dangerous friends and relatives. In *Riders of Destiny* a gang of outlaws is attempting to deny ranchers their water rights; in *Blue Steel* another unscrupulous group is bent on forcing ranchers off gold-rich land; in *'Neath the Arizona Skies* local toughs are trying to take oil land from a young Indiana girl; and in *Rainbow Valley* shady individuals are determined to prevent a road from being built from a small town to the county seat. Innocent people are shot at, beaten up, and left for dead; they are cheated, robbed, and chased off their land. And as often as not the leaders of the gangs are "respected" town leaders. As Richard D. McGhee noted in his study of John Wayne films: "These stories portray economic disasters as a result of deliberate strategies by capitalists to rob after reducing people to desperate need and mass hysteria."[42]

Watched through the lens of the Great Depression, the films suggested that the source of the country's problems was bad people, particularly bad businessmen. Too often they controlled a community's natural and financial resources, and they used their power clandestinely to enrich themselves further. The problem was not scarcity of resources but greed. All that was needed was a man on a white horse to ride into town and restore the community's natural balance. For millions of Americans in the South, Southwest, and West, it was a powerful message. One Saturday night each month growing numbers of them gathered at their local cinema to watch and cheer as John Wayne restored harmony and order.

The John Wayne they watched was an outsider—a son who had been away for years, a vagabond guitar player, a wandering rodeo cowboy, a falsely branded outlaw on the lam, a lucky prospector, a drifter searching for a lost relative or looking to settle an old score. He rides alone, and into trouble. He attacks problems head-on, his force and gun against his enemies' guile, deceptions, and guns. Although occasionally he is an undercover agent for the federal government or the sheriff of a small town, he is still a loner at heart, a man separated from all others and defined by a strict personal moral code. He may not always know what the law is but he does know the difference between right and wrong. It was a role John Wayne would play with complete sincerity for the rest of his life. He was so convincing that in time this screen identity fused with his own personality.

Projecting sincerity on the screen, however, hardly ever comes naturally for an actor, and it certainly did not for Wayne. In his early films his best as an actor was not very good. In fact, he probably had more aptitude for stunt work than acting. In his serials and early Monogram Westerns he appears uncomfortable in front of the camera, smiling too often and at inappropriate times, speaking too rapidly in a high flat voice that constantly threatened to spill over into a whine, and having no idea of what to do with his hands. He acts as if the camera was never far from his thoughts. Producer Paul Malvern recalled seeing Duke off by himself "going over his lines and practicing how to play things."[43]

Duke recognized his weaknesses. Lindsley Parsons, a writer on many of his early Westerns, said that after Duke would do a dialogue scene "he'd just cuss himself out terrible. He'd go off behind a rock and talk about how lousy he was." The anger made him work all the harder. He copied mannerisms from actors he admired. He learned to mount a horse in the same stiff-legged, stiff-backed swing as Tom Mix. He copied the relaxed, informal delivery of Harry Carey. But even more importantly, he sought the advice of Paul Fix, a friend from his days at Fox, Warner's, and Monogram. A versatile actor with a smooth delivery and relaxed manner, equally comfortable as good guy or heavy, Fix understood the mechanics of acting. During the 1930s he became Duke's informal acting coach. Early in his Monogram career, Wayne confessed to Fix that he felt stiff and self-conscious in front of the camera. "Duke was bright enough," remembered Fix, "but he didn't know how to move, what to do with his hands, and after three lines he was lost." Wayne particularly disliked the way his walk looked on screen. Fix told him to point his toes into the ground as he walked, an action that made his shoulders and hips swing in a distinctive manner. The walk, Harry Carey Jr. later said, was not unlike Marilyn Monroe's. "When Duke first did it, it was ballsey as hell." "Paul taught Duke to walk," Mary St. John recalled. "Duke's mannerisms were more studied than most people realize. He said it took him years before he could watch himself on the screen and not wince."[44]

About the same time he began to develop his familiar cadence. B dialogue was as difficult to deliver as serial dialogue. In a good A film the director allows the action and images to carry the story and develop the characters. Bs are more expository; often one of the central characters simply just tells the viewers what is about to happen in the story. "Most anybody can play anger or hysteria," Duke explained, "but try to do a long borin' speech like 'The stage from Albuquerque is due in at four and there's a shipment of silver and I hear that Joe and his gang are headin' for the Panamint so you take two men and be there to meet the stage and I'll keep my eye on Mike because he's fixin' to kidnap Maybell because she thinks her claim is worthless but it's a silver mine' and you got trouble."[45]

Duke attacked the problem from two directions. First, he avoided long speeches. Parsons was convinced that the basis of his friendship with the actor rested on his ability to keep Wayne's lines to a minimum. Second, he slowed down his speech and began to pause in the middle of sentences. "You say," Wayne said:

"I think I'll . . . (Now they're looking at you, and you can stand there for 20 minutes before you say) "go to town." If you say normally, "I think I'll go to town. Umm (pause) then we can go over and see something," the audience would have left you. But if you say, "I think I'll go (pause) to town and I'll (pause) see those three broads," now they're waiting for you. You can take all the goddamn time you want if you choose your time for the hesitation.[46]

Watching Harry Carey and listening to John Ford had taught him a basic lesson. Appearing natural, like appearing sincere, is artificial. "There's no way of being natural on the screen," he said. "You lose your tempo. You have to keep things going and try to get your personality through." The cadence he developed did just that. It permitted him to maintain an even tempo and present a character that at all times appeared deliberate, thoughtful, and deadly serious, a man who was normally considerate and friendly but dangerous when angered.[47]

He also learned to express honest screen emotions by watching Yakima Canutt. Although he was the best stunt man in the industry, Canutt was a terrible actor. Normally cast as a dog heavy, when he was called upon to show anger "he made grimaces and raised his voice and snarled." Duke noticed, however, that he reacted differently when confronted by real danger. More than once at some outback location some "rough customers" would challenge Canutt to a fight. When Yak was in "real trouble," Duke observed, "he had a half humorous glint in his eyes and talked very straight and very direct to his opponent. You had a feeling that there was a steel spring waiting to be released. . . . I tried to explain to him that his REAL attitude was better than his REEL attitude for motion pictures. He didn't react to it but I did."[48]

Before the end of his first eight-picture deal with Monogram, the basic screen persona of John Wayne was in place. Straight out of popular Western novels, the cowboy hero is a lean, tough loner, impatient with small talk and small matters, willing to implement justice and protect the weak. The physical mannerisms of John Wayne were also in place. The familiar rolling walk, the midsentence pauses, the double take after being floored by a powerful punch, the economical use of his hands to emphasize a particularly crucial point, the cold, dead stare when he was mad—all the movements and gestures that in a decade would be familiar to millions can be seen in *The Man from Utah*, *Randy Rides Alone*, and *The Star Packers*. Only refinement remained to be added.

By the end of his second series of films with Monogram, John Wayne was a B star, especially in the Midwest and Southwest. His name alone was enough to fill a rural theater on Saturday night, and Duke recalled that Monogram paid him $2,500 a picture. Monogram, however, was not doing as well. Not all of its films had been as successful as its Wayne pictures and its adaptations of such classic novels as *Oliver Twist*, *Black Beauty*, and *Jane Eyre*, and it owed money to its film processor, Consolidated Film Industries. Monogram was not the only B studio that was in debt to Consolidated; Nat Levine's Mascot owed money as well. In early 1935 Consolidated president Herbert J. Yates, a former American Tobacco Company executive, proposed a solution to the chronic debt problem: Monogram and Mascot would merge their production and distribution operations with Consolidated Film Industries' processing laboratories and investment capital to form a single entity, Republic Productions. Yates also suggested that the new company would then buy out Liberty Pictures, Majestic Pictures, and Chesterfield Pictures and dominate the B film industry. Since he knew little about making movies and planned to remain in New York, Yates wanted Levine and Trem Carr to handle productions. W. Ray Johnston would be president of the new company and take care of distribution, and Yates would assume the role of chairman of the board. It was a bold plan, one that would solve Johnston and Levine's financial problems and allow them to become major players in the industry. Johnston and Carr agreed almost immediately, and after some months of hesitation Levine also signed on.[49]

Herbert Yates was not even mentioned in the *New York Times* article that announced the formation of Republic Pictures Corporation. The move was viewed as a simple reorganization of Monogram to allow the company to increase its production. But that was only a part of the story—and a small part at that. Yates might not have known much about the business of making movies, but he had mastered the business of business. He had left the tobacco industry in 1915, bought into film processing, and gradually increased his market share through mergers and takeovers. A short man with a big belly, he looked like Harry Truman, constantly had a chew of tobacco in his mouth, and, as one employee remembered, "never missed a trick where money was involved." Whether the *New York Times* knew it or not, Herbert J. Yates was bent on running Republic. A little more than a year after the merger, he and Levine bought out Johnston and Carr; a year after that he did the same to Levine.[50]

The formation of Republic gathered together some of the best assets in the B film industry. Levine brought the old Mack Sennett Studios to the new company. For years he had held a lease with an option to buy, but, chronically short of cash, he had funneled profits into production rather than equity. Along with Levine came Mascot's serial technicians, stunt men, directors, and actors, including Gene Autry and Ann Rutherford. Monogram added its network of distribution exchanges and even more talent and experience. Joining Johnston and Carr were Bradbury, Malvern, John Wayne, and a fine group of Western actors and stunt men. Yates added film processing and, more importantly, money. One writer for Republic remembered that everyone was excited by the new company. They had yet to discover that Yates, their money man, "didn't know a camera from his rear end."[51]

In the fall of 1935 Republic settled into its new studio complex on Ventura Boulevard in the San Fernando Valley, but even before then the company was filming pictures. Less than a month after the official formation of the studio, Duke began to film his first Western for Republic. As far as he was concerned, Monogram had merely changed its name. His new eight-picture contract called on him to continue to work with the same people, playing the same roles he had been playing for the past two years. *Westward Ho* was a Monogram family reunion. Trem Carr headed the production team, which included Malvern, Bradbury, Canutt, writer Parsons, cinematographer Archie Stout, editor Carl Pierson, and technical director E. R. Hickson—all men Duke had worked with a dozen or more times at Monogram. The only difference was the film's budget. Republic had more money, and that translated into more character actors, more extras, more horses, more wagons, and more expensive sets.

More did not, however, mean better, and it certainly did not mean A. In 1935 Yates was only mining for B gold. *Westward Ho*, Duke recalled years later, took almost a month to shoot and included seventy-five white and seventy-five black horses. Budgeted at about $34,000, the film had elaborate chase and fight scenes and major production values, but it was hampered by a typical Monogram script that included murdered parents, long-lost brothers, a classic battle between good and evil, and, once again, John Wayne as a singing cowboy. Thanks to a healthier budget, Duke is joined in song by "the Singing Raiders," fellow vigilantes on white horses who announce their good intentions in their songs.[52]

If not better artistically, more did mean more success in this case. The added cost of *Westward Ho* was more than recouped at the box office. Wayne insisted that it made a fortune—"close to a half a million dollars, I guess." If that figure was high by one or two hundred thousand, his general point was true. The film demonstrated to Yates that the B El Dorado was no mirage. It was out there on the bottom of double bills and in the more than five thousand small-town theaters scattered across the United States. And all it took to reach it was the right formula. For Republic that formula was the Western and the singing cowboy. The singing cowboy meant Gene Autry and Roy Rogers. Autry's smooth voice and effortless manner redefined the singing cowboy, and neither poor scripts nor poor acting could dent his popularity. All he needed was a few new songs and the slightest pretext to sing them, and Republic had a hit. Supporters claimed that he revolutionized the B Western; critics charged that he destroyed it. In either case, his bland style, fancy clothes, and Boy Scout image had replaced Duke at Republic. Rogers played second fiddle to Autry at Republic. Born Leonard Slye in Duck Run, Ohio, Rogers could croon measure for measure with Autry, but his youthful face and slight build did not project enough strength or toughness to make his fights with burly bullies believable. Between 1935 and 1951 Autry starred in almost sixty Republic Westerns and Rogers in more than ninety. But neither singer ever made the transition into A films. Duke played a singing cowboy in one more film—*The Lawless Range*—then retired from the genre.[53]

Wayne continued to make the harder-edged, nonsinging, populist Westerns, the ones that said: If you put a banker, a lawyer, and a businessman in a barrel and roll it down a hill there will always be a sonofabitch on top. In the 1930s it was a message that Americans repeatedly heard on their radios and read in their newspapers. Millions read the charges of Sen. Gerald Nye (Dem. N. Dak.) that bankers and munitions makers—"the merchants of death"—had led the country into war in 1917. As many as thirty million people a week listened to Father Charles Coughlin, the Detroit radio priest, denounce the nefarious influence of bankers in the country's and the world's economy.

That message oozed out of Duke's early Republic films. In *Lawless Range* (1935) a banker attempts to force ranchers off of his land; in *The Lawless Nineties* (1936) one large rancher tries to prevent statehood and deny the will of "the people"; in *King of the Pecos* (1936) a land and water agent seeks to use his water hole monopoly to fleece ranchers; in *The Lonely Trail* (1936) a corrupt political appointee works to enrich himself at the expense of Southern taxpayers; and in *Winds of the Wasteland* (1936) a crooked stagecoach line owner fights to eliminate any possible competition. The moneyed interests versus the people: John Wayne, tall, forthright, and plainspoken, represents and defends "true Americans" against shyster lawyers, heavy-bearded outlaws, and vicious killers, a group best portrayed in the films by Cy Kendall, a soft, overweight, effeminate-looking yet sinister character actor destined in every picture to be done in by his own greed. Indeed, in *King of the Pecos* Salamander Stiles, played by Kendall, is crushed to death by his own safe.

Moviegoers responded to the morality plays, and as success followed success Yates modestly increased the budgets on Republic's John Wayne films. Although most were still shot in six days, they enjoyed bigger casts, more elaborate period costuming, and better editing. In the beginning of the eight-picture deal, only the major chases were scored, but by *The Lawless Nineties* the entire film received scoring. The increased production values moved Wayne before a new audience. Urban American met him for the first time in his reincarnated career, and reviewers for even the most influential newspapers liked what they saw. Bosley Crowther, lead reviewer for the *New York Times*, saw *The Lawless Nineties* at the upscale Rialto and praised the film's energy. "It is rare that a Western screen story affords so many legitimate and even logically necessary pretexts for action," he wrote. John Wayne, etched against the background of Mount Whitney and the High Sierras, was difficult to ignore. By the time his Republic contract expired, he was America's leading B Western star. In a nation that had long before enshrined the Western hero, John Wayne was America's leading film cowboy.[54]

But he wanted more. "I was ambitious and wanted to vary my pictures," he said. He was restless at Republic, and the young studio was undergoing management changes. Although the company was awash in profits, the men who had brought Duke to Republic were losing the corporate wars. Nat Levine replaced Trem Carr as head of production, Paul Malvern suffered a demotion, and Joseph Kane replaced Robert Bradbury as the leading director of Wayne films. By the end of 1936 Yates and Levine had bought W. Ray Johnston and Trem Carr's Republic Pictures stock for one million dollars. Duke liked Carr, he liked Malvern, and he hardly knew Yates, who spent most of his time in his New York office or his processing laboratory across the river in Fort Lee, New Jersey. One by one, Duke's ties to Republic were undone.[55]

In late spring 1936 Trem Carr offered him a chance to break out of his B straitjacket. Carr had turned down an offer from MGM to become a producer at Universal, reassembled part of his old Monogram team, and hatched a plan to make a series of non-Western action films. It was a heady time at Universal. Carl Laemmle had retired and sold his stock in the company in 1936, and the new management team announced plans to make an aggressive move into low-cost A film production. Specifically the company wanted to make films that fell between As and Bs. Their agenda called for fewer and less expensive sets and the introduction and cultivation of "new," lower-priced talent. John Wayne was exactly the sort of actor Universal producers had in mind. Carr offered him a six-film contract at six thousand dollars a picture to join the company. Duke agreed. He took off his Colt .45, turned down a new Republic contract, and moved to Universal. In 1936 and 1937 he was the leading man in *The Sea Spoilers, Conflict, California Straight Ahead, I Cover the War, Idol of the Crowds,* and *Adventure's End.* He played a Coast Guard commander, a lumberjack-turned-boxer, an owner of a trucking company, a newsreel cameraman, a hockey player, and a pearl diver.[56]

Wayne's primary reason for going to Universal was simple. He needed to act in something other than B Westerns. But Carr's series was poorly conceived and funded. In the 1930s, when only a handful of A Westerns were made, B Westerns were the only game in town. The star of a B Western was by default a major Western star. It was a different story with action films. The major studios regularly made action pictures with budgets in excess of five hundred thousand dollars. Such films as *The Lives of a Bengal Lancer, Captain Blood, The Charge of the Light Brigade, Mutiny on the Bounty, Anthony Adverse, San Francisco,* and *Captains Courageous* filled the theaters in the mid-1930s, and such actors as Clark Gable, Spencer Tracy, and Errol Flynn defined the action hero. Carr's adventures, budgeted at seventy thousand dollars each and shot in six days, could not compete in that market. Even as B offerings, they suffered by comparison. "We were trying to sell cotton socks in a silk stocking field," Duke later told Maurice Zolotow. "The exhibitors wouldn't touch a John Wayne movie with a ten-foot projector. Universal was losing. I was bleeding to death."[57]

Actually the project started well and received enthusiastic reviews. A *New York Times* reviewer believed that *Conflict* was a fine choice for "a dull, rainy afternoon," and critic Frank Nugent called *I Cover the War* "an ingeniously romantic fable." But the pictures just never found their audience. After a few lost money, Universal abandoned interest in the project, and by the end of the series even the reviewers had raised a white flag. Director Arthur Lubin recalled that the last of the pictures, a sea film called *Adventure's End,* was made simply because Universal had a boat on the lot that needed use. "That's the way pictures were made. They said, 'Well, what sets are up these days that we can make pictures on that won't cost us much money?'" Bosley Crowther called the ill-conceived film a "pale reflection of several recent Hollywood sea epics," adding that "the title is much more revealing than it presumably is intended."[58]

When his contract with Universal expired, Duke was back where he had been five years before. Once again he had failed at a major studio. It was useless to blame Trem Carr; he was a sweet man, not a "ruthless sonofabitch" like Harry Cohn. Duke had made the decision—and now he was out of work. Years later he told Zolotow, "I had lost my stature as a Western star—and got nothing in return."[59]

He had lost more than stature by 1937. Clyde's heart trouble worsened in 1936. On Sunday afternoons every fall, Duke, Josie, Clyde, Florence, and Nancy regularly drove to the Los Angeles Coliseum to watch professional football games. After graduating from USC in 1935, Wayne's brother Bobby had signed a contract with the Los Angeles Dons. Although Josie and Florence complained good-naturedly about the afternoon ritual, Duke and Clyde enjoyed watching him play. In the fall of 1936, Clyde had an increasingly difficult time negotiating the Coliseum steps. Shortness of breath forced him to rest several times before locating their seats. Nancy Morrison remembers how frustrated he had become at the beach, where he loved to bodysurf, because he had so little energy. "He just couldn't catch his breath anymore." On the morning of March 4, 1937, Clyde decided to stay home from work. "He had to be deathly sick to stay home," Nancy recalled. "He worked long hours, every day, never missed." He took a nap that morning and never woke up. Early in the afternoon, Duke, Josie, and Florence came over to Glendale High School, took Nancy out to the car, and told her Clyde was dead. "Duke was heartbroken, sobbing in the car, and so was I. He hugged me and we cried some more." Molly refused to attend the funeral.[60]

7

Stagecoach

Nine months after Clyde died, as Duke was finishing his last film on the Universal contract, he starred in *Born to the West*, a B Western for Paramount, which was released December 10, 1937, only five days after *Adventure's End*. *Born to the West* was a fitting punctuation mark to his failed experiment with not-quite-A A movies; it differed little from the dozens of pictures he had made with Monogram and Republic. It had a cattle drive and cattle rustling, chases and shoot-outs, poker games and a touch of romance. It had John Wayne and Johnny Mack Brown, and *Variety* predicted that it would be "a cinch for the outdoor fans." It was a B all the way. Perhaps it was the Universal experiment, perhaps it was a sense of aging brought on by Clyde's death, perhaps it was a realistic understanding of the limitations of a B career—but Wayne wanted to break the cycle and he was willing to give up steady work to do so. So, after finishing the film in early November, he waited for something better. To fill his time he went on several trips aboard the *Araner*. He relaxed with Ford and Ward Bond, fishing off the coast of the Baja Peninsula, enjoying the sight of Dudley Nichols being almost scared to death by a close encounter with a hugh manta ray. But mostly he just waited. Fall passed, then winter, then spring. And still he waited.[1]

Finally he had waited enough. He had a wife and two kids—and another on the way—to support, a mortgage on his recently purchased North Highland Avenue home and bills to pay, and he needed work. One day in the spring, Lindsley Parsons called, inviting Duke to rejoin the recently reorganized Monogram. "Oh my god, I couldn't think of anything better," Wayne said, "but I just got so desperate I signed with Yates again."[2]

Reluctantly he had returned to the only acting that had brought him any measure of success, trudging back to Republic with his proverbial hat in hand and no leverage for negotiations. Herbert Yates took him back, but not before trimming Duke's salary. On May 7, 1938, the actor signed a new five-year contract. The deal called for Wayne to be paid $461.54 a week, or $24,000 a year, and for that price Republic expected him to star in eight Westerns. The contract also contained four options that, over time, promised to move his weekly salary from the base of $461.54 to $961.54. By Hollywood terms it was quite modest. To sweeten the deal Yates made vague promises that Duke could star in an A film of the life of Sam Houston. Wayne signed the five-year contract. But a half year later, when Republic moved into A films with *Man of Conquest*, a biopic of Houston, the leading role went to Richard Dix. "You're not strong enough," Yates informed Duke.[3]

Making him a "studio star" was not what Yates had in mind for Wayne. Instead of featuring him in his own B Westerns, Yates shuffled him off into an ongoing series as just one of the boys. For the 1938 season Duke replaced Robert Livingston as the character Stony Brooke in the Three Mesquiteers series. "Christ, they were awful. They were kids' movies," Wayne later told an associate. It was an accurate assessment. The Three Mesquiteers, an Alexandre Dumas rip-off based loosely on a series of pulp novels by William Colt MacDonald, were Tucson Smith, Stony Brooke, and Lullaby Joslin, three frontier characters adept at finding and getting out of trouble. RKO Radio Pictures and Grand National had both produced Mesquiteer films, but the trio found a lasting home at Republic, where in 1936 the first of the studio's fifty-one Mesquiteers movies was made. During the initial two seasons the cast usually consisted of Crash Corrigan as Smith, Robert Livingston as Brooke, and Max Terhune as Joslin, but there was often tension on the set between Livingston and Corrigan. The replacement of Livingston by Wayne was in part an attempt to restore harmony on the set, although Corrigan, who felt he was being mishandled at Republic, resented Duke as much as he had Livingston.[4]

But there was another reason for the change. Republic believed that Livingston had star potential and wanted to feature him in higher budget, non-Western movies. Duke understood the politics of Republic and the film industry; he knew that by casting him as Stony, Yates and Republic were clearly telling him where he stood in the industry. He would be playing for the Saturday matinee crowd, sharing time with Crash Corrigan and Max Terhune—a daredevil actor and a ventriloquist—and at the end of the films he would swing into his saddle and ride off with his best friends, not embrace the heroine and ride into the sunset.

Max Terhune believed that the series offered something for everyone: "For the girls, it had the running gag of rivalry between Stony and Tucson. . . . It had plenty of action and fights, and the boys liked that. I like to believe the kids liked Elmer [the ventriloquist's dummy], too. And the adults, I think, liked the variety of plots and the scenery and beautiful horses." And box-office receipts backed up Terhune's claims. It was a popular series, and its popularity increased with the addition of John Wayne. Produced with Republic's large midwestern and southwestern audiences in mind, the Three Mesquiteers defended law and order against the attacks of meddling outsiders and city types, greedy bankers and businessmen, and corrupt politicians and government appointees.[5]

But not everyone liked the series. For John Wayne, each Mesquiteer film he starred in was another indication that he had sunk deeper than ever in the world of the Bs. *Pals of the Saddle*, *Overland Stage Raiders*, *Santa Fe Stampede*, and *Red River Range*—four times in 1938 John Wayne faced his public as Stony Brooke. They were "horrible monstrosities," he told writer Maurice Zolotow. They branded him as a "cheapie" actor, a kid's actor, hardly an actor at all. So what if they received good reviews? Such reviewer comments as "John Wayne more than fills the shoes, or rather the saddle, of Robert Livingston" and "Wayne . . . should please the juvenile trade" were at best backhanded compliments. So what if they were box-office draws and Duke was clearly the main character in the series? They did not inch him any closer to the world of the As. They were tickets to nowhere. Mary St. John, who had just begun to work at Republic in the secretarial pool, remembered that Duke moved about the lot like "a wounded puppy—sad, frustrated, and unhappy. He felt like his career had bottomed out."[6]

It may have been at the bottom in 1938, but what Duke did not realize was that a decade of starring in B movies had exposed him to a huge audience of young adults and children in rural and small-town America. Between 1930 and 1939 he made sixty-five films. For a later generation of Americans, television would bring such exposure to many actors and actresses, but John Wayne was the first to combine fame with comfortable familiarity. He was on screen so often during the 1930s that he almost became a member of the family. His young audiences would come of age in the 1940s, just as he graduated to A films. They would go off to World War II and Korea and return from battle watching his movies. By the 1950s and 1960s, after they had migrated to cities and suburbs, they would be the backbone of American society and Duke would still be their hero. And when their sons died in the jungles of Vietnam by the tens of thousands in the 1960s and early 1970s, Duke spoke up for them eloquently, powerfully, and unashamedly. The world of the Bs may have seemed like a dead end to Duke at the time, but it was actually a springboard for his eventual leap to superstardom and status as a pop culture icon and American hero.

But superstardom was far away in 1938. As he worked on the Mesquiteer series, Wayne knew that his only hope of escaping the B prison lay outside the Republic Studio gates. One of the people who could help him—John Ford—was one of the last he would ever ask. Duke had never pressed the limits of their friendship. He had never begged for favors, not even after he had been dropped by Fox and Columbia. Occasionally, half in jest, he would ask the director, "When is it my turn?" Ford would reply, "Just wait, I'll let you know when I get the right script." But Duke did not expect much. Their relationship was too pure for either man to exploit, and besides, professionally they moved in different circles. Ford was one of the leading directors in the industry. He made major films for major studios. Between 1935 and 1937, he had directed *The Whole World's Watching* (Columbia), *The Informer* (RKO), *Steamboat 'Round the Bend* (Twentieth Century-Fox), *The Prisoner of Shark Island* (Twentieth Century-Fox), *Mary of Scotland* (RKO), *The Plough and the Stars* (RKO), *Wee Willie Winkie* (Twentieth Century-Fox), and *The Hurricane* (Goldwyn–United Artists). He had won an Academy Award and a New York Film Critics Award. During the same years Wayne had starred in a string of horse operas that had had the staying power of a panhandle dust storm, and what stock he had once had as an actor was no longer trading on the big board.[7]

All that began to change one summer morning in 1938. The year before, Ford had purchased the film rights to "Stage to Lordsburg," a short story by Ernest Haycox that had been pubished in *Collier's* in April 1937, and Dudley Nichols had converted it into a screenplay. As the *Araner* moved out of the San Pedro breakwater, Ford gave Wayne an early draft of a script. "Read it," he told him. Sitting on the deck of the *Araner*, as the ketch sailed toward Catalina, Duke read the story of a stagecoach ride through Indian country, a simple story, but one that promised under Ford's direction to

raise the Western to a new level of emotional and psychological sophistication. Duke had read hundreds of Western scripts. But none had moved him
like Nichols's treatment of Haycox's story.[8]

That night after dinner, Ford and Wayne discussed the script. As they
played cards, Ford sought Duke's advice on casting the film. "I've got Claire
Trevor, George Bancroft, John Carradine, and Tommy Mitchell, but I need
your help on something," Ford said. "You know a lot of young actors. Do you
know anybody who could play the Ringo Kid?"[9]

Wayne considered the question for a moment. The Ringo Kid was the central character in the script, the archetypal Western hero—young, brave, fast
with his gun, gentle with women, democrat with a small d. "Why don't you
get Lloyd Nolan?" Wayne suggested. Nolan would be good. He had played
the heavy in Paramount's *The Texas Rangers*, perhaps the best A Western of
the mid-1930s, and the scene in which he murdered a friend—shooting him
from under a table while he smiled and talked of friendship—had impressed
several critics. Although in his mid-thirties, he looked younger, and he was a
versatile actor who had starred in a dozen action films.[10]

Ford considered the suggestion as he chewed on a cigar. Nolan wasn't quite
right. "Jesus Christ, I just wish to hell I could find some young actor in this
town who can ride a horse and act. Goddammit, Duke, you must know
somebody. But then you've been out at Republic. You're not likely to see a hell
of a lot of talent out there."

The verbal slap at Wayne ended the short conversation. Over the years,
Duke had become accustomed to Ford's cruel comments. Most of the time he
did not take them personally. Ford belittled almost all of his close friends, except for the ones with distinguished military records. The director's standard
line on Wayne was Duke's failure to escape the world of B Westerns. "Christ,
if you learned to act you'd get better parts," Ford said on numerous occasions,
usually when a half dozen or more people were listening. Wayne did not particularly enjoy the shots, but he did not complain either.[11]

The next evening, Ford resumed the casting discussion, with a twist:
"Duke, I want you to play the Ringo Kid."

Wayne felt as if he had been "hit in the belly with a baseball bat." His only
fear was that Ford would reconsider Nolan. For a decade Wayne had wandered in Hollywood's B wilderness. Now Ford was offering him passage to a
different environment. The "Stage to Lordsburg"—or *Stagecoach,* as the
Nichols script was entitled—would take him there.[12]

John Ford believed in *Stagecoach*, but he had a difficult time getting a producer to share his faith. Hollywood producers, then as now, did business on the basis of a bundle of myths and untested assumptions as if they were carved in stone, at least until one of their number took a chance and showed that the conventional wisdom was wrong. Harry Cohn, for example, asserted that he could tell with absolute certainty whether audiences would like or hate a film. Previewing a film alone in the projection room, the head of Columbia placed his faith in his backside: "If my fanny squirms, it's bad. If my fanny doesn't squirm, it's good." "Imagine," writer Herman J. Mankiewicz said, "the whole world wired to Harry Cohn's ass!"[13]

During the 1930s, unbelievably, the collective asses in the industry convinced themselves that there was no longer a market for A Westerns—a conclusion as wrong sixty years later as it was at the time. B Westerns might play well in the sticks, but the people who regularly went to A pictures wanted urban sophistication, glamour, and class, not horses, Indians, and cattle.

It was a self-fulfilling prophecy. Each year during the 1930s the eight major studios produced about 350 feature films. Slightly more than 10 percent of those features were Westerns, and most of those were B Westerns. In 1931, for example, the Big Eight produced only five A Westerns. That output shrank to two in 1932, one in 1933, and zero in 1934. For the next four years the production of A Westerns remained anemic—four in 1935, seven in 1936, three in 1937, and four in 1938. The halcyon days of the twenties—the era of William S. Hart, Tom Mix, Hoot Gibson, Ken Maynard, Harry Carey, Buck Jones, and Tim McCoy—had passed, and many of the leading Western stars had moved to Poverty Row. The frontier, producers insisted, was settled; vacationers now drove on highways that had once been the routes of cattle drives.[14]

Of course, the frontier was closed. As President Franklin Roosevelt noted, "Our last frontier has long since been reached. There is no safety valve in the form of a Western Prairie." But it had been all but closed even when the myth and entertainment genre first appeared in the dime novels of the 1870s. At any rate, during the 1930s and early 1940s, producers created urban dramas, often centered on depression themes, with the major studios developing individual styles. MGM emphasized the glamour of such stars as Greta Garbo, Joan Crawford, and Clark Gable. It was the Tiffany of studios, and its films dealt in quality. Warner Brothers sold gritty crime tales, with a clipped, cold mise-en-scène, that featured James Cagney, Edward G. Robinson, George Raft, and Bette Davis. Their tales were normally set in contemporary urban America. Paramount presented the urban comedy of the Marx Brothers and Mae West and the cool, European sophistication of Marlene Dietrich, Cary

Grant, and Maurice Chevalier. Fox (and, after the 1935 merger, Twentieth Century-Fox) turned Henry Fonda into a folk hero, a visible representative of the country's heartland. RKO portrayed the corruption and the enticements of the city in films as diverse as *King Kong* and *Citizen Kane* and *The Gay Divorcee*. Columbia depended on the populist screwball comedies of Frank Capra and Howard Hawks. Universal, home of Frankenstein, Dracula, the Werewolf, the Mummy, and the Invisible Man, placed its future in the hands of monsters. With few exceptions, the major studios left Westerns to Republic, Monogram, and the other Poverty Row outfits.[15]

Ford had begun his career directing Westerns, but after completing *Three Bad Men* in 1926 even he had deserted the genre. Yet the more he worked with Nichols on the screenplay of *Stagecoach*, the more committed to the project he became. The problem was finding a producer to finance the film and a distributor to market it. Darryl Zanuck, head of production at Twentieth Century-Fox, wanted nothing to do with it, refusing even to read the screenplay. MGM, Warner Bros., Paramount, and Columbia followed Twentieth's lead. They liked Ford's work but did not want a Western. The project attracted more interest at Selznick International Pictures, where Ford's friend Merian Cooper was vice president and a producer. Before joining forces with Selznick, Cooper was the head of his own production company, Pioneer, and he had signed Ford to a two-film contract. David O. Selznick definitely wanted Cooper to keep Ford under contract, and he wrote memos to his vice president expressing the hope that Ford would direct a movie of the life of Benedict Arnold and work on *Gone With the Wind*. Ford, however, wanted only *Stagecoach*.[16]

Making fast decisions—and holding to them—was never Selznick's strong point. Arrogance was. By 1937 he had begun to supplement his four or five packs of cigarettes a day with amphetamines, and the combination swept away all battle fatigue. But he was still indecisive. After dinner and a lengthy discussion with Ford and Cooper, Selznick voiced his support for *Stagecoach*; the next day he had second thoughts. A pattern developed. One day he would say that *Stagecoach* was "just another Western" and Ford and Cooper should stick with the "classics"; a few days later he would give them the green light; the next day he would suggest that without a Gary Cooper or Marlene Dietrich the project just was not commercial enough. Merian Cooper was caught between his boss and his friend. Finally Selznick made a decision to cut bait. "Ford apparently has no desire to go through with his commitment with us," Selznick wrote one of his executives, "evidently being annoyed because he could not do

The Stage to Lordsburg." Selznick wanted Ford but only on his terms. "He is an excellent man, but there is no point in treating him as a god."[17]

So through most of 1937 Ford kept searching for a producer. Then the independent Walter Wanger took an interest. Wanger had made a career out of going against conventional wisdom and taking chances. Educated at Dartmouth, Heidelberg, and Oxford, he had served on President Woodrow Wilson's staff at the Paris Peace Conference. One of the film industry's outspoken liberals, he wrote about the moral obligation to use movies to inform. In Hollywood he was reputed to care about a film's message as much as, though not more than, its box-office potential. Such rumors made him seem somehow graced, apart from the other grasping, selfish producers. In the early 1930s he was the production force behind *Washington Merry-Go-Round, Gabriel Over the White House*, and *The Bitter Tea of General Yen*, pictures that explored such subjects as political corruption, political apathy, and miscegenation in the Orient. Dangerous subjects for most producers, but not for Wanger who seemed to have the knack of producing movies that both said something and made money. He also gained a reputation for recognizing talent. Claudette Colbert, Walter Huston, Maurice Chevalier, Ginger Rogers, and the Marx Brothers are all listed as Wanger "discoveries." But he soon grew uncomfortable with the demands and limitations of the big studios, and in 1936 he formed Walter Wanger Produtions and signed a financing and distribution deal with United Artists. He was now free to take even more chances.[18]

Wanger's early films at United Artists did not inspire confidence. None of his first seven films returned a profit, and UA had become concerned about his budgets. *Vogues*, for example, had been budgeted at $800,000 but ran $600,000 over, a miscalculation that did not escape United Artists' accountants. The studio demanded supervisory control over Wanger's budgets. Wanger refused, and UA stopped financing his projects. The studio did, however, help arrange for Wanger to receive financing from other sources.[19]

Whether Wanger liked it or not, United Artists was sending the eternal message of "cultural" industries: Art and ideas are nice, but money is nicer. As he discussed the *Stagecoach* project with Ford, Wanger worried about the budget. He was willing to take a chance on an A Western, but it had to be as lean as a longhorn on the open range. No fat, no overruns, no hidden costs. Ford agreed. He knew how to make inexpensive movies and had a well-deserved reputation for shooting only what was necessary, doing it in one take, and bringing in a film on budget and on time. He could save money by shooting *Stagecoach* in black and white (the newly introduced color process added 30 percent to production costs), paying attention to the logistics of location and studio shooting, and employing less expensive talent. After going over the schedules and eliminating all excesses, Wanger and Ford agreed on a budget of $546,200. They signed the contracts in October 1937.[20]

The budget precluded such high-priced stars as Gary Cooper or Marlene Dietrich. Ford worked for a flat $50,000, $25,000 less than his going price at Fox and $50,000 less than he had made a year before for *Hurricane*. Dudley Nichols accepted $20,000 for the screenplay, and actors and actresses—most of whom were friends of Ford—worked for below their market value. Before the casting was done, Wanger had budgeted $35,000 for the female lead, $15,000 for the male lead, and between $4,000 and $5,000 for the supporting players, but Ford decided to pay less for the stars and more for the character actors. Claire Trevor received $15,000 to play the female lead, and in supporting roles Thomas Mitchell got $12,000, Andy Devine $10,624, Louise Platt $8,541, George Bancroft $8,250, Donald Meek $5,416, Tim Holt $5,000, Berton Churchill $4,500, and John Carradine $3,666. John Wayne, the male lead, agreed to do *Stagecoach* for $3,000, an amount only slightly over Poverty Row standards. But for Duke the film had nothing to do with money and everything to do with his career.[21]

He was the last important member of *Stagecoach* to be cast. Dan Ford has suggested that his grandfather was determined to cast Duke in the part of the Ringo Kid from the time he bought the rights to *Stage to Lordsburg*. "For some years," Dan Ford wrote, John Ford

> had believed that once Wayne shed his youthful callowness, once he put on some age, weight, and character, he could become a first-rate actor. . . . John noticed that Wayne "moved like a dancer." He sensed in him a charm, a charisma, a vulnerability with which he thought audiences could identify. John also knew that Wayne had the phenomenal, almost pathological drive that it took to survive in Hollywood. He was hungry.

Perhaps Ford had always intended to pull Duke out of the Bs and make him a part of his stock company; perhaps he had always intended to use him in *Stagecoach*; but the film's budget added a touch of necessity. He needed a Western actor—a man who was tall, handsome, and knew how to ride a horse and use a gun. And Gary Cooper simply did not star in risky films for $3,000.[22]

Wayne did not care about the money, but he had problems with Republic. Several points bothered the leaders of the studio. Paradoxically the low salary scale was one; Duke had agreed to work five weeks for Ford at the same rate that Republic paid him for a six-day B Western, and that created problems for everyone who made the comparison. Then there was the matter of quality. Executives at Republic insisted that they made the best Westerns in the industry. Their ignorance startled Wayne, who knew from his Mesquiteer series just how poor Republic's Westerns were. But he kept quiet, hoping to get a release. As time for shooting drew closer, Wanger pressed Ford to get a release or get another leading man. Finally, Republic relented, loaning out Wayne to Wanger for six hundred a week to make his "inferior" Western.[23]

On the last day of October 1938, Ford began to shoot *Stagecoach*. Ford set about building his usual cast and crew's family atmosphere, as if he had to construct one fictional world before he could create another. It started the morning before the first day of shooting, when everybody gathered for a complete reading of the script. Slowly the actors and actresses, leads and bit players, read through their parts. Ford knew from experience that often studios would have sent a secondary character only the few pages of a script that he or she was involved in, but he wanted everyone to have a feel for the entire script. During the reading Ford would separate himself a little from the rest and smoke a pipe, saying little but absorbing everything.[24]

Once they commenced shooting, work began at nine o'clock each morning. Ford wanted everyone on the set, even though most of the actors and actresses would probably not be in any scenes. Since he generally worked on picture after picture with the same basic cast and crew, nobody complained and the custom kept everyone involved in the making of the film. Why should anyone protest? The mood was light and jocular; cast members drank coffee and relaxed while crew members went about their duties. Ford discussed what he wanted to accomplish, but he never seemed rushed. Then he would step off to a quiet spot and ask his leading player for that day to join him. Duke recalled that Ford would sit with him and ask him to read his lines for the upcoming scene. Just Wayne and Ford—no other cast members, no camera. If Ford liked what he heard, he would say "Jesus, that was nice." Such comments pleased Duke. Then Ford would call over the camerman and run through the scene again. Finally he would call over the other players in the scene and run through it once more to establish the timing.

As Ford listened as the players read their lines, he suggested small changes. He regarded scripts as general outlines, not stone tablets. He cut lines, added lines, combined lines. Dudley Nichols was always on the *Stagecoach* set, even though all his contract called for him to do was deliver an acceptable screenplay. Ford was not a writer himself, but in his prime he was a superb editor, adept at eliminating all but the best of Nichols's dialogue. Ford and Nichols worked with the players, often for an hour or more, until Ford was satisfied with a scene. Then he shot it. By the time the camera started rolling, the kinks had been worked out, the players rehearsed, and the mood created. It may have taken Ford longer than other directors to prepare to shoot, but he seldom needed more than one or two takes. Probably no other major director made movies that wasted less film or needed less editing.

Most days on a Ford set followed the same meandering course. Nine o'clock coffee, rehearsals, shooting, more rehearsal, more shooting. Danny Borzage, as usual, played Ford's favorite songs on an accordion. Stars, stunt men, extras, crew members gathered for communal lunch, but the general rule was no shoptalk while eating. Every day at four there was a tea break. Ford never seemed rushed, but somehow he almost always brought his films in on time.

Also as usual, Ford's manner was not always gentle and casual. He got mad at Andy Devine and said: "You big tub of lard. I don't know why the hell I'm using you in this picture." "Because Ward Bond can't drive six horses," Devine shot back. In another scene he bawled out Thomas Mitchell until the actor said, "Just remember: I saw *Mary of Scotland*," reminding the director of his 1936 critical failure. Other times his insults were simply mean—designed, Ford's supporters insist, to draw the best performance out of an actor, but painful nonetheless. If he picked on many people, he tended to attack only one person each film. In *Stagecoach* it was Duke. No sooner had John Wayne gone to work for John Ford than Ford went to work on him.[25]

Ford was determined to make Wayne into his idea of an actor, and he did not do it gently. During an early screen test, "Ford took Duke by the chin and shook him," Claire Trevor recalled. "Why are you moving your mouth so much? Don't you know that you don't act with your mouth in pictures? You act with your eyes," Ford ranted. He belittled Wayne, ridiculing his work in B Westerns, calling him a "big oaf" and a "dumb bastard." He criticized the way Duke moved: "Can't you walk, for Chrissake, instead of skipping like a goddamn fairy?" He attacked the way Duke delivered lines and the way he held his body. "It was tough for Duke to take, but he took it," Trevor said.[26]

Ford's criticism did not end with the screen test. In one of the first scenes he shot, he went after Wayne again. It was a simple scene in which all Duke did was wash and dry his face. "Can't you wash your fucking face?" Ford yelled. "For Chrissakes, *wash* your face! Don't you ever wash at home? You're dabbing your face, you're *daubing* it! You're just splashing water on it." He made Duke do the scene again and again, until his face was "almost raw from rubbing it with the towel. "I was so fucking mad I wanted to kill him," Duke remembered. Finally Tim Holt, who had a small part as an army officer, had seen enough of Ford's brutality and said: "Why don't you lay off the poor guy?" Ford took a short break, returned in a better mood, and went back to work, but during the next few weeks he continued his assaults.

What was the reason for the attacks? Wayne has suggested that there was a motive behind Ford's actions. Duke was a young, untested actor whose only success had been in B Westerns. He was working with veterans: Thomas Mitchell and John Carradine had distinguished themselves on stage as well as screen; Andy Devine, Berton Churchill, Donald Meek, and George Bancroft were well-established character actors. They had worked with Ford before, and they knew each other. But they were all supporting a man who had failed in every A film in which he had starred. Perhaps Ford's attacks were designed to get the other cast members on Wayne's side. He became the much-abused un-derdog—kicked around, yelled at, and beaten up on. With Duke treated in such a manner by Ford, it was impossible for the cast not to pull for his success.

Some elements of the treatment clearly had a different—if equally be-nign—motivation. In one important scene Ringo expresses his love for Dallas (Claire Trevor) as they walk into a rough section of Lordsburg. The scene de-manded a long walk in muted lighting. "Keep your head up," Ford cautioned Wayne after one ruined take. "For God's sake, keep your face up! Don't look down!" he said after another. It was the same thing take after take, Ford accus-ing Wayne of ruining the scene and causing delays. Duke knew he was not looking down and was angry. After the scene was over, he walked away, count-ed to ten, and tried to control his temper. Ford walked by him and without stopping mumbled a hasty "Thanks." Only then did Wayne realize that it was Claire who was looking down, and that Ford, who tended to treat women with extreme kindness, had berated him in the hope that Claire would stop looking for her mark.

Contrariness was also at work, such as the time when he asked Duke if he would like to preview some early rushes. Struck by this act of kindness, Wayne said yes and went to the projection room. Afterward Ford casually asked, "Well, how do you like it?" "Well, it's just magnificent, Coach. I've never seen anything like it in my life," Duke replied. "How do you like Mitchell?" "Oh, he's great!" "How do you like Claire?" "Great," Duke replied. "How do the stunts look?" "Great." "The stage scene?" "Oh, great." After a few more "greats," Ford asked him, "Well, Jesus, Duke, you've looked at the whole goddamned thing, isn't there one criticism, one constructive criticism you can give me? You're acting like a schoolboy." "Well," Duke offered, "too bad on the close-up of Devine on the stage the prop man didn't use a few people with springs to give the scene a more realistic stage look." "Ah, huh," Ford mused. He then called the cast and crew together and announced, "I just sent our young star in to see his first effort. And he's very well satisfied with himself, and with the rest of the cast, but he thinks Andy Devine stinks."[27]

Duke tolerated the criticism, held his temper in check, did what he was told, and gradually came to believe that above all Ford was trying to pull the best possible performance out of him. His character, Ringo, is a combination of extremes—brutality and gentleness, hate and love, vengefulness and protectiveness, individualism and concern for a community of people. In addition, he is inarticulate, unable to express exactly what he feels or why he feels it. He does not understand, or only dimly understands, much of what happens—or has happened—in the story. Confronted with danger he is a resolute man of action, but he is awkward, confused, and uncomfortable in most social settings. It was a role that demanded more than Duke had ever given before, and Ford's treatment may have been necessary preparation. Ford confused Wayne, injured his pride, embarrassed him in front of others, and made him feel like an outcast and a fool. He made him feel like Ringo.

Ford had used this form of psychological preparedness before. In *The Informer* Victor McLaglen played Gypo Nolan, another inarticulate, complex, brutish, explosive character. Like Wayne, McLaglen had a reputation as a limited actor. Dan Ford wrote that during the filming of *The Informer,* John Ford:

> did everything he could to keep McLaglen off balance and thus inadvertently in character. He juggled the schedule without telling his leading man, so that McLaglen, a slow study under the best of circumstances, would have to learn his lines when he arrived in the morning. As the day progressed John hurried McLaglen on and off the set at dizzying speed, showering him with abuse if he dared to slow down. In the afternoons, under the pretext of rehearsal, John ran McLaglen through his "next day's" scenes, while the camera rolled away. McLaglen's tentative efforts with the unfamiliar dialogue resulted in some of the best takes.

At one point he even told Victor to go out and get drunk because he had the next day off; then woke him up early the next morning and made him do a crucial scene with a bad hangover. The treatment reduced McLaglen to a "trembling wreck"; he also won an Academy Award.[28]

Ford, of course, never explained his methods, and several men close to him felt that he liked meting out the brutal treatment. "You had to wonder where the line was in Jack's mind," said his brother-in-law and assistant director Wingate Smith. "Sure, he was getting great stuff from Vic, but I also think he enjoyed seeing him suffer. He was like a mean little kid playing with a bug."[29]

Was John Wayne the latest bug in Ford's collection? Ford never said, and Wayne never knew. But if being that bug was the cost of the lessons, Duke was willing to pay the price. Each night he went over to Paul Fix's house and worked on his lines. Each day he listened to and tried to follow Ford's instructions. "Just look into the camera," Ford told Wayne repeatedly. "Just look into the camera." He explained that there was no real need to pantomime anger, hate, or love—that context was everything and that the audience would read into his expesssion whatever emotion was called for. Sound man Walter Reynolds recalled Wayne having a problem in a love scene with Claire Trevor. "He couldn't get it right. Finally Ford said: 'Just raise your eyebrow and wrinkle your forehead.'" Duke did it, and it looked so good in the context of the scene that he made it one of his standard screen mannerisms.[30]

It took Ford almost two months to shoot *Stagecoach*, but the most important shooting took place in the first week. Somewhere Ford had heard about Monument Valley, a region of stark, epic grandeur. Exactly where Ford learned about this Navajo land is unclear. Never too concerned about literal truth, Ford himself advanced at least two stories. He told writer/director Peter Bogdanovich: "I knew about it. I had traveled up there once, driving through Arizona on my way to Santa Fe, New Mexico." At about the same time, Ford told director Burt Kennedy: "I knew this guy, Harry Goulding, who had a trading post there. Once he asked me, 'Did you ever think of Monument Valley for a location?' I said, 'Say—that's a good idea.'" John Wayne contradicted both stories. Monument Valley, he claimed, was *his* discovery, one he had made in the late 1920s when he was working as a prop man on a George O'Brien film. Duke said that he had told Ford about the location before filming started on *Stagecoach*, and that once the director saw the valley he immediately jumped Wayne's claim of discovery.[31]

Duke might have known about Monument Valley, and he might have told Ford about the location, but Harry Goulding probably did play the most crucial role. Ford led interviewers to believe that Goulding was an old friend of his. It was all part of the director's pose—the idea that he was friends with Indian traders was a smart affectation. In truth the two men had not met before 1938. In 1921 Goulding had explored and fallen in love with Monument

Valley, and a few years later he and his wife, "Mike," began homesteading in the region, where they lived in a tent for the first four or five years, raising sheep and trading food for Navajo jewelry and blankets. The depression, however, badly injured the wool market, and a drought curtailed the Navajo food supply. Times were desperate. In 1938 Goulding heard a rumor that a Hollywood movie was going to be filmed in the Flagstaff area, and, armed with pictures of Monument Valley, he invaded Hollywood, bent on selling the filmmakers on his site. It took some time to arrange a meeting with Wanger or Ford, but Goulding was patient. While Mike sat in their car reading and knitting, Harry staked out Ford's office. A secretary told him that the director was too busy to see him, and Goulding replied, "Well, I got plenty of time. I'll just stay in here and wait for 'em," and he began to untie his bedroll. The ploy worked, and he finally got a chance to talk with Ford. The pictures convinced the director that Monument Valley offered a perfect backdrop for a Western film, and Goulding convinced him that the Indians needed the work as extras and laborers.[32]

Stagecoach transformed Monument Valley into the archetypal Western landscape. The thirty-mile strip along the Utah and Arizona border resembles no other section of the United States. Millions of years of wind and water have carved its de Chelly sandstone mesas into rugged towers, many a thousand or more feet high. It is a dream landscape—arid, lonely, haunting. In the 1930s no other place in the country was as far away from a railroad, and it was not on any road to anywhere. It is a land, an environment, that dwarfs people, plays tricks on the human eye, and seems undaunted by civilization. All distances appear relative—a tower that is twenty miles away looks only a mile away. It even has its own sense of time. Edward Buscombe has observed that "no one can look at such a spectacularly eroded landscape without reflecting on the eons which separate us from the creation of the earth." It was the ideal backdrop for *Stagecoach*, the tale of a fragile, isolated coach wending its way across hostile Indian country.[33]

Though Monument Valley dominates *Stagecoach*, very little of the movie was actually filmed there, and most of the picture's cast and crew did not make the trip to the remote location. All Ford needed from Monument Valley was basic second-unit work—shots of the landscape and Indians strung out against high-desert buttes. All the interior stagecoach scenes were shot in the studio. "It would have been useless to try to shoot those scenes with the grinding and rattling of the wheels of the stagecoach and the clippity-clop of six horses," recalled Wayne. To give the illusion of the stage moving through

toleration would be intolerable. The head of the PCA, Joseph I. Breen, had not approved the script until two weeks before the film went into production, and then only after several significant changes. Everything about the script bothered him: He disliked the idea that a prostitute and a convict would be sympathetic characters, hated the fact that the sheriff would permit a triple revenge killing and then help a convict to escape justice, and was uncomfortable with the amount of on-screen drinking. Only after Wanger and Ford agreed to keep Dr. Boone's drinking down "to the absolute minimum necessary for plot and characterization" and never mention the words "prostitute or prostitution" did Breen give script approval.[37]

Strong performances by Trevor and Mitchell made Breen's dictates meaningless. After a half decade of weak roles and missed opportunities, *Stagecoach* was Trevor's chance to break into better films, and she imbued the character of Dallas with her own sense of desperation. There was no need to mention the word "prostitute." Whenever a "respectable" person shuns Dallas, her fragile, hurt eyes declare her occupation. Mitchell's Dr. Boone is equally convincing. As the film progresses, his character evolves beyond the broad comedic drunk to a poignant study of alcoholism, and his exchanges with Donald Meek—the good Mr. Peacock—shift from comedy to tragedy. Mitchell won an Oscar for his performance in *Stagecoach,* capping off a year in which he also had good parts in *Gone With the Wind, The Hunchback of Notre Dame, Mr. Smith Goes to Washington*, and *Only Angels Have Wings.*

Yet, for all the outstanding performances, *Stagecoach* is John Wayne's movie. Ringo is the moral center of the isolated group, and, though an outlaw, he has the most fully developed sense of community. His philosophy—"There's some things a man just can't run away from"—shows his clear moral compass. His world is black and white. He hates the man who shot his brother and loves Dallas because she is kind and gentle. After seeing the red-light district of Lordsburg, he asks a friend to make sure Dallas gets safely to his ranch because "This is no town for a girl like her." The irony of his statement is clear, but there is nothing humorous about it. His sincerity is palpable. Even when he realizes that Dallas is a prostitute, he still wants her to become his wife.

Ringo was John Ford's idea of a man, and Duke knew it. After Wayne viewed some early rushes, Ford asked him how he liked himself as Ringo. "Well, hell, I'm playing you, so—*you* know what that is," Duke replied. Years later he explained to Peter Bogdanovich that Ford was careful to place Wayne's Ringo "in a good light. . . . Anytime there was a chance for a reaction—which is the most important thing in a motion picture—he always took reactions of me, so I'd be part of every scene. . . . I knew [Ford] liked that particular character as well as me, and I think this is what he would have wanted a young man to be." Duke did not need lines in *Stagecoach*; indeed, many of the supporting characters had more lines than he did. All he needed was a presence as large as Monument Valley.[38]

Harry Carey Jr. had grown up around Ford and had worked with him in several of his greatest films. He felt certain that John Ford, John Wayne, and Ringo were all part of a complex tapestry. "Ford was a tender, loving man," Carey said, "and he was a delicate, artistic man. You could see that his hands and eyes were so gentle. Yet he was intrigued with machoism. He wanted to be a two-fisted, brawling, heavy-drinking Irishman. He wanted to do what John Wayne did on screen and clean up a barroom all by himself, which Ford couldn't do. There was a part of him that Wayne exemplified physically, something he always wanted to be. So he created that on the screen. No one had a presence on the screen like John Wayne did. Physically, he was overpowering." Years later, Maurice Zolotow asked Wayne what had set him apart from other cowboy idols like Bob Steele, Tim McCoy, Tex Ritter, Roy Rogers, and Gene Autry.

Wayne finished smoking a cigarette, extinguished it, and smiled: "John Ford."[39]

Two days before Christmas, Ford finished shooting. He had exceeded his schedule by four days but brought the film in under budget. But no one was quite sure if Duke or the film would be a success. Ford seldom viewed rushes, and only a few of the cast members had seen any. Even then the unedited and unscored footage was too random to give a complete sense of the film. Claire Trevor recalled that she thought the film would be good, but she "did not realize how great it would be. During our own scenes the actors didn't get any feel for great drama; the scenes were too fragmentary. But it was all shaping up in Ford's mind. He knew how all the pieces were going together." She was right; the film was in Ford's mind. Ford "cut in the camera," said *Stagecoach* editor Dorothy Spencer. Unlike more cautious directors, he did not bother to film each scene from a variety of angles. He knew the shot he wanted, filmed it, and then let the editor put the pieces together. When he turned the footage over to Spencer, Ford was satisfied.[40]

During January Spencer edited the film under the supervision of editorial supervisor Otho Lovering. A team of composers created a score based on period songs—"Jeannie with the Light Brown Hair," "Shall We Gather at the River," "Gentle Annie," "The Union Forever," "My Lulu," "The Trail to

Mexico," "Ten Thousand Cattle," and especially "Bury Me Not on the Lone Prairie." The music was nostalgic, a soft lament for the America of the Civil War era, and Ford was so pleased with the result that he used the film's primary composer, Richard Hagman, on many of his later films.

The finished film previewed on February 2, 1939, at the Fox Village Theater in Westwood, near UCLA. By then Duke was back at Republic, and Mary St. John, a young studio typist, remembered that he seemed edgy and nervous. But he had a few extra tickets for the preview and gave them to Republic executives Moe Siegel, Sol Siegel, and Leonard Goldstein. They joined a critical audience mostly made up of students. It was "the toughest place in the world to have a Western," Duke recalled. The film began, and the audience watched as all the main characters were introduced. Each stood in stark contrast with another: a prostitute and a lady, a Northerner and a Southerner, a pillar of the community and a social outcast. All the main players and plot lines had been introduced before John Wayne made his entrance, fifteen minutes into the film.[41]

"It's one of the most stunning entrances in all of cinema," wrote film historian Edward Buscombe. There is a mythic quality to Wayne's first appearance in the film. The stagecoach rolls through Apache country, where Geronimo, the chief, is on the warpath. Seated high and exposed in the driver's seat, Buck, the driver, tries to calm his fears by chattering idly to Curly, the marshal, who is riding shotgun. There's a shot. Curly jerks up his gun. The camera cuts suddenly to a cowboy standing by the trail, twirling a rifle and carrying a saddle. The camera dollies so quickly toward a tight close-up that it momentarily loses its focus. Then, in a fraction of a second, the focus adjusts perfectly on John Wayne's sweat-streaked face framed against the classic western backdrop—desert, sky, and the buttes of Monument Valley.[42]

"Hold it," he commands.

"Hey look, it's Ringo," Buck cries out with pure delight.

"Yea. Hello, Kid," says Curly in a cautious flat tone as he points his shotgun at Ringo.

"Hiya, Curly," Ringo replies just as cautiously. And then with a quick smile and a change in his voice, "Hello Buck, how's the folks?"

Duke is dressed in a manner that would become his trademark. The placket-front, button-paneled wool shirt, the army-style braces, neckerchief, the dusty jeans worn outside of the boots. His accent is an amalgam, a blend of sounds from the South, Midwest, and West. It is a pleasing combination made even more so by his singsong, halting delivery. In an age when most leading men cultivated East Coast or European accents, John Wayne speaks with a voice that was purely American.

The scene also establishes the role that Wayne would play in *Stagecoach*. If Buck is happy to see him, the marshal is wary. Throughout the scene the marshal keeps his shotgun leveled at Ringo, demanding that Ringo surrender his Winchester. "You might need me and this Winchester," Ringo tells the marshal. John Wayne's role is set within thirty seconds of his first major screen appearance. He is the outsider, a man of few words, vaguely distrusted by marshals and other representatives of authority but affectionately regarded by average Americans. He is armed and alone, ready to defend the defenseless but not to join any established community. Above all else, he prizes his independence. In a crisis he can be counted on by decent people—his Winchester will always be on the side of justice—but during all other times he simply wants to be left alone.

The college audience responded to Wayne's entrance, and to every bit of him after that. "They stomped, they screamed, they . . . goddamn, nobody ever enjoyed a picture more than these people enjoyed *Stagecoach*," Duke said. They were caught in Ford's magic. "They were quiet at all the right times. Jesus, it was like watching and knowing that this guy had them by the. . . . He just had them mesmerized with the picture."[43]

It seemed that Ford had mesmerized everyone but Wayne's bosses at Republic. Duke saw the trio sneak out of the theater after the preview, but none of them said a word to him the next day at Republic Studio. Duke waited a few more days for a comment. Nothing. Finally, three or four days later, he asked Goldstein, "How did you like *Stagecoach*?" "Well," the production manager replied, "the boys and I went out and had some coffee afterwards, and we decided if they want Westerns, they'd better let Republic make 'em." Years later Duke still found it difficult to fathom "that sort of ignorance." "I couldn't believe what I heard. . . . I mean here's probably the classic Western of all times. God, it sure had all of Bret Harte's characters in it. Boy! And these guys say, 'Better let Republic make it.'"[44]

After some more fine-tuning, *Stagecoach* was released nationally on March 2, 1939. The reviewers disagreed with the self-satisfied Republic producers. *Variety* called it "an exemplary picture," a match for "the best in western literature." "Brilliant direction, writing and acting," added the *Hollywood Reporter*. *Stagecoach*, reviewers emphasized, was more that a Western; it was "a

Grand Hotel on wheels," suggested *Photoplay*. Frank S. Nugent, the influential *New York Times* film critic, who saw *Stagecoach* at Radio City Music Hall, announced that the picture was a classic:

> John Ford has swept aside ten years of artifice and talkie compromise and has made a motion picture that sings a song of camera. It moves, and how beautifully it moves, across the plains of Arizona, skirting the sky-reaching mesas of Monument Valley, beneath the piled-up cloud banks which every photographer dreams about. . . . Here, in a sentence, is a movie of the grand old school, a genuine rib-thumper and a beautiful sight to see.

Nugent was particularly moved by Ford's celebration of the American landscape, and he praised the director for moving out of the studio to film a picture "beneath the clouds."[45]

Hailed as a critical success, *Stagecoach* became one of the top movies in 1939. Ford won the New York Critics Best Director Award, and the film was nominated for seven Academy Awards, including ones for best picture, director, supporting actor, cinematography, score, editing, and interior decoration. However, 1939 was the greatest year in Hollywood history, an *annus mirabilis* that saw the premieres of *Mr. Smith Goes to Washington*, *The Hunchback of Notre Dame*, *Elizabeth and Essex*, *Only Angels Have Wings*, *Destry Rides Again*, *Love Affair*, *Gunga Din*, *Dark Victory*, *Goodbye, Mr. Chips*, *Ninotchka*, *The Wizard of Oz*, *Wuthering Heights*, *Beau Geste*, *Juarez*, *Drums Along the Mohawk*, *Young Mr. Lincoln*, and *Gone With the Wind*, the last of which dominated the Academy Awards. *Stagecoach* won only the Best Supporting Actor (Thomas Mitchell) and Best Score Oscars.

John Wayne received no awards, not even a nomination, but in such a year it hardly mattered. He had starred in a major motion picture, and it had been a critical and financial success. *Stagecoach* had not been a repeat of *The Big Trail*. In less than one year after its domestic release, it had earned several hundred thousand dollars more than it cost to make, and during the next decade its domestic and foreign receipts exceeded its costs by almost 200 percent. And almost all the reviews of the film singled Duke out for praise, most echoing *Variety*'s comment that Wayne displayed "talent hither to only partially used." Even John Ford later grudgingly acknowledged his accomplishments: "Duke did okay. He knew his lines, and he did what he was told to do. Of course, I surrounded him with superb actors, and some of that glitter rubbed off on his shoulders. But he's still up there with the best of them. He's god-damn good." Judged by the standards of Hollywood, John Wayne had finally arrived.[46]

Even before all the reviews were in and the final accounting completed, Duke's life had changed. Shortly after the national release, he needed a letter typed and took it to the secretarial pool at Republic. When he walked into the room several of the secretaries stood and began clapping, and before long they were all standing and cheering the new star. He was clearly startled by the display and nervously fidgeted with the letter, but at the same time he was deeply moved. Mary St. John, who by then had been placed in charge of the clerical staff, left her desk to shake his hand and congratulate him. "Thanks. Thank you, so much," he kept repeating. It was his Academy Award ceremony.[47]

The applause was not confined to Hollywood. Three months after the *Stagecoach* premiere, Duke went back to Glendale for Nancy Morrison's graduation. He stopped by Florence's apartment to give Nancy a graduation present—a diamond-studded watch. Nancy opened it, thanked him profusely, and then unwrapped a present from Florence. Inside the small box was an elegant but relatively inexpensive woman's wristwatch. The coincidence embarrassed Duke. He insisted on exchanging his gift, telling Nancy: "Your mother's is the watch you want to wear and remember the rest of your life, not mine." He returned with a diamond-and-emerald ring. Later that afternoon the two of them strolled through the hallways of Glendale High School. Suddenly Duke looked down a hall, stiffened, and whispered into Nancy's ear, "My God, Nancy, is she still around?" Miss Soper, Duke's old civics teacher, was indeed still terrorizing students. She marched up to them and said: "Marion, you've done quite well for yourself. It doesn't surprise me."[48]

8

Foreign Affairs

John Ford sensed trouble on his 1939 Christmas cruise down the Baja Peninsula and into the Gulf of California. Everything was quiet, but something was not quite right. Playing cards aboard the *Araner*, Ford talked with John Wayne, Ward Bond, Preston Foster, Wingate Smith, and George Schneiderman about the war in Europe and the chances that the United States would be pulled into the fight. Japan, however, seemed even more threatening than Germany, and Ford, a lieutenant commander in the Naval Reserves, watched the waters and harbors for unusual activities, searching for signs of Japanese military intentions. He looked to find Japanese machinations, and not surprisingly he thought he found what he was looking for.[1]

Before the trip, Capt. Elias Zacharias, chief intelligence officer for the 11th Naval District, had asked Ford to write a detailed but unofficial report on Japanese activities in the Baja region. It was cloak-and-dagger stuff, and Ford loved it. His seven-page report reads like a spy's travelogue. He found no signs of Japanese military activity in the bald mountains that surrounded Magdalena Bay, nothing at Man of War Cove, and nothing in Mazatlán. At Cape San Lucas though he did discover an "unusual" Japanese photographer who was "impossible to contact," and at Las Freilas Bay he spied a Franco-American fishing boat with a Japanese crew.

Even more suspicious was a Japanese shrimp-boat fleet anchored in the harbor of Guaymas. "The crews [came] ashore for liberty in well tailored flannels,

worsted and tweed suits . . . black service shoes smartly polished. . . . The men
are above average height . . . young . . . good looking and very alert. All carry
themselves with military carriage . . . hair well cut." Aboard each trawler he
noted three or four young officers dressed in "regulation braid-bound Imperial
Navy uniform[s], smartly cut and well pressed." Not only were they all dressed
alike, Ford reported, they all looked alike: "These young men were tall, straight
as ramrods, high cheek boned, with aquiline features, definitely aristocratic.
For want of a better word I would call them Samurai or military caste." Seeing
men in uniforms with all the trappings and manners of officers, Ford stated
that he was "positive" they were "Naval men." Convinced that the Japanese
were on a reconnaissance mission, he wrote: "It is plausible to assume that
these men know every Bay, Cove and Inlet in the Gulf of California."

Ford and his companions' concerns deepened on the trip back to Los Angeles from Mazatlán. Traveling overland by train, they encountered other
Japanese who raised their suspicions. One, an "eagle eyed, hawk visaged,
straight and erect" army "type," was "sublimely indifferent" to the picturesque
Mexican countryside but took photographs of bridges and oil tanks with an
elaborate Leica. Another acted like a comedian on the train, but during one
brief stop barked orders at several other Japanese.

Had Ford and his friends uncovered an espionage ring working the West
Coast of Mexico? Dan Ford suspected that his grandfather was "fantasizing,"
that his military ambition and love of intrigue and storytelling had gotten the
better of him. John Wayne also tended to discount the importance of Ford's
observations, and so, no doubt, should we. But more certain—and more important—is the fact that as early as the winter of 1939 John Ford, along with
many liberals and radicals in America, believed that the United States had to
be prepared for war. And unlike many of his countrymen, Ford could do
something to influence American readiness. Ford told a *New York Times* reporter at the beginning of 1939 that he and his screenwriter Dudley Nichols
had for years wanted to make an antifascist film.[2]

Wayne, by contrast, despite the activist political stance that he later made
famous, did *not* follow his mentor's lead. He simply was not as personally interested in military service as his friend. In the period between the outbreak of
war in Europe and the Japanese attack on Pearl Harbor, Ford's concerns about
the world affairs grew into a consuming preoccupation, one that not even his
second Academy Award could abate. "Awards for pictures are a trivial thing to
be concerned with at times like these," he wrote Dudley Nichols. By the
spring of 1940 his greatest ambition was to create a reserve unit made up of

Hollywood professionals. Wayne, on the other hand, was more concerned with his own career.

Stagecoach had revived that career, and if he was not *at* the top of his profession, he had clawed his way to a position from which he could see the top. Fearing that he would slide back into the world of the B Western, he worked to secure his status as an A film star. From 1939 to 1942 he tried to move beyond Westerns and Republic. He wanted to attempt more challenging roles and work for the major studios. At that moment in his career, world politics, the fates of nations, and the advance of fascism were less important to him than Hollywood politics.

Looking at the arc of Wayne's career, the importance of *Stagecoach* is apparent; it clearly marked the end of his years as a B actor and his emergence as an A star. But at the time he finished the film, its impact was not readily apparent to his bosses at Republic. Even after its Westwood screening, the studio heads were convinced that neither the picture nor its leading man was anything special, and when Duke returned to Republic in early 1939 they treated him as if he was just back from a vacation. Without missing a beat or even a hasty "Welcome back," they assigned him to another series of Mesquiteers films. At Republic, Duke was Stony Brooke, who along with Crash Corrigan and Max Terhune made B Westerns designed and packaged for matinee audiences.

Before *Stagecoach* was premiered in early March, he had completed his work on *The Night Riders*, a Robin Hood tale set in the West of the early 1880s. While *Stagecoach* played before full houses and he attracted the attention of the fan magazines, he starred in three more Mesquiteers movies— *Three Texas Steers*, *Wyoming Outlaw*, and *New Frontier*. Unlike *The Night Rider*, his last three Mesquiteers films had contemporary settings and centered on vaguely contemporary concerns, ranging from political corruption to the price of progress.

"Duke was never very good at hiding his feelings, and you could tell he wasn't happy about returning to those awful six-day Westerns," Mary St. John recalled. "He felt that Republic was exploiting him and cheapening the work he had done in *Stagecoach*." He was correct. Overnight John Wayne had become a hot property, and Republic held the rights to him. "Hollywood has discovered talent in candy stores on Hollywood Boulevard, among movie extras in rare cases, in an Omaha Stock company, among headline news personalities, on the Broadway stage, in London, Berlin, Paris—in fact in every nook and corner of the world from Brooklyn to Capetown," wrote Sam Adams in *Screenland*, "but John Wayne's is the unique case of a *movie star* [being] discovered [and] re-discovered." Jerry Asher, a writer for *Movie Mirror*, agreed. After a decade in the industry but before *Stagecoach*, "John could have roped a steer in front of the Vine Street Brown Derby and no one would have known who he was. Now, 'The Ringo Kid' has to steer himself clear of being roped in by Hollywood lion hunters!" For Republic executives the articles in the fan magazines had the feel of crisp dollar bills they had done nothing to earn. Duke was their 1939 windfall, and they were determined to wring as much profit as they could from him.[3]

The four Mesquiteers films provided the quickest way to capitalize on the windfall and serve as a gauge to Republic's response to Duke's fame. As the reviews from *Stagecoach* appeared and as the movie magazines printed articles about Wayne, Republic expanded his roles in the Mesquiteers series. By *New Horizon*, Crash Corrigan and Raymond Hatton—an accomplished character actor who had replaced Max Terhune in the series—serve more as John Wayne's sidekicks than equal partners. The balance of the series is gone. Duke constantly occupies center stage in the crucial scenes, single-handedly saving the residents of New Hope Valley from a crooked real estate agent and a ruthless construction boss.

Wayne had hated the Three Mesquiteers before *Stagecoach*; but after his breakthrough film, there was no way that Republic could present him in the series that he found acceptable. With this in mind he approached Herbert Yates. Although there were still years left on his 1938 contract, he wanted to alter his position at Republic. His plan was simple: He would become the studio's feature A star. No more Mesquiteers or any other B pictures. In addition to making several films a year for Republic, Wayne would be free to work on other projects for other studios, which, of course, would bolster his status in the industry and increase his box-office appeal for Republic. From Yates's perspective, it was an ideal situation because he would make money for nothing by loaning Wayne out to major studios.[4]

John Wayne had made his last six-day Western, his last B film of any kind. But he had not made his last bad movie. *Allegheny Uprising*, his final film in 1939, proved that point. Laboring under the standard Hollywood assumption that what worked once would work again and again, RKO producers decided that the John Wayne–Claire Trevor team was box-office magic. Their love scenes in *Stagecoach* had been underplayed, but viewers sensed the depth of their passions. *Allegheny Uprising* brought them together again, for no other reason, it seems, than to bring them together again. Their relationship in the pre–Revolutionary War period piece has none of the subtlety and tenderness evinced in *Stagecoach*. Trevor plays Janie McDougle, a rifle-shooting, tavern-running frontier woman whose single ambition in life is to be "with my man." The only problem is that her man (Jim Smith, played by Wayne) champions independence—his own as well as his countrymen's.

Written and produced by P. J. Wolfson, *Allegheny Uprising*, commented Wayne, was an "awful stinker." It's a poor man's *Stagecoach*, minus the stagecoach. Jim Smith and his "Black Boys" face evil whichever direction they look. They are trapped between the uncivilized West and the overcivilized East, between barbaric Indians and crooked merchants protected by the British Army. The merchants in the film echo the sentiments of *Stagecoach*'s Gatewood: "What's the army for if not to protect business?" suggests one businessman. "And what's the government for if not to protect business? Certainly not to interfere with it," adds another. They insist on illegally selling rum and weapons to the Indians. Unfortunately the British Army is less efficient than the cavalry in *Stagecoach*. Effete and snobbish, Captain Swanson (George Sanders), the central British officer, shows the intelligence of a badly inbred poodle and unwittingly aids the contraband dealers. It takes frontiersmen Jim Smith and his followers to restore economic order and the rule of law to the region.[5]

A bad script was not *Allegheny Uprising*'s only problem. Its timing could not have been worse. It was released on November 10, 1939, exactly one week after the opening of *Drums Along the Mohawk*, John Ford's Technicolor Revolutionary War saga starring Henry Fonda and Claudette Colbert. Ford's first color film, *Drums Along the Mohawk* is far from his best, but it was good enough to win the battle of Revolutionary War–era films. *Allegheny Uprising* was only a modest success at the box office and a nearly unqualified critical failure. "For a picture which roots around in some of the most lively pages of American history, it is surprising and downright incredible that *Allegheny Uprising* . . . should be as stiff and unexciting as it is. . . . You would think that P. J. Wolfson and his collaborators at RKO could have come along with something better than a screen translation of a research worker's notes," sniffed a *New York Times* reviewer.[6]

The outbreak of war in Europe two months before the premiere of *Allegheny Uprising* contributed to the film's timing troubles. The movie was openly critical of the British. "You'll never learn. You'll never learn to know us," Jim Smith tells Captain Swanson, suggesting the fundamental differences between Americans and English and touching on a delicate political problem. Making matters worse, the film's heavies are merchants who engage in contraband trade. During the high tide of isolationism in the mid-1930s, when the Senate was investigating and excoriating the munitions industry, such isolationist sentiments were common, but in late 1939 Great Britain was at war with Nazi Germany and President Franklin Roosevelt was looking for ways to aid the British cause. In *Allegheny Uprising* Captain Swanson is presented as a mincing dictator, defending crooked merchants and placing honest Americans in irons and locking them away without warrants or trials. It was an embarrassment in the United States.[7]

Duke avoided these sensitive political issues by ignoring them and moving on to *The Dark Command,* his next picture. By 1940 Republic had ventured timidly into the A picture business. Explaining the new direction, Herbert Yates had told a reporter the year before that while Republic would continue to turn out B Westerns and serials, the studio planned to make two "big-scale" films each year. He expressed no plans to hire "name" actors because "for some reason or other . . . [they] feel as though they're lowering themselves by working for us." Nor would he try to develop his own A stars. "We'd rather farm out our promising players to other companies and let them do the experimenting. Take John Wayne, for instance. He's in our Westerns—which are cleaning up doubly because we loaned him out to Wanger for *Stagecoach*." Though Republic had done nothing to develop the A potential of John Wayne, he had achieved that status, and Yates stood ready to cash in on his luck.[8]

Budgeted at $750,000, *The Dark Command* was an expensive and ambitious project, and in its brief history, Republic had never spent as much on a picture. Like *Man of Conquest,* Republic's first A, *The Dark Command* is a historical drama, loosely based on the story of Missouri border raider William Quantrill and set against the backdrop of Bleeding Kansas and the Civil War. But the film is far more interested in drama than history. After breezing over the conditions that gave rise to Bleeding Kansas in its introductory moments, *The Dark Command* details a conflict between two men, both good but one tragically flawed. Bob Seton (John Wayne) is an illiterate Texan whose only ambition is to see the deserts and mountains of the West. Will Cantrell (Walter Pidgeon) is a schoolteacher, a decent, learned man who patriotically leads his class in singing "America" but is secretly obsessed with getting "to the top." The two men meet in Lawrence, Kansas, where Cantrell offers to teach Seton to read and write, but they soon become rivals for the same woman and the same job. When Wayne is elected town marshal and begins to attract the attention of Mary McCloud (Claire Trevor), Cantrell falls victim to his own "bad blood"—the same evil that had ruined his brothers. He turns slave-trader and gunrunner, and when the Civil War begins, he leads a band of guerrillas "loyal to no flag" and bent on fighting only "to take what's coming to you." They pillage and loot Southern as well as Northern border towns, even returning to sack and burn Lawrence. In the final showdown of good and good turned evil, Seton shoots Cantrell.

The Dark Command, in short, is an A picture that looks an awful lot like an expensive, well-produced B film. It contains the best elements of Wayne's Monogram Westerns, including Yakima Canutt's stunt work and George "Gabby" Hayes's sidekick character, with the added benefits of a good script, the expert direction of Raoul Walsh, and an experienced cast. To distinguish it from Republic's usual run of films, Yates launched an aggressive publicity campaign that teetered between chutzpah and farce. The grand premiere in Lawrence was fine, and even the claims to historical accuracy could be ascribed to standard Hollywood excess, such as publication of "A Guide to the Discussion of the Photoplay" prepared by the regional director of the Kansas Department of Secondary Education. The guide was a Cliffs Notes version of the movie and even contained a "Questions for Study" section, with such brain twisters as, "Do you feel that Cantrell would have made a good marshall [*sic*]?"[9]

Despite the film's suspiciously B nature, praise for *The Dark Command* from influential critics on both coasts outstripped even that for *Stagecoach*. "Republic moves definitely into the big league," trumpeted the *Hollywood Reporter*. "*The Dark Command* is one of the best and most tensely absorbing action pictures to reach the screen in many a day. . . . Producer Sol C. Siegel has scored a rare achievement of moulding a dynamic torrent of epic-scale spectacle and historic conflict into a moving personal drama. . . . This picture has boxoffice written all over it." *Variety* followed the same theme: "*The Dark Command* steps out as a big, spirited spectacular. . . . It is comparable to the best in this type of production from any major plant." Bosley Crowther in the *New York Times* could only add that the film was "the most rousing and colorful horse-opera that has gone thundering past this way since *Stagecoach*."[10]

John Wayne received special attention from the reviewers, most of whom were unfamiliar with his earlier B work. Duke's Bob Seton was vastly different from his Ringo Kid. Ringo is painfully innocent—inarticulate, uncomfortable in society, ever conscious of his prison record and lack of social graces. His Bob Seton lacks education but not confidence. He speaks too much when nervous and continually prefaces his remarks with, "We got a sayin' down in Texas, Ma'am. . . ." Wayne handles the role with the light comic touch. "The most pleasant surprise of the picture," commented Crowther, "is the solid performance of John Wayne. . . . With a long career of Westerns behind him, Mr. Wayne knows the type; and, given a character to build, he does it with vigor, cool confidence and casual wit." The other reviewers agreed. Wayne's performance in *Stagecoach* was no fluke. In *The Dark Command* he "more than fulfills all previous promise" (*Hollywood Reporter*) and "impressively carries off one of his best roles" (*Variety*). *The Dark Command* was critically important to Duke's career. He had proved to critics and studio heads alike that he could act *and* sell tickets by the millions. The film also established the fact that Westerns could be A films, capable of making money in big-city theaters as well as in the small towns of the South and West, and that John Wayne was the acknowledged champion of the genre.[11]

The Dark Command more than fulfilled its box-office potential, leading all Republic moneymakers in 1940. Producers and directors at the major studios began to give Wayne a second look. Even Cecil B. De Mille took notice. Four years before, when De Mille was casting *The Plainsman*, Duke had secured a meeting with the imperious director. "I sat outside that bastard's office and I could look in there and see him just thinking. So after about an hour—the son of a bitch kept me waiting that long—he came out and said, 'Well, I'm going for lunch.' My agent said, 'You asked John Wayne to come over for an interview.' De Mille said, 'Oh yeah, so I did. Come along.' That's what you say to a dog." He told Wayne that he had seen him in *The Big Trail* and thought he had done fine, but that "a lot of water had run under the bridge since then." Duke did not get the part he wanted; he did not even get a return call. But after Wayne finished *The Dark Command*, De Mille, suddenly all charm and good manners, asked Duke if he would be so kind as to have the studio send over a print of it. An ability to forgive had never been among Wayne's strong points. "Make him come over here if he wants to see it," he told Republic executive Sol Siegel. When Siegel pressed Wayne, Duke replied: "Just tell him that I said a lot of water's run under the bridge since I'd seen him last."[12]

"For the first time in his life," his secretary recalled, "he could say 'fuck you' to a few people in the business." "He didn't do it much," she said, "but he felt he could." Box-office success meant even more, however. It offered him a chance to join official Hollywood society—not just an anti-yacht-club yacht club—and to do business and mix with men of influence and power. What he soon discovered was that while he had been churning out Bs at Monogram, Universal, and Republic, Hollywood had discovered politics and developed a sense of social consciousness. In fact, by 1939 Hollywood had become one of the two most politically charged centers of internationalism and liberal causes in the country. Led by a small but dynamic group of communists, a steady stream of European political refugees, and an active and wealthy liberal community, Hollywood had become the "far West Side" of New York City.[13]

It had become a town of causes—the Scottsboro boys, the victims of the Dust Bowl, the struggle to organize labor, the plight of refugees, the fight against fascism, aid for the Republican forces in Spain—peopled by self-anointed saviors and well-meaning citizens. From 1935 to the autumn of 1939, Hollywood liberals and radicals had joined together in a popular front, a loose confederation of alliances ranging from the Motion Picture Democratic Committee, Hollywood Anti-Nazi League, and the Motion Picture Artists Committee to the Joint Anti-Fascist Refugee Committee, and the Hollywood Committee for Polish Relief. Actors and directors hosted fund-raising dinners in their homes and fund-raising cocktail parties by their pools; screenwriters organized rallies and staged benefits.[14]

"We're up to our necks in politics and morality just now," Mary McCall complained good-naturedly in a 1937 issue of *Screen Guild's Magazine*:

> Nobody goes to anybody's house any more to sit and talk and have fun. There's a master of ceremonies and a collection basket, because there are no gatherings now except for Good Causes. We have almost no time to be actors and writers these days. We're committee members and collectors and organizers and audiences for orators. When the director yells "Cut!" for the last time . . . life begins. Then we can listen to speeches, and sign pledges, and feel that warming glow which comes from being packed in close with a lot of people who agree with you—a mild hypnotism, an exhilarating pleasurable hysteria.[15]

Not everyone, of course, was caught up in the hysteria. In an effort to comfort McCall, screenwriter and leading Communist party organizer Donald Ogden Stewart assured her that he had personally attended "practically all of the 'radical' meetings, symposia, and benefits" and that "99.44 percent of Hollywood is still sleeping peacefully in its options." Most members of the film community, he said, were not "the least interested in anything political that does not concern their own studio or the abolition of the State and Federal Income Tax."[16]

The truth was somewhere between McCall's observations and Stewart's statistics. Historians Larry Ceplair and Steven Englund have estimated that during the 1930s the Hollywood film community, from the wealthiest moguls to the lowest-paid extras, fluctuated between fifty and sixty thousand people. Of that number perhaps fifteen thousand people, or about 25 percent, joined one or another of the many Hollywood political organizations. Most of the activity was the result of "a core group of about two hundred progressives," working "closely with, and following the lead of, fifty to seventy-five committed radical activists." The power of the group's members, however, was generated by their occupations, not their numbers. More than half of the leading radicals were screenwriters.[17]

The alliance of New Deal liberals, communists, and fellow travelers ended during the weeks after August 24, 1939, the day the Nazi-Soviet Nonaggression Pact was announced. After its years of antifascist leadership, the Soviet Union's *rapprochement* with Germany seemed to be a bad scene out of a bad movie. Antifascist liberals were outraged; American communists were shocked into momentary silence. Before the announcement such an about-face had been unimaginable. American party member George Charney felt "limp and confused," while another of his comrades "floundered in the dark for two days and did not know what to do." But when they overcame their initial surprise, they did what their leaders in Moscow ordered. They justified the pact, arguing that the conflict in Europe was an "imperialist war" and of no concern to socialists and communists. They also rationalized the subsequent Soviet invasions of Poland and Finland. And, in what can only be interpreted as an attempt to commit public suicide, they demanded that the United States remain neutral in the conflict. "That just wiped us out as far as our ability to influence anybody or anybody else's desire to remain united with us," recalled Hollywood party member Paul Jarrico.[18]

During the 1930s John Wayne brushed against members of the inner circle of activists. John Ford was an outspoken if quirky liberal, drawn to dramatic causes and closely associated with such politically committed activists as Walter Wanger, Dudley Nichols, and screenwriter Philip Dunne. His *The Grapes of Wrath*, shot in 1939 and released in early 1940, became an instant liberal classic, a celebration of the strength of the American folk and the work of the New Deal. In foreign affairs Ford, like almost every other liberal, supported antifascist causes, championed the Loyalist forces in Spain, and believed that isolationism and noninterventionism were akin to avoiding danger by hiding under a bedsheet. A July 1937 meeting with Ernest Hemingway, who was in Hollywood pushing his propaganda film *The Spanish Earth* and pressing stars for money to support the Spanish Loyalists, had a searing effect on Ford. After the meeting he joined the Motion Picture Artists Committee, served as a vice chairman of the Motion Picture Democratic Committee, and gave liberally to other "progressive" causes. "*Politically*—I am a definite Socialist Democrat—always left," he wrote his nephew Bob Ford, who had joined the Abraham Lincoln Brigade.[19]

But if Duke was friends with Ford and Nichols, he was also close to outspoken conservatives. Ward Bond was as idiosyncratic a conservative as Ford was a liberal, and screenwriter/producer James K. McGuinness was as committed to the right as Nichols was to the left. Actually, given the political infighting in Hollywood—the alliances, schisms, and partisan activity—John Wayne remained surprisingly outside it all. Henry Fonda exaggerated when he wrote that when he and Wayne first started to make movies together Duke "couldn't even spell politics," but he was closer to the truth when he claimed that in the 1930s Duke "never talked politics." Wayne avoided politics and politicians and kept most of his deepest beliefs to himself. He was a down-to-earth, hardworking man so preoccupied with making a living in the 1930s that politics was little more than an abstraction. He later claimed that he was a "socialist" for a time during his USC days and a "liberal" because he was willing to listen to all sides of any issue before making up his mind. During the mid-1930s, what politics he had were mildly progressive, going so far in 1938 as joining together with Melvyn Douglas, Philip Dunne, and other Hollywood liberals in supporting the successful gubernatorial campaign of Democratic state senator Culbert L. Olson. But by the end of the decade, he had become disenchanted with the Left and begun to drift right.[20]

The only organization in which he took much interest was the Screen Actors Guild, and it was there that his basic midwestern instincts began to evolve into a conservative political philosophy. Formed in 1933, when Franklin D. Roosevelt's New Deal openly supported the rights of workers, the Screen Actors Guild was a labor union for actors. It concerned itself with bread-and-butter issues—salaries, working conditions, and contractual rights. Over time, however, it developed into a strong, conservatively oriented union. Liberalism and radicalism found their home in the Screen Writers Guild. Hollywood writers were the best-educated people in the business, and they often assumed an air of intellectual superiority over everybody else—actors, producers, directors, and even studio executives. Duke had cast his lot with actors, most of whom came from decidedly working-class backgrounds, gave little thought to political ideology, and resented the smug arrogance of the writers. While members of the Communist party exerted considerable influence in the Screen Writers Guild, they never carried much weight in the Screen Actors Guild.

Still, they tried. "I noticed something was going wrong in this business around 1937, 1938," Duke told Maurice Zolotow in the 1950s. "The communists were moving in, and under the guise of being anti-fascist I saw they were hoaxing a lot of decent men and women on humanitarian grounds. I was on the executive board of the Screen Actors Guild and I noticed one or two of my fellow members whose hearts were always bleeding for the little fellow, but they never really helped him. They just talked about it and tried to stir up dissension between extras and producers and directors." He also began to notice that the level of political discussion in Hollywood had taken a leftist turn. At parties he heard screenwriters say that "Russia [was] the hope of the world" or "that the United States was shot to hell and patriotism was a big joke." He did not give voice to his changing attitudes, but they were changing nonetheless.[21]

It was possible in the late 1930s and early 1940s to live and work in Hollywood without joining any political organizations or contributing to any causes. It was possible to stay out of the small battles over the Spanish Civil War and New Deal reforms and the Nazi-Soviet Pact. It was difficult, but it *was* possible. It was not possible, however, to work in the industry—to perform in movies—and not become part of someone else's political agenda. Ford and Nichols endorsed one of the unstated messages of *Stagecoach*: America did not need another businessman president. Directors William A. Seiter and Raoul Walsh advocated the central themes of *Allegheny Uprising* and *The Dark Command*: Americans had to be prepared to defend their freedom. As the male lead in all three films, John Wayne became the representative of those beliefs and values.

As Duke ventured beyond the Western genre, the messages in his films became more politically focused. *Three Faces West*, his second Republic film in 1940, was a grab bag of Popular Front political correctness. Written by poet Joseph Moncure March, playwright F. Hugh Herbert, and novelist and screenwriter Samuel Ornitz, *Three Faces West* is *Casablanca* meets *The Grapes of Wrath*. It tells the stories of two different types of refugees: Austrian victims of Nazi persecution and American victims of the Dust Bowl. The refugees, European and American, look west for their salvation. To Austrians, Dr. Braun (Charles Coburn) and his daughter, Leni (Sigrid Gurie), the West is the United States, a land of freedom. Extolling the greatness of his adopted country, Dr. Braun lectures his daughter: "No soldiers do we see, no frontiers do we cross, no cats and mouse, no guards. . . . Here at last we find peace. . . . Our lives begin again in a happy land with happy people." To John Phillips

A summer job arranged by his football coach Howard Jones exposed Duke to filmmaking. At Fox Studio he met John Ford *(above left)*, a director who would play a crucial role in his life. Duke propped for Ford, received small parts in such Ford movies as *Salute (below)*, and became part of the director's extended family. Before too long, Duke was a guest aboard Ford's yacht the *Araner (above right)*, a sign that he was among the director's closest friends.

The film *The Big Trail* moved Duke from propping to acting. A big-budgeted Western directed by Raoul Walsh, *The Big Trail* promised to make Marion—renamed John Wayne—and Marguerite Churchill *(above)* stars. Fox released the film shortly after the stock market crash, and even an East Coast publicity tour by John Wayne *(right)* could not save *The Big Trail*. Both Wayne's and Churchill's careers suffered from the picture's failure.

The failure of *The Big Trail* convinced the leaders at Fox that the age of the Western was over and that John Wayne was not a Western star. Publicity stills show an attempt to remake Duke into a debonair, moody college student and football player, a popular type in the early 1930s.

Duke failed in his college playboy roles. He was cast with Loretta Young in *Three Girls Lost* (1931) *(above left)*, but the film did nothing to revive his sagging career or convince Fox to pick up the option on his contract. After brief stints at Columbia, Mascot, and Warner Bros., Wayne found a niche making B Westerns for Monogram, a Poverty Row studio. For millions of Americans in the mid-1930s he was the white-hatted hero *(above right)*, a man of action, not words. In films such as *Randy Rides Alone* (1934) *(below)*, he learned the tricks of stunt riding and gun play from Yakima Canutt (center).

Steady work at Monogram gave Wayne the financial security to marry. In June 1933 he married Josephine Saenz *(above)* at the home of Loretta Young's (at right) mother. Josie was uncomfortable in Duke's Hollywood world *(below left)*, just as he was in Los Angeles, Catholic society. They did, however, have four children together. Michael *(below right)* was the first born.

(John Wayne) and his fellow residents of Asheville Forks, a farmed-over, blighted outpost in the heart of the Dust Bowl, the West is Oregon, a land where farmers can remain farmers, not like California where farmers are transformed into exploited fruit pickers. Unlike *The Grapes of Wrath*, which premiered four months before *Three Faces West* and centers on the disintegration of Dust Bowl communities and families, the people of Asheville Forks pool their money and move west together.

The writers and producer of *Three Faces West* were not content with just the Dust Bowl and refugee themes. In the seventy-nine minute film, they also found room for a conventional love triangle and a commentary on the state of rural medicine, Nazi free spending, and the Nazi-Soviet Pact. The love triangle contains twists that look forward to *Casablanca*. Leni Braun's fiancé, Eric, helped her and her father flee Nazi oppression but is left behind and presumably dead. She then falls in love with John Phillips, only to later learn that Eric is still alive. Like Rick and Ilsa in *Casablanca*, John and Leni are torn between their desire for personal happiness and the pull of duty and obligation. "There's a lot of things stronger than duty," he tells her, but they both know the truth, that duty—though occasionally "bitter and hard and cruel"—is transcendent, and that in this crazy world the problems of three little people don't amount to a hill of beans and if they chose love over duty they would both regret it, maybe not that day, maybe not the next, but soon, and for the rest of their lives. This settled, Leni leaves John and travels to San Francisco to meet Eric, only to discover that he has become a leading Nazi who had played some vague role in the Nazi-Soviet Pact. The pat Hollywood ending allows Leni to follow her heart and her sense of duty.

"Had the authors of *Three Faces West* maintained the courage of their original theme instead of allowing it to fritter into the simplest melodramatic mode, the film . . . probably would have been a great deal more than it is at present, an only partially fulfilled and therefore oddly unsatisfactory drama," observed a *New York Times* critic. The film's major problem, as the reviewer notes, is that it moves from a "stripped, unpretentious and grimly honest" exploration of Dust Bowl conditions to "glib and stilted . . . fairy-tale version of *The Grapes of Wrath*. . . . Where the Okies . . . found only a cruel mirage, these settlers find an Eden which is apparently there for the taking. . . . [H]ow a community supposedly ruined by dust storms manages to acquire rich bottomlands in Oregon with hardly any trouble isn't explained. An economic impasse can't be evaded by a trick of mirrors."[22]

Reviewers did not blame Wayne for the film's problems; indeed, one praised his "conviction and casual assurance." But *Three Faces West* suffered from two production difficulties. First, it was shot and released after *The Grapes of Wrath*, which revealed it for what it was—a cheap imitation. Second, like other message films of the period, it failed in its attempt to mix melodrama and propaganda. Samuel Ornitz, undoubtedly the picture's lead screenwriter, was a Communist party member who tried to intertwine social themes with entertainment, an ambition that was easier to achieve before the Nazi-Soviet Pact. *Three Faces West* lacks the old Popular Front's antifascist, pro–New Deal neatness. The film deplores the conditions in Nazi Germany, but it is also critical of the Soviet Union. And its position on the New Deal is ambivalent. First, New Deal agents pass out books on how to reverse the effect of the Dust Bowl; then they tell the farmers that nothing can save their land. More than anything, a new message, unarticulated and perhaps even unrealized by the film's writers, runs through the picture. The world, it seems to announce, is more complex than anyone knows. New Dealers are human, capable of giving bad advice as well as good, and the Soviet Union is not the antifascist bastion the liberals thought it. It is a cynical message, delivered by a writer who still wanted to find a saving higher theory—a deadly combination. Had the cynicism led to a more human, less theoretical story of the importance of love and relationships, it might have worked.[23]

The day after Duke finished his work on *Three Faces West*, he began work on *The Long Voyage Home*. Unlike *Three Faces West*, however, *The Long Voyage Home* was a conscious—perhaps too conscious—work of art. For John Ford and Dudley Nichols it was a labor of love, a chance to show the United States and the world that not everything in Hollywood was schlock. Nichols had fashioned a screenplay out of four Eugene O'Neill one-act plays—*In the Zone*, *The Moon of the Caribees*, *Bound East for Cardiff*, and *The Long Voyage Home*. Although O'Neill had set his plays in World War I, Nichols and Ford updated them to the present. The film follows the tramp steamer *Glencairn* and its men as they sail eastward from the West Indies to an American port to pick up a load of explosives and then go through the Atlantic war zone to England. At sea they confront danger from Nazi ships and planes, but their greatest threat is their own inner fears and demons. This theme—that our greatest demons are within us—is brilliantly realized in the camera work of Gregg Toland, probably the most inventive cinematographer of the period. The world of the *Glencairn* is a landscape of night and shadows, of fog and knifeblade shafts of light, where disillusioned and lonely sailors and drunks dream of a home they will never again see and stoically face an uncertain future.

The war is likened to the wet fog that shrouds the sailors. "Is there any place on land or sea where there is no war?" asks Aloysius Driscoll (Thomas Mitchell), the unofficial leader of the crew. "Everywhere people stumbling in the dark. Is there to be no more light in the world? Is there no place in this dark land where a man who's drunk can find a decent bit of fog?"

Ole Olsen (John Wayne) is the only character who prevents *The Long Voyage Home* from being a grim piece of *film noir*. Ole, who is often framed stretched out in the sunlight, is childishly innocent and gentle, a man who after a decade at sea is untouched by its harsh conditions. It is his final voyage, his last Atlantic crossing before returning to his mother and brother in neutral Sweden. For the other crew members he is also a symbol of hope. Though they will never see home again, he will, and so through him they can still dream. In port they pamper and protect him, sewing his money into his pocket, pinning his ticket to the inside of his coat, preventing him from getting drunk, and finally saving him after he is shanghaied onto another steamer. Ole is the light in the fog.

The part was a heavy burden for Duke to carry. Once again Ford surrounded him with some of the best character actors in the industry—Mitchell, the brawling, hard-drinking Irishman; Barry Fitzgerald, the small, comic Irish boaster; Ian Hunter, the disgraced English alcoholic; Ward Bond, the rugged Yank; John Qualen, Ole's Swedish guardian; and Fitzgerald's brother Arthur Shields, the conscience of the crew. But as in *Stagecoach*, Ford needed a believable performance from Wayne. Ole is not the Ringo Kid; he is not a man of action. Though physically strong, his real strength is his kindness and gentleness.

Duke was nervous about the role. Not only was he unfamiliar with a Swedish accent, he knew that in most Hollywood films it had been used for low comedy. It was associated with El Brendel. And even in *The Long Voyage Home*, John Qualen played a comic Swede. But there was little broad humor in Duke's Ole. The first day on the set he knew something was wrong. Years later Duke could still recall that summer morning: "Now, there's one line, 'Ja, jag gå hem,' or something that Ford gave me. So I said OK. Christ, this is my mentor. So I said it, 'Ja, jag gå hem,' which I knew, my ear told me, did not sound right." Ford disagreed. It sounded fine to him. Duke was still unsure. Already he was looking forward to his most important scene where he tells his life's story to a whore in a waterfront saloon. "Think of that scene," he told Ford. "I've got to have help." "Well, Jesus, all right if you want to be a goddamn actor," Ford replied. "[But] you don't need it."[24]

Danish actress Osa Massen agreed to help Duke with the accent. "She had a beautiful accent," Wayne said. For about two hours a day he practiced his accent and read over his lines with Massen. Slowly he improved, but there were still times when he delivered a line that was "embarrassingly bad. . . . The hard thing about it was that Qualen with the same accent must be funny, and I must not be funny and have an accent. It was a tough spot to be in."[25]

Ford did not help matters. The mood on the set was more somber than usual. He did not ride his whipping boys as hard, nor was he as warm and gentle as normal. He went about his work with a grim determination to get the job done. Lewis Jacobs, a *New York Times* critic who somehow obtained permission to visit San Pedro Pier 195, where Ford was shooting a scene, was surprised by the serious mood of the cast and crew. "There was little of the kidding around during set-ups as is so common on the sets of most directors. Everyone was alert and quiet, attention focused on the immediate business at hand." Slouching in his director's chair, his eyes hidden by dark glasses and his teeth biting into his pipe, Ford spoke only to explain a scene and spent most of his time quietly watching the actors rehearse. On the day Jacobs described, Barry Fitzgerald had trouble with a scene, and Ford let him know it. But there were no compliments when the scene was done well, only a noncommittal "Print it."[26]

Later in his life John Wayne gave reporters the impression that reviews were unimportant to him, that there was nothing a movie critic could teach him about his profession. But that simply was not true. He cared about reviews at the beginning of his career, and at its end. He read all the major reviews, smiling at the good ones and cursing the bad. But in few films did Duke feel that the reviews were as important to his career as in *The Long Voyage Home*. He saw the film as a turning point, a chance to move beyond Westerns. If audiences laughed at his Swedish accent, if he was unconvincing in the role, then it was back to Republic, probably for the rest of his career.[27]

For his own career as much as Wayne's, producer Walter Wanger was determined to make the film a success. In his promotional campaign he sold the film as art. Not content to rest his campaign simply on the reputations of John Ford and Eugene O'Neill, while the film was still in production he negotiated an agreement with the Associated American Artists of New York to sponsor an exhibition of paintings inspired by *The Long Voyage Home*. Nine artists, including such well known painters as Grant Wood, Thomas Hart Benton, and George Biddle, contributed works to the exhibition and divided the fifty thousand dollars Wanger contributed to the joint effort. No one denied the mutual back scratching. The artists worked like screenwriters, knocking off their paintings during a two-week stay in Hollywood under the pressure of a deadline. Still, both the program for, and the reviews of, the exhibition stressed the novelty of the alliance between the motion picture industry and the art world, adding that it "may well be the forerunner of a whole new field of interest and income for the American artist. . . . It is hoped that the paintings will, in turn, serve the film well. [T]he artists' interpretations will encourage the public to search the film from an entirely new angle, from the artist's angle, seeking that which is especially significant in action and in characterizations. The exhibition opened in New York City, then went on the road.[28]

Whether because of the overall campaign or the New York exhibition or just Gregg Toland's cinematography, *The Long Voyage Home* was hailed as a work of rare artistic sensitivity and rated a "certain contender" for the 1940 Academy Awards for direction, photography, and screenwriting. *Variety* observed that it was "a great man's picture" with "dark beauty . . . in every foot of the film." "It is . . . about as high an art of motion pictures as one could find . . . ," judged the *Hollywood Reporter*. "Never has a story been told with such thoughtful and, at the same time, forceful direction. Every character in the picture actually lives before your eyes. There's not a phoney movement in the entire picture." Bosley Crowther etched it in stone in the *New York Times*: "John Ford has truly fashioned a modern Odyssey—a stark and tough-minded motion picture which tells with lean economy the never-ending story of man's wanderings over the waters of the world in search of peace for his soul. . . . [I]t is one of the most honest pictures ever placed before the screen."[29]

The unstinting praise embraced everyone connected to the film. No reviewer ridiculed Duke's accent, and a few even placed his performance on the same level as Mitchell's and Fitzgerald's. But almost every reviewer stated the obvious: *The Long Voyage Home* was real art, and real art never had played well outside the country's largest city. "Arty" was the only word that one reviewer could think of to describe the film, and he predicted that it would "take all the top honors but those at the boxoffice." Other reviewers concurred. The film contained too much dialogue for the "kiddies," either ignored women or treated them as "agents of evil," and contained nothing to recommend it to the family trade, all of which led one reviewer to suspect that "b.o. returns [would] be on the lee side."[30]

They were. It was a complex, uncompromising film for a time that sought pat answers, and it lost money. "Perhaps it was too grim," Dan Ford reasoned. "Perhaps it reminded people of events that they were trying to forget." Actually, by 1940, Hollywood studios had begun to make antifascist films that dramatized the issues of the day. As leaders in Germany and Italy slowly closed their countries to American films, Hollywood moguls stopped worrying about offending the fascists. In 1938 Walter Wanger's *Blockade* dramatized the plight of the Republican forces in the Spanish Civil War and advocated American interventionism. "Where can you find peace?" Henry Fonda, the film's star, asks at the end of the picture. "The whole country's a battlefield. There is no peace. There is no safety for women and children. Schools and hospitals are targets. And this isn't war, not war between soldiers. It's not war, it's murder. It makes no sense. The world can stop it. Where is the conscience of the world? Where is the conscience of the world?" *Blockade* generated an intense political debate, *and* it made money. So did *Confessions of a Nazi Spy* (1939), *The Mortal Storm* (1940), *The Great Dictator* (1940), and a handful of other antifascist, prointervention productions. The problem with *The Long Voyage Home* was not that it dealt with contemporary issues, or even that it was too grim. Its box-office trouble was the result of its political ambiguities. German fascists are not portrayed as evil in the film; in fact they form only a faceless, off-screen presence. And the only true heavies in the picture are waterfront British lowlifes out to exploit the sailors. Hollywood was in the business of manufacturing heroes, but Ford's picture offered moviegoers a collection of badly flawed humans whose only act of heroism was opening their eyes each morning.[31]

The Long Voyage Home lost money, but it did not hurt anyone's career. As many of the reviewers had predicted, it picked up several Academy Award nominations, including Best Picture, Screenplay, and Black-and-White Cinematography. It lost across the board, but again for John Ford that hardly mattered. At the award ceremonies Ford validated his reputation as Hollywood's leading artistic curmudgeon. Both the *The Long Voyage Home* and *The Grapes of Wrath* received Best Picture nominations, but Ford received a Best Director nomination only for the more financially successful *The Grapes of Wrath*. When Frank Capra presented the award, he called all the nominees to the podium. Alfred Hitchcock, Sam Wood, George Cukor, and William Wyler made their way uncertainly up to Capra. After a round of handshakes, Capra opened the envelope and announced that the winner was John Ford, who at that time was with Henry Fonda fishing off the coast of Mexico, where, he had told reporters, he planned to stay "for as long as the fish are biting."[32]

The awards were meaningless for Duke as well. By the time the Oscars were presented in early 1941, his life in B Westerns and relative obscurity had ended. As the United States moved tentatively toward involvement in the world conflict, John Wayne marched steadily toward the pinnacle of his profession. "You could see the difference in him when he was on the Republic lot," recalled Mary St. John. "He walked with more confidence, and he smiled more. He knew who he was." And so did the fan magazines. "He started as a football player. Now he's playing drama by Eugene O'Neill," wrote James Reid in *Screenland Magazine*. "He used to travel around with horses. Now he's making love to Marlene Dietrich."[33]

Reid meant making love on the screen, and Duke was making love to her there too. Only Hollywood could make such a match. Marlene Dietrich and John Wayne—Weimar decadence and American innocence. Their first meeting became a standard Hollywood legend. Tay Garnett, a crony of Wayne's in the Emerald Bay Yacht Club, had been assigned by Universal producer Joe Pasternak to direct Dietrich in *Seven Sinners*, a modern *Madama Butterfly* with a less tragic ending. With Dietrich as the female lead, Garnett needed "a big, rugged he-guy type with competent fists, plus sex appeal," Pasternak said. "T'aint going to be easy," especially given the fact that Dietrich had casting approval. But Garnett had an idea, or at least he claimed to have had it. According to his own testimony, he arranged for Duke to be in the Universal commissary when he arrived with Marlene. "Dietrich," Garnett wrote, "with that wonderful floating walk, passed Wayne as if he were invisible, then paused, made a half-turn and cased him from cowlick to cowboots. As she moved on, she said in her characteristic brasso whisper, 'Daddy, buy me THAT.'"[34]

"It may have happened just that way," Steven Bach commented in his biography of Marlene Dietrich. But Garnett never let truth stand in the way of a good story, and Dietrich always seemed determined never to allow truth to creep into any. More probably their first meeting was less theatrical   after all, "Daddy, buy me THAT," is a line from Somerset Maugham's *The Circle*, a play in which Dietrich had once performed.

The inspiration to cast Duke opposite Dietrich may also have been influenced by the wallet of agent Charles K. Feldman. By 1940 it was apparent that John Wayne was virtually unrepresented in the industry, and Feldman was one of the leading agents in the business. Duke's experience with the Leo Morrison Agency had been singularly unpleasant, and he believed that the agent collected 10 percent of his earnings and did nothing in return. "What's an agent?" Duke asked toward the end of his life. He had been around them for fifty years and was still uncertain about "what the hell they do." Studying

Hollywood in the late 1930s, writer Leo Rosten believed that they were the real sellers of the industry:

> They sell talents and stories; they get their clients jobs, contracts, raises, and concessions. They guard prestige and bargaining power. They are experts in marketing anything from a pair of legs to an unwritten synopsis. Agents get ten percent of the salary of their clients, by whom they are generally resented, and haggle, coax, plead, or fight with producers, by whom they are generally disliked.[35]

Agents were as much a part of Hollywood life as producers and taxes, and after telling Leo Morrison that his services were no longer desired, Duke began to get advice from Charles K. Feldman, a Los Angeles lawyer who had abandoned a conventional practice in the early 1930s to form, and become president of, Famous Artists Corporation, one of the leading agencies in Hollywood. Feldman was worth every penny of *his* 10 percent fee. An accomplished high-stakes card player, he knew when to bluff and when to press an advantage in both poker games and studio negotiation sessions. During the late 1930s and early 1940s, he had made fortunes for Irene Dunne, Claudette Colbert, Tyrone Power, Marlene Dietrich, Fred MacMurray, and George Raft. He was particularly attracted to two new business approaches. First, he believed in short-term studio contracts and picture-by-picture deals. He maintained that successful directors, writers, and stars were the only bankable commodities in Hollywood, and that they could make more money as free agents than they could tied to a long-term studio contract. Second, he was an early advocate of the package deal. By the end of the 1930s he had begun to dabble in buying film rights for books and plays, and arranging for his own clients to write, produce, direct, and star in the properties. Not surprisingly, by the early 1940s he had moved into independent production.[36]

After Dietrich brought them together, Duke tacitly agreed that Feldman should represent him. With this done, the agent promoted Wayne to get the role. The original plan had been to have Tyrone Power costar with Dietrich, but Darryl Zanuck at Twentieth Century-Fox balked at the deal. Since Feldman now informally represented Wayne, it was natural for him to try to keep the role in his extended family.[37]

In any case the timing of their meeting was more important than the circumstances. Dietrich was on her second tour in Hollywood. In 1930, just before the release of *The Blue Angel,* she had come to Hollywood under a contract with Paramount. Her name, she had told reporters, was pronounced Mar-*lay*-na, but she gave straight answers about little else. "She was twenty-five or twenty-three," wrote Bach about Dietrich's tendency to invent fresh biographical details during every interview. "She was born in Berlin or Weimar or Dresden. She had a baby who was four or two or new and a husband who was a producer or a director or an executive. Her real name was von Losch and Maria or Marie and Magadalena or Magdalene, and her father had been a Franco-Prussian War hero or major in the imperial cavalry— or both—who had fallen during the Great War fighting Russians."[38]

Dietrich became an immediate sex goddess. *Morocco* (1930), her first American film, was a box-office sensation, but then the English version of *The Blue Angel* (1930) died in a sea of good reviews. Her career followed the general course of a roller coaster, and it was as full of screams and excitement. *Dishonored* (1931) was "a fairly complete flop," but *Shanghai Express* (1932) was an unqualified success. Then *Blond Venus* (1932) was a titanic disaster. "There is no possible excuse for *Blond Venus*," wrote critic and filmmaker Pare Lorentz, "except that it supports the incredibly accurate prediction made in this department some months ago that Marlene Dietrich was due to explode with a loud hollow pop."[39]

For several years the prediction held true. Dietrich moved from one box-office failure to the next. The only consistent ability Dietrich and her director Josef von Sternberg demonstrated was for making films that alarmed the Hays Office. Hollywood's leading censors hated *The Scarlet Empress* (1934) and *The Devil Is a Woman* (1935); so did reviewers, and so did moviegoers. After *The Devil Is a Woman,* Paramount got rid of von Sternberg and attempted to halt the free-fall. The studio cast Dietrich opposite Gary Cooper in *Desire* (1936), a critical and modest financial success, but the film was not enough to breathe much life into her dying career. She made *The Garden of Allah* (1936) for Selznick-International, and the film's Technicolor photography received more praise than Dietrich. It did not come close to recouping its $1.4 million production costs. She next traveled to England to star in Alexander Korda's *Knight Without Armour* (1937), but the film proved hardly worth the trip. Back in Hollywood she made *Angel* (1937) and probably wondered why she had not remained in London. Three films, three failures. After *Angel* the Independent Exhibitors of America, theater owners with no studio affiliation, took out full-page advertisements in the Hollywood trade papers announcing that Dietrich was "box-office poison." Lorentz's "loud hollow pop" was heard from Sunset and Vine to Mulholland.[40]

By 1937 things appeared to be all over for her. Most of Hollywood had lost interest; as Steven Bach observed, Paramount paid her $250,000 *not* to make *French Without Tears*. Moviegoers and reviewers had also grown weary of her performances, which somehow all seemed to melt into one long, stilted, self-indulgent promotional. She departed America for Venice's Lido and the Hotel des Bains, where she ate her meals at "the exile table," gossiped with friends, and watched Europe speed pell-mell toward war. She traveled—Switzerland, Paris, Cap d'Antibes, New York, Los Angeles—and lived beyond her means. Then in 1939 her exile ended. Hollywood wanted her back. Joe Pasternak at Universal and Charles Feldman wanted to make Marlene a Western star.[41]

It was a far cry from the early 1930s, when Westerns were supposed to be over as major pictures—now they could even work with Marlene Dietrich in them. The Western was *Destry Rides Again*—Marlene Dietrich and Jimmy Stewart in the Wild West. Dietrich plays a dance-hall moll who takes a bullet meant for the man she loves, then dies in his arms. It was nearly perfect schmaltz, embraced by critics and moviegoers alike. Dietrich was back, no longer the unapproachable sex goddess, now an experienced barmaid, a bit worn around the edges but with a heart as large as the West. The success of *Destry Rides Again* convinced Pasternak and Feldman that they had discovered the secret of the Hollywood lottery. They had a formula: East meets West, experience meets innocence. As the box-office returns mounted, they began to search for another project for Dietrich and an American innocent.

They settled on *Seven Sinners* and John Wayne. Even if Tyrone Power had been Pasternak's first choice, Duke was better suited to the new Dietrich formula. Like Gary Cooper and Jimmy Stewart, Dietrich's most marketable leading men, Wayne had a relaxed, agreeable screen presence, a mixture of awkwardness in social settings and manliness in times of danger. *Seven Sinners* called for exactly that sort of man. Like *Destry Rides Again*, it traffics in love and sacrifice. Dietrich plays Bijou Blanche, a well-traveled chanteuse in the Seven Sinners Cafe on the South Sea island of Boni-Komba. Her sultry smile and breathy voice mesmerize sailors, inciting their passions for love and riot. Wayne plays Lt. Dan Brent, a young naval officer who falls under Bijou's spell and is willing to sacrifice his career for her. It is the Ringo Kid and Dallas, with the twist that Ringo is no longer a convict on the run but a ranking member of a privileged society. Rather than allow Brent to resign his commission, Bijou breaks off their relationship.

Seven Sinners is Dietrich's film. Anna Lee, a young blond actress who had a part in the film, remembers that Dietrich was in complete control. When she first saw Lee, Dietrich ordered, "No more blondes," and Lee had to dye her hair. She had a standing mirror on the set and was always conscious of how she looked at any given moment, even instructing lighting men which beam to use on her. The film advanced her new image as a woman who would sacrifice all for the right man. Although it took Duke off the range and put him in the navy, it did not ask him to play a different type of character. But his career was flying pretty high—not in the top tier of Cooper, Stewart, and Gable—but high enough to hold a formulaic Dietrich vehicle up to box-office scrutiny. The film, critics agreed, was made to please, and their reviews are studded with superlatives: "noisy, robust fun," "tremendous climax," "blustering, beguiling," "sexy, robust, comical," "top cut." After years of coldly admiring or actively disliking the old Dietrich, they liked—really liked—the new comical incarnation. And they treated Wayne like an old reliable professional who could be depended on every time. As he had begun to demonstrate toward the end of his B Western career, he had the timing and manner to handle light comedy.[42]

And off the set Duke was starring in a different production. Duke's publicists and Charlie Feldman's public relations agents started producing volumes of copy about John Wayne. The fan magazines portrayed him as the consummate family man. Around his neighborhood the Waynes were known simply as "the Bumsteads," noted one reporter. He was Dagwood, and his wife and children were his only concerns. "His entire family, including servants, the nursemaid, friends and physicians are in constant league against him. If he suspects Michael or Toni or Patrick has one degree of fever, he goes wild."[43]

The making of the John Wayne legend had begun—pure American, down-to-earth, loyal, and hardworking. In reality Wayne's home life was badly splintered. By 1940 Duke commented to Zolotow, he and Josie were "moving in two different channels." "I was part of the movie group and she was becoming part of the social set, the real society of Los Angeles. It was a group in which the men did nothing but wear evening clothes and say, 'Hello.' The women dominated the mood." After long days on the set and doing his own stunts, he found the frequent black-tie dinners and social events, punctuated by small talk and polite behavior, "interminably boring." Josie held the same low opinion of *his* friends. Many, she thought quite correctly, were alcoholics, others merely boorish and crude. Neither Duke nor Josie was able to comprehend the attractions of the other's world and friends. Between the priests and socialites and Ward Bond stretched an unbridgeable chasm. Almost as soon as they were married they began to drift apart. Feelings

of obligations and duty grew into quiet resentments and passionate arguments. "I don't know exactly when you stop loving each other," Duke said.[44]

Perhaps he was unsure precisely when he stopped loving Josie, but by the
end of his life a clear pattern toward wives had emerged. Simply put, he insisted on being their main interest. Whenever possible he wanted them to share
his world, his friends, his interests. When Josie refused to conform, they
fought. "We tried again and again to make it work and again we'd have bitter
quarrels." She complained about his drinking and coarse language, and he
was frustrated by her sexual inhibitions, which he blamed on the Catholic
Church. "I felt like I had to get permission from the priest before I could kiss
her." He also resented Josie's seemingly total lack of interest in his career. He
later told Pilar, his third wife, that Josie "didn't understand his frustration or
unhappiness" during his years of Poverty Row five-reelers. Duke especially
worried about his children. He had grown up around his parents' "petty bickering" and remembered how he had suffered. He did not want his children to
go through the same experience, but divorce did not seem a particularly appealing alternative. So he stayed married, spending less time at home, avoiding quarrels whenever possible, and drifting further away from his wife.[45]

"I couldn't be a philanderer. I tried it—but it made me feel cheap and
dirty," he admitted to Zolotow. Certainly during the late 1930s and early
1940s he "tried it" on several occasions, but he was discreet enough to keep
his affairs private. They almost never became public, but after *Stagecoach* rumors circulated freely. He was linked romantically with Claire Trevor, probably the inevitable result of their making three pictures together between 1938
and 1940. Duke remained a close friend of Trevor's all his life, but there is no
evidence that they were ever lovers. It is more likely, but not at all certain, that
Duke had brief affairs with Sigrid Gurie, his costar in *Three Faces West*, and
Osa Massen, his accent coach in *The Long Voyage Home*. Mary St. John, during those years, heard the rumors, but she never talked to Duke about them,
even after she went to work exclusively for him.[46]

"There are always rumors," St. John said. "It's just part of the business. Remember, a Hollywood set is a very small world. Most of the people on a set
have little to do during much of the day. A hairdresser, a makeup artist—their
work is mostly completed before the shooting begins. But they have to be
around in case someone's hair or makeup needs attending to. So while they
wait, they talk. Mostly gossip. Who came in late the night before. Who is
drinking too much. Who is sleeping with whom. Who *might* be sleeping with

whom." Years later, Duke admitted to Floyd Slate, the cook on his yacht, "Aw hell, Floyd. When I was your age I was screwin' everthing I could get ahold of." Back then, there was some gossip about Duke, but it was not on the same level as the stories that were exchanged about Gene Autry or Bob Hope, whose affairs were legendary in Hollywood. It is clear from delving into Wayne's life that he simply did not view women as potential conquests. In fact, after working with him for more than thirty years, Mary St. John remarked that Duke "never really understood women. He put them on a pedestal, and though he tended to be a romantic, he was uncomfortable around them. He didn't understand them and they scared him." He became "madder than hell" when one of his leading ladies "took liberties with him," rubbing against his crotch or "slipping him a tongue" during a love scene. The more famous he became, the more it happened. He never became accustomed to such advances. The fact that he did not reject them all probably says more about his inability to build a successful marriage than about his philandering. By Hollywood standards, he was gun-shy with almost all women.[47]

During the making of *Seven Sinners* Dietrich took more than a professional interest in him. For Marlene affairs with her leading men were almost standard operating procedure. Her marriage was as open as an all-night diner, and she and her costars regularly became lovers. Her daughter later claimed that she became Jimmy Stewart's lover in 1939 during the filming of *Destry Rides Again*, and she moved into George Raft's Coldwater Canyon home in 1941 during the shooting of *Manpower*. And in the summer of 1941, when she made *The Lady Is Willing* with Fred MacMurray, she asked the film's producer and director, Mitchell Leisen, why her leading man was not falling in love with her. "Listen, Marlene," Leisen replied, "Fred's so much in love with his wife, Lilly, he couldn't care less about any other woman, so you lay off. Just make the picture."[48]

Between Stewart and Raft—between Mr. Smith and the Wise Guy—in Marlene's take-your-number-and-wait-your-turn life came John Wayne. She was the female Don Juan, and he was no Fred MacMurray. Anna Lee remembers that "Dietrich was the one chasing Wayne. She was the aggressor. Not him. He resisted at first, but he couldn't hold out." How it began and when is uncertain. Pilar Wayne said that Duke told her that Dietrich had invited him into her dressing room even before *Seven Sinners* was cast. Unaccustomed to the luxury of a star's quarters at a major studio, he stood silently looking around, when she said: "I wonder what time it is?" Before he could answer, Marlene "lifted her skirt, revealing the world's most famous legs. Her upper thigh was circled by a black garter with a timepiece attached." She looked at it, moved toward Wayne, and said: "It's very early, darling. We have plenty of time." He saw his opportunity and took it. Given Dietrich's taste for men and the theatrical, it may have happened just that way. But regardless how it started, by the time shooting began in August 1940, Wayne and Dietrich had become lovers. Neither made any great efforts to hide their affair. "Dietrich was a very European woman, like Zsa Zsa Gabor," recalled Mary St. John. "Men really didn't mean much to her. They were means to an end—power, money, a part, a title, a night's pleasure. She was about as romantic as a cash register." But Duke was captivated by her. Duke never liked talking with Pilar about Dietrich, but he did say that she was "the most intriguing woman I've ever known." In January 1979, when Barbara Walters asked Duke if he had ever fallen in love with one of his leading ladies, he replied matter-of-factly: "Well, yeah, Marlene Dietrich." He was a bit more explicit with his closest male friends: "The best lay I've ever had," he told one.[49]

Those were the halcyon days of affairs in Hollywood. To a great extent, the studios controlled all news about the industry. With only a few exceptions, journalists who wanted to work in Hollywood played by the studio's rules: In exchange for interviews and access, they wrote puff pieces. Serious crimes were about the only activities that could not always be successfully covered up. Affairs that were common knowledge in the industry seldom filtered outside of Hollywood unless, of course, a studio head wanted the news to spread. Wayne and Dietrich therefore enjoyed a fairly public fling, which journalists tended to write off as publicity stunts between costars. They attended football games and prizefights, took trips up to San Luis Obispo and Santa Barbara, and drove into the mountains to hunt and fish. They showed up together at the leading night spots—Ciro's, the Brown Derby, Mocambo, and the Café Trocadero. For almost three years their affair survived Duke's marriage and Dietrich's other romances, ending only when Marlene headed off to entertain the troops and Wayne became more interested in another woman.[50]

Wayne had a new sense of confidence, perhaps as much because of his relationship with Dietrich as his blossoming career. She spent a great deal of time with Duke on location for his next film. Harry Carey's wife Ollie noticed that Dietrich would bring picnic lunches to Wayne, and that their lunches often lasted past dinnertime and into the early morning hours. It was not unusual to see Dietrich walking down the trail from Wayne's cabin before breakfast. He spent other nights at her hotel near the lake. (One morning, worried about being late on the set, Duke raced away from her hotel room and overturned his station wagon on a curve.) In later years Dietrich disingenuously wrote that she found Wayne nice but dull, and that she "helped as best [she] could" by introducing him to Charles Feldman and attempting, unsuccessfully, to introduce him to the world of books. She may have been important in introducing Wayne to Feldman, although the agent represented many of Duke's other friends as well. But Duke enjoyed reading long before he met Dietrich. And she had followed him to his location shoot, an effort for a man she found "not a bright or exciting type."[51]

John Wayne was becoming a star, and the powers in Hollywood knew it. The critical acclaim of *The Long Voyage Home,* followed by the critical and commercial success of *Seven Sinners,* helped to secure his place in the industry. A Paramount release noted that he was "picking up favor with fans throughout the country more rapidly than any other player in pictures." Perhaps even more telling, Marlene Dietrich was not in the habit of engaging in extended affairs with literary or show business second-raters. "At Republic, we don't attempt to develop personalities," Herbert Yates had said in 1939. He was content instead to farm out his best talent and let other studios "do the experimenting." Duke's rise had followed Yates's strategy. John Ford and Walter Wanger had taken a chance casting Wayne in roles where he had to appear rugged, masculine, *and* innocent. Tay Garnett and Joe Pasternak had taken another gamble, and now so did Henry Hathaway and Jack Moss in *The Shepherd of the Hills.* They had all believed that Wayne, like Gary Cooper, could be tender, rugged, masculine, *and* funny. Critics and moviegoers proclaimed that the gambles were successful. Yates, with five years left on Wayne's seven-year contract, was more than happy to claim some of the profits.[52]

There was nothing light about *The Shepherd of the Hills.* Less than a month after finishing *Seven Sinners* at Universal Duke was hard at work at Paramount. The film is a sentimental melodrama based on a novel by Harold Bell Wright, one of the bestselling writers of the 1920s. Always a preacher at heart, Wright turned all his novels into sermons, dispensing wisdom about the dangers of greed, ambition, hypocrisy, and other human failings. "Harold is always Wright," one critic complained about the author's excessive moralizing. *The Shepherd of the Hills* tells the story of Daniel Howitt (Harry Carey), a healer who shows up one day in an Ozark community. He nurses back to health a moonshiner shot by a revenue agent, saves a sick child from certain death, and pays for an operation that restores a woman's sight. His power to heal soon extends beyond the physical. He revives the bitterly divided community and labors to restore Young Matt Matthews's (John Wayne) psychological balance. Matthews is obsessed with punishing his father for leaving his mother. "Some one of these days I'll find him. Him that never came back to you," he vows over his mother's grave. Howitt, of course, is that father, and he had failed to return to his wife and son because he had once killed a man and been sent to prison. It is this fate—murder and prison—from which he is determined to save Young Matt, even if he has to shoot him in the process. In the final showdown, shoot him he does, but then he nurses him back to physical and emotional health.[53]

If the film was weighed down by religious symbolism and "too obvious" attacks "on the tear-ducts," Wayne's mood on the set was light and confident. He was the leading man in a big-budget, Technicolor film for a major studio. Henry Hathaway, who had recently made *The Lives of a Bengal Lancer* with Gary Cooper, was the director. Like John Ford, Hathaway was never tied to the exact words in the script. If a line did not fit a character, he changed it. Duke felt confident that Hathaway cared about him and his character, although the director had a difficult time getting Cooper out of his mind. He saw in Wayne another Cooper—reticent, tough, but sensitive. "Try to act like Gary Cooper. Be more like Gary Cooper," he kept telling Wayne. In addition to Hathaway, Harry and Ollie Carey helped make the set comfortable for Wayne. If Duke ever had an idol, he was Harry Carey. He had patterned his dress and acting style after Carey; he admired his no-nonsense, no-show-business approach to life. And he "loved" Ollie, a wonderful woman who chain-smoked, swore like a sailor, and always spoke her mind.[54]

On location at Big Bear Lake, Duke talked with reporters about his ambitions as an actor. He had become famous enough to be able to expose his professional goals without someone laughing. He wanted to play all kinds of roles, he said. He wanted to play character parts and heavies and avoid being typecast as the hero. A reporter for the *Los Angeles Times* observed that "the word around Hollywood had it that Wayne was the fastest-moving leading man among the come-uppers on the Coast. . . . No more Westerns for Honest John Wayne. He's right up there among them now." Ollie Carey heard Duke say the same thing to several cast members one night. She looked on, unusually quiet. After the others left, she gave her opinion. "You big stupid sonofabitch. Would you like to see Harry do all these things you were telling these people?" Duke shook his head no. "People have accepted you," Ollie continued. "They've taken you into their homes and their hearts now, and they like you as a certain kind of man." She predicted that if he changed his screen persona, his fans would resent him and stop attending his pictures. He never forgot Ollie's words, and for the rest of his career he accepted only roles that did not dent his accepted persona.[55]

Wayne starred in five films in 1940. But in early 1941 he returned to Republic. From January to early April he worked on two films, *A Man Betrayed*, with Frances Dee, and *Lady from Louisiana*, with Ona Munson. Actually it was more like working on one picture with two parts, for the plots of both productions were the same. In *A Man Betrayed*, Wayne plays a country attorney who travels to the big city to solve a mystery surrounding a friend's death. In the course of his investigation, he confronts a well-oiled political machine and falls in love with the boss's daughter. By the end of the film, he solves the mystery, rids the city of the machine, earns the respect of the boss, and marries the daughter. *Lady from Louisiana* transports Duke back to late-nineteenth-century New Orleans, where he plays a Yankee attorney come South to overthrow the notorious lottery and politically purify the wicked city. Once again he confronts a political boss, who is more of a dupe than actually corrupt, and his henchmen, who are thoroughly criminal. Once again he falls in love with the boss's daughter. But in *Lady from Louisiana* Duke breaks up the machine, marries the boss's daughter, and saves the entire city from flooding by instructing a ship captain to steer his boat into a breach in the levee.

A Man Betrayed and *Lady from Louisiana* are typical of Republic's A films of the period in that they amount only to dressed-up Bs. *A Man Betrayed* is a lame attempt at "screwball" comedy, a light, offbeat genre that was popular in the second half of the 1930s. It aims at being witty and urbane but hits in the neighborhood of trite and silly. In one scene Lynn Hollister (Wayne) tells Sabra Cameron (Frances Dee), "You know you'd be lovely if you had brown hair." When she replies that she does, he mutters, "Yeah," and kisses her. Then, in later scenes, the film turns into a political exposé, an action picture, and an exploration of the mentality of a mentally incompetent murderer. In its effort to move between light comedy to heavy moralizing—to steal the best from *It Happened One Night, Mr. Smith Goes to Washington*, and *Of Mice and Men*— the picture comes off as schizophrenic. A *New York Times* reviewer believed that if the film had more action and less talk it "might have amounted to something better than just a torpid exposé of a political boss." It might also have been strengthened by less action and better dialogue. In either case, by trying to provide something for everyone, it actually gives very little to anyone.[56]

Lady from Louisiana demonstrates other problems with Republic As. When the studio spent money, it wanted the public to be fully aware of it, a tendency that often turned a historical drama into an elaborate costume picture. The film showcases "extravagant costumes for an extravagant number of extras," and it boasts "sumptuous period interiors of old delta-town mansions." And since producers at Republic were convinced that any film benefited from song-and-dance numbers—a legacy of Gene Autry's success at the studio—the film contains a few of these gratuitous nuisances. Money lavished on costumes, sets, songs, and special effects, however, was money not spent on screenwriting, and the final product suffers from this misappropriation of funds. The film is "a veritable cornucopia of cliches," commented one generous reviewer, populated by a "spotless hero," a "shiny-eyed heroine," and a "nasty group of political grafters." Added to the clichés are a series of plot twists that can only be brought together by an act of God. The lightning bolt that splits open the courthouse just when the hero/prosecutor's case is falling apart and the flood that drowns the villain are poor substitutes for a tighter plot. But they are typical of Republic's approach to filmmaking.[57]

Reviewers seldom indicted Wayne for the shortcomings of Republic films. Instead, while panning the pictures, they observed that he was "exceptionally good," bringing a "simple and casual charm" to his roles. This was true enough, but one senses that he had already begun to regard his Republic career as day work. Though he had temporarily departed Westerns for historical dramas and urban mysteries, his Republic character remained fixed. He played the slow-talking, friendly but determined outsider come to the big city to solve some specific problem. It was the John Wayne character that he had developed in scores of B Westerns. "Nobody could play John Wayne like John Wayne," Mary St. John said. But he seldom gave more. Undoubtedly Republic directors, working on tight schedules, never asked for more. He gave his best to directors who demanded it, men like John Ford, who worked outside the Republic factory.[58]

Finished with his Republic commitment, Duke began to field offers from the industry's most ambitious directors. Once again Cecil B. De Mille was interested in his services. He was casting an adventure picture called *Reap the Wild Wind* and wanted Wayne to star in the film, with Ray Milland. Time and success had not taken the sting out of De Mille's earlier treatment of him, and Duke was not interested in working for the director. Yates, however, persuaded him to just talk with De Mille. At this meeting Duke was not kept waiting, and he was not treated like a dog. "Mr. Wayne," De Mille began, "I don't want to work with you if you don't like me, but I've admired your work and I'd like to see you in this picture. What is your reaction?"[59]

Duke hesitated. He knew that De Mille wanted to cast him as the heavy, and he worried about the impact that the role would have on his career. As Ollie Carey had told him, people had accepted him in a certain kind of role, and they might reject him in this. The film called for Milland to play a "panty-waist" who shows his character by outfighting a tough sea captain. Wayne was not at all sure it was a good idea to play a punching bag for Milland's adult Fauntleroy, and he had heard that De Mille could be brutal to his actors. "I'm a little worried about whether [we'll] get along," he told the director. "And besides that I'm from Republic and the only reason you're calling me over here is to make Ray Milland look like a man." De Mille tried reasoning, telling Duke that he had been fair to Preston Foster when he played opposite Gary Cooper in *North West Mounted Police,* and that he "would never put [Duke] in a spot where [he] would lose [his] human dignity." Wayne replied that getting "beat up by Ray Milland would lose anybody's dignity." But after a few more meetings, and after watching *North West Mounted Police,* Duke accepted De Mille's promises and took the part.[60]

Once filming began in June 1941, De Mille and Wayne got along fine. The director allowed Duke to select his own costume, against the judgment of the color coordinator, who objected to the actor's choice of an orange scarf. De Mille and Duke also ate lunch together regularly. Wayne admired De Mille's principles and the way he directed crowd scenes. "He was the only director I know of that could take a crowd and make them not be a mob," he later remarked. He had a lower opinion of De Mille's direction of his stars. Unlike Ford or Hathaway, De Mille either had a bad ear for dialogue or just did not care. He seemed unconcerned by stilted scenes, as if the special effects and epic quality of so many of his films would be enough to satisfy his viewers.[61]

Reap the Wild Wind shows De Mille at both his best and worst. Budgeted at four million dollars, it is an extravagant, flamboyant slice of Hollywood. Like many of De Mille's films, *Reap the Wild Wind* is a grand and improbable love story, a *Gone With the Wind* with sea storms and shipwrecks that uses history as a romantic prop. Set against a backdrop of salvage work and outright piracy in the Florida Keys in 1840, it is the story of Loxi Claiborne (Paulette Goddard) and the two men who love her, Captain Jack Stuart (Wayne) and Stephen Tolliver (Ray Milland). The two present a study in contrasts: Stuart, a rugged, independent salt; Tolliver, a Charleston-bred, foppish sea lawyer and devoted company man. They are rivals not only for the same woman but also control of the Devereaux Line. In typical Hollywood fashion, they develop a mutual admiration that survives a series of misunderstandings and Stuart's scuttling of the flagship of the Devereaux fleet, and ends only when

Stuart sacrifices his own life to rescue Tolliver from the tentacles of a giant squid.

The film begins with what may be a passing reference to America's undeclared war with Germany on the high seas: "Eighteen forty. America's lifeline is the sea. . . . The sea and the sea alone makes America one nation." Yet De Mille's only real object in *Reap the Wild Wind* was entertainment. Although most of Asia and Europe were engaged in war, De Mille made movies as if no world existed outside of Hollywood.

But by September 1941, when *Reap the Wild Wind* went into postproduction and Duke headed back to Republic for one more quick film before Christmas, America had lost its splendid isolationism. Increasingly, producers were advocating political positions in their films. Following the lead of President Franklin Roosevelt, they had begun to prod their countrymen toward intervention and war with Nazi Germany. *A Yank in the R.A.F.* (1941) and *International Squadron* (1941) show Americans joining the Royal Air Force to fight Nazis. Far more important, however, was *Sergeant York*, the top box-office draw in 1941, which told the story of America's most celebrated World War I soldier. Portraying the passage of Alvin York, played by Gary Cooper, from pacifist to defender of democracy and the American way, the film suggests that there are beliefs and institutions worth fighting and dying for. As a forceful plea for interventionism, *Sergeant York* had the unofficial endorsement of the White House. Eleanor Roosevelt, Selective Service Director Gen. Lewis B. Hershey, and Gen. John "Black Jack" Pershing attended its lavish New York premiere, and President Roosevelt invited Alvin York to Washington to compare notes on the film.[62]

American isolationists condemned the film, quite rightly labeling *Sergeant York* pro-Roosevelt propaganda. On a national radio broadcast, leading isolationist Sen. Gerald P. Nye of North Dakota argued that movies "have ceased to be an instrument of entertainment" and had become propaganda "designed to drug the reason of the American people, set aflame their emotions, turn their hatred into a blaze, fill them with fear that Hitler will come over here to capture them, that he will steal their trade, that America must go to war." Rather than show the horrors of war, the carnage and death and pain of war—"men crouching in mud" and "boys disemboweled, blown to pieces"—Hollywood only portrayed men "marching in their bright uniforms, firing the beautiful guns at distant targets." In the worst tradition of isolationists, echoing Father Charles Coughlin, Nye believed that a handful of Jewish moguls, the Roosevelt administration, and the importance of Hollywood's British market were behind the interventionist films. "Are you ready to send your boys to bleed and die in Europe to make the world safe for this industry and its financial backers?" he asked his listeners.[63]

In September 1941 the isolationists, armed with subpoenas and questions, summoned Hollywood leaders to Washington. The Senate Committee on Interstate Commerce's Subcommittee on War Propaganda, headed by D. Worth Clark of Idaho, charged that forty-eight films contained specific elements of interventionist propaganda. The subcommittee was stacked with isolationists and anti-Roosevelt senators, but Hollywood was unimpressed. Led by their chief counsel Wendell Willkie, the moguls counterattacked. Willkie admitted that Hollywood was guilty of making an occasional anti-Nazi film, but he applauded that fact. Neither he nor such studio powers as Harry Warner or Darryl Zanuck saw anything but evil in Hitler's regime, and to remain silent and do nothing in the face of German expansion and militarism would have been shameful. When Warner took the stand he echoed Willkie's opinions. Nazism was "an evil force," he said, and his studio had made films to warn Americans of the dangers posed by Hitler. Where was the propaganda in the truth, where was the crime in taking a moral stand? Commenting on the proceeding, liberal writer John T. McManus observed that Hollywood's greatest failure was making so few movies that alerted Americans to the dangers of fascism. During the previous two years Hollywood had turned out more than eleven hundred films, and less than one-half of 1 percent treated fascism.[64]

The isolationists' attempt to browbeat Hollywood ended in utter failure. Ernest McFarland of Arizona, the lone Roosevelt supporter on the subcommittee, conducted a vigorous examination of Nye and his charges. Unsatisfied with the North Dakota senator's broadbrush attacks on Hollywood, McFarland pressed for specifics. Where was the propaganda? In which films? In which scenes? Nye was unsure. He could not precisely recall. He confused one film with another. He appeared ignorant, anti-Semitic, and demagogic. On September 26, 1941, subcommittee chairman Clark beat a hasty retreat, announcing an adjournment of the hearings. They never reconvened. The day after the Japanese attack on Pearl Harbor, Clark abandoned the proceedings.

While Nye began an offensive that ended with him taking careful aim at his own foot, while industry heads counterattacked and left the field in triumph, while liberals talked of free speech and Nazi threats, while American communists discovered to their discomfort that they were temporarily aligned with conservative America Firsters—John Wayne was holed up at Republic making *Lady for the Night* with Joan Blondell. Few films could have been more out of step. Like so many of the studio's films of the 1930s and early 1940s, it emphasized the class and racial barriers that divided Americans. Its theme was: Stay with your own kind. Jenny Blake (Blondell), a successful 1880s dance hall owner and performer, yearns to escape her humble origins and enter Memphis society. After using her money to achieve her goal, she realizes that she deserted "real people, warm people" for "trash. Yes, trash that sits around hating, sits around waiting for slavery to come back, for cotton to come back, for the ghosts of their sons to come back. Zombies, the living dead who haven't the decency to lie down and stay buried."

There was nothing distinguishing about *Lady for the Night*, except perhaps its vague echoes of *Rebecca* and the level of its racism and sexism—one black servant boasts that "Mr. Lincoln done emancipated and proclamated me," and Jack Morgan (Wayne) tells Jenny that he will accept her back only if she will "promise to sew [his] buttons and cook [his] meals and darn [his] socks." And the film is more of a Blondell movie than a Wayne movie, although neither was anxious to lay claim to the picture. It was just a typical Republic quickie, the kind of film that Herbert Yates loved so much because it could be counted on to make money. *Lady for the Night* was not the last such film that Duke made at Republic, but it was the last film he made before Pearl Harbor. While it was being cut and edited, the Japanese attacked the United States. Hollywood interventionists had told Americans to be prepared for a crisis, and now it had occurred. What no one in the industry could have anticipated at that time was that the crisis would help to make John Wayne the greatest star in the history of Hollywood. His moment had finally arrived.

9

John Wayne and Hollywood
Go to War

December 7, 1941. The news reached Hollywood at 11:26 on a calm Sunday morning. The Japanese had attacked American naval and air bases in Honolulu. A few people refused to believe the news. It seemed impossible, almost like another "War of the Worlds" broadcast, and they waited for the soothing voice of an announcer to tell them that it was only make-believe. Everything about the day clashed with the brutal facts. The weather was perfect, even for a city where ideal weather was the norm. A cool night breeze blew off the desert from the northeast, but by 11:00 it was already in the low seventies. For the Hollywood elite, many of whom had gone to their vacation retreats in Malibu, Palm Springs, or the High Sierras, golf and swimming, not war, were on the day's agenda. Before the news reached Los Angeles, harmony reigned. Only the day before the UCLA Bruins and the USC Trojans had played to a 7–7 tie, and that very morning a *Los Angeles Times* headline announced FINAL PEACE MOVE SEEN.[1]

The attack stunned Angelenos. Responses varied. Some followed normal schedules. Thousands turned up at the "little world championship" football game and watched the undefeated Hollywood Bears, led by Kenny Washington and Woody Strode, defeat the Columbus Bulls. During the game, news updates reminded the spectators that the Bears' victory would probably not be remembered as the day's most important event. In another part of town, several hundred spectators watched Paramount Studio's baseball team defeat an "all-Jap aggregation." After the game the FBI took the Japanese team into custody. The attack, however, disrupted most schedules. Golfers finished the holes they were playing and returned to the clubhouse. Gossips ended their conversations about Harry Warner's new granddaughter or the removal of Eddie Albert's tonsils or the antiaircraft men who had set up shop at Hollywood Park and turned to more urgent topics. Thousands simply got into their automobiles—tanks full and rubber treads still good—and drove aimlessly through the city, leading to traffic jams in downtown Los Angeles and Hollywood.[2]

Soon the rumors started to ricochet like bullets. Air defense men had known the attack was imminent. Two squadrons of airplanes—thirty aircraft—had been sighted over the California coast. Japanese airplanes had reconnoitered the Bay area. They had bombed the Golden Gate Bridge. Pearl Harbor was only a stepping-stone. California was next. There would be an uprising of Japanese Americans. Sabotage was certain. Moved to action by the rumors as well as the need to take sound precautions, policemen went on twelve-hour shifts and sent extra security guards to dams, bridges, and power stations. Most people waited for FDR's announcement that the United States was now at war.[3]

Hollywood and the entertainment industry responded to the attack with sincere feelings of patriotism mixed with an equally sincere desire to cash in on the event. Studios abandoned a few films already in production with poorly timed themes or poorly chosen titles—the musicals *Pearl Harbor Pearl* and *I'll Take Manila* and the comedy *Absent Without Leave*, about a GI who goes AWOL. Just as quickly studios secured the copyrights for more promising titles—*Sunday in Hawaii*, *Wings Over the Pacific*, *Bombing of Honolulu*, *Remember Pearl Harbor*, *Yellow Peril*, *Yellow Menace*, *My Four Years in Japan*, and *V for Victory*. Tin Pan Alley produced topical songs within days of the attack. Although none muscled onto the Hit Parade, such tunes as "Let's Put the Axe to the Axis," "We're Going to Find the Fellow Who Is Yellow and Beat Him Red, White and Blue," "They're Gonna Be Playin' Taps on the Japs," "The Sun Will Soon Be Setting for the Land of the Rising Sun," "To Be Specific, It's Our Pacific," "When Those Little Yellow Bellies Meet the Cohens and the Kelleys," and "You're a Sap, Mr. Jap" expressed the angry mood of the country. The Metropolitan Opera Company, sensing that Americans did not want to see a sympathetic portrayal of any Japanese, dropped their production of *Madama Butterfly*. The Greenwich Village Savoyards followed the Met's lofty example and dumped their production of *The Mikado*.[4]

While Tin Pan Alley turned out its topical tunes and opera companies pruned their repertoires, Americans huddled close to their radios. On Monday morning and Tuesday night FDR delivered his impassioned war speeches before Congress. For a few days Americans—and particularly West Coast residents—moved through a fog of air raid alarms, blackouts, and tense expectations. They listened as commentators broke the news that Germany and Italy had declared war on the United States. They listened to the news that the Germans had sunk two British ships and that the Japanese had followed up Pearl Harbor with attacks in the Philippines, Hong Kong, Wake Island, Guam, and other Pacific strongholds.

For Hollywood parochial concerns came first. Many moaned that the war was a killer at the box office, echoing the literati's reaction to the international crises of the past several years. According to the story current at the time, in 1935, when Mussolini's troops stormed into Ethiopia and the world focused on the League of Nations, a Hollywood producer asked a friend, "Have you heard any late news?" Yes, the friend replied hotly, "Italy just banned *Marie Antoinette!*" In 1939, when Italy ruthlessly invaded Albania, Louella Parsons, Hollywood's leading gossip writer, began her column that week: "The deadly dullness of the past week was lifted today when Darryl Zanuck announced he had bought all rights to *The Bluebird* for Shirley Temple."[5]

By mid-December Hollywood spokesmen were complaining that Americans were too interested in the war to go to the movies. Attempting to demonstrate that Hollywood was concerned with other events, *Variety* observed that the war had also hurt Christmas shopping, but clearly the box-office crisis overshadowed all other concerns. *The Wolf Man*'s *Variety* advertisement announced: "Listen to That Box Office Howl!" but the only noise was the studios' cries of financial pain. The same was true for *The Great Dictator*, *Sergeant York*, *Citizen Kane*, and the season's other top pictures. Hand-wringing, along with speculation about the long-term impact of the war on the industry, was typical of the Hollywood response.[6]

John Wayne's reaction was similarly parochial. After years of struggle with bad scripts and tight budgets, by late 1941 he had come close to stardom. The reviews of *Stagecoach* and *The Long Voyage Home* had pushed him toward the top. Republic's Herbert Yates had responded by searching for better scripts, assigning first-line directors, and increasing the budgets for Wayne films. And less than four months before the attack on Pearl Harbor, Duke had finished his work on Cecil B. DeMille's *Reap the Wild Wind*, which Paramount had scheduled for a March 1942 release.[7]

At the age of thirty-four he was a player but not yet a major star. In late December 1941, *Variety* issued its annual review of the stars, which set down clearly where an actor or actress stood in a complicated pecking order. At the summit of the hierarchy were the performers whose pictures earned the most money for the year: Gary Cooper, Abbott and Costello, Clark Gable, Mickey Rooney, Bob Hope, Charlie Chaplin, Dorothy Lamour, Spencer Tracy, Jack Benny, and Bing Crosby. They had helped make 1941 the best year ever for domestic box-office receipts.[8]

Next came the individual studio reports. The stars and featured performers of the individual studios were listed and briefly discussed. The major studios controlled the major talent. MGM led the pack; its stars included Gable, Rooney, Tracy, Robert Taylor, Lana Turner, James Stewart, Hedy Lamarr, Judy Garland, Myrna Loy, William Powell, Joan Crawford, Nelson Eddy, Jeanette MacDonald, Greta Garbo, Norma Shearer, the Marx Brothers, and a host of other leading performers. If the other studios could not match MGM, they could all boast of their proven attractions. Warner Bros., king of the gangster genre, had James Cagney, Humphrey Bogart, Edward G. Robinson, John Garfield, and George Raft, as well as Errol Flynn, Bette Davis, Merle Oberon, and Ronald Reagan. Twentieth Century-Fox had a group of attractive leading men and women, which included Tyrone Power, Betty Grable, Gene Tierney, Henry Fonda, Randolph Scott, Maureen O'Hara, and Linda Darnell. Paramount had its comedians—Hope, Crosby, and Benny—as well as Lamour, Claudette Colbert, Veronica Lake, Paulette Goddard, Fred MacMurray, and Ray Milland. RKO featured Ginger Rogers, Orson Welles, Cary Grant, Carole Lombard, Ronald Colman, and Gloria Swanson. Universal had a great year in 1941, thanks to the success of Abbott and Costello. And Columbia featured Peter Lorre, Boris Karloff, Fay Wray, and the recently signed Rita Hayworth.[9]

At the bottom of the hierarchy were the smaller studios and their performers. There dwelled Monogram: "No pretenses. No ambitious production. Just bread and butter," noted *Variety*. Its older cowboy and action stars—Jack LaRue, Buck Jones, Tim McCoy, and Bela Lugosi—kept the studio afloat. Finally came Republic. *Variety* listed Gene Autry and John Wayne as Republic's "two corking box-office assets." Wayne's reputation derived from his "loanout" status. Like Monogram, Republic produced films for theaters outside the major distribution circles, and a star like Wayne, who was used by the majors, gave prestige to his Poverty Row home studio.[10]

Duke, always a clear-thinking realist, knew where he stood. He was a big star in the third-and-fourth-run theaters in the South and Southwest, in areas with more cattle than people. His success following *Stagecoach* introduced him to the first- and second-run palaces of the East, Midwest, and West. At the end of 1941 he was nowhere near the summit of the hierarchy, far from the status of such leading men as Clark Gable, Robert Taylor, Tyrone Power, Cary Grant, Gary Cooper, or Henry Fonda. And he was aging, with perhaps only a few years left as a leading man. He was ambitious, and no one in the industry had his capacity for work. But did he have enough time left to make it?[11]

The key question that seemed to follow Japan's bombers across the Pacific was that of enlistment. While Duke pondered his future and prepared for his next picture, other Hollywood stars put their careers on hold and their lives on the line. Pearl Harbor aroused deep emotions in Hollywood. During the next four years journalists and politicians would accuse the film industry of being cynical, opportunistic, greedy, and worse—charges that were often accurate. But in late 1941 and early 1942 scores of actors, directors, producers, and technicians enlisted out of a real sense of patriotism. Like millions of other Americans, they were shocked by the Japanese attack and wanted to help win the war.

Henry Fonda, one of Duke's boon companions on vacation cruises to Mexico, felt the pull of patriotism. He was thirty-seven—three years older than Wayne—and had a wife and three children. For all practical purposes, he was exempt from the draft. But he had a baby face and did not want the wives and mothers of soldiers and sailors to see him on the screen and ask, "Why isn't he out there?" Besides, as he told his wife, "This is my country and I want to be where it's happening. I don't want to be in a fake war in a studio or on location. . . . I want to be on a real ocean not the back lot. I want to be with real sailors not extras." After he finished *The Ox-Bow Incident*, in which he was then starring, he drove to the Naval Headquarters in Los Angeles and enlisted. No photographers were present; his press agent had not tipped off any reporters. Fonda wanted it simple, no different than other Americans.[12]

John Ford, the man Duke admired the most, also felt the pull. During the late 1930s he had followed with growing uneasiness the spread of fascism in Europe. That spring he organized the Naval Field Photographic Reserve Unit, which Washington officially recognized. The forty-six-year-old Ford was ordered to report to Washington for active duty the month before Pearl Harbor. Immediately and without publicity he left Hollywood—the money, the fame, the career, the glamour.[13]

When the Japanese attacked Pearl Harbor, Ford was eating lunch at the eighteenth-century Alexandria, Virginia, home of Adm. William Pickens. He watched the admiral take the urgent phone call; he saw the blood drain from his face. After they heard the news, Pickens's wife, Darrielle, showed Ford the place on their home where a Revolutionary War musket ball had torn through a wall. "I never let them plaster over the hole," she said. Throughout the war and for the rest of his life Ford would remember the story. He wanted to be part of that tradition.[14]

Tradition and patriotism pulled Jimmy Stewart into the war. Stewart's grandfather had fought for the Union during the Civil War. His father had fought in the Spanish-American War and in World War I. In February 1941 Stewart attempted to enlist in the Army Air Corps but was rejected because his weight (147 pounds) was ten pounds too light for his six-foot-four-inch frame. He went on a diet of candy, beer, and bananas. In a month he had put on the ten pounds and he was sworn into the army. He left his fifteen-hun-dred-dollar-a-week movie salary for a private's wages.[15]

Other Hollywood personalities also felt the pull. One leading man at Republic said that on the day after Pearl Harbor, half the men at the studio enlisted, and that the joke around the lot was that anyone who left Republic to go to war was a coward. But most went anyway. Wayne's fellow star at Republic, Gene Autry, joined the Army Air Corps. The major studios also felt the exodus. Robert Montgomery enlisted in the navy. Tyrone Power joined the marines. William Holden went into the army. After the death of his wife, Carole Lombard, in January 1942, Clark Gable also enlisted in the army. David Niven, Laurence Olivier, and Patric Knowles returned to their native Britain and enlisted. Ronald Reagan, Sterling Hayden, Burgess Meredith, and Gilbert Roland all signed up. So, too, did directors Frank Capra, William Wyler, Anatole Litvak, John Huston, and William Keighley; producers Hal Roach, Jack Warner, Gene Markey, and Darryl F. Zanuck; writers Garson Kanin and Budd Schulberg; cameraman Gregg Toland; and thousands of other Hollywood workers. By October 1942 more than 2,700—or 12 percent—of the men and women in the film industry had entered the armed forces. Some, like Fonda and Stewart, enlisted quietly and without fanfare. Others, like Reagan, Zanuck, and Gable, made the process of enlistment and service an act of public theater. But they all served.[16]

In 1941 professional baseball players were the only men who received as much attention and adulation as Hollywood stars. When the war started they, too, laid down their bats and picked up service-issue weapons. Joe DiMaggio, Hank Greenberg, Bob Feller, Ted Williams, Bill Dickey, Pee Wee Reese, and most of the game's other legends from the 1930s entered the service. More than 4,000 of the roughly 5,700 players in the major and minor leagues served in the armed forces during the war. Some were killed or seriously injured during the conflict. Others experienced the loss of crucial skills because of a lack of practice. And even the players who returned to the big leagues after the war lost several years from careers that at best were painfully short.[17]

Movie stars and baseball stars, boxing champions and politicians—they took their place with millions of other less famous Americans. More than any other war in America's history, World War II was a popular, democratic war. In the five years between December 1941 and December 1946, 16.3 million Americans entered the armed forces. All males between the ages of eighteen and sixty-four had to register for the draft, although the upper age limit for service was set at forty-four, later lowered to thirty-eight. One out of every six American men wore a uniform during the war. The wealthy fought alongside the poor, the single beside married men with children. Relatively few men tried to avoid military service. For a man in his twenties or thirties not in uniform, the central question was, "Why not?"[18]

It was a question John Wayne had to face for the next four years. Duke's case was not a matter of draft dodging. Although by late 1941 his marriage was falling apart and his visits to his home and children were becoming more infrequent, he was technically married and had four children. This, coupled with his age, meant that he was not a prime candidate for the draft. Only weeks after the war began, FDR announced that Hollywood had an important role to play in the war effort: "The American motion picture is one of our most effective media in informing and entertaining our citizens. The motion picture must remain free in so far as national security will permit." Unlike steel, automobiles, and other vital American industries, which were heavily controlled by the government during the war, the controls on the film industry were comparatively light. Although several of FDR's advisers counseled him to take over Hollywood production, he believed that the industry leaders would perform their duty better if they remained in charge. But the subtext of Roosevelt's message to Hollywood was clear: The moguls could continue to make money, but their product had better serve the war effort. They had to combine propaganda with entertainment. If they did not, the government would take over the industry. Adding to Hollywood's special position, in February 1942 Gen. Lewis B. Hershey, director of Selective Service, called the motion picture industry "an activity essential in certain instances to the national health, safety and interest, and in other instances to war production." In accordance with his statement, he instructed Selective Service officials in California to grant deferments to men vital to the industry. Although Hershey's order was not meant as a blanket deferment, and although the Screen Actors Guild announced that it did not want privileged status, the California draft board was liberal in its application of the ruling. Many Washington and California officials argued that Gary Cooper was more valuable to the war effort as Sergeant York than as Sergeant Cooper.[19]

The most visible Hollywood commodity in need of protection during the war was the leading man. Out of sincere feelings of patriotism or the fear of being branded as a slacker, many of Hollywood's youngest and most famous leading men enlisted. In fact, George Montgomery, the popular Republic and Twentieth Century-Fox actor whose career never really recovered from his service absence, recalled that Duke was about the only leading man who did not do a tour in uniform. The shortage created a ticklish problem for studio public relations staffs. Leading men were supposed to project youth, sexuality, virility, and strength. But a movie star projecting those traits on the screen during the war faced the painful question, "Why isn't he in the army?" As *Variety* commented, "No more he-man build-up of young men as in the past, for these might kick back unpleasant reverberations. If the build-up is too mighty, [the] public may want to know if he's that good why he isn't in the Army shooting Japs and Nazis. This is a particularly touchy phase and p-r has to be subtle about it." The irony of the situation was best expressed by an agent who told a producer about his latest discovery: "I've got a great prospect for you—a young guy with a double hernia."[20]

A leading man during the war needed a good profile and an adequate voice, but more importantly he either had to be over forty, married with two or more children, or 4-F. Gary Cooper, Bing Crosby, James Cagney, John Garfield, Don Ameche, and Joel McCrea all "had a brood at home to call [them] 'Pop.'" Warner Baxter, Neil Hamilton, and Nils Aster—all forty to fifty—led the new crop of "semi-romantic" leading men. Sonny Tufts, the handsome, ex-Yale football player who starred in the hit *So Proudly We Hail,* was safely classified as 4-F.[21]

John Wayne's draft status was a family present. Like other actors with two or more children, he could have enlisted. Like his friends Henry Fonda or John Ford, he could have placed his concern for his nation above his concern for his family, status, and career. Wayne never spoke to the press about some aspects of his life; some he rarely (if ever) even spoke to his family or closest friends about. His decision not to enlist was a part of his life that he did not discuss. Pilar Wayne, whom he met and married a decade after the war, said that the guilt he suffered over his failure to enlist endured long after the war was over. "He would become a 'superpatriot,'" Pilar wrote, "for the rest of his life trying to atone for staying at home." Catalina Lawrence, a script supervisor at Republic during the war who sometimes doubled as Wayne's secretary, remembers writing letters of inquiry to military officials for Wayne, but he never really followed up on them. Mary St. John agreed. She recalled that he suffered "terrible guilt and embarrassment" because of his war record. "Every time he visited a military hospital or a base over the years, some young kid would ask him which branch he had served in. It embarrassed Duke terribly to tell him he had not served. That's why he made up a story about the football injury keeping him out." Aissa Wayne, Duke's oldest daughter in his second family, concluded that "with four children at home, and a lifelong anxiety about money, my dad never went to war. To a man who believed that life largely meant testing one's self, this was an ultimate test untaken." The fact that his brother, Robert, served in the navy only exacerbated Wayne's sensitivity. "He felt so bad," Catalina Lawrence recalled, "especially after Robert was drafted into the Navy." His mother, who always openly favored Robert, was not above reminding him that Robert, and not he, had served his country during the great crisis. On the screen Wayne was the quintessential man of action, one who took matters into his own powerful hands and fought for what he believed in. Never before or after would the chasm between what he projected on the screen and his personal actions be so great.[22]

He did not set out to avoid military service. Throughout 1942 and 1943, as he made one picture after another and as his reputation as a leading man soared, Duke flirted with the idea of enlistment. He was particularly concerned about his stature in Ford's eyes, and he suspected rightly that the director had little respect for celluloid soldiers. In early October 1941, shortly after he went on active duty, Ford wrote his wife that Wayne and Ward Bond's frivolous activities were meaningless in a world spinning toward total war. "They don't count. Their time will come." Three months after Pearl Harbor, Ford again mentioned Wayne in a letter to his wife. In words soaked in contempt, he remarked that he was "delighted" to hear about Duke and Bond sitting up all night on a mountaintop listening through earphones for signs that the Japanese were attacking California: "Ah well—such heroism shall not go unrewarded—it will live in the annals of time."[23]

A pattern developed in Wayne's letters to Ford during the first two years of the war. Repeatedly he wrote his friend that he wanted to enlist—planned to enlist—as soon as he finished just one or two pictures. In the spring of 1942, he inquired if he could get into Ford's unit, and if Ford would want him. If that option was closed, what would Ford suggest? Should he try the marines? Plaintively he insisted that he was not drunk and that he hated to ask for favors, adding, "But for Christ's sake, you can suggest can't you?" A year later little had changed. After he finished one more film he would be free. "Outside of that," Duke said, rephrasing a line from *David Copperfield,* "Barkus is ready, anxious, and willin'."[24]

But "Barkus" never did enlist. Toward the end of his life, Wayne told Dan Ford that his wife, Josie, had prevented him from joining Ford's outfit. According to his story, OSS head and Ford's superior, William J. Donovan, had sent a letter to Wayne explaining when Duke could join the Field Photographic Unit, but Josie never gave him the letter. He also confessed that he considered enlisting as a private, but rejected the idea. How, he pondered, could he fight alongside seventeen- and eighteen-year-old boys who had been reared on his movies? For them, he said, "I was America." In the end he concluded that he could best serve his country by making movies and going on an occasional USO tour. Such a weak justification, provided a quarter of a century after the end of the war, can be taken on the surface as flimsy, arrogant rationalization. But Duke was not an egotistical or arrogant person. He was an honest man without delusions of grandeur or self-importance. The World War II issue was simply the most painful episode of his life. He postponed making a decision about joining until it was too late to join. The fact that he had become a war hero without serving gave every explanation a false, self-serving ring.[25]

The problem with any discussion of Wayne's "war record" is that it depends too much on statements he and others made long after the war ended. Did his wife hide Donovan's letter? There is no such letter in Donovan's public and private papers. Did he believe that he was such an American institution by 1942 that he could not enlist as a private? This statement is difficult to take at face value, when one considers that Gable, Power, Fonda, and Stewart—far more important stars than Wayne—were willing to share a foxhole or a cockpit or a ship deck with teenage American soldiers or sailors. Did Wayne, in fact, try to enlist?[26]

The closest one can come to the truth is his Selective Service record, and even here there are a few problems. The government has destroyed full individual records; all letters between Wayne and his draft board have long since been turned into ashes in official incinerators. The skeleton of Wayne's record, however, remains. When the war started, Marion Mitchell Morrison—Selective Service Serial Number 2815, Order Number 1619—was classified 3-A, "deferred for dependency reasons." A continuation of that classification was requested and granted on November 17, 1943. Local draft boards periodically reviewed all classifications, and depending on their needs the government changed some classifications. To maintain a deferment or obtain a different deferment, a person or his employer had to file an official request. After returning the initial Selective Service questionnaire, he never personally filed a deferment claim, but a series of claims were filed "by another." Although the records have been destroyed, Republic Pictures was almost certainly that "other." After Republic's leading money earner Gene Autry enlisted in 1942, Yates was determined to keep Wayne out of uniform and in front of the camera. Therefore in April 1944 another deferment claim was filed and granted, reclassifying Wayne 2-A, "deferred in support of national health, safety, or interest." But a month later, with the war in Europe and the Pacific reaching a critical stage, he received a 1-A classification, "available for military service." This generated a series of new deferment claims, and on May 5, 1945, he was once again classified 2-A. His last classification came after the war ended when he received a 4-A deferment on the basis of his age.[27]

Wayne could have appealed his classification at any time during the war. At no time did he do so. Always an active man, the war years were particularly frantic for him. With his career bolting forward, he worked at four different studios and starred in thirteen pictures. In addition he divorced his first wife, met and courted his second, and led an active social life. When he was not working, the absence of a uniform gnawed at his self-respect and sense of manhood. It was then that he wrote Ford that "Barkus is willin.'" But then would come another movie, another delay, another link in a chain of delays that stretched from Pearl Harbor to Hiroshima.

Perhaps he believed that his single-minded pursuit of his career meshed with his sense of patriotism. If so, he was not the only person in Hollywood who expressed such beliefs. In March 1942, shortly after the premiere of *Reap the Wild Wind,* he attended a luncheon for the Associated Motion Picture Advertisers. Cecil B. De Mille addressed the audience on the subject of the role Hollywood should play in the war. De Mille, his voice charged with moral urgency, remarked: "The job of motion pictures is to help bring home a full realization of the crisis and of the deadly peril that lurks in internal squabbles. Ours is the task of holding high and ever visible the values that everyone is fighting for. I don't mean flag waving, but giving the embattled world sharp glimpses of the way of life that we've got to hang on to in spite of everything." In De Mille's mind the civilians who worked in the motion picture industry had a job and a duty every bit as important to the war effort as that of the American marines fighting on Pacific islands or American sailors battling the Germans on the Atlantic. Victory demanded unity and dedication by all Americans—at home and abroad, civilian and military.[28]

Washington's liaison with Hollywood was Lowell Mellett, a former editor of the *Washington Daily News* who had the good looks of an older Hollywood character actor. After considerable bureaucratic reorganization, in June 1942, Mellett was placed in charge of the Bureau of Motion Pictures (BMP), which was nominally under the Domestic Branch of the Office of War Information (OWI). While Mellett, dubbed the "white rabbit" for his less than forceful character, administered the BMP from his Washington office, the bureau's Hollywood office was run by Nelson Poynter. A close friend of Mellett's as well as a newspaperman, the dark-haired, frail-looking Poynter had unassailable New Deal and interventionist credentials but lacked even basic knowledge of Hollywood and filmmaking. Nevertheless FDR charged the team of Mellett and Poynter with making sure that Hollywood produced the kind of pictures deemed important to the war effort.[29]

If he was uncertain about the process of making pictures, Poynter was very explicit about what kind of films he expected Hollywood to produce. In his tiny office in Hollywood, he and his small staff compiled *The Government Informational Manual for the Motion Picture Industry*. According to Poynter the central question every producer, director, and writer should ask was: "Will this picture help win the war?" Every film should contribute to that end by presenting America's effort and cause, its allies and friends, in the most generous possible terms. The manual emphasized that the United States was engaged in nothing less than "a people's war" to create a "new world" where want and fear were banished and freedom of religion and speech were birthrights.[30]

In practical terms *The Government Informational Manual for the Motion Picture Industry* codified a long list of dos and don'ts for Hollywood. Although adherence to the code was technically voluntary, most Hollywood producers and directors tried to take them into account and even allowed for revisions if government officials were uncomfortable with a movie. Whenever possible, the code argued, films should "show people making small sacrifices for victory"—bringing their own sugar when invited out to dinner, carrying their own parcels when shopping, travelling on planes or trains with light luggage, uncomplainingly giving up seats to servicemen or others travelling on war priorities. Americans on the home front should be portrayed as happy, busy, productive, rationing-loving patriots, planting victory gardens, taking public transportation even when they could afford to drive, and generally pitching in to win the war. Heading the list of don'ts was disunity on the home front or the battlefront. America was not to be presented as divided along any racial, class, or gender lines. Scenes of strikes were frowned upon; plots which suggested that the United States was anything less than a paradise for black Americans were verboten; and resorts to ethnic or religious bigotry were censored. Similarly, the allies of the United States had to be presented as paragons of national virtue. Poynter instructed Hollywood to use its magic to manufacture a classless Britain, an efficient and incorruptible China, and a democratic Russia. Noting the irony of Hollywood's whitewash of the Soviet Union, *Variety* commented, "War has put Hollywood's traditional conception of the Muscovites through the wringer, and they have come out shaved, washed, sober, good to their families, Rotarians, brother Elks, and 33rd Degree Masons." In short the U.S. government, not the large cadre of Hollywood communists, was the most successful pro-Soviet agitator in movie history.[31]

John Wayne became a de facto propaganda machine during the war. To be sure, the producers of Wayne films occasionally clashed with the BMP, but the conflicts were usually caused by the BMP's narrow interpretation of individual scenes or insistence that a specific propaganda message appear in the film's dialogue. Of course Duke believed in the BMP's message: He *was* its message.[32]

During the first four months of 1942, before the manual or even the bureau, as American forces experienced painful losses in the Pacific and the Atlantic, Wayne made two pictures—*The Spoilers* and *In Old California*. Both films have similar plots. *The Spoilers*, based on the Rex Beach novel, is set in Nome in 1900 during the Alaska gold rush, centers on a claim-jumping scheme, and features a love triangle between Wayne, a society woman, and a dance hall girl. Wayne thwarts the claim jumping and discovers that the society woman is heartless and the dance hall girl has a heart as pure as a Klondike nugget. *In Old California* is set in Sacramento in 1848–49 during the California gold rush, features a land-grabbing scheme, and highlights a love triangle between Wayne, a society woman, and a dance hall girl. By the end of the film, not only does Wayne foil the land-grabbing scheme and discover that the society woman is heartless and the dance hall girl has a heart as pure as a nugget from Sutter's Mill, but he also saves the entire region from a particularly nasty typhoid epidemic.

The message of both films was simple: Defend your property with every fiber of your being. Neither film expresses any sympathy for men who traffic in appeasement or legal niceties. In *The Spoilers* two prospectors announce in a saloon that they were "just working along kinda peaceful like," when at least twenty claim jumpers forced them off their stake. What could we do? they ask. "Ya still have five fingers on your gun hand, ain't ya?" comes the immediate reply. All at the bar nod in agreement at the sage advice. Even the sexual innuendo revolves around claim jumping and force. Crooked gold commissioner Alexander McNamara (Randolph Scott) plans to jump both Roy Glennister's (John Wayne) Midas Gold Mine and his woman, Cherry Malotte (Marlene Dietrich). He tells Cherry that he might "move into [Glennister's] territory." "Could be tough going," Cherry cautions. "But worth it," McNamara replies. Glennister's use of brutal force defeats both forms of aggression. In one of the longest fistfights in film history, Glennister outlasts McNamara. Force—not the impotent and even dishonest representatives of the law—proves the only solution to aggression.[33]

The same conclusion is expressed in *In Old California*. When the good but timid citizens of Sacramento are attacked, Tom Craig (John Wayne), the otherwise peaceloving town pharmacist, asks: "Doesn't anybody fight back around here?" "Angry men defending their home," he asserts, can never be defeated. For Americans embroiled in a war to prevent land-grabbing aggression, the significance was obvious.[34]

In Old California was little more than an inexpensive Republic formula picture. Without John Wayne, wrote *New York Times* reviewer Bosley Crowther, the picture "would be down with the usual run of strays." *The Spoilers*, however, received favorable reviews. "The he-men are back," noted the *New York Times*. "John Wayne is . . . virile," commented *Variety*. "John Wayne is a valuable piece of property," judged the *Chicago Tribune*. The acting characteristics which Wayne had spent a decade perfecting—the sideways glance and smile at his female lead, the tight-lipped, shark-eyed stare at his evil rival—found worthy recipients in *The Spoilers*. Dietrich's seething sexuality and Scott's oily villainy contrasted nicely with Wayne's cocky masculinity.[35]

Wayne was maturing as an actor, and he knew it. On the set he was more self-confident. He was occasionally rude and impatient with Scott, who took a more artistic approach to his craft than did Wayne. Scott, a southerner with courtly manner, disliked Duke. On and off the set of *The Spoilers*, Dietrich occupied Wayne's attentions. On and off the set they were constantly together, dining at trendy restaurants, attending sporting events, and taking weekend hunting and fishing trips.[36]

At Republic Pictures, Herbert Yates was not so interested in Wayne's emotional and intellectual growth as in his burgeoning box-office power. Paramount released *Reap the Wild Wind* in March 1942, and it opened in the first-run theaters and music halls throughout the country. Bosley Crowther saw the Technicolor epic in Radio City Music Hall. Always a generous reviewer for De Mille's films, he was particularly lavish in his praise for *Reap the Wild Wind*. It was "the essence of all [De Mille's] experience, the apogee of his art and as jam-full a motion picture as has ever played two hours upon a screen. It definitely marks a DeMillestone," Crowther wrote. The review, and others like it, echoed like gold coins in Yates's mind. *Reap the Wild Wind* was a hit—reviewers compared it with *Gone With the Wind*—and John Wayne was one of its stars, even if he was killed in the movie by a giant squid and therefore failed to win the heroine. And Wayne belonged to Yates and Republic. If Yates had been unimpressed by Duke's success in *Stagecoach* and *The Long Voyage Home*, he now fully understood the worth of his star attraction.[37]

With profits and the war in mind, Yates put Duke into his first war film. Were it not for the fact that *Flying Tigers* was a shameless ripoff of *Only Angels Have Wings*, the film might be considered as the prototype for World War II combat films. It possessed everything but originality, not a point of serious concern for an action-oriented studio like Republic. Howard Hawks's *Only Angels Have Wings* (1939) contained all the motifs that film scholar Robert B. Ray has labeled as basic to Hollywood's World War II combat films: "the male group directed by a strong leader, the outsider who must prove himself by courageous individual action, the necessity for stoicism in the face of danger and death, the premium placed on professionalism, and the threat posed by women."[38]

Only Angels Have Wings centers on a group of pilots in a South American jungle, contracted to deliver the mail over a range of dangerous, jagged mountains of unearthly appearance. In this group of flying mercenaries is a brave leader called "Pappy," who emphasizes teamwork, another man branded as a coward who has to prove his courage to win acceptance, a woman who threatens to destroy the chummy fraternity atmosphere, and pilots who share a common Hemingwayesque code of life and language. They speak with their actions, resist expressing their emotions, and demonstrate their deep bonds in such nonverbal ways as asking for a cigarette or a match.[39]

Flying Tigers contains all the same elements. This time the mercenary pilots are part of Col. Claire Lee Chennault's American Volunteer Group, flying against the Japanese for China on the eve of Pearl Harbor. Once again the leader stresses the value of teamwork and is called "Pappy" by his men. Once again there is a suspected coward who must prove himself, a flamboyant individualist who on the surface seems to care about only himself, and a woman who threatens the harmony and effectiveness of the male unit. There is even the same language of cigarettes and matches and painful grimaces when talk turns to matters of the heart. The similarities of plot and structure are so striking that Ray commented that "Hawks should have sued for plagiarism."[40]

But for all the similarities—and there were many—there was a major difference. *Flying Tigers* went into production shortly after Pearl Harbor, during America's darkest months in the Pacific, and dealt with the most urgent topic in the world: the war. It was filmed from May to July 1942, months that saw the Japanese take Corregidor and the United States win the Battles of the Coral Sea and Midway. It capitalized on the nation's mood. At a moment when the nation demanded a hero, Republic responded with John Wayne. At a time when Americans longed for good news from the Pacific, *Flying Tigers* recounted the heroics of Chennault's American Volunteer Group. During a crisis when the country wanted to believe the best of its allies and the worst of its enemies, the film presented Chinese straight from the pages of Pearl S. Buck's *The Good Earth* and robotic Japanese fresh from hell. In addition the film touched the rawest of American nerves—Pearl Harbor. FDR's full war speech is replayed in the film, and the climactic scene occurs after the Japanese attack on Pearl Harbor. Thus, despite its similarities to the earlier film, *Flying Tigers* was successful.

The film was an ideal vehicle for Wayne. The role of the solid, quiet leader around whom all the action and all the other parts revolve played to Duke's strengths. Increasingly in his movies, he was developing a screen presence that could dominate without dialogue, often even without movement. In one scene in *Flying Tigers*, the pilots listen to FDR's war speech on the radio. Slowly the camera moves in for a close-up on Wayne, who stands silent, listening, a cigarette in his left hand. During the entire message, he never moves. His eyes and mouth do not change expression. The only movement is the smoke drifting upward from his unsmoked cigarette. At the end of the speech, he takes a deep breath and walks off screen. Roosevelt had said it all; Wayne could have added only a trite cliché. Yet Duke played the scene with controlled passion and utter sincerity. It is a powerful scene that underscored his screen presence.

Republic believed that *Flying Tigers* conveyed the message advocated by the OWI's BMP. The film emphasized teamwork. Government officials, however, had mixed reactions to the film. Harry B. Price, a government consultant on China, noted that although the film was generally of a high caliber, it left "much to be desired from the standpoint of an adequate portrayal of our Allies, the Chinese." Like so many other Hollywood films, wrote Price, *Flying Tigers* presented the Chinese as "likable, but slightly ludicrous," and there is "little in the picture to suggest that the Chinese people are human beings just as varied and many sided in their natures as Americans." In addition the film did not explore Chennault's tactical innovations. The assessment of the BMP staffer who reviewed *Flying Tigers* agreed with Price's. Marjorie Thorson complained that the film's glorification of individual heroics muted its theme of teamwork and cooperation, that the Chinese were presented as harmless and slightly incompetent people, and that the major issues of the war were not discussed. She noted that although there were Chinese nurses and doctors in the movie, only American nurses were shown changing bandages and "the final decision in any matter of a flier's health is left to the non-professional American squadron leader . . . just being an American presumably qualifies him to make medical decisions over the head of the trained Chinese." Even worse, "no Chinese men are shown fighting." "Altogether," she concluded, the "picture attempts a great deal more than it accomplishes."[41]

Official complaints often demonstrated an ignorance of both filmmaking and the war. Members of the American Volunteer Group charged that *Flying Tigers* was "unbelievably bad" because it contained several factual errors and employed as technical advisers two former members of the AVG who had been dishonorably discharged for being "suspected of perversion" (that is, homosexuality). But their parochial concerns were just as misplaced as the bureau's. Contentions that filmmakers distort history by focusing on the individual or the small group at the expense of historical reality reveal a deep misunderstanding of the industry—they could be made, no doubt, about every historical movie ever shot. As for the treatment of Chiang Kai-shek and the Chinese in *Flying Tigers*, "blindly generous" rather than "inhuman" is the best description. The fact is that, divided by warlordism and civil war, plagued by corruption and inefficiency, Chiang's Kuomintang government dismissed "aggressive action" against the Japanese before Pearl Harbor. After December 7, 1941, they left any serious fighting to the United States. As one American military official noted in late 1941, "The general idea in the United States that China has fought Japan to a standstill and has had many glorious victories is a delusion." If the film's portrayal of the Chinese was historically inaccurate, it was closer to reality than the line adopted by the BMP. And the assertion in the film that Americans provided the combat muscle in the war did reflect actual conditions.[42]

The entire debate was irrelevant at Republic. Yates believed in the picture and disregarded the bureau's criticism. He was not interested in the veracity of *Flying Tigers*. His was a bottom-line studio, and his only concern was ticket sales. From its first preview, the film exceeded Republic's usual modest expectations. The *Hollywood Reporter* announced: "*Flying Tigers* marks an all-time production high for Republic. It is a smashing, stirring, significant film. . . . It will be a record grosser in all engagements, and no theater in the land should hesitate about proudly showing it." *Variety* agreed: "In *Flying Tigers*, Republic has its best picture." Even though the film was released late in the year, *Flying Tigers* became one of 1942's leading box-office successes and the only picture in the top twenty not produced by one of the major studios.[43]

No one at Republic had to search for the reason: It was John Wayne. If Republic executives needed confirmation, they found it in every major review. *Hollywood Reporter*: "John Wayne is at his peak." *Variety*: "John Wayne matches his best performance." *New York Times*: "Mr. Wayne is the sort of fellow who inspires confidence." Republic had a hit and a star. Yates was now convinced, and so was the rest of the industry. And during the next three years of war, Wayne would reconfirm repeatedly his star status as his name alone came to guarantee a film's success.[44]

Now more than ever, Yates was determined to keep Wayne. Shortly after the release of *Flying Tigers* the film's producer, Edmund Grainger, and director, David Miller, entered the armed services. Neither would make another picture until the late 1940s. Duke believed that he, too, should enlist, but Yates refused to release him. The loss of Gene Autry, whose contract to make eight straight pictures for Republic had to be shelved when the singing cowboy enlisted in the Army Air Service, devastated Yates. When Duke raised the issue, Yates became apoplectic. "You should have thought about all that before you signed a new contract," Yates bellowed. "If you don't live up to it, I'll sue you for every penny you've got. Hell, I'll sue you for every penny you hope to make in the future. God damn it! Nobody walks out on me." But Gene Autry did, and Duke could have. He just did not. Yates told Wayne that he would sue him for breach of contract if he enlisted. Furthermore, Yates announced, if Duke enlisted he would make certain that he would never work for Republic or any other studio. Although his threat went against government policy—every person in uniform was guaranteed his or her civilian job once the war ended—Duke did not press the issue. He feared poverty and unemployment, and perhaps he feared even more losing the status he had achieved and sinking into obscurity.[45]

His boss was Republic, but Yates was happy to loan him out to other studios. With the scarcity of leading men becoming more pressing every month, he was never in greater demand. It was an ideal situation for Wayne. He was a man who never made peace with inactivity. He loved his work and he hated the time between pictures. Mary St. John said that part of his problem was that he had no hobbies, nothing to do to fill the empty days. His daughter Aissa commented that he "was a slave to his energy." On location he always awoke by 4:30 or 5:00 A.M., and even when he was not working on a picture he was up at dawn. "He never slept late. Ever," Aissa remembered. Once up, and wired by his morning coffee, he was ready for work, and when there was no work, he simply had to endure long periods of restless rest. In 1942 such stretches were painful but infrequent. His home life was empty, his marriage almost over, many of his friends in uniform. When he worked, his life had structure and purpose. When he was not working, he had time to mull over the irony that without serving a day in the armed forces he was becoming a World War II hero. It was during these periods that he penned "Barkus" letters to Ford.[46]

Throughout 1942 Duke worked at a hectic pace. *The Spoilers* was shot in January and February, *In Old California* in March and April, and *Flying Tigers* in May, June, and July. While *Flying Tigers* was in post-production, Duke moved on to other films. Between the end of July and September he starred in *Reunion in France* for MGM, and in September and October he worked in *Pittsburgh*, another Universal film with Marlene Dietrich and Randolph Scott. Both *Reunion in France* and *Pittsburgh* were released in December. In one year Wayne had made five films, all released that same year. In addition, *Lady for the Night* and *Reap the Wild Wind* had also premiered in 1942. There were few empty periods.

Like *Flying Tigers*, *Reunion in France* and *Pittsburgh* were war films. *Reunion in France*, however, was a peculiar sort of war film, the product of MGM's odd but predictable slant on life. MGM, noted Warner Bros. executive Milton Spalding, "was a studio of white telephones." Quality—or at least the illusion of quality—mattered, and studio head Louis B. Mayer spent money to obtain it. As a result at MGM nothing was what it seemed; everything was idealized. Reality never entered the MGM lot. Women especially had to look perfect. Cameramen "had to photograph the movie queens and make them look damn good," said MGM director George Cukor. If such

MGM women as Greta Garbo, Joan Crawford, Jean Harlow, Norma Shearer, Lana Turner, Greer Garson, and Myrna Loy had individual styles, they all shared a common glamour and elegance. Regardless of the role they were called on to play, they always projected beauty.[47]

After Pearl Harbor and the start of the war, Hollywood wags exchanged jokes about how the conflict would be portrayed at MGM. "The Japs may take California but they'll never get in to see Louis B. Mayer," quipped one wit. When an industry personality remarked that the United States needed a positive slogan that articulated what the country was fighting for, a less earnest listener replied, "Lana Turner." There was truth in both jokes. Louis B. Mayer called the shots at MGM, and as long as he did so, only movies that presented a highly stylized version of World War II would be made. As long as Mayer approved all projects, MGM would fight a war to make the world safe for Lana.[48]

Reunion in France created a stark glamour out of the war. The film centers on the trials and clothes of Michele de la Becque (Joan Crawford), a wealthy French socialite who loses her mansion and carefree life when the Germans invade France in 1940. With the Nazi blitzkrieg, her comfortable, insulated world is shattered. Her industrialist fiancé turns collaborationist, her wealth is confiscated, and she is forced to work for her former dressmaker—a job that pays poorly but allows her to remain the best-dressed woman in Paris. Resisting Nazi occupation, she befriends Pat Talbot (John Wayne), an American RAF Eagle Squadron flier who has been shot down and wounded behind enemy lines, and helps him escape. The film ends with Michele's reunion with her fiancé, who turns out to be a resistance fighter in collaborationist clothing. Far from helping Germany, he had been sending the Nazis faulty war matériel to foil their efforts to dominate Europe.

The BMP reacted angrily to MGM's sanitized version of the war. "If there were ever a perfect argument for OWI reading of scripts before they are shot, this picture is it," wrote BMP staffer Marjorie Thorson in her review of the film. The picture failed the war effort on a number of counts. Count one: It presented the Gestapo as "cruel, suspicious, and sadistic" but contained a *favorable* portrayal of all other Germans. The German military governor of Paris is depicted as a courtly, sweet, and charming older gentleman, an echo of the European aristocracy of decency and integrity. Furthermore, the German soldiers were disciplined and polite. Count two: It suggests that any greedy, opportunistic collaborationist may really be an upstanding, patriotic member of the French resistance. "It is a well known fact," the reviewer reported, "that many of the great French industrialists were pro-fascist long before the present war began; that they helped the Nazis conquer France; that they are now reaping the blood-stained rewards of their betrayal." Count three: It shows nothing of the misery that the Germans brought to the French people. MGM portrays a France that "falls with great elegance. Everyone we see is beautifully gowned, comfortably housed, and apparently well fed." Nazi occupation of Paris, the film insinuates, means only that the swastika hangs on the railroad stations and dumpy German women get the first crack at the latest Parisian fashions. Count four: It misses the chance to contrast Nazi and democratic ideologies. Beyond the heroine saying that democracy is not dead and will live again in France, the film fails to explore the vital issue. In the context of the film, democracy suggests only that thin French women will someday reclaim their own fashions.[49]

The serious charges led to the final verdict: *Reunion in France* "is a very poorly conceived picture. It misrepresents France, the French underground, the Nazis. Far more serious, it unintentionally gives aid and comfort to the enemy in the peace offensive that will surely, and perhaps soon, be launched." That was the crux of the matter. The OWI predicted a German peace offensive in January 1943, and it believed that *Reunion in France* would work to the Germans' benefit. At the time when the OWI was pressing the BMP to get producers to discuss the issues of the war seriously in their films, MGM suggested that the war was between fat German fraus and thin French mademoiselles, with fashion hanging neatly pressed in the balance. Reviewing the film, the OWI's Bureau of Intelligence commented, "the most striking feature of France as shown in the picture is a genius for designing and wearing women's clothes. . . . The preservation of this genius from the bad taste of the Germans is the big issue."[50]

Newspaper reviews, which were entirely uninterested in propaganda values, nonetheless agreed with the government's assessment. One review commented that Joan Crawford behaves in the film "like nobody except an MGM movie star," and the *New York Times* found Wayne "totally unconvincing as an American flyer." Most reviews agreed with the government on aesthetic grounds, noting that the war was a serious affair and should not be used as an MGM costume drama. Such criticisms, however, did not manage to kill *Reunion in France* at the box office. It was one of MGM's top fifteen grossers for 1943. And this time the film was seen as a *Wayne* movie, not a Joan Crawford or Marlene Dietrich or Claire Trevor or anyone else movie. The message in Hollywood: Even a bad Wayne film made money.[51]

Duke's last film of 1942 was his most ambitious attempt to aid the war effort. As originally planned by agent/producer Charles K. Feldman, *Pittsburgh*, like *The Spoilers*, was to be a vehicle for three of his clients—Dietrich, Wayne, and Scott. But it soon turned into a tribute to the industrial home front. Associate producer Robert Fellows worked closely with the BMP to ensure that the film conveyed the government's exact propaganda message. It focuses on the Markham-Evans Coal Company, and its heroes are industrialists and workers in the coal and steel industries. In the film Duke plays the flawed hero, Charles "Pittsburgh" Markham, a man who rose from the depths of a coal mine to the ownership of the company. In a role that he was to develop more fully in such films as *Red River*, *Hondo*, *The Sea Chase*, *The Searchers*, and *The Man Who Shot Liberty Valance*, he portrays a man obsessed, driven by his own inner demons. Pittsburgh willingly uses anything and anyone to acquire power. On his way to the top, he abandons the woman who loves him (Marlene Dietrich) and his trusted partner (Randolph Scott). But the same ruthlessness that allowed him to rise in the coal business, leads to his downfall, causing him to lose his wife, his company, and his self-worth. World War II provides a rebirth for Pittsburgh. Once again he rises from the mines to manage the company. Only this time he works for his nation, not himself. He is redeemed by submerging his own ego into America's crusade for a better world.

When Nelson Poynter and his BMP staff previewed *Pittsburgh* at Universal Studios on December 1, 1942, they were delighted. The picture was a preachy epic of coal and steel that appealed to the BMP's wordy sense of effective propaganda. It contained long semidocumentary sections of the coal and steel industries, and it rarely said anything visually that could be put into flat dialogue. But there was no mistaking its message: Every American—soldier and industrial worker alike—could and should contribute to the war effort; victory would only result if "all the people" worked and fought as one. The BMP applauded the results. "Pittsburgh succeeds in making many excellent contributions to the war information program," noted the BMP review of the film. In fact, much of the dialogue "appears to have been culled directly from the OWI Manual of Information for the picture industry." Nevertheless the picture was "highly commended for an earnest and very successful contribution." As far as the BMP was concerned, *Pittsburgh* was "one of the best pictures to emerge to date dealing with our vital production front."[52]

Poynter, who had worked closely with Bob Fellows on *Pittsburgh*, thought he had scored a real coup. Often ignored by the more important producers, Poynter actually believed that *Pittsburgh* was a good film and that his contributions to the film had been significant. As soon as he saw the final cut, he shot off a series of letters complimenting everyone involved with the movie including himself. "Magnificent. . . . It shows what can be done if the creative unit sets out to help interpret the war and at the same time put on a helluva good show," he wrote Fellows, Feldman, and several Universal executives. He wrote Lowell Mellett, his BMP superior in Washington, telling him to see *Pittsburgh* and to take other OWI and War Production Board people with him.[53]

Mellett went, but he did not share Poynter's enthusiasm. "The propaganda sticks out disturbingly," Mellett responded to Poynter. Most newspaper reviewers shared Mellett's opinion. "This business of instructing and informing intrudes at times at the expense of the entertaining," noted the *Motion Picture Herald*, but the film "yields realistic results when not hampered by dialogue freighted with purpose." From West Coast to East, the reviews were the same. *Pittsburgh* was not exactly a bad film, but it was certainly "not in the inspired class," or, more to the point, it was "routine entertainment at best." In a New York theater, a cartoon entitled *Point Rationing*, which explained the use of the new rationing book, drew a more positive review than *Pittsburgh*.[54]

The critical and financial failures of *Pittsburgh* reinforced the belief in Hollywood that if FDR and his alphabet agencies could not get America out of the depression, they certainly could not make a hit movie. The resistance against Poynter and his staff that was present in the industry from the beginning stiffened even more in the months after the release of *Pittsburgh*. Hollywood was right. The BMP was not film-literate. Both Mellett and Poynter were newspapermen who thought in terms of words. They wanted dialogue that sounded as if it had come straight off an editorial page. As far as they were concerned, if a movie did not use dialogue to present the government's message, then the message was not delivered. They had difficulty thinking visually. The major studio executives realized that the government approach toward propaganda would mean death at the box office. They were willing to make propaganda pictures that served the interests of the country, but they wanted to make them in their own way.[55]

No film better demonstrates Washington's lack of understanding of movies than *Casablanca*. The classic film ran into trouble in Washington. Various sections of the OWI were disappointed by the movie. Most were upset with Rick's (Humphrey Bogart's) cynicism. Others were dissatisfied with the treatment of the French, the Germans, and the North Africans. And the last line—"This could be the beginning of a beautiful friendship"—well—as far as the OWI was concerned, it said nothing about the Atlantic Charter or why the United Nations were fighting fascism. As film historians Clayton R. Koppes and Gregory D. Black observed, Washington "was not content to let meaning emerge from the interaction of the characters and the overall story line . . . it would have preferred a two-paragraph sermonette explaining Nazi aggression and the justice of the Allied cause."[56]

The battle between Washington and Hollywood would drag into 1943 and would last, in a more limited way, for the rest of the war. It was a war fought by studio heads and producers, not actors, and as he did with the larger war, Wayne avoided the conflict. Making the most of his opportunities, Duke worked at a frenetic pace, piling up as much money as he could, trying to secure his place in the industry and his financial future. More than most actors and actresses, he knew how fickle Hollywood could be, how quickly some stars can be eclipsed, how easy it was to wake up on Poverty Row. And military service was still a possibility. Perhaps Duke worked so hard in 1942 because, in case he did enlist, he would have enough money to support Josie and kids for the duration. Whatever the reasons, between late 1941 and the end of 1942, Duke starred in seven films: *Lady for a Night, Reap the Wild Wind, The Spoilers, In Old California, Flying Tigers, Reunion in France,* and *Pittsburgh.* He even undertook a series of twenty-six radio programs for NBC, starring as an alcoholic detective in *Three Sheets to the Wind.* But his hectic activities of 1942 had begun to undermine his health. On January 21, 1943, he collapsed on a movie set and was rushed to the hospital. Doctors told him he had influenza and needed rest. That was the bad news. The good news was that his collapse was reported in the *New York Times.* Duke was a star.[57]

10

In the Catbird Seat

John Wayne and Hollywood were in the catbird seat in 1943. For a nation of thirsty people, the film industry was an ice-cold Coca-Cola. The war had ended the depression, and the country enjoyed nearly full employment, but Americans with money in their pockets confronted a pitiless consumer nightmare. Wartime prosperity quickly devoured the nation's inventory of automobiles, tires, refrigerators, ovens, and other durable goods, and most of the steel, aluminum, and rubber needed to replenish the supplies were diverted to the war effort. Silk stockings, nylons, furs, and other luxury goods became scarce, as did beer, whiskey, chocolate, and cigarettes. Meat and sugar were also in short supply. Across the country, the slogan "Use it up, wear it out, make it do or do without" played like a stuck record. In New York City, columnist Walter Winchell lamented:

Roses are red, Violets are Blue,
Sugar is sweet. Remember?[1]

The shortages ushered in boom times for Hollywood. "Every night is Saturday night," boasted *Variety*. Ticket sales increased from slightly over fifty million each week to more than ninety million during the war. The nation's sixteen thousand theaters, with a seating capacity of 11 million, entertained nearly two-thirds of the American population each week. Domestic rentals—

the amount of money theaters in the United States and Canada paid to run films—of the major eight studios reflected the prosperity, jumping from $193 million in 1939 to $332 million in 1946. Even more impressive, the Big Eight made more money at the same time as they were producing fewer pictures: They released 338 pictures in 1939 and only 252 in 1946. One journalist noted, "The basic explanation of the movie boom is the obvious one—more people with more money to spend, and fewer things to spend it on. In addition, the strains and pressures of war work and war news are goads that drive millions into the movie theaters, where for a little while they can escape from the world of reality and relax in the comfortable darkness." The lure of the movies was so overwhelming that in towns where factories operated around the clock, movie theaters never closed their ticket booths or doors, catering to shift workers.[2]

Hollywood, like these theaters, never slept. For servicemen heading out to sea or coming back from some Pacific outpost, for defense workers from one of the huge aircraft plants—Douglas, Lockheed, North American, Northrop, and Hughes—or one of Henry Kaiser's shipyards, Hollywood was the place where people gathered, wandered the legendary streets, and looked for action. During the week civilian workers ruled the streets, but on weekends servicemen predominated. Thousands of them slept in Hollywood's theater lobbies and parks rather than return to their boats or bases. As the war lengthened, the city's residents supported the "Bed for Buddies" drive that provided a free night's lodging for men in uniform.[3]

The film industry extended a warm welcome to the troops. After Pearl Harbor the studios had closed their doors to tourists, but within a few months they reopened their lots and provided tours for servicemen with overseas records. At night men in uniform headed for the Hollywood Canteen, at 1451 Cahuenga Boulevard, where they could meet the stars. Canteen president Bette Davis made sure that a name band played every night and that servicemen got to dance with such stars as Hedy Lamarr, Betty Grable, Olivia de Havilland, or one of the 700 other "hostesses" on the canteen's list. While the female stars danced, John Wayne and other male stars, such as Spencer Tracy, Humphrey Bogart, and Walter Pidgeon, washed dishes, bused tables, or jumped onstage for an impromptu number. All the while the news cameras rolled, and the publicity photographers snapped pictures. The American public was not denied a glimpse of their favorite stars acting like just one of the folks.[4]

Wayne's busy work schedule meant that he visited the canteen less frequently than most of the stars not in uniform. On important occasions he would drop by, such as on Thanksgiving 1943, when he carved the turkeys. But Mary Ford, who worked religiously at the canteen throughout the war years, complained to her husband that Duke's work record was marginal. At a time when it was fashionable in Hollywood to join war committees—ranging from the Hollywood Victory Committee for Stage, Screen, and Radio and the Volunteer Army Canteen Service to Bundles for Bluejackets and the Civil Air Patrol—Wayne was not a joiner. He never had been. He preferred the company of his prewar friends, spending his occasional free nights drinking at the Hollywood Athletic Club and playing cards with Ward Bond and his other boon companions.[5]

For all the enjoyment the canteen provided servicemen, Hollywood and Wayne's primary contribution to the war effort was keeping the nation entertained. The business of Hollywood was making movies, and seldom did the Hollywood Canteen stints or the USO tours or the defense bond campaigns or the war rallies interfere with that business. After the shock of Pearl Harbor began to dull, Hollywood could even joke about the war. When Fox's hot-tempered production manager, Darryl F. Zanuck (John Ford said the F stood for "Fuck 'em"), was commissioned as a lieutenant colonel in the signal corps, Hollywood strategists announced: "That settles it! Hitler may have taken Poland and France—but now he's got to deal with Zanuck." And Warner Bros., whose Burbank studio was located close to the Lockheed plant, painted a twenty-foot arrow on the roof of a sound stage with the message: LOCKHEED—THATAWAY.[6]

But, jokes aside, the Hollywood that John Wayne had become accustomed to was changing. The industry's major concern during the war was whether it could continue to do business. "War," said the General Sherman of Hollywood, Samuel Goldwyn, "is L-41." In Hollywood L-41 was the economic equivalent of hell. It designated the end to the industry's heroic waste. After FDR declared war, the War Production Board told Hollywood that profligacy was no longer acceptable, that it was unpatriotic and a hindrance to the war effort. The board's L-41 rule forbade a studio to spend more than five thousand dollars on new materials for set construction on any picture. To be sure, the moguls expected some restrictions; they all agreed that the three hundred thousand dollars D. W. Griffith had spent back in 1916 to build the Babylonian set for *Intolerance* was a mite extravagant. But five thousand dollars was miserly—worse, it smacked of being un-Hollywoodian. With set costs of an average A picture running at fifty thousand dollars—of which 30 to 40 percent represented the cost of new materials—industry leaders worried about how they could stay in business, let alone make another *Gone With the Wind*.[7]

The War Production Board ordered Hollywood to use less raw film stock (unprocessed film). Cellulose, the primary component of raw stock, was needed for gunpowder, and, even more important, the government needed increased supplies of film for its own propaganda campaign. Order L-178 first froze raw stock in the hands of manufacturers and then allocated it on a controlled basis. To make do with less film, the studios produced shorter films, limited the length of advertising trailers, reduced screen credits, and ordered directors to rehearse scenes more before shooting to reduce the number of re-takes. There was even an unsuccessful attempt to end that most sacred of de-pression staples, the double feature.[8]

Other shortages similarly constrained Hollywood. Camel-hair brushes used for applying makeup were needed by the aircraft industry for dusting precision instruments; breakable bottles used in fight scenes were made of the same resin that was needed for a variety of war jobs; breakable windows were made with sugar, which was on the rationed list; breakable chairs were made of balsa, which went on the priorities list after the fall of the Philippines elim-inated the main supply; silk wigs became scarce after the government froze silk supplies. From cheesecloth and wallpaper to metals, lumber, paints, and burlap, the materials needed for set construction were either difficult or total-ly impossible to obtain. To stay in business Hollywood had to salvage and reuse nails, hoard razor blades, reduce the number of sets in a picture, do more location shooting, and employ more toy planes, submarines, and ships in combat scenes. Indeed, the dark tones of *film noir* owe as much to wartime shortages as to the somber themes of the pictures.[9]

But Hollywood muddled along, bitching all the way. There was never enough of anything to satisfy anyone. Producers complained constantly. Most leading men had gone to war. The technicians had enlisted or been drafted. The war had drained the pool of extras. The war had stolen pigments for makeup, hair for wigs, and cloth for costumes. The war had made films look cheap and sent a swarm of bureaucrats to Hollywood to plague the industry with forms and guidelines. The war, the war, the war—it was always the war that was to blame. Yet the war had also fostered a level of prosperity previous-ly unknown in the industry.

Stars complained that the war had disrupted their way of life. The night-club and restaurant scene dropped off precipitously. Ciro's, owned by the *Hol-lywood Reporter*'s editor W. R. Wilkerson, closed and reopened intermittently during the war. The Ambassador Hotel's Coconut Grove, the night spot with a wild interior of palm trees and stuffed monkeys with electrically lit eyes, opened only for Friday- and Saturday-night trade. Big spending and ostentatious displays lacked patriotism. For John Wayne and the other stars left in Hollywood, nightlife became even more intensely private than it had been before the war.[10]

The war also curtailed daylight pastimes. The U.S. Coast Guard commandeered the great Hollywood yachts. John Ford's *Araner*—the heart of the "Young Men's Purity Total Abstinence and Yachting Association"—was transformed into an antisubmarine patrol vessel during the last two years of the war, and it prowled the waters off the coast of California rather than cruising to Catalina. To make matters worse, for part of the war the government closed the Santa Anita, Hollywood Park, and (farther down the coast) Del Mar racetracks. For an industry obsessed with gambling, one where luck seemed the very *deus ex machina* that made and destroyed careers, the sight of thoroughbreds running aimlessly around the Santa Anita track just for exercise was a chilling experience. As one journalist wrote after the first raceless season, "It has been a bleak winter for people in the studios, who are forced to make wagers on strange horses in Miami and have been deprived of their chief pleasure in life."[11]

It was a rich person's nightmare. The situation amounted to a "Hollywood Holocaust," noted one insider, with typical abusive hyberbole. Japanese gardeners were in Rocky Mountain internment camps. Chauffeurs and butlers were either in uniform or working at Lockheed, Hughes, Douglas, or one of the other aircraft plants. Even the female servants were gone: "Defense plants have taken them in thousands. Cooks are running drill presses at Douglas or North American; second maids have become riveters." One advertisement announced: "Maid wanted; will pay Lockheed wages." Without the servants the mansions of Hollywood's elite were no longer so comfortable and polished, their grounds no longer so manicured.[12]

The domestic war against the automobile, however, was Hollywood's greatest concern. Cars were as much a part of life in Southern California as the sun and surf. Nobody who was anybody in Hollywood lived close to anybody or anything of importance. Public transportation was anemic, and walking was a breach of station. Highways were the arteries of life. Gas rationing and the shortage of rubber for tires posed a grave threat for the elite, especially the ones who lived in the canyons. "Why, this gas rationing. It's—it's worse than being bombed!" a famous actress told reporter Kyle Crichton. "Four gallons of gas a week for a Hollywood movie worker means precisely as much as a pint of water a month for a Marine on Guadalcanal. People living up in the canyons of Beverly Hills might as well be on a raft in the Pacific. There is no bus service; there are no stores for miles; there is no delivery service—nothing but cliffs, crags and nightly fog. . . . They wanted to be different and now they are not only different but stranded," Crichton wrote.[13]

With the specter of no gas and flat tires, with talk of a salary cap for the richest Americans, with butlers gone to war and maids to Lockheed, with restaurants and racetracks closed, with shortages at every turn, Hollywood limped into 1943.

While industry leaders bemoaned their circumstances, John Wayne continued to make films and refused to complain about shortages or the lack of entertainment opportunities. It helped that his home on Highland Avenue was only a short drive from Republic Pictures and Universal Studios, and that his gambling centered on poker, not ponies. The loss of John Ford and several other close friends to the army and navy and the *Araner* to the Coast Guard diminished his social outlets, but Ward Bond, an epileptic 4-F, remained in Hollywood. And Bond, as always, was a one-man social event. As long as he was around, Duke knew where to go for a drink and a laugh.[14]

Work, not play, dominated his life at the beginning of 1943. The bout with influenza had disrupted his schedule. In the early spring, before he was fully recovered, he made *A Lady Takes a Chance* for RKO, a comedy with Jean Arthur that followed the same pattern as *It Happened One Night*. Rather than dwell on war and scarcity, *A Lady Takes a Chance* is set in 1938, long before Americans began to ration sugar and plant victory gardens. Recalling the halcyon days before the Japanese attack on Pearl Harbor "when people drove sixty miles an hour, drank three cups of coffee at a time, and ate big gobs of butter," the film follows *New Yorker* Mollie Truesdale's (Jean Arthur) trip to the West, where she meets and falls in love with rodeo star Duke Hudkins (John Wayne). The two share several awkward nights, Mollie demonstrates her hitchhiking abilities, and Hudkins gradually surrenders his freedom for marriage. The film revolves around the classic American film theme of commitment. Hudkins finds the specter of married life frightening and the loss of his horse, tumbleweed behavior, and male sidekick unacceptable. In one scene he flees Mollie in terror when he catches a glimpse in the mirror of himself wearing an apron. But in the end, he travels to New York to "claim" his woman, whom he promptly takes back to the West.[15]

The top pictures of 1943—*For Whom the Bell Tolls, Song of Bernadette, Random Harvest, Madame Curie, This Is the Army, Stage Door Canteen,* and *Hitler's Children*—were either uplifting celebrations of America and military life or somber tragedies. *A Lady Takes a Chance* was an airy, well-written and -acted, low-budget comedy—"a plain, ordinary good time," noted the *New York Times*. Arthur's "uncloying coyness" and Wayne's fine performance—one praised by James Agee, America's leading critic—made the film RKO's third leading grosser for 1943. It also showcased Wayne's maturing sense of comedic timing. As he had demonstrated in *The Spoilers*, he could do more than simply look good and fight. He could deliver believable comedy dialogue, and, matched with Jean Arthur, whose touch was far lighter than Dietrich's, Wayne excelled.[16]

The success of *A Lady Takes a Chance* indicated that after a year and a half of serious films, the nation was beginning to tire of moral rectitude. The change in America's mood that registered in the films of 1944 and 1945 actually began in mid-1943 in Washington. A conservative Congress began to eat away at the edges of President Roosevelt's domestic programs. Believing that the president was using the OWI to distribute pro-Roosevelt propaganda, Congress gutted the OWI budget by almost 75 percent, providing enough money to avoid, said OWI director Elmer Davis, "the odium of having put us out of business and carefully not enough to let us accomplish much." Both Lowell Mellett and Nelson Poynter of the OWI's BMP resigned.[17]

Washington set the tone for the rest of the nation. In New York a young band singer with a punctured eardrum and a 4-F deferment shattered a fifteen-year attendance record at the Paramount Theatre during an eight-week engagement. During one performance a girl in the twelfth row fainted—the press said "swooned"—causing another to stand up and scream. Frank Sinatra, who had confronted more daunting obstacles in his rise from a cold-water Hoboken tenement, kept singing, even as the number of standing and screaming females increased. Journalists dubbed Sinatra "the Voice," "Frank Swoonatra," "the King of Swoon"—and an epidemic of screaming followed him from the Paramount Theatre, to his next engagement at the exclusive Waldorf-Astoria, and then across the country. With American soldiers fighting and dying from Italy to New Guinea, American bobby-soxers concentrated their emotions on a paper-thin crooner in a bow tie. Observing the irony, historian William Manchester wrote: "The hero of the hour was supposed to be a strapping, steel-helmeted GI in full battle array, leaping through surf to storm an enemy shore. Frankie . . . looked as though he had been strained through a condom."[18]

Signs of restlessness surfaced. Americans weary of rationing, shortages, victory gardens, and car pools turned to the black market for relief. Illegal marketing of commodities soared in the summer of 1943. The country was flooded by counterfeit gas ration coupons—especially the generous C coupons—and travel vouchers, black-market beef, alcohol, rayon, and other commodities. Although enforcement officials complained about the activity and Gallup polls indicated that a majority of Americans did not patronize the black market, the police and courts generally winked at the violations. Few black marketeers were arrested, and even those who were convicted usually received light fines rather than prison sentences.[19]

Clothes reflected the changing social climate. In an attempt to save cloth, many men abandoned vests, wide lapels, and a second pair of suit pants. But black and Hispanic males defied conservation and popularized the zoot suit, an outfit that featured a wide-lapeled, knee-length suit coat and loose-fitting, pegged pants. It was an ideal outfit for doing the jitterbug, but the excessive cloth in the balloon pants and long jackets seemed to mock the country's war effort, enraging sailors on leave in Los Angeles or New York. On a hot June night in 1943, a band of some three thousand whites, led by sailors, attacked zoot-suited Hispanics in downtown Los Angeles. When Hispanics responded in kind, police arrested them, and one newspaper ran the headline: ZOOTERS THREATEN L.A. POLICE.

Fashion in Hollywood moved toward "patriotic chic." Women conserved cloth by exposing more flesh. Bare shoulders, backless dresses, plunging necklines, short skirts, and two-piece bathing suits became the rage. If fashion made a political statement, it also carried a social message. Millions of women on the home front were no longer willing to drape themselves in frumpish clothes and wait by the hearth for their men to return. Like the "Victory girls" who crowded near the gates of military posts, women were also asserting their sexuality, a trend that contributed to rising divorce, prostitution, and venereal disease rates.[20]

John Wayne, like millions of other Americans, backed off the hectic pace he had maintained in 1942. In the first ten months of the war, he starred in five pictures. During the remaining years of the war, he starred in just seven more. His personal life occupied more of his time. He drank, played cards, and took trips with Ward Bond and several other friends. But, more important, he developed close relationships with Bo Roos and Esperanza Baur. The first relationship would cost him millions of dollars. The price tag on the other was his marriage.

Bo (pronounced Boo) Christian Roos, observed one person who knew him well, "was the sort of man that once you shook his hand you wanted to take a shower." With his hair slicked straight back, his pencil-thin Errol Flynn mustache, his mouth full of straight white teeth, and his perfect tan, Roos was pure Hollywood. He was groomed to please, quick to smile and make a new friend. From the mid-1930s until the 1960s, he was one of Hollywood's leading business managers. When it came to handling the money of the top talent in Hollywood, five men—Roos, Morgan Maree, Noel Singer, Myrt Blum, and Charles Goldring—controlled ninety percent of the action. They were not agents, they were accountants and investors, but they were far more powerful than either label suggests. Each handled about forty accounts, taking five percent off their clients' gross income for the financial protection and investment and tax advice they offered. Damned by some stars as smooth operators and praised by others for the same slick practices, business managers lived in the worlds of both show business and finance. As middlemen operating outside the studio system, they acquired considerable power and influence, but their reputations suffered from the occasions when a member of the brotherhood would abscond with his clients' money. Certainly even some of his own clients did not trust the husky, blue-eyed, cigar-smoking Roos.[21]

An air of European aristocracy surrounded Roos—perhaps because of his name, or the rumors that his wife was from the nobility. But Bo was neither European nor aristocratic. He was born in 1903, the son of a Swedish engineer who had immigrated to Southern California in search of work. His father died when Bo was five, leaving his wife and four children strapped for money. Bo dropped out of school at age fifteen and took a job as a secretary to help support his family. In 1922 he married Gladys L. "Billie" Holmes, daughter of a wealthy contractor. The marriage was Bo's first inspired financial move. Entering his father in law's construction business, he was in the right job at the right time in the right place. He made a small fortune in the mid-1920s real estate and development boom in Southern California. By the age of twenty-four he was rich enough to get out of the construction business and gamble on another career.[22]

Too young to retire and too bored to continue in construction, he searched for another profession, one that promised excitement as well as money. When his accountant suggested that he consider becoming a business manager for Hollywood's new millionaires, Bo immediately entered the developing field. Since most Hollywood celebrities had only the vaguest idea of what a business manager should do, Roos had little difficulty persuading stars to become his clients. The business of Hollywood was illusion; the industry trafficked in deception, surface appearances, and lies. In Hollywood, persona took precedent over personality. Frequently greatness was the result of convincing others of one's greatness. Bo wore expensive suits, and, along with a portable tape recorder, his car was equipped with one of the West Coast's first mobile phones. He was a complete package—more than enough to convince leading actors, actresses, directors, and writers that he could manage their money. By the mid-1940s his Beverly Management Corporation's list of thirty clients included some of the biggest names in the industry—Marlene Dietrich, Joan Crawford, Merle Oberon, George Brent, Red Skelton, Johnny Weissmuller, Fred MacMurray, Lloyd Nolan, Ward Bond, Patric Knowles, Ray Milland, and the Andrews sisters.[23]

Wayne and Roos had known each other socially long before Bo took over the management of Duke's money—in fact, years before Duke had any money to manage. Roos, a fringe member of the Young Men's Purity Total Abstinence and Yachting Association and a regular at the Hollywood Athletic Club, moved in the same circle as Wayne. Although Roos did not go on the Mexican cruises with Wayne, Ford, Bond, and Fonda, he did attend the association's formal drinking occasions, and he had visited Mexico often enough to swap stories about Mexican jails and prostitutes. In early 1941, as Wayne approached stardom, Marlene Dietrich convinced him that he needed someone to manage his money. She suggested Roos, her business manager. Always fearing a return to poverty, and never very good with money, Wayne saw the need for a manager and signed on with Roos. In Roos he saw a kindred spirit, a man who loved to drink, play cards, hunt, and fish, a man with whom he could share a drink and a story. All the better that this man could also provide him with financial security and perhaps even make him rich.[24]

But the first order of business between Bo and Duke was pleasure. Most Hollywood celebrities—and Roos was certainly one—needed time away from the insecurities and pressures engendered by the spotlight. Some fled to the mountains or desert, others to a home in Connecticut or an apartment in New York. Mexico City and Acapulco were Roos's favored retreats. He believed that Mexico was the last frontier of both American capitalism and the American libido. He liked to go there with clients so that he could pay for his trip from their accounts. In August 1941 Roos and a few of his clients—Ray Milland, Fred MacMurray, and Ward Bond—traveled to Mexico City to appraise several investment opportunities and to sample the nightlife. Wayne, exhausted from his work in *Reap the Wild Wind*, went along.[25]

Holed up in Mexico City's exclusive Del Prado, Team Roos relaxed in style, drinking day and night. Wayne and Milland had been friendly since the mid-1930s, and their wives were particularly close. During the shooting of *Reap the Wild Wind* they had developed a warm working relationship. In Mexico City they spent even more time together. One night, Milland introduced Wayne to Esperanza Baur Diaz Ceballos. She was Milland's "Mexican woman," his escort and lover when he was in town. Once she met Wayne, however, Milland became yesterday's gringo, and the friendship between the two actors abruptly ended. After the trip Wayne and Milland did not work, socialize, or even talk together. Only more than a quarter of a century later did Milland break their years of silence. Then, after Wayne won his Academy Award for *True Grit*, Milland sent him a warm, conciliatory congratulation letter. By then the fires of Mexico City had destroyed a friendship, a marriage, and a person had grown cold.[26]

Everyone called Esperanza Baur *Chata*, a Spanish word that translates into "pugnose" but that in Mexico more often means "cutie" or "sweetie." She was beautiful, captivating, and mysterious. Her beauty was warm and irregular, the product more of an inner vitality than physical perfection. She was tall and thin, almost gangly, with long arms and legs. Her eyes and hair were dark, but she was far from the ideal of a dark, Latin beauty. Her mother was of French descent, and that blood dominated her features. Her face was long, rather than round, and she had a poor complexion which she covered with thick makeup. When she smiled, however, her imperfections vanished. Her smile attracted men; it made them laugh and aroused desire. Mary St. John described Chata in a phrase borrowed from Rudyard Kipling: "In every man's life there is always a woman whom other women don't understand. Chata was that woman in Duke's life."[27]

Chata's life before 1941 is a mystery. She was never accepted in Hollywood, and rumors circulated that at the time she met Wayne, she was working as a high-priced call girl and a bit actress in the Mexican film industry. Pilar Wayne later wrote that Chata was born in the slums of Mexico City and became a prostitute to escape poverty. Others said that when Chata and Duke met she was married to a Mexican student named Eugenio Morrison. After she married Wayne, a leading fan magazine commented that Chata was a Mexican film star in 1941. Two things are certain: She was not a leading Mexican actress, and she was involved with Milland. The rest is lost.[28]

They met at a party thrown for Roos and his stars by Mexican movie people. Before he was introduced to Chata, Duke was bored and restless, but that ended with their first conversation. He was enchanted by her. She was taken by his manners. While Milland treated her like a prostitute, Wayne was courteous and kind. Chata's past was unimportant. It was like the Ringo Kid courting Dallas. A romantic all his life, Wayne saw in women what he wanted to see. He constantly put them on pedestals of nobility and virtue. And his was a world in which prostitutes often embodied goodness, in which pasts did not necessarily impinge upon futures. Over the next several days, he fell in love with her. (More than a decade later, when he and Chata were fighting bitterly, Wayne still believed that she was "the love of [his] life.") When he left Mexico, he did not forget her.[29]

They met several times during the next two years. Either he took short trips to Mexico City or they rendezvoused in Yuma, Arizona. What he felt for her was different from his feelings for Marlene Dietrich or the other women with whom he had flings. And Chata offered Wayne something that Josie could never give—freedom and pleasure. Her joy in life seemed pure and uncomplicated. The scars of her past were invisible in the early 1940s, and she had a total lack of pretense. Only twenty when she met Duke, Chata viewed Hollywood and movies as a child did, full of wonder and enthralled by the magic. She loved to talk about movies and to listen to Wayne discuss his profession. Of course, she was sensual and beautiful, but Hollywood was awash in sensuousness and beauty. Chata's attraction was her basic innocence.[30]

The contrast with Josie was stark. Chata was light and airy, Josie moored securely to the ground. Josie had little interest in Duke's world of make-believe. She offered commitment and stability, not freedom and pleasure. Her life centered on her family, her religion, and "respectable" Los Angeles society. Although Wayne loved his four children, he chafed at Josie's commitment to the Catholic Church and high society. After early morning calls and long days on the set, he hated the idea of returning home, putting on formal clothes, and attending a party or social function crowded with people with whom he had nothing in common. He seldom even attempted to conceal his feelings, gaining a reputation for sulking, silent rudeness. "He'd silently wander around parties," one person remembered, "looking sleepy, unhappy, and, oh, so bored."[31]

The social occasions meant not only L.A. benefactors but also priests. Josie, along with Loretta Young, Dolores Hope, and Irene Dunne, was one of Los Angeles's leading benefactresses of Catholic charities. No party she hosted or function she attended was without priests. "I was up to my ass in Catholics," Wayne later privately confided to a friend. Increasingly he viewed the church and the priests as rivals. In his marriage to Josie, as in his future marriages, he expected to play the leading role; he brooked no rivals. He expected his concerns to be Josie's concerns, his interests to be hers. As in his future marriages, he was not particularly interested in compromise. While Josie occupied her time with family, church, and charities, he drifted out of her orbit.[32]

During the late 1930s and the early 1940s, Wayne spent less and less time at his and Josie's Highland Avenue home. After a day on location or at the studio, he would get together with Ward Bond, Grant Withers, Beverly Barnett, or one of his other friends and drink. Dissatisfied with both his career and his marriage, he would drink until he was drunk, sleeping at the Hollywood Athletic Club or at a friend's. After his career began to rise, his mood lightened, but his marriage continued to deteriorate, and he continued to drink and stay away.[33]

In the spring of 1943 Chata moved to Hollywood. To keep the tabloids quiet, Republic put Chata under contract, describing her as a budding young star. Late in 1942 the studio secured a visa for her and then legal residence papers, and her contract paid $150 a week. During the next ten years, Republic paid Chata more than $80,000 without ever giving her a film role. Duke was no longer content to remain in an empty marriage, no longer willing to drink with his friends at night and see his children on Sundays. He wanted a fresh start, including a new wife, new home, and even another family. By that summer he had moved out of his home and had taken rooms at the legendary Chateau Marmont hotel on Sunset Boulevard. Making no secret of his relationship with Chata, he asked Josie for a divorce.[34]

Divorce raised a number of thorny issues. To begin with Josie's Catholicism was deeply held. In the fashion of a B Western, Hollywood's Catholic community circled the wagons around Josie. The Catholic wives of Hollywood stars tacitly accepted their husbands' occasional affairs, but they refused to allow the affairs to destroy their marriages. Rumors—and often strong evidence—constantly linked Ray Milland, John Ford, and Bob Hope with other women, but they stayed married. John Ford, for example, had a serious affair with Katharine Hepburn in 1936, but it did not lead to a divorce. Ford's grandson Dan noted, "Mary seemed to have given John a free rein to indulge in extramarital affairs—her only stipulations being, first, that she wasn't to know about them, and second, that they were not to become public knowledge." And Bob Hope was said to be famous in Hollywood for his affairs. He allegedly gave out so many mink coats to lovers that at one point in the 1930s Hollywood starlets fretted about wearing their own minks because they were afraid everyone would assume that they were sleeping with Hope.[35]

Even when Duke's affair with Chata did become public, Mary Ford, Dolores Hope, and Barbara Milland advised Josie not to grant the divorce. Given Wayne's close friendship with her husband, Mary Ford struggled the hardest to keep the Waynes together. She had a reputation as a good-natured but strict moralist. As the head of the female volunteers at the Hollywood Canteen, she was ever vigilant against any impropriety. The iron rule of the canteen was that a volunteer's relationship with a serviceman ended at the canteen's door: No dating. No liaisons that would tarnish the canteen's reputation. Furthermore Mary had a strong sense of duty. Several of her uncles and cousins had gone to Annapolis or West Point, and her husband and only son were in the navy during the war. That Wayne should be so self-absorbed at a time when the world was at war and so many were sacrificing so much was intolerable to her.[36]

Once it became clear that Wayne wanted a divorce, Mary wrote her husband, asking him:

> Can't you write and try to beat something into Duke's head. . . . He has gone completely berserk over that Esperanza Bauer [*sic*] and cares for no one. Thinks he is the hottest bet in pictures and says he is madly in love and nothing else matters. It's a damn shame that with a war going on he has to think about his lousy stinking tail. I only think of those gorgeous kids. It's really tragic.

Toward the end of her letter she again implored Ford to write "that big Western Star," adding that one of her friends believed that Wayne was "too stupid and conceited to save."[37]

It was not the sort of assignment that Ford relished. He was probably closer to Duke than any other man, but their friendship was based on shared experiences and mutual interests, not moral instructions. Both were uncomfortable talking about their deepest feelings; neither put much stock in private or public confessions. There were certain things, both believed, that men simply did not talk about. When Ford finally wrote Wayne, he couched his advice in vague phrases. He suggested that Duke was too busy "playing with Mexican jumping beans" to write, and that—for no specifically stated reason—Wayne was a "damn fool." Ford's counsel failed to sway Wayne. His marriage was over, he wrote to Ford, and he did not "give a four letter word, if I can see my kids." What was more, he had had enough of "the local board of busy bodies."[38]

Of Josie's close friends, only Loretta Young advised her to give Wayne the divorce. More than her other Catholic friends, Young believed that she understood the hopelessness of the Wayne marriage. In 1930 she had married Grant Withers, a man who became one of Duke's closest friends. During the late 1920s Withers was one of Hollywood's most promising leading men, a matinee idol, tall, handsome, and dashing. Loretta starred with Withers in *The Second-Floor Mystery* when she was only sixteen, fell in love, and eloped to Yuma with him the following year. From the first it was an unfortunate marriage. The charming Withers was twenty-five, divorced, irresponsible, and a heavy drinker. Unlike the normally staid and dependable Loretta, he passed bad checks, refused to pay bills, and generally acted as if he were life's only child. In a year of marriage, he was sued several times, arrested several more, and dumped by Warner Bros. In 1931 Loretta divorced him, and the next year he declared bankruptcy. The marriage was a mistake, and Loretta Young's most intelligent decision was the divorce. Although Wayne was not as bad as Withers, "the Steel Butterfly"—Withers's description of Loretta—nevertheless felt that Josie would be better off without him.[39]

Wayne also had reason to consider the Withers-Young debacle. Loretta was known in the fan magazines as the "baby star," and her messy relationship with Withers created a sensation. It was a Hollywood soap opera, replete with an elopement, an attempt by her mother to force an annulment, and an unhappy ending. The scandal it caused crippled Withers's career and threatened Loretta's. It was difficult to play the virgin when the papers were dragging her through the gutter.

Wayne faced a similar dilemma. Image determined a star's value. After the Fatty Arbuckle rape scandal in the early 1920s, the studios instituted formal rules and mechanisms to protect their own images as well as those of their stars and the industry. The centerpiece of this protective shield was the morals clause of the standard studio contract. It read:

> The artist agrees to conduct himself with due regard to public convention and morals and agrees that he will not do or commit any act or thing that will tend to degrade him in public or bring him into public hatred, contempt, scorn or ridicule, or that will tend to shock, insult or offend the community or ridicule public morals or decency or prejudice the product or the motion picture industry in general.

Violation of the morals clause could, and often did, lead to a swift end of a career.[40]

The public and the interpreters of the morals clause judged behavior on a sliding scale. Some stars could get away with more than others. It was expected that urbane, sophisticated actors and actresses would lead urbane, sophisticated lives. Errol Flynn's and Jean Harlow's careers, for instance, were almost scandal-proof. And European stars were judged more leniently than their wholesome American counterparts. Wayne, however, was particularly sensitive to attack. As the classic American hero, he projected an image of the hard, moral man, tough as chaps leather on the outside but unapproachably decent and considerate on the inside. The hard, moral man did not avoid just wars, and certainly he did not leave his wife and four young children and take up with a Mexican prostitute. Leaving Josie for Chata, Wayne risked more than his marriage.

Of course, studios had more to gain by protecting their leading stars than by hounding them out of Hollywood for the slightest infraction of the morals clause. The clause was concerned primarily with "public" exposure that created scandals and degraded the industry. Studio officials did not care what their stars did in private. They were only concerned when one of their leading men was *publicly* caught in bed with a dead woman or a live boy. If at all possible, they preferred to remove the body and tidy up the mess before the police arrived and the cameras flashed. Damage control was the studios' primary motive. Each studio had a publicity director whose job it was to control the flow of information by lobbing sops to the fan magazines and newspapers and by suppressing damaging news. Perhaps the best in the industry was MGM's publicity director, Howard Strickling, known to every cop, gambler, drug pusher, and madame in Hollywood as "the Fixer." "Mild, meek and unassuming," noted one member of the MGM family, Strickling

> held down the lid on sin: his was the voice that muted the scandals and quieted the gossip nobody was supposed to hear. It was 'business as usual' with him to defuse the rumors of domestic mayhem between married stars, fix drunk-driving raps that piled up against studio workers every weekend, handle the tempers that snapped when newspaper photographers caught personnel in places where they were never supposed to be.

Gossips speculated that Strickland's greatest cover-up involved the death of Paul Bern, an MGM producer and husband of Jean Harlow. Strickland got into the house before the police arrived, making what was rumored to be a murder appear to be a suicide.[41]

If the Fixer could cover up the murder of an MGM producer to protect Jean Harlow, Herbert Yates's Republic Pictures team could put the best face on Wayne's marital problems. The studio director had more than a passing interest in the potential scandal. John Wayne had emerged as Republic's biggest single star and moneymaker. Recognizing the fact, Charles Feldman had demanded a new contract for Duke, which raised his salary considerably and gave him more room to make money outside Republic. Under one option of his 1938 contract, he had been earning $807.69 per week, plus a small fortune for Republic on loan-outs. Fearing that if he did not renegotiate Duke's contract, he would lose him to another studio when it expired, Yates agreed to new terms. Duke's May 3, 1943, five-picture deal called for him to be paid on a per-film basis, starting at $3,125 a week and escalating in later pictures. Even with the raise, however, Yates still stood to make millions off Wayne, but only if the actor remained popular. By that spring the Republic boss was looking for ways to keep his star's messy personal life out of the newspapers.[42]

Yates's solution involved two simple steps: First he gave Chata a screen test and placed her under contract. Although she never appeared in a Republic film, it was not Yates's object to make her an actress. The screen test and contract simply gave her a legitimate reason for being in Hollywood in the company of John Wayne. With Wayne and Chata both contracted to Republic, the studio's publicity director could easily explain away any sensitive questions about their relationship.[43]

The second step in keeping Duke relatively scandal-free was to put him back to work and get him out of Hollywood. Even Wayne must have sensed that he needed to escape town. It had been more than three months since he had worked on a picture, and his civilian status was once again making him uneasy. In the spring of 1943, Catalina Lawrence typed a letter in which Duke inquired about openings in John Ford's Field Photographic Unit. A navy official replied in May that although the navy and marine allotment for Ford's outfit was full, there was room for Duke to enlist in the Field Photographic Unit under the army's allotment. Duke acquired the necessary enlistment forms and even began to fill them out, but before he could complete them Republic sent him to Parreah, Utah, to star in *In Old Oklahoma*. "Fifty miles of dust from Kanab, Utah," Parreah seemed on a different planet than Hollywood. Located in the high-plateau, red-dirt area of southern Utah, there were more national parks than people in the region. It was in the heart of nowhere—"hell," Wayne wrote Ford, "the Indians won't take it back." In the letter Duke also told Ford about his enlistment plans, promising to be ready to serve sometime in October 1943, when shooting for *In Old Oklahoma* was complete.[44]

He left behind a Hollywood in heat. It was the season of sexual scandal, as careers went on the chopping block. Hollywood's steamy 1943 had started as 1942 had ended—with the eyes of the nation focused on the Errol Flynn rape trial. Flynn was charged with two counts of statutory rape, one involving seventeen-year-old Betty Hansen and the other fifteen-year-old Peggy LaRue Satterlee. It was a circus trial, brimming with lurid accounts of Flynn's sexual exploits, and in early 1943 he was found "innocent," a particularly ironic judgment given his hedonistic lifestyle. Americans were still talking about being "in like Flynn" when Charlie Chaplin, the Great Dictator and the Little Tramp, went to court. Chaplin was fighting federal charges that he had violated the Mann Act by bringing a woman across state lines for immoral purposes, and a paternity suit brought against him by Joan Berry. Chaplin won the first case but lost the second, and both trials injured his career. And when, later that year, the fifty-four-year-old Chaplin married eighteen-year-old Oona O'Neill, his reputation took a further slide. Hollywood, critics charged, was sex mad, and the release of such movies as *The Outlaw*, featuring Jane Russell's cleavage, and *Double Indemnity*, featuring an adulterous affair between the two leads and the murder of the heroine's husband, only seemed to confirm the allegations.[45]

The heat and dust of Utah were better for Wayne's career in mid-1943 than the heat and dirt of Hollywood. And *In Old Oklahoma* enhanced Duke's public image of the hard moral man. In the film he plays Dan Somers, a former sergeant in the U.S. Army who was the first American to reach the top of San Juan Hill and who continued to fight for his country in the Philippines after the Spanish-American War. Domestic rather than military battles provide the driving force of the film. Somers battles rival Jim "Hunk" Gardner (Albert Dekker) for both the love of Catherine Allen (Martha Scott) and the oil under the land near Sapulpa, Oklahoma. In the first half of the film, Somers is only concerned with his fight for Catherine and seeks to avoid any larger commitments. When Gardner ruthlessly drives the smaller oilmen out of business and they appeal to Somers for help, Dan refuses, commenting: "It ain't my money and it ain't my oil land." Only after Hunk slugs Dan does it become his fight. Then he agrees to champion the "little fellers" by going to Washington for them and attempting to win a lease to drill for oil on Indian land. Hunk, who has the support of the Bureau of Indian Affairs, seeks to cheat the Indians out of the profits from the oil. Dan argues for a "square deal" for the Indians and the wildcatters. For the "little fellers," he asks only for "a chance to take a chance." Seeing in his plea the essence of American democracy and capitalism, President Theodore Roosevelt grants the lease to Somers's group. Although Hunk continues to attempt to thwart the wildcatters' efforts by destroying their equipment and monopolizing the only pipeline, in the end the "little fellers" prevail. The film ends with a peaceful resolution: Hunk decides to stop fighting Dan and join forces with him. Everyone wins—the big entrepreneur, the small entrepreneurs, and the budding Indian entrepreneurs.

Although the film seemed a harmless traditional Western, the BMP believed that it was littered with ideological land mines. When the BMP read the script in March—before Congress slashed the OWI's budget and Lowell Mellet and Nelson Poynter left the BMP—it warned Republic that despite the project's "excellent potential," problems existed. In terms of domestic and overseas distribution, the most serious problem was the presentation of American Indians. The bureau did not want to paper over the government's ill treatment of Indians—just the opposite. Reviewing the script, BMP staffer Peg Fenwick noted, "There is never any repudiation of [the white man's] unjust treatment of the Indians." She believed that a film faithful to the submitted script would incite disunity in the country at a time when cooperation between all Americans—white, red, and black—was essential. It has been well documented that the war did much to advance the civil rights of African Americans, since many whites realized that blacks could not be asked to fight for freedom abroad without enjoying it at home. Here, however, was a case of the war doing something to advance whites' self-admitted guilt for the Indians' plight. And the problem was exacerbated by one of the script's leading characters, the Cherokee Kid, a "brutal, treacherous and disloyal" half-breed.

Added to the unfair portrayal of Indians, the ideological thrust of the script also troubled the BMP. Dan Somers occasionally uses illegal means to achieve his moral ends, Hunk Gardner is never punished for his ruthless economic behavior, democracy is defined simply as "a chance to take a chance," and the American people "are presented as money-mad, fawning on Hunk who can help them achieve wealth, sacrificing every real value in their mad scramble to get rich."[46]

A BMP official observed:

> At a time when we are fighting for equal rights for all men, this type of presentation of an American minority, which suggests that Americans as a whole are completely indifferent to the plight of one of their minorities, can only serve to arouse antagonism and resentment among other races throughout the world. Furthermore, it unwittingly confirms the Nazi propaganda contention that Americans condemn the fascists for ill-treatment of minorities while practicing the same things ourselves.

In addition the script's portrayal of Americans as greedy "only serves to confirm the Nazi world propaganda line that Americans are only interested in making money . . . [and] plays into the hands of the enemy." The script reviewer asks, "Is this the picture we want to give other peoples of the world of the American heritage? At a time when people in other countries are eager to learn more of America, its history, and its way of life, this type of presentation does nothing to contribute to their confidence in our ability to participate in the creation of a better world."[47]

Republic followed most of the BMP's recommendations, ignored a few, and made a successful film. *In Old Oklahoma* was Republic's only picture to break into the top grossers list for 1943. The government was particularly pleased, calling it "an excellent example of successful cooperation" between government and studio. The film also generally pleased the reviewers. Although the *New York Times* critic complained that the film changed the landscape of eastern Oklahoma by giving the region "desert arroyos and high eroded mountains," and that it was "full of stale phrases about up-and-coming tycoons and their greedy dreams of empire," he liked Wayne's performance and many of the film's action scenes. The *Hollywood Reporter* could find no fault with the film: "a picture that cannot fail. . . . It has no aim except entertainment and that it hits with uncanny accuracy. . . . it is an almost perfect example of good motion picture technique and craftsmanship."[48]

Wayne was singled out for his performance in the film. One reviewer commented that he had "never [been] better. . . . It is hard to believe that there is anything studied about the performance, it rings so beautifully with sincerity." The reviewer noted Duke's adroit use of his "quiet eyes, winning grin [and] expressive hands" in achieving the desired effect. This was the Wayne Republic wanted America to see and hear about: sincere, truthful, manly.[49]

In early August Wayne returned to Hollywood from Utah determined to bring his personal life more into line with his screen persona. He was weary of fantasy, tired of playing a hero in the movies while other men fought in a real war. He finished and mailed the enlistment form he had begun before going to Utah. But Republic was already lining him up to star in another film—*The Fighting Seabees*. Duke loved the script and knew it was going to be a winner, so he postponed enlisting again. He let Republic file another draft deferment request for him, and told Ford that he needed one more "fling before going off to battle."[50]

But before that time he would fight once again in Hollywood's version of World War II. Shooting began in mid-September for *The Fighting Seabees*, a film dramatizing the work of the Construction Battalion of the U.S. Navy. It was a safe film for Republic to make. The shake-up in the Office of War Information had made Hollywood producers cautious. When Mellett and Poynter left the BMP after Congress cut the OWI's budget, power shifted from the Domestic Branch of the BMP to the Overseas Branch. Headed by Ulrich Bell, a hard-nosed former Washington bureau chief for the *Louisville Courier-Journal*, the Overseas Branch of the BMP determined which films were distributed outside the United States. Bell was aggressive and opinionated, better at political infighting than either Mellett or Poynter. Not nearly so liberal as the other BMP leaders, he believed that no film should show "the sordid side of American life." He opposed any dramatization of class, race, or labor conflict, and he absolutely condemned any movies that showed lawlessness. He felt so strongly about this last point that he initiated a crusade against the gangster film. Realizing that he would need help, and understanding that the only true leverage in Hollywood was the dollar, he enlisted the support of the Office of Censorship. By the summer of 1943 his office had become the "advance guard of the Office of Censorship." In effect, he determined which films got export licenses.[51]

Exports and profits were interchangeable in Hollywood. Most pictures were lucky to recover production costs in their domestic run. Studios depended on foreign distribution for their profits. Canada, Mexico, Central America, South America, and Great Britain were hungry for American movies. And as Allied forces rolled back the German and Japanese frontiers, old markets were reopened for Hollywood's product. As the *Motion Picture Herald* asserted in August 1943, it makes "dollar-and-cents sense for producers to shoot at the greater and growing market." The road to the lucrative foreign markets started in Bell's office. To obtain an export license, Hollywood had to follow his rules.[52]

Republic was especially concerned during the first weeks after the change of the BMP's guard. Bell harbored no love for the B picture. Shot on shoe-string budgets, often without fully formed scripts, B pictures were difficult for the BMP to control. Earlier in 1943 Bell had objected to an inexpensive Republic feature, the *London Blackout Murders*, a film that suggested that "the British government would accept a negotiated peace, took some mild swipes at Lend Lease, and showed an overworked doctor accidentally cutting off a woman's head during a blackout instead of amputating her leg." Bell attempted to block the export of the *London Blackout Murders* but failed, which only increased his dislike of sensational B pictures. The standard plots of B Westerns centered on crime and presented weak portrayals of American law-enforcement officials. As an earlier OWI report remarked of the formula Western: "This plot is becoming a Hollywood habit, the men who should be the town's leaders are bandit leaders instead, and some itinerant cowboy has to administer justice for the people." *The Spoilers, In Old California,* and *In Old Oklahoma*—the OWI appraisal could have been directed at each of Wayne's previous three Westerns.[53]

The Fighting Seabees was Republic's peace offering to Bell. Unabashedly patriotic, it wrapped itself in the American flag and sang hosannas to the unheralded Seabees. "We build for the fighters. We fight for what we build," was the Seabees' motto, but the film contains far more fighting than building. Originality was not Republic's strength; years of being a modestly profitable studio had taught Republic not to take chances and to stay with a proven formula. Although *The Fighting Seabees* treated a new subject, at its core it is a formula picture whose dramatic conflicts and themes followed the same pattern as *Only Angels Have Wings* and *Flying Tigers.* The action centers on a small group of professional builders, Americans all but of multinational origins. At a welcome-home party early in the film, they take turns singing the verses of a song; one sings with an Irish brogue, another with a Scottish accent, the next in proper English, the last in Polish. Their voices are separate, their accents distinct, but their song is the same. The melting-pot motif was one of the most popular of World War II, one officially endorsed by the *Government Information Manual for the Motion Picture Industry* and supported by Bell and other BMP officials.

The Fighting Seabees' tightly knit group of professionals is not only multinational in origins, it is led by a short-tempered, individualistic man. Wedge Donovan (John Wayne) is the prototypical can-do American, impatient with delays and bureaucratic red tape. Described by the heroine as "a hot-headed ape with a hair-trigger temper," his uncontrollable individualism creates most of the problems in the film. Rather than follow orders, he leads his men into the wrong battles at the wrong times. Although the movie preaches cooperation and teamwork, he never seems able to harness his temper. To be sure, he learns to speak the language of teamwork, and he even develops a certain fondness for navy forms, but under pressure he reverts to type. In the end of the film, he disobeys orders, leads his hard hats into a Japanese trap, and then redeems himself with an even more impetuous act: a suicide mission in a bulldozer. As in all the formula war films, cooperation and teamwork are praised in the abstract, but woe to the outfit without at least one individualist ready to save the day with a really foolhardy, heroic act. To Bell, undoubtedly, it was perfectly acceptable to have a rash can-do in uniform; it was only when the character's role fitted his personality—that is, when he was outside the law and the establishment—that problems arose. Aesthetic sense made bad patriotism.

As in most war films, women in *The Fighting Seabees* threaten men almost as much—and occasionally even more—than does the enemy. The enemy can kill a soldier, but that soldier will continue to live as part of the larger group, an indestructible entity. A woman, however, can tear at the very fiber of the group, disrupting the esprit de corps, setting soldier against soldier, friend against friend. In the original script war correspondent Constance Chesley (Susan Hayward) continually disrupts the group's activities. She gripes about being stranded on the tropical island, complains about the navy's bureaucratic procedures, brags about her previous assignments, and becomes bored and restless when she is not the center of attention. Even worse, both the "outsider" hero Donovan and the official hero Lt. Cmdr. Robert Yarrow (Dennis O'Keefe) fall in love with her. Her character also underscores the true nature of the film: It is not as much about war as about men's relationships with each other, relationships that can only be complicated and threatened by women.

Republic knew that *The Fighting Seabees* followed a successful formula and thought that it would please Bell's office. Early in the project the studio sent the script to the Overseas Branch of the BMP. The BMP liked everything about the film—except Constance: "The Heroine—demanding, pouting, self-centered, intolerant of importance attributed to anything but herself—would give audiences overseas a derogatory picture of an American woman correspondent." Republic thereupon made an about-face. The character of Constance received a thorough scrubbing and emerged clean, pure, and without a hint of selfishness. Rather than threaten the group of men, she became the central figure, a means to bring Donovan and Yarrow together. Bell complimented Republic on the new script, expressing his delight with "the way in which [Republic] dramatized the contribution of the different nationalities in this great democracy to the fighting construction battalions." In fact he was so impressed by the script that he said that he hoped to send the finished film into the newly liberated countries. In short, he was saying, if the script were followed, the BMP would guarantee that the film would make money.[54]

Republic remained faithful to the revised script. The BMP recommended *The Fighting Seabees* for "special OWI distribution in liberated areas." But even without this distribution, *The Fighting Seabees* was a solid hit. If critics claimed that Republic's war films employed stock western formulas, substituting sadistic Japanese for bloodthirsty Indians, Republic knew its audience and catered to its tastes. "Republic Aims Its Films at Heart of America," accurately declared a World War II *Variety* headline. Sometimes described as "the hicks in the sticks," Republic's audience did not demand sophisticated comedies or psychological thrillers. Republic delivered simple plots filled with heroes, heroines, villains, and plenty of action, and now, during the war, it simply added a heavy dose of patriotism. The only effect the war had on the Republic audience was to enlarge it. Before the war Republic films had played largely in theaters located in the small towns of the South, Midwest, and West. During the war, however, defense jobs pulled millions of rural and small-town Americans to the major industrial cities. Just as this migration opened a new market for country music, it broadened Republic's market. Yates and Republic responded to the new opportunities with the same cheap formulas. More than anyone else, John Wayne benefited from the windfall.[55]

With each war film Wayne increasingly came to embody the American fighting man. Before the war Gary Cooper, Humphrey Bogart, or Spencer Tracy could play a war hero but none could move beyond his well-known persona; moviegoers were always aware that they were watching Cooper, Bogart, or Tracy. Wayne's screen persona, however, was not as well developed on the eve of the war, especially in the larger markets. According to Republic's schmaltzy formula, his screen image and public persona emerged entirely intertwined with the role of the American hero. His war pictures were really little different from his Westerns; he played only variations of the same hard moral man—ornery and uncompromising, but truthful, loyal, and likable. Now, however, he was the only one available to play it, and America desperately needed a hero to celebrate.[56]

Increasingly, as many have discussed, his screen persona would merge with his personality, off-screen would merge with on. But that transformation was not yet complete in early November 1943, when he finished his work on *The Fighting Seabees*. On November 17, he learned that the Selective Service Board had extended his 3-A deferment. Off the set he lived in a storm of moral controversy. Continuing to press Josie for a divorce, he lived openly with Chata. For a time they stayed in the guest room at Paul Fix's house, then they moved into the penthouse apartment at the Chateau Marmont. And even more frequently than before the war, he spent nights carousing with Ward Bond.

Like Wayne, Bond had left his wife. Like Wayne, too, Ward had never been the ideal husband. To Wayne and Ford, Bond's chief faults were endearing. They laughed at his constant complaining and firm belief that he knew the best way to do anything; they baited him, and laughed more when his face turned red with rage. Best of all, they knew that as long as he was the center of attention he was happy; his temper subsided as quickly as it rose, and no insult could do permanent damage. They knew that Ward's ego was indestructible. As a husband Bond—with his complaining and tendency to bully—was far from amusing. Doris Sellers Childs Bond, his "socially prominent wife," charged him with cruelty, telling Superior Court Judge George A. Dockweiler that her husband "continually nagged her about the way she ran the house and reared her child by a previous marriage." But the most serious obstacle to the continuation of their eight-year marriage came on October 15, 1943, when Ward told Doris that he no longer loved her and promptly left home.[57]

He took a room at the Beverly Hills Hotel and commenced to live and enjoy a bachelor's life. Wayne was in an "uproar" because his "commission didn't materialize." The fact is that Wayne could have forced the issue and enlisted. He chose instead to join Bond. Saddened that the two men had left their wives, Mary Ford tried to patch up both marriages. Duke and Ward refused. Duke's "off his head about that Mexican," Mary wrote her husband, and Ward "can't stand Doris and her sloppiness any longer." In both cases, she finally decided, there was no chance of reconciliation.[58]

Mary condemned Wayne's and Bond's behavior, but their generosity soon reclaimed her affections. Duke put in a carving stint at the Hollywood Canteen on Thanksgiving—Ward was supposed to help but got drunk and "couldn't make the grade"—and both men were "over-generous" on Christmas, filling Mary's house with flowers, perfume bottles, and presents. Even though she spent the night before Christmas "helping Josie and Doris keep their chins up," Wayne and Bond's friendship lightened her holiday. The two men were willing to break their commitments to their wives, but they remained faithful to their friendship with the Fords.[59]

Indeed, over the course of his life, Duke would walk out on three marriages, but he never failed a friend. As much as he needed a wife, one suspects that he needed his friends more, and during the war no friend was more important to him than Bond. Boisterous, conceited, self-centered, thick-skinned, hard-drinking—Bond was Wayne's safety valve, always there to help relieve pressures.[60]

Their friendship was often sophomoric, as if they were still involved in USC fraternity pranks. Drunk, they were apt to do or try anything. One night they stood on the roof of the Hollywood Athletic Club and threw billiard balls at the cars moving along Sunset. Another night Wayne attempted to wake Bond to go drinking. When traditional approaches failed, he poured vodka on his friend's chest and lit it. On yet another occasion, drunk and improvising, Ward bet Duke that "he could stand on a newspaper and Wayne couldn't knock him off it." As soon as the wager was accepted, Bond put down the newspaper in a doorway and shut the door with Wayne on the other side. "Ok, you dumb son of a bitch, now hit me," Ward called. Wayne smashed his fist through the door and won the wager. Somehow they survived it all.[61]

But his failure to be involved in the war still bothered Duke, though it never seemed to have troubled Bond. Popular with Americans at home, Wayne was not so popular with the soldiers and sailors who were fighting the war. Edward Ludwig, the director of *The Fighting Seabees*, recalled that while most of the film was shot on Iverson Ranch in California, a few of the scenes were shot

> on location in the South Pacific, where the Japanese had vacated. There was a saloon near our location frequented by servicemen and every time Wayne would go in there, some guy would pick a fight with him, wondering why he wasn't in uniform instead of play-acting that he was in military service for his country. Wayne would lose more fights than he won and I had to forbid him going in there if I expected to get him through the picture in one piece.

Undoubtedly, Ludwig's story was exaggeration, but there were a few fights, and Duke was painfully conscious of his draft status. He knew that his films were important to some aspect of the war effort, but he thought he should do more.[62] By December 1943 he probably knew that he would never enlist. He had stopped talking about the possibility after his 3-A deferment. There were no more "Barkus is willin'" letters, no more "one more movie, then" promises. There were only a career and a cluttered personal life. Besides his movies his primary contribution to the war effort was a USO Camp Shows tour of the South Pacific and Australia he made in late 1943 and early 1944. USO tours gave stage, screen, and radio stars not in uniform a chance to make a personal contribution to the fight. Between Pearl Harbor and the end of the war some 3,500 performers entertained the troops. The USO organized four tours: The Victory Circuit put on revues, plays, and concerts at the largest army posts and naval stations in the United States; the Blue Circuit played the small U.S. bases; the Hospital Circuit entertained troops in military hospitals; and the Foxhole Circuit took leading acts to soldiers and sailors stationed overseas.[63]

The Foxhole Circuit was the most popular tour for Hollywood stars, and such entertainers as Joe E. Brown, Bob Hope, Jack Benny, Bing Crosby, Ann

Sheridan, Paulette Goddard, and Gary Cooper made repeated trips overseas to entertain the troops. In the damp jungles of the Pacific islands and Southeast Asia or close to the front lines in North Africa and Italy, entertainers attempted to bring Main Street to American soldiers and sailors. Weary of battle and homesick, the troops appreciated the entertainers' efforts. Popular singer Ella Logan once gave a performance in an oversized Nissen hut in North Africa. She did her hour show and then performed requests for another hour. Finally she called out: "Fellows, am I keeping you from anything?" "Yeah," came the immediate reply. "Suffering."[64]

The alleviation of suffering was only one of the reasons Wayne made his tour. The other was to collect information. William J. "Wild Bill" Donovan, Ford's commander in the OSS, wanted Wayne's impressions of the officers and the men in the South Pacific. Poor relations with Gen. Douglas MacArthur continually plagued Donovan's Pacific network, and he hoped that a celebrity like Wayne could provide information denied his own operatives. Donovan was particularly interested in Duke's assessment of MacArthur himself. Wayne's mission was only partially successful. He never met MacArthur, and although he filed a report with Donovan when he got back to the States, he had nothing substantial to offer. Donovan, he later recalled, "gave me a plaque saying that I had served in the OSS. But it was a copperplate, something that Jack [Ford] had set up. It didn't mean anything." When the certificate was sent to Ford's home, Duke never bothered to pick it up.[65]

Wayne was more successful as an entertainer. For almost three months he toured southwest Pacific bases and battle lines from Brisbane, Australia, to New Britain and New Guinea. He performed two shows a day and visited hospitals, where he talked to the injured troops, asking them where they were from but never how they felt. Wearing a Colt .45 automatic on his right hip, he visited soldiers in areas of New Guinea where nightly bombing raids and enemy infiltration made any performance dangerous. Through long nights he sat with the troops, swapping stories and drinking their potent "jungle juice." Describing those areas and the servicemen, he said, "They're where 130 degrees is a cool day, where they scrape flies off, where matches melt in their pockets and Jap daisy-cutter bombs take legs off at the hip. They'll build stages out of old crates, then sit in mud and rain for three hours waiting for someone like me to say, 'Hello, Joe.'" He was deeply moved by the suffering and endurance of the troops, convinced that those at home owed the soldiers their most profound thanks.[66]

At the press conference after his return to Hollywood, he spoke to America about their boys overseas. "What the guys down there need," he said, with the air of a man who had returned from the front with the real poop, are letters and snapshots, cigars and lighters, phonograph needles and radios. They needed the support and love of Americans back home. It was a message that had been delivered by others but never grew stale.[67]

By 1944 a star coming home from the war zone received almost as much publicity as those who served overseas in the military. In a story of his homecoming, *Screen Guide* ran pictures of Duke and his four children—photographs of him hugging them, giving them presents, showing them where bullets pierced his pants. The article did not mention that he no longer lived with them or was pressing their mother for a divorce. It did mention, however, that his next starring role would be in RKO's *Tall in the Saddle*.[68]

By the time Duke returned from the extended USO tour, the Department of War was planning the two great offensives of World War II—the invasion of Europe, scheduled for June 1944, and the assault on the Philippines, slated for later in the year. Manpower needs increased dramatically, and 3-A deferments based on family needs were harder to come by. Based on Duke's willingness to do the USO tour, Republic filed for a 2-A deferment—"deferred in support of national health, safety, or interest." In April 1944 the Selective Service gave Duke the new classification.[69]

With the USO tour over and a new deferment in hand, Wayne was anxious to get back in front of the camera. During the spring and summer, he starred in two Westerns—*Tall in the Saddle* and *Flame of the Barbary Coast*. Although the government's overseas censors were upset by the lawlessness in *Tall in the Saddle* and the political corruption in *Flame of the Barbary Coast*, neither film had an overt political message. Lawlessness and political corruption were generic themes of Westerns; they had become the essential components, whatever men like Bell might think of them. Noted an OWI official about *Flame of the Barbary Coast*: "Any picture which takes historic episodes as a background is certain to be accepted overseas as reasonably authentic. Hence our concern to see the widespread graft and corruption counterbalanced by the feeling that the people, once aroused, are determined to clean up the city." The scripts of both films were altered, but the changes were cosmetic. They remained true to the John Wayne Western formula, featuring a hard-fisted, fearless hero who rides into a dangerous and corrupt town, restores law and order, makes the land safe for "decent people," and, almost as a form of compensation, wins the heart of the "prettiest girl in town." The OWI's fears that both productions made John Wayne symbolize America's role in world affairs were precisely what these films intended to do, for the good of both the film and Wayne's career.[70]

Duke received little satisfaction from making *Flame of the Barbary Coast*. Formulaic and trite, it lacked imagination and was only a step above the B Westerns he had starred in for a decade. *Tall in the Saddle* was different. On December 15, 1943, shortly before he left Hollywood for his USO tour, he had signed a six-year, six-picture deal with RKO, the normally economically strapped studio, which was enjoying a short period of good luck. *Tall in the Saddle* was his second film for RKO, and he later said that he had found the magazine story and helped in script development and production. He also claimed that in order to get control of the film, he had agreed to work for half price. Actually Duke was paid $6,250 a week for his work—his standard RKO salary—but he undoubtedly did play a part in development. *Tall in the Saddle* was produced by Robert Fellows, with whom Duke would later go into the production business, and its screenplay was written in part by his old friend Paul Fix. Working with Fellows and Fix convinced Duke that he wanted more control than he was getting at that time at Republic.[71]

Tall in the Saddle was the finest pure Western Duke had made since *Stagecoach*, and it foreshadowed the sort of roles he would play after the war. Wayne plays Rocklin, a misogynist—"I never feel sorry for anything that happens to a woman"—with no first name and no past. He rides tall in the saddle and lives by a Western code that stresses truthfulness, prizes absolute courage, and prefers silence to talking. Although he asserts: "No woman is going to get me hog-tied and branded," he falls for a woman who follows the same code, but not before she attacks him, first with a gun and then with a knife. By contrast *Flame of the Barbary Coast* is a weak Republic product that tries—and fails—to make up for its lack of plot with more than the usual number of Republic songs. Its only similarity with *Tall in the Saddle* is its attitude toward women, who are compared to liquor, cards—"Usually when you pick one up, you wish you hadn't"—and "horseflesh."[72]

Both *Tall in the Saddle* and *Flame of the Barbary Coast* were filmed in or around Los Angeles. For six months Duke had escaped his personal difficulties by either leaving Hollywood or, when in town, spending his nights drinking with Bond. In the spring and summer of 1944, however, his work kept him near home. Worse, after appearing *Tall in the Saddle*, Bond's career was nearly destroyed in a terrible accident. A large automobile hit Bond in July on a Hollywood street, fracturing his left shin. He was rushed to the hospital, where physicians prepared to amputate his leg. Before the operation, however, an attendant recognized him and the hospital called his studio, where the decision was made to try to repair the leg and risk gangrene rather than amputate and kill the actor's career. Surgeons successfully reconstructed his leg and hoped for the best. By the third day after the operation, much to everyone's relief, it was clear that his leg, life, and career had been saved. Before the week was over his sense of humor had returned and he began pestering nurses and planning a coup of the hospital administration.[73]

Republic lawyers worked as hard on Duke's draft status as the nurses and doctors did on Bond's leg. In June 1944, a week after the D-day invasion of Europe, Duke received a surprise in the mail. With the assault on Guam and Saipan in the Pacific just three months down the road and military manpower needs increasing daily, the Selective Service reviewed its classification system and automatically eliminated most 2-A deferments. Duke learned that he had been reclassified 1-A—"available for military service." Republic's attorneys immediately went to work, filing a series of appeals on Wayne's behalf, arguing that his film work was more important to the war effort than any actual military service he might perform. Selective Service eventually agreed, restoring Duke's 2-A status.[74]

Nothing, however, could restore Duke's marriage. He wanted a new life with a new wife, and Josie stood in the way. Josie had moved cautiously toward a divorce, hoping at every step that Duke would change his mind. They separated in May 1943, but she did not file for divorce until October. Finally, in November 1944, her case went to court. To comply with California divorce law, which required a specific reason to dissolve a marriage, she charged Duke with "extreme cruelty" that caused her "physical and mental suffering." Before Superior Court Judge Jess E. Stephens, she recounted the last years of her marriage—the nights he did not return home, his refusal to explain his activities, his cautions against her checking on his movements. She told about finding a "lady's coat" in his car on his return from a trip to a resort. And when she threatened to divorce him, he only replied: "Hurry up and get it over with." Duke did not contest her account, and on November 29, 1944, the judge granted her the divorce.[75]

The details of the settlement had been agreed on before the case went to court. Josie received custody of the four young children—Michael was ten in 1944, Toni eight, Patrick five, and Melinda four. Duke agreed to generous support payments for Josie and the kids, recalling nearly a decade later that Josie had received the house, the car, one hundred thousand dollars in securities, insurance, and a 20 percent claim on his gross earnings. Duke also agreed to put two hundred dollars a month into a trust fund for each of his children. "She damn well deserves it," he told a *Look* reporter. "She's done a wonderful job with the kids." Even after his death in 1979, his estate continued to pay Josie a yearly income. Even more important for her, she received permission from the church to obtain a civil divorce. In her only public discussion of the event, she asserted that the divorce was "the only means of clarifying the position of my children." However, she emphasized, the divorce was "a purely civil action in no way affecting the moral status of a marriage." In other words, in her eyes and in the eyes of the Catholic Church, she remained Mrs. Marion Morrison. She never remarried or even dated another man. She remained steadfastly faithful to her marriage vows, devoting her life to her children and her religion.[76]

Years later, after he married and divorced Chata, Duke called his divorce from Josie the "the stupidest damn thing I ever did in my life." Not only had he deserted the first woman he loved, a woman whose weaknesses seemed insignificant compared to her strengths, but he also left four young children whom he loved. Some friends of the Waynes took Josie's side and never forgave Duke. Wayne believed that his oldest son, Michael, never forgave him for deserting Josie. Pilar described the intensity of Duke's guilt: "Duke told me that Michael, more than any of his other children, had judged him harshly when Duke divorced Josephine. Duke suffered lifelong guilt in the aftermath of the divorce as a result." "He's still angry at me," Duke told Pilar in 1953. "I'm afraid he always will be. It breaks my heart." Although in later years Michael ran Duke's production company, the father and son had a distant, often strained relationship. "Duke had even taken to calling Michael 'Khrushchev,'" Pilar wrote. "You know, Michael has never forgiven me for leaving his mother," Wayne told Mary St. John. There was not a hint of bitterness in the statement. Duke respected Michael for holding tight to his anger, and he knew that Michael was right to be angry. Duke had been tragically wrong, and he never believed that he deserved Michael's forgiveness. Just as he never fully forgave his mother for her treatment of his father, Duke understood that Michael could never forgive him.[77]

The guilt, however, had to wait on his career, as the marriage had. Wayne's focus in November 1944 was on making another film that would aid the war effort. He also found himself entering a new, private battle of his own. The film was *Back to Bataan*. The battle was Duke's first confrontation with communists.

Back to Bataan started with an idea of Robert Fellows's, an idea inspired by a dramatic gesture. At one o'clock on the afternoon of October 20, 1944,

Gen. Douglas MacArthur, cutting a dignified figure in his freshly pressed khakis, field marshal's cap, and dark sunglasses, clutched a corncob pipe between his teeth and waded onto the beach off Leyte Gulf. While Japanese snipers fired shots from their perches on tops of palm trees, MacArthur walked slowly through the knee-deep surf. When the Japanese had forced him out of the Philippines in 1942, he had promised to return. And now he had kept his word. He savored the moment, inspecting the beachhead and talking with his officers. Then he found a radio transmitter and delivered his message: "People of the Philippines, I have returned! By the grace of Almighty God, our forces stand again on Philippine soil." MacArthur's stagey entrance and his memorable lines, combined with the important U.S. victory at Leyte Gulf, seized the attention of the country. Americans shifted their focus from the Allies' push toward Germany to the Pacific. They were reminded once again of the bleak days in the spring of 1942 when the Japanese crushed American and Filipino forces on Bataan and Corregidor. They remembered that thousands of American and Filipino soldiers had been taken prisoners. Like MacArthur, they savored the sweet reversal of fortunes.[78]

Leyte Gulf was only the opening engagement in America's battle to reclaim the Philippines, but few Americans doubted the certainty of the final victory. RKO producer Robert Fellows shared the majority opinion, and he believed that a film that recounted the war in the Philippines—from the Japanese invasion and the fall of Bataan to MacArthur's return and the final liberation of the islands—would make a splendid tribute to American and Filipino fighting forces and a profitable movie. But timing would be everything. The film would have to be completed and released shortly after America's final victory over the Japanese in the Philippines.[79]

Fellows moved quickly. In Washington he won the support of the War Department and the OWI. The army agreed to provide technical advisers, and the OWI promised to throw its considerable propaganda weight behind the project. In Hollywood he lined up the talent he needed to make the film. Ben Barzman agreed to write a script, and Edward Dmytryk said he would direct the film. Fellows's friendship with Wayne brought Duke into the project. He told his team that there could be no delays, no lengthy rewrites or reshooting of scenes. He gave Barzman five weeks to complete a screenplay and Dmytryk ten weeks to shoot the film. With American forces moving toward the main islands of the Philippines, Fellows pressured everyone to work fast.[80]

The speedup in production affected Wayne less than the other men. Compared to a typical Republic project, a ten-week shoot was leisurely. Duke's personal life, however, made him edgy and short-tempered. Filming started the month of his divorce and continued during a period when Josie and he were trying to establish a livable, nonmarital relationship. Eventually they worked out an amicable arrangement that was the best for the children, but the bitterness and anger were still too fresh at the end of 1944 for there to be any peace between the two. Complicating matters, Wayne's relationship with director Dmytryk and writer Barzman started badly and got worse. In late 1944 and early 1945, politics was again beginning to resurface as a divisive issue in Hollywood. The awkward Popular Front era that saw conservatives, liberals, and communists unified against America's fascist enemies was drawing to a close, and the older Hollywood political order was re-forming. John Wayne—anti-FDR, anti–New Deal, and very much anti-the higher war income taxes—found little in common with Dmytryk and Barzman, both of whom were later named as members of the Communist party (USA).[81]

Wayne managed to work out an uneasy truce with Dmytryk, but he did not attempt to hide his contempt for Barzman. The Canadian screenwriter sensed the hostility from the moment Fellows introduced him to Wayne, who unsmilingly stuck out his hand and said that he was "Duke" to his friends. As they shook hands, Wayne added, "Also to people I work with." The message was clear: Barzman might work with him, he might even call him "Duke," but that did not confer friendship. During most of the time that they worked together, Barzman and Wayne engaged in a private cold war, in which insults and script alterations were used as weapons. Since *Back to Bataan* was a rush job, Barzman was continually writing scenes the night before they were shot. He was bound to make mistakes. Dmytryk told him, for example, to go easy on all "s" sounds, "which when uttered by a Filipino slithers out 'sibilant,' and the sh sound comes out a funny esss." In one scene in which Wayne discusses plans to fight a rear-guard action against the Japanese, Barzman gave a Filipino leader the unfortunate line, "With knives and bolos against machine guns." Spoken with admirable passion but questionable articulation by the Filipino leader, the line emerged, "With nifesssss and bolosssss against masss-sine guns." Everyone on the set laughed, but Wayne bellowed longer than the rest. He and his friends never allowed Barzman to forget his mistake, whispering, "With nifesssssssss and bolosssss against massssine guns," whenever the screenwriter was on the set. And each day when Duke would read over his fresh dialogue, he would comment, "Now let's see what kind of golden hero our boy genius has made me today."[82]

Barzman returned fire with his typewriter. Early on he noticed that Wayne took an inordinate pride in performing his own stunts. He considered the use of doubles for even dangerous stunts as unmanly. It was a manifestation of hubris that gave a decided advantage to a plotting writer. As Barzman later wrote: "Eddie and I started inventing stunts that we were sure would make [Wayne] cry uncle and ask for a double." Barzman's desire for revenge was magnified by the director. Dmytryk was known in the industry as a director who was fascinated with violence, sadism, and pain; no stunt was too extreme for him, and he threw them all at his star. They put Duke in a leather harness and had a crane lift and drop him, making it look as if he had been blown sky-high by an enemy shell. One cold night toward the end of the shooting, they broke ice off a pond on the RKO ranch and had Wayne lie under the water sucking air through a reed. The scene had to be shot again and again until a way was discovered to keep Duke from floating to the surface of the pond. To the last he stubbornly refused to use a double, even during the painful pond scene. He was trapped. He did not want to play a fool for some "lefty screenwriter," but he did not back down. At one point though, a blue-lipped, shivering Wayne took a drink of whiskey and warned Barzman: "You better be goddamn sure we don't find out this is something you dreamed up out of your little head as a parting gift."[83]

Barzman's stunts did not bother Wayne as much as the way Dmytryk and his aides treated the film's technical adviser, Col. George S. Clarke. The army assigned Clarke to the project to give advice on the nature and tactics of the guerrilla war in the Philippines. One of the last Americans to leave the Philippines in 1942, he was a serious, conservative, career soldier with an underdeveloped sense of humor. When Wayne was out of sight, Dmytryk and his friends rode the churchgoing, patriotic Clarke unmercifully, taking shots at his religion and singing the "Internationale." When Wayne heard that the "pro-Reds" were belittling Clarke, he confronted Dmytryk. "Hey," Duke asked, "are you a Commie?" Dmytryk said he wasn't, adding, "But if the masses of the American people want communism, I think it'd be good for our country." The word "masses," Wayne believed, was not part of "Western terminology," and anyone who used it had to be a communist. From then on he avoided Dmytryk as much as possible."[84]

Back to Bataan survived the political tensions and frantic schedule. It is a classic propaganda feature, touching on most of the issues that the OWI had been pushing since 1942. It presents the Filipino resistance movement as a true "people's war" fought by men and women, adults and children. "There are no civilians in the Philippines," notes one of the resistance leaders. *Back to*

Bataan suggests that the central issue in the war is freedom—for the United States, for the Philippines, for the world. In school Filipino students learn that the Spanish brought Christianity to their country, while the American gift to them was the concept of freedom, along with baseball, hot dogs, and soda pop. Japan, by contrast, exports only slavery and terror to the lands it controls.

Like other films about the Pacific war, it depicts Asians in stark black and white. The Filipinos are goodness incarnate. Throughout the film Dmytryk focuses on the gentle faces of the Filipino peasants and recounts their many acts of courage and sacrifice. A school's principal chooses death over hauling down the American flag. A young boy sacrifices his life rather than betray the location of the guerrilla force. Dmytryk's visual and emotional treatment of the Filipino peasants recalls John Ford's depiction of the Okies in *The Grapes of Wrath* and foreshadows Elia Kazan's portrayal of the Mexican peasants in *Viva Zapata!* All three films ennoble their peasant subjects, investing them with an earthy dignity, virtue, and grace.

The Japanese are irredeemably vile. Unlike the distinction some films made between good Germans and evil Nazis, films centered on the Pacific war uniformly portrayed all Japanese as evil. Ernie Pyle, America's most famous war journalist, who was transferred from the European theater to the Pacific theater in February 1945, noted the contrast: "In Europe we felt that our enemies, horrible and deadly as they were, were still people. But out here I soon gathered that the Japanese were looked upon as something subhuman or repulsive; the way some people feel about cockroaches or mice." U.S. magazines published articles with such titles as "Why Americans Hate Japs More than Nazis." In the Pacific, Adm. William F. "Bull" Halsey, commander of the U.S. South Pacific force, told the press, "The only good Jap is a Jap who's been dead six months."[85]

In 1943 Dmytryk had directed *Behind the Rising Sun*, perhaps the only war film that even attempted to treat the Japanese as human. In *Back to Bataan*, however, he joined the mainstream. In ruthless jungle warfare, in which the rules of civilized behavior go unenforced, the Japanese commit unspeakable crimes. They mechanically shoot and bayonet American prisoners of war during the Bataan Death March. They hang schoolteachers, brutalize young boys, and smilingly mutter ominous threats against entire populations. Their leaders take a sadistic pleasure in this cruel behavior. Dmytryk cast Richard Loo, Philip Ahn, and Abner Biberman as the Japanese. The three actors had played Japanese heavies so often during the war that audiences understood from the onset that the characters they portrayed would be sadistic killers. Richard Loo was particularly effective in *Back to Bataan* as the sociopathic Mayor Hasko.[86]

Good and brave Americans and Filipinos fighting for freedom, ruthless Japanese bent on world domination, the arch of the Pacific war from Corregidor to the liberation of the Philippines—*Back to Bataan* satisfied the OWI. Although the OWI found a few nagging problems, it still labeled *Back to Bataan* "an American tribute . . . to our Filipino allies." As proof of its propaganda value, the film broke all attendance records in Manila. After watching *Back to Bataan,* Mrs. Sergio Osmeña, wife of the president of the Philippines, announced, "*Back to Bataan* is a picture all Filipinos as well as Americans should see as an epic presentation of that Filipino-American pact of friendship sealed by the blood of our heroes and martyrs of Bataan and Corregidor."[87]

Back to Bataan also satisfied the American public and most film reviewers. Released shortly after V-E Day, when the nation turned its entire attention to the Pacific war, the film's themes of sacrifice and sweet revenge reflected national concerns. The *Hollywood Reporter* called it "a credit to picture makers and an ace-in-the-hole for the State Department on the question of colonial peoples." The reviewers who saw the film before the end of the war agreed that all Americans should see it. Only after the war was over did a few reviewers question its authenticity. Bosley Crowther found the movie full of clichés and formula action. "Unless you are easily susceptible to Hollywood make-believe, you will probably find it a juvenile dramatization of significant history," Crowther wrote.[88]

After the war, of course, critical judgments would sharpen. In the heat of the conflict, however, John Wayne had already taken the front rank of stardom that he would maintain for the next thirty years. Since the stock market crash in October 1929, he had appeared in some ninety movies. A whole generation had grown up watching him foil corrupt businessmen and criminals during the depression and Germans and Japanese during World War II. His great success was cemented by the fact that he fulfilled the country's need for a hero, which was made possible only by his refusal to play the ordinary soldier in real life. He achieved so much in the war years that he became virtually critic-proof. Sadly, his greatest critic in the years ahead would be himself.

John Wayne had emerged as an important Hollywood star in World War II movies. He brought a believable authenticity to the most cliché-ridden role: the rock-hard American who through dint of personal activity ensures the victory of good over evil. He gave form to the values Americans cherished, and dramatized their aspirations. In his war films he battled for justice and liberty in Europe, Asia, and America. True to the form of the classic Hollywood star, he played one variation after another of the same character. Jim Gordon in *Flying Tigers*, Pat Talbot in *Reunion in France*, "Pittsburgh" Markham in *Pittsburgh*, Dan Somers in *In Old Oklahoma*, Wedge Donovan in *The Fighting Seabees*, Col. Joseph Madden in *Back to Bataan*—they were all the same character. By the end of the war, Americans totally identified John Wayne with that idealized American figure. At no other time did so many Americans go to the movies as during World War II. And at no other time in his career did John Wayne make so many feature films. Americans came to know him through his wartime films, and they absorbed his character with the films' message. His draft status and his divorce were unimportant to his audience. What he represented on the screen was all that mattered.

11

New Beginnings
and Dead Ends

How big a star was John Wayne in 1945? Richard Fleischer remembered his first days in Hollywood, recalled vividly his first visit to RKO Radio Pictures Studio. He had just finished a three-year stint with RKO-Pathé News in New York, where he had advanced from a $35-a-week assistant title writer to a $100-a-week head writer for a newsreel and a writer/editor/producer/director of a series called *Flicker Flashbacks*. Finally he had received his call to Hollywood, where he became a $150-a-week contract director. It was 1945. Allied forces were close to victory in Europe, and United States troops were tightening the circle around Japan. Times were good. Fleischer had a spartan office, a title, and enough faith in his own abilities to believe that even better times lay ahead. Sid Rogell, a veteran producer of B films, gave Fleischer his first tour of the RKO lot. "The studio was humming with activity. It was the Golden Age of RKO, and every stage was crammed with famous stars and directors."[1]

First stop on the tour was a large soundstage where *Back to Bataan* was in its last weeks of production. As he glanced at the exterior of a large house, dirt, and real trees and plants, Fleischer was impressed. "But," he thought, "something was wrong." It was 10:30 in the morning and everything was quiet. "Nothing was happening. The crew, and it was a large one, was lounging. Small groups were sitting around, talking in subdued tones, and playing cards." The bustle and activity of filmmaking were absent, replaced by an eerie stillness. An assistant director saw Rogell and hurried over to explain. "John Wayne hasn't shit yet," he announced.

"What . . . is that supposed to mean?" Rogell wondered.

"Well, you see, the Duke can't work until he has a bowel movement. Looks like he's constipated today. He usually shits much earlier than this." Pointing toward Wayne's trailer, he added: "As soon as he comes out of his dressing room we'll go to work."

And so it happened. When Duke made his entrance, the soundstage swarmed alive. "Bells rang. A voice yelled out, 'Hit 'em all!' and the huge arcs sputtered to life. Lights all over the place flickered on. The crew scattered to their various posts." The assistant director ran over to Rogell and Fleischer. "He's shit! He's shit!" he proclaimed happily and then scurried off to perform some task. Wayne strode toward the set: "Big as life. Big as all outdoors. Big as the wheat fields of Kansas, the oil fields of Texas. America's hero . . . This episode gave me pause," Fleischer wrote. "What I had witnessed was a display of unadulterated, raw power. Who else could halt production for hours, at great cost to the studio, by peristalsis alone? It was too awesome to think about. This was not someone you wanted to offend."[2]

Not everyone was as concerned about offending Wayne as Fleischer. John Ford had never spent much time worrying about the actor's feelings. When he returned to Hollywood in the summer of 1944, Ford entertained a low opinion of movie people in general, but particularly of the men who were not in uniform. He had seen the war at close range. Ford and his photographic unit had made films of America's Panama Canal defenses and the state of the Atlantic fleet. They had made *The Battle of Midway*, a film President Roosevelt said he wanted "every mother in America to see." They had made a film about the attack on Pearl Harbor and documented America's 1942 landing in North Africa and the 1944 D-day invasion. Ford had been wounded at Midway, provided invaluable aid to Wild Bill Donovan in the China-Burma-India theater, and received an out-of-line promotion to captain. He had forged friendships with important leaders—Donovan, Chennault, Gen. A. C. Wedemeyer. His sense of self had changed. "Increasingly," wrote grandson Dan, "he was adopting the attitudes of the professional military men around him. He was beginning to see himself as an OSS. operative first, a naval officer second, and a Hollywood director third. More and more he was looking at Hollywood with scorn and distaste."[3]

Ford left the front for Hollywood on a mission personally requested by Secretary of the Navy James Forrestal. After four years of making documentaries, he had agreed to direct a feature film on the war. His distaste for Hollywood and nonserving actors had to be overcome; his old friendship mingled with Wayne's star power to bring the two together on the project. It was an assignment he had ducked for two years. In 1942 MGM had purchased the rights to W. L. White's best-selling nonfiction book *They Were Expendable*, the story of a squadron of PT boats led by Lt. John Bulkeley in the early months of the Pacific war. Ford's close friend and MGM producer James McGuinness had developed the project, and another Ford friend, Lt. Commander Frank "Spig" Wead, had written the screenplay. McGuinness believed that only Ford could direct the patriotic story of duty and sacrifice. The director had his doubts. He had little confidence in MGM—writing Wead that if that studio made the film it would be "ske-rewed up"—and even less in war films. Sensitive to the criticism Darryl Zanuck had received for attempting to mix service and business, he contended that if he made a commercial picture while still on active duty, "every congressman in America would be after my ass."[4]

McGuinness had pressed his point. He did not want just another war movie, even a financially successful one. "The story of the expendables seems to me as much a part of America's heroic tradition as The Alamo, the Green Mountain Boys at Ticonderoga, Valley Forge, or any of the other great patriotic heroics of our national life. It could be a picture . . . that would be available generation after generation for our youth." The producer saw a chance to record history while it was "still fresh in the minds of those who lived it." Still Ford resisted.[5]

Then he met Bulkeley. Ford's assistant Mark Armistead had worked with Bulkeley in preparation for the D day invasion, and one morning, shortly after Ford arrived in London, Armistead took Bulkeley to Claridge's to introduce him to the director. Armistead banged on Ford's door until a voice said to come in. Ford was in bed, but when he saw the naval hero he stood up, naked, and saluted. On June 6, 1944, Ford witnessed the Allied landing on Omaha Beach from Bulkeley's PT boat, where he spent the next five days. He was impressed by the Congressional Medal of Honor winner's quiet professionalism and modesty. Bulkeley downplayed his own accomplishments, insisted that White exaggerated the *Expendable* story, and remarked that he hoped that MGM "never made the goddamn [book] into a movie." That was enough for Ford; there had to be a movie about Bulkeley, and he had to direct it. If MacArthur could return to the Philippines, John Ford could return to Hollywood.[6]

Ford insisted, however, that *They Were Expendable* be an honest war picture, not a typical guts-and-glory, win-one-for-the-Gipper, John Wayne–Errol Flynn Hollywood war film. And to avoid any criticism of capitalizing on the war, he arranged for his entire three hundred thousand dollar salary to go toward the establishment of a "living memorial" for his Field Photographic Unit, a clubhouse and picnic area where his men could gather with their families to relax or to pay tribute to their comrades who had died defending their country. He was determined to make a navy film, using navy personnel whenever possible. Frank Wead was a commander in the navy, second unit director James C. Havens a captain in the marines, and director of photography Joseph August a lieutenant commander in the navy. Ford cast members of his own unit in small roles and chose Robert Montgomery to play Bulkeley (Lt. John Brickley in the film). By Hollywood standards it was an odd choice. Montgomery had spent his film career in a tuxedo, a charming, debonair leading man playing opposite Norma Shearer, Greta Garbo, Myrna Loy, and Joan Crawford. During World War II, however, he had been first an assistant U.S. naval attaché in London, then commanded a PT boat in the Pacific, and finally served aboard a destroyer during the D-day invasion. He had been awarded a Bronze Star and was a Chevalier of the French Legion of Honor, and as far as John Ford was concerned he had earned the right to play a naval hero.[7]

Not all of the cast and crew were military men. Ford gave a choice supporting role to Ward Bond, who was still recovering from his leg injury. It was an act of loyalty and friendship. Bond needed the money, but his leg still hurt and his mobility was limited. Ford solved the problem by shooting scenes around Ward, choreographing them so that everyone else moved about and Bond delivered his lines standing still. Only once does he walk in the film, and then only two steps. Ford cast Wayne as Lt. Rusty Ryan, Brickley's quick-tempered, individualistic second in command, a toned-down version of the character he had played in *The Fighting Seabees*.

In many ways Duke's part was better than Montgomery's. The role of John Brickley is static; he is a professional officer committed to the chain of command, an iron bond that seldom allows him to question orders or to show emotional conflict. Rusty Ryan, like all of Wayne's characters, does question. He is volatile and impulsive, ready to swing for the fences when the manager tells him to bunt. The idea of sacrifice does not disturb him, and he is more than ready to die performing some heroic deed, but he hates the notion of retreat. Throughout the film Brickley continually reminds Ryan that he has a duty, one that he might not find appealing but a duty nonetheless. Even when Ryan tries to give up his seat on the last American plane out of the Philippines to a man with a family, Brickley reminds him that his orders call for *him* to leave. "Rusty, who are you working for?" Brickley asks. "Yourself?" Ryan does not respond. He knows that his duty is to die when the navy orders, not when he fancies it. The film ends with an ironic but terrible very un-John-Wayne-like sacrifice: Brickley and Ryan are ordered to Washington while their men are left to die on Bataan.

The themes of sacrifice and duty pervade *They Were Expendable*. The story recounts America's rear-guard action against the Japanese in the Philippines in the months following Pearl Harbor, a struggle that culminated with Gen. Douglas MacArthur fleeing the islands and defeats at Bataan and Corregidor. The Americans who fought there, the expendables, battled for time, not victory. Outnumbered 5–1, they made the supreme sacrifice while their countrymen prepared to take up their struggle. Ford made the film because he believed that more sacrifice loomed on the horizon. When he began to shoot in late February 1945 in Key Biscayne, Florida, World War II seemed far from over. Hitler was alive, Auschwitz had only been liberated the month before, and Allied troops were pushing toward Berlin. In the Pacific the fighting was even more intense. In the week before the first scenes were shot, American servicemen were fighting to recapture Bataan and Corregidor and had raised the American flag on top of Mount Suribachi on Iwo Jima. Everywhere U.S. forces were on the offensive, but there seemed so much left to accomplish. Ahead lay Okinawa and then the home islands of Japan. If all went according to plan, the United States would commence its invasion on November 1, 1945. Few officials doubted that the invasion would be successful, but many agonized over what a victory would cost in American lives. Historians still debate the predictions of American casualties that circulated, but it was argued by all that there would be a terrible price to pay.[8]

Ford believed that it was his duty in *They Were Expendable* to prepare Americans for the invasion by telling the truth. He wanted no improbable heroics, no scenes of one man taking out a company of Japanese. Nor did he want any race-baiting. No Japanese soldier or sailor ever appears on screen. Ford concentrated his efforts on steeling his fellow countrymen to further sacrifice. The message he offered was the same that W. L. White advanced in his book. "It's like this," a young naval officer had explained to White:

Suppose you're a sergeant machine-gunner, and your army is retreating and the enemy is advancing. The captain takes you to a machine gun covering the road. "You're to stay here and hold this position," he tells you. "For how long?" you ask. "Never mind," he answers, "just hold it." Then you know you're expendable. In a war, anything can be expendable—money or gasoline or equipment or most usually men. . . . You know the situation. . . . So you don't mind it until you come back here where people waste hours and days and sometimes weeks, when you've seen your friends give their lives to save minutes.[9]

Perhaps surprisingly, officials in the Motion Pictures Division of the OWI supported Ford and Wead's realistic approach to the war, something they might not have done in the early, headier days of U.S. involvement. After reading the script, OWI. staffer Peggy Gould was sure the film would be "an outstanding contribution to the Government's War Information Program." The only character in the script that concerned her was a black enlisted man who expressed muted criticism of racial conditions in America. Reflecting on the loss of the Philippines, he says: "It's gonna be bad back dere in de South—no hemp—what'll dey do for lynchin's?" Wead and Ford followed their orders and whitewashed the script, removing both the lines and the black character.[10]

Later in his life Ford told English film critic and director Lindsay Anderson that he had never wanted to make *They Were Expendable*. "I was ordered to do it," he insisted. But in mid-February 1945, he was in Miami Beach and looking forward to the project. He wrote his wife that it was "as hot as blazes," but the entire cast was growing beards, getting tans, and "rearin' to go." He was amused watching the "old ladies" swoon over Duke and Ward, and he was pleased to be reunited with his two friends. But he was still edgy and intense, as if he were having trouble getting the war out of his bones.[11]

Having Bond on the set relieved some of the tension. As usual, Ward was "a pain in the ass," moving about the set as if he were the star of the show and trying to bed every attractive woman he saw. Duke and Ford laughed at him. Robert Montgomery was less amused and quickly developed a strong dislike for Bond. To relax the tension between the two, Wayne persuaded Montgomery to play an elaborate practical joke on Bond. Always well connected socially, Montgomery let it slip that he had been invited to an exclusive party thrown for members of British royalty in the Bahamas. Soon it turned out that Wayne and Ford had also been invited. Duke kept casually mentioning the affair to Bond, once even remarking that he had not packed his white dinner jacket and asking if he could borrow Ward's. Bond hated nothing more than being left out of something, especially something that seemed important. Duke made sure that the topic of the party came up frequently. The more it was mentioned, the bigger and more important it got. All the talk drove Bond to distraction; he spent days worrying about it and trying to discover a way to get invited. Only after a few weeks did Bond realize that there was no party, but by that time Montgomery had learned to abide him.[12]

Wayne enjoyed the joke, but once shooting began there was little pleasure to be had. Just days before production started, Ford received word that "Junior" Stout and Francis Wali, sons of two of his friends, had been killed in action. Other friends and their sons, many members of Ford's own unit, served on the front lines of the war. Perhaps it was his awareness of those dangers, those risks, that made it impossible for Ford to relax. Perhaps, too, he resented that his friend John Wayne's only uniform had been issued by MGM's wardrobe department. Whatever the reason, he rode Duke hard. It was *Stagecoach* revisited. Montgomery was his golden boy who could do no wrong, and nothing Wayne did was right. He picked on the way Duke moved, calling him a "clumsy bastard" and a "big oaf." He said that Duke did not know how to walk or talk like a sailor, which upset Wayne because he knew that, if nothing else, at least he *moved* well.[13]

One day Ford's criticism crossed the fine line to verbal humiliation. It started with a comment on the way Duke saluted. Ford just would not let it die. He kept insulting Duke. Normally quiet and always professional, Montgomery finally intervened. He walked over to Ford, placed his hands on both sides of the director's chair, leaned into the old man's face, and said: "Don't ever talk to Duke like that. You ought to be ashamed." For a moment, the set was absolutely still. Then everyone took a break to allow tempers to cool down. One person on the set later told Harry Carey Jr. that Montgomery's rebuke made the director cry.[14]

But Montgomery's outburst only temporarily quelled discord on the set. During the shooting of one scene, a technician made a serious mistake. "It was while we were shooting a process scene where my boat is strafed by an airplane," Wayne remembered. "A special-effects guy was shooting ball bearings at my boat, and he had forgotten to replace the windshield with a nonbreakable plexiglass one. Real glass went flying into my face." Never one to suffer fools silently, Duke grabbed a hammer and went after the man. "No you don't. They're my crew," Ford said as he stepped in front of Wayne. "Your crew, goddamnit, they're my eyes," Duke replied.[15]

Then on May 17, not long before the scheduled completion of filming,

Ford slipped off a camera scaffolding and fell awkwardly onto a cement floor. "Jesus Christ, you clumsy bastard," Wayne called out, but Ford was in too much pain to respond. He fractured the upper end of his tibia and was put in traction for two weeks. While Ford rested, Montgomery finished the film. Duke could have directed the final scenes, but Ford gave the assignment to Montgomery. It was a final swipe at Wayne's service record, or perhaps a compliment for Montgomery's. Just before shooting concluded, Duke received another 2-A deferment.[16]

The result of Ford's efforts is a sustained paean to the navy. Lindsay Anderson called *They Were Expendable* "a heroic poem." It celebrates the traditions, rituals, tactics, and men of the navy. At the heart of a cruel war it posits Ford's vision of an ideal family—patriarchal, structured, and caring. Bulkeley is the perfect father; judicious, unflappable, and devoid of histrionics, he is a natural leader. Lieutenant Sandy Davyss (Donna Reed), the film's only important female character, is Ford's quintessential woman, moving effortlessly in Ford's soft light from nurse to mother to Madonna. The men in the squadron are the children—some young, others old, some impulsive, others dutiful, but all loyal members of the family; they follow orders even when they do not understand or disagree with those commands. And looming above all the rest, one short step from God, is the great man, Gen. Douglas MacArthur. Ford treats the leader of America's Pacific forces like a deity. In the novel MacArthur is quite human, even to the point of suffering seasickness. In the film he loses all contact with the earth. Ford films MacArthur's departure from Luzon in an extended low-angle shot. It is almost as if Ford was filming Moses' departure from Egypt. In the scene MacArthur becomes, commented one film critic, "a statuesque image of ultimate right and superiority, staring from behind his sunglasses toward the horizon and the future." As he walks toward a PT boat, "The Battle Hymn of the Republic" plays on the soundtrack, linking him with Abraham Lincoln, another savior of the nation.[17]

In short *They Were Expendable* was artfully made and confidence inspiring, if uncritical and didactic. It was intended to be viewed by a nation still at war, but as it turned out, its timing was lousy. In late April, while Ford was shooting the film, Hitler committed suicide, and Germany surrendered early the next month. Still while Ford was shooting, after a costly eighty-three-day fight, American forces took Okinawa in June. Then, in July, as U.S. pilots bombed the main islands of Japan, American scientists successfully tested an atomic bomb. The war ended the next month in the flames of Hiroshima and Nagasaki. On August 15, 1945, the day Emperor Hirohito informed his nation that the fighting was over, *They Were Expendable* was still in post-production.

When the war ended, Ford was back in Washington. In Hollywood, James McGuinness was nervous about the fate of the film. He wired Ford that MGM had made the decision to rush *They Were Expendable* into release. The film premiered the week before Christmas to near-unanimous praise. Critics cheered the directing and the acting, the special effects and the battle sequences, the authentic little details and the grand panorama. They labeled it "an enthralling tribute" and "a labor of understanding and love," neither of which gave comfort to MGM executives concerned with the box office. Reviewers deemed nearly everything "outstanding," "superior," and "exceptional." But they could not overlook the one inescapable fact: This was a movie aimed at a nation at war. "It is in no wise depreciatory of . . . *They Were Expendable* to say that if this film had been released last year—or the year before—it would have been a ringing smash," wrote Bosley Crowther. "Now, with the war concluded and the burning thirst for vengeance somewhat cooled, it comes as a cinematic postscript to the martial heat and passion of the last four years."[18]

Crowther, a reviewer with a strong sense of public tastes, had again hit the mark. The force of the critical praise failed to stir the apathy of American moviegoers. For several months it did good business, and it even grossed enough to put it twenty-ninth on *Variety's* list of the year's top-grossing films. But it generated more curiosity than sustained interest and seemed out of touch with the most popular films of 1945. "After eight million war stories, people were tired of them," Wayne later said. The hit of the year was *The Bells of St. Mary's*, a Christmastime feel-good movie, with Alfred Hitchcock's *Spellbound* and Billy Wilder's *The Lost Weekend* receiving the most critical acclaim. The war was over, and Americans were more interested in watching Frank Sinatra and Gene Kelly sing and dance in *Anchors Aweigh* than seeing Robert Montgomery and John Wayne glorify sacrifice in *They Were Expendable*. They were tired of gas rationing and food shortages, exhausted from fighting and saving and sacrificing. They wanted something new—in their kitchens, their garages, and their theaters.[19]

Duke probably sensed the public mood better than Ford. During the filming he had lobbied the director to expand the emotional range of his character, and several of his best scenes, including his final attempt to remain behind with his men, were the results of these requests. Ford revered military behavior—tradition and ritual, blind loyalty and unquestioning obedience. Wayne, however, understood that the director's ideal type had become Montgomery's character, not his. As he had learned so well, his audience expected him to be independent and rash, whether Ford was sympathetic or not.[20]

Those same characteristics were beginning to surface more regularly in Duke's professional life. Between the late 1920s and Ford's death in 1973, his relationship with his friend served as a barometer for his career. Duke believed that he owed his success in the industry to Ford, and he treated him with sincere respect. But over the decades the relationship underwent subtle shifts as Duke's career moved steadily upward and Ford's leveled off and then began to decline. In 1945 Wayne was still the dutiful son, Ford the stern father. But Duke had moved far beyond the set of *Stagecoach*. More confident and mature, only partially intimidated by Ford, he was more likely to say what was on his mind, fight for better scenes, and demand roles that bolstered his accepted image.

An indication of his professional growth and power came a month after finishing work on *They Were Expendable*, for he began to negotiate control over some cast and crew jobs in his future movies. Returning to Republic, he starred in *Dakota*, a typical John Wayne vehicle set on the Dakota frontier of 1870. Herbert Yates's plan was to use Duke to advance the career of Vera Hruba Ralston, one of the studio's newest leading ladies and Yates's future wife. At exactly what point in their relationship Ralston and Yates became lovers is unclear, but it was probably early on, for almost from the first he evinced a willingness to promote a career that every objective observer agreed was doomed.

Born Vera Helena Hruba in Prague, Czechoslovakia, she achieved modest fame as an ice skater. In their promotional campaign for her, Republic claimed that she had finished second to Sonja Henie in the figure-skating competition in the 1936 Garmisch-Partenkirchen Olympics, a detail still repeated in some biographical sketches. In fact the sixteen-year-old Hruba placed a distant seventeenth. But she *was* an Olympic skater, and to Hollywood Sonja Henie had demonstrated that there was more gold in the movies than at the games. As her homeland was overrun by Nazi Germany, Hruba turned to the United States and the Ice Capades, where in 1941 she attracted Yates's interest. Although the studio boss prided himself in not developing his own stars, he lavished attention and money on her. After featuring her in several Ice Capades films, he added Ralston to her name and placed her in such unmemorable and unsuccessful films as *The Lady and the Monster, Storm Over*

Lisbon, and *Lake Placid Serenade*. They were terrible. Hruba's command of English was so limited that she had to learn her lines phonetically. Undaunted by the film failures and her shortcomings, which included bad acting as well as a thick accent, Yates pressed forward.[21]

By the end of the war, Ralston's understanding of English had improved, though her accent remained a problem. Joseph Kane, who directed nine of her films, said that she never became a good actress but was anxious to please. "She was in the same sort of position with Yates as Marion Davies was with William Randolph Hearst. So . . . she could have made it rough on everyone. . . . She never took advantage of that situation. She was always very cooperative, worked very hard, tried very hard." She just never captured the public's interest.[22]

Yates hoped that by teaming her with Republic's main attraction, moviegoers would take note of her. Duke accepted the arrangement, but he insisted that he exert some control over casting the other roles. Like John Ford, he wanted to work with friends, especially character actors whom he could depend upon to give consistently good performances. Already in 1945 the John Wayne Stock Company was taking shape. Choice supporting roles in *Dakota* went to Ward Bond, Paul Fix, and Grant Withers. Yakima Canutt served as second-unit director, and stuntman Cliff Lyons had a small part. Though these men had talent, which they would repeatedly demonstrate over the years, none of them could make *Dakota* into a hit.

Duke was not even in the mood to try. Midway through the production schedule he received news that his son Michael had fallen off a cliff at a summer camp and badly hurt his back and left shoulder. Mary Ford wrote her husband that it was a "terrible accident," that Michael had injured a lung and was in serious condition, though the doctors assured Duke that his son would pull through. Wayne, however, was frantic. *Dakota* and Yates's concerns for Vera Ralston seemed meaningless.

The results were predictable. Irredeemably bad, the film is handicapped by a plot that is at once too complicated and too trite, and the overuse of rear projection. The OWI, in its last months of film reviewing, criticized the extensive use of negative race humor in the film, and at least one reviewer was struck by how good acting "can almost make a hit out of an old, tired story and overcome the banalities of poorly-staged direction." The plot problems alone caused one reviewer to ask: "What's come over Republic anyhow?"[23]

Wayne might have asked the same question. The studio was changing, and although the change would better serve Duke's career, it was not evident in *Dakota*. By the mid-1940s Yates had initiated a new production strategy aimed at upgrading his studio's product. With production costs rising and the market for B films declining, he called for greater diversity of filmmaking and devised four classifications: Jubilee, Anniversary, Deluxe, and Premiere. Each classification denoted a different type of film. Jubilee pictures were standard Republic Bs; almost all were Westerns shot in seven days on a budget of $50,000. Anniversary pictures were dressed-up Bs, shot on fourteen- or fifteen-day schedules on budgets ranging from $175,000 to $200,000. Deluxe pictures were the major films made by Republic personnel. Many were directed by Joseph Kane, the studio's leading director, and they were shot on twenty-two-day schedules on budgets of about $500,000. Premiere pictures were intended to compete with the best films made at the top studios. Most would be made by outside directors, men like John Ford, Orson Welles, Allan Dwan, Lewis Milestone, Fritz Lang, or Frank Borzage, who had gone into independent production or wanted to have more control over a project. Budgets for Premiere pictures could run one million dollars or more, and shooting schedules varied. These were the films Yates believed would make Republic into a major studio.[24]

The new system at Republic marked a significant step in Duke's career. On September 24, 1945, he signed a new seven-picture nonexclusive contract with the studio, under which he was to receive 10 percent of the gross profits on his films with a guaranteed minimum. Duke now stood to make $200,000 or more on a successful film, a considerable jump. Under his 1943 contract he had made *In Old Oklahoma, The Fighting Seabees,* and *Flame of the Barbary Coast,* for which he had been paid $43,229.20, $31,770.83, and $35,000.00, respectively. Even with the money he had made working on pictures for other studios, he was grossly underpaid. In a memo on Duke's earnings, his agent Charles K. Feldman noted Duke's acting income as $128,000.00 in 1942, $116,169.46 in 1943, $167,291.66 in 1944, and $220,000.00 in 1945. He was far from being on the dole, but not anywhere near the top of his profession. Now he had a contract that would allow him to make more than a million dollars a year.[25]

After 1946 he was effectively through with anything below Republic's top films. There would be no more *Dakota*s or *In Old California*s for him. He would make only six more pictures at the studio. He produced two of those, had virtual production control on two more, and made the last two in cooperation with John Ford and Merian C. Cooper's Argosy Pictures. From 1946 on, he determined what pictures he would make, and with whom. His days of being controlled by Herbert Yates had ended. He would still make an occasional bad picture, but with one possible exception, they would not be Yates's fault.

But Republic was just one of Duke's studio commitments. He also had a six-year, six-picture deal he had signed in 1943 with RKO, a studio with an unstable past, which was experiencing a brief era of high profits. Instead of taking an early Christmas break that year, he accepted second billing (not yet unheard-of for him) to Claudette Colbert and made *Without Reservations*, a screwball comedy directed by Mervyn LeRoy. In the 1930s LeRoy had earned a reputation at Warner Bros. for making gritty social drama with such films as *Little Caesar*, *Five Star Final*, *I Am a Fugitive From a Chain Gang*, and *They Won't Forget*, but toward the end of the decade he went to MGM, where he directed movies ranging from romances (*Random Harvest*) to biographies (*Madame Curie*) to action dramas (*30 Seconds Over Tokyo*). He was a thorough professional who had been in show business since he was twelve years old, and he was adept at getting the most out of actors and scripts.[26]

Neither original nor particularly well plotted, *Without Reservations* is a wonderful period piece that reviewers liked in spite of its many flaws. Modeled closely after *It Happened One Night*, the original screwball comedy, starring Claudette Colbert and Clark Gable, *Without Reservations* is a road tale. Rusty Thomas (John Wayne), a marine flyer en route from New York to an air base in San Diego, meets Christopher "Kit" Madden (Claudette Colbert), best-selling author of *Here Is Tomorrow*, on her way from New York to Hollywood. Rusty is a man's man, Kit a proponent of the modern new age guy. For Rusty the attraction between a man and a woman is simple: "He's a man. She's a woman. That's all." For Kit the psychology of human attraction is complex, subtle, and burdened by continual analysis. Yet for some unexplained reason she views him as the perfect embodiment of her fictional creation Mark Winston. During the three-thousand-mile train and car trip to the West Coast, they fall in love and struggle with their emotions. Both learn, as a Mexican farmer tells Kit, that love is "brutal, selfish, and turbulent," not gentle and kind, but for all that, love experienced is better than love imagined. Predictably, after they separate and suffer briefly, they are reunited.[27]

The strength of the film is not its script, and certainly not the themes, but rather its mood. It captures the energy and joy of America returning to peace—men in uniforms, crowded cross-country trains, love on the move. *The Best Years of Our Lives*, *Crossfire*, and scores of other films detailed the painful adjustment to postwar life; *Without Reservations* touched on the fun. Inexpensive to make, it made *Variety*'s list for top-grossing films, finishing 1946 in forty-third place and making an outstanding profit for RKO.[28]

There was little fun, however, on the set. To begin with, Colbert was get-

ting a little old to play an ingenue. She had turned forty a month before filming began, and the best part of her career was behind her. But she had experience and a fine sense of comedy, which she was ready to share. LeRoy was not
interested in her views, however. It seems he took gender roles seriously, and
he objected to Colbert's suggestions on ways to improve the flat script. Duke
felt uncomfortable in his role and admired Colbert's comedic abilities, but, as
he later said, "Mervyn wasn't letting any woman tell him what to do." The
more Colbert offered opinions, the more her little idiosyncrasies bothered
LeRoy. He complained that she never watched where she was walking and
bumped into cameras and lights. He objected to her insistence on only having
her left profile shot. "I thought she looked very good on both sides, but she
was adamant about it," LeRoy wrote.[29]

More than anything else *Without Reservations* was a picture everyone just
wanted to finish and move on from. In December, shortly before the end of
the shooting schedule, Duke was in the news. *They Were Expendable* and
Dakota were released within a week of each other, and though the films did
not receive consistently strong reviews, Wayne did. A critic for the *Hollywood
Reporter* offered reservations about *Dakota* but said of Duke's performance,
"You'll love the big lug all over again."[30]

And he was in the news for other reasons. On December 25, 1945, the interlocutory decree on his divorce became final. As he was finishing his work on
Without Reservations, Louella Parsons told readers of the *Los Angeles Examiner*
that Duke would not remain single for long. She was right. On January 17,
1946, he married Chata Baur at his mother's Unity Presbyterian Church in
Long Beach. A small gathering of family and close friends witnessed the ceremony. Ward Bond, still walking with a cane, was best man; Ollie Carey was
matron of honor; and Herbert Yates gave the bride away. After the wedding,
Duke's mother hosted a reception at the California Country Club.[31]

Neither Hedda Hopper nor Louella Parsons, Hollywood's two leading gossip columnists, told their readers that Duke and Chata had been living together for several years before the marriage. Given the circumstances of their
meeting and their life together, the coverage of the wedding was as antiseptic
as possible. Hopper, in fact, claimed that Duke had only met the "comely
Mexican screen actress" a few months before the wedding. And Parsons, continuing the charade that Chata had come to Hollywood to star in movies,
commented that "it is doubtful if she will continue her movie career after becoming Mrs. Wayne." The only unusual aspect of the marriage that the reporters noted was the coincidence of Chata becoming Mrs. Morrison for the

second time. She had married Mexican college student Eugenio Morrison in 1941, and Duke used his real name, Marion Morrison, in the ceremony.[32]

After a brief honeymoon in Hawaii, the couple returned to 4735 Tyrone Street in Van Nuys, the house they had been living in for more than a year. Duke had bought the one-floor bungalow in 1944. Located in the San Fernando Valley, Van Nuys was outside the bustle of Hollywood and the elegance of Beverly Hills, but it was only a short drive from Republic Studios. For two people the house was fine, not stately, and modest by Hollywood standards, but comfortable. It had one large bedroom, one good-size bathroom, a living room, dining room, and kitchen, and two smaller rooms. Built on a narrow lot with a garage facing Tyrone, the house was under two thousand square feet but was set back off the street, giving it a sense of privacy.

One of the problems the couple faced, at least as far as Duke was concerned, was that they needed even more privacy. Waiting for the newlyweds on their return home was Chata's mother, Esperanza Baur Ceballos, who was unmarried, unattached, and given to spending extended vacations with her daughter. At the beginning of their relationship, Wayne liked Chata's mother, but her lengthy visits took their toll. Mrs. Ceballos was a beautiful woman with brownish red hair and green eyes, and she was less than ten years older than Duke. But she spoke little English, and he little Spanish. Catalina Lawrence, who had been born in Barcelona, helped Duke out when she could, taking Chata's mother shopping and getting her out of the house from time to time. But there was no getting around the fact that three adults were one too many in Wayne's small house. And when Duke complained about the arrangement all Chata would say was "Why don't you buy me a bigger house?"[33]

Duke had married Chata against the advice of Ward Bond, John Ford, Bo Roos, and several of his other friends, who claimed that her years as a fun-loving party girl did not bode well for a long-term relationship. He loved her deeply enough to ignore the rumors about her past and to put up with her mother. And at first, Chata was easy for him to love. She enjoyed exactly what he did, whether it was watching or talking about movies, spending the night drinking with him and a group of his friends, attending a prizefight, or going to a party. Though she had an accent, her English was excellent, and she joked and laughed easily. Those in Hollywood who knew her best said that she was a totally natural person, guileless and innocent, a woman who loved all children, Duke, and a good time.

But life between the two was seldom ideal and frequently difficult, and their problems ranged from cultural ones with solutions to emotional ones without. Duke, for example, was fastidiously clean, well groomed, and had great taste in clothes. He liked the feel of his skin after he had taken a hot shower with Neutrogena soap and put on freshly laundered clothes. Chata, however, often took a laissez-faire attitude toward how she was dressed. She cut her own hair, bought her own clothes, and put on her own makeup— none of which Duke thought she did particularly well. "She sometimes looked a bit peculiar and out of it," Mary St. John remembered. In addition, she did not always bathe as often as Wayne would have liked, a circumstance that he believed added to her acne troubles. He had particular difficulty dealing with the fact that like many Latin and European women, she did not shave her legs. She had thick, dark hair and was given to wearing sports clothes and dresses without stockings. "It drove Duke nuts," Mary St. John said, "but he was afraid to say anything to her, afraid that he would hurt her feelings." Finally, after Chata came to a Sunday brunch at Charles Feldman's home wearing a short, white tennis skirt, Duke begged people to intervene, and Chata began shaving her legs.

Other problems were not so easily handled. Within months Chata's mother became a greater source of friction. Both Chata and Mrs. Ceballos liked to shop and drink, and there were times when they did too much of both. Many times Duke would return home after a long day at Republic and find both well into their cups, arguing about something or other, or about him. Chata's mother was particularly convinced that an actor and an actress could not engage in a love scene without real feelings. The subject was like waving a red flag in front of Chata. Once started, it usually led to a fight. Angry at her mother for raising the issue and mad at her husband on the off chance her mother was right, she frequently pulled Duke into the battle. It was like living with his parents again. Emotional outbursts were part of the fabric of life at 4735 Tyrone.[34]

If Duke did not know it when he married Chata, he soon discovered that she was an alcoholic and a mean drunk. The problem would get worse in the later years of their marriage, when she began to drink more regularly, but there were early signs of her condition. Mary St. John vividly remembered Duke coming into his Republic offices one day in late 1946 with a nasty gash on his cheek. "Looks like someone really got even with you," she said as a joke. Duke did not laugh. "Yeah, my wife," he said, and shortly called Mary into his office to explain. The night before he and Chata had been invited to a party for a prominent Mexican businessman visiting in Los Angeles. The people hosting the party thought that the famous actor, who loved Mexico, and his Mexican wife would be ideal guests. But Chata got drunk and belligerent and insulted everyone from both north and south of the border. Embarrassed, Duke suggested they leave. Chata refused, shouting that she was having a good time. Duke insisted. Chata ignored him. Finally, he lifted her up, put her over his shoulder, and carried her out to their car. When they were both inside, she reached over and deeply scratched his face. Duke told Mary that he did not say a word, just drove home and locked his wife in their bedroom. The next morning at breakfast Chata insisted that he, not she, had been drunk and that he had no right to remove her from a perfectly good party.

It was a sign of worse to come, but in early 1946 Wayne was married to a woman whom he felt he loved. If there were occasional bad times, there were far more good times when they laughed and had fun and thoroughly enjoyed each other's company. "Duke deeply, deeply loved Chata," Catalina Lawrence said, "and Chata was devoted to him." Focusing only on their battles, at least in their first few years of marriage, as some books on Wayne have done, distorts their relationship.[35]

His career was entering a happy phase as well. Under the terms of his new contract, Wayne became an independent producer at Republic. He had the right to find and develop projects, hire talent, and control the editing of his films. As soon as he returned from his honeymoon, he began planning for his debut as a producer. His first decision was to hire Mary St. John. Mary had been born in Missouri and had planned a career in law, enrolling in a law school after graduating from high school. But on her first day in class, a professor who felt that there was no place for women lawyers set out to embarrass her. She was the only female in the class, but she was the one he chose to ask: "In rape cases, to what extent must penetration occur in order to constitute rape?" She turned red, picked up her books, walked out of the class, and dropped out of school. She then entered the University of Missouri and graduated four years later. For three years she worked for a prominent Kansas City attorney who specialized in personal injury cases and made it a general rule not to believe anyone who walked through his door. In one important case, scheduled for trial January 2, 1936, he needed someone to work with him on New Year's Day. Mary volunteered. After he won the case, he rewarded her with a month-long vacation to anywhere she wanted to go. Mary left a blizzard in Kansas City and discovered sun in California, and her Hollywood vacation lasted for forty years. She could type, take dictation, and manage an office, and she got a job in the Republic secretarial pool. Since 80 percent of the women in the pool had no secretarial skills and only wanted to be discovered for the movies, she was soon in charge of the pool. On the day in 1939 when she congratulated John Wayne for his performance in *Stagecoach,* he told her that if he ever needed an assistant, he wanted her for the job. In 1946 he offered her that position, and she remained loyal to Duke through his marital and economic troubles, his triumphs and political controversies, until he died.[36]

The second person he brought onto his production team was James Edward Grant, a former Chicago newspaperman who had joined the army of journalists that had invaded Hollywood after the introduction of sound. Irving Thalberg had summoned Grant to the West Coast after buying the rights to one of the writer's magazine stories. Grant, noted one writer, looked like "a successful gangster or a shrewd metropolitan detective." With his compact build and crew cut, he seemed to have stepped out of the pages of a Mickey Spillane novel. As a screenwriter he had enjoyed several hits; Spencer Tracy starred in his *Whipsaw* (1935) and *Boom Town* (1940), and Van Heflin won an Oscar in *Johnny Eager* (1942). John Ford introduced Grant to Duke in the early 1940s, and the two became friends. Both were consumed with the industry, and both were drinkers—Duke a hard social drinker, Grant a full-fledged alcoholic.[37]

Early in 1946 Grant handed Duke a script he had written entitled *The Angel and the Outlaw,* the story of a gunfighter who falls in love with a Quaker and renounces violence. It was an offbeat Western, different from the ones Wayne had done in the past. It lacked substantial action and was decidedly wordy, but Duke liked its compelling story and strong hero. He was particularly struck with Grant's writing, which combined colorful Western language with a good dose of moralizing. Grant made only one request: He knew the screenplay better than anyone else and wanted to direct it himself. Like Wayne, he wanted to explore other aspects of the industry. For Duke's initial move into production, however, it was probably the wrong script and the wrong director. He might have been better served by a more traditional Western—one that lacked ambiguity and was strong on gunplay and stunts—and a more experienced director. But his career was moving steadily upward—he was on a roll—and he decided to take a chance. Ford had taken a chance on him, Duke told Louella Parsons, now it was his turn to take a chance on a friend.[38]

Throughout the early spring Duke and Grant worked through the preproduction details. Both reveled in the tasks of developing the script and hiring the cast and crew, and they frequently worked from early morning at Duke's Republic offices to late at night at the actor's home. "Our two families were practically so close we might as well have been living in the same house," Duke later recalled. Duke's interest in the project bordered on an obsession. "My husband is one of the few persons who is always interested in business," Chata explained. "He talks of it constantly. When he reads, it's scripts. Our dinner guests always talk business, and he spends all his time working, discussing work or planning work." Like John Ford, Wayne rounded up his friends. He gave nice supporting roles to Harry Carey and Bruce Cabot; hired Yakima Canutt to coordinate the stunt work and handle second-unit chores; and employed Archie Stout, who had shot so many of his Lone Star and Republic Westerns, as the cinematographer. Also like John Ford, Wayne was a temperamental leader, given to frequent outbursts and finding it difficult to give an order without shouting, swearing, and insulting someone. But once he realized that he had offended a member of his crew or cast, he was just as quick to apologize. "I'm always apologizing to somebody," he told a reporter.[39]

One person he seldom had to apologize to was Gail Russell, a beautiful brunette with large, sad, dark-blue eyes, whom he cast in the lead female role. Catalina Lawrence, the script supervisor for the film, recalled that none of Republic's leading ladies suited Wayne, so he paid $125,000 to Paramount for Russell. "She was just so beautiful. No one, not even Elizabeth Taylor, was as beautiful as Gail." She had started her career in Hollywood before graduating from Santa Monica High School, and although she was only twenty-one when she went to work for Duke, she had already been in the industry too long. "Everything happened so fast," she later said. "I was going to Santa Monica High and the next thing I knew I was being groomed for a picture." There "was always a sense of pressure, no time to think, to relax, to take stock." During her three years in the industry, producers, directors, and actors had taken advantage of her, demanding sexual favors and casting her on the proverbial couch. She was just too fragile and insecure to say no. Wayne was kind and gentle with her, something she probably had not experienced from males in the business, and she became emotionally and physically attracted to him, though he did not take advantage. Shortly before she died in 1961, of natural causes but in a vodka stupor, at the age of thirty-six, she told a producer: "You know, the one word that defines Duke is 'honest.' He's an honest man. He can't be otherwise." Wayne became her unofficial therapist and father figure, listening to her for hours at a time. He wanted to protect her and take care of her. "Gail, you just got to learn to say no to some of this shit," he kept telling her.[40]

Duke began shooting *Angel and the Badman* in April. Although Grant was the director, Wayne controlled how the film was shot. Throughout his life

Duke maintained that he did not act, he reacted. By this he meant that he played off the other actors. His breakthrough role in *Stagecoach* was essentially one with few words and strong reactions. Ford had the camera linger on Wayne because he spent most of the film listening and reacting to what the other characters said. Now he followed Ford's philosophy in positioning his own camera. In any given scene, he was more interested in the reactions of the listener than the speaker. Viewers, after all, can sense the speaker's emotions from his or her words, but they have to see the listener. Wayne was not interested in the camera always focusing on him. Unlike other stars, he never counted the minutes of camera time he received in a film, because he knew that strong supporting performances made the star look even better. Here, too, he never forgot the lessons he learned making *Stagecoach*.[41]

On the surface it appears that Wayne patterned his filmmaking closely after John Ford's. *Angel and the Badman* begins with a pan of Monument Valley, and it emphasizes reaction shots. But ultimately it does not have the look or the feel of a John Ford film. Its black-and-white camera work does not have the subtlety of a Ford movie, and it lacks Ford's humor and meandering pace. The film has the stark simplicity of a Monogram Western—which is hardly surprising given the fact that Stout was the cinematographer—or a 1920s William S. Hart picture, and the moral tone of the more melodramatic silent era. Like many of Grant's later scripts, it deals in simple maxims. "Only the doer can be hurt by a mean or evil act," says one character. "The gun is the symbol of force, of evil," says another. A sampler reads, "Each human being has an integrity that can be hurt only by the act of that same human being, and not by the act of another human being." A crusty rancher is emotionally reborn after doing a good deed, and an outlaw becomes enthralled with reading the Bible. The theme of salvation, of hope, runs throughout. Quirt Evans (John Wayne) is a Western Odysseus who finally discovers the peace of home. Penelope Worth (Gail Russell), whose loom is in the same room where she nurses Quirt back to health, is portrayed as the ideal woman—loyal, steadfast, willing to follow her man anywhere.

But *Angel and the Badman* is a better film than its long stretches of moralizing would suggest. A *New York Times* critic called it "different from and a notch or two superior to the normal sagebrush saga." The outdoor camera work is superb, and at times the direction is of so high a quality that several critics suspected that John Ford might have spent some time on the set, though there is no evidence that he did. Bruce Cabot and Lee Dixon turn in strong supporting performances, and Harry Carey shows his skill in a tailor-made role as the patient, laconic marshal. Finally, *Angel and the Badman* may be Gail Russell's best film. For perhaps the only time in her career she demonstrates "the haunting mixture of sweetness and sex appeal she possessed, and was either unable to control properly or unwilling to submit to proper guidance," noted one critic. Although the reviews of the film were mixed, and it was not a great box-office success, Duke was satisfied with the results.[42]

If producing *Angel and the Badman* was an important step in Wayne's career, it further disrupted his marriage. From the first, Chata felt uneasy with Gail Russell's interest in her husband, and the more time he spent away from home the more suspicious she became. She resented Duke's treatment of his costar, his willingness to listen to her problems and to help her out. "Chata got so jealous that anytime Gail even came toward his office Duke would head out the back door," Mary St. John said.[43]

Chata's suspicion and resentment reached a boiling point on the night of the wrap party at Eaton's, a restaurant opposite Republic Studios. Just cast and crew were invited, no spouses, and most people drank too much and enjoyed themselves, feeling certain that they had made a hit. Duke, who had been burdened by the pressures of being both the producer and the star, drank more than the rest. When the party ended around 8:30 P.M., a few people decided to go to another bar for more to drink, and they left in two cars. Duke offered to drop Gail off at her family's apartment and drove her car. They got separated in traffic from the other automobile, searched for their friends in several bars, then stopped at Carl's Restaurant, on the beach near Santa Monica, for food and more drinks. They stayed for a while. Duke saw several old Glendale friends, who called him Marion, and an artist made a charcoal sketch of Gail. It was almost midnight when they reached Gail's apartment and Wayne was drunk, but not so plastered that he did not know he was drunk. Gail's mother was in a robe, and Duke apologized for arriving late. He talked for a while with Gail's mother and brother, had another drink or two, then called a taxi to take him home. About 1:00 A.M. Gail's brother helped Duke into a cab, which took him from Santa Monica to his home in the San Fernando Valley.[44]

The door to Wayne's home was locked when he arrived there, and he did not have a key. He knocked and rang the bell, and though no one answered, he could hear Chata and her mother "whispering—buzz, buzz, buzz—inside." He called out: "Chata, come on—open the door. It's Duke." When there was still no answer, he broke a glass panel, reached inside, and unlocked the door. Then he lay on a couch. He could hear his wife and mother-in-law "yabba-yabba-yabba-ing" in another room. The next thing he remembered, Chata was pointing a .45 automatic at him, and her mother was shouting: "Don't shoot, that's your husband."[45]

Chata, not surprisingly, would later tell a slightly different version of the story, one that suggested that Duke and Gail Russell were engaged in an affair. In court she claimed that her husband had promised to return for dinner, and when he failed to show up she had become concerned because "at a party like that Mr. Wayne usually drinks very, very much. I was afraid he was in an accident." Chata called Eaton's, only to be told that her husband had left hours before. She then called Duke's production assistant, Al Silverman, who was supposed to be his driver for the night, and got his wife, Jewel. Chata asserted that Jewel gave her the number of a hotel where Al said he could be reached, but she was unable to get in touch with either Duke or Silverman. Eventually she went to bed but was awoken at about 6:00 A.M. by the crash of breaking glass. "I grabbed a gun and went down the hallway," adding that Duke kept two loaded automatic weapons on the nightstand by his bed and had told her "not to be afraid to use a gun if anyone came into the house." And after seeing shattered glass on the floor and the door open, she was prepared to fire. "I was positive someone had broken in. I saw somebody on the couch and I was just about to shoot when my mother grabbed me." She said that her husband was "disheveled and quite intoxicated," so drunk in fact that he could not even walk to their bedroom. The next day, she said, he told her that he and Gail Russell had spent the night together, alone, at her home. Duke's attorney later asked him if there was any truth to Chata's allegations, and Duke assured him emphatically: "Absolutely not!"

Chata's story had the details the tabloids love, but it was illogical. Why was she worried about her husband drinking too much and having an accident when she believed he had a driver? Why would an intruder break into the house and fall asleep on the couch? Both Duke and Chata agreed that he had come home very late—though how late was disputed—and very drunk, that he had gone to sleep or passed out on the couch, and that she had pointed a gun at him. Duke, however, insisted that he had not been alone with Gail Russell in her apartment, and that he certainly had not had an affair with her. Mary St. John knew Duke, Chata, and Gail—knew them all well—and was certain about one thing. There was no affair between John Wayne and Gail Russell—not then, not ever. Two years later Duke told Pilar, his new wife, "I told Mary St. John to set Gail straight. Make sure she understands how I feel, but do it gently. The poor kid's having a tough time."[46]

The whole episode might have been forgotten, or at least kept out of the newspapers, had it not been dredged up by Chata during her 1953 divorce proceeding against Duke. At the time it had not had a profound impact on either of their lives. Their marriage was so tumultuous, so given to passionate extremes, that one major blowup, one way or the other, hardly seems to have mattered. Within a few days of the fight they had moved on to another crisis. Chata discovered that Wayne and Grant had each given Russell an additional $500 above her salary so that she could put a down payment on a new car. Again Chata became enraged. "I wondered why unless there was some relation between them, some friendship or closeness," she said. Again Duke explained that he was not "running around" with Gail Russell and the money was for the work she had done on his film. Although he paid Paramount $125,000 for her services, that studio was only paying her $125 a week. All totaled, he said, he had given out $2,500 in gifts to members of his cast and crew. This incident, like so many others, soon passed.[47]

In the context of 1946, the flare-ups over Gail Russell entailed just a few bad days. They certainly did not weigh heavily on Duke's mind. He was more concerned with the postproduction details of *Angel and the Badman* than with Chata's occasional emotional outbursts. By the time the film was cut, edited, and ready for release, it was time to make his 1947 RKO film.

The films he had made at RKO from 1943 to 1947 had all done well at the box office. One senses, however, that despite everything RKO producers did not have full confidence in Wayne's drawing power. They had starred him in a low-budget Western (*Tall in the Saddle*) and a World War II film (*Back to Bataan*), both fairly secure bets given Duke's career and the popularity of such films during the war years. They had matched him with better-known female leads—Jean Arthur in *A Lady Takes a Chance* and Claudette Colbert in *Without Reservations*—and given him second billing. By 1947, however, they finally felt that he could carry a high-budget, Technicolor spectacular, and they gave him top billing in *Tycoon*.

The film was intended to fill a wide screen. But from the first there were problems. Initially Maureen O'Hara had been named to play opposite Wayne, but RKO producers assigned her to another film and cast Laraine Day in the part of Duke's strong-willed lover. It was a mistake. As would subsequently become obvious, O'Hara and Wayne were perfectly matched. They had the same powerful screen presence, the ability to dominate scenes and not be swallowed by each other's performance. It was exactly what *Tycoon* called for. Day, by contrast, had emerged as a star in the Dr. Kildare film series and was best suited for domestic drama. She did not have the presence to play opposite John Wayne in a big adventure film. RKO also shifted locations for the film. It had intended to shoot the film at its new studio in Churubusco, Mexico, a suburb of Mexico City, but less than a week before the start of production there was a change in plans. Doubts about the lighting facilities in their Mexico studio, and perhaps a few concerns about the political stability south of the border, prompted the decision. Instead of shooting in an exotic Latin location, most of the outdoor scenes were filmed in Lone Pine.[48]

Laraine Day's recent marriage added to the problems. Shortly before filming began on *Tycoon*, she had been granted an interlocutory decree in her divorce proceeding against Ray Hendrick in California. But instead of waiting the mandatory year before remarrying, she went to Juarez, Mexico, obtained a "quickie divorce," then recrossed the border into El Paso and married Leo Durocher, the controversial manager of the Brooklyn Dodgers. The press had a field day with baseball's bad boy and his new Mormon bride, who neither drank nor smoked. Though the marriage did not hamper *Tycoon*, Durocher did. When shooting began in early February, before spring training, the manager became a frequent visitor on the set, and he never adjusted to seeing his wife in Duke's embrace. He just sat there day after day, Wayne recalled, watching him like a base runner who was preparing to steal home. Perhaps his presence, as much as anything else, was responsible for the decided lack of passion in the love scenes.[49]

Little could have helped the lackluster plot, however. *Tycoon* is the story of Johnny Munroe (John Wayne), the head of a railroad construction company laying tracks through the Andes. In the course of the film he falls in love with and marries Maura Alexander (Laraine Day) and battles her wealthy, possessive father (Cedric Hardwicke). Empire building, forbidden love, money, and enough dynamite to blow away the Andes—the film had potential. Duke's character, however, is poorly developed. For reasons difficult to understand, he begins the film as a gruff but good-hearted boss, changes into a maniacal Ahab, and ends up as a sweetheart. It made no sense, and the reviewers said as much. "*Tycoon* emerges as a halting, wordy and escapist item hardly worth all those expensive trappings," commented a *New York Times* critic. And James Agee in a "Midwinter Clearance" review summed the movie up in one sentence: "Several tons of dynamite are set off in this movie; none of it under the right people."[50]

Tycoon did not do badly at the box office; *Variety* listed it thirty-sixth for 1948's top-grossing films. It just did not do well enough to recover its costs, running $1,075,000 in the red. Mary St. John remembered that Duke was disappointed by the film and the reviews, and that he was beginning to have doubts about his career. It was not a question of talent but of age. He turned forty-one in 1948. He was losing his hair and having trouble keeping weight off. He was still handsome, but not *as* handsome as he had been a decade earlier when he was making *Stagecoach*. And a new crop of young, handsome, talented leading men were storming Hollywood. Duke was not sure how many years he had left as a leading man, and he was uncertain if he could play anything else. Unlike so many other actors, he had rarely played character or secondary roles. In good films and bad, he had always been the leading man. Looking around, he saw only one other avenue for aging leading men: producing and directing. No one cared if a producer was bald or a director fat, and the footsteps of younger men did not seem as loud. Age, he reasoned, might thin his hair, but it could not take away his knowledge of the profession. And so as 1948 approached he planned for new directions.[51]

What he did not plan for, what he did not anticipate, was becoming the greatest box-office attraction in the history of motion pictures.

12

"All I Can See Is the Flags"

66 It was a boiling hot day, really nastily hot," remembered actress Anna Lee. Born and raised in England, she was not accustomed to the brutal, late-summer heat of Corrigan's Ranch in California. John Ford was setting up a key shot in *Fort Apache*, the moment when Lt. Col. Owen Thursday's (Henry Fonda) regiment rides away from the safety of the fort to battle the Apaches. It took three hours for the director to line up the shot. He wanted everything just right. The horses had to be lined up straight, the regimental colors had to be blowing just so, the clouds had to be perfect. Finally it was time for Lee's big scene. As the regiment moves out, her character, Mrs. Collingwood, receives news that her husband, Capt. Sam Collingwood, has been transferred to West Point. The other women encourage her to give the news to him immediately to save him from the ordeal he is about to face, but she refuses. Once before in his career Collingwood had been falsely suspected of cowardly behavior, and his wife refuses to provide the cause for more rumors. No, death would be preferable to that. So instead of calling her husband back, she watches. Flanked by Philadelphia Thursday (Shirley Temple) and Mrs. Mary O'Rourke (Irene Rich), she watches her husband ride out of sight, until finally she says: "I can't see him. All I can see is the flags."[1]

The line offended Shirley Temple's sense of proper English. "I don't think that's good grammar," the nineteen-year-old star said after the scene was shot. Temple might as well have told Ford that he was a lousy filmmaker. Almost everyone on the set stopped breathing as they waited for the director to explode. Anna Lee and Irene Rich just looked at each other as if Temple had just put a match to the American flag. But Ford truly liked the sweet, young actress, and he remained calm. "Now where did you go to school, Shirley?" he asked. "Did you graduate? Do you think that you could write a better script?" Sensing that she had committed an unpardonable sin, Shirley mumbled an apology, and Ford laughed.[2]

There was nothing wrong with Shirley Temple's grammar, but John Ford did not need anyone to point out good or bad writing to him. The line "All I can see is the flags" is the single most memorable sentence in a powerful, beautiful film. It is the heart of *Fort Apache*, and Ford felt its truth in his bones. After living with soldiers and sailors, officers and noncommissioned men, during World War II, he knew that wars were less about men than about symbols. It was the symbols and timeless rituals that glued men from different ethnic groups, races, religions, and classes together. By the thousands they had died for the flag, and Ford loved the simple ceremonies that surrounded it. *Fort Apache*, his classic war movie, is a stirring, patriotic reaffirmation of that flag and those military traditions.

The film began the most consistently productive phase of John Wayne's career. Between the summers of 1947 and 1950, Duke starred in eight films. The roles he played in those movies presented him as a unique American hero. In four of the films he was a military hero, in three an empire builder, in one a religious icon. With a single exception, they were all superior films and roles, and Duke made the most of each. At the end of 1947, after one mediocre and one terrible film, he had worried that his career had reached a critical stage. By 1950 he had received an Academy Award nomination and was Hollywood's leading box-office attraction. By that year too, his image had become fused in the public's mind with America's past, present, and future. More than ever before, he was John Wayne, American.

Like any Hollywood image, it was the end result of the work of many men. But of the many, John Ford was the most important. Even before Duke had completed *Tycoon*, he heard that Ford was casting a new picture. In 1946 Ford and Merian Cooper had formed Argosy Productions and signed a three-picture deal with RKO. Their first film, *The Fugitive*, had been a financial bust, and Argosy needed a hit. The commercial success of *My Darling Clementine*, which he had made two years earlier at Twentieth Century-Fox, convinced him to return to a Western theme. In March 1947 he had bought the rights to James Warner Bellah's short story "Massacre," which had appeared in *The Sat-*

urday Evening Post the month before. Combining Ford's two favorite subjects, the West and the military, "Massacre" is the tale of two officers, Owen Thursday, a major general and hero in the Civil War who after the war had been reduced to the rank of major and put in command of a Western post, and Flintridge Cohill, a first lieutenant who had been raised on Western posts. Thursday is Gen. George Armstrong Custer thinly disguised, proud, vain, ambitious for honor and glory, frustrated that he has been banished to an insignificant frontier outpost. Cohill is everything that is noble about the army; he is strong, competent, and devoted to honor and duty. The mood Bellah created, the raw, honest sketches of the main characters, was perfect material for John Ford, who preferred to develop films from short stories rather than novels.[3]

Ford followed his usual procedure in casting the film. He sat in his office and waited for his regulars, one at a time, to come in to see him, at which time they would chat for a while about anything but his upcoming film and then toward the end of the aimless conversation Ford might say, "Oh yes, by the way," and offer the person a part. Or he might not. "That's the way it worked," said Harry Carey Jr. "No one ever asked him anything about the picture—not John Wayne, not Victor McLaglen, not Ward Bond—not anybody. You sat there until he told you, and when he did, he usually told you a little about the story and a little about your part in it."[4]

Ford offered Wayne the role of Cohill (changed to Captain Kirby York in the film). Although it was a major part, it was not *the* major part. Ford believed that he needed a real actor, a man with emotional range and a solid reputation, to play Owen Thursday. In 1947 he had only one "leading man"—Henry Fonda. Fonda was proven goods, and his work was unassailable. From *Young Mr. Lincoln* (1939) and *Drums Along the Mohawk* (1939) to *The Grapes of Wrath* (1940), *My Darling Clementine* (1946), and *The Fugitive* (1947), he had delivered the performance that Ford desired. Wayne's parts in *Stagecoach*, *The Long Voyage Home*, and *They Were Expendable* had been limited in their emotional range. The director liked Duke, but was still not sure he was a good enough actor for a psychologically complex role. More than a year later, after Ford saw Wayne in *Red River*, he told director Howard Hawks: "I never knew the big son of a bitch could act."[5]

The part of Captain Kirby York, however, was far from the typical John Wayne role. Former *New York Times* film reviewer Frank Nugent's screenplay did not call on Duke to play an action hero or a romantic lead: York does not wipe out the enemy, save the day, or win the heart of the heroine. John Agar plays the romantic lead, and the film's major action occurs in the climactic massacre scene, an engagement in which York does not even participate. York's most heroic attribute is restraint. He is called upon to follow orders, even when he knows that those orders will lead to disaster, and in the end it is his duty to bury the dead, cover up the mess, and "for the good of the service" tell the world that Owen Thursday died a hero. Before filming began, Duke was frankly concerned about the subtlety of his role. While Fonda got to "strut" around like a martinet, Agar got to make "moon eyes" at Shirley Temple, and Victor McLaglen, Pedro Armendariz, and Ward Bond got "every goddamn humorous line in the script," Duke had to quietly display a sense of honor, duty, and service. It was not his idea of a great part.[6]

But that was what Ford offered, and Duke was not about to question his judgment. He knew what Harry Carey Jr. would later learn: "There was absolutely no chain of command with John Ford. There was him, and there was us. There was no star except him, and he treated us all the same." Instead in June 1947 Duke packed his bags and went to Monument Valley—Ford's "lucky spot"—with the rest of the cast and crew and did what he was told. Although Duke, as one of the film's three stars, was assigned a room at Goulding's lodge and did not have to live in a tent like lesser ranked members of the cast, he was subject to the same heat and winds as everyone else. There was nothing simple about making a film in Monument Valley. It was hot dirty work. Desert storms and high winds caused delays, upset schedules, created budget overruns, and made Ford's temper sharp.[7]

John Agar felt the force of the director's anger more than the rest. The son of a meat packer, in 1946 Agar had been honorably discharged from the Army Air Corps, signed to a film contract by David Selznick, and married to Shirley Temple. He was tall, had a rugged jaw, and a smooth, unlined baby face. *Fort Apache* was his first film, and he was totally unprepared for John Ford's attacks. Gil Perkins, a stuntman on the film, recalled that Ford just "ate him alive. Oh, there was nothing this poor kid could do that was right; he just chewed him up one side and down the other." Biographer Ronald L. Davis wrote, "Psychologists might suggest that Ford feared the feminine side of himself . . . and lashed out at 'pretty boy' types. An even darker interpretation might infer that the director's need for dominance was a form of seduction." Or maybe Ford resented Agar's marriage to Shirley Temple, or was testing the man's grit, or was trying to pull out his best performance, or was just in a bad mood. Or perhaps Ben Johnson was closer to the truth when he charged that Ford "just did it for damn meanness." Whatever the reason, the director verbally jumped on Agar at the start of the film and made him hate life.[8]

Duke had been there, and he knew what Agar was feeling. After one particularly brutal attack Agar walked off the set and said he was going to quit the
picture. Duke had threatened to do the same thing almost a decade before on
the set of *Stagecoach*, but he had stuck with it, and he encouraged Agar to do
the same. Ford was under severe pressures, Duke explained, and did not mean
anything personally. "You're the whipping boy now, but give him time. He'll
get around to the rest of us soon enough." Agar stayed, and Wayne's prediction came true. Dan Ford said that a few days later Ward Bond arrived in
Monument Valley, but not before he convinced the pilot of the private plane
to buzz the set, ruining a take and causing another delay. "Well, you can relax
now, he's found another whipping boy," Duke told Agar.[9]

Ford spared no one. Duke accepted his methods as a basic characteristic of
the man, but the director's brutal side bothered Fonda. Michael Wayne, who
had gone to Monument Valley with his father, recalled seeing tears in Fonda's
eyes after one confrontation with Ford. "He just turned and walked away," said
Michael. Ford's minimal directions to his actors also frustrated Fonda. The director did not like to discuss scenes or motivation or particulars; he just wanted
his orders followed. "If an actor came up to him and wanted to talk about a
scene, he would change the subject or tell him to shut up," Fonda said.[10]

But even with Ford's frequent bursts of anger, life on the set of *Fort Apache*
was not without its finer moments. Michael Wayne remembered the hard
work—the six-day workweeks and the eighteen-hour workdays—but he also
fondly recalled the long, quiet Monument Valley nights, the sound of Danny
Borzage's accordion or a lone singer's voice floating across the desert air, and
the flash lightning in the pitch black sky. He remembered his father and John
Ford playing cards well into the night. Duke thought Michael brought him
luck in games of pitch and would "shoot the moon" when his son was around.
"Get that goddamn kid out of here," Ford would shout. He also remembered
Sunday masses that everyone—Protestants and Jews as well as Catholics—attended and Ford passing the hat and watching to make sure nobody let it go
by without contributing something.[11]

In mid-August, after Ford finished the location work in Monument Valley,
the cast and crew returned to California for interior shooting at the Selznick
studio in Culver City and some additional outdoor filming at Corrigan's
Ranch. On October 2, 1947, Ford finished work on *Fort Apache* and boarded
the *Araner* for Mexico.[12]

Duke, Bond, and Fonda joined him in Mazatlán. After the long difficult
shoot, everyone unwound in their own way. Ford spent most of his time

aboard the *Araner*, too drunk to make it into town. The others hired a mari-
achi band and roamed from "bar to bar, saloon to saloon, whorehouse to
whorehouse." They drank, listened to the music, and talked. "You didn't
fuck," Fonda later recalled. "You didn't think you should. Those whores
looked grungy." But they did laugh and enjoy themselves. One night, Fonda
said, they all got drunk at the bar in the Central Hotel, spotted an American
couple on their honeymoon, and invited them over to their table for a drink.
"Now Duke, who was a great talker and a great storyteller, was holding forth.
. . . Like Ford, it was impossible for him to say two sentences without using
words that would put a dockworker to shame. He was telling a story to the
young bride and her groom and suddenly out popped, ' . . . and then, the
cocksucker . . . oh, shit! I'm sorry.'" Fonda laughed loud and hard. "Oh, shit!
I'm sorry," he repeated.[13]

  Drunk or sober, they had earned their vacation. *Fort Apache* put both
Wayne's and Ford's careers back on solid ground and set a new standard for
war films by adding depth and complexity to the issues of combat and service.
Although some critics and moviegoers considered *Fort Apache* a Western, the
only thing Western about it is its setting. Otherwise the central characteristics
of the Western—especially the independent, tough outsider who rides into
town, solves the problems of the community, and then rides out of town—are
absent. What is present is the sense of combat and military traditions Ford
had experienced during World War II. He had met officers like Owen Thursday, men obsessed by glory and publicity; he had also served with men like
Kirby York, for whom duty and the integrity of their regiment was everything. As Dan Ford has claimed, his grandfather had fallen in love with military service and traditions—or at least in love with the idea of being in
love—and that love lies close to the heart of the film. The movie begins with a
bugler playing "Officer's Call," and some of the finest sequences in *Fort
Apache* lovingly depict life on the outpost—the observed formalities of
dances, the traditions of training recruits, the interaction of experienced noncommissioned officers, the arcane knowledge of frontier officers. Scored with
such traditional cavalry songs as "Gary Owen," "The Girl I Left Behind Me,"
and "Regular Army O," the film creates a powerful sense of nostalgia for the
lost world of the army, a world of absolute order and harmony, governed at
once by a rigid code and an unshakable faith in democracy. The mood Ford
creates is similar to Rudyard Kipling's celebrations of the British empire.[14]

  The threat to this world comes from inside, not outside, the compound.
The Indian threat is inconsequential; they are, after all, reasonable men with

legitimate grievances. Owen Thursday is the only real threat. He is the fanatic, not the Indian leader; he is the racist, not his soldiers; he is the caste snob without honor, not his officers. And of course his prejudice, ignorance, and pride leads to his death—through suicide in Bellah's original short story and a suicidal decision not to retreat in the film.

But Thursday's faults are covered up by Capt. Kirby York "for the good of the service." He tells several reporters, "No man died more gallantly. Nor won more honors for his regiment," adding that the painting "Thursday's Charge" was "correct in every detail." Although most critics have interpreted York's defense of Thursday as ironic, Ford meant no irony. York's lies were not meant to convey but to conceal the truth, for Ford believed that the reputation of the regiment was far more important than the simple falsification of history. With the "Battle Hymn of the Republic" playing in the background, York praises the officers and soldiers who died with Thursday but live in the collective memory of their regiment: "They aren't forgotten, because they haven't died. They're living. . . . And they'll keep on living, as long as the regiment lives. The pay is thirteen dollars a month, their diet beans and hay—they'll eat horsemeat before the campaign is over—fight over cards or rotgut whisky, but share the last drop of their canteens. The faces may change, and the names, but they're there, they're the regiment, the regular army, now and fifty years from now."

In the end Ford affirms the military's, not Hollywood's, sense of the happy ending. Years later Peter Bogdanovich asked Ford: "The end of *Fort Apache* anticipates the newspaper editor's line in *The Man Who Shot Liberty Valance*, 'When the legend becomes a fact, print the legend.' Do you agree with that?" "Yes," the director answered, "because I think it's good for the country. We've had a lot of people who were supposed to be great heroes, and you know damn well they weren't. But it's good for the country to have heroes to look up to." Although John Ford could see more than the flags, it was the flags which were the most important.[15]

John Wayne delivered Ford's message to America. More than any other character in the film, he represented the director's love of the military and his country. And Duke did so with complete sincerity. His low-key, almost understated portrayal of Kirby York was one of the finest in his career. Reviewers praised his work, audiences responded, and *Fort Apache* finished twenty-second on *Variety*'s list of leading moneymakers for 1948.[16]

Before Duke even saw the final cut of *Fort Apache*, however, he was putting the finishing touches on another film. Actually he had done most of his work on it before *Fort Apache*, though various complications prevented its release.

In December 1945 director Howard Hawks had declared his independence of the Hollywood studio system and formed his own company, Monterey Productions. Although Hawks had made films ranging from action and adventure to crime and comedy, he had never made a Western, but for Monterey's first—and only—independent production he purchased the rights to Borden Chase's story "The Chisholm Trail"—even before it was serialized in the *Saturday Evening Post*—and began work on the film *Red River*. From the first it was an ambitious project. He budgeted the picture at two million dollars, a huge sum for an independent production in 1946, and planned to make an epic about the first cattle drive along the Chisholm Trail.[17]

The Chase story was a sprawling epic, strong on action and incidents but weak on characterization and psychological depth. "It is simply amazing that Hawks could make such a good movie out of such terrible material," wrote an authority on Hawks's films. But together with Chase, screenwriter Charles Schnee, and executive producer Charles Feldman, Hawks brought a focus to the material, structuring the epic tale within an equally epic confrontation between Thomas Dunson, a strong-willed cattle baron, and his surrogate son, Matthew Garth. In the final screenplay the cattle drive serves as the backdrop for the intensely personal story of two powerful men.

Hawks initially planned to cast Gary Cooper as Dunson and Cary Grant as the gunfighter Cherry Valance, a part that was more important in the original script than it was in the completed film. Both men were Hawks favorites. Cooper had won the Best Actor Oscar in Hawks's *Sergeant York* (1941), and Grant had worked for the director in *Bringing Up Baby* (1938), *Only Angels Have Wings* (1939), and *His Girl Friday* (1940). But neither Cooper nor Grant wanted anything to do with the parts Hawks offered. Cooper thought Dunson's ruthlessness did not suit his screen image, and Grant just did not like the idea of playing a secondary part.[18]

At the urging of Charles Feldman, Hawks turned to Duke and offered him $75,000 and a share of the film's profits to play Dunson. Wayne was perfect for the role, better probably even than Cooper. No Western star in Hollywood commanded the screen quite as he did. By the end of World War II he simply dominated his films. The role, however, was also perfect for Wayne, although at first he did not think so. Thomas Dunson is strong and virile, but he is older and not the film's romantic lead. When Hawks talked to him about the part, Duke said he was not sure he wanted to play an "old man." "Duke, you're going to be one pretty soon, why don't you get some practice?" the director replied. Duke accepted the part.[19]

Casting Duke as Dunson was comparatively simple; more difficult was casting a younger actor who would not be dwarfed by Wayne. Hawks favored Montgomery Clift, a young New York stage talent trained at the Actor's Studio, to play Matthew Garth. The director had seen Clift the year before in the Broadway production of Tennessee Williams's and Donald Windham's *You Touched Me!* and been moved by Clift's sensitive portrayal of Hadrian. In February 1946 he offered Clift the part of Garth. The idea of playing opposite John Wayne in a Western intrigued Clift, but he initially refused. Hawks persisted, flying Clift out to Hollywood, discussing the script, and offering $60,000, a fabulous sum by Broadway standards. Finally, after considerable discussion with friends, Clift accepted.[20]

Duke was out of touch with Broadway, and the name Montgomery Clift meant nothing to him. When the two met in Duke's office at Republic, he was not impressed by the frail five-foot-ten-inch actor. Instead of sitting in a chair and talking with him man to man, Clift perched on the back of a sofa, put his feet on its cushions, mumbled inaudible responses to Duke's questions, and avoided making eye contact with anyone in the room. "He's a little queer, don't you think?" Duke asked Mary St. John after Clift left. "Christ, how does Howard expect that kid to stand up to me in a movie? He can't even look me in the eye."[21]

Wayne later told Hawks as much, "Howard, this is not going to work. . . . This kid isn't going to stand up to me." The director tried to explain that Clift had an intense quality that would translate well onto the big screen and that he felt, almost intuitively, that the slender actor could somehow pull it off. Duke shook his head, still not convinced.[22]

When shooting began in June 1946, in Rain Valley, a desolate area east of Tucson, Arizona, Duke learned to trust Hawks's instincts. Clift was determined to play his scenes with Wayne as resolutely as possible to demonstrate to viewers that he was a match for Duke. But Hawks said: "No, don't try to get hard, because you'll just be nothing compared to Wayne." Instead, he told Clift to underplay his scenes and give the impression that more was going on in his mind than his actions indicated. "The effect was electric," commented biographer Robert LaGuardia. Throughout the film Clift plays his scenes with a cool aloofness which contrasts wonderfully to Wayne's passionate intensity and still conveys a strength of character. When Wayne saw the first rushes he knew that he had made a mistake, that Clift would not be lost in his shadow. But he still worried about his climactic fight scene, confessing to Hawks: "He can hold his own, anyway, but I don't think we can make a fight."[23]

Wayne's attitude infuriated Clift, adding to the submerged rage and intensity he brought to the fight sequence. When Matthew Garth lifts himself off the ground and hits Dunson with a savage punch, one senses that Clift was striking back at Wayne. "We took four days [to film the fight], and my arm's still sore from trying to show Montgomery Clift how to throw a punch, every move," Hawks later recalled. But the scene worked. It was choreographed so that the size difference between Wayne and Clift is not apparent, and the finished product was convincing.[24]

On the set Clift learned film technique from Hawks and Wayne. He was almost too intense and precise for the two Hollywood veterans. "Monte, you don't have to study lines, you don't have to have them exact," Hawks told him. Calling Wayne over, the director said to Clift: "Just give us a situation." Clift did, and Hawks and Duke played the scene. "I'll be goddamned," Clift said. "I know you didn't know about this beforehand because I picked out the scene."[25]

Clift wanted to teach as well as learn. He particularly looked forward to the scene when Garth takes control of the cattle drive away from Dunson. On a personal level he saw the scene as the point where he would take control of the film. But taking a film away from John Wayne was never a simple task. Clift, observed Hawks, "thought he had a great scene," but Wayne played his part in an unexpected manner. As Clift delivered his speech about why he had assumed control over the drive, Duke looked away from him. Then in a flat, calm voice he called Garth "soft" and said: "I'm going to kill you, Matt." "Monte didn't know what to do," Hawks said. "Finally, he came out of the scene and came around to me and said, 'My good scene certainly went to the devil, didn't it?' I said, 'Anytime you think you're going to make Wayne look bad, you've got another thing coming.'"[26]

Off the set Duke and Clift had little in common. Unlike Ward Bond and the other actors Wayne was accustomed to working with, Clift was withdrawn and moody, given to fits of depression and silence. "Clift is an arrogant little bastard," Duke told a *Life* editor.[27]

Web Overlander, Duke's makeup man, was a particularly harsh Clift critic. Web was part court jester, part "pain-in-the-ass," but a permanent member of the Wayne entourage. A habitual liar, he was a constant source of amusement to Duke. He claimed to have been a coxswain at Yale, and he regularly read entries in the *Encyclopaedia Britannica* and then steered conversations around to those subjects. Bruce Cabot had dubbed him "the Assassin" because of his constant, behind-the-back attacks on his fellow workers. One night on the set of *Red River* an actor made a positive comment about Hawks's ability as a director, which prompted Web to say: "Hawks couldn't direct traffic." And if, in Web's opinion, Hawks was a bad director, Clift was a worse actor. "Christ, everyone knows Duke is carrying the picture. Clift couldn't take a piss by himself. Hawks must be an idiot if he thinks that s.o.b. can act."[28]

For his part Clift respected Wayne's and Hawks's professional abilities but disliked them on a personal level. He told a friend about Duke's and Hawks's nightly card games: "They laughed and drank and told dirty jokes and slapped each other on the back. They tried to draw me into their circle but I couldn't go along with them. The machismo thing repelled me because it seemed so forced and unnecessary."[29]

The relationship between Duke and Clift, however, was the least of Hawks's troubles. Budget miscalculations led to eight hundred thousand dollars or more in overruns, Rain Valley lived up to its name, writer Borden Chase drank more than he worked, and supporting actor John Ireland (Cherry Valance) was a constant problem. According to Hawks, he drank too much, smoked marijuana, carried on an affair with female lead Joanne Dru, kept losing his hat and gun, and could not remember his lines. "I just cut the hell out of his scenes and gave them to someone else," Hawks said. But the problems led to delays. Scenes had to be reshot, and the production, which was scheduled to be completed by the end of 1946, dragged on into 1947.[30]

Millionaire filmmaker Howard Hughes made matters worse when he sued Hawks for stealing the climactic fight scene from *The Outlaw*, a film the director had helped to develop but had left for another project. Hughes never forgave Hawks for running out on *The Outlaw*, and his suit came only one week before *Red River* was scheduled to open nationally and the same day as Hawks was leaving for Europe. Hawks instructed Christian Nyby, the film's editor, to take care of the problem. In an effort to please Hughes, Nyby cut and recut the final sequence. Hughes was not satisfied. Nyby cut some more. Sixteen times he reedited the scene, and Hughes was still dissatisfied. He then turned the process over to Hughes, who edited a version of his own. For hours Nyby and Hughes cut, reedited, and negotiated until they had something they both could live with. Altogether they cut twenty-four seconds from the fight scene. Nyby then redubbed the scene, sent the piece of film to the lab with an order for 450 copies, and hired "24 or 25 assistant editors and editors" to go to the various film exchanges and splice in the new final scene. The last-minute changes were successful and the picture opened on schedule.[31]

The result was worth the effort. *Red River* is an American epic, part *Odyssey*, part Old Testament Exodus, part *Huckleberry Finn*, part *Mutiny on the Bounty*. Film historian Gerald Mast believed that Hawks intentionally made an epic. Why call the film *Red River*—a title that no one else on the project liked or thought was relevant—unless he meant it as a reference to the Red Sea? "As in Exodus," Mast noted:

> the travelers cross a body of water called the "Red." . . . Once the travelers in both *Red River* and Exodus reach the wilderness on the other side of the Red, their troubles increase. Like Moses's reaction to the prostrate Israelites at the feet of the Golden Calf, Dunson's inflexible commitment to duty, honor, and the written law keeps him from understanding the weaknesses that have driven his weaker but equally mortal followers to the false idol. Like Moses, Dunson condemns his erring followers justly but harshly and, like Moses, he is repaid for his hubris, his harsh and inhuman sense of justice, by being deprived of his command. Joshua, not Moses, takes the children of Israel to the Promised Land, and Matthew, not Dunson, takes the men and the herd to Abilene.[32]

It is impossible to say if Hawks meant such conscious parallels. Nyby did not recall Hawks making any such reference, but he did believe that *Mutiny on the Bounty* was on Hawks's mind. It was certainly on Duke's: "I was playing [Charles] Laughton's part in *Mutiny on the Bounty* in *Red River*. It's just the story of *Mutiny on the Bounty* put into a Western, and the guy who wrote it did it that way." Hawks did, however, know he was making an epic Western, which was "America's guiding historical myth, our cultural equivalent of the Trojan War and the exodus from Egypt." He realized that by telling the story of the first cattle drive to Kansas he was enshrining an important chapter in the story of his country.[33]

Several critics have suggested that *Red River* is a badly flawed film, that it promises more than it delivers, and that in some respects it is a remarkably actionless action film. Throughout the first half of the film there is talk about Missouri border gangs and savage Indians, but Dunson's and Garth's drive never encounters a Missouri gang and easily and quickly dispatches the Indians they confront. The film seems to promise a gunfight between Garth and both Cherry Valance and Dunson, but delivers neither. Even the grand love between Matthew and Tess Millay (Joanne Dru) seems singularly underdeveloped and anticlimactic. The original Borden script was filled with action and adventure; it delivered all the anticipated fights. But Hawks used almost nothing Borden wrote, and he removed most of the violent action.[34]

Instead of gunfights and Indian attacks, Hawks focused on the psychological clash of opposites: the uncompromising, physically powerful Dunson and the flexible, seemingly soft and gentle Garth. Everything else, from the spectacular stampede and river crossing to the relationship between Dunson and Groot (Walter Brennan) and Garth and Tess Millay, is incidental. Like Hawks's later Westerns, *Red River* is a study of relationships between men—how they act, how they interact, how they work, and how they get the job done. Like so many literary epics—and unlike so many Hollywood epics—*Red River* had less to do with its panoramic canvas and everything to do with the human heart.

Many reviewers missed the central point of the film and judged it by the standards of a typical Western. Kyle Crichton, a Hollywood journalist, felt *Red River* was an example of a filmmaker attempting to avoid the issues of his day: "When things get tough in Hollywood they start the horses galloping. It is always a sure-fire formula, and famous directors like John Ford and Howard Hawks know when to use it. Nobody can yell 'propaganda' at a motion picture full of cows, horses, gun play, brave women and daring men." Bosley Crowther, the influential film critic of the *New York Times*, also assumed that *Red River* was only a Western, writing that "up to a point" the film was "on the way towards being one of the best cowboy pictures ever made. And even despite a big let-down, which fortunately comes near the end, it stands sixteen hands above the level of routine horse opera these days." What Crowther praised were the incidentals on Hawks's canvas, the cattle, cowpokes, rivers, and dust. It was the ending, the reconciliation between Garth and Dunson, that bothered him. Other reviewers also failed to notice the main theme but still accepted the film as a Hollywood epic. "Monumental in stature; sweeping in scope; and powerful in historical content, 'Red River' combines fact with fiction; action with dialogue; and enormity of subject matter with vastness of background to emerge as one of the screen's supreme examples of motion picture art and entertainment," claimed a *Variety* reviewer. Other critics agreed, sprinkling the words "epic," "monumental," "grand," and "lavish" throughout their reviews.[35]

A few of the reviewers singled out Wayne's portrayal of the aging, graying Dunson for special praise. *Variety* called Duke's performance "magnificent," and *Showmen's Trade Review* labeled it "one of the most potent characterizations of which Hollywood can boast." But no reviewer noted what Hawks—and later critics—realized: The part of Thomas Dunson was incredibly complex and difficult to play. Hawks called upon Duke to be hard, mean, cruel, headstrong, and as ruthlessly obsessed as Ahab and as unbending as

Capt. William Bligh. But without ever giving an inch, he also had to be somehow sympathetic. For the film to be successful, the audience had to want to see him live in the end. "We were walking a tightrope in telling a story like that," Hawks said. "Are you still going to like Wayne or not?"[36]

Wayne succeeded. "It may seem a hyperbolic claim," wrote Gerald Mast, "but no star in the history of film other than John Wayne could play this role in *Red River* and make it mean what it does and make the story mean what it does." At all times he commands the viewers' attention, even, as in the scene in which Garth takes the drive away from him, when he does nothing. His looming presence dominates the film even in the scenes from which he is absent. Such scenes as when he wades through an ocean of longhorns to get to Garth inspired film historian Jeanine Basinger to define "a nonmovie lover [as] the person who walks out of *Red River* talking about Montgomery Clift." Mast credited Hawks with creating John Wayne's screen character, the "rock-solid, firm, slightly over the hill, unbending in his stated commitments and intentions, using that inflexibility to mask his vulnerability and insecurity," and he further asserted that Duke had never played that character before *Red River*. In fact Wayne had already developed the character; Thomas Dunson is simply an extension of such earlier screen roles as Young Matt Matthews, Capt. Jack Stuart, Roy Glennister, Pittsburgh Markham, Wedge Donovan, Rocklin, and Johnny Munroe. But that is a little like saying that a Mercedes is an extension of the Model T Ford. Although he had played the Dunson type before, Duke had never breathed so much life into the character; he had never transformed the type into such a believable person. And it was a character he could play again and again, one that was not constrained by the same biological imperatives as the romantic lead. If Hawks's makeup artists could make Duke look in his mid-fifties to play Dunson, Wayne knew that when he was in his fifties—or sixties—he could still play Dunson.[37]

Red River was a smash hit. It finished second on *Variety*'s list of the leading moneymakers for 1948 with domestic rentals of $4,150,000. As far as Duke was concerned, however, he had been shortchanged financially on the film. The production and postproduction problems bankrupted Monterey Productions, and not only did Wayne not receive a percentage of the film, but as late as 1951 he was still trying to get his full $75,000. But the money was irrelevant to his career, and he could have written off all his salary on *Red River* as seed money. Hawks had given him something more valuable than a share of a popular film. Along with John Ford, he had revitalized Wayne's career, making viewers and critics forget about *Dakota* and *Tycoon*. In its review of the year 1948, the editors of *Variety* commented that although John Wayne was not on any of the "smart 'most popular' lists" his three films during the year grossed $9,650,000, impressive by any standards, and especially in Hollywood where box-office appeal meant power.[38]

The 1948 *Motion Picture Herald* poll of Hollywood's most popular stars ranked Duke thirty-third, but *Red River* was released too late to affect his ranking. Shortly after the poll was published and *Red River* went into general release Gladwin Hill, a feature writer for the *New York Times*, commented on an emerging John Wayne phenomenon. In the decade following *Stagecoach*, Duke had been popular, but suddenly he had become the hottest property in the industry. "Even the home-bound little-old-lady-in-Pasadena—the mythical ex-owner of every used car sold in California—can hardly peek out of the door these days without coming into figurative contact with that amiable, shambling, six-foot-three pillar of the Hollywood community Marion Michael Morrison, alias John Wayne, alias 'Duke'," wrote Hill. It seemed as if his name was everywhere. "Theatre marquees blazon *Fort Apache* and *Red River*. . . . The dailies report that John Wayne, having finished *Three Godfathers* and at the moment engrossed in *Wake of the Red Witch* is about to start work in *She Wore A Yellow Ribbon*." Adding to that impressive list, *Stagecoach* was doing boom business in reruns.[39]

"What gives?" Hill wondered. Why had Wayne's career lasted so long? Why after two decades in the industry was it continuing to rise? John Ford offered one explanation: "Duke is the best actor in Hollywood, that's all." But Hill did not accept that line; he probably knew that Ford either underplayed or overplayed every hand and was given to hyperbole. A more likely explanation, Hill believed, was that Duke was "Hollywood's hardest working and least ostentatious star." But beyond Duke's gritty work habits, the writer was mystified about why the refugee from unmemorable horse operas had become such a "hot shot." The article reflected a more general attitude about Wayne in the late 1940s. Yes, he was popular. Yes, he worked hard. Yes, his movies were successful. But . . . well, cowboy stars are not real actors. When the 1948 Academy Awards nominations were announced, the name John Wayne was nowhere on the Best Actor list. Nor, for that matter, was either *Fort Apache* or *Red River* nominated for the Best Picture Oscar, and neither Ford nor Hawks received a Best Director nomination. The Motion Picture Academy of Arts and Sciences was more interested in art and angst, casting their votes for Laurence Olivier (Actor), *Hamlet* (Picture), and John Huston (Director) for his work in *The Treasure of the Sierra Madre*.[40]

Hill was right about one thing: While the members of the Academy were voting, Duke was working. Before the end of 1948 he had finished three more films, *Three Godfathers*, *Wake of the Red Witch*, and *She Wore a Yellow Ribbon*, all released in 1949. Most of the leading men in Hollywood in the late 1940s would have considered the three films—two of them John Ford productions—a solid foundation for a career. For John Wayne, they represented seven months of work.

On one level, *Three Godfathers* was John Ford's tribute to Harry Carey; on another, it was his tribute to silent movies. When Carey died on September 21, 1947, Ford felt he should do something. The two had made twenty-five films together at Universal during the silent era; they had helped to shape Western films and the Western hero. Then Ford left for Fox and the two ended their collaboration. Perhaps something happened, perhaps not. The two remained distant friends, but their friendship was strained, as if there was something that neither wanted to discuss. One day, Harry Carey Jr., whom everyone called Dobe because his hair was the color of adobe brick, asked his father why he stopped working with Ford. Carey took a deep drag on his cigarette, exhaled the smoke through his nose, coughed, blew his nose, wiped his eyes, and said: "He won't ask me?" Then he added: "But you will [work for Ford]—not till after I croak—but then you will." About a year after that conversation Carey died after an agonizing fight with cancer. Ford was with him at the end. Duke was in the next room. "God, it was a terrible day," his son recalled. "Duke brought me a tumbler of whiskey. I think it was the first time I ever turned down a drink. I don't know why. . . . No one should have gone through the agony my father went through those last weeks."[41]

At Carey's wake Ford told Ollie Carey that he was going to remake *Marked Man*, his favorite silent film, which he and Harry had made in 1919 and which had been reworked a decade later by William Wyler as *Hell's Heroes*. Furthermore, he told her that he wanted Dobe to play one of the badmen. "I'm sure John Ford thought this was a wonderful surprise for my mother; that it would take away some of the pain of her loss," wrote Dobe. A few months later, at a dinner party for Ford at his Odin Street home, the director talked to Dobe about the project. "You're going to hate me when this picture is over, but you're going to give a great performance," he kept repeating.[42]

Ford kept his word. In May 1948, when he took his cast and crew to Death Valley, California, to begin work on *Three Godfathers*, he was in an ornery mood. The film—a story of three outlaws on the run who come across a pregnant woman alone in the desert, deliver her baby, and then after she dies display a willingness to sacrifice their liberty and lives to save the child—had three stars: John Wayne as Robert Marmaduke Hightower; Pedro Armendariz as Pedro "Pete" Fuerte; and Harry Carey Jr. as William "the Abilene Kid" Kearney. Once on location Ford did not seem happy with any of them.

Armendariz, "the Clark Gable of Mexico," who had worked for Ford in *The Fugitive* and *Fort Apache*, made a critical early mistake of telling Ford that he had brought his own costume for the picture. Wayne and almost everyone else who ever worked with Armendariz loved the warm, friendly Latin actor, who seemed to take an unusual joy in even casual conversation. After his first breakfast at the Furnace Creek Ranch in Death Valley, Pedro told Ford, "Jack! Jack! I have brought to you from Mexico the most fantastic outfit for this picture you have ever seen! I had eet especially made for thees role!" He explained that clothes were important to him, that he was "the symbol of Mexico," and that he had to dress in a manner that would reflect well on his people. Ford said he would take a look, and Armendariz left to change clothes. He returned dressed like Leo Carrillo, the star of the Santa Barbara Fiesta Parade, decked out in a white silk shirt, skintight black leather pants with silver studs, and a colorful sombrero. Ford told him that the outfit looked great, that it would look great in a movie—"but not in this movie." Compounding his first mistake with a second, Pedro argued: "Jack! I *have* to wear this outfit! I have to dress for the people of my country! Also the people of Latin America! They expect me to look like this. It's my goddamn image for Christsake, Jack." Ford explained that he was playing a dusty, hard-riding desperado, not "the symbol of Mexico," and he ended the conversation with a parting shot: "Wardrobe! Fit this guy in a tuxedo! He's going to play a pimp in my next film!" In the end Armendariz wore the outfit Ford wanted, but after *Three Godfathers* he never worked for the director again.[43]

But Ford's verbal swipes at Armendariz paled next to his treatment of Dobe Carey. Dobe's career was only a few years old. Duke had gotten him a nice small part in *Red River*, and he had appeared in several other productions, but he had never come close to a lead role. *Three Godfathers* was his chance to prove himself, and he was nervous. He knew that what small career he had was a by-product of his father's fame, and he had little confidence in his own abilities. Polite and anxious to please, he followed every order Ford gave him, tolerated repeated indignities, and tried his "damndest," but he rarely satisfied the temperamental director. On several occasions Ford told Dobe to "bend over" then gave him "a swift, hard kick in the ass" just, Ford said, "to keep him on his toes." Sometimes Ford ordered Duke to do it, which embarrassed Wayne, who did it anyway. In later years, Dobe was willing to write off the treatment as a joke, but there was nothing funny at the time. Nor was there any humor in Ford's constant references to Audie Murphy, the World War II hero who had become a cowboy actor. Whenever Dobe made a mistake, Ford lamented, "My God, Audie Murphy begged me for this part!" or "Christ, maybe it's not too late to get Audie Murphy!" At one point the director became so angry that he threw a jagged rock the size of a cantaloupe at Dobe's face. Ford "was about twelve feet away, and directly on target, too, but I ducked," remembered Carey. "It didn't hit me, it hit the 'Symbol of Mexico' about four inches from his cojones. He was almost an instant soprano."[44]

Inexperience accounted for part of Carey's difficulty. He had no "feel" for the lens, a problem that caused him to miss his marks, stand where shadows obscured his face, and disrupt stage directions by blocking another actor out of the camera. Also, unlike Montgomery Clift, he had a relaxed, effortless acting style that Ford believed needed improvement. So Ford attacked—day after day, scene after scene. Perhaps he was trying to throw the young actor off balance; given Dobe's role as the Abilene Kid, this interpretation makes sense. The Kid is shot early in the picture and dies gradually. In the past Ford had attacked actors whom he wanted to appear confused and scared on the screen. Dobe admitted that the criticism improved his performance, but the treatment hurt nonetheless, and many times it was simply unwarranted.

When Ford was in one of his bleak moods he was almost impossible to work with. As soon as he became angry, out popped his white Irish linen handkerchief, and he commenced chewing. During best of times, he mumbled, and when he was "steamed" and "eating that damn handkerchief" his speech became incomprehensible. Carey was often in the dark concerning what Ford wanted him to do. Not only could he not understand what the director was saying, Ford's tinted dark glasses prevented anyone from reading his eyes. All Dobe could see was the tendon throbbing in and out on the right side of Ford's neck; all he could hear were wild rants about Audie Murphy.[45]

"I don't remember the Old Man being nice to me for one whole day during the location shooting in Death Valley," Carey wrote. "He was bearable or unbearable—never nice." At night Duke would tell Dobe about how hard Ford had been on him in *Stagecoach,* and that "Pappy was only mean to people he really liked." Wayne told him that Ford's favorite line in *Stagecoach* was "Christ, I should have got Gary Cooper to play Ringo." But even those words did not help much during the days of criticism. Once, however, Duke did come to the rescue. They were filming a scene in a place called the Devil's

Golf Course. It was hot and dusty, and no one was in a particularly good mood. Carey was leading Wayne and Armendariz in a trek across the desert. Ford carefully instructed Dobe to head out toward a big rock on his right, then veer off toward a little rock on his left. "Yessir," Carey answered, then did exactly as he was told. "Cut!" Ford screamed before the take was finished. Ford "was yelling all kinds of terrible things at me," Dobe recalled. "He pantomimed masturbation with an expression so loathsome that even in my early teen years, I could never have looked so demented. Everyone giggled."[46]

Then Wayne said very loudly: "He went right where you told him to!" The giggling stopped. Everyone was quiet, expectant. Ford said calmly, "Ah ha—I forgot. Mr. Wayne here once produced a picture. So now he's decided to direct this one." But that was all. Without admitting that he had made a mistake, Ford told Dobe to walk toward a different rock. "I could have kissed him," Carey said of Duke.[47]

The long, hot days added to the stress on the actors. *Three Godfathers* was a terribly difficult shoot for Wayne, Carey, and Armendariz. One of the central scenes in the film has the three men walk through a windstorm, an effect created by two huge, wooden airplane propellers. The scene took days to shoot, and the sand lodged itself in the actors' pants, shirts, boots, ears, and eyes. Even when the propellers were turned off, the actors had to work outdoors, exposed to the desert conditions. They worked each day from 8:00 to 11:00, broke for a long lunch during the hottest part of the day, then worked again from 3:00 to 6:00. Duke drank gallons of Poland Spring Water from Maine, which prevented dehydration but was of little help to his lips and skin.

If the days were the worst, the nights were the best. Carey recalled the satisfaction of knocking off work and heading back to the Furnace Creek Ranch. There were no pampered stars on a John Ford picture, no private limousines and palatial quarters. The three stars and Ford rode back to the ranch in one station wagon, Ford seated in the front next to the driver, and Duke, Dobe, and Pedro cramped in the back. At the ranch the stars slept two to a room; Pedro and Duke bunked together, as did Dobe and Ward Bond. The ranch had a pool, and when they returned from the set Ford took a nap and his stars relaxed and swapped stories. Often they would just sit in a screened porch, discuss the day's activities, drink Poland water, smoke cigarettes, and laugh. "It was wonderful," Carey wrote. "I didn't get any sympathy, either, just warm compassion, and love, and understanding.[48]

After dinner they played dominoes late into the night. Early on Armendariz announced that he was the finest domino player in all of Mexico, where, he claimed, the game was played better than anywhere else. "They say in my country that it is wiser to fight the bravest bull at the Plaza de Toros than to play dominoes with Pedro Armendariz," he asserted. Duke, who had scores of friends in Mexico, later said that in that country the standing joke was: "What's worse than going to hell?" Answer: "Playing dominoes with Pedro Armendariz as your partner." In any case, at the Furnace Creek Ranch, Ford and Duke played Bond and the Symbol of Mexico every night, with Dobe keeping everyone supplied with water. Ford played dominoes like he played every other game—he cheated. With his eyes obscured by his tinted glasses, he would lean back and try to peek at his opponents' tiles, an action that offended Armendariz's sense of fair play. On one occasion Pedro caught him in the act and shouted, "Ah-hah! You want to see my hand? You want to see my hand? Well, have a good look at eet!" He then threw his rack of dominoes at Ford's chest, which ended the game for the night.[49]

At other times Bond sent Armendariz into a rage. Pedro tried to be gentle; he tried to teach the rugged Yankee the finer points of the game. But Bond just did not catch on, and by the end of an evening Armendariz was usually screaming oaths at his partner. To make matters worse, Duke always tried to put the water bottle next to Bond so that his friend would have to pour. This, added to Armendariz's insults and Ford's cheating, could be counted on to set Ward off on a round of cursing—to the great amusement of Dobe and Duke.

As far as Wayne was concerned, the only problem was that losing put Ford in a foul mood, and he was apt to take it out the next day on the actors. Several times he attempted to get Armendariz to throw the games. Pedro refused: "Are you keeding, for Christ's sake! To hell with heem!" So much for pleasing Ford. Wayne accepted the victories and the punishments. He laughed and he bitched, and all things being equal, there probably was nowhere else in the world he would rather have been. For all the humiliation and mental torment, Dobe Carey would have agreed.

When they returned to the RKO-Pathé lot in Culver City to shoot interiors and work on a studio set, Ford's mood lightened. By then Carey had learned to read the director's disposition by his dress and body language. If he wore his dirty, slouch hat with the brim slanting toward his eyes, that was a bad sign. If he chewed on his handkerchief, that was trouble. If the tendon came alive in the right side of his neck, "Well, shit! Everybody overboard; man the lifeboats." But if he wore the St. Louis Cardinals baseball cap Stan Musial had given him, or his Irish tweed cap, and if he held a pipe between his teeth, then all was right with the world. Back in Hollywood he wore a cleaner coat and a tweed cap, and he smoked his pipe. Sometimes when some MGM studio bigshot visited the set, Ford would say something nasty to Duke just to show off, but Wayne took no offense, and none was really intended. With Ford in a chipper mood, the cast relaxed.

Mildred Natwick, a Ford regular who had a small part in the film as the mother of the baby, also recalled the easy mood in Hollywood. Her part did not call for her to go to Death Valley, and she finished it in one morning at the studio. Ford only became mildly upset one time, when he stopped the filming to tell Duke: "You look as if you're just watching Millie act." Wayne immediately knew what the director meant. His part called for him to listen to Natwick's dying words, and although the camera was usually on her, he was not giving her the emotional support she needed. Duke delivered. "I just felt such sympathy from John Wayne then for the character," Natwick remembered.[50]

Time passed quickly. Finally there was only one scene left to shoot. Before shooting it Ford sent Harry Carey Jr. home. Then Cliff Lyons dressed up like Harry Carey, mounted Harry's horse, Sunny, rode up the crest of a hill, stopped, and looked into the sunset. *Three Godfathers* started with the scene and the dedication: "TO THE MEMORY OF HARRY CAREY. BRIGHT STAR OF THE EARLY WESTERN SKY."[51]

Filmed in Technicolor—a decision forced on Ford by MGM because the movie did not have a leading lady and the studio believed it therefore needed something a little extra—*Three Godfathers* is visually stunning. Winton Hoch's camera work is superb. In fact, the film's visual impression is much more lasting than its dialogue or story line. Like Ford's early silent films, there are long stretches in *Three Godfathers* where dialogue would only detract from the images. The story line itself is remarkably simple, and there is almost no character development. The three godfathers are never portrayed as truly bad men. They are cattle rustlers and bank robbers, but really quite decent, and there is never a doubt that they will do the right thing. Similarly, the lawmen, led by Perley "Buck" Sweet (Ward Bond), are competent, hardworking, decent men. Instead of a dramatic showdown of good versus evil or the tension of a love story, Ford infused the film with a sort of paint-by-numbers religious symbolism and meaning. Bibles fall open to meaningful passages, the three godfathers follow the stars to New Jerusalem, and the birth of a child leads to redemption. In the end *Three Godfathers* is an *It's a Wonderful Life* set in the West.

Yet even with its ham-handed treatment of religious themes, it is still a fine movie. But reviewers generally either ignored it or thought it was boring, and even a sympathetic Ford scholar called it "a minor movie, its long stretches of desert monotony redeemed by magic moments." It is, however, a fitting tribute to Harry Carey and a lost era of motion pictures—one dominated by images and simple moralism. That may have been enough to please Ford, never driven exclusively by commercial success.[52]

Only weeks after finishing *Three Godfathers* Duke returned to his home studio for a quick film. *Wake of the Red Witch*, a panoramic tale about fortune hunters in the South Pacific, was not a Howard Hawks or John Ford film. It was a Republic product, and its purpose was to entertain, not elevate, educate, or motivate. The film's story line resembles a series of Chinese boxes, with the secret of the conflict between Captain Ralls (John Wayne) and Mayrant Sidneye (Luther Adler) in the last one. The film unfolds in a complex chain of first-person narratives. Sam Rosen (Gig Young) is the primary narrator, but inside his narration are the stories of Sidneye and his niece Teleia Van Schreeven (Adele Mara). Together, the tales recount Ralls's consuming interests in gold and Angelique Desaix (Gail Russell). Like most Republic films, *Wake of the Red Witch* derives from other movies. The love affair between Ralls and Angelique, for example, follows the same general pattern as that of Catherine and Heathcliff in *Wuthering Heights*. Angelique falls in love with Ralls, and although she marries another man, her love for Ralls remains strong. As she's dying, Ralls makes his way to her bedroom for a death scene straight out of *Wuthering Heights*. She says, "Ralls, don't forget me. Never forget me," then asks to look at the sea one last time. Lifting her into his arms, he carries her to a balcony where she looks at the sea and dies with the words, "This isn't the end, [it's] the beginning." The *Wuthering Heights* theme is continued in the last scene of the film. After Ralls dies he and Angelique are seen sailing the *Red Witch* across the sky.

In addition to its *Wuthering Heights* love story, *Wake of the Red Witch* had a treasure box full of pearls, $5 million in gold in a sunken ship, tribal orgies, witchcraft, and a giant squid. Everything about the film is larger than life, including John Wayne's role. Captain Ralls is a man who inspires passionate extremes—hated by his enemies, loved by his friends, and worshiped by South Pacific islanders. His past is largely a mystery, but he is a hard, driven, obsessed character. He is a Thomas Dunson gone completely over the edge, a swaggering Captain Ahab with an eye for the ladies. With the film coming so close to *Red River*, Duke knew the type, and he threw himself into the role.

Critics generally panned the film's rambling story line, and one reviewer said the special effects were poorly done: "The ships are obviously models, the pearls and palm-trees are make-believe, and the sleepy lagoons of the enchant-

ed islands are plainly tanks on the studio lot." But the low-budget film performed well at the box office and finished forty-third on *Variety*'s list of the
top moneymakers in 1949. Duke also liked the film. He later named his independent production company Batjac after the fictitious Batjak Trading Company in *Wake of the Red Witch*, and eventually he linked the film's plot with
his own fight with cancer. At the end of the film, when Ralls dies trying to recover gold from the sunken *Red Witch*, his right-hand man says, "She's got
him. . . . She was waitin' for him all this time." For John Wayne cancer became his *Red Witch*, lying submerged in his system, waiting patiently year
after year, but determined to get him.[53]

After finishing *Wake of the Red Witch* Duke had hoped to be able to take an
extended rest, but Ford did not give him the chance. He had offered editing
suggestions to Howard Hawks about several sequences in *Red River* and had
viewed Wayne's work in that film. The performance surprised him. "Jack
never respected me as an actor until I made *Red River*," Wayne recalled.
Duke's performance convinced Ford that John Wayne alone was enough of an
actor to carry a film, and he decided to showcase his friend in another cavalry
film. Like *Fort Apache*, *She Wore a Yellow Ribbon* was based on the short stories of James Warner Bellah. Ford and screenwriters Frank S. Nugent and
Laurence Stallings took elements from Bellah's "War Party" and "The Big
Hunt"—both of which had appeared in the *Saturday Evening Post*—and
crafted a narrative about the last week in the military career of Nathan Brittles, a cavalry captain who is retiring at the statutory age of sixty-four after
forty-three years in the service. The story called for Duke to play a man a generation older than himself—a dignified officer, an Indian fighter grown weary
of battle, and a widower. It also called for him to give a sensitive, nuanced performance. He could bluster his way through *Red River*; *She Wore a Yellow Ribbon* was all finesse.[54]

She Wore a Yellow Ribbon, like *Fort Apache*, was shot in Monument Valley,
but unlike the earlier film it was shot in color. Impressed by Winton Hoch's
work in *Three Godfathers*, Ford hired the industry's leading Technicolor artist
to capture the rich earth tones of the director's dreamscape. Before any filming, however, Ford, Hoch, and art director James Basevi studied the subtle
hues and authentic scenes in the western paintings of Frederic Remington.
When they started shooting the picture in late October 1948, Ford patterned
entire scenes after the Remington paintings, and Hoch captured the tones of
the artist's works. "I tried to get in his color and movement, and I think I succeeded partly," Ford later told Peter Bogdanovich.[55]

After a decade of shooting in Monument Valley, Ford knew the territory; he knew the best places to set up his cameras and the best times to film different areas. The knowledge allowed him to work at a furious pace and to finish his location shooting in thirty-one days and under budget. But he did not work so fast that he was unable to take advantage of a new opportunity. While he was shooting one cavalry scene the sky suddenly darkened and bolts of lightning began to cut through the rain clouds. "Lightning hit this butte right beside us," Ben Johnson said, and Hoch wanted to get everyone into a shelter. But Ford liked the effect and wanted to keep filming. Hoch protested. He was the expert, and he said there was not enough light. Ford told him to keep shooting, which Hoch finally did, although he later sent a letter of protest to the American Society of Cinematographers. Johnson recalled: "It was pretty scary, and everyone was mad at Ford because he was making them stay out in the rain." But the results were memorable. The shoots of the long cavalry line with the thunderstorm in the background were among the most striking in the film, and they contributed to Hoch winning an Academy Award for his work on the movie.[56]

After the hell of *Three Godfathers*, *She Wore a Yellow Ribbon* was a vacation for Dobe Carey. What he recalled most were the primitive conditions of Monument Valley. The Goulding Trading Post made the Furnace Creek Ranch look like a luxury resort hotel. After the train trip to Flagstaff, Arizona, it was a day's journey to Goulding's over the rutted, red clay roads of the Navajo reservation. Carey shared a station wagon with John Agar and Victor McLaglen. After learning that Dobe had just recently finished his first picture with Ford, McLaglen asked: "Mean to ya', was he?" Carey answered yes, and the veteran actor nodded and said: "Yeah-yeah-yeah. I know, lad, I know. He's a sadist, he is. A sadist. . . . he's a bad one. A fucking sadist, he is. But ya' can't let it bother ya', lad." For the rest of the ride the three actors swapped stories about working with Ford and admired the rugged scenery. Once at Goulding's the film's "stars" slept three to a room in a dirt-floor cabin—only Ford and Wayne had private rooms—and shared a toilet and a five-gallon-oil-drum-cold-water shower. Altogether, the conditions did not encourage good hygiene.[57]

If the conditions were rugged, Ford was gentler than usual. Ben Johnson was Ford's newest star. Although Ben had a small role in *Three Godfathers*, he had a substantial part in *She Wore a Yellow Ribbon*, and he was not at all sure he liked the change. Unlike Duke, Carey, and Agar, Johnson never aspired to being an actor. Born in Pawhuska, Oklahoma, he was the real thing: a range cowboy and a rodeo champion. What he did best was ride a horse, and he cared more about those animals than about Hollywood producers and directors. What he liked about the movie industry was the wages—not the glitz, not the glamour, not the attention. Ford probably sensed that Johnson was a different breed, that he was always only a half step away from leaving show business, and treated him "tenderly." Ford encouraged, he praised, he advised; he led Ben through his scenes with consideration, gentleness, and good humor. And he pulled a fine performance out of him.

But Johnson never tried to be one of Ford's "boys." Ford asked him to play cards one night, and Johnson knew that if he played well he would be asked every night. So he just lost hand after hand, playing so badly that he took all the fun out of the game even for Ford, who liked to win but did not relish beating an idiot. From Johnson's perspective, for very little money he bought a permanent pass out of the director's nightly competitions. It is entirely possible that Ford finished *She Wore a Yellow Ribbon* ahead of schedule because of the lack of good nightly card games. Johnson, Agar, and Carey were inept players; Bond and Armendariz were not part of the cast. That left Duke and Ford and two empty seats that were filled by such assistants as Wingate Smith or such stuntmen as Cliff Lyons and Frank McGrath. Smith was fine, but Lyons hated the games and McGrath was too unpredictable. McGrath was half American Indian, half Irish; he was short, wiry, tough, and good at his job, but he loved nothing more than drinking and fighting and was singularly unimpressed by John Ford. In one game he caught Ford cheating and said: "Hey, One Eye! Stop peeking at my damned hand." Then he kicked the director in the shins. Duke roared with laughter while Ford grumbled about McGrath being a "useless" drunk. "Go ahead, Boss, send me home," the stunt man added, concluding: "De Mille wants me, anyway."

Recalling the nightly games years later, Dobe Carey wondered: "When I think back on it, it must have been pretty hard on Duke. Here's a man who's carrying the whole picture on his shoulders, who has to know his lines perfectly, never miss a mark, and play cards every night, and lose." But Wayne was not one to complain, and having McGrath or Lyons at the table more than made up for the sleep he missed. In addition he appreciated Ford's genius. One day Ford was filming the scene in which Sergeant Quincannon (McLaglen) tells his troops that he has "a special announcement": Women are going on a trip with them and they had best "watch them words." As Ford prepared the scene, a shaggy mongrel was sleeping in front of the line of soldiers. Instead of chasing it off, Ford decided to write it into the script. He told

McLaglen to start his announcement, then pause, spot the dog, ask whom it belonged to, and say: "Nice dog. Irish setter!" Coming from McLaglen, the perpetual Irishman, it was an ideal line, one that would breathe life into the routine scene. Unfortunately McLaglen did not initially get the joke, and on the first take he said, "Nice dog. Cocker Spaniel!" "There was a moment of silence, then I thought Duke was going to have a stroke from laughing," Carey said. But the moment explains why Wayne enjoyed working with Ford: In the end the abusive outbursts became mere anecdotes.[58]

When *She Wore a Yellow Ribbon* went into general release in October 1949 it was an immediate hit. Critical response ranged from "the finest outdoor picture produced in Hollywood for a very long time" to "another of John Ford's classics" to "John Ford outdoes himself," and it was one of the year's leaders at the box office. Yet only one thing raises the picture above being a beautifully photographed, relatively slow-moving period piece: the performance of John Wayne. Dobe Carey was right: Duke carried the film. He dominates almost every scene. Unlike *Fort Apache*, in which he could play off Henry Fonda, in *She Wore a Yellow Ribbon* there are virtually no heavies. Ford's army life had become an ideal world of Irish sergeants, gallant soldiers, judicious officers, and noble wives. Making Wayne's job even more difficult, the film has surprisingly little action and an underdeveloped romance.[59]

Duke's portrayal of Capt. Nathan Brittles—a symbolic name—is certainly one of the finest of his career. It was a most un-John-Wayne-like role. Duke's central scenes called for him to be passive and reflective, not active and aggressive. He has to counsel peace, offer sage advice to younger officers, and demonstrate strength of character more than physical power. And he did it all beautifully. His graveside monologues with his dead wife are touching without crossing into maudlin, and his brief "Lest we forget" speech after being presented with a silver watch is magical. Reviewers agreed that they had never seen Wayne better.

She Wore a Yellow Ribbon also further developed Wayne as an American icon. Capt. Nathan Brittles was Ford's ideal leader—the best parts of George Washington, Robert E. Lee, and Douglas MacArthur. Lest his nation forget, Ford constantly underscores that Brittles is part of a proud tradition. Brittles's words, "I'll be back, men, I'll be back," conjures up images of MacArthur leaving the Philippines, and his retirement speech is a copy of Washington's Newburgh Address. (At Newburgh, Washington, confronted with a potentially mutinous army, had advocated restraint. At one point in his talk, he took out his spectacles to read a letter. There was a murmur among his troops, most of whom had never seen him in eyeglasses. Noticing this, he said: "Gentlemen, you must pardon me. I have grown gray in your service and now find myself growing blind." His words ended any chance for a mutiny or military coup.) Wayne tapped into that rich American iconography when he fumbled with his glasses before reading the inscription on the silver watch his troops had presented him. For Americans raised on tales of Washington's sacrifice and service at Valley Forge and Newburgh, for Americans who had followed the career of MacArthur and knew sacrifice and service firsthand, Captain Nathan Brittles was a civics lesson, and John Wayne was a class in American history. He was Washington in the Revolution; Grant, Sherman, and Lee in the Civil War; MacArthur in World War II. He was old, stiff, and wise.

Duke liked everything about the movie but its ending. He thought the film should have ended right after he had led his men through the Indian village, chasing off the Indian horses and preventing a war. Remembering the scene a quarter of a century later, Wayne said: "And then [Brittles] takes out his watch and he says, 'Well, what time is it by my brand new silver watch and chain? Three minutes after twelve. I've been a civilian for three minutes. Hard to believe,' then rode off down the hill. That was the end of the goddamn picture." Instead Ford tacked on another ending in which Brittles is made a Western scout, and then the director added the moralistic epilogue about the heroic service men like Brittles performed "and only a cold page in the history books to mark their passing." Everything considered, Duke was correct; it *was* "something of a bullshit ending." But it seemed to hardly matter to anyone but a few critics.[60]

After finishing three pictures in just over six months, Wayne told Hedda Hopper: "I guess I'm pitching for the record." In Hollywood industry insiders were asking unprecedented questions: Can a star be billed to death? Is there such a thing as too many play dates? How much exhibition can a player survive? Where, on the scale of mushrooming demand, is the point of diminishing return? William R. Weaver, a *Motion Picture Herald* journalist, was not sure, but he suggested that John Wayne might soon answer the questions. At one point in 1949, before the release of *She Wore a Yellow Ribbon*, nine different John Wayne films were playing in Los Angeles in the same week. The pictures ranged "from great to awful," from Republic Three Mesquiteer films to his most recent releases, and they all were doing outstanding business.[61]

Wayne, however, was unconcerned by talk of saturation. "I think four a year, which due to delays probably means three and a half, is about right," he told Weaver. "Who can complain if a man sees a chance to make a buck? That's business."

Business had never been better. He had written contracts with Republic, Warner Bros., and RKO, and an ironclad, unwritten commitment to John Ford's Argosy Productions, and all the studios wanted him in their films. In 1949 he would be ranked fourth in the *Motion Picture Herald*'s poll of most popular stars; only Bob Hope, Bing Crosby, and Abbott & Costello were ahead of him. But long before the polls were announced, Duke knew he was on a roll. His career was reaching a new plateau, and he was not about to slacken his pace. After a brief break in early 1949, he returned to the job of making money and building his reputation as a symbol of America.[62]

During the first half of the year he worked exclusively at Republic. He produced the first film, a quickie called *The Fighting Kentuckian*. Once again Duke teamed with Vera Ralston in a film that suffered from a convoluted plot, bad acting, and weak comic relief. Just about everything about it was forgettable. Marie Windsor, one of the female leads in the film, didn't even know until decades later that Duke had produced it. "When I went on the interview, he was there," she recalled. "But I didn't realize at the time that he was one of the producers." The best that could be said about *The Fighting Kentuckian* was that it starred John Wayne, and it made money.[63]

Duke's next Republic film was different in intent and results. *Sands of Iwo Jima* was producer Edmund Grainger's pet project. By the late 1950s World War II had once again become a popular subject in Hollywood, and in that year and the next such films as *Battleground* (MGM), *Task Force* (Warner Bros.), and *Twelve O'Clock High* (Twentieth Century-Fox) drew rave reviews and made huge profits. Grainger was on the cutting edge of the war film revival. In 1948 he ran across the phrase "sands of Iwo Jima" in a newspaper and immediately thought of the famous Joe Rosenthal photograph of a group of marines planting the American flag at the summit of Mount Suribachi. With a title and a climax, he wrote a quick treatment that was later turned into a script by Harry Brown and further developed by James Edward Grant. The story line was a basic, classic war tale: A tough but decent sergeant turns an ethnically diverse group of individualists into a crack marine unit. Though his men initially resent his harsh methods, they learn that everything he did was designed to save their lives, and by the end of the film they love him.[64]

The U.S. Marine Corps, caught in a political struggle for funding and survival, thought highly of the idea. The army, navy, and air corps had been glorified in such films as *Air Force, Thirty Seconds over Tokyo, The Story of G.I. Joe*, and *They Were Expendable*, but except for *Wake Island, Guadalcanal Diary*, and a few other weak imitations, Hollywood had not told the marines' story in a cinematic classic. Yet from the earliest days of Hollywood, the corps had encouraged the making of movies about the marines and had used those movies in recruitment and public relations campaigns. Grainger promised the corps that *Sands of Iwo Jima* would portray the valor, heroism, and sacrifice of the marines and that it would make money as well as win friends and influence legislators in Washington. After some initial reservations—there was some doubt that a studio like Republic could deliver anything but schlock—the corps signed on, promising Camp Pendleton as the location for filming and all the equipment and technical advice Grainger needed.[65]

After securing marine cooperation, Grainger hired veteran Allan Dwan to direct the picture and began casting. He later claimed that he had wanted Kirk Douglas to play Sgt. John Stryker, and that Wayne had approached him about the part. Duke wanted the role so badly that "he could taste it," Grainger told a technical adviser. Michael Wayne had a different memory. He said that his father was uncertain about the script's potential and reluctant to do the film, and only when the Marine Corps asked him personally to play Stryker did he agree to make the film. Given the fact that Grant, Duke's house screenwriter, was brought onto the project, it is likely that Wayne was more in a position to make demands than ask for favors, but regardless of how it happened he was cast as Stryker, and once signed to the part he became one of the film's strongest supporters. It was a "beautiful personal story," he told film historian Lawrence H. Suid; the tale of Stryker and his men was "the story of Mr. Chips put in the military. A man takes eight boys and has to make men out of them." If one can imagine Mr. Chips cracking the jaw of one of his students with the butt of a rifle, the comparison is an apt one.[66]

In the summer of 1949 the Republic team traveled a hundred miles south of Hollywood to Camp Pendleton to make *Sands of Iwo Jima*. On a $1 million budget, Grainger and Dwan made the technically difficult picture. They reenacted two battles—Tarawa and Iwo Jima—and the assault on Mount Suribachi. Their technicians built hundreds of plaster palm trees, pillboxes, and gun emplacements, laid thousands of feet of barbed wire, and covered the sand with oil and lampblack to make it look like volcanic ash. The marines provided troops, Corsair planes from their air base at El Toro, amtracs, cruisers, destroyer escorts, and LSTs. "Without Marine cooperation," Grainger said, "the picture would have cost at least $2,500,000."[67]

The idea was to make the film as realistic as was possible, or at least as was commercially possible. "There will be no heroics in this picture, but it will show the heroism of the average American as he readjusted from civilian life to the war," Grainger told a reporter. Unlike the war pictures Duke made during World War II, he was not called on to commit foolish acts of sacrifice and heroism—no bulldozer attacks on enemy positions or suicide missions. War, the film said, was dangerous enough; there was no need to make it more so. As Stryker told his recruits, his job was to teach them to survive, not die.[68]

By the time shooting began, Duke was fully committed to his role, and he wanted to get it right. He grilled the technical advisers and studied the movements and behavior of a tough warrant officer. "Duke *became* Stryker," Mary St. John said. "He really believed in the part." John Agar, who was cast as Stryker's most important convert, agreed. "Sgt. Stryker was right down Duke's alley. It showed the tough part about him, the soft part about him, it really was very much like him." Agar recalled how easy it was to play opposite Wayne in *Sands of Iwo Jima*. "His eyes expressed such conviction, and when I spoke my lines it just seemed as if I was talking to him. And he was so encouraging." Unlike Ford, Wayne constantly complimented Agar, commenting repeatedly that the younger actor was doing a fine job.[69]

When it was released during the Christmas season, *Sands of Iwo Jima* was Republic's most expensive production. It had run four hundred thousand dollars over budget, but even Yates believed that he had a marketable product. With the "Marine Hymn" playing in the background, the film's trailer boasted that the movie was "One of the Truly Great Motion Pictures Ever to Reach the Screen." Walter Winchell, America's most influential columnist, agreed, adding, "The original story was written in blood by the glorious United States Marines! John Wayne must be everyone's idea of a good actor! He's immense in *Iwo Jima*, the best of the war pictures." This heroic chord was sounded throughout the advertising campaign. When the picture premiered at Grauman's Chinese Theater, Duke used the opportunity to put his bootprint in the cement outside the movie palace. His boots, however, made his footprint look small, almost like the foot of a dancer. To lay all such notions to rest, in a gesture worthy of Chesty Puller he jammed his fists into the cement beside his boots.[70]

If some reviewers complained that the film presented the usual bundle of stock clichés, almost all the critics praised Duke's performance. "Wayne is especially honest and convincing, for he manages to dominate a screenplay which is crowded with exciting, sweeping battle scenes," wrote a *New York Times* reviewer. "His performance holds the picture together, lessening to some extent the hackneyed devices employed by the authors in their poverty-stricken personal fiction about the men." His portrayal of Sgt. Stryker was so powerful that even the Academy of Motion Picture Arts and Sciences' voters took note and nominated Duke for his first Academy Award. Although he did not win the Oscar for best actor, and although his performance in *She Wore a Yellow Ribbon* was probably superior to his work in *Sands of Iwo Jima*, Duke appreciated the nomination. Though he seldom said as much, he cared about reviews, awards, and public acceptance.[71]

He also cared about money, and *Sands of Iwo Jima* finished eighth on *Variety*'s 1950 list of the top moneymakers. It made $3,900,000 in domestic rentals and was a huge success. On the basis of *Sands of Iwo Jima* and his next film, *Rio Grande*, at the end of 1950 the *Motion Picture Herald* listed John Wayne as Hollywood's most popular star. He had reached the summit of his world.[72]

The timing was important. The spectacular rise of John Wayne had occurred at a time when the United States was at the height of its postwar power. In America, as well as abroad, Duke had become a symbol of that power. His swaggering confidence and his identification with the American West and the Marines in World War II assumed an iconographic dimension. Assessing the importance of John Wayne as an image, Suid wrote, "Not until John Wayne created the role of Sergeant Stryker in *Sands of Iwo Jima* and then merged his own personality with the character did Americans find a man who personified the ideal soldier, sailor, or Marine. More that twenty-five years after he appeared in *Sands of Iwo Jima*, Wayne and his military image continued to pervade American society and culture." During the war other actors played soldiers or marines, but no actor symbolized the idea of duty and service to their country like John Wayne. In that single arena, he was transcendent.[73]

Already Duke was beginning to live in the shadow of his own image. He had never served a day in the military and he was America's ideal marine; he disliked horses and he was the country's favorite cowboy. From the disappearing flags of a cavalry regiment to the raising of the flag on Mount Suribachi, John Wayne's image had become tightly intertwined with the destiny of the United States.

Rio Grande, the only new John Wayne film to be released in 1950, further cemented his image. The last and least significant of John Ford's cavalry trilogy, *Rio Grande* is something of an afterthought. It is common to refer to Ford's cavalry trilogy as if each film was a piece of a planned whole, but in truth he never planned to make three John Wayne cavalry films. It was more of a case of demand creating product. In 1950 Ford's Argosy Productions began a brief, turbulent relationship with Herbert Yates's Republic Studios. Ford wanted to make *The Quiet Man*, but Yates disliked the director's Irish romance and demanded that he make a solid box-office hit before he sank Republic's money into some foolish, artistic project. As a result Ford returned to a proven formula. He bought the rights to "Mission With No Record," another Bellah *Saturday Evening Post* short story about the cavalry, hired John Wayne and most of his regulars, and had James McGuinness craft a script along the lines of *Fort Apache* and *She Wore a Yellow Ribbon*. Then in the summer of 1950 he took his cast and crew to Moab, Utah, to make the picture.[74]

No one, least of all Ford, took the film too seriously. Harry Carey Jr. called it one of the director's "vacation pictures." It was budgeted at $1,238,000, only half as much as the budget of *Fort Apache*, and was shot in thirty days. He used several of the same Victor McLaglen Irish gags he had used in his previous two cavalry pictures, and filmed most of the movie in loose shots. "The filming was extremely easy for him—no strain at all," commented Carey. Most of the time, he was even in a good mood. It was as if he had so little respect for Yates and Republic that he felt no compulsion to make a classic. *Rio Grande*, his attitude said, was a money picture—nothing more, nothing less.[75]

There were only two major incidents during the three weeks of shooting along the Colorado River. The first was more comical than serious. One day Yates and Rudy Ralston, Vera Ralston's brother, whom Yates had made a producer at Republic, showed up unannounced in Moab. Literally scores of things would put Ford in a foul mood, and near the top of the list was studio executives walking onto his set. Chuck Roberson, a stuntman and Duke's double, claimed that when Yates walked on the set at ten o'clock one morning, he discovered no one working. Pointing out the time, he asked Ford, "When are you going to start shooting?" "Just as soon as you get the hell off my set," Ford supposedly replied. Harry Carey Jr., however, insisted that Ford did reluctantly allow Yates on the set on one of the two days the studio head was in town—though he refused to permit Ralston on the set. Then Ford exacted his revenge by having Alberto Morin, one of his actors, dress as a waiter and serve Yates and Ralston dinner. Speaking half-French, half-English, Morin proceeded to "break a few dishes, knock over their water, and spill the soup all over the poor guys." Neither caught on to the joke, and neither became angry. "That's what made the whole thing sad and very unfunny," recalled Carey.[76]

The other incident was more serious. One evening, after a day of shooting an Indian attack on a Catholic church, everyone was eating dinner in an open tent. The atmosphere was light, and conversation was free. Ford, with Duke on his left and Maureen O'Hara on his right, was at the head table, and Dobe and Ben Johnson were sitting at another. "Well, there was a lot of shootin' goin' on today, but not too many Indians bit the dust," Johnson drawled. It was an off-the-cuff comment, dinner small talk, and nothing was meant by it. Johnson knew that Ford would film the attack one day and the stunt falls another. It was just a joke, directed only to his good friend. But he made the comment at a quiet moment, and Ford heard it. So did almost everyone else. The room was quiet for several painful seconds.[77]

"What did you say?" Ford asked.

"I was just talkin' to Dobe, Mr. Ford," Johnson replied.

"I know. What did you say?"

"I was just talkin' to Dobe."

It was an awkward moment, one that called for Ford to back off a step. But he didn't. In his "nastiest tone" he asked again: "Hey stupid! I asked you a question. What did you say?"

Johnson stood up and left the mess, stopping by Ford and saying something quietly on his way out. "I wasn't very smart," Johnson remembered, "but I told him what he could do with his damn picture."

"There was an embarrassed silence—an uncomfortable, deadly silence all around the table." Then Ford said: "Oh, Jesus Christ, Dobe, go get him, for God's sake." Ford had always known that Johnson was not like Duke or Dobe or Bond or even John Agar. Johnson was quieter and more polite, a product of a code in which men watched what they said or were ready for the consequences if they didn't. Ford knew that he had "screwed up."

"I've never seen Ben so unhappy before or since," Dobe recalled. Johnson would not return to dinner, but he remained in the film. The next day life returned to normal on the set. Ford joked a few times with Johnson; Ben did not brood, and neither mentioned the incident. Maybe they should have. Ford dropped Johnson from his stock company. It was thirteen years before the two men worked together again.

When *Rio Grande* was finished it seemed more of a Republic than a John Ford film. It has more songs than a Gene Autry movie, a simplistic view of Indians, and a contrived story line. But Ford's decision to return Wayne to a romantic role was well calculated, and his choice of Maureen O'Hara as Duke's love interest was inspired. "Maureen," said Mary Loos, "was the sort of woman [Ford] would have invented." Beautiful, tall, opinionated, and strong willed, she was the perfect match for John Wayne. Perhaps Duke's son Patrick best explained the success of the relationship between Wayne and O'Hara and Ford: "Ford saw himself as my father. He saw himself as a Western character and identified strongly with that. Maureen O'Hara was the perfect mate for John Wayne and so was the perfect mate for John Ford."[78]

If *Rio Grande* was the weakest of Ford's cavalry films, it was the one that seemed the most relevant to Americans. In June 1950, while Ford was in Utah making the movie, North Korean forces had invaded South Korea. When the film was released in November, U.S. soldiers were deep into North Korea and American policy makers were debating under what conditions the war should be carried into Communist China. Finally, in late November, while *Rio Grande* was enjoying box-office success, Chinese forces attacked U.S. positions in North Korea. In Korea, Gen. Douglas MacArthur suggested that it might be necessary to use atomic weapons against the Chinese; in Washington, President Harry Truman said that he would do no such thing. The central concern in *Rio Grande* is the frustration of diplomatic niceties and the untenable nature of borders. After two cavalry films in which Ford preached peaceful coexistence with Indians, *Rio Grande* advocated defense through aggression. Col. Kirby Yorke (John Wayne) is tired of watching marauding Apaches escape punishment by fleeing across the Rio Grande into Mexico, and he yearns to solve the Indian problem by the brutal application of force.

Rio Grande reflects the politics of Bellah and screenwriter McGuinness. Both men were politically conservative. Bellah's own son said that his father's "politics were just to the right of Attila. He was a fascist, a racist, and a world-class bigot." But he was no more conservative than McGuinness, one of the most vocal leaders of the right wing in Hollywood; indeed, McGuinness was so outspoken that he had been forced out of his producer's job at MGM. Between Bellah's short story and McGuinness's script, there was no room for political ambiguity. *Rio Grande* had a political message: America faces enemies, ruthless men who murdered women and children and then sought cover in "neutral" countries. For the two writers the Apaches of the 1870s were no different than the Communists of their own day. Loyal Americans, Bellah and McGuinness believed, should not permit such enemy activities; they should root out the evil, destroy it, and the devil with the consequences. In the film Gen. Philip Sheridan tells Yorke, "I want you to cross the Rio Grande, hit the Apache and burn them out; I'm tired of hit and run, I'm sick of diplomatic hide and seek." Though the mission threatens Yorke's career, he welcomes the chance to confront his country's enemy.[79]

By 1950 the politics of *Rio Grande* had become Wayne's politics. In 1948, when he began his rise to the top of his profession, he had been one of the more politically inactive stars in Hollywood, remaining distant from the debate that was consuming the industry. But by the end of 1950 he was in the middle of the fight, searching for enemies, naming names, and taking stands. Five years before he died Duke told a reporter: "I've played the kinda man I'd like to have been." Before 1950 he had not tried very hard to be the kind of man he played. All that, however, was about to change.[80]

13

A Different War

Despite his reservations about agents, John Wayne generally liked Charlie Feldman—but not all the time. Sometimes he just could not fathom how the agent's mind worked. In October 1948, for example, Feldman sent him a script to read. Robert Rossen planned to produce and direct a film based on *All the King's Men*, Robert Penn Warren's novel about the rise and fall of a thinly fictionalized Huey Long, and he wanted Wayne in the lead role. Duke read the script carefully, and by the time he finished he was throwing ashtrays and knocking over furniture.

In a letter to Feldman, Wayne was not content to say that he had no interest in the part; he wanted his agent to understand how much he despised the entire project. Before Feldman sent the script to any of his other actor clients, Duke told him to ask them if they wanted to star in a film that "smears the machinery of government for no purpose of humor or enlightenment," that "degrades all relationships," and that is populated by "drunken mothers; conniving fathers; double-crossing sweethearts; bad, bad, rich people; and bad, bad, poor people if they want to get ahead." Everything about the film struck an exposed nerve. How could any director want to make a movie that threw acid on "the American way of life"? How could any director want to destroy people's belief in family life, human dignity, and the desire to better themselves? If Feldman had such clients, Duke wrote that the agent should "rush this script . . . to them." Wayne, however, offered Feldman another course of action: "You can take this script and shove it up Robert Rossen's derriere. . . ."[1]

The day he received the letter, Feldman wrote Wayne in an attempt to explain his reasoning. Given Duke's frontal assault, this took some backbone. Of course Duke was entitled to his opinion, Feldman wrote, but so was he entitled to his ideas. He felt that the script had merit. It was "a faithful adaptation" of a Pulitzer Prize–winning book, Columbia had paid $200,000 for the property and budgeted it at $1,750,000, and Rossen was "one of the best talents in this business." Had he not submitted it to Wayne, he believed he "would have been derelict." But that said, Duke had the absolute right of refusal.[2]

Feldman, of course, was correct about the script's potential. *All the King's Men* won rave reviews. In 1949 *Life* called it "the most exciting film to come out of Hollywood this year," and it was nominated for a handful of Oscars, including Best Picture, Best Actor, Best Director, and Best Screenplay. Broderick Crawford, who was said to have based his portrayal of Willie Stark on Harry Cohn, the infamous head of Columbia, won the Best Actor award, and the movie captured the Oscar for Best Film. Duke had turned down one great role.

Wayne never regretted his decision. He knew Rossen's reputation—he remembered that he had been targeted by the House Un-American Activities Committee (HUAC) in 1947 for his ties to the Communist party. And though Wayne had worked with Communists in the past, the script bothered him even more than Rossen did. He had reached the point in his career and life where there were some things he just would not do. His letter to Feldman was as close to a political manifesto as he ever wrote. Full of passion born of outrage, it said exactly what he believed was right and wrong about America and Hollywood. He said it at a time when across the land battle lines were being drawn.

In the domestic Cold War, Hollywood was one of the front lines. Even before the last shots of World War II were fired, when the United States and the Soviet Union were allies, tension between Hollywood Communists and liberals on one side and conservatives on the other was mounting. Part of the split revolved around domestic politics. Most Hollywood liberals and Communists had long revered President Franklin D. Roosevelt and the New Deal. Even when they criticized Roosevelt, their misgivings focused on his unwillingness to push the country even farther to the left. But Republicans, out of power in Congress since 1930 and the White House since 1932, were ready to make a political comeback, and they targeted the New Deal legacy of high taxes, deficit spending, and big government. In the presidential election of 1940, Douglas Fairbanks Jr., Humphrey Bogart, Melvyn Douglas, Henry

Fonda, Groucho Marx, Lucille Ball, Joan Bennett, and John Garfield campaigned for Roosevelt, while such conservatives as Robert Montgomery, Ginger Rogers, George Murphy, Adolphe Menjou, Irene Dunne, Hedda Hopper, Gary Cooper, John Wayne, Ward Bond, and Mary Pickford backed Republican Wendell Willkie. The lineup was the same in 1944, when Roosevelt sought a fourth term and ran against New York governor Thomas E. Dewey. In both elections Americans voted to keep Roosevelt for the duration.

But the political debate in Hollywood over the merits or demerits of the New Deal was mild compared to the visceral hostilities generated by communism. Conservatives resented the rebirth of the Hollywood Popular Front and opposed organizations which preached the idea of "one worldism." They believed that such groups as the Hollywood chapter of the internationalist Free World Association was dominated by Communists, and they charged that Communist screenwriters and liberal producers were using their talents and positions to advance their own far-left agenda. During the early years of the war the battle between right and left had been waged sub rosa in studio boardrooms and writers' offices. But by late 1943 the war had taken on a public dimension. Increasingly Jack Tenney, chairman of the Joint Fact-Finding Committee on Un-American Activities of the California legislature, and Hollywood executives openly aired their opinion that Communists were gaining control over filmmaking. The first engagement in the public war contained elements of farce. The Free World Association scheduled a meeting for the evening of February 5, 1944, at the palm-lined Beverly Hills Hotel, and liberal Vice President Henry Wallace agreed to address the organization. In an attempt to show that not every member of the film community was a Free Worlder, a group of conservative screenwriters, producers, directors, and actors scheduled a dinner of their own the night before at the Beverly Wilshire Hotel. Somehow Wallace's driver and motorcycle escort were given the wrong instructions, delivering the vice president to the Beverly Wilshire—devoid of liberals and full only of lingering cigar smoke from conservatives—rather than the Beverly Hills Hotel. The error was quickly detected. Wallace was "rushed at pre-rationing speed over to the Leftists' Beverly Hills," commented the *Time* magazine reporter.[3]

When Wallace finally arrived at the correct hotel, he was greeted by some of the leading stars in the motion picture industry. James Cagney, Charles Boyer, Rosalind Russell, Dudley Nichols, Walter Wanger, and some two to three hundred more show business personalities listened as Governor Earl Warren introduced Wallace and the vice president called for Hollywood to understand and portray "the unexpressed hunger in the souls of moviegoers." In keeping with the goals of the Free World Association, he called on all Americans to maintain their good faith in the country's alliance with the Soviet Union and work toward the brotherhood of all men. Wanger, president of the Motion Picture Academy of Arts and Sciences, also made a brief speech. Aiming his remarks at the anti-Communists who had met the night before, he noted: "Let's keep the record straight. We, too, find home-grown communism as odious as home-grown fascism. . . . [But we do not] intend to be misled by the familiar Hitler line by which communism is made the bogey . . . to confuse us."

Wanger's remarks were prompted by charges that the Free World Association was doing the work of the Communist party. Less than twenty-four hours before Wanger's impromptu comments, Hollywood's most outspoken conservatives had officially announced the formation of a new political action organization, the Motion Picture Alliance for the Preservation of American Ideals. "We believe in, and like, the American way of life," announced the alliance's "Statement of Principles." The signers confirmed their belief in freedom—"to speak, to think, to live, to worship, to work and to govern ourselves, as individuals, as free men"—and "the right to succeed or fail as free men, according to the measure of our ability and our strength." All they wanted was to preserve what they believed was their heritage as Americans. "We have no new plan to offer. We want no new plan, we want only to defend against its enemies that which is our priceless heritage." They resented the growth in influence of Communists within their own profession, and they proposed to battle the "un-American" ideology: "We pledge ourselves to fight, with every means of our organized command, any effort of any group or individual, to divert the loyalty of the screen from the free America that gave it birth."

They elected Samuel Grosvenor Wood as the first president of the alliance. A veteran director who had learned his craft as an assistant to Cecil B. De Mille, Sam Wood was known throughout the industry for his solid work and anti-Communist beliefs. His directorial résumé was impressive. During the decade before 1944 he had made such hits as *A Night at the Opera* (1935), *A Day at the Races* (1937), *Madame X* (1937), *Goodbye, Mr. Chips* (1939), *Kitty Foyle* (1940), *Our Town* (1940), *King's Row* (1942), *The Pride of the Yankees* (1942), and *For Whom the Bell Tolls* (1943), and he had directed some scenes in *Gone With the Wind*, although he had received no screen credit. Wood had a kind-looking round face and a quick smile. Jeane Wood remembered her father as "a charming man—gentle, generous, dear . . . until 'It' came up. 'It' invariably transformed Dad into a snarling, unreasonable brute; we used to leave the dinner table with our guts tangled and churning from the experience." "It" was communism. The older he got, the more obsessed with "It" he became. Things reached a point where he put an instruction in his will that all his heirs, save his widow, could not inherit a penny until they filed an affidavit with the clerk of the probate court swearing that they "are not now, nor have they ever been, Communists."[4]

Historians of the Hollywood political scene have suggested various reasons for Wood's strident anticommunism. Personally close to William Randolph Hearst, by the early 1940s he had developed an abiding hatred of President Franklin Roosevelt and the New Deal. Added to this was his frustration at not winning any professional honors. He had received Academy Award nominations in 1939, 1940, and 1942, but had lost each time. Convinced that politics had interfered with art, he believed that Hollywood liberals had scuttled his chances.[5]

Other Hollywood leaders, especially at MGM, shared Wood's conviction that many of the guilds and craft unions were at least partly controlled by Communists. Communism was more actively opposed as un-American at Metro-Goldwyn-Mayer than any other studio. Under the guiding hand of Louis B. Mayer, MGM had long been the most politically conservative studio in Hollywood. Mayer loved America. Claiming that his birth records had been lost during immigration, he chose to celebrate his birthday on the Fourth of July, and his films idealized America and its people, much in the manner of a Norman Rockwell painting. The actresses at MGM—from Greta Garbo to Norma Shearer—were almost like Greek statues, beautiful but distant. The actors—Robert Taylor, William Powell, Walter Pidgeon, Melvyn Douglas—"all were tall, stylish, and rather aestheticized," wrote film historian Neal Gabler. "With the glaring exception of Spencer Tracy, these were men who didn't muss their suits." Even the mothers at MGM were idealized. "Metro's mothers never did anything but mothering," complained one actress. "They never had a thought in their heads except their children. They sacrificed everything." Perhaps the perfect embodiment of the MGM vision of America was the mythical town of Carvel, home of the Hardy family series, a community of white frame houses, white picket fences, church steeples, and a stately library. There was no place for Communists in Carvel.[6]

Six weeks after the formation of the alliance, FBI agent R. B. Hood estimated that about 200 of the 225 members of the organization worked at MGM. The Metro connection was particularly evident in the alliance's leaders, whom Hood characterized as "responsible persons." Wood, third vice president Norman Taurog, and treasurer Clarence Brown were all MGM directors; second vice president Cedric Gibbons was an MGM art director; and executive secretary George Bruce was an MGM writer. James K. McGuinness, head of the Executive Committee, was an MGM producer, and the majority of that committee were employed by or had strong ties with MGM. Of the major figures in the alliance, only Walt Disney, first vice president, was not on the MGM payroll. Head of his own studio, Disney was especially concerned about the ties between the Communist party and labor unions in Hollywood. As early as 1941 he had told a *Variety* reporter that he was "positively convinced that Communist agitation, leadership, and activities" had led to a strike at his plant.[7]

As the alliance's attacks on Hollywood Communists increased and it forged ties to the American Legion and other anti-Communist groups, it became clear to FBI investigators that the "wheel horse" of the organization was not Wood as much as it was McGuinness. When he was not talking about communism, James K. McGuinness liked nothing more than a friendly drink and a good conversation. "Away from political discussions he was one of the most charming men I ever met," recalled a liberal MGM writer. John Wayne said that McGuinness was "pleasant company" but a "lousy drunk." When he was around John Ford, McGuinness wore the mask of the professional Irishman, slipping into a brogue, addressing Ford as Sean, and signing his letters Seamus. But when any conversation turned political, he lost his genial Irishman pose and accent and became quite serious. In the early 1930s he had fought a losing battle against Communists in the Screen Writers Guild. McGuinness organized the Screen Playwrights, a rival union, in 1935 because he hated the presence of Communists in the Screen Writers Guild. But in 1938 the Screen Writers Guild defeated the Screen Playwrights in an NLRB representation election, and the studios then had to negotiate exclusively with the more left-wing union. McGuinness remained genuinely concerned about the influence of radicals in Hollywood, and he never slackened his attacks, even though his career suffered as a result. "He was conscientiously trying to do what he thought was right," said actor and politician George Murphy. "He was trying to blunt the efforts of the opposition to take over the industry."[8]

The alliance declared war against Hollywood Communists, who responded in kind. For the next three and a half years it was a conflict of nasty political infighting, name-calling, and campaigns of misinformation. In early March, for example, a letter was sent to conservative Democratic senator

Robert R. Reynolds of North Carolina, signed "A Group of Your Friends in Hollywood." It called his attention to such films as *Mission to Moscow* and *The North Star*—"eulogies to Communism and the Red Army"—and warned him of the crisis in the motion picture industry. Something, the letter suggested, had to be done, and soon. Reynolds expressed enough interest in the letter to have it placed in the appendix of the *Congressional Record*, but not enough to read it on the floor of the Senate. Liberals and radicals claimed that members of the alliance had sent the letter, and *Variety* printed an editorial telling the alliance to name names or shut up. The alliance, however, bought newspaper space to disclaim the letter. Claiming their purpose was "to educate, not to smear," leaders of the organization said: "Any statements made, or any letters written by the Alliance have been and will be signed by the members of its Executive Committee." Nevertheless, on the basis of that one letter, the alliance was accused of inviting Washington to investigate Hollywood and starting a witch-hunt in the industry. If that were not bad enough, Communists branded the alliance as anti-Roosevelt and anti-Semitic, charges that could ruin a career in Hollywood. A series of articles in the *People's World*, a Communist-controlled newspaper, pressed the anti-Semitism issue, claimed that the alliance was a front organization for William Randolph Hearst's brand of domestic fascism, and commented that the group was filled with "labor baiters." Behind most of the smear campaign against the alliance was screenwriter John Howard Lawson, whom the FBI identified as a member of the Executive Committee of the northwest section of the Communist party in Los Angeles, and a small group of men that included screenwriter Robert Rossen and labor organizers Herbert Sorrell and William Pomerance.[9]

Organizations on both the left and right actively recruited stars for their publicity value, although screenwriters and directors normally controlled the agendas of the groups. *People's World* boasted that the Free World Association had "a dazzling roster of film names," including Jimmy Cagney, Orson Welles, John Garfield, Walter Pidgeon, Rita Hayworth, Olivia de Havilland, Joan Fontaine, Bette Davis, and Ingrid Bergman. While the alliance could not match the association in number of stars, its leaders did manage to attract a few major box-office draws. Gary Cooper signed on early. By early spring Clark Gable had joined the organization. At a March 28, 1944, meeting of the alliance at the Hollywood Chamber of Commerce, both of these leading men made brief speeches. Cooper scolded "the luke-warm Americans who dally with sedition in the guise of being liberals" and suggested that they would benefit from careful study of the pledge of allegiance to the flag. Gable, a captain in the army who had only recently returned from overseas duty, made an even more dramatic statement. He declared that he was happy to learn of the formation of the alliance to campaign against the Communist influence in the motion picture industry. "It has been said that there are no atheists in foxholes," he claimed. "There were no Communists either in the foxholes where I was. The boys sit around and talk about home and what they want to find when they get back—and it's not communism."[10]

John Wayne would later be closely identified with the alliance, but during the early years of the organization he played no active role. Busy making several films and touring the Pacific war fronts with the USO, he seldom even attended alliance meetings. Fundamentally conservative in his point of view by the end of the war, he nevertheless disliked politics and had a midwesterner's suspicion of all true believers. His personal guilt over not enlisting was only in its infancy, and he felt no need to atone. In a few more years his sense of guilt would deepen, and by that time he had grown weary of the excesses of the Left in Hollywood. Only then would he take a stand. Also, Duke was his own man. Unlike Cooper and Gable, he did not like reading speeches written by someone else. On the one occasion when he did go to a meeting, McGuinness asked him to read a canned address. Duke insisted that he had not come to the meeting as an actor but as an American, and if he spoke he would express his own ideas in his own words, not read from a script. McGuinness was his friend, he recalled many years later, but, "Christ, I wouldn't have done it for anybody." McGuinness understood and turned to Ward Bond, who agreed to give the speech as written. Duke probably only attended a few meetings and did not join the alliance during the war years.[11]

During the early years of the alliance the FBI carefully scrutinized its activities, commenting on its leaders and its followers. At no time before 1948 does the name John Wayne appear in the agency's reports. In fact, historians have probably exaggerated the influence of the alliance in the mid-1940s. In February 1945 an FBI field agent reported: "At the present time the MPA is not very active although the organization formed to combat it, the [Communist-dominated] Council of Hollywood Guilds and Unions, is comparatively extremely active." Critics on the left claimed that McGuinness and his friends were trying to "Red Wash" liberals and radicals alike, then accused the members of the Alliance "collectively and individually" of being anti-Semitic, fascistic, antilabor, anti-FDR, reactionary, and promoters of disunity. Duke's sympathies were clearly with the alliance, but he watched the mudslinging from a safe distance.[12]

He continued to remain on the sidelines of the Hollywood political war during the 1947 congressional investigations of the influence of Communists in the motion picture industry. The alliance, however, did not. By that year their recruitment campaign boasted, "FIRST . . . WE ORGANIZED. THEN . . . WE SURVIVED. THEN . . . WE GREW. NOW . . . WE ATTACK." How many members cooperated with House Un-American Activities Committee (HUAC) investigators is uncertain, but what is perfectly clear is that Sam Wood, James McGuinness, Walt Disney, Adolphe Menjou, and others told all they knew about communism in Hollywood. When HUAC sent out its pink-slip subpoenas, it correctly targeted the leading radicals and Communists in the industry. Altogether, J. Parnell Thomas's committee issued forty-three subpoenas, nineteen to left-wingers. "Between fifty and sixty high-profile activists composed the core of the Hollywood radical movement of the thirties and forties," wrote the leading authorities on the politics of the film industry. "Without question these nineteen men qualified to a man for membership in this group on the basis of their long-term dedication either to the guilds, the Communist Party, or the myriad organizations and causes of the Popular Fronts." With very few exceptions, they qualified on all three grounds.[13]

When the hearings began in Washington on October 20, 1947, the "friend-ly" witnesses included McGuinness, Wood, Menjou, and Disney, but also writ-ers Rupert Hughes, Morrie Ryskind, and Fred Niblo Jr. and director Leo McCarey—all leaders in the alliance. Some of Hollywood's leading men—Gary Cooper, Ronald Reagan, Robert Montgomery, Robert Taylor, and George Murphy—also testified. They came well prepared to discuss the foothold the Communists had gained in Hollywood. They named names. To them communism was a threat, and the intervention of Congress was welcome.

In the second week of the hearings the "unfriendly" witnesses took center stage. The committee questioned eleven of the nineteen radicals who received subpoenas. Of the eleven, eight—John Howard Lawson, Dalton Trumbo, Al-bert Maltz, Alvah Bessie, Samuel Ornitz, Ring Lardner Jr., Lester Cole, and playwright Bertolt Brecht—were screenwriters; two—Herbert Biberman and Edward Dmytryk—were directors; and one—Adrian Scott—was a producer. Rather than candidly discuss their political beliefs and associations, or even plead the Fifth Amendment, they chose to stand awkwardly on their First Amendment right of free speech, not refusing but avoiding the question: "Are you now or have you ever been a member of the Communist party?" They knew that a Fifth Amendment refusal would get them blacklisted. "We used to say if you want to be a martyr you've got to expect to get your side pierced," screenwriter Herman Mankiewicz's liberal anti-Communist son Frank observed. "They wanted it both ways: they wanted the glamour of being a martyr and they wanted $5,000 a week for writing trash for the screen." It was a risky, obfuscatory strategy that was almost certain to draw a contempt citation. And in the end it failed. Ten of the eleven "unfriendly" witnesses received citations and prison terms; one, Brecht, was allowed to leave the United States after testifying. A lengthy appeal process ended in April 1950 when the Supreme Court refused to review John Howard Lawson's and Dalton Trumbo's contempt convictions, and the Hollywood Ten were sent to federal penitentiaries.[14]

By then John Wayne had left the sidelines and become the quarterback for the alliance. In 1948 both he and Ward Bond had been elected to the Executive Board of the alliance. The following year Duke succeeded Robert Taylor—who had been asked by executives at MGM not to run again—as the president of the organization. He took office on March 30, 1949, at the sixth annual meeting of the alliance at the Hollywood American Legion Auditorium on Highland Avenue. Robert Stripling, HUAC's chief investigator, who had just retired, delivered the keynote address. Stripling's message was that the barbarians were at the gate and that Hollywood, America, and the world had better respond. In his short acceptance speech Wayne agreed that Hollywood and the nation faced a crisis, and he saw no reason why the United States should tolerate a political party that was controlled by the country's Cold War rival and opposed to the country's existing political and economic systems.[15]

Explaining his position a few years later, Wayne told Maurice Zolotow that Communists

> were rotten and corrupt and poisoned the air of our community by creating suspicion, distrust, hatred. We [members of the alliance] were called anti-Semite, although [Morrie] Ryskind [a Jewish screenwriter] was one of our leaders. We were called anti-labor, although Roy Brewer [head of the Los Angeles division of the International Alliance of Theatrical and Stage Employees, AFL-CIO] and three other AFL leaders were in with us. Actually we were the real liberals. We believed in freedom. We believed in the individual and his rights. We hated Soviet Communism because it was against all religion, because it trampled on the individual, because it was a slave society.[16]

A complex mix of personal concerns and international events inspired Duke's decision to jump off the political fence. Politics had long been an abstraction to him, even during the late 1930s and early 1940s when his own innate political conservatism took shape. He had flirted with liberalism and even socialism as a young man. "When I was a sophomore at USC," Duke recalled in 1971, "I was a socialist myself—but not when I left. The average college kid idealistically wishes everybody could have ice cream and cake every meal. But as he gets older and gives more thought to his and his fellow man's responsibilities, he finds that it can't work out that way—that some people just won't carry their load." Duke was almost forty-two years old when he assumed the presidency of the alliance, and like many middle-aged people, he had become more skeptical about human nature. Socialism, he later argued, "isn't going to stop the selfishness of human behavior. It isn't going to stop the greed. If you take twenty dollars and give a dollar to every son of a bitch in a room and come back a year later, one of the bastards will have most of the money. It's just human nature, and you're not going to whip it with a lot of laws."[17]

Concrete financial concerns contributed to his deepening conservatism. He had listened, with detached sympathy, over the years to Ward Bond's complaints about the federal government, but by the end of the war, the threat of big government was no longer an abstract issue for Wayne. During World War II, personal income tax rates skyrocketed, just when Duke began to earn large sums of money. When Congress passed its major tax bill of 1944, he discovered that individuals earning more than one hundred thousand dollars a year owed 68 percent of it to the federal government, and that people with incomes in excess of five hundred thousand dollars owed 88.6 percent. With existing surcharges, the marginal tax rate was a whopping 94 percent. Wayne found the brackets ludicrously high. "From the time I first went to work for him in 1946," Mary St. John remembered, "Duke complained about taxes. Sometimes he felt there was no point working anymore when so much went to the government." Joe De Franco, one of Duke's closest friends, remembered that Wayne "hated politicians and big government. They wasted too much money, including too much of *his* money." For the rest of his life, he supported political candidates who believed in reducing tax burdens and the cost of government." In 1957 John Ford wrote Duke that he had seen Wayne's income tax returns: "Ouch! Gawd! . . . What the hell are we working for?" Duke's Republican party loyalties, first formed in the midwestern conservatism of Iowa, became hard as steel in the late 1940s, when the rebellion against New Deal taxation and spending policies first began.[18]

His strident anticommunism and high-profile activism in the Cold War at home, however, was of more recent origin. During the 1930s and early 1940s, the conservatism of the Screen Actors Guild stood in sharp contrast to the liberalism and radicalism of many members of the Screen Writers Guild, and Duke sympathized with the actors. When Jim McGuinness launched his crusade against the Screen Writers Guild and later formed the Motion Picture Alliance, Duke believed he was on the right track. "I was invited at first to a coupla [communist] cell meetings, and I played the lamb to listen to 'em for a while," but as he later told an interviewer, "It was just a bunch of Commie bullshit." Several years later, with his star rising in Hollywood, his friends on the right—people like Ward Bond, Robert Montgomery, Jim McGuinness, and Robert Taylor— worked hard at stimulating his latent conservatism. When they first offered him the presidency of the alliance in 1948, Duke turned it down. Tempers were short and hyperbole long in Hollywood at the time, and he wanted to make movies, not political capital. But they kept after him, especially after *Red River* (1948) had thrust him to the top of Hollywood's pecking order. They told Duke they needed him to take a stand, to assume a very public profile, that his country needed him. America was heading into another war, a Cold War, and the stakes were high. "It was a confused time," Duke recalled in 1977. "Dissension because one clique wouldn't go along with another. Hysteria on the right, the liberal writers wanting to run people out of the business on the left. But there was substance to the MPA's allegations."[19]

In discussing his reasons for accepting the lead role in the alliance, Wayne was apt to underscore the atmosphere of the time and the fates of his friends. But it is entirely possible that his World War II record, and the guilt it inspired, played a part. "He regretted not serving," Mary St. John recalled. "He was not the kind of man to dwell on it or talk about it, but you knew he did. You could see it in his face when anyone asked him about his war record. He would tell them that he had not served, and it made him feel like a hypocrite." Did that nagging sense of not doing the right thing at a crucial time make him more willing to stand up for his country during the Cold War? Did he want to make sure that he did not sit out this war? Whatever the case, his stand put him more directly in harm's way than ever before. He did not want to be embarrassed again as a result of his failure to act.[20]

Duke ascended to the presidency of the alliance just when the Cold War entered its hottest phase. "In those days," he told an interviewer in 1976, "it looked like the communists were willing to go to war to achieve the objective of winning the world by destroying our system." Duke served four one-year terms as president of the alliance, taking office in March 1949 and leaving in June 1953. They were the most crucial years in the Cold War, years that witnessed the victory of Mao Zedong's Communist forces in China, the Soviet

Union's successful detonation of an atomic bomb, the convictions of Alger Hiss and Ethel and Julius Rosenberg, the emergence of Joseph McCarthy, and the outbreak of the Korean War. It was a time of security leaks and loyalty oaths, of the enemy at our doorstep and the evil inside our house. It was an age of the paranoid style, a manner of perception that, as defined by historian Richard Hofstadter, trafficked "in the birth and death of whole worlds, whole political orders, whole systems of values" and saw the entire globe locked in a mortal struggle between "absolute good and absolute evil." It was, in short, a period that almost demanded that individuals take sides.[21]

At least some of Duke's success in navigating the political shoals of Hollywood in the late 1940s was due to Beverly Barnett. A quiet, unassuming man, Barnett was working in the publicity department at Republic during the late 1930s when he met Duke. Scrupulously honest and at the same time very tactful, he won Wayne's trust and the respect of the Hollywood press corps. If anything, Barnett's press releases were paragons of understatement, and reporters learned to accept them at face value. In an age of Hollywood hype and shrill political infighting, Duke's publicity had the ring of truth, and it solidified his reputation as a man of his word.[22]

No American community was more torn apart by the forces of history than Hollywood, which housed a proportionally large Communist population. Since most members of the Communist party in the United States did not advertise their political affiliation, it is impossible to state exact numbers, but Larry Ceplair and Steven Englund, the most thorough scholars on the subject, estimate that during the 1930s and 1940s there were about 300 Communists in the film industry—approximately 145 screenwriters, 50 to 60 actors, 15 to 20 producers and directors, 50 or more in various "animation departments, composing departments, back lots, and front offices," and 10 to 30 who were never identified. After watching the performance of the "unfriendly witnesses" at the 1947 hearings, members of the Association of Motion Picture Producers held a closed-door conference at the Waldorf-Astoria Hotel in New York, discussed the Communist problem, and then issued a statement promising a full housecleaning. Not only did they decide to dismiss the Hollywood Ten, they proclaimed: "We will not knowingly employ a Communist or a member of any party or group which advocated the overthrow of the Government of the United States by force or by illegal constitutional methods."[23]

The problem, as Wayne saw it at the time of his presidency of the alliance, was that the producers had not delivered on their promise. True, they had fired and blacklisted the ten, but very few others. In fact, Alliance members believed that they, not the Communists, were suffering at the hands of the producers. By continuing to press the issue of communism in Hollywood after the hearings, they drew attention to the studios' failure to make good on its "Waldorf Statement," embarrassed the moguls, and undermined public confidence in the industry at a time when attendance was dropping. As far as the leading executives were concerned, alliance members were not team players. At least the Communists kept quiet about their beliefs. Wayne and others maintained that during the late 1940s and early 1950s there was an unofficial and unstated anti-Communist blacklist.

"Jim [McGuinness] was taken out by the Commies," Duke told Dan Ford almost thirty years after the event. For years McGuinness had been a capable writer and producer for MGM, but in 1949 he was forced out of the studio during a staff reorganization. Some of his friends blamed liberal Dore Schary, who in 1948 had become chief of production at MGM. Others, including labor leader Roy Brewer, thought that Louis B. Mayer had personally given the order because McGuinness "defied him" by continuing his anti-Communist crusade. McGuinness died less than a year later, and in conservative circles he became a martyr. In December 1950 Duke announced that the alliance had voted to create a James Kevin McGuinness Americanism Award in honor of the late producer's anti-Communist efforts.[24]

McGuinness was not the only right-winger who had suddenly found himself unemployable. Roles for Adolphe Menjou slowed to a trickle, and Morrie Ryskind's screenwriting career abruptly ended. In the early 1930s Ryskind had shared a Pulitzer Prize with George F. Kaufman and Ira Gershwin for the stage musical *Of Thee I Sing,* and he had written or collaborated on the screenplays for such hit comedies and musicals as *Palmy Days* (1931), *Animal Crackers* (1931), *A Night at the Opera* (1935), *Anything Goes* (1935), *My Man Godfrey* (1936) *Stage Door* (1937), *Room Service* (1938), and *Man About Town* (1939). But by the late 1940s, he was out of work. "He was a tremendously successful writer who . . . was blacklisted by the communist sympathizers," Duke told reporter Roy Bryant.[25]

Given the fates of McGuinness and Ryskind and his interpretation of events inside and outside Hollywood, Duke felt he had to take a stand. In this, he stood with the vast majority of the country. Taking a stand was not without risks. In early 1949, his career had just moved to a new plateau. *Fort Apache* had gone into general release in March 1948, *Red River* in September 1948, *Three Godfathers* in January 1949, and *Wake of the Red Witch* in March

1949. "Duke, you're a goddam fool," Herbert Yates told him. "You are crazy to get mixed up in this. It'll put you on the skids in Hollywood." Charles Feldman and Bo Roos agreed; both advised him to stay out of politics. But he ignored their counsel.[26]

"I was a victim of a mud-slinging campaign like you wouldn't believe," he told Zolotow. "I was called a drunk, a pervert, a woman-chaser, a lousy B picture western bit player, an unfaithful husband, an uneducated jerk, a tool of the studio heads." By 1950 Duke and the alliance were ready for a counteroffensive. While he was in his second term in office, the alliance demanded that the Los Angeles City Council register all Communists in the community. Roy Brewer, head of the Executive Committee of the alliance, charged that Communists constituted a "clear and present danger" which "the United States Supreme Court recognizes as justifying action for the protection of our lives and institutions."[27]

They saw registration as only a first step toward the "complete delousing" of Hollywood. "Unfortunately we have received little support from top executives," noted an alliance press release. "Some, stupidly, have even opposed us, and a few have tried to destroy us. We know that, within the next year, motion pictures will again come under Congressional fire because of our Communists." In the absence of self-regulation, alliance members welcomed the intervention of Washington. "We know pretty well ourselves who they are, and our estimate is that the total number of actual, hard-bitten revolutionary, subversive Communists in Hollywood is not much above 100. . . . Let us, in Hollywood, not be afraid to use the D.D.T. on ourselves. We don't need much of it."[28]

If the alliance wanted another round of investigations, it did not have long to wait. In early 1951, during Duke's third term as president, HUAC resumed monitoring Hollywood. The composition of the committee had changed since 1947. J. Parnell Thomas had been convicted of padding his payroll and sent to a federal penitentiary in Danbury, Connecticut, the same prison where Hollywood Ten members Lester Cole and Ring Lardner Jr. were serving time. (Ironically, as Cole relates in his memoir, he had a brief encounter with Thomas while the former HUAC chairman was cleaning out the prison's chicken coop. Thomas saw Cole with a scythe cutting hay and said: "Hey, Bolshie, I see you still got your sickle. Where's your hammer?" Cole replied, "And I see just like in Congress, you're still picking up chickenshit.") John S. Wood, a Georgia Democrat, had replaced Thomas as the chairman of the committee. But its mission remained the same, and its success in the Hiss case, coupled with the rise of Cold War passions, had increased its power and popularity. Many liberal groups and individuals in Hollywood had vocally opposed HUAC in 1947. In 1951 there was nothing but silence from the Left. The Screen Actors Guild, the Screen Directors Guild, and even the Screen Writers Guild expressed support for HUAC and offered their complete cooperation.[29]

Once again HUAC had done its homework. As journalist and authority on the subject Victor Navasky commented:

> The overwhelming majority of HUAC's immediate targets *were* Communists and former Communists. Although it served the Party's interest to present the 'witch-hunters' as indiscriminate smearers, in fact HUAC came to specialize in red-baiting reds and former reds. The real vice of HUAC was not that it bagged the wrong quarry but that it had no moral, political, or constitutionally legitimate hunting license in the first place.

Before HUAC swore in its first witness, it knew who the Hollywood Communists were, and those served subpoenas faced a simple but painful choice: Plead the Fifth Amendment, refuse to name names, and find themselves blacklisted; or act contrite, make a full confession, renounce their radical pasts, and name names. It was a lose-lose proposition. Of the 110 Hollywood workers who testified before HUAC between 1951 and 1953, 58 decided to name names.[30]

Some, like director Elia Kazan, justified their decision to inform "because secrecy serves the Communists, and is exactly what they want." After telling the committee about his brief stint in the Communist party, he took out an ad in the *New York Times* explaining his decision to inform and calling for others to do the same. "The Communists automatically violated the daily practices of democracy to which I was accustomed," he wrote. "They attempted to control thought and to suppress personal opinion. They tried to dictate personal conduct. They habitually distorted and disregarded and violated the truth. All this was crudely opposite to their claims of 'democracy' and 'the scientific approach.'" In an odd way, he seemed glad that he had been a Communist, for from the experience had come insight:

> It . . . left me with the passionate conviction that we must never let the Communists get away with the pretense that they stand for the very things which they kill in their own countries. I am talking about free speech, a free press, the rights of property, the rights of labor, racial equality and, above all, individual

rights. I value these things. I take them seriously. I value peace, too, when it is not bought at the price of fundamental decencies.

Kazan's statement could have been written by James McGuinness or John Wayne, and although some critics have dismissed it as a shabby attempt to save his career, Kazan continued to express the same ideas in his films. *Man on a Tightrope* (1953) contained an anti-Communist message, and *On the Waterfront* (1954) justifies the act of informing. Three of the leading forces behind *On the Waterfront*—director Kazan, screenwriter Budd Schulberg, and actor Lee J. Cobb—were former Communist party members who had named names before HUAC.[31]

Other members of the Hollywood community who named names did so only to salvage their careers. Lee J. Cobb had been named as a Communist by another actor in 1951, but he did not testify before HUAC until 1953. In the two intervening years, he was unable to get a part, he ran out of money, and his wife was institutionalized for alcoholism. He was "shocked" by Kazan's testimony, and "offended." The committee, he thought, would never break him. But the blacklist and the phone taps and the constant surveillance did. Years later he told Navasky, "The human animal is not noble. . . . I didn't act out of principle. I wallowed in unprincipledness. One of my closest friends pleaded with me not to do a thing like this, as he ran to catch a boat for England. He was fleeing the country, but I was the coward." David Raksin, a leading Hollywood composer, agreed. He, too, named names, although he said later: "The only thing a decent person could do was not talk—I still believe that. . . . I said to myself, 'This is like the Spanish Inquisition, so maybe the best I can do is come out alive.'"[32]

Those who pled the Fifth faced stark, immediate, and irreversible consequences. Although dozens of books have been written about the blacklist in Hollywood, and the subject has provided material for hundreds of magazine and newspaper articles, movies, television programs, and plays, it is important to bear in mind that there was nothing unique about it. Americans, conservatives and liberals alike, worried about the inroads communism had made throughout the United States, not just in the movies, and the Red Scare was a broad-based political phenomenon that extended well beyond the membership of the Alliance for the Preservation of American Ideals, and the House Committee on Un-American Activities. During that decade, purging Communists was as American as motherhood, baseball, and apple pie.

Both of the country's leading labor unions—the American Federation of

Labor (AFL) and the Congress of Industrial Organizations (CIO)—purged Communists from their ranks. The AFL had been anti-Communist since the 1920s, and it had vehemently opposed U.S. recognition of the Soviet Union in 1933, but during the 1930s the CIO had actively recruited Communists. By the end of World War II several of the CIO's constituent unions were Communist-controlled, including the Mine, Mill and Smelter Workers; the Fur and Leather Workers; the Food, Tobacco and Allied Workers; the Marine Cooks and Stewards' Association; the Fishermen's Union; the International Longshoreman's and Warehouseman's Union; and the American Communication Association. Collectively the Communist-controlled CIO unions had a membership of more than two million. Beginning in the late 1940s and early 1950s the CIO turned against its Communist brothers. Led by Walter Reuther of the United Automobile Workers and Philip Murray of the United Steelworkers, the CIO called for a purge. "If Communism is an issue in any of your unions," Murray told the CIO Executive Council, "throw it the hell out . . . and throw its advocates out along with it. When a man accepts office . . . paid office in a union . . . to render service to workers, and then delivers service to outside interests, that man is nothing but a damned traitor." By November 1950 the *CIO News* proudly announced: "To put it bluntly—and factually—the CIO in a year has broken the back of the Communist party in the United States."[33]

Purges were common even on the Left. In the early 1940s, in one of the great ironies of the Cold War, the American Civil Liberties Union (ACLU) imposed a ban on Communists serving in leadership positions. In 1947 a national conference of liberals met in Washington and formed the Americans for Democratic Action (ADA), which was soon recognized as one of the most liberal political-interest groups in the country, but the ADA declared that communism and liberalism were incompatible and banned Communists and "fellow-travellers" from membership. And such groups as the Congress of Racial Equality (CORE), the American Jewish Committee, and the American Jewish Congress—all among the most liberal organizations in the country— worked diligently in the 1950s at blacklisting attorneys from the left-wing National Lawyers Guild. Communists were attacked and blacklisted in America's most liberal ivy universities and the halls of government, in the back rooms of union meetings and the classrooms of public schools, in newspaper offices and scientific laboratories. It was a simple, undeniable fact that during the early years of the Cold War about the only organization open to American Communists was the Communist party of the United States of America.[34]

In short, John Wayne, and the other members of the alliance, were well within the mainstream of American political rhetoric. In April 1951, Albert Maltz wrote his fellow member of the Hollywood Ten Herbert Biberman, suggesting that times had changed since the 1947 hearings: "The new Hollywood business is very grim, very savage. I watch it with inner sickness. . . . Oh the moral horror of this parade of stoolpigeons, what a sickness it spreads over the whole land. That which we predicted is here—the complete triumph of the Motion Picture Alliance for American Ideals. My God."[35]

If anything, Hollywood was more forgiving of former Communists and more willing to bring them back within the fold than was the rest of the country. Once a Communist or radical had renounced his or her past and named names, it was the job of his or her lawyer, often Martin Gang, to send out the word that a client was again employable. Gang, for instance, worked quite well with the leadership of the alliance, Roy Brewer's Motion Picture Industry Council, the American Legion's national office, and the Anti-Defamation League of the B'nai B'rith. Nonetheless, many Hollywood leftists preferred the blacklist to the humiliation of explaining their actions to the American Legion or asking Roy Brewer or Ward Bond for forgiveness.[36]

Bond, not unexpectedly, was particularly arrogant with former radicals. John Ford, a liberal, hated the idea of a blacklist and deeply resented Senator Joseph McCarthy and his political cronies. On one occasion, when Bond invited Ford to a party honoring McCarthy, Ford told his old friend: "You can take your party and shove it. I wouldn't meet that guy in a whorehouse. He's a disgrace and a danger to our country." Ford refurbished his old epithet for Bond when he told Harry Carey Jr. that Bond simply could not help himself: "Ward would do anything to make himself feel important, even at the expense of stomping on people, 'cause he is just too thickheaded to really analyze it and see what a phoney thing it is. Let's face it. Ward Bond is a shit, but he's our favorite shit." Other liberals did not find Bond such a likable shit. Screenwriter Nunnally Johnson reflected on the horror of Bond in power: "I saw so many things happen, so many outrageous things went on, that made me ashamed of the whole industry. . . . Think of John Huston, having to go out and debase himself to an oaf like Ward Bond and promise he'd never be a bad boy again, and Ward Bond would say, 'Alright then we clear you, but we've got our eye on you.'" But the ones who wanted to work again took a deep breath and acted contrite.[37]

John Wayne, to his credit, was one of the quickest members of the alliance to extend his forgiveness, despite the problems that caused him with other anti-Communists. Borden Chase, who wrote the screenplay for *Red River*, claimed that "we had a split in the group . . . the once-a-Commie-always-a-Commie group and the group that thought it was ridiculous to destroy some of those who, say, joined the party in the '30s in Nazi Germany. Duke and I were in the latter group." On March 21, 1951, when HUAC began its second round of hearings on subversive activities in the entertainment industry, Chairman John S. Wood called Larry Parks as his first witness. Best remembered for his portrayal of Al Jolson in *The Al Jolson Story* (1946) and *Jolson Sings Again* (1949), both big hits, Parks had been subpoenaed as an "unfriendly" witness during the 1947 hearings but not called to the witness stand. But there was no way he could avoid the spotlight in 1951. When asked if he was or had ever been a member of the Communist party, he answered yes, that he had joined the Party in 1941 and left it in 1945 because of a "lack of interest." He detailed his involvement with the Party but hesitated about naming names. "I would prefer, if you would allow me, not to mention other people's names," he told Chairman Wood. "This is not the American way. To force a man to do this is not justice." Some members of the committee agreed with Parks, but others insisted that he give the names of other Hollywood Communists. "Don't present me with the choice of either being in contempt of this Committee and going to jail or forcing me to really crawl through the mud to be an informer," he pleaded. The committee denied Parks's request, and finally in a closed session he gave HUAC "four or five" names. The committee was satisfied, commenting to reporters that Parks had been "very cooperative."[38]

In 1947 Parks would have been able to go back to work. In 1951 his renunciation was not necessarily good enough. Executives at Columbia announced the day following Parks's testimony that the studio would not use him in 1951, even though he had been scheduled to star in a comedy entitled *Small Wonder.*[39]

The question of blacklisting Parks was soon put to John Wayne. HUAC asked him to say a word on the actor's behalf, and Duke agreed. He sympathized with Parks, later telling Zolotow: "I wanted to say something good about him. I realized this was a crucial issue. Parks was breaking not just with the Party but all of his friends. He needed our moral support so other witnesses would be encouraged to break." He told reporters that although he could not speak for other members of the alliance, he believed that Larry Parks had done a "courageous thing" and should be "commended as a good American." "Duke just felt sorry for Larry," Mary St. John recalled. "When Parks appeared at a Screen Actors Guild meeting and said that he had made a mistake and asked for forgiveness, for a second chance, Duke felt that Larry should be given that chance. He even understood Larry's reluctance to rat on his friends."[40]

Not all the members of the alliance were so free with handing out second chances. At an alliance meeting at the Hollywood American Legion Hall the day after Parks's testimony, Hedda Hopper, the powerful and conservative gossip columnist, asked to speak. Duke introduced her and began to move toward his seat, but she asked him to remain on the stage. Before a crowd of more than one thousand motion picture workers, she tore into him. Suggesting that she spoke for the mothers of the 55,000 men who had been killed or injured in Korea, Hopper said: "I have read the papers. I have listened to the radio. And then I was shocked as I read the statement of our president John Wayne." She said that Parks "read the best script of his career" in front of HUAC, and she believed that his career was meaningless next to the lives of the men who were fighting and dying in Korea. "Larry Parks says he felt he'd done nothing wrong," Hopper continued. "I feel sorry for him. And I'm wondering if the mothers and families of those who've died and the wounded who are still living will be happy to know their money at the box office has supported and may continue to support those who have been so late in the defense of their country?"[41]

Duke did not reply, but he later remembered that "fifty women went after her" for her criticism of him. Many more members of the alliance, however, applauded her strident address. As a body, after much disagreement, the alliance voted unanimously "to withhold comment on the Washington hearings until the complete facts are known." Some members, such as Ward Bond, Hedda Hopper, Sam Wood, and Adolphe Menjou, maintained that it was almost impossible to trust any person who had ever been a Communist, and the best strategy was just to blacklist the entire lot. Menjou was so extreme, in fact, that he once told a friend that if the Communists ever threatened a takeover of America, "I would move to the state of Texas . . . because I think that Texans would kill them on sight." And at the same meeting that Hopper attacked Wayne's generosity toward Parks, newspaper columnist Victor Riesel was loudly cheered when he urged an immediate "preventive war" against the Soviet Union and called for President Harry Truman to order the military to drop atomic bombs on Russia and China. Others, such as John Wayne and Roy Brewer, felt that any person who cooperated with HUAC, even a former Communist, should be free to work in the industry.[42]

The political difference between the left and right wings of the alliance might have seemed razor thin to Hollywood liberals and radicals, but it represented the line that separated conservative from reactionary. And anyone who ever heard a political discussion involving John Wayne and Ward Bond immediately sensed the difference. Geraldine Page was accustomed to liberal New York politics when she went west in the summer of 1953 to star in *Hondo*. Director John Farrow shot the film in 3-D in Carmago, Mexico, and Page recalled that the heat was terribly intense and the 3-D machine was "very temperamental" and constantly broke down. "So we had lots of time to sit under the broiling Mexican summer sun" and talk. Sitting in a tiny shelter with Duke, Bond, and Farrow, she listened to their political discussions with a growing sense of "horror. I couldn't get up and run or anything." But gradually she noticed differences between the three. "John Wayne would talk so sensibly, but that Mr. Farrow was very much a Machiavellian sort of syllogist . . . and Ward Bond was just an oversimplifying bully. It seemed to me that John . . . would wander out towards something that made sense to me—but that Farrow, in his clever way, would take what John said and weave it back into this pattern of what horrified me." By the end of the film she had concluded that all three men were "reactionaries," but that Duke was "a reactionary for all sorts of non-reactionary reasons. . . . I swear that if John Wayne ever got transplanted out of this circle of people that are around him all the time, that he would be the most anti-reactionary force for . . . good." Despite her own leanings, she had hit upon a truth. He was indeed a force for good—putting decency above all else. Neither an activist nor an ideologue by nature, Wayne's politics revolved around a simple issue: He felt protective of his country and its way of life.[43]

Throughout the blacklist years Wayne found it easy to forgive a person for what he perceived as a personal political mistake. He was less tolerant, however, with men who made films that were critical of American institutions and traditions. In his mind Robert Rossen's greatest offense was not being a member of the Communist party but rather making the film *All the King's Men*. "To make Huey Long a wonderful, rough pirate was great," he said; "but, according to this picture, everybody was shit except for this weakling intern doctor who was trying to find a place in the world." The film was unforgivable. So was Carl Foreman and Stanley Kramer's *High Noon*, a film, Duke believed, which portrayed a town whose citizens, courts, and churches lacked moral fiber. While his screenplay for *High Noon* was being filmed in 1951, Foreman was called to Washington to testify. He took the Fifth Amendment before HUAC and knew he would be blacklisted as soon as *High Noon* was finished. Foreman decided to get even by rewriting enough scenes in the film to make sure people knew he was protesting HUAC and the Red Scare. "I became the Cooper character," Foreman later wrote. The sheriff (Gary Cooper) is abandoned by everyone, left alone to fight his battles for law, order, and civil rights.

Producer Stanley Kramer let the changes stand, as did Gary Cooper. Duke was a forgiving man—toward people who wanted to be forgiven. Foreman sought forgiveness from no one. He was unrepentant. The alliance publicly attacked Foreman, and Hedda Hopper urged that "he never be hired here again." Life imitates art. Stanley Kramer cut his ties to Foreman, Cooper apologized but caved in as well, and Foreman relocated to England. Gary Cooper won the Oscar as Best Actor for *High Noon*, and, ironically, he asked Duke to accept the award for him. Wayne politely agreed and behaved himself at the Academy Awards ceremony. But he hated the film. "It's the most un-American thing I've ever seen in my whole life," Wayne told one interviewer. Misremembering the final scene, he added, "The last thing in the picture is ole Coop putting the United States marshal's badge under his foot and stepping on it. I'll never regret having helped run Foreman out of this country."[44]

Disliking messages in the movies of liberal and radical filmmakers, by the early 1950s Duke was increasingly trying to make political statements in his own films. He did so in two different genres: World War II films and Cold War dramas, in which he starred at Warner Bros. and RKO. From the winter of 1949 to the summer of 1952, while he was still president of the alliance, Duke played the lead in four message films—*Jet Pilot, Operation Pacific, Flying Leathernecks*, and *Big Jim McLain*.

His first overt message film almost failed to make it into the theaters. The problem was not Wayne, who turned in a credible performance, or even the film, which was trite but still probably better than most anti-Communist movies. The real problem was Howard Hughes, the new head of RKO and about as unpredictable a filmmaker as ever purchased power in Hollywood. Tall, thin, handsome, his hair parted in the middle and slicked neatly to the sides, Hughes had an enigmatic smile and dark, expressionless eyes that always seemed to see more than what was in front of them. "Everything about him needed a sharp edge," wrote RKO producer Richard Fleischer. When he was eighteen his father died, leaving him the controlling interest in the Hughes Tool Company, a prosperous oil-drilling-equipment business. The money from the company allowed him to dabble in his primary hobbies—aviation and filmmaking. From 1926 to 1948 he was something of a bête noire in both fields, and people were not sure if he was a genius or an idiot savant. In both areas he enjoyed great successes and suffered even greater failures. In Hollywood, he produced *Front Page* (1931) and *Scarface* (1932), launched the career of Jean Harlow, and went to war with industry censors over Jane Russell's breasts in *The Outlaw* (1943). In the field of aviation, he broke the world speed record, the transcontinental speed record, and the around-the-world speed record, and poured millions of dollars into his white-elephant Hercules (aka the Spruce Goose) plane. Then in 1948 he returned to Hollywood as a mogul, buying the controlling interest in RKO from Floyd Odlum for almost $9 million.[45]

RKO had never been a particularly stable studio, and it had overwhelmed every executive who tried to establish order on the lot. But for all the disorder, the studio had turned out a number of quality movies, including Fred Astaire and Ginger Rogers musicals, Katharine Hepburn and Cary Grant comedies, and such occasional classics as Alfred Hitchcock's *Suspicion* (1941) and Orson Welles's *Citizen Kane* (1941). Hughes's regime, however, made RKO's previous history seem tranquil and orderly. Part of the problem was that he was becoming increasingly reclusive. He avoided the studio, spending most of his time at his offices at Goldwyn Studios on Santa Monica Boulevard, and months after his takeover many department chiefs had not met him. In September 1948 the *New York Times* noted that it had been reported but not confirmed that late one night Hughes presented himself to an RKO policeman on guard at the gate and demanded a tour of the studio. When the owner saw some of his company's mobile equipment parked haphazardly, he inquired: "Have I bought a movie company or a parking lot?" and departed. Another story made the rounds in Hollywood that after remaining silent for a two-hour tour of the RKO facilities, Hughes exited with the simple instruction: "Paint it."[46]

Once in charge of RKO, Hughes proceeded to steer the floundering studio onto sharp financial rocks. Dore Schary, the imaginative head of production, resigned, and other executives followed him. Hughes fired many more, including Sid Rogell, who could not tolerate phone calls from his boss at three in the morning. Production dwindled, failures mounted, losses multiplied. At a time when the entire industry was in a tailspin, RKO seemed ready to crash and burn. It was a nightmare. Lengthy and costly production delays—most the result of Hughes's caprice—became the order of the day. One producer said: "Working for Hughes was like taking a ball in a football game and running four feet, only to find the coach was tackling you from behind."[47]

Into this Howard in Wonderland world stepped John Wayne. The two had been friends for years. During Duke's early years with Chata, Hughes occasionally flew him to Mexico City to see his lover, and they shared strong anti-Communist sentiments. Liberal director Joseph Losey claimed that Hughes had his own off-beat test for Red directors at RKO. He would give them a perfectly dreadful script entitled *I Married a Communist,* and if they turned it down, it proved, at least to Hughes, that they were radicals. It seemed natural that Hughes and Wayne would make movies together, and natural that those movies would have conservative messages. Unfortunately it also seemed natural that there would be problems along the way.[48]

In 1949 Duke agreed to star in *Jet Pilot,* an uninspired attempt to update *Ninotchka.* Jules Furthman's story line was both hopelessly complex and badly simpleminded. Allen Eyles, an authority on Duke's films, called it "the most ludicrous film of Wayne's career," a bold statement given the actor's B Westerns and such feature films as *The Conqueror.* The plot centers on the adventures of Colonel Shannon (John Wayne), a crack jet pilot in the U.S. Air Force, and Anna (Janet Leigh), an experienced Soviet jet pilot and spy who defects to America to gather U.S. military secrets. From that rather improbable beginning, the plot turns silly. While Shannon and Anna pump each other about their respective jet programs, they take trips to Palm Springs, compare political philosophies, and, of course, fall in love. They marry, escape to the Soviet Union, and then return to the United States and presumably live happily ever after.[49]

Wayne's misfortune far exceeded the obvious script problems. It was clear early on that Hughes was determined to use the film to explore three of his obsessions: anticommunism, women's breasts, and aviation. His first two obsessions were more on the order of odd tangents than serious obstacles to production. Throughout the film Janet Leigh wears bras that look as if they had been built out of reinforced concrete, and, if needed, could be used as weapons. Looking at Anna's hard, perfectly cone-shaped breasts beneath only a Soviet issue undershirt, Shannon remarks to a fellow officer: "This might be some new form of Russian propaganda. . . . Maybe they are actually trying to make friends and influence people." Scene after scene in *Jet Pilot* either highlights Anna's breasts or makes reference to them. When Anna remarks that Shannon's father was a "bird-stuffer," he says: "You're pretty well stuffed yourself." And when they are discussing political philosophy, he looks at her breasts and proclaims: "We both believe in uplifting the masses." Shannon refers to Anna as his "silly Siberian cupcake" or his "Soviet Tootsie Roll."

The film's ideological message is equally shallow. Politics are reduced to the level of taste and sight. The difference between capitalism and communism, the movie implies, is the difference between a thick steak and a blintz. After

Anna sees Palm Springs, samples the foods and fashions of America, and witnesses the material advantages of the United States, she can no longer tolerate the drab life of a Soviet citizen. As for Shannon, Anna's body overcomes his disdain for her beliefs. "I hate your insides and vice versa," he tells her. But he soon discovers that beneath every hardened Communist is a budding capitalist yearning for the freedom to spend.

Had the film simply had a bad script and a silly message it might have just been an average flop. What made it a heroic failure was Hughes's self-indulgence, his unlimited willingness to waste his money and time on the project. The real problem—the serious, fatal flaw—was that *Jet Pilot* was filled with information about jets and aviation, subjects close to Hughes's heart. He had never gotten over the exhilarating experience of making *Hell's Angels*, his 1930 classic about World War I pilots, which included state-of-the-art aerial photography, and he wanted to make the same sort of film about Cold War flyers. Expense was as irrelevant as plot. Hughes had envisioned whole aerial scenes, erotic shots of jets banking in and out of cotton-like cumulus clouds and twirling in near-erotic patterns, and he sent second-unit director Paul Cochrane with his large crews of pilots, technicians, and cameramen across the country to film the movie that existed in his mind. They shot footage in California, Nevada, and Colorado, spending weeks and hundreds of thousands of dollars on the ground because the clouds were not right. They traveled to Fargo, North Dakota, then back to Denver. They encountered snowstorms in Great Falls, Montana, and Rapid City, South Dakota. Hughes "went crazy," wrote one of his biographers, "now dispatching second and third camera crews in zigzags across thousands of miles, looking for fuckable clouds."[50]

One location blended with the next—Lowry, Great Falls, Reno, Las Vegas, Oakland, Burbank, Rapid City, Toulonne Meadows, Mount Shasta, Mount Lassen, Sacramento. Weeks became months. Hughes fired Cochrane and hired Byron Haskin, who was almost burned to death in a B-29 fire and then dumped from the project. There were also troubles at his RKO studio. Veteran director Josef von Sternberg, long past his prime, was hired, fired, rehired, and refired. Like Hughes, he was a perfectionist who demanded seemingly endless rehearsals and had a rude remark for everyone. Duke told Leigh at one point that if he allowed his temper to explode "I'd kill the S.O.B." Between von Sternberg and Hughes there seemed no end to the petty nonsense, and the project, like a bad faucet that leaked dollars, continued to drip. In May 1951, seventeen months after shooting began, it ended—the longest shooting schedule in RKO history.[51]

But that was not the end of the story. Once the primary shooting was over, Hughes continued to tinker and tinker and tinker. Years rolled by, and jet technology changed. Hughes continued his elusive search for the pictures in his head, tapping his contacts in the Air Force and the aviation industry. Finally, in October 1957, more than a year after Hughes had sold RKO to General Teleradio and almost eight years after the film went into production, *Jet Pilot* was released. Unfortunately film critics had calendars. "Wars have been fought and airplanes have been improved since 'Jet Pilot' . . . went before the cameras in 1949," wrote Bosley Crowther. "John Wayne, the hero, has grown grayer; Janet Leigh, the heroine, has become more blond; and a good many better motion pictures about jet pilots have gone over the dam." But even if Duke's and Janet's hair had not changed colors, Bosley believed the film would still have been "silly and sorry." "Mr. Wayne and Miss Leigh play their quaint roles like a couple of fumbling kids. Others are even less impressive."[52]

If Duke wanted to get his Cold War message on the screen, he discovered that it was best not to run on Howard time. In 1951 *Operation Pacific* and *Flying Leathernecks* put the message in conventional World War II genre films. *Battleground* (1949), *Task Force* (1949), *Sands of Iwo Jima* (1949), and *Twelve O'Clock High* (1950)—all box-office hits—demonstrated that there was still an audience for war films, and once this had been established studio executives, desperate for moneymakers, returned to World War II with a vengeance. Once again movie theaters came alive with the buzz of British Spitfires and the roar of American B-17 bombers, the rat-a-tat-tat of machine-gun fire, and the explosion of hand grenades. During the Korean conflict, a war mired in limited offensives and stalemate, such films as *Halls of Montezuma* (1951), *Flat Top* (1952), *Above and Beyond* (1952), and scores of others showed how the "good war" was fought by "real men" and for keeps. Most of the films glorified the American sailors and soldiers who fought World War II, though a few, such as *From Here to Eternity* (1953) and *The Caine Mutiny* (1954), had more ambiguous messages. Always hating ambiguity, Wayne chose scripts that used World War II to present role models for Americans during the Cold War.[53]

Operation Pacific was the first film Duke did under his new Warner Bros. contract, which called for him to be paid at least $150,000 per film plus 10 percent of gross receipts. Like Warner's successful *Destination Tokyo* (1943), *Operation Pacific* is a submarine film, but unlike the earlier movie it tries to mix war with domestic romance, casting Patricia Neal opposite John Wayne. In the course of the film, Duke Gifford (John Wayne) rescues a unit of children and nuns, solves a problem of dud torpedoes, makes a sizable dent in the Japanese Imperial Fleet, and woos back his former wife from the arms of a "fly boy." Along the way he also finds time to instruct Americans about duty and sacrifice, about putting one's country and mission above one's happiness. Duke Gifford places service above his marriage, and Pop Perry (Ward Bond) gives his life to save his crew.

Some critics scoffed at Hollywood's return to World War II. When Gifford puts the nose of his submarine on a reef so that he can personally save the life of the pilot who is his rival for the hand of his former wife, a wag commented: "The things these Hollywood guys can do with a submarine." And other critics complained that submarine films should concentrate on the men at sea and forget trying to work in a love interest. Most reviewers, however, overlooked the contrived melodrama and praised the film, one giving it the dubious compliment of being one of the finest submarine pictures ever made. More rewarding for Wayne than even the best reviews was the fact that the navy approved of the film's message and showcased it on their bases.[54]

Flying Leathernecks contained the same message: The price of freedom is dear. In *Operation Pacific* the commanding officers of the *Thunderfish*—Pop Perry and Duke Gifford—are best of friends and demonstrate a marked willingness to sacrifice their own lives to save their men. *Flying Leathernecks* is more grim. The film was an undisguised attempt to capitalize on *Sands of Iwo Jima*, and, like many such efforts, it lacked the original's fire. The two leaders of a marine fighter squadron, Maj. Dan Kirby (John Wayne) and his executive officer Capt. Carl Griffin (Robert Ryan), are at odds throughout most of the film. Griffin, popular with his men and sympathetic to their needs, resents Kirby's willingness to sacrifice his flyers in close air support of Guadalcanal ground operations. He believes that Kirby is a martinet who cares more for his strategic theories than his men. Kirby knows that his executive officer cares more for his men than winning the war. Although he considers his men expendable in the larger framework of the war, he tries to explain that he is not insensitive to the young men he commands. "I knew him," he says of a downed pilot. "I knew a whole squadron of him at Midway." In a series of confrontations between the two men, the film explores the nature of leadership and sacrifice, which reaches a resolution when Griffin is given command of the squadron and promptly sacrifices his brother-in-law for the good of the mission.

The problem with the film is less its theme, which is the central command conflict in any war, than its treatment of that theme. *Flying Leathernecks* was the first RKO film to contain the credit "Howard Hughes Presents." Hughes's primary concern, of course, was the movie's aviation sequences, which were filmed in Technicolor and in 1951 were considered spectacular. He was less interested in the film's content. James Edward Grant's screenplay is a stockpile of war film clichés, devoid of dramatic tension. All the major characters in the movie are motivated by their sense of duty, though they occasionally define duty different-ly. Throughout the film officers do their duty and make tough command deci-sions, soldiers grumble but do their duty and follow, and wives do their duty and keep the hearth warm. "The old *Dawn Patrol* story of the subordinate who comes to loathe his commanding officer as a heartless butcher of 'kids' and then finds himself put in the same unrewarding spot has never been so sophomoric," commented one reviewer, charging that Grant's screenplay ranges from the bor-ders of the "absurd" to "downright embarrassing." Another critic concurred, adding that the film had potential that "under the weight of a confused and rambling screenplay" is "only infrequently fulfilled."[55]

Reviewers agreed that the film had only one saving grace: John Wayne. Named by the *Motion Picture Herald*, *Showman's Trade Review*, *Modern Screen*, and *Photoplay* magazine as the most popular box-office attraction in 1950, Wayne was considered to have a back sufficiently broad to carry even Grant's badly executed scripts. Somehow his pictures seemed immune to the economic troubles that were infecting the rest of the industry. Both *Operation Pacific* and *Flying Leathernecks* finished in the top twenty-five in *Variety*'s list of 1951's most profitable films.[56]

Despite two uninspired films in 1951, at the end of the year the *Motion Picture Herald*'s annual poll of film exhibitors once again named Duke as America's leading box-office attraction. Nothing, it seemed, could diminish his appeal—not his leadership of the alliance, not the filmmaking eccentrici-ties of Howard Hughes, not the scripts of James Edward Grant. "He was just on top of his world," Mary St. John recalled. "He had been in the industry for twenty-five years, and he knew the business from top to bottom." What he wanted was more control. Perhaps he had wanted it for years. Although he had nothing personal against studio owners like Herbert Yates and Howard Hughes, he was not terribly impressed with the money men who controlled his career. More than ever he wanted complete control, the power to take his own risks and make his own mistakes, the power to put his own dreams on film. It was beginning to dawn on him that Hughes and Yates, victims of their own dreams and ambitions, did not share his.[57]

14

The Unquiet Man

John Ford, John Wayne, and Herbert Yates all had dreams, plans, and ambitions. Ford planned to return home, to a mythical place he imagined as Ireland, and then to chart the territory in a film. Duke also longed to make a film, one that spoke to Americans about their past and present and future, about what was wrong with the world and right with the United States. Yates, sensing the death of B pictures, sought a new profile for Republic Pictures; he wanted his studio to compete in the A market, and he wanted to do it on the cheap. In the early 1950s these three reached a crossroads together, and they enjoyed a brief period of harmony and success. But the same dreams and desires that brought them together soon drove them apart.

Sometime in 1933 or 1934 Ford read a short story entitled "The Quiet Man" in the February 1933 issue of the *Saturday Evening Post*. Maurice Walsh's short story proved so popular that in 1935 he expanded it and included it in a series of stories entitled *Green Rushes,* which became a best-seller. In its more developed form, Walsh's Irish tale narrates the story of Paddy Bawn Enright, a Kerry native who emigrated to the United States to seek his fortune and returned home fifteen years later planning to live the rest of his years quietly in a small croft on Knockanore Hill. But even the longer version had problems. Except for a one-sided, five-minute fight at the end, the tale lacks any dramatic action, and its story line and characters are underdeveloped. Yet it is drenched

in the atmosphere of peat fires and pubs, and although it lacked the political
and psychological aspects of *The Informer* and *The Plough and the Stars*, Ford
loved it. In February 1936 he bought the screen rights to "The Quiet Man" for
ten dollars, but he was unable to interest Darryl Zanuck at Twentieth Century-
Fox (or any other studio heads) in the charming property.[1]

For more than a decade "The Quiet Man" incubated in Ford's mind. Oc-
casionally during the next decade he would think of the project. Back in Hol-
lywood on leave from the navy in 1944, he visited Maureen O'Hara on the
RKO lot and told her about his plans to make the film. She agreed to play
Mary Danaher, the female lead, and gave him a "handshake contract." By that
time he had also received handshake contracts from John Wayne, Barry
Fitzgerald, and Victor McLaglen. Seventeen years before he filmed *The Quiet
Man*, he had already cast it.[2]

But casting *The Quiet Man* proved easier than finding a studio to bankroll
it. In March 1946 Ford and Merian Cooper incorporated Argosy Pictures,
their independent production company, to allow the director more control
over the selection and the making of movies. From the start of Argosy "The
Quiet Man" was in the front of Ford's mind. That summer he wrote Lord Killanin, an Irish friend and later head of the International Olympic Committee,
informing him that he planned to make the film in Ireland and in Technicol-
or the next summer and asking Killanin to work with him on the project.
Ford said that Sir Alexander Korda, chairman of London Films Productions
and one of Britain's most successful producers, would finance the film. But
the deal between Ford and Korda bogged down in conflicts over "money, per-
centages, credits and what not" and finally fell through, and the summer of
1947 came and went.[3]

When Korda bowed out, Ford turned to RKO for financing. RKO executives were anxious to sign a deal with a director of Ford's stature, but they had
their doubts about his Irish project. They signed Ford to a three-picture deal,
whose key provision said that if the director's first RKO film showed a profit
then he could make *The Quiet Man*. For some odd reason, for his first RKO
film Ford decided to make a film based on Graham Greene's novel *The Power
and the Glory*. It would have been difficult to have chosen a less likely story
line, or one more objectionable to Hollywood's Catholic censors. The story involves an alcoholic priest, fleeing Mexican anticlerical authorities, who becomes sexually involved with a prostitute. Hardly the stuff of Hollywood, and
Ford knew it. "It is really not a sound commercial gamble but my heart and
my faith compel me to do it," he wrote Zanuck in 1946. Henry Fonda recalled

that Ford had read the novel in 1939 aboard the *Araner* and had wanted to make the film before the war, but had been unable to secure studio support. "It had been rejected all over town because there were too many censorship problems, but Jack felt that if he took out the love affair he could make the story acceptable to them and be left with a beautiful Christ allegory."[4]

Ford titled his film *The Fugitive*. There are critics who insist that the film's composition, lighting, and editing are remarkable. There are others who insist that it is self-indugent, vulgar, and maudlin. Ford loved the movie; American moviegoers, sensing an art film, stayed away in droves. Allegorical tales had never been particularly popular. At the bottom line, something Ford professed not to give a damn about, *The Fugitive* was a flat bust. As far as RKO executives were concerned, Ford's plans to make *The Quiet Man* no longer involved them.[5]

The years passed. John Ford continued to make films for RKO and for other studios, and most of them were quite successful. Maureen O'Hara and John Wayne also made profitable films, and they aged beyond their *Quiet Man* characters. But Ford continued to dream about and plan to make *The Quiet Man*. "Each year we would hold the summer open and each year there was no money and we wouldn't make the movie," O'Hara remembered:

> The script was taken to Fox, RKO and Warner Brothers and all the studios called it a silly, stupid little Irish story. "It'll never make a penny, it'll never be any good," they said. And the years slipped by. John Wayne and I used to go to the studio and say: "Mr. Ford, if you don't hurry up I'll have to play the widow-woman and Duke will have to play Victor McLaglen's role because we'll be too old!"[6]

Finally Duke offered Ford a chance to make the film. "As long as I was stuck at Republic, I thought I might as well try to get Jack to come out there too," Wayne later told Ford's grandson Dan. "I knew that Yates was worried about television taking the audience away from B pictures. I knew he wanted to start making A pictures. I went to him and told him he should get Jack Ford to come to Republic. If he got him, then the other big directors would follow." Actually Yates had already begun making A pictures, but the chance to sign Ford was a real opportunity. "OK, what do I have to do?" he asked Wayne. "Let him make a property he owns called 'The Quiet Man.' Give him fifteen percent of the gross and tell him nobody checks his budgets," Wayne replied. Yates agreed, took out a pencil, wrote a three-page contract, and signed it. "Give this to Ford the next time you see him," he told Duke.[7]

That night Duke met Ford and several other friends for an evening of bridge. "Coach, before we start, I've got something I want you to read." Ford took the contract and, holding it "an inch or so" away from his good eye, read it. When he finished he "wadded it into a ball and threw it into the fireplace" without saying a word to Wayne. The actor recalled: "He never said, 'Jesus, Duke, that's a hell of a deal, but I don't trust that bastard Yates.' He never said another word. I thought he was mad at me for buttin' into his personal affairs where I had no business." More likely, he simply resented the fact that Wayne had reached a position in the industry where he could pass out favors.[8]

Not long afterward, of course, Ford did sign a three-picture deal with Republic. Yates followed the RKO philosophy by insisting that Ford make a profitable picture before he made some foolish Irish romance. But this time Ford had learned something from the ill-conceived *The Fugitive*. His first Republic film, *Rio Grande*, was a solid box-office hit, finishing thirty-fourth on *Variety*'s list of top grossers for 1950. Yates was so pleased with the results that he gave Ford the go-ahead to make *The Quiet Man*, and the director made a reconnaissance trip to Ireland to scout sites and visit family and friends.[9]

Before he could fully turn to the project the navy asked him to make a propaganda film about the Korean conflict. In late December 1950 Ford flew to Korea, where he met Gen. Douglas MacArthur and then led a camera crew in filming around the Pusan area. By February 1951 he was back in Hollywood working on the final editing of *This Is Korea*, which was released by Republic in August. It was a critical and commercial failure, and few theaters wanted any part of it. It also made Yates nervous. Ford, he believed, was unpredictable, a box-office giant one moment and unconcerned with the commercial success of a project the next. Yates appreciated businessmen and no others; he trusted directors who made formula films that turned a predictable profit. To his mind there was a touch too much of the bohemian artist in Ford.[10]

The closer Ford came to taking his crew to Ireland, the more nervous Yates became. By the spring of 1951 he had convinced himself that the film would be "a phoney art-house movie" and a financial disaster. Everything about the project bothered him, from the script and Ford's casting to every detail of the budget. Unlike other Republic pictures, *The Quiet Man* would be shot outside the United States and the budget was a very un-Republic $1,750,000. The more he thought about it, the more he feared utter disaster. Before the cast and crew left for Ireland, he told Wingate Smith, Ford's brother-in-law and chief assistant, "Wingate, you're going to Ireland to make a picture that nobody will go and see."[11]

He even called Wayne into his office and warned him about the film. Although the part of Sean Thornton (Paddy Bawn Enright in the expanded version of the short story) had been carefully developed first by Welsh novelist Richard Llewellyn and then by screenwriter Frank Nugent with Duke in mind, Yates insisted that it was all wrong for Wayne. "He sat there with his boots on his desk, spitting tobacco juice into an ashtray, [and] told me that *The Quiet Man* was going to hurt my career. He wanted me to know that he had nothing to do with it and refused to take any responsibility for it," Duke recalled. Yates's constant complaints failed to diminish Ford's commitment to the project, but they did rattle his confidence. He agreed to cut costs and got Wayne and O'Hara to work for well below their standard rates. While Duke was touring South America with Chata and the Grants—a present from Howard Hughes for Wayne's work in *Flying Leathernecks*—Ford wired him: AFTER MUCH FUSS AND FEATHERS, MUCH WRANGLING, FIST-FIGHTS AND HARSH WORDS THE BUDGET IS SET EXCEPTING, OF COURSE, FOR YOUR SALARY WHICH YOU WILL HAVE TO TAKE UP WHEN YOU GET BACK. I'M A NERVOUS WRECK. Duke was not anxious to waive his standard Republic salary plus 10 percent of the profits, but to help Ford out he agreed to do the film for a flat one hundred thousand dollars. Still, Ford remained shaken from his bouts with Yates.[12]

The sight of Ireland, of the rocky shores of Connemara, and of the village of Spiddal near Galway, where his father had been born and where he still had relatives, only temporarily lifted Ford's spirits. Everything should have been ideal. Much of his family had made the trip with him—son Patrick, daughter Barbara, soon-to-be-son-in-law, Ken Curtis, brothers Francis Ford and Eddie O'Fearna, brother-in-law Wingate Smith. His best friends surrounded him—Duke, Ward Bond, Victor McLaglen, Maureen O'Hara. Indeed, the set often resembled a family gathering. Duke had brought over Chata and his four children; McLaglen was accompanied by his son Andrew; Maureen brought along her seven-year-old daughter Bronwyn and found a small off-screen job for her brother, Charles FitzSimons; Ford regulars Barry Fitzgerald and his brother, Arthur Shields, had major parts. But Ford was uneasy about the script, worried that it just did not hold together. The short story and the script were set during the Troubles, when Republican Irishmen fought bloody battles with the British Black-and-Tans. But the atmosphere of deadly politics mixed badly with the lighthearted, nearly comic love story. Something had to give, and Ford jettisoned the politics, still worrying that the love story alone was not enough to tie the picture together.[13]

Nor did the weather help his mood. When Wayne asked what kind of weather to expect, he was told look across a lake toward some distant mountains. If he "could see the mountains early in the morning it was sure to rain; if [he] couldn't see the mountains, it was raining." Director of photography Winton Hoch said that during six weeks of shooting in Ireland there were only six days of intermittent sunshine, the rest being rainy and overcast. Several locals who worked as extras on the film recalled that the summer was actually fairly dry by Irish standards, but with constantly shifting clouds and light. Lord Killanin said that Hoch spent much of each day with his back to the actors while he checked his light meter. "Never employ a cameraman to direct a film because he never sees what's going on," Ford remarked. Filming the movie in Technicolor added to Hoch's troubles. "Most of the time the clouds were moving across the sky, and the light was constantly changing. I had to light each scene three different ways: for sunshine, for clouds, for rain. I worked out a set of signals with the gaffer, and we were ready no matter what the light was. But I'll tell you, it wasn't easy." Though Hoch's system worked, the photography did not please Yates when he screened the rushes back in Hollywood. "But it's all green," he commented after one session, a remark that did nothing for Ford's deepening depression.[14]

Even the locals themselves created problems. Most of *The Quiet Man* was filmed in and around Cong, a scenic small village located on an isthmus between Lough Mask to the north and Lough Corrib to the south, in County Mayo. Cong and its surrounding countryside are a patch of Ireland straight out of an Irish Tourist Board brochure. It has the ruined twelfth-century Cong Abbey, Ashford Castle manor house, a trout stream that runs through the village, and acres of green countryside and parkland. In 1951 the closest most of the residents of Cong had ever come to Hollywood was a Saturday-evening visit to a movie theater, and the arrival of the "great John Wayne and the great John Ford" was "an event of epic proportions," commented Joe Mellotte, a tall Irishman who acted as a stand-in for Wayne. Everything that happened on the set or involved the cast was news, dutifully reported in the *Connacht Tribune*.[15]

Ford's unit invaded an Ireland where postwar scarcity was still an everyday fact of existence. Jobs, cash, and entertainment were scarce. The talk that spring was about the prospect of a potato blight, the electrification of the rural areas, and the chances of a cinema strike. Ford's arrival changed all that, and rumors, not entirely unfounded, circulated that Republic Pictures planned to spend £225,000 locally. Unemployed and underemployed men and women from Galway to Athlone flocked to Cong looking for work and "a wee bit of excitement." Jack Murphy, owner of the general store that became "Cohan's Bar" in the movie, said:

> The film created work for so many people, not just the extras. Technicians, mainly brought in from London, filled the local Ryan's Hotel and guest houses. Local tradesmen were employed, some using their skills to make Celtic crosses and headstones out of cardboard so we could carry them about for different scenes. The shops did well because, with it being just after the war, many things were still rationed though in Ireland the likes of tinned fruit and chocolate were plentiful and the visitors bought up everything to post home in parcels.

"They bought and they bought. They bought up practically the whole area," added Cong postmistress Mary Gibbons. And the jobs—extras, stand-ins, technicians, and carpenters—paid well: "The great thing about it was that we were paid cash up front at the end of each day's filming. . . . My wage was £1 4s [one pound four shillings] a week and here were the film people giving me £1 10s a day," noted another local worker. Free box lunches, plenty of free time to gawk, a chance to meet John Wayne or Maureen O'Hara or Barry Fitzgerald—employment on the set of *The Quiet Man* seemed the best deal in Ireland.[16]

Joe Mellotte, from Neale, a few miles north of Cong, was judged by most, including himself, to have acquired the best job in town. He was chosen as a finalist for the job from hundreds of hopefuls. "We stood in a line that morning and it was John Wayne himself who appeared, to carry out an inspection of the troops. He walked back and forth a couple of times, pointed at me and said in that drawl of his: 'That's him.'" Mellotte got £3 a day for the work, and besides standing in for Duke, his only vital function was to show up for work each day with two hundred Camel nonfilter cigarettes, which Wayne bummed one at a time every five minutes or so. Mellotte found Wayne to be intense and serious about his work, but also devoid of pretense and friendly. "He was the same in real life as he was in the movies. Everyone liked him."[17]

Nevertheless, without meaning any harm the local sightseers got in the way and created continuity troubles and delays. "I had to start watching for points of continuity—people looking out windows, that sort of thing, which no one else noticed," Ford told British filmmaker/writer Lindsay Anderson. "Then, of course, our technicians work a lot faster than yours. It was really too big a job for one man to tackle on his own." *Connacht Tribune* writers cautioned Cong residents to stay away from the set. After talking with production manager Lee Lukather, one warned that "an untimely sneeze after 'quiet please' is . . . likely to cost Republic Pictures a few hundred dollars." The cautions and warnings mostly went unheeded.[18]

The bickering with Yates, worries about the script, concerns about the weather, and other small problems exacted a toll on Ford. About a third of the way through the shooting schedule he became ill (it is unclear exactly what he suffered from). Duke said that he had a cold; Ford told Anderson that his war injuries had caused him some pain; and Dan Ford remarked that during the filming of *This Is Korea* his grandfather had once again begun to drink heavily. Although Duke and Ford made a pact not to drink during the shooting of the film, both men broke it from time to time—Duke with friends in a pub, Ford alone in Ashford. He was in sorry shape, and his physical condition worsened his psychological condition. "Jack had always worked at studios where people had respect for his work, where they understood that he was the brightest, sharpest director in the business," explained Duke. "But now, here he was at Republic, where everything had always been second class, and he was getting a lot of flack from Yates. The 'but-it's-all-green' thing epitomized it." When Ford became ill Wingate Smith asked Wayne to talk to the director. "Duke, I don't know what to do. I'm just not sure about the script. I don't know whether I've got a picture here or not," Ford said. Later Wayne recalled: "In all the years that I knew and loved Jack Ford, I never saw him so down and so willing to admit his fears as he was that morning."[19]

Duke told him to rest for a few days. While Ford was in bed, Wayne took the second-unit crew over to Connemara and shot action scenes for the horse-race sequence. Lord Killanin had scouted a beautiful stretch of country along Tully Strand—all tall grass, sand, and rocks—and with a strong breeze bending the grass, Duke got some great footage. Wayne's excitement about his progress had had the desired effect on Ford: The director could not stand not being part of the action, and after a few days of rest, he was ready to go back to work.

By that point in the film, however, Wayne was having troubles of his own. One problem surfaced soon before shooting began: When Ford trimmed his budget to the bone to satisfy Yates, he decided not to take Web Overlander to Ireland. Instead he asked Wayne to use Maureen's makeup man. Duke's face was sensitive to makeup, and after one treatment from Maureen's assistant it puffed up like a blowfish. So much for penny-pinching. Within days Overlander was in Cong.[20]

A more pressing problem centered on how Ford wanted him to play his part. In the original the character Wayne played was a small ex-fighter whose courage was evident in his willingness to fight with the IRA against the Black-

and-Tans. He does not want to fight his brother-in-law because he is uninterested in contesting a dowry and because (politics aside) he prefers peace to violence. Writing the part for Wayne, Frank Nugent had to make several fundamental changes. First Sean Thornton became a heavyweight, close in size and weight to his brother-in-law Red Will Danaher (Victor McLaglen). Second, Thornton's motive for not fighting had less to do with his attitude toward his wife's dowry or desire for peace than the fact that he had killed a friend in the ring in America. That motive, however, is not revealed until toward the end of the film. As far as Wayne was concerned, through much of the film Sean Thornton lacks backbone.

Duke and Ford had several open disagreements on the set. Joe Mellotte remembered that Wayne seemed like a perfectionist; when he thought he could do a scene better, he insisted that it be reshot. Duke said that his major confrontation with Ford had to do with the actions of Sean Thornton. "It was . . . a scene where Maureen goes and slams the door and locks me out. The way they had written it, I go over, pick up my boxing gloves, and throw them into the fire. Well, shit! They had me kowtowing and saying 'Yes, Ma'am' and 'No, Ma'am' all the damn time. I was beginning to wonder if they were ever going to let me show some balls! I brought this up with Pappy and he just gave me a dirty look. But later he changed the scene and said, 'Duke, I'm going to let you do what you always do when a broad locks you out. I'm going to let you kick the fuckin' door down.'"[21]

Fighting for his part was just business as usual for Duke, and his head-butting with Ford did not bother either man for very long. Most of his memories were pleasant. He was happy to have his kids around, and his relationship with Chata, while not ideal, was fairly stable. And, of course, he enjoyed working with Ford and Bond. Charles FitzSimons remembered one story that demonstrated how much sheer pleasure Duke received from Bond. Leading cast members stayed in Ashford Castle, which had the ruins of a tower on its extensive grounds. One day Bond climbed to the top of the tower and, on the inside of the wall, carved: "FUCK HERB YATES." "Then in a roundabout way he got someone to tell John Wayne about the spectacular view to be had from the tower. Wayne swallowed the bait and his face was priceless when he saw the message in such an unlikely spot. He came back roaring and laughing when he realized the joke that had been played on him. He laughed himself silly."[22]

Once Ford had regained his confidence, the long Irish summer days allowed him to finish shooting ahead of schedule. Late on the morning of July 14, he wrapped up his location work. That night Wayne and several of the members of the crew went to O'Reilly's pub and drank hard late into the night. Unlike most members of the cast, he seemed in no hurry to leave Ireland. "I believe he was the last to leave," Mellotte remembered. "I can't say he had a tear in his eye—he talked so much about America you knew where his heart was—but I am certain he was still under the influence of the Guinness."[23]

Back in Hollywood Ford went to work shooting interiors at Republic. Within shouting distance of Yates once again, he became edgy and short-tempered. In the horserace scene he ordered the wind machine to blow Maureen O'Hara's hair from back to front, which reversed the conventional way to shoot such a scene with a long-haired woman. Maureen's hair whipped against her face and cut across her eyes, and she squinted to save her vision. Ford screamed and swore at her, telling her to "open your so-and-so eyes." But by then she had had enough of his abuse. "What would a bald-headed son-of-a-bitch know about hair lashing across his eyeballs?" she answered back. Ford laughed, but he continued to drive his actors.[24]

At dinner at Ashford Castle the night before he finished the Irish shooting, he told his cast that he would be happy if *The Quiet Man* was the last film he ever made. His weeks in Ireland and the reunion with old relatives had moved him deeply. "It seemed like the finish of an epoch in my somewhat troubled life," he wrote Lady Killanin in October 1951. "Maybe it was a new beginning." In August and September he pieced his masterpiece together.[25]

Yates liked nothing about the film, starting with the title, which he considered too mild for a John Wayne picture. During the preproduction stage he tried to get Ford to change the title to *Uncharted Voyage* or *The Man Untamed*; during postproduction he fixated on *The Prizefighter and the Colleen*. Ford refused to consider any change. Yates also pressured the director to trim the film down to 120 minutes: "My experience has taught me that no matter how good a picture is, audiences won't sit longer than two hours," he intoned. Ford tried. After close to two months of work he got the picture down to 129 minutes, too long for Yates but perfect for just about everyone else.[26]

The charm of the film rests in its pace and its mood. "What makes *The Quiet Man* the most agreeable film ever shot about village life is the relaxed mastery of its making. Nothing could be better done in the best of all possible film worlds," wrote Ford biographer Andrew Sinclair. From the first the story progresses naturally. Nothing is contrived; there are no trick camera angles. The decision to use Father Peter Lonergan (Ward Bond) as the narrator was a stroke of genius, and from his first line—"Now, I'll begin at the beginning."—the story unfolds as an adult fairy tale. Although Ford bragged that he remained true to Irish customs, *The Quiet Man* presents an imagined Ireland, a dreamland enshrined in the minds and memories of Irish-Americans, where, save for a donnybrook now and again, peace and harmony reign and Catholic parishioners cheer for Protestant bishops.[27]

Throughout the filming the story bothered Wayne. Until the end of the film, he is little more than a straight man, setting up punch lines for Maureen O'Hara, Victor McLaglen, and especially Barry Fitzgerald. "Wayne's low-energy, suppressed, dead-rhythmed performance . . . marks Sean Thornton as a dead man emotionally," commented film historian Tag Gallagher. Maureen O'Hara remembered that "it was a different role for Duke. He was a romantic lead, not a cowboy with two guns in his hands." For Duke it was a professionally taxing experience: "That was a goddam hard script," he told an interviewer. "For nine weeks I was just playing a straight man to those wonderful characters, and that's really hard." But he trusted Ford, and the persona he had already established was enough to give strength to his character. Although John Wayne played Sean Thornton, audiences knew that Sean Thornton was John Wayne, and that sooner or later the quiet man from the States would roar.[28]

Even before Ford had finished editing the film, its dream landscape and Fitzgerald's and Wayne's performances were the talk of Republic Studios. "People were walking around shaking their heads in awe," said Mary St. John. "They said, 'John Ford had done it again.' They said, "This might be his best.'" But Herbert Yates was unconvinced. He thought *The Quiet Man* was too green and too long. Repeatedly he commanded, "No longer than 120 minutes." Finally the day came to screen the film for Republic's distributors. Yates had decided that if they liked it, he would pump money into the advertising campaign; if they did not, he would advertise only the fight scene, release it into mass distribution, and hope to recoup his costs before the public learned it was a dog.[29]

The screening went well—very well. From the opening scene of the train pulling into Castletown and a request for directions to Innisfree, the distributors were enthralled. Even Yates began to suspect that the film was something special. Then at exactly 120 minutes, and just as the big fight between Sean and Red Will Danaher was beginning, the film abruptly stopped. The distributors did not know what had happened. Ford looked at Yates: "There you are Herb. Exactly 120 minutes. I couldn't figure out how to cut nine minutes out without ruining it, so I figured, what the hell? Why knock myself out? I just cut out the fight and got it down to 120 minutes." His point was made. Republic released the 129-minute version.[30]

Yates was starting to have second thoughts. On the off chance that he was wrong—or, more precisely, that his original prediction had been right—he had a midweek showing of *The Quiet Man* at New York's Capitol Theatre. Critics raved. The *New York Times* reviewer called it "as darlin' a picture as we've seen this year." That success gave him the confidence to book the film into Radio City Music Hall, an unprecedented step for Republic. Across the nation the reviews were the same. Critics praised the film's lush photography, outstanding performances, and sense of humanity; they singled out Barry Fitzgerald and John Wayne for special praise. But they all agreed that Ireland and Ford were the stars of the picture: "Never before, I'm sure, have you seen a movie quite like this one, nor will you again, unless you go see it twice or more. Which, incidentally, is what I recommend you do," wrote Kay Proctor in the *Los Angeles Examiner*.[31]

After the overwhelmingly positive August reception, Yates became a true believer. In September he traveled to the Venice Film Festival to accept the acclaim of the international film community. "Thunderous ovation," he wired Ford. "Audience consisted of three thousand persons in formal dress from every free country. It was a sight I do not ever expect to see again." *The Quiet Man* won three awards in Venice and claimed a strong position in the Oscar race. It received nominations for Picture, Supporting Actor (McLaglen), Director, Screenplay, Cinematography, Art Direction, and Sound Recording. On Oscar night, March 19, 1953, *The Quiet Man* earned Academy Awards for John Ford and cinematographers Winton Hoch and Archie Stout. At the time Ford was in Africa making *Mogambo*, and Duke accepted the director's fourth Oscar.[32]

He accepted another Oscar that night. Gary Cooper won Best Actor for *High Noon* and asked Duke to represent him at the ceremony. The fact that Duke had not been nominated as best actor for *The Quiet Man* was not lost on Hollywood insiders. After the HUAC hearings in 1951, tempers were running short, and people were playing for keeps. Ward Bond was convinced that Communists in the industry made sure that Duke did not get a nomination because of his leadership of the Motion Picture Alliance. Though not as conspiratorial in her assessment, Mary St. John felt that "Duke's politics definitely hurt him that year. *The Quiet Man* was his best performance to date, in a film that was nominated for a half-dozen awards. And they ignored him."[33]

Yates was happy, but his late-discovered faith in *The Quiet Man* did not change Ford's conviction that he ran a "cheap poverty-row bullshit" operation. In addition the director believed that Yates was bilking Argosy on overhead charges and manipulating box-office returns. *The Quiet Man* finished twelfth on the *Variety* list of 1952 top-grossing pictures, with rental fees of $3,200,000, but for some reason little of the profits were returning to Ford and Merian Cooper's company. "Somewhere between the theaters and Republic's accounts the money was disappearing," wrote Ford's grandson Dan, "and John had a pretty good idea where it was going: right into Herb Yates's pocket." Money was never the driving force in Ford's life, but he did not like the idea of being cheated either. Angry, he lashed out at his friends, blaming Cooper for not paying enough attention to the contracts and Wayne for getting him involved with Republic in the first place. Although Ford did not remain angry at Wayne for very long, his fight with Cooper ended their relationship. In the end Yates was forced to pay up. The law firm of Argosy and Ford's World War II boss, Bill Donovan conducted an audit of Republic's books and found indications of "enormous fraud." Three years after the start of the audit, Yates paid Ford and Cooper $546,000 each. The controversy, of course, ended Ford's relationship with Republic. When Yates tried to get back with Ford, the director wired Lord Killanin: "Absolutely impossible for me personally to do business with him."[34]

Yates's business practices also upset Wayne. As far as Duke was concerned, there was no excuse—ever—for cheating John Ford. Ford's name stood for quality and integrity; he never padded budgets or chiseled employees. Ford had called Republic "a back of the bus operation" and worse, and Duke had to acknowledge that he was right. In fact, at the same time that Yates was trying to cheat Ford he was backpedaling on a promise he had made to Wayne. If *The Quiet Man* was Ford's dream project, *The Alamo* was Duke's. He liked the idea of a film rooted in American history, a film about men willing to take a stand and die for their dream of a republic. He had wanted to make the film for years, and Yates had given him a tentative okay. "Yates promised me I could do the picture," Wayne later said. "I had found a location in Panama. . . . a really perfect setting, that just looked exactly like San Antonio back then." Duke reasoned that it would be less expensive to make the film in Panama, and he told Yates that the location he had found was close to an airstrip. With *The Quiet Man* finished and successful, he wanted to turn his complete attention to the project, which he and Bob Fellows had budgeted at $3 million.[35]

Three million dollars was more than enough to make Yates start crawfishing. Suddenly he was full of suggestions and reservations. Why not make the film on the Republic lot? Why not cut down on the number of extras? Why not shoot the film in black and white? Every "why not" was designed to cut costs and, to Duke's way of thinking, cheapen the final product. At one point the two men got into a "terrible shouting match" in Duke's Republic office. The fight ended when Yates "stormed" out of the office.[36]

Duke also marched out, without a word to Mary St. John. Less than half an hour later, Duke called and told her to start packing. "Pack everything. We're moving," he said. He added that he had called a moving company and a truck would be around shortly to move his files and personal belongings. Mary did as she was told, and before long Republic employees started to peek in to see what was going on. By the time the moving van arrived, Yates decided to take a personal look. Mary explained what her orders were, but Yates demanded to talk to Wayne. "He's gone," she said as she continued to pack. Chewing a wad of tobacco, a bit of juice in the corner of his mouth, Yates lost his temper and told Mary to stop packing. She refused. "Who are you working for, him or me?" he screamed. "Wayne," she answered. Then she picked up her purse, walked out of the room, and departed the studio.

She never returned. Nor did Wayne. Herbert Yates had lost America's most popular movie star. By the end of the decade Yates's Republic Pictures would be out of the moviemaking business.[37]

Wayne might have left Republic even if Yates had not cheated Ford and frustrated his plans to make *The Alamo*. *The Quiet Man* was the last picture on his seven-film, six-year contract with Republic. In the *Motion Picture Herald*'s annual poll of film exhibitors, Duke had been named the most popular star in 1950 and 1951, and although his ranking slipped to number three in 1952, there was no question that he was the country's top box-office attraction. Perhaps he would have used his popularity to negotiate a better deal with another studio. But perhaps not—loyalty was important to him, and he had many friends at the studio. In addition his contract at Republic allowed him to produce his own films and work for other studios.[38]

In any event the fight over *The Alamo* eased Wayne's departure from Republic. Since at least 1946 he had been producing pictures at Republic. He had received credit as producer for *Angel and the Badman* and *The Fighting Kentuckian*, and he had functioned as the virtual producer on several other Republic films. In addition in 1950 he had teamed with Robert Fellows, whom he had worked with at RKO during the war, to produce *The Bullfighter and the Lady* (1951). He cast Robert Stack in the lead role and did not appear onscreen himself. Released shortly after Robert Rossen's *The Brave Bulls*, the Wayne-Fellows film suffered by comparison; Bosley Crowther in the *New*

York Times wrote: "By comparison with *The Brave Bulls*, this latest arrival might be said to bear just about the same relation as do the works of Burt Standish to those of Ernest Hemingway." (Throughout the film Stack appeared a clean-cut all-American, as if he stepped out of the pages of one of Standish's Frank Merriwell novels.) Yet even Crowther admitted that the action sequences were well done, and the film made money.[39]

When Duke left Republic he decided to form an independent production company with Fellows. It was a predictable move. Independent production had always played a role in Hollywood, but it gained greater force after World War II. Several factors accounted for the development. Internally the 1940 consent decree (which outlawed blind selling and block booking in packages larger than five films) and the 1948 *Paramount* decision (which ordered the breakup of the major studios' monopoly over production, distribution, and exhibition) placed an increased emphasis on talent and spectacle. Externally the decline in movie attendance and the rise of television and other entertainment forms contributed to the same development. In the decade after 1946 ticket prices rose almost 40 percent, but annual box-office receipts dropped 23 percent. As a result the major studios made fewer pictures and employed fewer actors. In 1947 Hollywood as a whole released 369 pictures; by 1956 the total number had fallen to 272. During the same period the number of actors and actresses under contract to a studio fell from 742 to 229—with a similar decline in contract directors, writers, and skilled and unskilled laborers—and more than four thousand theaters went out of business. The bad news, however, was not evenly distributed. Stars with consistently high box-office appeal were the most prized commodities in the industry, and their power increased proportionately.[40]

Even before the end of the war, such men as James Cagney, Walter Wanger, Sam Jaffe, Fritz Lang, Hal Wallis, and Lewis Milestone had ventured into independent production. The decade after the war witnessed an unprecedented rise of star-controlled companies. The boom was evident in the numbers as well as the names. There were an estimated 40 independent producers in 1945, 70 in 1946, 90 in 1947, and about 165 in 1957. John Ford and Merian Cooper incorporated Argosy Productions in 1946, the year before Humphrey Bogart formed Santana Pictures. Burt Lancaster joined his agent Harold Hecht to form Hecht-Lancaster Productions in 1948, and Kirk Douglas incorporated Bryna Productions in 1955. Constance Bennett, Frank Capra, Gary Cooper, Bing Crosby, Joan Fontaine, John Garfield, Paulette Goddard, Bob Hope, Hedy

Lamarr, Fred MacMurray, Ginger Rogers, George Stevens, Hunt Stromberg, and Sam Wood were but a few of the leading actors and directors who also went into business for themselves. Other major talents gained semi-independence within individual studios. Cecil B. De Mille and Hal Wallis at Paramount; Bette Davis and Errol Flynn at Warner Brothers; Dudley Nichols and Leo McCarey at RKO; and Mervyn LeRoy and Mark Hellinger at Universal made their own artistic decisions and shared in the profits of their productions.[41]

Although independent production involved some risk, there were important artistic and economic reasons for taking that course. Actors and directors had more control over script selection and development; they determined what they made—and how they made it. Most important, their earning potential shot up dramatically. Under the draconian wartime tax code, individuals with high salaries were taxable up to 90 percent. If, however, a star formed his own company, did not pay himself a salary, listed his profits as capital gains, and sold his interest in the film as a capital asset, he would have to pay only a 25 percent capital gains tax. And even if he chose to claim a salary, as the head of the company he could reduce his tax rate to 60 percent. In addition, since corporate tax rates were substantially lower than individual ones, a production company became a lucrative place to postpone tax liabilities and shelter capital. Although some individuals, such as John Ford, hated having to focus constantly on the bottom line and play financial games with the government, others enjoyed the opportunity to keep more of what they made. "Look, Ma, I'm a Corporation," the title of a *Variety* article on independent production, captured the sense of joy and liberation that many stars felt as they went into business for themselves.[42]

Both the artistic freedom and the money attracted Duke. For all his years in the movie industry, he did not consider himself a wealthy man. In early 1953 he told a writer for *Look*: "I made over $500,000 last year, and taxes and expenses took all but $60,000. Though I live conservatively in a three-bedroom house and throw no big parties, I spend $65,000. You see where that leaves me. Sure, I'm broke, but I don't owe a dime in taxes. I have a good reputation with money." Though he was not quite as strapped as he suggested, his point still held true. His day-to-day existence was not what Americans would expect from Hollywood's leading box-office attraction. It was his hope that independent production would close the gap between the illusions of his fans and the realities of his life.[43]

The plan for Wayne-Fellows was for Duke to make the creative decisions and Bob Fellows to take care of the financial details. Fellows had been making

Duke received his first Academy Award nomination for his portrayal of Sgt. John Stryker in *Sands of Iwo Jima* (1949) *(above left)*, the classic movie about World War II. The Oscar, however, went to Broderick Crawford for his performance as Willie Stark in *All the King's Men,* a part Wayne had turned down. But even without the Oscar, John Wayne was the leading box-office draw in Hollywood. In *The Quiet Man* (1952) *(below)*, perhaps his most loved film, Duke once again played opposite Maureen O'Hara. Not even his sensational divorce trial detracted from his popularity, although Chata *(above right)* did her best to destroy his image.

a living in Hollywood as long as Wayne had. "I got my start as a chair boy for Cecil B. De Mille when he was making *King of Kings*," Fellows told a reporter. "He always had a dozen people following him around—you know, with scripts, pencils, megaphones and such. And when he got tired, he'd just sit down. It was my job to see that there was a chair under him every time he looked as if he was going to relax." That was at the old Pathé Studios in 1926, the same year Duke became an assistant prop man at Fox. About the same time as Wayne moved into acting, Fellows shifted into production as an assistant director and unit manager at Warner Bros. and Universal. In 1938 he was promoted to a producer at Warner's, and he produced such hits as *Virginia City* (1940), *Santa Fe Trail* (1940), *Knute Rockne—All American* (1940), and *They Died with Their Boots On* (1941). He left Warner's in 1942, had a brief stay at Universal—where he first worked with Wayne when he produced *Pittsburgh*—and then signed on with RKO as a unit producer. At RKO his relations with Duke became stronger, and the two worked well together on *Tall in the Saddle* and *Back to Bataan*. Fellows never stayed at one studio or in one position very long, and in 1946 he moved once again, this time to Paramount, where he produced such solid successes as *A Connecticut Yankee in King Arthur's Court* (1949), *Red, Hot and Blue* (1949), *Streets of Laredo* (1949), *Let's Dance* (1950), and *Appointment with Danger* (1951). By February 1952, when he went into business with Wayne, Fellows had been involved in well over one hundred productions, and had produced films ranging from musicals to crime thrillers, Westerns, and war and action films.[44]

"What Bob doesn't know about the business," Duke said in 1953, "isn't worth knowing. He's been a stage manager, actor, assistant cutter, prop man, writer and director—just name it." Even more important, he had been Wayne's friend since 1940, when they had met on the set of *Seven Sinners,* and they shared a common faith in Hollywood. Unlike so many other executives in the industry, neither feared the spread of television or worried about the future of their business. Looking every inch a Hollywood executive with his West Coast tan, slick hair, and pencil moustache, Fellows told a reporter: "The only thing that can menace Hollywood is a succession of bad pictures."[45]

Wayne-Fellows's first business move was a conservative one that reflected the trends of their day. Although a few independent production companies worked on picture-to-picture deals, moving back and forth from one studio to another, most companies found it safer to sign multipicture contracts with a single studio. The postwar decline of the industry made bankers leery about financing productions, and the multipicture deal made it easier for independent producers to obtain studio financing as well as distribution. Major studios favored the arrangement because it freed them from the expense of employing contract talent and allowed them to collect rent on their production facilities. Shortly after going into partnership with Duke, Fellows worked out a deal with Warner Bros.[46]

Wayne already had a multipicture deal with Warner's, and he thought highly of Jack Warner and the studio. The contract Fellows negotiated, however, bothered him. Fellows had tentatively agreed to an exclusive seven-picture contract that would have prevented Wayne-Fellows from making films for other studios. Duke believed that defeated the purpose of independent production, and he argued for a nonexclusive five-picture arrangement. After the normal dickering, Wayne-Fellows signed a nonexclusive multipicture deal. Warner's agreed to finance and distribute the Wayne-Fellows productions and to pay Duke at least $150,000 per film and 10 percent of the gross receipts.[47]

Showing the direction that his life would increasingly take, Wayne hoped to use his new position as an independent producer for political purposes. As president of the Alliance, he had become increasingly interested in national politics. The Hollywood Left thought he was wired into the national conservative scene. After one early Saturday morning meeting with Duke, Carl Foreman was convinced that the actor "sure had a lot of inside information." In truth, Wayne was only beginning to move beyond the local political squabbles. But he did take an emotional interest in the 1952 presidential race.[48]

Although he did not enjoy politics, Wayne told Mary St. John that world issues had become too serious not to take a stand. With the country mired in a bloody stalemate in Korea and President Harry Truman's popularity plummeting, Republicans sensed that a generation of Democratic control of the White House was close to an end. The question was not whether the Republicans would win but rather *which* Republican would win. Duke joined Ward Bond, Cecil B. DeMille, Adolphe Menjou, and other leaders of the alliance in support of Sen. Robert Taft of Ohio, the darling of the Republican right, who promised to cut taxes, reduce government spending, and dismantle the New Deal. Although Taft had maintained an icy distance from Sen. Joseph McCarthy, a disappointment to Motion Picture Alliance members, the rumor that General Douglas MacArthur might serve as his running mate reassured those who feared the spread of communism.[49]

Taft's chief rival was General Dwight Eisenhower, whose more moderate positions attracted the support of such leading Hollywood producers as Jack Warner, Samuel Goldwyn, and Darryl F. Zanuck. Moderate Republicans asserted that Taft was too strident to win, and they argued that by backing Ike they could keep Democratic front-runner Adlai Stevenson out of the White House. Duke, however, was not interested in compromise candidates, and he campaigned vigorously for Taft during the spring primaries.

"This man would make such a good president," he told a friend, "and if he would stop acting so fucking stiff he might get elected." It was a sentiment that occurred to other Taft backers. In an age when image was becoming increasingly important, "Mr. Republican" acted as if he dined exclusively on cardboard. His speeches struck those who could stay awake as well reasoned, but his Hollywood supporters knew that he vitally needed work on his delivery. On the radio he projected uncertainty; in person he radiated dullness. Menjou told him to "pause at the end of phrases to let [his] points sink in." Others told him to relax, smile, and remember that the delivery was more important than his message. Taft listened, then promptly forgot.[50]

Before the Republican convention, Duke went to work for Warner Bros. and himself. If Taft could not deliver an effective message, he thought he could. *Big Jim McLain* was the type of film Duke often claimed he hated—an open, frank, preachy propaganda film. It called on all "real Americans" to be vigilant against communism. By early 1952, when *Big Jim McLain* went into production, the anti-Communist genre had become well established; indeed, between 1947 and 1954 the major studios had released more than fifty such films. According to one student of the genre, most anti-Communist films were as financially unsuccessful as they were artistically impoverished, but as second features on twin bills they were widely seen. "They were part of Hollywood's ritual of atonement and appeasement," claimed cultural critic Nora Sayre, "and were aimed at an uninformed audience in a decade when almost anything that middle America feared could be related to Communism."[51]

Even the most popular films of the genre—such pictures as *The Iron Curtain* (1948), *The Red Menace* (1949), *I Was a Communist for the FBI* (1951), *The Whip Hand* (1951), *Walk East on Beacon* (1952), and *My Son John* (1952)— dealt in cartoon stereotypes. "These movies instruct us especially on how American Communists look: most are apt to be exceptionally haggard and disgracefully pudgy," wrote Sayre. "Occasionally, they're effeminate: a man who wears gloves shouldn't be trusted." Nor were gloves the only sign of subversion. In anti-Communist films, viewers quickly learned "that there was something terribly wrong with a woman if her slip straps showed through her blouse; . . . it meant treason." The films suggested that the Communist party was populated by female blonds of questionable authenticity, "impressionable" and overly sensitive young males, and men and women devoid of even the slightest hint of a sense of humor "who grimly demand explanations of 'jokes.'" As a group they dressed like gangsters, treated animals dreadfully, never had normal families, were completely untrustworthy, and, as Sayre observed, could be detected by the way they exhaled smoke: "They expel smoke very slowly from their nostrils before threatening someone's life, or suggesting that 'harm' will come to his family." In short the typical Reds in Hollywood anti-Communist films were not very different from the average Hollywood hit man, even down to their tendency to kill each other. "All in all," noted Sayre, "the movies suggest that Communists were so adept at eliminating one another that there was little work or glory left for the FBI."[52]

The quintessential anti-Communist film was Leo McCarey's *My Son John.* A member of the Motion Picture Alliance for the Preservation of American Ideals who had been one of HUAC's "friendly" witnesses in 1947, McCarey wrote and directed this attack on American Communists, which centers on the effects of ideology on one family. The father (Dean Jagger) is a rough, loud American Legionnaire who claims that if he even thought his son was a Communist, "I'd take you out in the backyard and give it to you with both barrels!" His mother (Helen Hayes) is a gentle, devout Christian. The son (Robert Walker) is a smug, confident intellectual who lies with his hand on a Bible and mocks his father's outspoken patriotism. The film pits Christianity against communism, fundamentalist beliefs against prideful intellect. In the end the mother tries to convince her son to join the fight against communism. Comparing the crisis to a football game—a game her other sons played—she pleads, "You listen to me, John, you've got to get in *this* game, and you've got to carry the ball yourself. . . . Take the ball John! Time's running out. We can't stop the clock! I'm cheering for *you* now!" Then she chants: "My son John. My-son-John. *My son John!*" When he fails to renounce the Party and carry the metaphorical ball, she collapses onto a sofa and shouts to the FBI agents: "Take him away! He has to be punished!" Eventually John decides to confess, but before he gets to the FBI Building, his own comrades shoot him on the steps of the Lincoln Memorial.[53]

Big Jim McLain has the same message—and the same campy trappings— as *My Son John.* Based loosely on a *Saturday Evening Post* article entitled "We Almost Lost Hawaii to the Reds," the film follows the activities of two HUAC investigators sent to Honolulu to smash a Communist ring. John Wayne plays Jim McLain, the lead investigator, who narrates the film in voiceovers. *Big Jim McLain* emphasizes the need for all loyal Americans to join the fight to save the Union. It even begins with the Stephen Vincent Benét question from *The Devil and Dan'l Webster*: "How stands the Union?" Or, as Mal Baxter (Jim Arness) puts it to a local businessman, "You want to stay in business? Co-operate." The film suggests that America's greatest threat is not so much the Communists—who mostly shout orders at each other and bump each other off—but the freedoms guaranteed by the Constitution. *Big Jim McLain* begins and ends with Communists escaping "justice" by claiming their Fifth Amendment rights, and McLain says that the Constitution is being "used and abused" by the very people who want to destroy it.

Although the film falls short of actually calling for the abolition of the Fifth Amendment, it does indicate that all too often such technicalities do more harm than good, and its strong political stand raised problems at Warner's. Carl Milliken, the studio's head of research, wrote another executive that he was concerned about the script. It showed HUAC officials breaking and entering, intimidating witnesses, conducting illegal wiretaps, and being physically violent. It "also show[s] them as expressing more than once the wish that the protective mantle which American law throws about all individuals on trial be cast aside in the case of 'these scum.'" Milliken feared the film might "backfire . . . even to the possible extent of placing us in contempt of Congress."[54]

Duke was unconcerned about the film's political ramifications. But the script had more basic problems, the most important of which was that *Big Jim McLain* never attempts to go beyond the stock characters of the anti-Communist genre. Every Communist in the film is either a humorless dictator waiting to come to power, a psychologically flawed individual, or a bully. Sturak (Alan Napier), the leader of the ring, is a tall, thin, passionless ideologue who views the lives of even Party members as a means to an end. Dr. Gelster (Gayne Whitman), a vital member of the ring, is devoid of any personality. And Communist bully Poke (Hal Baylor) calls McLain a Texas cotton picker and says such things like: "Choppin' cotton is for white trash and niggers." Written by the committee of James Edward Grant, Richard English, and Eric Taylor, the film features almost every Cold War cliché and seldom rises much above the weakest of Wayne's B efforts, factors that prompted one film critic to wonder "how many loyal Americans may actually have converted to communism out of embarrassment that their country could produce" such films as *Big Jim McLain*.[55]

The film was designed to excite controversy, and it did. Even before Duke finished location shooting, the FBI had taken an interest in the project. On May 5, 1952, the *Honolulu Advertiser* printed a story in which it indicated that the film was about an FBI investigation of Communist activities. J. Edgar Hoover had always been sensitive to how the media portrayed his organization—in fact, more than a decade later, he would personally review every script of *The FBI* television show—and he was concerned about the Wayne film. After a brief investigation, however, an agent reported to Hoover that the film concerned HUAC investigators, not FBI men. Satisfied, Hoover closed his file on *Big Jim McLain*.[56]

However, the problem with the film, liberal critics argued, ran deeper than a bad script and poor acting, deeper than the lack of action and continuity troubles. Its approach to communism was based more on reflex than analysis. It attacked without understanding and offered simple solutions to complex issues. "The over-all mixing of cheap fiction with a contemporary crisis in American life is irresponsible and unforgivable," observed Bosley Crowther. Although he normally praised Wayne, Crowther felt: "No one deserves credit for this film."[57]

Although eastern critics hated the film, West Coast trade reviewers found it hard-hitting and truthful. The *Hollywood Reporter* called it "an angry film" and "a successful motion picture from any angle." The reviewer predicted a box-office bonanza. Though less enthusiastic, *Variety* also praised the film's "documentary-styled account of the Communist peril." Writing for the *Los Angeles Examiner*, Kay Proctor noted that *Big Jim McLain* was "a walloping good movie" that was apt to make the viewer "boiling mad." She praised the film as entertainment—especially Wayne's "I mean every word of this!" quality—and supported its political message.[58]

As for the public, the film played to enthusiastic audiences, and the conservative reviewers were more accurate than the liberals. But if Duke's politics were out of touch with those of eastern critics, they were mainstream everywhere else. Released in August 1952, during a slow season for Hollywood, *Big Jim McLain* was a solid hit, ranking twenty-seventh on *Variety*'s list of top-grossing films for 1952. In 1952 Wayne-Fellows and Warner Bros. earned $2,600,000 in domestic rental fees for the film, only $800,000 less than *High Noon*. Considering that Duke made the film for $825,554—only slightly over its $750,000 budget—and that it received few positive reviews, its success was remarkable, a clear signal that John Wayne was exempt from the general decline in the motion picture audience. His image and politics might not be endorsed by major reviewers, but they were well received throughout large sections of the country.[59]

It was a pattern that would hold for much of the rest of his career. Republican politics, bad East Coast reviews, successful movies. Only—and fortunate-ly—the quality of the films was usually much higher. Sadly, another pattern was evident for Wayne that year. While he was making the film, his marriage to Chata made a sharp turn from unstable to disastrous. The final fight took place in Hawaii. Duke and Chata had taken a boat to the islands in an at-tempt to patch things up. It would be a second honeymoon, he told her, a chance to "rediscover each other." What they discovered was that they did not like each other very much. No sooner had the ship left port than Chata start-ed to drink, and the couple began to fight. They argued across the Pacific, and when they landed in Honolulu they continued to argue. Duke had a week be-fore shooting started, and he and Chata filled most of the days and nights with more arguments.[60]

The day before shooting was scheduled to begin, George and Anita Van-derbilt threw a party in honor of the couple. Duke had an early call and did not want to go, but Chata had bought a new dress and wanted a chance to show it off. Reluctantly Wayne went along but told the Vanderbilts that he would have to leave early. At 9:00 P.M. he tried to get Chata to go back to their hotel with him, but she was drinking heavily and refused. For the next two hours he continued to press her to leave, and she continued to drink and say no. Finally, around 11:00, he told the Vanderbilts that he had to leave and asked if they could call a cab for Chata when she was ready to go.

At 4:00 A.M. Duke's phone rang. Chata was drunk and sitting in the mid-dle of the floor, Anita Vanderbilt said. "We're tired of her. We're bored with her. Could you please get her to leave?" Duke said he would send over a stu-dio driver. The driver had no better luck than Duke or the Vanderbilts. An hour later Anita called him again: "Duke, will you come over and get this Mexican bitch out of my house." Wayne apologized and asked if Chata could stay there the rest of the night. The Vanderbilts agreed.[61]

Shortly before 7:00 A.M. Chata staggered into the Edgewater Beach Hotel as Duke was about to eat breakfast before going to work. She had hitchhiked back to the hotel, and she was a mess. She was carrying her heels, her dress was torn and stained, and her hair was disheveled. He asked her if she wanted to talk about what had happened. "Nothing happened," she answered. "I had a great time. You just left me at the party." Then, after having trouble hitting the correct elevator button, she went up to their room, and Wayne went to work.

A few days later, on May 7, they attended another party, a luau at the home of Nat Norfleet, a sportswear manufacturer. Again Chata drank too much, and Duke tried to get her to leave. Chata stalled—she later said it was because she was looking for her purse—and Duke became angry. He threw her shawl in the mud and forced her to leave. Back at the hotel they fell into a heated argument. Chata said that Duke pounded the wall of their room, called her "vile" names, and threw two upholstered pillows at her. The next day she booked a flight to L.A., which developed engine trouble and had to return to Honolulu. She stayed alone that night in a separate room at the hotel, departing again the next morning.[62]

Duke had had enough. The battles had become too painful, the peaceful reunions too brief. In the three years before their final clash, during Duke's most productive years, his marriage had gotten steadily worse. In the summer of 1948, after living for more than two and a half years in a small house with both Chata and her mother Mrs. Ceballos, he had given his wife an ultimatum: "Choose between your mother and me." After a major blow-up and a brief separation, Chata told Wayne, "I want you." Duke bought a house for his mother-in-law in Mexico City, but the arrangement never really worked. An only child who had lived with her mother almost all of her life, Chata had trouble adjusting to the separation. "I've got to see my mother," she claimed, and began taking frequent trips to Mexico City. At first she would leave for a week; then a month; then several months. She spent more time away from her husband in the second half of 1948 and early 1949 than with him. But with Duke off on location most of that time, it did not seem to make much difference in their marriage.[63]

Chata returned to Duke in early 1949, and they spent most of the year together. Her mother came for a Christmas visit, and the three got along well, but when Mrs. Ceballos returned to Mexico City, Chata went along and remained there through the summer. Duke visited her often, asking her repeatedly to return to Los Angeles. The problem, as he saw it, was that although Chata loved and emotionally needed her mother, the relationship was the worst thing for her. Chata seemed to drink more and have more violent outbursts when she was with her mother. Wayne thought that if she could only sever the emotional cords, their marriage would improve. Finally Chata returned, but a nervous ailment caused her skin to break out, and an illness—perhaps alcoholism—forced her to spend two months in Scripps Clinic. Before Christmas in 1950 she told Wayne that she had to see her mother, insisting that a visit to Mexico City would cure her nervous problems.[64]

Chata did not return to Hollywood until the summer of 1951, shortly before she and Duke departed for Ireland and *The Quiet Man* set. She seemed happy. She seemed to get along well with Duke's daughters during the family's stay in Cong. She drank less and seemed to be at ease with herself. But when they returned to Los Angeles, she insisted that her mother come live with them again.[65]

For once they talked about their marriage. Chata was clearly jealous of his work and friends; she resented the hours and days they took him away from her. When he was off on location in Monument Valley, where John Ford barred wives, she became lonely and depressed, even more in need of her mother. Duke did not want to walk out on another marriage. Without actually changing the rhythms of his life, he tried to please her, but his offerings were mostly material—presents, flowers, surprise gifts.

The couple's search for a new home illustrated Duke's method of pleasing his wife. From the first weeks of their marriage, Chata had complained that their Tyrone Street home was too small. She wanted an estate, something big and grand that reflected her husband's status in the industry and was large enough to suit her mother. Periodically they had gone house hunting, but Duke never found exactly what he was looking for. Before leaving for Ireland, they had located what Chata believed was the ideal house, a lovely eight thousand-square-foot, fourteen-room, two-story colonial on Louise Street, sitting on a five-acre lot in the foothills of Encino close to where Clark Gable lived. It had everything—including a pool, a guesthouse-cabana, stable, and riding ring. Duke said that it was too big. Chata countered that it would give her something to do when he was off on location. He agreed to think about it while they were in Ireland. But when they took a second look after they had returned, the FOR SALE signs had been taken down. Chata was furious. "We should have bought it," she kept insisting. Duke just shook his head and accepted the criticism. Finally he said: "We did."[66]

For a while the surprise put their marriage back on track. Both enjoyed the excitement of furnishing and decorating their new home, and Chata's mother moved back in with them. But after several months they started fighting again. Duke complained that Chata's mother was a lush and an embarrassment, and that with her mother around he had no privacy. Chata accused him of being insensitive. Every day was a struggle. Their lives seldom meshed. Duke, for example, woke early, ate breakfast, and went to work. Chata rose later and ate breakfast at about 11:00 A.M. Her mother seldom ate hers until 2:00 P.M. One day Duke returned home at about 3:00 P.M. and asked the Mexican houseboy to make a sandwich for him. Putting down a dish, he replied, "I've just finished serving my third breakfast in this house. I quit."[67]

Chata's failure to become pregnant was yet another problem. She loved children, and she desperately wanted a family. Duke, she said, was at fault, and she charged that he was infertile, though several trips to a physician for tests produced no evidence for her contentions. (Wayne later told his third wife that Chata "was too evil to conceive.") Frustrated, Chata wanted to adopt children, but he had no interest in that solution. "Perhaps he just sensed that his marriage was too unstable," a close friend speculated.[68]

Duke worried about Chata's drinking. Too many of his friends were alcoholics for him not to recognize the signs. Chata and her mother would go on binges and get sloppy drunk, leaving Wayne or one of his assistants to take care of them. "The longer they were married, the more of a problem it became," Mary St. John recalled. "The mother was long past saving, and Chata was not far behind. I don't know if it was the drinking, but she seemed to age unusually fast. Her complexion got worse, and she lost that quality—a kind of innocence—that she had in the mid-forties."

In late December 1951, they got into an argument over something—two years later neither remembered the cause—and Duke threw a glass of water at her. She threw a bucket of ice at him and started to attack. He ended the fight by splashing her face with another liquid. "It blinded me for a moment, and I said it wasn't water," Chata said. "Of course it wasn't water, it was alcohol," Duke replied. She left soon afterward for Mexico City, then returned to Los Angeles and consulted a local divorce attorney. But by mid-January the two were back together. "I blame myself for our troubles," Duke told the press. "I devoted too much time to business and not enough to making a home for Esperanza and me."[69]

Chata ran off again in February. In a feature cover story on Wayne, a *Time* writer reported that Chata had become "fed up with the inroads Duke's work has made on their private life." Duke made several visits to Mexico City to talk with her, and by the end of the month she had returned. A writer observed that Duke held her hand and "grinned boyishly at this latest proof that in a well-ordered world, everything turns out right in the end." But Duke's world had never been well-ordered, and happy endings occurred mostly in his movies.[70]

After their fight in Hawaii, Duke had no interest in reunions. A few weeks after Chata had left the islands she sent her husband a present for his forty-fifth birthday. "Send it back," he told Mary St. John. "Don't open it, just send it back." For the next few months while he finished shooting *Big Jim McLain* in Hawaii, Chata stayed in Encino. There was no communication. Then, the day before Duke was scheduled to arrive back in Los Angeles, she flew to

Mexico City. "I'll be damned if I'm going to go get her," he told several friends. "If she thinks that, she's crazy."

Duke's feelings that his marriage was over were confirmed when he got back to his Encino home. J. Hampton Scott, Wayne's longtime butler and doorman, said that another man had stayed with Chata while Duke was in Hawaii. Then he gave the actor a sheet filled with Chata's "doodling." Written over and over were "Esperanza Hilton," "Chata Hilton," "Mrs. Nick Hilton," and "Chata and Nick." It turned out that Nicky Hilton, the former husband of Elizabeth Taylor, had spent a week in Wayne's house. When asked later what his reaction was to the doodling, Wayne replied: "I went into the bathroom and threw up."[71]

Once again the newspapers reported Duke's marital problems. Louella Parsons told her readers that the source of the couple's difficulties was Wayne's concern for his first family. "Mrs. Wayne is desperately jealous of John's devotion to his four children by a previous marriage," Parsons wrote, adding that she would not be surprised if Duke and Chata divorced and he went back to his first wife. Jerry Giesler, Chata's attorney, told the press that Chata hoped that "a permanent separation may be averted."[72]

While columnists speculated on the future of Duke's marriage, Ernie Saftig, Duke's friend who worked as a production assistant for Wayne-Fellows, convinced his boss to go to Peru to get away from his trouble with Chata and to scout locations for future films. Shortly after he left, Chata called Mary St. John in an attempt to find out where her husband was. "Peru," Mary answered. Chata was furious. "That bastard. He always knew I wanted to visit there," she said. As far as she was concerned, their current fight was no different than the others. She might threaten to leave him, might actually even leave for a few months, but eventually they would reunite.

Events, however, were spinning out of her control. In Lima, Duke was introduced to Richard Weldy, a tall, handsome, hard-drinking Irishman who worked for Pan American but also led occasional safaris up the Amazon. Duke liked Weldy. Along with Saftig, they explored the nightlife of Lima, and after a few days they decided to visit a more exotic site. A remake of *Green Hell* was being shot in Tingo Maria, a remote community on the border of a jungle, and Wayne was interested in seeing the location. When he arrived on the set, he watched a young Peruvian actress in a low-cut Gypsy costume dance barefoot. After the scene was shot, the film's director introduced him to the actress, Pilar Pallete Weldy, the estranged wife of Duke's guide.[73]

Before that moment, Pilar had only vaguely heard of John Wayne. She knew he was an actor, but she could not match a face to his name and had never seen one of his films. She enjoyed Joan Crawford or Ava Gardner romances, not Westerns. But she did not need anyone to explain to her why Duke was the most popular star in Hollywood. "All I could do was stare," she later wrote. "He was the handsomest man I'd ever seen. I couldn't believe anyone's eyes could be so blue." "That was quite a dance," Duke said. Pilar felt awkward. According to her, she was powerfully attracted to Wayne, but she was married to, though separated from, the man who was his guide.

That night Duke's party joined the cast of the film for dinner and drinks. Against a backdrop of a "pale jungle moon" and candlelit tables, Pilar entertained the gathering by playing the guitar and singing a collection of Latin American and American songs. Duke, she said, kept asking for more. He especially appreciated her singing "As Time Goes By," one of his favorites. When she finished, her husband tried to pull her aside to talk to her about patching up their marriage, but she brushed him away. He had cheated on her, and she told him their marriage was over. Besides, she was more interested in the visiting American. That night she had dinner at Duke's table. Pilar told him that she had thought he was "wonderful" in *For Whom the Bell Tolls*. He said she had him confused with his friend Gary Cooper, and asked if she liked Westerns. "Not really," she answered without thinking. Duke laughed, and everyone, save Richard Weldy, seemed to enjoy the evening.

Pilar was only twenty-three when she met John Wayne. Although she had been raised a strict Catholic in a prominent family, her father had died when she was in her teens, and she had married young and embarked on a movie career. *Green Hell* was only her second film. In many ways she was like Josie. She was short and thin, almost frail, with large dark eyes and a warm smile. Laraine Day met Pilar a year and a half later on the set of *The High and the Mighty* and thought she was "delightful; very shy, and certainly not what you would think of as a South American star, because she had none of the obvious attributes of an actress. She was not out-going, sort of a shell, . . . a little withdrawn." Mary St. John agreed. Duke introduced her to Pilar a few weeks after he had met her. "There was an innocence about Pilar which I think attracted Duke," Mary said. "Remember, Chata had turned into something of a raving bitch, making Duke's life a hell, and Pilar was so sweet and so obviously in love with him. Compared to the women in Hollywood who were after him, she was positively passive. I think Duke liked her quiet nature, liked the idea that she might bring a tranquillity to his life."[74]

Duke left Peru shortly after meeting Pilar, but the two were not separated long. By her own account Pilar went to Hollywood in the fall of 1952 to dub her dialogue in *Green Hell,* and quite by accident ran into Duke on a Warner Bros. soundstage. Dave Grayson, a makeup man for Wayne-Fellows, told a slightly different story. He said that after visiting Peru and several other South American countries, Duke showed up in Mexico City, where Wayne-Fellows was making *Plunder of the Sun,* starring Glenn Ford. Pilar was with Duke, Grayson remembered, and Wayne had John Farrow direct her in a screen test. Whatever the truth—whether Pilar came to the United States with Duke or whether he had nothing to do with her trip—shortly after she arrived in Hollywood, she began—or continued—an affair with him. As early as March 1953, Louella Parsons announced to her radio listeners that Pilar Pallete was John Wayne's "new romance."[75]

Professionally Duke ruled Hollywood. He had just been named the top box-office draw in the industry for the second straight year, a position of great power. And he loved every second of the attention. Watching him host a group of writers at a buffet, Pilar thought: "This man will break my heart. He belongs to his fans, to the press, to the world." He seemed comfortable only when he was surrounded by friends and admirers, when everyone was talking and drinking and having a good time. Unlike Pilar, he reveled in crowded, smoky rooms.[76]

Perhaps the smoke obscured the mess of his private life. The same man who dominated the film industry was living in a small rented house on Longbridge Avenue in Sherman Oaks in the San Fernando Valley. After his final fight with Chata, he had rented out his Encino estate and told his wife that she could live in their Van Nuys house. At the same time he told Pilar: "I'm not a rich man." He said he owed half a million dollars, and had no idea how much Chata would end up costing him. But of one thing he was certain: He was in love again and he was determined to get out of his marriage. Just as he had a decade before, he set up his lover in Hollywood while he maneuvered to obtain a divorce from his wife. He moved Pilar into an apartment in a building owned by Fred MacMurray, close to Duke's own rented house, and he signed her to a movie contract with Wayne-Fellows to avoid any immigration troubles. Both moves were designed to conceal their relationship. Pilar spent most of her days and nights in his house, and he never planned to cast her in one of his movies. She was his mistress, and as soon as possible he planned to marry her. "That's the way Duke was," Mary St. John said. "He wasn't a man to move around from one woman to next. He liked the idea of permanence. It was one woman at a time. When he fell in love with Chata, he just wanted to be with Chata. When he fell in love with Pilar, she was the only woman he wanted."[77]

Chata now stood in the way of the order he desired. Only weeks after Duke met Pilar, Chata began to rattle to the press about her desire for a legal separation from Wayne. This was nothing new. In the past, when the two had troubles, she had retained Jerry Giesler and threatened legal action. Each time Wayne had convinced her to give their marriage another try. In September, however, he called her bluff. "A man has to have some self-respect," he told Louella Parsons. "I've taken all I can take. I refuse to be a doormat any longer." This said, he filed for divorce, charging general cruelty. Not to be outdone, Chata countercharged for separate maintenance on the grounds of physical and mental cruelty. Although Giesler and Wayne's attorney, Frank Belcher, told the press that both their clients hoped for a peaceful settlement, leading Hollywood columnists were not fooled. "This will be one of the hottest contested battles of anytime," Parsons told her readers.[78]

Parsons was right. Chata used the divorce court as a battlefield and lawyers as weapons. She seemed grimly determined to injure her husband by taking his money, undermining his image, and destroying his career. There seemed nothing she would not say or do. In the spring of 1953 she hired lawyers to file suits against Duke and private investigators to report on his every movement. She demanded temporary alimony pending a separate-maintenance hearing. She wanted $9,000 a month for living expenses, including $650 a month to support her mother. Duke balked, and Belcher told the court that he had never heard of a man having to support his wife and mother-in-law. They made a $600-a-month counteroffer. Chata responded by telling the press that Duke had been an abusive husband who frequently struck and threatened her. She asked the court for a restraining order to keep her husband at a safe distance. Duke denied her allegations: "Mrs. Wayne's charges are fantastic," he told reporters. Not only had he not hit his wife, in the past year he had only seen her twice, once from a distance and once in the presence of other people.[79]

All Wayne wanted was out. While Chata moaned to the press, he busied himself making pictures. From October to December, 1952, he starred as a pool-shooting, divorced football coach at a financially strapped Catholic college in *Trouble Along the Way* at Warner Bros. Then, in early 1953, he went on location to Donner Lake near Truckee, California, for the Wayne-Fellows production of *Island in the Sky*, a rescue film directed by William Wellman. Finally, from June to August he was in Carmago, Mexico, making *Hondo*.

The last two pictures kept him away from Hollywood, but he was never really able to get Chata out of his mind. Chata, his "psychiatric opponent," dominated his letters to John Ford. He fretted about how much the divorce was costing him and the damage it was doing to his reputation. His temper was short, and he was given to sudden outbursts.[80]

Melville Shavelson, the producer of *Trouble Along the Way*, had no doubt that Chata's activities were having their desired effects on her husband: Chata had "put a detective on his tail, and if she could catch him with Pilar that would change the size of the settlement tremendously. So he was going out of his mind. One day he shook the detective and didn't show up on the set for a week. . . . We had to close the picture, and when he did show up he said, 'I want you to change all the dialogue, all the scenes. Whenever I'm in a scene with a woman she's got to go and make a play for me.'" Shavelson knew it was wrong for the character. He and screenwriter Jack Rose rewrote Duke's scenes, but behind his back they reshot the film as it was originally written. "One day [Wayne] showed up on the set on the wrong day and he grabbed me. That was a real confrontation. Boy, if you've never been grabbed by a guy who is six foot five [and] running the goddam picture!"[81]

Shortly after he finished *Trouble Along the Way*, Pilar gave him another problem to worry about. She thought she might be pregnant. Pilar did not know who to go see, and neither did Duke, but Bo Roos did. A visit to a doctor confirmed her fears. Wayne told Belcher to rush through his divorce, no matter what the price, but Chata would not budge. "She wanted more than money, she wanted to humiliate Duke, and the best way to do that was to put him through the three ring circus of a name-calling public divorce trial," Pilar wrote. "Nothing else would satisfy her."[82]

Duke told Pilar that it was her decision. If she wanted to have the child, he would stand by her. She was confused and scared and saw no chance for a happy Hollywood ending. If she had the baby the scandal might destroy Duke's career as surely as it had Ingrid Bergman's after she had Roberto Rossellini's child. Years later Pilar noted: "I knew Duke loved me, but his deepest commitment was to making movies. I could not and would not endanger his happiness." After a few agonizing days, she went to a doctor who was practicing without a license and had an abortion. It was, she said, a decision that "almost destroyed" her.

Pilar's decision may have saved his career, but it did not improve his mood. Geraldine Page, his costar in *Hondo*, recalled that he was often "grouchy and grumpy." And when Duke was grumpy he was apt to snap at anyone. Lee

Aaker, the boy who played Page's young son in *Hondo*, made the mistake of ruining an unusual number of scenes in the film. He turned right when the script called for him to turn left, opened a door at the wrong time or forgot to open it at the right time, and blew line after line. Wayne was merciless. "What are we going to do about that God damned kid?" he asked anyone who would listen, unconcerned if Aaker heard him or not. Aaker was not the only one who felt his wrath. Every morning, Page said, he "would scream and just destroy somebody," but usually he would know just how much abuse he could administer, stopping just before his target said: "Duke, you can take your movie and shove it."[83]

Sometimes, however, he crossed the line. When he went to Carmago, he sent Pilar to Peru. He feared that if Chata's detectives saw him living openly with his mistress she would use it in the divorce proceedings. The decision made sense, but Pilar still felt as if she had been exiled. During her stay in Lima she lost weight, turned yellow from jaundice, and was miserable. When Duke wired her to join him in Mexico City, she felt as though she had been issued a reprieve, but the man she found there was edgy and mean. At one meal with the Saftigs he seemed particularly remote, as he sat silently smoking cigarettes and drinking tequila. When his steak came he cut off a piece and shoved it at Pilar, bruising her lip with his fork. She fled the restaurant in tears. Ernie Saftig followed her, explaining that Duke was "half crazy" over the publicity his divorce was attracting. Wayne later apologized: "I don't know what the hell got into me." But clearly he was feeling the pressure.[84]

Chata would have had it no other way. Her legal strategy seemed carefully planned to humiliate her husband and tarnish his reputation. Reporters detailed her every step. Unwilling to accept any sort of out-of-court settlement, she openly wooed the press. First she exposed Duke's financial position, a subject he did not like to discuss publicly. Raising her request for temporary maintenance to $13,091 a month, she forced him to open his financial records to the court and press. He called her requests "ridiculous" and emphasized that he was nowhere near as wealthy as his wife claimed, a strategy designed to minimize his final settlement. "Making money—big money—in Hollywood isn't as easy as it was in the old days," Duke said. If his gross income seemed high, taxes, publicity, and other expenses whittled it down to a more modest sum. Although Chata claimed that he made more than half a million dollars a year—and he had admitted as much before the court proceedings began—he produced his income tax statements, which showed that he made $347,998 in 1952, $285,710 in 1951, and $392,364 in 1950, but he paid taxes in those same years of $180,239, $125,536, and $187,258. In addition he paid expenses on several homes, supported Josie and his children, made "bad" loans to a series of friends, bought gifts for members of his casts and crews, and paid for his own publicity. By the end of the year there was not much left. Duke's attorneys claimed that his net worth was only $160,000, with a mere $4,601 in the bank. "We spent everything I made," Wayne told the judge at his alimony hearing.[85]

Wayne blamed Chata for his financial state. "I told my wife we had been spending too much and that my manager wanted us to live on a budget. I asked her to confer with him." But conferences with Bo Roos had failed to curb her spending, or, for that matter, his. As a star he was simply expected to pick up checks and leave large tips. "An actor has to put up a good front," he said. "If you went into a barber shop and didn't tip the barber a few dollars, he'd tell his friends you were a heel and the news would get around." As a result he had had to borrow on insurance policies to pay his taxes.[86]

Duke was embarrassed by the entire affair, but Bo Roos and Frank Belcher told him he had to fight Chata on the temporary alimony issue. If they could trim down Chata's demands, it might force her to accept a quick, out-of-court divorce settlement. But pleading "poverty" and fighting Chata did nothing for Duke's image. The press had a field day, printing headlines about the movie star who "COULDN'T MAKE ENDS MEET ON $160,000," and Chata took an obvious delight in recounting how she and her husband spent their money. She even itemized their monthly spending: $1,245 for maintenance on their primary home; $1,938 for household expenses; $3,654 for personal expenses; $948 for auto upkeep and traveling expenses; $1,513 for health and insurance; $746 for personal clothing; $261 for gifts; $499 for furs, jewelry, and personal effects; $1,023 for charities; $794 for train and travel fares; $301 for telephone; and, of course, $650 for her mother. At a time when most Americans were making less than $4,000 a year, Chata's hard luck story was designed to attract more ridicule than sympathy—and more headlines than both.[87]

Duke struggled to keep his temper. During the temporary maintenance hearing Jerome Rosenthal, who had replaced Giesler as Chata's attorney, suggested that he could "prove that John Wayne is a liar," that he hid income and that he used all sorts of tax dodges, including having RKO pay for his vacations in lieu of part of his salary and writing it off as a publicity campaign. Duke's face turned red and he smashed his fist on the court's guard railing, made a move toward Rosenthal, then rushed out of the courtroom. After smoking a cigarette, he returned, but he resented being called a liar almost as much as he resented opposition lawyers examining his financial records.[88]

He resented the loss of control even more. "He hated feeling as if he'd lost control of his life," Pilar wrote. "It brought out the worst in him." During the maintenance hearing in late May 1953, Wayne-Fellows lost $10,000 for each day Duke was not on the set of *Hondo*. To make matters worse, Chata and her lawyers snapped at him constantly, filing suit after suit. Attorneys Jerry Giesler and Thomas Mercola said that they had spent more than four hundred hours on Chata Wayne's case before she fired them, and they demanded that Duke pay their $25,000 fee. Rosenthal wanted $15,000 for the work he had put into Chata's case and another $25,000 to $30,000 for future work. In addition he requested $15,000 for appraisers, $20,000 for auditing, and $10,000 for private detectives. Not only did Chata want to destroy her husband, she wanted him to pay for it.[89]

The hearing fascinated the public. Reporters and curious spectators filled the courtroom and halls outside Superior Court Judge William R. McKay's chambers. Occasionally demonstrations were held outside the court. One man carried a large placard that read: "Some use B-Girls. Some use Gambling Devices. Some use Guns. Some use our Superior Alimony & Divorce Courts *to commit robbery*." Wayne hated the circus atmosphere, worried that he was being cast as a clown in Chata's domestic drama, and he knew that it would only get worse the closer they came to the real divorce trial.[90]

After a fifteen-day preliminary hearing, Judge McKay awarded Chata only $1,100 a month in maintenance pending the trial, and said Duke only had to pay his wife's attorneys $10,000. She bit her lip, blanched, and appeared shaken as she heard his ruling. Duke grinned, and most of the spectators in the jammed courtroom applauded the decision. As Wayne attempted to leave City Hall, a group of teenagers, mostly female, surrounded him and offered their congratulations. "I am a very happy man," Wayne told reporters.[91]

But it was hardly a victorious moment. Chata continued to badger him. She told reporters that her husband was a drunk and that he frequently struck her. Duke denied both charges, especially insisting that he had never hit his wife. "In fact," he said, "I was woman-handled. On many occasions I had to protect myself from her temper. I often had to grab her arm or hold her foot." The phrase "woman-handled" caught on, and reporters poked fun at the six-foot-four-inch action hero being physically abused by his Latin wife. And Chata's dramatic antics made sure that the case remained in the headlines. After her Cadillac was repossessed by a collection agency representing an Encino market, where she had an outstanding $2,367 food and liquor bill, she drove to court in a beat-up pickup truck. A picture of Chata wearing a $90 hat and $300 silk suit stepping out of the truck appeared in the *Los Angeles Times* and several other newspapers. "Jesus Christ," Duke muttered when he heard the story.[92]

Through the summer, while Duke was in Carmago, Chata pressed her suits and fought bill collectors. Though Judge McKay refused to reconsider her temporary maintenance arrangement, she did not stop asking. Unable to obtain a larger monthly income, she made do by refusing to pay most of her bills. "Let Duke pay," was her attitude. She owed thousands of dollars to stores ranging from Sales Markets in Encino to Saks Fifth Avenue in New York. Ignoring collection agents and court judgments, she told reporters that she would be fully vindicated—and her bills would be paid—after her October divorce trial.[93]

The trial was docketed to begin on Monday, October 19. The *Los Angeles Times* noted that it promised to be "the year's most bitter domestic tiff," a major Hollywood divorce, "a 3D production with Technicolor to spare." It promised everything that pumped up the sales of tabloids and newspapers—adultery, violence, and a mother too drunk to walk. Wayne had wanted to avoid the confrontation, but he said his wife had been "an unreasonable woman." "I have already offered my wife more than she could possibly win in court, no matter what the outcome of the trial," he told a reporter. He had offered her a large financial settlement, which included bonds, houses, cars, oil leases, and a percentage of his future earnings. But she had refused every offer. "I'm all set to fight—and fight hard," he added. "I deeply regret that I'll have to sling mud. But I'm ready and willing to begin."[94]

Chata, however, picked up the first fistful. Still driving a pickup truck, she arrived at court an hour late for the first day of the trial. Traffic was bad and her truck was so slow, she said. Although she was only thirty-one, she looked older, and she appeared ill at ease on the witness stand as she toyed nervously with her white gloves. But she did not back down from any of her twenty-two charges against Wayne. According to her, Duke had been an abusive husband from the first, and his violent behavior was always triggered by alcohol. She said that in 1946, during a trip to Hawaii with James and Josie Grant, she had lain down on a bed while her husband and friend were talking. Then, for no specific reason, Duke had "grabbed [her] by the foot and dragged [her] to the floor." When she asked him what was the matter, he had "insulted and berated" her. Chata claimed that he became even more violent a few years later.

They were in the Hotel Del Prado in Mexico City during the filming of *The Bullfighter and the Lady*, and again for no apparent reason he attacked her. "He grabbed me and threw me against the wall and pulled my hair. He kicked me, then dragged me the full length of the corridor. He called me terrible things, then punched me in the eye. Next morning my eye was black and swollen. I wore dark glasses to hide it."[95]

For hours Chata continued her litany of the sins of John Wayne. She said he was a man of excesses—alcoholic, violent, and profane. One night in 1950, she testified, "he punched me in the nose." The same year, at the home of actor John Carroll, she objected to Duke's drinking and "he knocked me down, hit me while I was on the floor, and kicked me." She described a man who was frequently out of control and given to sudden bursts of anger, a man who threw objects at her and humiliated her at social gatherings. She said he tripped her, threw rubbing alcohol in her face, and generally mistreated her from their first days of marriage. While Wayne listened, occasionally shaking his head at her charges, she described a man whose private behavior varied widely from his public image.

Arriving late again on the second day of the trial—somehow her slow truck was ticketed for speeding—Chata complained of laryngitis and spoke in a husky whisper, which prompted Superior Court Judge Allen W. Ashburn to move the case to a courtroom with better acoustics. But the change in her voice did not lead to a change in her story. She dwelled at length on what she believed were her husband's infidelities. She recounted the fights the two had over Gail Russell, prompting Russell's counsel to say that his client was "outraged at the untruths concerning her at this trial." She also told about the night Duke showed up at a Hollywood party with "a big, black bite on his neck." When Rosenthal asked if it was a "spider bite," Chata replied emphatically: "No. This was a human being bite—unmistakably." She also recounted the many times she had left her husband, and how he would "stage a big crying scene to win her back."

All Wayne could do was sit, watch, and chew gum. "No question, the first two days were the worst," Mary St. John remembered. "Chata was reckless. She simply told the wildest stories." And the newspapers dutifully detailed them all. "The divorce trial was as bad as we all feared," Pilar wrote. "In her testimony Chata described Duke as a drunken, vicious brute. She listed twenty-two specific acts of physical cruelty, giving dates and places, using the word 'clobber,' over and over. According to Chata, Duke had clobbered her in California, Hawaii, Mexico, London, Dublin, and New York. She called him a drunk and blamed him for turning her into one too." By the third day Wayne was "at an all-time emotional low, suffering from the flu, looking and feeling terrible."[96]

On Wednesday, October 21, however, Chata was silent. Perhaps she realized that she had almost no reliable confirmation for her tales of abuse. Perhaps, too, Duke and his lawyers decided to up the ante. Mary St. John recalled that Judge Ashburn had simply become "sick and tired of all the crap and controversy, disgusted with all the salacious details, and brought both of them into his chambers and instructed them to reach a settlement and do it soon." For whatever reason, when Chata arrived on the nineteenth floor of City Hall—again late—she did not resume her testimony. Instead she and her people went behind closed doors with Duke and his people and worked out an agreement. Nothing was actually signed, but the attorneys felt certain that they had an agreement in principle. "We are very close," Frank Belcher told the press. "It's like working a cross-word puzzle." "There has been a change of views," Jerome Rosenthal added. "We are closer together." It appeared that the trial, which was expected to take close to two months, was almost over. To give everyone time to work out the final details, Judge Ashburn recessed the proceedings until the following Wednesday.[97]

Duke never wanted a trial in the first place, but after listening to Chata for two days he believed that he had to respond. She had told too many lies, she had done too much damage to his image and reputation, for him to allow her charges to go unanswered. Even if the lawyers could come to terms on the financial details, he wanted his day in court. "My wife has put me in the position of being forced to defend myself and to clear the names of friends she has needlessly dragged into the case, particularly Miss Russell," he said. "I am afraid now that I have no choice but to talk about my wife. It's going to be distasteful to me. It's going to be bad for her. And I'm afraid the public's reaction might be bad. But what else can I do under the circumstances?"

During the next week, while the lawyers hammered out a settlement, Wayne agonized about what to do. Discussing the case with Aline Mosby, a Hollywood columnist, he admitted he was in a "tough spot." He worried that while Chata's accusations had made headlines, his response would "probably be in small print." He expressed concern for the impact the stories would have on his children and admitted that the entire affair had made him sick. He even felt sad for Chata. "Maybe the worst part of it is that everyone will think there were no good times or laughs during our marriage. But there were," he added.[98]

By the following Wednesday the details of the divorce had been settled, but Duke still demanded a chance to tell his version of married life. For two hours he talked. His voice was hoarse from a heavy cold, but it was strong enough to contradict every one of Chata's accusations. His first concern was to distance Gail Russell from the sordid proceedings. He "absolutely" denied that there had been any improprieties between the actress and himself. They did not have an affair; they did not go to a motel room together. They were friends and only friends.

He also denied that he had ever slapped, punched, kicked, or in any way physically abused Chata. Their problem, and especially Chata's, was alcohol. When she drank she drank hard and turned into a nasty drunk. He told about the parties they had attended, how they were always the last ones to leave because she could never stop drinking. Typically he would try to get her to leave, and she would take a swing at him or try to kick him. Her behavior put him in an awkward position. "I had to cover up for the fact that she was not acting like my wife," he said. "I had to keep up the public relations for us. It was humiliating to have her get drunk, fall down in cafes, cause disturbances at private parties. It affected my work and embarrassed me on many occasions." Although he denied that he had ever struck Chata, he did not say he was a saint. He admitted he had called her a "bum" and a "motherfucking streetwalker" and worse. He admitted that he had thrown a drink at her and that he had been "bit" at a stag party, though, as he told Chata at the time, it had been a surprise, an unwelcome bite.

Close friends and employees of the Waynes supported Duke's testimony. James and Josie Grant, John Lee and Barbara Mahin, Andy McLaglen, Budd Boetticher, Robert Fellows, Bo Roos, Ernie Saftig, Jewel Silverman, Duke Woods, and Hampton Scott—each had seen one or more of Chata's scenes. Although they were not all called to testify, the ones who were sworn in confirmed Duke's tale. They had all seen Chata drunk, loud, and out of control. Jim Grant called her "a wildcat"; Josie Grant said she was "quarrelsome"; they all agreed that she was the wrong woman for John Wayne.

By noon Duke had had his say, and there was no need to drag the case out any longer. After all, the money had already been divided, at least on paper. Leaks to the press indicated that Duke had agreed to give Chata "close to $100,000 during the year following their divorce" and $35,000 and $40,000 in each of the following years. And to dwell further on the details of his testimony would do neither his career nor his ego any more good. Therefore Judge Ashburn applied the seldom used "humane principle," which made it unnecessary to declare either party as right or wrong, and awarded interlocu-tory decrees to both parties. Simply put, he called it a draw and ended the short, nasty trial.

Chata vanished from Duke's life, though she resurfaced from time to time during the next year to create legal problems. She died thirteen months later, "alone," Pilar Wayne wrote, "in a tiny hotel room in Mexico City, surrounded by empty liquor bottles." Harry Carey Jr. knew a Mexican who knew Chata toward the end. "It was not pretty," the man said.[99]

15

"That'll Be the Day"

A smiling portrait of John Wayne, with Monument Valley and a cash register as backdrops, graced the cover of *Time* magazine's March 3, 1952, issue. For the second year in a row, the *Motion Picture Herald* had named him Hollywood's number one box-office star, and he now commanded $250,000 per film. He was the most popular man in the country, perhaps in the world. By the early 1950s, it was common in many cities to have several Wayne films playing simultaneously. "To millions of moviegoers and televiewers," the *Time* writer claimed, "in whose private lives good and evil often wage dreary, inconclusive little wars, John Wayne's constant re-enactment of the triumph of virtue is as reassuring as George Washington's face on a Series E bond." Almost as an afterthought, the writer added, "And virtue, in Wayne's case, brings just as solid returns." It was going to be a very good year. Duke made *Big Jim McLain*, *Trouble Along the Way*, and *Island in the Sky* in 1952, and *The Quiet Man* achieved critical and box-office acclaim. The Motion Picture Alliance's anti-Communist crusade eased much of his pain about not serving in World War II, and he was delighted that the Republicans, including anti-Communist Richard Nixon, had triumphed in 1952 and kept Adlai Stevenson and the Democrats from capturing the White House.[1]

His private life, however, was far from triumphant. Failure there continued to stalk him. His family seemed in shambles. He could see "I told you sos" in the faces of his closest friends. Secrecy shrouded the affair with Pilar, including the abortion and the breakup of her marriage to Richard Weldy. His children seemed more distant than ever. A week after the election he wrote to Florence Morrison, his stepmother, apologizing for not staying in better touch and worrying that in the process of making movies and playing politics, he had lost touch with his friends and even his children. John Wayne had achieved professional triumph; private redemption still escaped him.[2]

With the divorce proceedings looming, he welcomed the opportunity to hide out in Camargo, Mexico, shooting *Hondo* for Wayne-Fellows in the summer of 1953. Much as he would miss Pilar, he shuttled her back to her mother in Peru for the duration of *Hondo* in the summer, away from the inquiring eyes of Chata's private investigators. "Camargo is a one-horse border town," Duke explained. "A beautiful woman like you would stick out like a sore thumb down there. I don't want your name used in my divorce." Chata's detectives followed him to Mexico, but Pilar was nowhere to be found. To keep them off track, Duke and Pilar communicated by cable using assumed names.[3]

Several of Chata's private detectives made their way down to Camargo. When they started nosing around, asking questions, local officials approached Wayne and learned how upset he was about being trailed. *Hondo* was a boost to the local economy, and they wanted him back. They asked him if he wanted the police to "take care of" the private investigators, a euphemism for murder and permanent disposal of the bodies. Duke didn't want anything quite so drastic. He told the police just to lock them up in the local jail. They obliged. A few days later, when one of the detectives came down with acute appendicitis, Duke got them released—"I thought I'd return good for evil"—on the condition that they leave the country.[4]

Hondo was one of Hollywood's attempts to deal with its postwar decline. The falloff in attendance had been accompanied by suburbanization. In major cities first-run theaters were located downtown, often in trashy, crime-ridden areas with limited parking. Young adults, giving birth to the "baby boom" generation after World II, stayed close to home, changing diapers rather than watching movies. With television providing free entertainment at home, movie attendance eroded even more. Desperate producers searched for answers, and a frustrated Jack Warner remarked: "What they're all trying to say is that there's nothing wrong with this damned industry that a dozen John Waynes couldn't cure."[5]

But there was only one John Wayne, so Hollywood tried to provide entertainment that could not be duplicated on television. One gimmick was 3-D. MGM had experimented with three-dimensional projection as early as 1935, but not until the crisis of the early 1950s did Hollywood return to the idea. The process required two shootings of each scene. Theaters then projected both films on the screen simultaneously, from different angles, and moviegoers donned special glasses, which matched the double images and added depth perception to the film. A spate of 3-D films came out of Hollywood in 1953—*Bwana Devil, House of Wax, Kiss Me Kate, The Charge at Feather River*, and *Dial M for Murder*. Action movies, with fights and falls, were especially suited to the process. Keenly aware of the shrinking box office, Wayne and Fellows decided to give 3-D a try. *Hondo* was their contribution.

Warner Bros. agreed to distribute *Hondo*, and Bob Fellows borrowed two cameras especially fitted for 3-D from the studio. Setting up the sequences required much more effort and entailed longer delays than normal filming, and retakes were more common, not because of actors or direction but because of camera breakdowns. "It was a very temperamental machine," costar Geraldine Page recalled. The summer dust and heat of Camargo clogged the camera, requiring frequent repairs, and Duke appreciated having a backup ready to go. But midway through the shooting, Warner Bros. began pestering Wayne and Fellows to return one of the borrowed cameras. Duke worried that with only one camera on the location, mechanical problems would lead to a nightmare of delays. A battle of wills set in, with Wayne holding the machines hostage in Camargo, and Warner Bros. threatening breach of contract. He complained that production costs exceeded thirty thousand dollars a week, and he needed both cameras in case one broke down. Delays on location cost money, and since Wayne-Fellows was producing, Duke did not want to have to cough up any more cash. In several letters to Warner Bros., he complained bitterly about their lack of faith, subtly letting them know that perhaps the ten-picture arrangement they had made in 1952 was not going to work. "If you don't want to cooperate," he told Warner Bros., "just call me back . . . [and] cancel our relationship—I'm goddamned mad enough to." Duke kept the cameras in Camargo, swearing and bitching at them on a regular basis.

Working with Geraldine Page did nothing to improve his mood. In casting her for the film, he had wanted to bring a new face to Hollywood, but he had no interest in breaking in an inexperienced actress. *Hondo* demanded an attractive woman with firm, strong features, but he was not looking for a sexy starlet. The actress had to play Angie Lowe, a married but abandoned single mother scratching out a meager existence in the hot, dusty desert of Apache country. The West Texas frontier had never tolerated pretty women; after a few years in the hothouse, pioneer women acquired the sandblasted, blank look of their adobe houses. Duke wanted a weathered, hardened, almost handsome face. Page's performance in *Taxi* (1953) had caught Bob Fellows's attention, and her acting credits, accumulated in more than a decade of successful stage performances, were above reproach. In addition Duke's agent, Charles Feldman, was guiding her career. Fellows offered her the part over the telephone, without a screen test, and she accepted.

When she arrived in Hollywood late in May, a few weeks before the company relocated to Camargo, Mexico, Fellows took one look and winced. Her teeth looked as if she had already spent a lifetime on some frontier where toothpaste and dentists were unknown. Visible cavities pocked her front teeth; some of the gaps were big enough to see through. Appallingly ugly smiles posed no problems on the Broadway stage, where even first-row viewers were too far away to notice, but a big screen would magnify the carnage. Duke could only imagine what 3-D might do to her smile. Fellows immediately sent her to a Beverly Hills dentist who crammed twenty years of dental work into three days—cleaning, picking, filling, pulling, and capping away until Page's mouth could stand the scrutiny of a zoom lens.

Once shooting was under way in Camargo, Duke learned why Page's teeth had been in such miserable shape. She not only had the look of a frontier woman; she reeked with the odors of one as well. Mary St. John remembered that Page had the hygiene habits "of a five-year-old boy who loathed toothpaste and bathwater. You could literally smell her on the set." Pilar Wayne was a bit kinder, claiming that "Geraldine didn't care much for makeup—or soap and water for that matter." Her table manners were not any better. One evening she ate mashed potatoes and gravy with her fingers. Duke got so irritated in the dining hall a week later that he dumped a plate of food over her head.

The script called for several love scenes between Hondo Lane (John Wayne) and Angie Lowe, complete with long embraces and deep kisses. Duke dreaded them. "Jesus Christ," he complained to Ward Bond, "I'm afraid I might puke the next time I have to kiss her. Maybe if I hold my breath it won't be so bad." In Duke's misery Bond found an opportunity. Carefully planning his prank, Bond waited until director John Farrow called for action and Duke took Page in his arms and touched his lips to hers. Bond "accidentally" slipped into the camera, budging it off center and forcing Farrow to do a retake. Laughing uproariously, Bond beat a hasty retreat before Duke could get to him.

On another occasion John Ford showed up suddenly on the set and observed Farrow shooting a love scene. He told Farrow that audiences would not believe that John Wayne on screen had fallen in love with such a homely woman. Farrow had the lines rewritten, requiring Page to say: "I know I'm a homely woman, but I love you." Pilar Wayne later wrote that "it never occurred to Ford, Duke or John Farrow . . . to consider how she would feel about having to redo the love scene with the additional lines they wanted her to say."[6]

"Do you want to know how bad she smelled?" Mary St. John asked years later. "Page did not have the best morals I have ever seen, and hard-up stunt-men stumbled out of her room every morning. But even Ward Bond wouldn't take advantage of her availability. That's how bad it was." Andy MacLaglen, production manager on the movie, remembered Page in Camargo. "She was fresh off the New York stage and had a beautiful body. I remember one day when it was raining she lay out on a director's chair like this . . . her nipples were just shining through the blouse. She couldn't care less."[7]

Actually there may have been more than her body odor to Bond's celibacy. When he arrived at Camargo fifteen pounds lighter than usual, he strutted around proudly, patting his belly, showcasing his new waistline, and bragging about his need for a new wardrobe. He attributed the weight loss to the miracle of sucaryl, a new sugar substitute that had recently made its way out of chemistry labs and into coffee cups and cereal bowls. Bond touted its virtues at every meal, ceremoniously pulling packets of the sweetener out of his pocket to dump in his coffee and driving everyone crazy with his unctuous self-righteousness. A man without any sense of boundaries, he often crossed over from propriety to impropriety, and his penchant for repetition could quickly turn him into a frightful bore. Duke had had enough. After dinner one evening, Bond promised Duke he could lose a few extra pounds by substituting sucaryl for sugar in his coffee. Dressed in his *Hondo* buckskins and breeches, and looking every inch a real man, Duke deadpanned to the rest of the crew: "I don't take sugar with my coffee."

Mary St. John got the best of Bond one evening in the dining hall. He started in again, hailing the sweetener's miraculous powers, and Mary innocently, or perhaps not so innocently, mentioned that she had read about some of the side effects of sucaryl. Bond's ears perked up and he asked, "Like what?" "Well," Mary said, "Apparently it can cause impotence in men." Duke's face brightened instantly and he let out a deep cough. "What did you say about Ward and sucaryl?" Duke boomed. "Yeah, what did you say?" queried Bond. "All I said," Mary intoned, "is that *Reader's Digest* claims that men who use too much sucaryl can become impotent." Duke laughed again, and Bond looked stricken. Mary recalled: "We all decided he might already be suffering from one of sucaryl's side effects." As Duke wrote John Ford, when Bond heard

Mary's report, he "dropped the bottle [of sucaryl] as if it were a rabbi's knife." The next day Bond was putting sugar in his coffee.[8]

Duke may not have warmed to Geraldine Page, but he charmed her completely. Coming from a different world—the small stages and theaters of New York—she found him, like the landscapes he occupied, larger than life. "He's a fantastic, fantastic man," Page recalled years later. "He's an enormous man. With the boots and the hat he's about seven feet tall—I felt so dainty next to him." She had never encountered another man quite as big, rugged, strong, loud, critical, mean, sensitive, short-tempered, quick to ask forgiveness and quicker to give it, profane, intelligent, and supremely gifted, a man who knew himself, whose self- confident assurance produced an all-but-irresistible charisma. "I loved him," Page told an interviewer. "We all did. Everybody just adored him in a most hysterical way. It gets to the point where I wouldn't be at all surprised if somebody would lie down in front of a truck and say, 'Run me over, for you I'd do anything,' you know."

She also admired him because "he would scream himself hoarse" and then apologize and seek forgiveness. "He'd never yell at me," Page recalled:

> He'd get sarcastic with me when he was out of temper and hung over, and start making snotty remarks about Stanislavsky and you New York so and so's. . . . And like everybody else, I was just about to say I'd had enough. He'd sense it, and he'd come over and sort of breathe down my neck and say, "Aw, Geraldine, you're not mad at the old Duke, are you?" And I would melt and say, "No." Then I'd go back to the motel and say, "What have I done? I'm so stupid. I'm the same as everybody else, I get taken by that charm, that tremendous charm." I just loved him.

Duke's kindnesses and charm also endeared him to the crew. Like John Ford, he accepted people as they were and treated them all—from stars to gaffers—the same. "He hates all kinds of hypocrisy and folderol," Page claimed. Late one evening on the Camargo set, they were shooting a scene in a dried-up lake bed when a big storm blew in. Farrow and Fellows quickly removed the American cast and crew before the lake bed flooded but left the Mexican crew behind to take care of the equipment. Hours later, in the middle of the night, with the Americans dry and warm, tucked away in their motel beds, Duke started worrying about the Mexican crew, who were spending the night outside in the wet cold. He awakened the caterer and together they hustled together hot coffee, sandwiches, and several bottles of tequila. Duke spent the rest of the night eating, singing, drinking, and telling stories with the crew. George Coleman, according to Page, said: "Oh, if you could have seen . . . those poor guys out there. . . . It was a great thing, like out of the movies, because he had gone to bring them a sandwich." Page waxed even more eloquent about Duke's charm. "You wonder how people like Caesar and Napoleon and Hitler would get this kind of fanatic following, but I think that John has some of that leadership quality, so that people just revere him."

She also stood in awe of his acting abilities. When asked about his skill, Page remembered that "he's terribly bright, terribly intelligent, and he learns so quickly. He knows how to do everything." Duke's laugh, she claimed, proved his talent. Throughout the Camargo shooting, Page observed people telling Duke jokes.

He has the most wonderful joke-appreciating laugh that is the warmest, the most spontaneous, the biggest most beautiful laugh—and it is exquisite technique, because it's the same for everyone. But you cannot believe it because it sounds so spontaneous. I have never heard a more beautiful spontaneous laugh in my life—until you hear it three hundred times a day, because of all the jokes. It's incredible.

She even fell in love with his profanity. At the Camargo motel, Bond's room adjoined hers, and every night during the location, Duke, Bond, and a couple of stuntmen gathered to drink and play cards into the early morning hours. The cheap motel walls did not filter much sound, and Page could hear most of what they said. "All night long I had such a refresher course in all the foulest language. I'd heard bits of it at different places, at different points through my life, but I never had had it all gathered together, you know. And endless . . . an endless stream of it, you know, it's like rhythm, like music . . . on and on and on, it's fantastic."

The actress had no trouble explaining John Wayne's screen presence and popularity. "He's a terribly honest man, you see. And that comes across, underlined by the kind of parts he plays. He always plays an honest man, and his own honesty feeds into it, and the simplicty of his acting." Big stars, she went on, "are a combination of their own personality and the parts they play, and if the combination of the two symbolizes something that's very dear to all of our hearts, we want to see them again and again, and that makes them stars."

Hondo provided exactly that type of role for Duke. Americans wanted to see him again and again because he symbolized something very dear to them. The film also appeared simultaneously with the beginning of novelist Louis L'Amour's career. Wayne-Fellows purchased film rights to the short story in 1952, and while they made the movie a year later, L'Amour turned the short story into the novel *Hondo*. It was his first of many best-sellers, and during the next thirty years, he sold more than two hundred million copies of his Western novels. By the 1980s Hollywood would routinely try to orchestrate the releases of books and movies to maximize sales, but the simultaneous release of *Hondo* as a film and *Hondo* as a novel was purely accidental. Nevertheless, millions of Louis L'Amour fans came to picture John Wayne as the protagonist of his stories.

Hondo was vintage John Wayne. As literary critic Jane Tompkins wrote, the West of John Wayne films and Louis L'Amour novels offers

> escape from the conditions of life in modern industrial society: from a mechanized existence, economic dead ends, social entanglements, unhappy personal relations, political injustice. . . . The desert light and the desert space, the creak of saddle leather and the sun beating down, the horses' energy and force— these things promise a translation of the self into something purer and more authentic, more intense, more real.[9]

The opening scene of *Hondo* reveals a stark southwestern landscape—a hot, harsh desert devoid of green trees and shrubs, shade, and water. An aura of death shrouds the land, just as Louis L'Amour described it in his novel:

> It was hot. A few lost, cotton-ball bunches of cloud drifted in a brassy sky, leaving rare islands of shadow upon the desert's face. Nothing moved. It was a far, lost land, a land of beige-gray silences and distance where the eye reached out farther and farther to lose itself finally against the sky, and where the only movement was the lazy swing of a remote buzzard.[10]

The movie revealed a little more movement than that. Off in the distance, barely visible at first, a lone man approaches on foot, saddle in one hand, carbine in another, a mangy dog following behind. Tall and lanky, covered by a buckskin shirt and working pants with turned-up cuffs, the stranger wears a blue neckerchief that appears color-coordinated with his eyes and the sky. His pants ride low on his hips, the gunbelt even lower. Hondo Lane is a dispatch rider for the U.S. Cavalry in 1874, crisscrossing the southwestern deserts from camp to camp and outpost to outpost, dodging Apaches all along the way. The land is merciless, the environment hostile, and human beings who have endured it have acquired its austerity. There were no weaknesses in Hondo Lane, L'Amour wrote. "He was a big man, wide-shouldered, with the lean, hardboned face of the desert rider. There was no softness in him. His toughness was ingrained and deep."[11]

Out in the middle of nowhere, his horse dead, Hondo stumbles on the Lowe ranch, a tiny cattle operation about to be swallowed up by the desert. Ed Lowe (Leo Gordon) has abandoned his wife Angie (Geraldine Page) and son Johnny (Lee Aaker). In return for a couple of meals, Hondo tends to the missing man's chores—sharpening blades, shoeing horses, breaking broncos. He is as tough as the desert he rides, a single man whose most precious possession is independence. When Angie tries to feed Hondo's dog, Sam, Lane cautions her: "If you don't mind ma'am, I'd rather you didn't feed him. . . . I don't feed him either. Sam's independent. He doesn't need anybody. I want him to stay that way. It's a good way." Taken aback, Angie retorts: "Well, everyone needs someone." "Yes, Ma'am" Hondo replies: "Most everyone. Too bad, isn't it?" A short time later, after watching Hondo break the horse he wanted to buy, Angie warns him: "You chose the most savage one. He's always been a fighter." With an understanding nod, Hondo reasons: "I wouldn't give a plug nickel for a horse who isn't a fighter. They let you down when the going gets tough." He teaches Johnny about the harsh reality of the desert. When the little boy asks Hondo for the third time if he can pet Sam, Hondo allows the boy his independence but warns: "I told you twice not to, but you do what you want to do." Of course, Johnny touches Sam, and Sam bites him. When Angie protests, Hondo delivers the desert code: "People learn when they get bit. The boy just learned."

Without the presence of a few hard men like him, the world Hondo occupies would have been absolutely unforgiving, an amoral universe where capricious, random events made jokes out of justice and fairness. Hondo can do nothing about the cruel landscape, but he can do something, and does, about renegade Apaches, incompetent soldiers, vulnerable women and children, and irresponsible husbands and fathers. In an act of self-defense, he shoots and kills Angie Lowe's derelict husband. He then falls in love with her himself. He also battles Apache warriors to preserve a place for civilization in the wilderness. Indefatigable in his own struggle with hardship and pain, and more than willing to answer cruelty with cruelty, Hondo Lane makes sure that justice prevails. He was a worthy successor to the Ringo Kid.

Wayne-Fellows released *Hondo* in mid-November 1953, just two weeks after the divorce, and the reviews were positive, the first decent newsprint about Duke in a while. The film, however, did not live up to expectations. If 3-D was an inconvenience for producers, it was a nightmare for theater owners. Handing out and then collecting 3-D glasses from patrons required extra personnel, increasing costs without increasing revenues, and ticket buyers were less likely to go to the concession stand for popcorn and candy while wearing the spectacles. Theaters had to run two projectors at once, increasing breakdowns and delays. When film in one of the cameras broke, projectionists had to mutilate the other film in the same spot and then splice exactly or risk a blurred image. Even slight differences of speed between the two projectors caused loss of synchronization and blurring. When *Hondo* was released, angry theater owners were threatening to boycott 3-D films, and ticket buyers had already tired of the cumbersome novelty. Only a week into *Hondo*'s release, Wayne-Fellows replaced it with a regular, flat-projection version.[12]

Hondo eventually returned $4.1 million in domestic rentals, guaranteeing Wayne-Fellows a decent profit, but the real Western hit of 1953, with more than $9 million, was *Shane*, a Paramount production starring Alan Ladd, Van Heflin, Jean Arthur, and Brandon de Wilde. The two films had much in common. Both cost about $3 million to produce. Both feature vast Western landscapes—*Hondo* the parched deserts of Arizona, *Shane* the high plains of Wyoming. Both revolve around a tough, solitary man who comes out of the wilderness to protect the innocent and to punish evil. Both present tough, blond women in the female leads and star small, tow-headed boys. But America loved *Shane* more than *Hondo*, perhaps because Shane was the more archetypal Western hero than Hondo Lane, an unattached loner free of the claims of women, family, and civilization. Hondo Lane softens in the end, falling in love with Angie Lowe and surrendering his freedom, readily taking on the responsibilities of fatherhood, riding off into the sunset toward his ranch in California, bringing Angie and Johnny with him. Shane leaves as he came, riding a roan pony into the sunset, the little boy pleading with him, "Come back, Shane, come back." "*Hondo* was a fine film," Mary St. John recalled years later, "but *Shane* was better. *Hondo* got lost in the shuffle."[13]

When *Hondo* was released in November, Duke was already filming *The High and the Mighty*, a Wayne-Fellows production that Warner Bros. would distribute. Early in 1953 William Wellman learned that Ernie Gann, who had written *Island in the Sky*, was working on another aviation story. After Gann told him the story line, Wellman told the writer, "Stay right there, baby, I'll make the quickest sale you've ever had in your life." Waiting until he was sure Duke and Fellows were in the office, Wellman called and relayed *The High and the Mighty* plot summary. Duke bought the project on the spot, agreeing to give Wellman 30 percent of the profits to direct and Gann $55,000 plus 10 percent for the story and screenplay. He told Wellman, however, that he wanted the movie shot in CinemaScope.[14]

Although 3-D had busted, Hollywood's box-office anxieties throbbed like a bad headache, and the compulsion to provide viewers an entertainment experience unavailable on television intensified. Other gimmicks, like odor-producing Smell-O-Vision and Aroma-Rama, would come and go, but the most enduring technological innovation was CinemaScope, a wide-screen projection process patented by Twentieth Century-Fox and first used in *The Robe* (1953). The CinemaScope camera was fitted with an anamorphic lens capable of squeezing a wide picture on to regular 35 mm film. Although the technique required the installation of wide screens in theaters, the visual effects dramatically distinguished CinemaScope from anything available on television.

William Wellman found the CinemaScope camera bulky and unwieldy, especially in composing scenes. Instead of scanning a scene with a moving lens, he found it much easier to station the CinemaScope camera in one place and let the actors move in and out of the picture, almost a reversion to the cinematic techniques of the silent era. Fortunately *The High and the Mighty* set consisted of little more than the cramped cockpit and passenger cabin of a DC-4 aircraft, and Wellman did not need to employ the same variety of cinematic techniques he used in action pictures. At the end of the filming, he had a new respect for the skills of cameraman William Clothier, and Clothier spent much of the rest of his career with Duke.

Casting was a nightmare. *The High and the Mighty* was the first in a long series of disaster movies that would later include *Abandon Ship* (1957), *A Night to Remember* (1958), *Airport* (1970), *The Poseidon Adventure* (1972), *Earthquake* (1973) and *The Towering Inferno* (1974). And like Edmund Goulding's *Grand Hotel* (1932), the film hosted an ensemble cast of troubled characters dealing with individual crises. Because the script explored those crises and the effects on other passengers, the film did not really have a central character whose part eclipsed all others. A number of big-name stars, including Joan Crawford, Ida Lupino, Barbara Stanwyck, Ginger Rogers, and Dorothy McGuire, turned Wellman down; the individual parts did not appear big enough. Eventually, Wellman decided "to hell with those other big stars. They think they know so much! I decided we could do without 'em. I decided to get competent, fine actors and actresses." He hired Claire Trevor, Laraine Day, Robert Stack, Jan Sterling, Phil Harris, Robert Newton, David Brian, Paul Kelly, Sidney Blackmer, and Julie Bishop, all competent but none giants.

Wellman did get Spencer Tracy to accept the part of Dan Roman, the copilot who emerges as the hero of the film. "We had lunch and shook on the deal." But Tracy then pulled out. Part of the problem was Wellman. Andy

McLaglen remembered Wellman as the best-prepared director he had ever met, but he was also a strict disciplinarian known for browbeating his actors. Friends who had worked with Wellman warned Tracy that he was in for an ego-bruising experience, and the actor decided to back out, telling Wellman he thought the script was "lousy." Wellman had a different explanation. "He changed his mind. Didn't think the role was good enough for him, I guess." Tracy's departure left Wellman, and Wayne-Fellows, without a marquee star for the film, and Jack Warner got nervous, threatening to pull Warner Bros. out of the distribution deal. Duke had no choice but to take the part of Dan Roman himself.[15]

Dan Roman is the copilot of Trans-Orient Pacific Airlines Flight 420, bound from Honolulu to San Francisco. At the beginning of the flight, the passengers are caught up in their own problems. Roman is dealing with the guilt of losing his captain's license, and his entire family, when a plane he was piloting crashed. Lydia and Howard Rice (Laraine Day and John Howard) are returning to the mainland to get a divorce. Flaherty (Paul Kelly) is a physicist obsessed by his role in developing weapons of mass destruction. May Holst (Claire Trevor) is the proverbial loose woman with a heart of gold. While these and other individual dramas unfold during the 2,400-mile flight, the DC-4 develops a series of mechanical problems, eventually resulting in a burned-out engine, a fuel-leaking hole in the gas tank, and the likelihood of a deadly, nighttime crash into the Pacific.

Under the stress of their plight, Captain Sullivan (Robert Stack) has a nervous breakdown and Roman takes control. Although Duke had worried that the role might be too much of a departure from his usual persona, Dan Roman is Sergeant Stryker dressed in the uniform of a commercial airline pilot. Cool, competent, and fearless, a man of few words who acts rather than talks, Roman beats some sense into Sullivan when the captain goes berserk. Confronted by death, the passengers resolve, or at least suppress, their individual problems, respond to Roman's determined leadership, and begin dismantling the aircraft cabin, jettisoning as much cargo and luggage as possible in order to lighten the load and extend the fuel supply. In the end, flying on fumes, the DC-4 sputters safely into San Francisco International. The passengers go their separate ways, and Dan Roman, with Dmitri Tiomkin's haunting score playing in the background, walks away, whistling, into the dark.

From his own look at the rushes, Duke worried about the film, and especially his own performance. Wellman loved what he saw. "Do you mean to tell me you don't think you were good in that?" Wellman asked incredulously.

"You couldn't ask for anything better." A few weeks before the release, Wellman told a reporter: "He [Wayne] thinks his performance is lousy and I think he's crazy." Wellman was right. *The High and the Mighty* was a smash hit, a huge moneymaker for Wayne-Fellows. The trade papers were lavish in their praise, *Variety* calling it "socko screen entertainment," and *The Hollywood Reporter* describing it as "one of the great pictures of our time." More important, given Hollywood's box-office doldrums, "It gives the public something it cannot get on television. It makes a trip to the movies a big event for any family and it restores to the screen a place of importance in our national experience." Audiences concurred. *The High and the Mighty* eventually earned more than $8.5 million in domestic and foreign rentals, and Wayne-Fellows had put only $1.465 million into the production.[16]

The film was the last project for Wayne-Fellows. A domestic drama drove the partners apart. Fellows had fallen in love with one of the secretaries at work, and, in the middle of January 1954, he told his wife Eleanor that he wanted to leave her. She had guessed as much. She approached Duke for help, asking him to talk some sense into her husband. His response, born of a midwesterner's desire to leave people alone, was immediate: "It's none of my business," he told Eleanor Fellows. "Well, I guess you approve of it," she replied. "I don't approve or disapprove," he countered. "It's none of my business." She kept up the pressure, eventually prevailing upon him to preside over a mediation session between the estranged couple. Always uncomfortable with the expression of intimate feelings, he was not the stuff of which marriage counselors are made. The meeting deteriorated quickly, confirming his worst expectations. Eleanor and Bob Fellows were soon screaming and shouting at each other, and Duke was resenting his part in the encounter. He abruptly stood up, pushed out his chair, and left, protesting to the couple: "I am very uncomfortable here. This is none of my business. Settle it yourselves."[17]

The marriage could not be salvaged. Convinced that divorce was imminent and that he would need to liquidate his assets, Fellows asked Duke to buy him out, and Duke agreed. He needed a new name for the company. For several months Duke used the "Fifth Corporation," but he did not much like the name; it sounded too much like whiskey or the Fifth Amendment. Michael Wayne, Duke's oldest son who worked part-time and summers for Wayne-Fellows while attending Loyola University, suggested "Batjak," the name of the Dutch shipping company featured in *Wake of the Red Witch*. Inadvertently it became Batjac. When a legal secretary was examining the incorporation documents, she wondered if there had been a typographical error in Batjak. Perhaps it should be Batjack? She called up Bob Fellows and asked if a "c" was missing from the title of the company. He replied, "No c." But she thought he meant, "No, c." So she typed it Batjac. When the final documents came back and everyone noticed the mistake, Duke responded, "I like it better with a 'k,' but it's no big deal. Leave it alone." On May 25, 1954, he rented office space at 1022 Palm Avenue in Hollywood and Wayne-Fellows became Batjac.[18]

After forming the company, Duke and Pilar made their way to St. George, Utah, where they spent the summer of 1954 on location for *The Conqueror*. Set in the Central Asian steppes in the twelfth century, *The Conqueror* details the early victories of Genghis Khan (John Wayne) and the Mongol horde over the Tartars. Susan Hayward, who had worked with Duke before in *Reap the Wild Wind* and *The Fighting Seabees*, was the female lead. RKO budgeted $4 million for the movie, and Howard Hughes hired Dick Powell to produce and direct it. Powell tried to get Marlon Brando on loan from Fox to play the lead, and Oscar Millard wrote the screenplay thinking Brando would do it. "I decided to write it in stylized, slightly archaic English," Millard remembered in 1981. "Mindful of the fact that my story was nothing more than a tarted-up Western, I thought this would give it a certain cachet and I left no lily unpainted. It was a mistake I have never repeated." Brando might have been able to deliver the lines, but Fox refused to loan him out to RKO.[19]

Powell had to cast for a new lead. Early in 1954 Duke had a business meeting at his office and noticed a script summary for *The Conqueror* on the desk. After a cursory review, he asked to do the film, thinking the part might give him the chance to stretch as an actor. "At first I was completely surprised," Powell recalled. "Wayne as the barbarous Genghis Khan? I asked him if he was serious and he said he was. . . . We discussed the matter thoroughly, and the more we talked the more the idea intrigued me. Besides, who am I to turn down John Wayne?"

He should have turned him down. A film written for Brando but starring John Wayne was a disaster waiting to happen. Duke also should have waited until he had seen a complete script before signing onto the project. When Powell told Millard that Brando was out and Wayne was in, the writer panicked. "When he starts mangling those lines," Millard told Powell, "he's going to be a joke." Powell was unperturbed. "He's promised to work on them with a coach and a tape recorder," Powell lied. "He's very enthusiastic." Duke had no intention of spending even a minute with a voice coach. The wasted hours on voice lessons for *The Big Trail* lingered in his memory.

He did not even look at the script until the location shooting began in St.

George, Utah. Early in May, on the evening before the cameras rolled, he read through the script to memorize lines and discovered the stilted dialogue. He got on the phone immediately, telling Millard: "You gotta do somethin' about these [expletive] lines. I can't read 'em." Millard protested that it was too late. "I'd have to rewrite the entire script for you. Why didn't you speak up sooner?" Millard complained. In Duke's pause-filled drawl, the dialogue was ludicrously stilted, riddled with silly, awkwardly delivered lines as, in one scene Genghis Khan tells his brother, "Let us have . . . no more of this . . . I will need . . . your wisdom . . . henceforth."

Hayward's lines were not much better. In the film she plays the petulant Tartar princess Bortai, and she behaved like a petulant princess off the set as well. Acutely preoccupied with her image, she scrutinized each day's rushes, examining them for even the slightest flaws. Cameraman Joe LaShelle lost his job, at her insistence, when he inadvertently allowed sunlight to glint off her nose. Even though the script called for wild horse rides through dusty desert landscapes, she refused to appear disheveled, berating the makeup artists for incompetence. In every scene of the film, Princess Bortai looks like Cinderella at the ball, her makeup impeccable and every strand of hair in place.

Against her better judgment, the perfect princess falls in love with Genghis Khan and betrays her Tartar father, all because, in the words of Oscar Millard: "I am consumed with want of him." Off the set, life imitated art. Powell had rented houses on opposite sides of the same street in St. George for the two stars, and *The Conqueror* was Pilar's first location. Hayward drank too much and frequently wandered across the street to flirt with Wayne. One night, Pilar remembered, Hayward stumbled over to their house, kicked her high heels into the corner, and challenged Pilar: "Take off your shoes and fight me for him." Duke politely escorted Hayward back home, but the next day, while Powell was shooting a scene, she made another play. Bortai is lying full-length on a lounge when Genghis Khan sits down and forcibly kisses her. Powell had the camera at Duke's back, shooting over his right shoulder. Hayward placed her right hand in Duke's crotch during the kiss, gently squeezing, and plunging her tongue deep into his mouth. Not wanting to waste the scene, Duke played it straight. But in his set trailer, he fumed to Mary St. John, "That goddamn bitch just stuck her tongue halfway down my throat." Ever polite to women, he never mentioned the incident to Hayward, and she never lost her affection for him. "He was tough and strong, just like his screen image," she told her biographer, "but there was a tremendous gentleness about him. Of all my leading men, he was my favorite."

Wayne and Hayward did share something offscreen, along with 89 other members of *The Conqueror*'s cast and crew. Of the 220 people Dick Powell brought to St. George, Utah, in 1954, 91 came down with cancer later in their lives, a number three times higher than actuarial tables would suggest. Forty-six people had died of the disease by 1980. Duke survived lung cancer in 1964 but later succumbed to stomach cancer. Pedro Armendariz came down with kidney cancer in 1959 and then committed suicide in 1963 when diagnosed with cancer of the larynx. Dick Powell fell victim to lung cancer. Agnes Moorehead would die of uterine cancer, and Hayward ended up with cancers of the skin, breast, uterus, and brain. Dr. Robert Pendleton, a radiologist at the University of Utah, claimed that with "these numbers, this case could qualify as an epidemic."[20]

Epidemiologists searching for an explanation noted that most of these people were heavy smokers, but they also knew that *The Conqueror* was filmed in the Escalante Valley of southern Utah. The Atomic Energy Commission detonated eleven atomic bombs in the dry lake bed of Yucca Flats, Nevada, in 1953. Two of the bombs were especially "dirty" with strontium 90 and cesium 137 isotopes. "Dirty Simon" exploded on April 25, and "Dirty Harry" went off on May 19. Both fireballs covered the surrounding desert with a fine gray ash. An aberrant wind carried Dirty Harry's fallout more than 150 miles to the east, blanketing St. George, Utah, and the Escalante Valley. The "hot" ash soon disappeared into southern Utah's red sands, but winds blew heavy amounts of the radioactive material into the rolling dunes of Snow Canyon, which served as a natural reservoir for the dust. Most of *The Conqueror*'s battle and chase scenes were filmed in Snow Canyon. The levels of strontium 90 and cesium 137 were still high enough in 1954 to set off wild ticking in Geiger counters. Crew members were covered in dust by the end of each day's shooting, and cast members had to be frequently blown clean of dust with compressed air and given time to rinse the dirt out of their mouths and eyes. Powell then trucked more than sixty tons of Snow Canyon dirt back to Culver City, California, to make sure the interior scenes had the same color and texture, and for another two months the cast and crew wallowed in the radioactive mix.[21]

Just as he had done with *Jet Pilot*, Howard Hughes refused to give *The Conqueror* a quick release. With almost manic compulsiveness, he toyed with the film, editing and reediting it, hoping to perfect what was hopeless imperfection. RKO did not let go of the movie until February 1956. For artistic reasons the studio should have kept *The Conqueror* locked permanently in its vaults.

Reviewers trashed the film and Duke's performance. The critic for *Time* magazine wrote that Wayne "portrays the great conqueror as a sort of cross between a square-shootin' sheriff and a Mongolian idiot." Idiotic or not, the critics were again out of step with audiences—*The Conqueror* scored at the box office, eventually bringing in $12 million in foreign and domestic sales.

The cast and crew of *The Conqueror* left Utah in August 1954. Under California law, as long as Chata's attorneys threw up no new legal obstacles, the divorce would be final on November 1, 1954, and Duke and Pilar would be free to marry. He had a contract with Warner Bros. to make *The Sea Chase* in the fall, and he asked Pilar to join him at the Hawaii location. They planned to get married there the day the divorce was final. Still technically married to Richard Weldy, Pilar had her attorney file for an annulment, claiming that the marriage was invalid because Weldy's January 1950 divorce from Katherine Weldy had not been final when he married Pilar.[22]

They sailed for Hawaii late in August. Warner's put the company up at the Kona Inn, on the big island of Hawaii. A hotel and spa, the Kona Inn attracted tourists from all over the United States, and Duke found himself hounded for autographs and pictures. Always conscious about his image and the need to be polite to fans, he graciously responded to every request. On the first night he stood for twenty-five pictures and signed seventy autographs. Unwilling to leave abruptly after a photograph or autograph, he made sure to linger for a few moments of small talk. Fans deserved the attention, but the routine was tiring, and he worried that at the end of long days in front of a camera, he would not be able to relax in his room. "Perhaps other actors can walk away from people and not be friendly and gracious. I cannot," Duke wrote to Steve Trilling at Warner Bros. After a week at the Kona Inn, he asked Carl Benoit of Warner's to secure him a private residence.[23]

The Sea Chase teamed Duke for the first time with Lana Turner. He plays Karl Erlich, the anti-Hitler captain of a German freighter caught in Australian waters when World War II breaks out. Intent on sailing back to the fatherland to help overthrow Hitler, Erlich is pursued by a British cruiser. In Sydney he takes Elsa Keller (Lana Turner), a German spy, on board, and they make their escape. The British navy pursues them around the world. During the journey Karl and Elsa fall in love. Both on and off the set, however, there was no chemistry between Lana and Duke. She was already on bad terms with director John Farrow. On the first night at the Kona Inn, Turner accused the director of planning to seduce her because they had adjoining rooms. He protested innocence and kept his distance. A deeply troubled woman whose recent years had been pockmarked by soured love affairs, migraine headaches, divorces, miscarriages, a suicide attempt, and IRS problems, Turner found solace by drinking herself into oblivion every night. Nursing disabling hangovers, she arrived late on the set and did not know her lines. She later recalled that she got along well with Duke, and that she put icepacks on the side of his head between takes when he developed an ear infection. But he had little sympathy for her plight. As far as he was concerned, professionals keep personal problems off the set. On the fifth day of shooting, Turner missed her third morning call, and Farrow fired her. She was genuinely surprised and asked Duke to intervene. "You've not been behaving like a professional," he told her, "but if it was up to me I would want to give you another chance." Farrow took her back, and Turner tried to mend her ways, but the film suffered. "*The Sea Chase* . . . was pieced together from a novel by Andrew Geer," claimed the film critic for *The New Yorker*. "Mr. Geer's novel, I'm told, was an exciting, straightforward bit of work. You'd never guess it from this interpretation."[24]

While working on *The Sea Chase*, Duke and Pilar made wedding plans. Chata was not making it easy. She may have been out of the Encino house, but she was hardly out of their lives. When she packed her bags and left, she absconded with Duke's prized fifteen-volume set of American Indian photographs. He valued the books almost as much as his collection of kachina dolls, and Chata knew he would miss them. She ignored repeated requests to return the books, and in desperation he offered her $1,000 per volume in cash. Chata needed the $15,000. Bills for booze, clothes, hotels, and restaurants ate quickly into her divorce settlement, but the ability to inflict further misery on Duke was even more precious than money. She eventually returned the books, one by one over the course of a year, in the mail, cutting each volume into thousands of pieces and sending them in a manila envelope. "She is one sick human being," Duke remarked to a friend.[25]

By the summer of 1954, Chata realized that her money was not going to last. With the tastes of a princess, she was chronically short of cash, and as her checkbook balance dwindled, her resentment of Duke's $250,000-per-picture salary mounted. In the eight years of their marriage, he had earned millions, and her settlement, especially after deducting lawyers' fees, seemed increasingly paltry. She asked Duke for more money, and when he refused, she threatened to go to a lawyer. The intimidation did not work, and his anger over the Indian books raged unabated. Chata had signed a carefully executed divorce settlement and was unable to extract more from the judge. What Duke and

Pilar feared, however, was that Chata would go to court, demand a renegotiation of the settlement, and delay the final divorce decree past October 1954—which was exactly what she tried to do. In August 1954 she retained attorney S. S. Hahn, asking him to reopen the case. Hahn's press conference announcing the action upset Duke and Pilar, who were looking forward to November 1. Nothing came of the lawsuit. Chata returned to Mexico City a few weeks later and became a virtual recluse, spending time only with her mother and her bottles. Mary St. John remembered it as "a pathetic attempt to get even by a very troubled woman."[26]

Duke and Pilar wasted no time getting on with the wedding. Late in October, attorney George M. Henzie secured the annulment of Pilar's first marriage, and two days later Duke's divorce was final. Farrow finished shooting *The Sea Chase* the same day. Duke's attorney called him immediately on learning that the final divorce decree had been issued. The wedding, held at the home of Sen. William H. Hill in Kona, was a simple one. Former senator Francis Brown served as Duke's best man, and Mary St. John was Pilar's only attendant. In ninety seconds, they exchanged vows, and a local magistrate declared them man and wife. At Pilar's request the word "obey" was dropped from the vows. "None of the others ever obeyed me anyway," Duke chuckled to Mary. They spent the night at the Royal Hawaiian Hotel in Honolulu and returned to California the next day to begin an extended honeymoon.[27]

They interrupted the honeymoon to spend the holidays in Encino. Duke wanted to have Christmas at home, a real Christmas, a Norman Rockwell kind of Christmas, with Pilar and all the kids opening gifts under the tree, talking and playing games, gorging on a holiday spread, just like the few family Christmases he had enjoyed with Josie so many years before. A new mother was in the portrait now, but it did not matter to Duke. Michael, Patrick, Toni, and Melinda came over for the Christmas celebration, and the day fulfilled his expectations. The house reverberated with laughter, congeniality, and affection. Later that evening, when his kids had left, Duke remarked to Pilar, "This is what it's all about, what I've always wanted—a successful career, a wife I love who loves me back, my family around me."[28]

Duke and Pilar then went to New York for the last leg of the honeymoon, but their stay in Manhattan was cut short by production problems on *Blood Alley*. A Batjac production, directed by William Wellman and starring Robert Mitchum and Lauren Bacall, *Blood Alley* started shooting in San Rafael, California, early in January 1955. Duke did not want to be bothered with the details. He desired a few months with his new wife. He did make sure that the movie, like *Big Jim McLain*, fired another salvo in the anti-Communist wars. The film centered on "Blood Alley," a three-hundred-mile stretch of the Formosa Straits on China's southeastern coast. The script called for Captain Wilder (Robert Mitchum) to lead Cathy Grainger (Lauren Bacall) and 180 villagers on a daring escape from Communist China to freedom in Hong Kong. At first Wilder is a reluctant participant. "Someone pinned the bleeding heart of China to your sleeve," he tells Grainger. He soon witnesses the evils of communism, however, and at journey's end tells Grainger, "The bleeding heart of China. You can pin one on my sleeve, baby." It was Batjac's first film, and Duke hoped it would be as big a hit as *The High and the Mighty*, but his financial thoughts were elsewhere.

Duke was about to experience the perils of independent production. Without a distribution arm, independents found themselves completely dependent on the studios. Cost overruns forced them to go back to the distribution companies, often pleading for enough money to finish production. Warner Bros. had advanced Wayne-Fellows $750,000 for *Big Jim McLain*, but the production cost $826,000. They got $900,000 from Warner's for *Island in the Sky*, but spent $967,000. *The High and the Mighty* exceeded its production by $145,000. In each instance Duke had to beg, hat in hand, more money out of Jack Warner.[29]

There were other risks as well. Independents were always destined to lose a large piece of revenues for their films because in most cases studios charged a standard 35 percent distribution fee. Studios without any financial stake in a production had no incentive to promote it effectively. When studios did help with production financing, they were entitled to retrieve their investment first from the revenues, before the independent got anything. Independents were at the mercy of the distributor, a lesson Duke learned only too well when Robert Mitchum left the cast of *Blood Alley*. Wellman and Mitchum had a falling-out three days into the shooting. He had given Mitchum his first real break in the industry when he directed him in *The Story of GI Joe* (1945), and he expected Mitchum to be suitably grateful for the rest of his life. Mitchum was not ungrateful, but he was not obsequious either. Mary St. John did not like Mitchum. "He always had this 'I don't give a damn' attitude. Whether it was real or posturing, I don't know. But it sure was obnoxious." The Waynes were in New York, and Wellman called complaining that Mitchum was drinking too much and raising hell. If anybody understood drinking and raising hell, it was John Wayne, who told Wellman to try to work with the actor. The next day, when transportation manager George Coleman vetoed

Mitchum's request for a bus to take the cast into San Francisco, Mitchum pushed Coleman off a pier into San Rafael Bay.[30]

It was the last straw. Wellman gave Duke an ultimatum: "It's either Mitchum or me. Either you star or I'm out of the picture." Duke agreed to get rid of Mitchum, but he did not want to interrupt his honeymoon. When Jack Warner learned that Mitchum was gone, he called Duke himself, threatening to pull out of the distribution deal unless Duke starred in the film or got another major star, such as Gregory Peck or Humphrey Bogart, to take the part. Peck was not interested and Bogart demanded a $500,000 salary, too much for *Blood Alley*'s $2.5 million budget. The honeymoon ended, and Duke flew out to San Raphael to go to work. To keep Batjac afloat, just as he had done for Wayne-Fellows when Spencer Tracy pulled out of *The High and the Mighty*, he took the role on short notice.

Batjac released *Blood Alley* in October 1955. *Newsweek* summed up the picture as "Good ship, shallow draft," and *Time* claimed that the "blunt point of the picture is to display John Wayne to best advantage—stripped in a bathtub, bloody at the wheel, phlegmatically stirring his bayonet inside a Communist. As usual, he makes a more convincing display than most of Hollywood's he-men." Although the film was not exactly a box-office smash, it more than returned Batjac's $2.5 million investment.[31]

In June 1955, a month after wrapping *Blood Alley*, Duke and Pilar arrived at Goulding's Lodge in Monument Valley to go to work on *The Searchers*. Cornelius Vanderbilt "Jock" Whitney, heir to the Minnesota Mining and Manufacturing Company fortune, had been a fan of Western novels and films since childhood. Anxious to make some of those films himself, and possessing enough money to finance his fantasy, in 1954 he formed his own film production company. With the assistance of producer Merian C. Cooper, who had already optioned Alan LeMay's short novel *The Searchers*, Whitney set out to make his first movie. The novel had been a popular one, serialized in the *Saturday Evening Post* and condensed in *Reader's Digest*.[32]

Cooper got Ford to direct and signed Duke for $125,000 plus 10 percent of the profits to star. Ford was anxious to make another Western. "I've been longing to do a Western for quite some time," he wrote a friend. "It's good for my health, spirit, and morale." When Hollywood learned that Whitney was making a John Ford–John Wayne Western, the bidding started, and Warner Bros. eventually won the distribution rights after offering a 65–35 percent split and waiving studio overhead costs. Ford and Frank Nugent produced a screenplay, and in February, the second unit began shooting winter scenes in

Gunnison, Colorado, and a buffalo hunt in Canada. After fifty-nine days in Monument Valley, the first unit went back to the Warner Bros. lot in Burbank in August 1955 to complete the interiors.[33]

Set in West Texas three years after the end of the Civil War, *The Searchers* tells the story of Ethan Edwards (John Wayne), a Confederate veteran who returns home to a Comanche uprising that ends in the slaughter of his brother's family and the kidnapping of his nieces Debbie (Lana Wood as the young Debbie and Natalie Wood as the older Debbie) and Lucy (Pippa Scott). Accompanied by a posse of neighbors and Texas Rangers, led by Captain Reverend Samuel Clayton (Ward Bond), Edwards sets out on a quest to punish the Comanches and rescue the girls. They soon locate the mutilated body of Lucy, but Debbie is nowhere to be found. Over the course of several weeks, as the chances of finding Debbie become more remote, the posse dwindles in size, down to two men. For the next five years, Ethan Edwards and Martin Pawley (Jeffrey Hunter) doggedly continue the search, scouring the high deserts and mountains of the Southwest for the single Comanche band. Ethan's anger turns into rage and his commitment into obsession, pushing his war-damaged psyche to the brink of insanity. It is a dark, brooding Western, a film that reflected Ford's deepening pessimism.

To make the film, Ford assembled his stock company—Wayne, Ward Bond, John Qualen, Ollie Carey, Ken Curtis, Harry Carey Jr., Hank Worden, Jack Pennick, Chuck Roberson, and Cliff Lyons. The preparations to shoot in Monument Valley were by then routine, bringing together equipment, arranging for Navajo extras to portray Comanches, taking care of the horses. Mike Goulding set up Ford's room as he wanted it, with a double bed and a refrigerator crammed with fruit juices. Bond was up to his usual antics. Within days of the company's arrival in Monument Valley, he developed a raging lust for Vera Miles, who played Laurie Jorgensen in the film. She roomed with Ollie Carey, and Bond, making up excuses to visit with Carey, would pick the oddest times to knock on their door and come in for a chat. Occasionally he would just walk in unannounced, without knocking, hoping to catch Miles in a nightgown or toweling off after a shower. The embarrassing possibility of catching Ollie Carey in a similar state did not deter him in the least. Convinced that women responded to naked men the same way men reacted to naked women, Bond sometimes disrobed and pulled open the curtains of his room, waiting for Miles to walk by. He was certain that once she had seen his nude body in all its glory, she would no longer be able to resist his advances. "Ward would say dirty things around her," Harry Carey Jr. remembered, "because he thought the way to a woman's heart was to be as crude as possible." Somehow Miles did manage to resist Bond's boorish behavior, and Duke and Ford ridiculed him incessantly about his spurned advances.[34]

Back in Burbank doing interiors, Bond also ruined a first shooting of one of the film's most powerful scenes. Early on in the search, Ethan, Pawley, and Brad Jorgensen (Harry Carey Jr.) come upon a Comanche camp. After scouting out the encampment, Brad returns jubilantly, thinking he saw his fiancée, Lucy Edwards, among the Indians. Earlier in the day, however, Ethan had found Lucy's naked, mutilated body, but he had kept the discovery to himself. Ethan does not describe what he saw, bluntly trying to convince Brad that what he had seen is a "buck" wearing Lucy's dress. As it dawns on Brad that Lucy is dead, he presses Ethan for details. Ethan squints his eyes and clenches his teeth, trying but failing to erase the hideous memory, and in a menacing, guttural voice warns Brad: "Don't ask me. Long as you live don't ask me no more." Harry Carey Jr. remembered being captivated by Duke's performance. Ford was delighted with the scene, smiling and clapping his hands in appreciation: "Print it."

But as Ford lit his cigar, he noticed mumbling and commotion in the background. Then Winton Hoch came up to him and sheepishly confessed, "The camera stopped, Mr. Ford. . . . It just stopped running." A hush descended on the set, but Ford, ever unpredictable, calmly told everyone, "Sorry, kids. That was fine, but we're going to have to do it again. When you're ready, do it just the same way." They did, and Carey came away even more impressed with Wayne's talent: "It was even better the second time." Later they all learned that Bond was the culprit. At the moment Ford had called for action, Bond had wandered into the shooting area, unplugged an electrical cord, hooked up his shaver, and removed his morning stubble. The cord he had unhooked was the lead to Hoch's camera.

More commonly Ford was his unpredictable self on the set. For some reason he took a dislike to Michael Wayne and treated him wretchedly. Sixteen-year-old Patrick Wayne, the director's godson, had a small part in the film. As he remembered years later: "Someone was always in the barrel with John Ford. Everyone had their turn. They were the brunt of his jokes or the object of his wrath—except me. I was the apple of his eye and could do no wrong." On one occasion, when Duke left his hand on a saddle horn, Ford bellowed: "When will you learn to ride a horse? You ride like a goddamn sissy." A distracted Ward Bond, depressed about a death in his family, missed some lines and Ford exploded: "Get your goddamned mind off that funeral." Yet just as often Ford was genial, kind, and even loving to his close friends.[35]

But it was not really business as usual on the set. In *The Searchers* John Ford reached the pinnacle of his career, making what film historians hail as the greatest Hollywood Western and among the all-time great American films. Duke delivered his finest performance. Harry Carey Jr. sensed that "*The Searchers* was extra special from the minute we started work on it. It was a different movie from anything I'd seen Ford do. From the first day of shooting it had a mood about it. Wayne was so powerful in that picture; he had really done his homework. He *became* Ethan Edwards. I think it was the greatest performance Duke ever gave." In his own autobiography Carey recalled one scene in particular, where he has come upon the family's prize bull, which the Comanches had slaughtered. "When I looked up at him [Wayne] in rehearsal, it was into the meanest, coldest eyes I had ever seen. I don't know how he molded that character. . . . He was even Ethan at dinnertime. He didn't kid around on *The Searchers* like he had done on other shows. Ethan was always in his eyes." Brian Huberman, a film historian, recalls meeting Wayne in London eighteen years later. Huberman was studying under Richard Attenborough; Wayne was in England making *Brannigan*, and Attenborough introduced the two. The night before, *The Searchers* had been shown on BBC television. Trying to make small talk with the star, Huberman said to Wayne: "That was a great part you had as the villain." Suddenly, Huberman remembers, Wayne clenched his jaw, gritted his teeth, and narrowed his eyes. The dark, ominous visage of Ethan Edwards consumed his face. "He was no villain," Wayne corrected. "He was a man living in his times. The Indians fucked his wife. What would you have done?"[36]

The closing shot of the film, the apotheosis of the Ford-Wayne combination, moved Ollie Carey to tears. Ford composed the shot very carefully, framing it in the doorway he had used so often in the film. "Jack made you feel that every scene was one of the high spots of the movie," Ollie remembered, "even if it was walking through a door." All Duke had to do was walk up to the door, turn around, and walk away. He had initially patterned his cowboy-hero persona after Ollie's husband, Harry Carey, who had died in 1947. She had known and admired Duke for several decades when they made *The Searchers*. "I think Duke has the grace of Nureyev," she later recalled. "He really is the most graceful man I've ever seen, his coordination is so fantastic. I love to watch him move around." They rehearsed the scene only twice. After Ethan's five-year search, he brings Debbie home. He stands alone on the porch, framed by the doorway, looking inside. The camera was set inside the house looking out the door. Duke, as Harry Carey Jr. remembered, "had a hangover from the night before. . . . There he was! The big man standing alone in the doorway. . . . He was to look and then walk away, but just before he turned, he saw Ollie Carey, the widow of his all-time hero, standing behind the camera. It was as natural as taking a breath. Duke raised his left hand, reached across his chest and grabbed his right arm at the elbow. Harry Carey did that a lot in the movies when Duke was a kid in Glendale, California. He'd spent many a dime just to see that. He stared at my mother for a couple of minutes, then turned, walking away into loneliness across red sand." Harry Carey Jr. later thought that a sign should be placed on Duke's room at Goulding's Lodge: "In this room John Wayne got drunk before he shot one of the most famous scenes in motion picture history."[37]

The Searchers was made at a time when the Western was reaching new heights in popularity. Three years after *The Searchers'* release, the weekly television lineup sported no fewer than thirty-five Westerns, and by the late 1970s Louis L'Amour had nearly 150 million copies of his books in print. In the novels of Zane Grey and Louis L'Amour, the films of John Ford and Howard Hawks, and the screen persona of John Wayne, the Western did for manhood what carnival rides did for thrill-seekers. And *The Searchers* was the ultimate Western. Film critic Andrew Sarris wrote that Wayne "acts out the mystery of what passes through the soul of Ethan Edwards in that fearsome moment when he discovers the bodies of his brother, his beloved sister-in-law, and his nephew. Surly, cryptic, almost menacing even before the slaughter, he is invested afterward with the implacability of a figure too much larger than life for any genre but the western."[38]

In terms of landscapes, religion, language, and human relationships, *The Searchers* took the traditional elements of the Western and pushed them to their cultural limits. The West of American popular culture was a place of wide-open spaces, a landscape without limits, with nothing to stop a man's movement across the earth. There he could choose how he lived, how he died, and how far he had to go to do both. Western novelists and filmmakers avoided deep forests and high mountain canyons, where nature closes in and geography imposes boundaries. The perfect settings for Westerns were the deserts of the Southwest or the high plains of the Missouri Breaks, places where horizons extended infinitely in every direction, where sky and earth connect at every horizon.[39]

John Ford picked Monument Valley for his landscape. Ethan Edwards and Martin Pawley search for Debbie in a vast red-and-yellow desert, where massive sandstone monoliths puncture the sky and nature stands poised to test a man's capacity for pain. They endure windstorms, blizzards, pouring rains, dust, cold, and heat—blistering heat that reddens necks, cracks lips, squints eyes, and weathers faces. Weaker men succumb, abandoning their homesteads, as Aaron Allen tells Ethan, when the desert drives "them back to choppin' cotton." During the course of their five-year quest, Ethan's commitment hardens into something ugly. "An Injun doesn't know," Ethan whispers to Pawley, "that here's a critter that will just keep coming. . . . We'll find her [Debbie], just as sure as the turning of the earth."

Such landscapes and feelings trivialize religion, language, and culture, because strength matters more than faith, action more than words, individual men more than women and families. Brute force—not faith, hope, and charity—determines survival, and the Westerns all but reject Christianity. So it is in *The Searchers*. Ethan respects the Texas Ranger badge of Captain-Reverend Samuel Clayton but exhibits contempt for his Bible-beating religious faith. A few days into the search for Debbie, Ethan comes across a dead Comanche, draws his six-gun, and shoots out the Indian's eyes. The good reverend protests, asking Ethan: "What good did that do?" "By what you preach, none," Ethan counters. "But what that Comanche believes, ain't got no eyes he can't enter the spirit land. Has to wander forever between the winds." His voice dripping with sarcasm, his lips curling in disgust, he ends the conversation: "*You* get it, Reverend." For Ethan the Comanche's religion is just as good, just as bad, and certainly just as irrelevant as Clayton's Christianity.

Just as certainly as it rejects Christianity, the Western abandons language. Action, not words, and doing, not talking, provide force: The Western distrusts language because the ability to manipulate language bestows power on the hated elites. For the Western hero, silence is power, conferring independence and dominance by preventing inspection, criticism, and dialogue. John Ford made sure that Ethan was a man of few words. His wrinkled, leathered, stubble-bearded face, his squinting eyes and controlled movements, and his ominous stare, speak a mute language of pain and endurance, of a bone-deep determination to see things through. Ethan does not have to speak. When his family asks him why he has been gone for so long, or where he has been, or how he acquired so much money, he keeps his own counsel.[40]

The intersection of language and religion, and wholesale repudiation of both, is revealed at the funeral for the slaughtered Allen family. With Samuel Clayton preaching, and the mourners singing "Shall We Gather at the River," Ethan, with a bellyful of the meaningless drivel, cuts short the service, blurting out as he puts on his hat and walks away, "Amen! Put an end to it. There's no more time. Amen!" The funeral is over, and the men mount up to begin the search. As Ethan prepares to lead the posse, Mrs. Jorgensen (Ollie Carey) carefully approaches, needing to talk and to give voice to her fears. Impatient with words anyway, especially while Indians are carrying Debbie farther away, he abruptly interrupts her: "I'd be obliged, ma'am, if you would get to the point." Mrs. Jorgensen does. "Ethan . . . Martha'd want you to take care of the boys as well as her girls. Don't let the boys waste their lives in vengeance. Promise me, Ethan!" Cinching up his saddle while she speaks, his back to her, he offers no reassurance, not even a nod of the head or a glance, not the slightest acknowledgment. Vengeance is redemption, a perfectly good way to die.

Like other Westerns *The Searchers* rejected women and families as well. Western heroes tended to be unattached, independent men, free from family responsibilities, free even from the encumbrances of friends and neighbors. They appear suddenly out of the vast landscapes and disappear back into them. Only unattached men are capable of the violence required out West; families and communities come with strings attached, knotted by law, culture, and civilization. Screenwriter Frank Nugent's introduction establishes Ethan Edwards's character from the very beginning of the film: "The camera frames and moves with the lone horseman. He is Ethan Edwards, a man as hard as the country he is crossing. Ethan is in his forties, with a three-day stubble of beard. Dust is caked in the lines of his face. . . . Rider and horse have come a long way, and strapped onto his saddle and roll is a sabre and scabbard with a gray sash wrapped around it."[41]

Ethan Edwards is a man to be reckoned with. The film reveals little about his past, but war, pain, and hardscrabble deserts have leathered him into a tough loner. The edges of his personality are sharp, and he is quick to anger. The vigilante inside is poised, ready to explode. Buried deep within him, however, is one small shred of tenderness. When he arrives at the isolated homestead of his brother Aaron (Walter Coy), Ethan is welcomed with open arms. It is soon obvious that Ethan is in love with his brother's wife, Martha (Dorothy Jordan), and that she shares his feelings. He gently kisses her forehead, assists her with a chore, and gazes nostalgically after her; she lovingly unfolds and pets his coat before giving it to him. Sometime before the Civil War, a generation ago, for unknown reasons, Ethan turned away from Martha, and she married Aaron. He still loves her, and she him. It was his first and only chance at a family.

When the Comanches slaughter her, Ethan loses even that shred of affection. His hatred of Comanches blossoms into a megalomaniacal compulsion, a racism of frightening proportions. "I seen his eyes," Martin Pawley declares. "He's a man that can go crazy." Ethan does. He mutilates Comanche corpses, scalps their dead, wantonly slaughters their buffalo, and attacks their villages. When he discovers that his niece Debbie has become the wife of Scar, the Comanche chief, he decides to kill her as well. She has become the enemy. "These are my people," she says. For Ethan the betrayal becomes an obscenity. He wills all of his belongings to Pawley, claiming he has no blood kin. When Pawley protests: "What do you mean you don't have any blood kin? Debbie's your kin." "Not no more she ain't," Ethan intones. "She's been living with a buck." Pawley, who began his search to rescue Debbie from the Comanches, continues it to protect her from Ethan, who, in the words of Pawley's fiancée, will "put a bullet in her brain."

In the climactic scene, Ethan kills Scar and corners his niece in the mouth of a cave. He moves forward menacingly, ready to slaughter her. He grabs her, lifting her over his head. But Ethan steps back from the brink of madness, remembering that Debbie is the daughter of the only woman he ever loved. She is terrified, certain that her obsessed, Comanche-hating uncle is set to kill her. Instead Ethan enfolds her in his arms: "Let's go home, Debbie." French director Jean-Luc Godard once recalled that that was the moment when he realized the power and complexity of John Wayne. A Marxist, Godard hated Duke's politics, and he was determined to dislike the actor's films. Then in 1957 he saw *The Searchers* and its climactic scene when Ethan's relentless, joyless, murderous, compulsive quest is transformed into a poignant reunion: "How can I hate John Wayne upholding Goldwater and yet love him tenderly when abruptly he takes Natalie Wood into his arms in the last reel of *The Searchers?*" In a darkened theater in Paris, Godard was moved to tears.[42]

Wayne's career peaked in 1956. He made thirty-eight more films before his death in 1979, but none matched his performance as Ethan Edwards. Some came close—John T. Chance in *Rio Bravo*, Tom Doniphon in *The Man Who Shot Liberty Valance*, Rooster Cogburn in *True Grit*, and J. B. Books in *The Shootist*—but none of them possessed the emotional range and screen presence of Ethan Edwards. "We watched some of the rushes together," Mary St. John remembered. "Duke was special in the film, and he knew it. Remember that scene when Ethan's looking at the white women who have spent years with the Indians? You could see sympathy and hate in his eyes at the same time. He was never better."

The Searchers was first released in March 1956, and its $10.2 in domestic ticket sales more than earned back Jock Whitney's investment. In the *New*

York Times, Bosley Crowther declared Wayne "uncommonly commanding as the Texan whose passion for revenge is magnificently uncontaminated by caution or sentiment." Although *Variety* complained that "despite its many assets, there is a feeling that "The Searchers" could have been so much more," most reviewers were more enthusiastic. The *Hollywood Reporter* called it "undoubtedly the greatest Western ever made," and *Look* dubbed it "a Western in the grand manner, the most roisterous since *Shane*." For Edward Schallert of the *Los Angeles Times*, it was "a superior John Ford western film. . . . He has penetrated more deeply than usual into life on the frontier." Over time, the film grew even more in stature. Few critics in 1956 picked up on its dark, brooding ambiguities. Edwards is not just a hero, he is also an obsessed maniac. White settlers are not simply the advanced vanguard of civilization; they are racists. Indians are not just noble savages; they are savage killers. The frontier is not a place of opportunity; it is a wasteland.[43]

It would take another decade, one filled with social upheaval and the rise of a new generation of Hollywood filmmakers, before *The Searchers* would be recognized as a classic. In the character of Ethan Edwards, John Wayne had extended the Western hero to the border of evil. If Tom Dunson had been homicidal in *Red River*, Ethan Edwards had upped the ante to genocidal. Duke had pushed the John Wayne persona way past the implacable, laconic good guy of earlier films; Ethan was melancholy and willful. Gene Autry and Roy Rogers, now relegated to Saturday-morning television, were still singing melodies atop Champion and Trigger; Duke had entered another realm.

In *The Searchers*, he transformed the Western gunman into an antihero worthy of the James Dean and Marlon Brando rebels of 1950s. Critics may have been lukewarm, but younger audiences identified immediately with Ethan's truculence. Throughout the film, when Ethan disagrees with the criticism of others, his catchphrase is: "That'll be the day." Within weeks of *The Searchers*' release, the phrase had surfaced in the slang of American teenagers. Buddy Holly, the West Texas rock-and-roller, penned a tune with the same name, and by the summer of 1957 it was at the top of the charts. Some Hollywood veterans immediately recognized the film's power. Twenty years after the film's release, an interviewer mentioned to Howard Hawks that *The Searchers* was one of the best American films ever made. Hawks bluntly responded: "I don't care what they rank it. I rank it as the best color picture that I've ever seen." Young filmmakers-to-be were also mesmerized by the movie. John Milius, who wrote the screenplays for *Jeremiah Johnson* (1972), *Judge Roy Bean* (1973), *Magnum Force* (1973), and *Dillinger* (1973), hailed *The Searchers* as "the best American movie—and its protagonist Ethan Edwards as the one classic character in films. . . . I've seen it sixty times." Director Martin Scorsese remarked: "The dialogue is like poetry! And the changes of expression are so subtle, so magnificent! I see it once or twice a year." Steven Spielberg, who has seen *The Searchers* dozens of times, never tires of it. It "has so many superlatives. It's John Wayne's best performance. . . . It's a study in dramatic framing and composition. It contains the single most harrowing moment in any film I've ever seen."[44]

Having created such a long-living masterpiece, it was only fitting that Duke cap off 1956 with a similarly astounding announcement from the home front. Pilar had already discovered that marrying John Wayne was not without its challenges. Plucked out of a respectable Peruvian family and transplanted into strange, new surroundings, she encountered all the emotional, if not financial, challenges of an immigrant married to an American man. She had an engaging personality, physical beauty, and a fine mind, but her English-speaking skills were limited, as was her formal education. She felt uncomfortable among strangers, and as the wife of one of the most famous personalities in the world, she found herself in the eye of Hollywood's social hurricane, trying to cope with an endless series of luncheons, press conferences, parties, and film debuts.

She was also lonely, suffering from too many acquaintances and too few friends. A month after the wedding, Duke and Pilar had left Encino for San Rafael, California, to shoot *Blood Alley*. During the next three months, she lived in a motel while Duke worked day and night. In June they went to Monument Valley for *The Searchers*, living at Goulding's Trading Post and putting up with 115-degree days. Location meant excitement, money, and good, hard work for Duke, but long hours in a small-town motel bored Pilar. In between locations he worked incessantly, shooting interiors for his movies and planning new projects for Batjac. She needed a life of her own, and for her that meant children.

Duke was more than willing. He needed to make some amends of his own, to address his own failures as a husband and a father. Life was fraught, he believed, with an inexplicable capriciousness; real men did the best they could and then tried to make up for mistakes committed along the way. America, he felt, was a great country because it gave men second chances—and third and fourth ones. After the disaster of *The Big Trail* and the serials in the 1930s, Hollywood had given him another chance. In the Cold War crusade of the Motion Picture Alliance, he had worked to compensate for his failure to serve in the military during World War II. Now, with Pilar, the opportunity to start another family was at hand.

A month after arriving in Monument Valley, and just eight months after the wedding, Pilar missed her period. She kept the news to herself until Duke finished *The Searchers* and they had returned to Encino. A few days later a gynecologist confirmed Pilar's suspicions—and her hopes. Duke was ecstatic. Fortune had smiled on him again. "This is my second chance at being a father," he confessed to Pilar. "It isn't often a man gets a second chance in life. This time, Pilar, I swear I'll do it right."[45]

16

Second-guessing

Duke welcomed the pregnancy as if he were a first-time father, strutting around the house, sketching out plans for a nursery, and buying boxes of expensive Cuban cigars to slip into the hands of close friends. He naively expected the older children to share his excitement. At a family dinner with all four of them in October, he stood up at the table, smiled broadly, and proclaimed that the stork was bringing a baby—a new Wayne—to the family next April. He was beaming, ready to toast the new arrival. What he got was a swift reality check. He was about to become the father of five children in two families, and the potential complications did not dawn on him until that moment. Deafening silence greeted the announcement until, as Pilar later recalled, an anguished Toni "wailed" to her father, "How could you, Dad!" Taken aback, and momentarily speechless, Duke struggled helplessly for a response and then lamely exclaimed, pointing at Pilar, "Don't scream at me. She's the one who's pregnant."[1]

Mary St. John later speculated that a bewildering mix of anger, frustration, and envy inspired Toni's outburst. She loved her father but probably had difficulty swallowing such enthusiasm for a second family when he had done so poorly by the first. The divorce continued to exact its emotional toll. Their private resentments contrasted sharply with America's unabashed adulation of Duke. Toni was the daughter of Hollywood's most popular star, a man who cast a shadow so large that it sometimes darkened the lives of those closest to him. Movie star John Wayne was going to become a father again in April 1956, and in Hollywood that would be big news, fodder for newspapers, fan magazines, and gossip columns. Toni wanted some limelight of her own. Engaged to Don LaCava, a law student at Loyola University, she and Josie were already planning a huge May wedding, complete with a nuptial mass by James Francis Cardinal McIntyre of Los Angeles and a trendy, social-event-of-the-season reception at the Beverly Hills Hotel. Perhaps, Mary recalled, Toni worried that the birth of John Wayne's newest child would upstage the wedding of his oldest. Mary also guessed that Wayne's convoluted private life probably seemed out of order. Pilar was only six years older than Michael and eight years older than Toni; Wayne's new children would be the same age as his grandchildren. Such a menagerie of stepchildren and half-siblings, and the infinite permutations of relationships they would eventually spin off, seemed to defy the natural rhythms of life.[2]

On March 31, 1956, Pilar gave birth to a beautiful, healthy daughter, whom they named Aissa Wayne. Three weeks later Toni's invitation arrived in the mail, announcing a wedding at the Blessed Sacrament Catholic Church of Hollywood on May 27, 1956. She asked Duke to escort her down the aisle, give her away, and then retire to the front pew and sit next to Josie. Pilar was not invited. Duke begged Toni to reconsider, but she was adamant. The wedding was for the first family, not the second. Angry and frustrated, he half-heartedly considered not attending, but boycotting would be small and petulant. Pilar harbored no doubts about the children's feelings. "Here I was," she later wrote, "having a baby at the very time they wanted him to pay attention to their marriages and the children they hoped to have. It must have seemed terribly unfair to all four of them. They couldn't accept the fact that their father was entitled to a new life, a new family."[3]

Duke's new life included new fame in 1956. *The Searchers* premiered two weeks before Aissa's birth in March, and his riveting performance raised his popularity another notch. After *Hondo*, *The High and the Mighty*, *Blood Alley*, *The Sea Chase*, and *The Conqueror*—a collage of mixed-quality films that had all made money—he was the most bankable property in Hollywood. And with production costs skyrocketing, studio accountants persuaded studio executives to stay away from lesser talents and to channel their funds toward certifiable stars. In June 1956 Buddy Adler of Twentieth Century-Fox cut a deal that shocked the industry. He signed Duke to star in three Fox pictures during the next four years, and in return the studio agreed to pay him

$200,000 annually over a ten-year period. The studio also covered Charlie Feldman's $200,000 commission. Trade papers and tabloids treated the news incredulously: John Wayne would be getting $666,666.66 a picture. When UP reporter Aline Mosby inquired about the deal, Duke smugly blamed the studios for their own plight: "I'm glad the producers were stupid. They won't spend any money to make stars. They won't take a chance on these kids."[4]

Rich and famous, Duke had his way in Hollywood, but his influence at home was far more limited. In spite of a deep yearning to be a better husband and father the second time around, he soon encountered familiar tensions and frustrations. His priorities had not changed. His first love, as it had always been, was still work—making money and motion pictures—not his family. At the height of his career in 1956, he read more scripts and fielded more offers than ever. He was busy, very busy, too busy, with long stretches away from home. Restless and easily bored, he wanted Pilar to keep him company on location, even though Aissa was a tiny baby. In the past, to be near her husband and fulfill his fixed vision of the good wife, she had tolerated the discomforts, inconveniences, and boredom. Pilar would get up, eat breakfast with the company, pull up a folding chair near the camera, watch Duke perform, and then enjoy dinner and the evening with him.

But that was before Aissa came along. Going on location with a baby upset the routine. For the first few months, traveling was relatively easy, especially if the locations were somewhere in the civilized world. Two adjoining hotel rooms, a crib, a hotplate, and a nanny allowed Pilar to spend time with Duke and Aissa. But the older and more active the baby, the more inconvenient locations became, and she did not want to raise her daughter in hotel rooms. Pulled between the contradictory demands of husband and child, she became increasingly unhappy.

The first location after Aissa's birth was Pensacola, Florida, where John Ford directed Duke in *The Wings of Eagles*. Pilar agreed to bring Aissa along. The baby was three months old and quite manageable when they left for Florida in June 1956. Air-conditioned hotel rooms made the heat and humidity of the summer tolerable. The Waynes remained in Florida until early October, except for a few days when Duke did a cameo role, playing himself, in RKO's *I Married a Woman*.

The Wings of Eagles was John Wayne and John Ford's tenth collaboration. The movie was a biography of Frank "Spig" Wead, an early pioneer of naval aviation. Known to schoolmates as "Smart Wead" for his brains, he had volunteered for the navy's first aviation class in 1919, and during his first solo, an unauthorized flight taken on a dare, he had crash-landed the aircraft into an admiral's swimming pool. Of such antics are legends made, and Wead became a legend. Late in the 1930s, however, he fell down a flight of stairs at his home in Santa Monica, California, and broke his neck. The resulting paralysis forced him out of the navy. Eventually, he regained partial use of his legs and learned to walk with braces and crutches. He tried his hand writing aviation stories for popular magazines and came to the attention of John Ford, who brought him to Hollywood to write screenplays. The two men became close friends, and during his career Wead produced a number of successful scripts, including *Test Pilot, Hell Divers, They Were Expendable, Air Mail,* and *Ceiling Zero.* After Japan bombed Pearl Harbor, Wead returned to active duty, helping to promote the idea of constructing small aircraft carriers to ferry planes back and forth to the battle line. He died in 1947.[5]

MGM suggested the film to Ford in 1956, but the director was skeptical. "I did not want to do it," he told Peter Bogdanovich, "but I didn't want anyone else to do it either." Ford loved Wead. For more than a decade, an autographed picture of Wead had adorned a wall in Ford's home, bearing the inscription: "To Jack in memory of birchrod . . . the Carleton . . . a coupla wars . . . a coupla lousy landings . . . air mail. . . . Expendable. . . . Lotsa bull and plenty of good times . . . affection. . . . Spig." Ford finally agreed to take on the project, but years later he recalled: "I have never approached a subject with such fear and trepidation as I did the story of Spig Wead. How can you make a picture out of the life of a guy whom you've loved and admired for forty years?"[6]

Playing Spig Wead appealed to Duke because he identified so closely with the man. Wead was a workaholic whose devotion to the navy had all but ruined his marriage. When he resurfaced in his children's lives, they barely recognized him, and when he disappeared again they hardly missed him. Spig Wead was a "man's man" who preferred the company of aviators to his wife and children. In the film, when Spig tries to reconcile with his wife, Min, (Maureen O'Hara), and explain himself, it could have been Duke pleading with Josie or Chata or Pilar: "When I do something, I go all the way—living—gambling—flying—I tap myself out. I guess that's the way I want it to be. Maybe it's the way I am." That's the way Duke was. So were the Ringo Kid and Tom Dunson and Sergeant Stryker and Ethan Edwards. Duke also admired Wead because there was no self-pity in the man. Real men accept the hand life deals them. Wead neither bemoaned his paralysis nor exploited it. "You couldn't help him," Duke remembered. "You couldn't. If you tried to lift him out of the chair, he'd hit you over the head with a crutch."[7]

In spite of John Ford's direction and the presence of John Wayne as Spig Wead, Maureen O'Hara as Min Wead, Ward Bond as John Dodge (the John Ford character), and Dan Dailey as Jughead Carson, Wead's friend and aide, *The Wings of Eagles* was a box-office disappointment, Duke's first in years. The reviews were solid, but MGM's publicity department misrepresented the film in its advertising campaign. War movies filled Hollywood coffers in the early 1950s, and ticket buyers expected to see John Wayne in aerial dogfights with Japanese Zeros. Ford had tried to get MGM to change the film's title, but the studio refused. Instead of a war movie, moviegoers were treated to an aging John Wayne, sans toupee, fighting the war from a wheelchair and a desk. In mid-December, Ford previewed the film with MGM executives. Some of them felt the film had too many laughs. "How the hell can a movie have too many laughs," Ford wrote Wayne on the day after Christmas. Actually, it had too many awkwardly composed comedy scenes. "Its humor," wrote Ford biographer Ronald Davis, "resembled the antics of the Keystone Cops." Ford felt better when he wrote Wayne a month later, after previewing the film aboard the aircraft carrier *Lexington*. The Navy pulled out all the stops—"dinner inspections, the works. . . . The Bluejackets were with it every minute, and during dramatic moments there was complete silence in that great big hangar deck which, as you know, is bigger than St. Peter's." Sailors might have liked *The Wings of Eagles*, but word of mouth among civilians was disappointing and audiences stayed away.[8]

In true Spig Wead fashion, Duke had not been back from Florida for a week before preparations began on *Legend of the Lost*, a Batjac film to be shot in Libya. Batjac, in conjunction with Robert Haggiag Production and Dear Film, Inc., had a contract from United Artists to produce the film, and it called for two months on location in the Sahara Desert, followed by twelve weeks of interior shooting at Cinecittà Studio in Rome. The film would require Duke's attention from January to August of 1957. He was to play Joe January, a desert guide leading Paul Bonnard (Rossano Brazzi) in search of a fabled lost city. Dita (Sophia Loren) is a prostitute who falls in love with Bonnard and follows him into the Sahara. Henry Hathaway, hired as producer and director, decided to shoot the movie in and around the village of Ghadames, an isolated Sahara oasis four hundred miles from Tripoli, Libya, which would give him access to the Leptis Magna ruins. Cast, crew, and supplies arrived in Ghadames by private plane, camel caravan, and off-road vehicles. They bunked in tents and slept on cots. Radios and telephones did not exist, nor did indoor plumbing, except for one toilet in one building. Temperatures

peaked at more than one hundred degrees in the afternoons and then plum-
meted to thirty degrees at night. Hathaway's brutal schedule, designed to keep
everyone at work from five in the morning to nine each night, was sure to
match the spartan existence.[9]

Duke expected Pilar to come with him to Africa. He expected her to tend
to Aissa in a desert pup tent or dingy room in the middle of nowhere. It was
an unreasonable request, but not out of character. Pilar thought she had a
ready-made excuse when Aissa's pediatrician said the baby was too little for
the required inoculations, but Duke insisted. "Damn it, Pilar, you're my
wife," he argued. "The nurse is perfectly capable of taking care of Aissa, and I
need you with me." Pilar held her ground, agreeing to cross the Atlantic only
when the company had settled down in Rome. But a few weeks into the
shooting, Duke sent her an urgent cablegram, pleading with her to come.
Worried that something was wrong, that perhaps he had been hurt on the set,
she made the journey. Ford cabled Wayne that she was coming. "She is an
adorable gal, Duke, and you're lucky." When she arrived in Ghadames, he
smiled and said: "I just wanted you here so you could see the sunsets." Instead
of a pup tent, Pilar got the most luxurious accommodations in Ghadames—a
mud-plastered room whose dirt floor had to be watered down each morning
to keep the dust at bay. She stayed until the desert shooting ended and then,
at Duke's insistence, accompanied him to Rome.[10]

She was far better company than Duke's costar. He never warmed up to
Sophia Loren. Tall, statuesque, with an exotic, almost Oriental face, Loren
projected an extraordinary sensuality on screen. She had first appeared as an
extra in several Italian films in 1950, enjoyed increasingly larger roles during
the next several years, and made her international mark in 1955 in *Woman of
the River*. Duke celebrated when Batjac signed her. Sex appeal, he was convinced, sold tickets. But according to Henry Hathaway, Loren "was a one-di-
mensional actress. It's just the beauty. She has no depth. Never did have, never
will have." Wayne had little to do with her during the shooting. Loren was
engaged to Carlo Ponti at the time, but Duke suspected her of having an ongoing affair with Rossano Brazzi, a married man. The two were inseparable
off camera. Guided by the prevailing double standard, Duke got along quite
well with Brazzi, but he had little use for two-timing women, and he kept his
distance from Loren.[11]

Loren may have been a screen goddess, Duke an international icon, and
Brazzi a European idol, but their combined sex appeal failed to boost *Legend
of the Lost* at the box office. Hathaway blamed Batjac for the problems, espe-

cially adding several clumsy crowd and bazaar sequences to the beginning of the film. The production was "a fiasco," he remembered, and "everybody tried to change it [the script] from what it was. I only wanted to see three people through the whole thing and they tried to make it more." Its rentals generated a small profit for Batjac, but nowhere near what Duke had anticipated. Gross ticket sales never reached *Variety's* coveted $8 million mark, and *Legend* was swamped by such 1957 hits as *Bridge on the River Kwai* ($34.2 million), *Peyton Place* ($23 million), *Sayonara* ($21 million), *Old Yeller* ($19 million), and *Raintree County* ($12 million). Even *Island in the Sun, Gunfight at the OK Corral, Pal Joey,* and *Heaven Knows Mr. Allison* did better. Added to *The Wings of Eagles,* Duke had put together back-to-back disappointments. Complicating matters, RKO finally released *Jet Pilot* in October, and critics savaged the film, setting off rumors that perhaps John Wayne's star had started to set.[12]

The decline in Wayne's career was a subject of some concern at Twentieth Century-Fox. The studio wanted its money's worth, and in October 1957, Duke arrived in Kyoto, Japan, to make the first in his three-picture deal. After *The Wings of Eagles, Jet Pilot,* and *Legend of the Lost,* he wanted to justify Fox's investment. Insecurity was a Hollywood epidemic, and John Wayne was not immune. Four losers in a row could tarnish Duke's luster and compromise future salary demands.[13]

For a thousand years Kyoto had been the capital city of Japan, and its back drop of Buddhist and Shinto shrines provided a breathtakingly beautiful location. Charles Grayson's screenplay, based on a true story by Ellis St. Joseph, revolved around Townsend Harris, the American diplomat who served as U.S. consul general to Japan from 1856 to 1860. In the mid-1600s, the Tokugawa shoguns, paranoid about the corrupting influences of foreigners, had sealed Japan off from the outside world, and Harris was the first American to breach their legal and military barriers. Duke had never worked with John Huston, but the director's solid reputation was impressive. Huston wanted Duke to play Townsend Harris because "his massive frame, bluff innocence and rough edges would be an interesting contrast to the small, highly cultivated Japanese . . . the physical comparison would help serve to emphasize their dissimilar viewpoints and cultures." Duke liked the part because Harris, armed only with an engaging personality, lived in Japan by himself, confronting the Japanese throne on his own. The fact that U.S. forces still occupied Japan in 1957 gave the story of the first American there a unique symbolic effect. Success seemed certain.

The film fell far short of Duke's hopes; indeed, *The Barbarian and the Geisha* was among the most frustrating experiences of his career. Within days of their introduction, Duke loathed John Huston. The feeling was mutual. A committed liberal, Huston hated Wayne's politics, especially his leadership of the Motion Picture Alliance. In an unsuccessful attempt to irritate Duke, Huston hired Sam Jaffe, a political radical, to play Townsend Harris's interpreter. To cast the female lead—a Japanese woman who falls in the love with the American she has been hired to spy on—Huston spent a month in Japanese geisha houses, sampling the women and finally bestowing the part on Eiko Ando, a twenty-three-year-old beauty whose only experience in show business was performing for a Ginza burlesque house. Defending her selection to an Associated Press reporter, Huston cited the fact that he had cast Marilyn Monroe, another unknown actress, in *The Asphalt Jungle*. "Marilyn Monroe and this girl both started with no acting experience," he argued. "Miss Ando is doing her part and what we ask her to do as well as Marilyn did hers." Whether Monroe spent any time on Huston's casting couch is a matter of conjecture, but Ando warmed Huston's bed throughout the location. They frequently arrived late on the set and could not keep their hands off each other. Duke was used to working with John Ford, Howard Hawks, William Wellman, and Henry Hathaway, directors who insisted on discipline and structure, who carefully planned each day's shooting, scene by scene and hour by hour. Huston was completely unstructured. He had three full-time staffers rewriting dialogue and redesigning scenes on a daily basis. When Wayne asked about the next day's shooting schedule, he would shrug him off, saying: "Spend more time absorbing the beauty of the scenery and less time worrying about your part." When Wayne protested that he could not learn lines unless he knew what they were, Huston would remind him, "Don't worry, we'll improvise." "He [Huston] can quote chapter and verse on the price of a god-damned piece of Japanese porcelain," Duke complained to Pilar, "but he won't tell me how he wants me to do a scene." "It's a little frustrating," Duke wrote Ford, "trying to arouse the, I presume, sleeping talent of our leader Mr. Huston."

Huston's carelessness almost ended in disaster. One scene called for a forty-foot barge, loaded with the bodies of cholera victims, to be burned at sea. Huston's technicians ignited the barge just off the coast of Kawana, a fishing village on the Izu Peninsula, but the wind changed and the smoldering barge drifted back toward shore, destroying three fishing vessels and threatening hundreds of highly flammable wood and rice-paper homes. "We worried that the whole town would go up in flames," Huston remembered, "and God knows what the cost in life would have been." The crew managed to stop the burning barge before it rammed several shoreline buildings, but enraged Japanese locals rioted, attacking crew members and beating some of them into unconsciousness. Duke had been watching the scene from a distance, and when the melee started, he made his way down to the docks and began waving his hands and shouting for silence. In an instant the rioters were transformed into fans. The riot was over. He promised to reimburse all financial losses, either from Twentieth Century-Fox or out of his own pocket. The incident only alienated him further from Huston. Three months later, when the location shooting ended, Duke could not stand the sight of John Huston. "The son of a bitch," he told Pilar, "can't make a good movie without his father or Bogart to carry him."[14]

For the first time since his quickie serials of the 1930s, Duke had no idea how the final version of the film would look. In May, when the interiors were finished, Hedda Hopper interviewed him. He acknowledged that *The Barbarian and the Geisha* was technically beautiful, "like a Japanese print," but complained that Huston "extemporized largely, so I never knew where we were script-wise." He speculated that the film, thick with plot but thin on action, would not be a very good vehicle for his screen persona. "I'm accustomed to making action films and I'm hoping there's enough action in this one to carry me." When Hopper asked him how the film was going to turn out, he shrugged: "We'll wait and see." Actually he had learned enough about John Huston's methods, and he had seen enough insipid rushes, to sense that *The Barbarian and the Geisha* would be a flat bust, perhaps not quite as flawed and incompetent as *Big Jim McLain, Blood Alley, The Conqueror,* and *Jet Pilot*—films that would have buried a less popular star's career—but still bad enough. He could not get over the fact that Huston had never delivered on his promise to write a decent script. "The movie just doesn't have a plot," he kept complaining; it was static, flat, boring. And the actors were like Japanese screens, not warm flesh and blood, just "things in the foreground."[15]

Duke's misgivings were well founded. Twentieth Century-Fox released *The Barbarian and the Geisha* nationwide late in September 1958, hoping to recoup a $4 million investment quickly. Its reception was disappointing. Critics agreed that Huston's penchant for historical accuracy and scenic backgrounds overwhelmed the characters. "It is an exotic and visually impressive picture," *Variety* claimed, "but the human story it tries to tell has been all but swallowed up by the weight of its production." The film barely broke even, giving Wayne his dreaded fourth straight box-office disappointment. Huston agreed that it "turned out to be a bad picture," but he tried to blame Wayne. "When I brought it to Hollywood, the picture, including the music, was finished, as far as I was concerned." But then he left, off to Africa to make *The Roots of Heaven*, and during his absence, he claimed: "John Wayne apparently took over. . . . He pulled a lot of weight at Fox, so the studio went along with his demands for changes. . . . By the time the studio finished hacking up the picture according to Wayne's instructions, it was a complete mess."[16]

As Duke's professional concerns mounted, Pilar's alienation deepened. After leaving the baby with a nurse during *Legend of the Lost*, Pilar had asked her mother to come to Encino and tend Aissa during *The Barbarian and the Geisha*. She felt better about leaving Aissa with her grandmother, but throughout the location, Pilar battled a vague, ill-defined anxiety. At first she wrote it off as a bad case of maternal guilt, but her uneasiness lingered and escalated, dominating her thoughts during the day and keeping her awake at night. She called home frequently, and Duke kept reassuring her that all was well. But two weeks after Christmas, he told her they would both be better off if she went home. The timing of her return could not have been more fortuitous. On January 14 the pet dog, Blackie, barking furiously, awakened Pilar, who immediately smelled smoke. By the time she grabbed Aissa from an adjoining bedroom, smoke engulfed much of the second story of the house. Seven engine companies fought the flames for more than an hour. Pilar, wearing a robe, watched the battle from the lawn. When it was over she took Aissa to Web Overlander's, who lived next door, and slept for a few hours. She called Duke the next morning and asked: "How do you like one-story houses?" The last thing he wanted was to break off shooting and come home. "Duke wouldn't want anyone to say he'd run out on John Huston, no matter how valid his reason for leaving might be." Instead of coming home he sent her a blank check accompanied by a note: "For the girl who really has nothing to wear."[17]

When Duke returned from Japan early in 1958, his outlook was bleak. The house could be fixed; he was not so sure about his career. He knew that a few bad films, even a few really awful ones, would not injure his career if he continued to make exceptionally good ones along with the mediocre and bad. Although he was reluctant to admit it, he was at his best only when he surrendered control of a script and the set to such strong, experienced directors as John Ford, William Wellman, or Howard Hawks. Thus when Hawks approached him with a new project, Wayne quickly accepted. It was a chance for both men to leave the exotic East and return to the West and Westerns.

Hawks's previous film, *Land of the Pharaohs* (1955), had been the worst of his long, distinguished career. "I didn't know how a Pharaoh talked," Hawks said, explaining the primary reason for the film's stilted dialogue. Nor did he have a feel for Egyptian characters. "I should have had somebody in there that you were rooting for," he later said. "Everybody was a son of a bitch." After spending a few years in Europe and taking time to "sit back and take a good look at the way things were going," he was ready to return to filmmaking.[18]

Several films kept running through his mind during his three-year hiatus. The first was *High Noon*, Stanley Kramer and Fred Zinnemann's 1952 Western about a sheriff who is deserted by his friends and the citizens of his town and forced to confront a gang of killers alone. The film, a ham-handed allegory about the impact of the Red Scare on community values, had enraged John Wayne, and it had bothered Hawks as well. "I didn't like [the] picture," Hawks told an interviewer. "I didn't think a good sheriff was going to go running around town like a chicken with his head off asking for help, and finally his Quaker wife had to save him. That isn't my idea of a good western sheriff." The second film which bothered Hawks was Delmer Daves's *3:10 to Yuma*, a 1957 psychological drama that deals with a lawman escorting an outlaw to Yuma prison. In the film the outlaw talks about the loyalty of his gang in an attempt to frighten the lawman. Hawks simply refused to believe that a real sheriff would fear the outlaw's taunts. As he told several friends: "That's a lot of nonsense, the sheriff would say, 'You better hope that your friends *don't* catch up with you, 'cause you'll be the first man to die.'"[19]

As a reaction to *High Noon* and *3:10 to Yuma*, Hawks decided to make *Rio Bravo*, the tale of Sheriff John T. Chance. Unlike the sheriffs in the other two films, Chance arrests a brutal murderer, then holds him in jail pending trial. Every inch a Hawks hero, Chance does not decry his fate or scour his town in search of help. He simply does his job, stoically and without fuss. In the process his friends respond. Without asking for it, he receives help in every crisis, and during the course of the film he is saved by a drunken friend, a crippled old man, a young gunslinger, a dance-hall girl, and a Mexican hotel operator. In *Rio Bravo*, Hawks directly defied *High Noon*. In the earlier film the sheriff (Gary Cooper) constantly appeals for assistance, but needs very little; in Hawk's film Chance never asks for help but constantly, and fortuitously, receives it. The townspeople in *High Noon* are timid, frightened, and totally self-absorbed; in *Rio Bravo* the secondary characters are occasionally timid and frightened, but they are not totally self-absorbed, and they risk their lives to defend Chance. What he stands for—duty, decency, the integrity of the individual, and rule by law—are the only things worth believing in.

Wayne was perfect for the role of Chance. In one form or another he had been playing the part for the last thirty years, and Hawks never seriously entertained casting anyone else for the role. Similarly, he could think of only one person to play Stumpy, Chance's old, crippled, comical sidekick. Walter Brennan had been playing that role almost as long as Duke had been playing Chance. In addition Brennan had worked for Hawks in such successful films as *Barbary Coast* (1935), *Sergeant York* (1941), *To Have and Have Not* (1944), and *Red River* (1948). Hawks demonstrated his genius in casting the other parts. He gave the part of the young gunslinger, Colorado, to Ricky Nelson, who on the surface seemed little more than a lightweight sitcom actor and bubblegum rock-and-roller. And he cast Angie Dickinson as Feathers, the dance-hall girl with a past. Before *Rio Bravo* she had enjoyed only limited success in bit parts and small roles in a string of undistinguished films. But Nelson and Dickinson succeeded in transforming their roles in *Rio Bravo* into something more than stock Western clichés.

The key part in the film, however, was Dude, Chance's alcoholic deputy sheriff. He is central to the action. It is his humiliation that sets the story in motion, and his heroic struggle with alcoholism that gives the film its heart. *Rio Bravo* revolves around Dude even more than around Chance. John T. Chance is as constant as John Wayne; he might get shot or even die, but he would never betray a friend or go back on his word. Dude, on the other hand, battles psychological demons; his great fear is not so much that he will betray a friend as that he might betray himself. Hawks knew that everyone who saw the film would be rooting for Dude's salvation, and the person who played the role had to give it the proper depth and feeling, the kind of depth Thomas Mitchell had given to the role of the drunken doctor in *Stagecoach*.

Hawks wanted Montgomery Clift for the part, but Clift was not interested. MCA, the powerful talent agency, pushed Dean Martin, and for reasons known only to himself, Hawks decided to test the singer. It was a strange choice. Until their breakup a few years before, Martin had been considered the untalented half of Martin and Lewis, the crooner straight man for the creative and frenetic Jerry Lewis. Although he had received good reviews for his performances in *The Young Lions* (1948) and *Some Came Running* (1949), most critics believed that he had demonstrated little else in film or in his life to suggest substance or anything beyond casual singing talent. But Hawks agreed to meet with him to talk about the role. He told Martin's agent that he would meet with Dean at 9:00 the next morning. Without offering an explanation, the agent said that his client could not get there that early. The next day Martin showed up about 10:30, and Hawks asked him why he could not make it at 9:00. "I was working in Las Vegas, and I had to hire an airplane and fly down here," Martin replied. He hired Martin on the spot. No screen test. No talk of contracts. Just go down to wardrobe and pick out a costume.[20]

For once Martin was called on to stretch his acting talents. It was a "very good role, more dramatic than anything I've ever done," Martin told a reporter. Marlon Brando read the script for him and offered some advice. "He didn't tell me how to play the part. He just told me what to think about. I play a drunk with DTs. I'm fighting the bottle, the bad guys, and John Wayne, the sheriff who makes me his deputy." He dug beneath the surface and worked to create a believable character. Some scenes were difficult for him, especially one where he had to cry. The idea of "even pretending to cry was something that unnerved him," wrote his biographer Nick Tosches, but eventually he got even that right. Hawks was impressed. "Dean's a damn good actor," Hawks later said, "but he's a fellow who floats through life. He has to be urged. He has to get some kind of a hint, something going, otherwise, hell, he won't even rehearse his shows. He wants to get on and play golf."[21]

There was no golf on the Old Tucson set of *Rio Bravo*—Hawks and Duke made sure of that. Wayne and Martin developed a warm friendship, one that continued until the end of Duke's life, and both enjoyed the boyishness of Ricky Nelson. On May 8, 1958, when Ricky turned eighteen, the two older actors presented him with a three-hundred-pound sack of steer manure; then, after dumping it on the ground, they threw the singer into his own gift. But far more time was spent listening to Hawks and trying to get their parts right.[22]

Even Wayne listened to Hawks. He knew that when working with Hawks or Ford, listening was more important than memorizing the script, which was likely to be changed anyway. Hawks later recalled that Duke never read the script; instead, he would ask the director, "What am I supposed to do in this thing?" Hawks would answer, "Well, you're supposed to give the impression of this and this." That was all Wayne needed. He could memorize two pages of lines in three or four minutes. With Hawks as with Ford, Duke was uninterested in the larger story line and how individual scenes would fit into the whole. If Hawks tried to explain, Duke was apt to say: "I don't want to hear it. I never like your stories and they always turn out good." For Hawks John Wayne was an ideal actor: "He never squawks about anything. He's the easiest person I ever worked with. Because he never says anything about it, he just goes ahead and does it."[23]

Occasionally, however, Wayne did not like a scene, and then Hawks listened to him. When he would see the actor shake his head, he would ask him what was wrong. Often Duke had trouble articulating the exact problem, but Hawks trusted his instincts. Together they would tear a scene down bit by bit until they discovered the problem. When the problem was located and corrected, Duke would "beam all over" and say: "That works good." And Hawks would resume shooting.[24]

"John Wayne represents more force, more power, than anybody else on the screen," Hawks remarked in the 1970s. "When Ford was dying we used to discuss how tough it was to make a good western without Wayne." *Rio Bravo* is a perfect case in point. John Wayne's image of the hard, stoic, decent man provides the immovable foil for all the other characters. Because of his well-developed image as the toughest son of a bitch on the range, he does not have to win every fight or dominate every scene. His mere presence, even on the periphery or offstage, is enough.

The opening scene in *Rio Bravo* is a case in point. In less than five minutes and without a word of dialogue, Hawks establishes the film's story line. He begins by cutting back and forth between Dude and Joe Burdette (Claude Akins). Dude, unshaven and disheveled, slinks through a saloon eyeing Burdette's bottle. With his eyes and the tilt of his head, Burdette acknowledges Dude and offers him a drink. With his eyes and a twitch of a smile, Dude accepts. Then Burdette, suddenly turned sadistic, takes a silver dollar and tosses it into a spittoon beside Dude. As Dude reaches for the dollar, however, John T. Chance kicks the spittoon away, refusing to allow even a pathetic drunk to sink to such an indignity. In a series of cuts that pay homage to Hollywood's silent era, Hawks sets the film's plot in motion with a fight and a murder. Before the first word is spoken, he establishes the characters of Chance, Dude, and Burdette—but the power of the sequence stems from Wayne's overwhelming screen presence. Every action, every detail, every nuance, speaks for itself. It is perhaps the finest opening sequence in the history of the Western, one that critics have praised and other directors imitated. And throughout *Rio Bravo* Hawks maintains the same high quality. One English film critic even went so far as to write: "If I were asked to choose a film that would justify the existence of Hollywood, I think it would be *Rio Bravo*."[25]

Sadly, the greatness of Hawks's and Wayne's accomplishments went unobserved by the film's earliest critics. Few recognized that in *Rio Bravo* Hawks carefully manipulated and altered the stock Western characters to create a fresh amalgam, and that Wayne had seldom so fully mastered a role. Philip

Scheuer of the *Los Angeles Times* wrote: "You could describe it as a folk come-dy-drama and not go too far wrong." The trade journals treated it as just an-other Western, "a big, brawling western," said *Variety*, or "a large, sprawling hulk of a Western" according to *Film Daily*. A. H. Weiler of the *New York Times* wrote: "It is hardly likely that anyone will sleep through *Rio Bravo*, but chances are that a wide-awake viewer will not be particularly startled by its random fireworks. [I]t is well-made but awfully familiar fare."[26]

Fortunately, and not surprisingly, *Rio Bravo* also made money at the box office, generating more than $10.5 million in ticket sales and easing some of Duke's concerns. He felt more comfortable talking about his salaries now that one of his recent films had done well. Early in 1958, while he was making *Rio Bravo*, Mahin-Rackin Productions tentatively offered him $750,000 plus 20 percent of the profits to work with John Ford and William Holden in *The Horse Soldiers*. Holden received the same contract, and Ford got $200,000 plus 10 percent to direct. Duke knew exactly why the studios coughed up such huge sums. "It's hard to get audiences away from other forms of recre-ation. A few of the older favorites like myself may have given them pleasure in a movie, so some people are more willing to go out of the house to see us." Refusing to apologize for his good fortune, he justified every nickel he earned: "I'm not taking money away from the exhibitor or the producing company. This money used to go into overhead for phony executives. I used to go by the big executive building at M-G-M and see all those people sitting there getting fat and rich, and I wondered to myself why not give the money to the people who are making it. I . . . get paid a lot now."[27]

Finally, then, after four failures—and despite the critics' yawns (a pattern that he would come to know only too well)—his career was back on track. His home was rebuilt. His assets were rocketing. But a new problem arose.

In 1958, after the fire, a deep depression swallowed Pilar. "What ifs" filled her thoughts. What if she had not left Duke in Africa and returned home early? What if the dog's barking had not awakened her? What if it happened again? Some "whys" sounded as well. Why did he insist that she come with him? Why did he make so many movies? Why did he work so hard? Her mother was pulled, Aissa Wayne remembered, "between marriage and moth-erhood, between following around her globe-trotting husband and rushing back to Encino to be with me. The stresses took their toll." Isolated, lonely, and frustrated, Pilar fought sleepless nights and lonely days, and she became uncharacteristically short-fused and demanding. A friend recommended a Beverly Hills physician whose practice flourished on the moods of depressed

Hollywood women. "You need to get some rest," he reassured Pilar. "A little sleep will work wonders." He prescribed Seconal, a sedative, to calm her frayed nerves and ward off the insomnia. Barbiturates imposed a temporary truce on Pilar's inner battles, but she soon escalated the war, consuming Seconals whenever she felt nervous, anxious, or depressed. Pilar Wayne had bought herself a habit.[28]

Unhappiness bewildered John Wayne. He could not understand it, at least not in people free of grinding poverty and gross physical infirmities. He relished his own life—working hard, playing hard, drinking hard—doing exactly what he wanted to do and receiving staggering rewards for it. Pilar's moods were a complete mystery: How could a woman with a loyal, hardworking husband; a beautiful, healthy daughter; a large, lovely home; and available cash be unhappy? Mary St. John recalled that Duke "just did not have a clue about what was going on in Pilar's head. She needed a life, an identity, of her own, and his lifestyle would not permit it." In September 1958 they decided to separate. News of the separation leaked out to the press, and Duke confessed: "It's true that she's moving out. It's been coming for some time. The going has been pretty rough for us because of my picture schedule and the fact that I'm all wrapped up in my career. Sometimes I'm gone for three or four months on a stretch when I make a picture on foreign location. I suppose it will end in a divorce." The matter-of-factness with which Wayne assumed, and spoke of, the worst, was telling—and wrong. They patched things up a few days later, but none of Pilar's frustrations had been addressed.[29]

In October Duke was scheduled to shoot *The Horse Soldiers* in Louisiana. He expected Pilar to be there. Putting the production together had been a legal nightmare. Screenwriters Martin Rackin and John Lee Mahin had formed their own production company and for one dollar optioned *The Horse Soldiers*, Harry Sinclair's novel about a Union cavalry raid during the Civil War. Walter Mirisch agreed to provide $3.5 million to produce the film if Rackin and Mahin could sign several bankable stars. They put together the John Wayne–William Holden–John Ford package. United Artists came on as the distributor. Paramount sued to keep Holden off the film, arguing that he was under contract to them, but lost the case. Lawyers from United Artists, Rackin-Mahin, the Mirisch Company, Batjac, John Ford Productions, and William Holden Productions eventually crafted a 250-page contract that was longer than the script.[30]

Rackin should have spent as much time working on the script as he did on the contract. Ford hated the first version, telling William Clothier: "Well, if you think I'm gonna make their god-damned script you are mistaken. Because there are some things in there I don't like." Set in 1863, the film told the story of Col. John Marlowe (John Wayne) and Maj. Hank Kendall (William Holden), who lead a Union cavalry regiment deep into Mississippi, where they destroy a railroad, cut Confederate supply lines, and allow Gen. Ulysses S. Grant to take Vicksburg. On the way to the railhead at Newton Station, they bivouac at a plantation and decide to take Hannah Hunter (Constance Towers), the mistress of the plantation, with them after she threatens to reveal their position. After the raid the troops fight their way out of Mississippi and into Union-occupied Baton Rouge, Louisiana. Ford insisted on several script changes, especially the film's ending. Rackin and Mahin originally had a completely upbeat ending, with the cavalry returning triumphantly and entering Baton Rouge to the welcoming trumpets of a military band. Ford wanted a darker, more subdued ending, one befitting the real pain real wars inflict on real people. With changes, he agreed to do the film, although he remained quite skeptical of its outcome. "You know where we ought to make this picture," he told Rackin. "No. Where?" Rackin replied. "Lourdes," Ford said. "It's going to take a miracle to pull it off."

Pilar needed Lourdes as well. She crashed just before they left for Louisiana. When the remodeling on the house was finished and they moved back in, the Waynes had a housewarming party for a few close friends. They invited Ward and Mary Lou Bond and Jimmy and Josephine Grant to watch a film in the new screening room. Pilar had swallowed the last of her Seconals earlier in the day and forgot to get a refill. Midway through the screening, she started withdrawing from the barbiturates, suffering an anxiety attack, sweating profusely, and losing any awareness of what was going on around her. She ran upstairs and Duke followed her. Physically sick and emotionally desperate, she insisted that Duke get to a pharmacy immediately. Pointing to empty prescription bottles clogging a drawer in her dressing table, she insisted: "You've got to get the druggist to refill my prescription now—tonight." Ignorant of her condition and caught completely off guard, he demanded: "Who the hell gave you this crap?" When she explained how much the drugs helped, Duke scoffed, scooped up all of the empty bottles, and refused to refill them. "They don't help you, Pilar."[31]

The next morning a family physician diagnosed a raging drug addiction and prescribed several weeks of constant surveillance until the barbiturates had washed out of her system. But Duke wanted her in Louisiana, not in a private sanitarium for drug addicts and alcoholics. "Pilar and I will conquer this ourselves," he insisted. Turning to Pilar, he promised to stay by her side during the location, to be with her "every minute, every step of the way. As soon as the picture wraps, we can go down to Mexico for a vacation. All you need is a little rest, a little good food." Duke asked Mary St. John to move into the Encino house for a few days and look after Pilar until she was ready to come out to Louisiana.

Pilar arrived with Aissa and two maids at the end of the week. But *The Horse Soldiers* location was no better than any other. If anything, because of John Ford's unpredictable moods, it was worse than most. Duke was up before dawn and not home until after dark. He controlled neither the film nor his own time. Ever solicitous of the old man, he did Ford's bidding, not Pilar's, and Ford was a nasty taskmaster that fall. On the wagon himself, he insisted that Duke and Holden stay off the bottle, and he watched them like a hawk. To get away from Ford, Holden rented lodgings in Shreveport, a good distance from Alexandria, and commuted back and forth in his Thunderbird. Duke was left behind in Alexandria to take Ford's verbal blows. After several weeks Holden and Rackin took pity on him and concocted a scheme to get Duke out of Ford's way, at least for a day. Rackin complained to Ford that Duke's teeth appeared off color in the first rushes and needed to be cleaned. Holden and Rackin made an appointment with a Shreveport dentist and drove him there. With a large bottle of Wild Turkey, the three men drank the rest of the day away. Ford had a temper tantrum when he found out, and he took to sneaking into Wayne's room searching for bottles. Duke had to hide his liquor in cameraman Bill Clothier's room.

By that time Pilar was in trouble. Sneaking around to get some booze or jumping at every one of Ford's whims, Duke could not find the time for Pilar. His promise to be with her "every minute, every step of the way" was an empty one. Without her husband or the Seconals, Pilar nosedived several days after arriving in Louisiana, hallucinating demons and taking a razor to her wrists. The suicide attempt was more a cry for help than a serious effort. Mary St. John was with her, and called an ambulance. Not wanting to interrupt the shooting—with six production companies involved and $3.5 million at stake—Duke felt that he could not afford to keep Pilar on the location. He chartered a private plane and hired two nurses to take Pilar back to an Encino hospital, where she recovered from both the suicide attempt and the drug addiction. Aissa remained in Louisiana, cared for by a maid and Mary St. John.

Pilar's suicide attempt was not the only disaster to strike *The Horse Soldiers*. Fred Kennedy, a forty-eight-year-old former stuntman, had a bit part in the film only because he had worked many times for John Ford, and the director knew he needed the money. Anxious to earn even more, Kennedy begged Ford to let him double Holden in a fall. Two years earlier, Kennedy had broken his neck in a stunt, but he insisted it had healed completely. Overweight and badly out of shape, he was in no condition to do the stunt, but Ford eventually acquiesced. To play a trick on his old friend, Ford told Constance Towers to rush in after the fall and plant a big kiss on Kennedy's lips. They set up the scene, Ford called for action, and Kennedy galloped the horse toward him and took the fall on cue. But he hit the ground off center, snapping his head back sharply. Towers ran out to him, took his head and shoulders into her arms, and leaned down for the kiss. He was sucking air desperately through a broken neck. Abruptly she looked back to Ford and screamed: "This man is dying." Kennedy succumbed before reaching the hospital in Natchitoches.

Kennedy's death killed any interest Ford had in the film. Guilt-ridden about letting Kennedy do the stunt, the director simply gave up. He went off the wagon and started drinking again. He had neither the physical strength nor the creative energy to finish the job. Instead of wrapping up the shooting in Louisiana, he dismantled the location and sent everybody home. When Duke returned to Encino he complained to Pilar: "Ford just doesn't seem to care any more. Hell, he looks and acts like a beaten man." Although the original schedule called for nineteen more days of shooting in Los Angeles at the Goldwyn and MGM lots, Ford could not do it himself. Three weeks after leaving Louisiana, he reassembled the cast and crew on vacant land in the San Fernando Valley and finished all the remaining exteriors in one day.[32]

With Ford's troubles, Pilar's troubles, and the downs and ups of his own films, it was a difficult period for Wayne. Perhaps the only piece of good news in 1958–59 came from his investments. Back in 1958, Wayne had purchased four thousand acres of cotton land in Stanfield, Arizona. He paid $1,000 an acre for it—a total of $4 million—even though the land was appraised for only $2.6 million, and set up the Clari Land Company to manage the farm. But the farm manager he hired was not much of a cotton man. The first year's yield was a paltry one bale an acre, and the entire operation lost money. Duke decided to go into Phoenix and meet with representatives of Anderson-Clayton, one of the country's biggest cotton brokers. He asked them if they could recommend somebody to take over his operation. Anderson-Clayton told him the best cotton farmer in the world was Louis Johnson, who also lived in Stanfield. Johnson owned six thousand acres next door to the Clari Land

Company. In fact, the year before Johnson had actually made a $1 bet during a casual lunch in Stanfield that Clari would only bring in one bale per acre and whoever owned the company would go under.[33]

Duke approached Johnson in December 1958 and asked him to manage the farm. He was impressed by Johnson's knowledge and manner. After a generation of dealing with Hollywood hype, he appreciated Johnson's realistic discussion of the ranch's economic troubles and his plans for putting it in the black. Johnson knew cotton and hard work. Wayne noticed his weathered face, skin made thick and full-colored from a lifetime outdoors. Johnson had a self-confidence not corrupted by arrogance. Few people impressed him, and he felt absolutely no need to impress anyone else. He was unassuming, smart, and not afraid to speak his mind, just the kind of person John Wayne liked. They agreed on a salary of $14,000, and Wayne put the cotton business out of his mind.

The cotton harvest season exceeded Johnson's expectations. But harvesting the crop presented problems. Johnson had Clari purchase ten large mechanized cotton pickers, which the Casa Grande Valley Bank in nearby Casa Grande, Arizona, financed with no money down. The First Interstate Bank in Phoenix financed the purchase of eighty cotton trailers to haul the harvest to the gin. The local wholesaler for the Union Oil Company agreed to sell Clari the fuel needed for the harvest. But the Clari Land Company had no money. When the Arizona bankers discovered just how tenuous Clari's financial situation was, they backed out of their deals. Just before starting the harvest, Johnson learned that the Casa Grande Valley Bank had sent out repo men to seize the ten cotton pickers, while the First Interstate Bank had made a similar move on the eighty trailers. The Union Oil Company wholesaler told Clari Land Company that all fuel purchases would require a cash payment. Bad news spreads fast in a small town like Stanfield.

Johnson tried to get through to Wayne, to let him know that his cotton business was unraveling by the minute, but it was no use. Wayne was too busy to take messages, and Don LaCava at Batjac did not return Johnson's calls. A crucial decision faced Johnson. From the porch of his stately white brick ranch home, he looked out on a sea of white—an unprecedented yield of 4.2 bales per acre, tens of thousands of bales in all. There were bills to be paid—interest and principal on the land, taxes, fuel and fertilizer costs, equipment payments, wages, and the cost of irrigation water—but it was still a great year.

Johnson had always considered himself a shrewd judge of character, and Duke impressed him as someone he could trust. Instead of letting Wayne's cotton rot on the bush, Johnson went to the Casa Grande Valley Bank, the

First Interstate Bank, and Union Oil Company and personally guaranteed Clari Land Company payments, an amount in excess of a half-million dollars. The cotton pickers and cotton trailers, loaded with fuel, rolled onto Wayne's land and brought in a bumper crop. Clari Land Company paid its bills.

Wayne was dumbfounded. Over the years he had been fleeced by one con man or friend after another, people who spun grandiose schemes and promised huge profits but who never delivered. Louis Johnson had made few promises but had delivered more than Duke had any reason to expect. He bailed Wayne out even though he had little to gain himself, except the satisfaction of having done an extraordinary job. Wayne asked Johnson to manage the farm for another year and Johnson agreed, but more important than that, Duke had found a man he could trust, absolutely and completely. In 1961 he suggested that they form a partnership, combining their acreage into a single operation. Johnson was reluctant, recalling: "I was not sure Duke was ready for the ups and downs of farming." When he expressed that concern to Wayne, Duke confidently replied: "What the hell, I've stubbed my toe before." Johnson then agreed. They formed a 50–50 partnership and did not take a penny out of the operation, plowing the profits back into the farm. During the next several years their business relationship blossomed into a deep, abiding friendship.

While his friendship with Johnson matured, his relationship with his "investment adviser" Bo Roos deteriorated. Johnson and Roos had nothing in common. The bounced checks and foreclosures from Clari Land Company before the cotton harvest embarrassed Wayne. Multimillionaires should not be bouncing checks and dodging foreclosure notices. He angrily upbraided Roos, and Bo apologized profusely, promising to liquidate some assets and improve Duke's cash flow. Quick to forgive a friend, Duke tried to put money out of his mind and return to more interesting projects.

But the money worries would not go away. Duke lost nearly $700,000 in the Panamanian revolution of 1959. Early in the 1940s Bo Roos had introduced Duke to Tony and Roberto "Tito" Arias. The Arias family, one of Panama's most distinguished, traced its roots back four centuries to Pedro Arias de Avila, the Spanish conquistador who founded Panama City in 1519. The family played a key role in Panama's rebellion against Colombia in 1903 and the Revolution of 1931. In 1955 Tito Arias, a former Panamanian ambassador to Great Britain, had married Margot Fonteyn, the British prima ballerina, and both were members of the international jet set. Out of power in Panama by the late 1940s, the Arias family played a constant game of intrigue, profiting handsomely from various family businesses and trying to regain control of the government from President Ernest de la Guardia. In November 1957, on advice from Roos, Wayne invested $525,000 in several Arias enterprises, including a large shrimping operation. Subsequent payments increased the investment to $682,850. Greed, not politics, motivated Duke, but he also enjoyed the company of Tony and Tito Arias, drinking whiskey, smoking Cuban cigars, and trading stories over the years. He considered them good friends, especially Tito.[34]

But in 1959 Duke found himself caught up in the labyrinth of Panamanian politics. Tito's father, Harmodio Arias, was a powerful newspaperman in Panama City and a vociferous, outspoken opponent of the Guardia regime. To quiet Arias the regime went after Tito, accusing him of landing a "ten-man" army on the west coast of Panama to overthrow the government. Knowing that sedition carried the death penalty, Tito fled the country before police could arrest him, but his wife was detained, questioned for a day, and deported. They both ended up in London.

While searching the Arias family estate at Santa Clara, police discovered a memorandum from Duke to Arias, outlining his investment of $525,000 in "Panamanian operations." Government officials speculated publicly that John Wayne might be involved in the conspiracy, a charge Duke vehemently denied. "Roberto never talked politics and I never heard him say anything about overthrowing the Panamanian government," Duke told an Associated Press reporter. "I've known Tito for twenty years on and off. I've got businesses in Panama with him and without him. It's a shrimp business, not just he and I, other people are in it. But he's a big stockholder." J. Edgar Hoover immediately put the FBI on the case, trying to determine if Duke had any involvement in the alleged sedition, finally concluding that there was insufficient evidence to implicate him in any conspiracy. Duke survived the incident politically, but his Panamanian investments were doomed. Panamanian officials made it impossible for the company.[35]

Two months later *The Horse Soldiers* was released, and Duke started worrying about money again. It was a rare reception: Reviewers were kind, but the film died at the box office, barely covering costs and rendering Duke's twenty percent worthless. Of Duke's previous six films, only *Rio Bravo* had succeeded. Even its take came nowhere near the megahits of the late 1950s. *The Ten Commandments* (1956) astonished Hollywood with more than $43 million in rental earnings, and Charlton Heston scored again in *Ben Hur* (1959), which earned $36.2 million. Duke might be able to dismiss his critics, but tepid box-office receipts disturbed him. He had turned fifty in 1957. Not for the first time, he feared that perhaps his days as an action hero were numbered. He was trapped by his own creation. If his future in the business was going to be offscreen rather than on, he needed to establish a different set of credentials, to market himself as something more than an aging action hero.[36]

In 1959 he was the most famous movie star in the world, but he was still not much more than that. Clark Gable, Kirk Douglas, Burt Lancaster, William Holden, and Charlton Heston were leading stars as well. Americans were drawn to their charisma but did not yet revere any of them. It would take the political firestorm of the 1960s to separate Duke from the pack of leading actors, to elevate him from star to icon. The winds of political change were blowing in 1959, and he was among the first to sniff out liberalism's resurgence. His response, naturally, was to make a film—this time, a political film entirely on his own impetus: *The Alamo*. Like the defenders of the Alamo in 1836, he drew a line in the sand and stood his political ground. The transformation from big star to cultural hero had begun.

17

"The Country's Going Soft"

John Wayne was broke. Considering the fact that he thought he was quite wealthy, the news was more than a little disconcerting. During the 1950s he was the top box-office draw in Hollywood, and since making *Stagecoach* in 1939, he had earned millions of dollars. The truth began to unfold early in 1959. Duke and Pilar spent several days shopping in New York City, where they ran up a $3,200 bill at Saks Fifth Avenue and told the store manager to send it to Bo Roos, who would pay it. Three months later the credit department at Saks sent an overdue notice to Wayne's Batjac office, not-so-politely demanding payment. Duke called Roos and shouted into the phone, "Jesus Christ, Bo, would you please pay the bill. I look like a goddamn deadbeat!" Roos maneuvered through a litany of excuses and apologies, promising to take care of it right away. Wayne mentioned the conversation to Mary St. John, who remembered hearing Ward and Mary Lou Bond express concern about Roos's investment strategies. Duke also recalled a conversation a few months earlier with actor John Howard, who asked him, "Is Bo Roos screwing you like he's screwing me?" He had laughed the comment off as a joke, but somehow the line had now lost its humor.[1]

The more he thought about it, the more concerned he became. He told Mary to go to Roos's Beverly Hills office and take a look at his investment portfolio. Roos tried to stall her, insisting she come back at a more convenient time, but Mary was tenacious, demanding access to the file. What she discovered dumbfounded her. Except for mortgages on some Culver City property and the Flamingo Hotel in Acapulco, the file was empty. Wayne met with Roos several days later and asked a simple question: "Bo, exactly how much money do I have?" "Well, Duke," Roos replied, "not a great deal of cash. Your money isn't sitting in the bank someplace. It's all invested—real estate, various business ventures." As Roos squirmed, Duke became irritated, impatient, and scared. "I know that," he replied testily. "Just tell me how much money I could raise if I had to." Still noncommittal, stalling for time, Roos mumbled: "That'll take a couple of weeks."

Two weeks later, and only at Duke's insistence, they met again. "Well, Bo, how much am I worth?" Evasive and worried, Roos insisted: "It isn't that simple, Duke." Wayne was out of patience. He stood up, slammed his fist on Roos's desk, and screamed: "For Chrissake, I've given you a goddamn fortune over the years. It's a simple question. What the hell have you done with the money?" The charade was finally over. Roos slumped into his chair, put his head down, and confessed: "It's all gone." Duke had his house, his personal possessions, and Batjac—and a few scattered, virtually worthless properties. He stormed out of the office and went straight to see his lawyer, Frank Belcher. Duke thought about the millions he had given Roos. He refused to believe it was gone. His accountants conducted a thorough investigation but discovered no evidence of fraud, just grotesque mismanagement. When Belcher told Wayne the news, Duke just shook his head. "I'll be god-damned," he sighed. "I was sure Bo had stolen it. Nobody's stupid enough to *lose* that much money."

Some of Roos's Hollywood clients made fortunes. Fred MacMurray, for example, kept close tabs on the business manager, calling him every week, scheduling frequent meetings, demanding monthly statements, personally inspecting every investment Roos recommended, and keeping him on a very tight rein. He paid standard commissions and refused to put Roos on any type of expense account. MacMurray was committed to a conservative, long-term investment strategy—blue-chip companies, U.S. government securities, and quality real estate. Concerned about irregularities in Roos's recommendations, MacMurray dumped the Beverly Management Company in 1956. It paid off: When Fred MacMurray died in 1990, his estate was valued at nearly $500 million.

Red Skelton, on the other hand, lost a fortune. Roos managed Skelton's investments, but Skelton did not keep track of the balance sheet. The comedian discovered something was wrong in 1957 when his eleven-year-old son Richard died of leukemia. Expecting a $50,000 payoff on the boy's life insurance policy, Skelton learned that Roos had been regularly borrowing against his clients' insurance policies, investing the money in high-interest commercial paper, repaying the low interest rate policies, and pocketing the difference. The boy's policy paid very little because Roos had borrowed against its equity. Skelton soon learned that Roos played similarly loose with his clients' income taxes. He would take money from their accounts to pay taxes, secure postponements from the IRS, invest the money in his own name, and keep the interest. Along with 10 percent management fees, 10 percent "accountancy fees," and a number of bad investments, Roos lost more than $10 million of Skelton's money.

Like Skelton, Duke never gave his investments a second thought. Roos lost Wayne's money gradually over the course of nearly two decades, dumping it into bad real estate deals, overpriced Mexican hotels, Panama shrimp, brokers' fees, empty natural gas leases, dry oil wells, Hollywood parties, and fees and inflated expense accounts for his Beverly Management Company. Mary St. John remembered that "Roos had a passion for free trips. If Wayne was home for six or eight weeks, Roos would not even call him, but as soon as he was on location, Roos would invent some reason for a visit, and they would talk about nothing of consequence. In 1957, when Duke was in Japan filming *The Barbarian and the Geisha*, Roos spent more than a month in a high-rise Kyoto penthouse, having sex with geisha girls, eating in the finest sushi restaurants, and charging it all to Duke's account." The cotton farm in Arizona would eventually restore Duke's fortune, but in 1959, he was all but broke.

Duke wanted to go to court to recover some of his losses, but attorneys advised him to meet with Roos, mutually decide on an arbitrator, and try to settle out of the public eye. They both trusted Howard Meacham of CBS Television, who agreed to mediate. Actually there was not much to mediate; Roos was all but bankrupt as well. Meacham finally told Wayne: "There's nothing left and it's your fault. How the hell could you give a guy millions and not ask any questions, never follow up on him? If you go to court it's going to make Bo Roos look like a fool and you like a complete ignoramus. Just forget about it and start over."[2]

Two days later, in August 1959, Wayne flew to San Antonio, Texas, to start work on *The Alamo*. The financial catastrophe could not have come at a worse time, since he needed money—big money—to make the movie. For more than twenty years he had dreamed of putting the story of the Texas freedom fighters on film. He loved San Antonio, Texas. It was a city of brown-skinned faces, Spanish sounds, and brightly painted houses, reverberating with the rhythms of its Hispanic past. His favorite area was several historic acres downtown, where modern buildings dwarfed the old adobe mission and presidio.

The Alamo was the place where 184 Texans sacrificed their lives in 1836 during the war for independence from Mexico. On several visits there, Wayne noticed the behavior of the tourists. They acted as if they had walked into a cathedral. They moved along somberly, silently, across the Alamo's hallowed ground. The defenders of the Alamo did not have to die. They could have left without a fight, turning it over to General Antonio López de Santa Anna and scattering across the countryside to live out their lives. But they stood their ground. They were tough men, willing to fight and ready to die for their country.

For years, Wayne had thought about the Alamo. He dreamed of a grand gesture—a movie imbued with patriotism and a love of country, a movie so grand, so oversized, that it would eclipse all previous epics. The story of Texas and the Alamo was perfect—rebels, freedom fighters, outnumbered and beleaguered, sacrifice their lives for the cause of liberty. Linda Crystal, the female lead in *The Alamo*, later recalled, "John Wayne loved *The Alamo* like a man loves a woman once in a lifetime—passionately." And as he had with all his women, Wayne put the movie on a pedestal.[3]

Duke was not the first Hollywood producer fascinated by the Alamo. The Texas rebellion had inspired dozens of novels, beginning with Anthony Ganilh's *Mexico versus Texas* in 1838. The first film version—*The Immortal Alamo*—was produced in 1911 in San Antonio by Gaston Méliès, but its distribution was limited. Five years later D. W. Griffith did for the Alamo what he had done for Reconstruction in *The Birth of a Nation*. Triangle Films made *The Martyrs of the Alamo* in 1916 and rereleased it in 1921 under the title *The Birth of Texas*. Walter Long, who played the leering, sex-starved mulatto in *Birth of a Nation*, played General Santa Anna. Overtly racist, the film portrays Mexican soldiers as uncouth misfits who spent all their time dancing, betting on cockfights, and defiling Anglo women, just as the emancipated slaves had done to southern white women in *Birth of a Nation*. Santa Anna appears as a perverted drug addict prone to debauchery and corruption, and one of the subtitles tells the audience: "Under the dictator's rule the honor and life of American womanhood was held in contempt." The stereotypes were so blatant, the racism so palpable, that Mexican-American audiences in a number of Texas cities boycotted the film. Wayne saw the movie when it played at the Glendale Theater in 1923. Three years later he saw a new Alamo film—*Davy*

Crockett at the Fall of the Alamo—at Loew's Theater in Los Angeles. In this version Davy Crockett and Jim Bowie assume mythic proportions. Sunset Studios produced a B western entitled *The Heroes of the Alamo* in 1936 to take advantage of the national attention afforded the centennial of the siege.[4]

For Wayne no previous version did justice to the story. In September 1948 Patrick Ford, son of John Ford, drafted a preliminary script. By 1950 Duke was in love with Mexico and had been married to two Hispanic women. He refused to portray Mexico and Mexicans as anything less than proud and noble. He was also committed to producing a big-budget film, complete with elaborate outdoor sets and a cast of thousands. Anything less, he maintained, would demean the sacrifice of the Texas freedom fighters. He was determined to avoid the racism and production problems that plagued the previous efforts.

In 1951, after completing *The Quiet Man*, Wayne approached Herbert Yates about *The Alamo*. Yates liked the idea, assuming that Duke wanted to make the film on the studio lot, telling him to take it to a studio screenwriter and schedule a set. But Wayne had something much bigger in mind. During his voyages down the Pacific Coast with John Ford, he had searched for suitable locations, and he had found a small settlement on the Pacific side of Panama that was perfect. Yet the more he talked to Yates about building realistic sets in a believable location and spending millions to produce the greatest movie ever made, the more nervous the tightfisted Yates became. He did not like risks, he did not like novelty, and he hated high-priced epics. "Who the hell is going to pay to see a picture where all the heroes die?" he asked Wayne. Finally, despite all they had been through together, despite the many years during which Wayne could have left but chose to stay at the second-tier studio, his ambition for this great story overcame his loyalty to Republic.[5]

After leaving he made *Big Jim McLain*, but a film about the Alamo was always on his mind. The dream depended on money. At union rates he estimated $70,000 to $90,000 a day to film the movie in Texas, and he thought it would take at least two months of shooting to complete the film. He could film it at half the cost south of the border—perhaps $35,000 a day—where labor unions and extras had a less exalted view of their worth. Late in 1951 he passed up Panama for an ideal site in Sonora, Mexico, and began issuing contracts for set construction. As usual he rushed ahead before he studied the potential problems. When word reached Texas that he was going to film *The Alamo* in Mexico, influential Texans yelped in protest. The Sons and Daughters of the Republic of Texas were up in arms. The latter were the official custodians of the Alamo in downtown San Antonio. For them the old mission was more than a historic site on a tourist map. It was hallowed ground purchased with the blood of heroes. Making a film about the Alamo in Mexico was sacrilegious. Foremost among the rebels were Jesse Jones and Bob O'Donnell. Jones was publisher of the *Houston Chronicle*, the financial developer of the Houston skyline, and the godfather of the Democratic party in Texas. He was in love with money and power, nurtured an incorruptible sense of personal ethics, and gave no quarter to rivals. He once bragged that he had read only one book in his entire life—a biography of Sam Houston. Robert J. O'Donnell was the most powerful individual in the Texas entertainment industry. As general manager of Interstate Circuit, Inc., he controlled hundreds of movie theaters throughout the state. The two men told Duke that shooting *The Alamo* in Mexico would offend every native Texan, and that if he persisted, they would see to it that he would receive no financing from any Texans—individuals or banks—and that the film would not play in any major Texas theater.[6]

Reluctantly—but only temporarily—Duke abandoned his plans again. It was clear that he would have to plan on a Texas location and pay a much higher price tag. Soon the huge success of Walt Disney's *Davy Crockett, King of the Wild Frontier* in 1955 freshly whetted his appetite, but by that time Herbert Yates had a scheme of his own. Wayne's departure after fifteen years at Republic was, of course, the worst blow the studio could have suffered, and, as an actor known for his fierce loyalties, he must have known that his decision would stick in the craw of the miserly yet independent Yates. The studio head suddenly chose revenge over finance and decided to make his own film about the Alamo on location in Texas. He carefully researched Texas history, and his screenwriters built the story around Davy Crockett, Jim Bowie, and William Travis. Sterling Hayden landed the role of Davy Crockett; while Richard Carlson played William Travis; Arthur Hunnicutt, Jim Bowie; and J. Carroll Nash, Santa Anna. They shot the film in Brackettsville, Texas, to take advantage of the buildings on the old cavalry stockade at Fort Clark. Yates released the film in 1956 as *The Last Command*. Though it was flawed by stiff performances from Hayden and Carlson, it broke even, barely, at the box office, and Yates must have celebrated the financially mediocre splurge as a preemptive strike against Wayne's dream. But Wayne was undeterred. He later told Hedda Hopper that Yates tried to "steal the idea. [He] came up with *The Last Command* which was a quickie. Nuff said."[7]

Between 1953 and 1959, Duke made sixteen films, divorced Chata, married Pilar, and fathered Aissa, but his obsession with the Texas freedom fighters did not diminish. He continued to worry about his age, about how long audiences would accept him as a cowboy-soldier-action character. Universal, Warner Bros., Twentieth Century-Fox, and Paramount all offered to coproduce the film, but only if he agreed to star in it, not direct it. But he wanted to direct the film himself: It was an obsession to end all obsessions. Everyone he trusted warned him against the project. Bob Fellows opposed the idea because of the financial risk, and Bo Roos counseled against it because he did not want Duke to try to liquidate his nonexistent assets. John Ford cautioned him about trying to produce and direct a film of such scale. But he was determined, telling a Hollywood reporter:

> My problem is I'm not a handsome man like Cary Grant . . . who will be handsome at 65. I may be able to do a few more man-woman things before it's too late, but then what? I never want to play silly old men chasing young girls, as some of the stars are doing. I *have* to be a director—I've waited all these years to be one. *The Alamo* will tell what my future is."[8]

Finally, in 1956, United Artists gave Wayne the chance he was waiting for. They agreed to invest $2.5 million *and* allow him to direct and produce, but only if he would star as Davy Crockett and sign a three-picture, nonexclusive contract with them. United Artists also wanted Batjac to put $1.5 to $2.5 million into the film. Duke estimated a budget of $7.5 million and knew he would have to raise the rest of the money through private investors. He hoped to come up with $5 million from the outside, which would not require any Batjac money.[9]

While trying to put together the financing, he decided on a location. He liked Yates's Brackettsville. It was a sleepy little Southwest Texas town of two thousand people whose best days had ended after the Indian battles and border wars of the late 1800s. The cattle industry drove its economy, and its high school football team provided the most exciting entertainment in the county. Duke met with Happy Shahan, who offered to let him build the set on his 22,000-acre ranch outside town. They began discussions about the location, which continued for more than a year. Shahan wanted to be the general contractor on the set and to retain ownership of it after filming. Wayne was reluctant to hand over so much responsibility to Shahan, since he had never worked with him. But in September 1957, Wayne gave Shahan what he had wanted. Late on the day of their agreement, Duke met Chato Hernandez, a Mexican with a third-grade education whom Shahan wanted to supervise the set construction. Skeptical of the man's abilities and worried, Duke said to him: "Mr. Hernandez. Do you think you can build the Alamo?" In halting

English Hernandez replied: "Señor Wayne. Can you make a movie?" Roaring with laughter, he turned to Shahan and said: "That's good enough for me."[10]

But he still needed $1.5 million to cover construction costs and another $5.5 million to shoot the film. Perhaps patriotism would help. To Wayne the message of the movie was that Americans needed to be ready once again to take a firm stand against aggression and dictatorship. At the state capitol in Austin, he appealed to Gov. Price Daniel to put him in touch with well-to-do men anxious to make some money in a good cause. Most Texans felt a profound loyalty, indeed a reverence, for Texas and its history, and many shared Wayne's conservative political values. Armed with Daniels's introductions, he approached prospective investors, and the money began to roll in. Oilman Clint W. Murchison wrote out a check for the $1.5 million and told Wayne: "Duke, if you make the movie you say you'll make, I don't care whether I get my money back or not." Another $1 million soon came from Clint W. Murchison Jr. and John Dabney Murchison. I. J. and O. J. McCullough, two Dallas oil equipment men, committed $3 million to the project. Five rich patriots, $5.5 million. With the $2.5 million from United Artists, he had more than enough. The time had finally arrived.[11]

In 1958 Hernandez and his workers started building the set. It was an enormous production. Ironically, given the Daughters of the Republic of Texas's concern about keeping the location on U.S. soil, they hired several dozen Mexicans to make twelve million adobe bricks, which were used to build more than two hundred thousand square feet of permanent buildings, virtually re-creating downtown San Antonio as it existed in 1836. They drilled six deep wells to guarantee a daily supply of 12,000 gallons of pure water and built fourteen miles of heavy-duty tarred roads between Brackettsville and the set. They laid twelve miles of underground water and sewage lines on the four hundred-acre set. In addition Batjac ordered the construction of five hundred acres of corrals for the stock. To make sure that he could get in and out of Brackettsville at a moment's notice, and that each day's film could be developed in San Antonio, Duke even built a large landing strip on the ranch. Michael Wayne remembered they made sure the set would allow for interior shooting, since Duke did not want to have to return to Hollywood and pay "horrendous rates" to rent space at a major studio.[12]

While the set was being constructed, Duke began a search for big-name talent. He wanted Clark Gable to play William Travis. He acknowledged Gable as "the King," but he also made fun of the star, laughing that it was "too bad Gable's brain wasn't as big as his ears." They talked several times, but

Gable could not manage to schedule the film. He had a prior commitment to *The Misfits*, which turned out to be his last film. Instead Wayne hired Laurence Harvey, and then had to calm the troubled hearts of the Daughters of the Republic of Texas, who were not sure they wanted somebody with a British accent portraying their hero. He hoped that Burt Lancaster would be Jim Bowie, but Lancaster was under contract to star in *Elmer Gantry*. He turned to Richard Widmark. Richard Boone, star of the hit television series *Have Gun, Will Travel*, agreed to play Sam Houston. Wayne then, of course, signed his friends and buddies—people like Hank Worden, Chill Wills, John Dierkes, Denver Pyle, Chuck Roberson, and Ken Curtis—for the remaining parts. Patrick Wayne, Duke's second son, and Aissa Wayne, his four-year-old daughter, also received parts.[13]

There were other casting problems. When Sammy Davis Jr. heard there was a part for a black—playing the role of Jethro, Jim Bowie's slave—he lobbied for the role. Davis was interested in broadening his career beyond the song-and-dance man he had been forced to play. Wayne was initially receptive to the idea, primarily because of Davis's star quality, but Duke's Texas investors were less excited. Davis seemed too "uppity" for them, too proud of who he was, too closely associated with the "Rat Pack"–Frank Sinatra–Peter Lawford–Las Vegas crowd. Hollywood was also rife with rumors in 1959 that Davis was having an affair with Swedish actress May Britt, and most Texans had little patience for interracial romance. Duke gave the part to Jester Hairston.[14]

He also had a casting dispute with Michael Wayne, who was coming into his own at Batjac. In his mid-twenties at the time, Michael had good business instincts, and sensed that the torch in the entertainment industry was being passed to a new generation of heartthrobs, many of whom were making the transition from music to films. He was convinced that if *The Alamo* was going to make any money, his father had to tap into the youth market. John Wayne was not so sure. He felt comfortable around the small group who had almost become an ensemble cast to him over the years. He had no choice, of course, for the major roles—he needed proven stars—but the idea of signing a rock star bothered him. Michael prevailed, however, and Duke gave Frankie Avalon, whose song "Venus" had skyrocketed to the top of the Hit Parade, the role of Smitty. Naively hoping that Mexicans would want to see the film, he also signed Carlos Arruza, one of the world's premier matadors, to play an aide to General Santa Anna.[15]

Shooting started on September 9, 1959. He assembled the entire cast and crew and had Father Peter Rogers of St. Mary's Catholic Church in San Antonio deliver a blessing and invocation. The blessing pleased Duke: "O, Almighty God . . . We ask thee . . . that the film 'The Alamo' will not only be the world's outstanding production, but will also be a tribute to the spirit of the men who first built it, who lived in it, who died in it." Then they went to work.[16]

Near the newly built Alamo, Wayne had stocked a small universe. At the suggestion of J. Frank Dobie, the legendary Texas historian, more than three hundred Texas Longhorn steers were gathered from around the state. Dobie also helped Wayne capture Davy Crockett's character. "Dobie once said that Crockett never ate on an empty stomach nor drank on a full," Wayne remembered. "That gave me an attitude of how to make a human being out of [one of] the great heroes." Duke also leased sixteen hundred horses. The permanent cast and crew of 342 people were housed at Fort Clark in Brackettsville, an old U.S. Cavalry installation once used to chase marauding West Texas Indians. Each of the bungalows had been refurbished before shooting began. Costumes for more than six thousand extras had been prepared. The catering outfit kept forty-five full-time workers on the set, and during the shooting they served nearly 190,000 meals. Wayne wanted to make sure everybody was well fed, and he defined well fed in his own protein-rich terms. He ordered nearly sixty tons—120,000 pounds—of steak, roast beef, veal, hamburger, and sausage, as well as nearly 500,000 eggs, 400,000 bottles of milk, and 1.5 million pieces of bread and rolls.[17]

The logistical problems proved to be the easy challenges. Personnel difficulties were not so simple. Duke had heard rumors that Richard Widmark was difficult to work with, and the rumors proved to be understatements. As soon as Widmark signed his contract, Wayne took out an ad in the *Hollywood Reporter*, saying simply: "Welcome aboard, Dick. Duke." But Widmark was nobody's Dick. The next time the two men met, Widmark bluntly said: "Tell your press agent that the name is Richard." Duke was furious. The remark was like "pissing on a friend when he tries to shake your hand." Duke's lips thinned, his teeth and fists clenched, and he slowly, deliberately told Widmark: "If I ever take another ad, I'll remember that, Richard."[18]

Two days after shooting began in September, Widmark burst into Wayne's room at Fort Clark, where Duke was just sitting down to dinner with Pilar and the kids. Widmark wanted out of the film. He felt miscast. Wayne politely told him, "Richard, I want to have dinner with my family. We can discuss this later." Widmark persisted until Wayne got up out of the chair, put his nose in Widmark's face, and told him to get out. But as much as he disliked Widmark, he needed him. If Widmark quit, the whole production would slow down until a new star was signed and a new wardrobe made to order. With location expenses running $90,000 a day, Wayne could not afford it. He went over to Widmark's cabin after dinner, and they got into a shouting match, with Duke threatening a lawsuit if Widmark broke his contract. Widmark relented, but he was difficult on the set, criticizing Wayne in front of the rest of the cast. After three weeks Wayne finally lost his temper and went after Widmark, threatening bodily harm as well as a lawsuit. Both men calmed down after that, but they remained off each other's Christmas lists.[19]

The murder of twenty-seven-year-old actress LaJean Ethridge added a whole new dimension to the pressures of the set. Ethridge—along with her boyfriend, Charles Harvey Smith, and three other men—was part of a troupe of actors making their way through small-town Texas theaters in 1959. They all signed on as extras for *The Alamo*. Wayne was impressed with Ethridge's performance and decided to give her a better part, casting her as the wife of one of William Travis's officers. Instead of paying her scale as an extra, he put Ethridge on salary and got her a membership in the Screen Actors Guild. Jealous of her success, Smith picked an argument with her on the evening of October 11, and she decided to move out of the small house they were sharing. After packing her bags, she returned to the living room and sat down next to Smith to explain why she was leaving. Suddenly he plunged a twelve-inch butcher knife deep into her chest, killing her in a matter of seconds. Her last words—"I love you"—bubbled out through the blood in her mouth. Duke reacted like an egocentric director, shouting: "Jeeeesus Kee-rist. This is all I need!"[20]

The location was also a problem. Frankie Avalon remembered: "I was a street kid. I'm from the neighborhoods of South Philadelphia. When I got to the wide open spaces of Texas . . . I didn't know where I was. I didn't know what to do. I'd never seen anything like that place. I had no idea. To be exposed to the elements of scorpions, skunks, and rattlesnakes. I knew about rats." Hank Worden remembered that "there were something like thousands of rattlesnakes every square mile." The heat was oppressive. In September the temperature was already 84 degrees by 10:00 A.M., and by 3:00 in the afternoon it was a blistering 98. The humidity was terrible, not at all the dry heat they had expected. Decked out in his costume and coonskin cap, Wayne poured sweat, sometimes so profusely that he had to change clothes before going in front of the camera. He had to get rid of the coonskin; it itched so much he almost scratched his forehead raw. He lost eight to ten pounds a day in fluids, and he had to drink water constantly. More than once dehydration left him weak and dizzy, and he suffered from muscle cramps in his legs. The constant sweat also moistened the glue keeping his hairpiece in place.[21]

Worries made the discomforts worse. He worried about everything—the heat, the $90,000-a-day budget, the cast, and producing, directing, and acting in an epic film. Something was always going wrong, always demanding his attention, always requiring a decision. By the end of September he was smoking 120 cigarettes a day. With so much at stake, emotionally and financially, he was in no mood to tolerate mistakes or distractions. On a hot afternoon, during a complicated scene, he was bothered by chatter behind him. Simultaneously shouting and turning around, he exploded: "Jesusfuckingchrist! Shut up back there," only to see that the culprits were a group of habit-frocked Roman Catholic nuns on an excursion to the location. Wayne apologized profusely and returned to the scene. One of the actors recalled: "After the outburst, you could have heard a rat cough."[22]

Perhaps the worst problem of all was the presence of John Ford. In 1950, when Wayne had become serious about taking on *The Alamo,* the press had reported that Ford would help him direct, and the rumor had stalked him for the rest of the decade. Over the years, in Duke's mind the rumor became more pernicious. *The Alamo* was *his* film, and its success would guarantee his future. Having Ford on the set was a no-win proposition. If the film got bad reviews, critics would blame him. If the film was good, critics would attribute its success to Ford. William Clothier remembered Duke confiding in him: "I'm directing this picture; it's my picture, good or bad or indifferent—I'm gonna rise and fall with this film; it's costing a lot of money and I've got the money and I don't want anybody else to run me."[23]

Ford showed up, uninvited but full of advice, soon after the shooting began. Each morning he pulled up a director's chair next to the camera and started giving unsolicited advice. "Goddamnit, Duke, that's no way to play it," he bellowed. "Here, try it this way." Each night, he wanted to eat dinner with Wayne and several stuntmen and then play bridge and tell jokes into the early hours. Ford wanted a return of the John Ford Stock company. He wanted to erase a decade and have all the "boys" dance once again to his music. But all Wayne wanted to do was take a shower, get a massage, have a quiet dinner with the family, and go to bed. He could not confront Ford. As far as he was concerned, Ford had given him a good life, and he could not be disloyal. He followed Ford's nightly script, though it exhausted him and irritated Pilar. She was fourteen hundred miles from home in the middle of nowhere, and John Ford was monopolizing what little time she might have had with her husband.[24]

Duke worried about Ford. The old man was entering the winter of his career, and opportunities to direct were more infrequent. After finishing *Sergeant Rutledge*, he did not have another film project to start. In earlier years Mexican vacations, with Wayne and Bond aboard the *Araner*, had filled the time between films. But now his friends were too busy with *The Alamo* and *Wagon Train*. Ford slipped into a deep depression, hiding out in his room for weeks at a time, refusing to get out of bed. Without exercise, his muscles lost tone. He ignored his hygiene: His fingernails grew long and dirty, his teeth yellowed with plaque and nicotine, and his hair and beard acquired a greasy, unkempt luster. Only on the set could he live again.[25]

Everybody breathed easier when Ford left for the University of Maine to receive an award from the film and drama department. The card games stopped, and Wayne slept more regularly. But two days later, when he was filming a night scene in which Davy Crockett and several Alamo defenders raid the Mexican camp to get beef and supplies, a disembodied voice resounded out of a grove of trees: "You didn't film that right. Duke, you can do better than that." Wayne knew instantly who it was. He grimaced to himself, politely turned around, and said: "Well, Pappy, what do you think I ought to do?" Ford gave him some advice. Early the next morning Duke confided to William Clothier, his cameraman: "I don't know what I'm going to do." Clothier suggested keeping Ford busy with a second unit, and Duke agreed. He told Jimmy Grant to write some additional action scenes and assigned Michael Wayne as Ford's assistant. "That was a rough position my father put me in," he recalled years later, "to try to keep Ford happy. My father said: 'Look, let him do anything he wants, but don't let him talk to any of the principals.' So we did stuff with extras and stock shots, shots of the Mexican army charging and retreating. I worked with Ford every single day, and we had a lot of run-ins. I would never give him the principals, and he always wanted to do something with them. So I had rubs with Mr. Ford." Ford stayed busy for several weeks, even though most of the old man's scenes ended up on the editing floor. Ford returned home at the end of September. Ever polite, and genuinely concerned about his mentor's health, Duke sent him a telegram on October 1, expressing appreciation for the director's help and inviting him back anytime.[26]

Wayne also had problems with Jim Heneghan, the first publicist for *The Alamo*. Duke gave Heneghan a contract for $100,000, or 2.5 percent of the profits, and Heneghan came out to Brackettsville and went to work. The deal soon soured. He brought writers from all over the country out to the set, but

Mary St. John claimed that he started supplying them with booze, parties, and companionship. The writers were showing up on the set hung over and bleary-eyed, late in the morning if at all, and Wayne noticed some strange women coming out of the cabins in the morning. When he found out what was going on, he first confronted, then hit, and finally fired Heneghan. He wanted nothing to do with the sleazy business. The idea of loose women on *The Alamo* set was unthinkable, a sacrilege, a dishonor to history and the men whose blood had been shed. Even though Heneghan filed a lawsuit against him, Duke still paid him the $100,000 fee. He replaced Heneghan with Russell Birdwell, providing a personal fee of $125,000, agreeing to pay all the expenses for Birdwell's offices in New York and Beverly Hills for one year, and setting aside $1 million for radio and television time and newspaper and magazine space.[27]

Laurence Harvey posed no acting problems as William Travis. Duke had known for years that Harvey was talented, but he had been unaware of the depth of his professionalism. One scene proved it. Crockett and Travis are standing next to a cannon atop an Alamo wall. Travis takes a cigar out of his mouth and ceremoniously lights the fuse. But when the cannon fired, the explosion toppled the two-hundred-pound artillery piece off its support frame and onto Harvey's foot, crushing several bones. Knowing that the cameras were rolling, and not wanting to ruin a take, Harvey did not even wince. Duke was impressed. But he found himself avoiding Harvey when they were not shooting. The acclaimed actor, who was bisexual, had developed a huge crush on Wayne, and he made a nuisance of himself, following Duke around like a puppy. Halfway through the shooting Harvey cornered Duke one evening and begged, "Please, Duke. Tonight. Just one time. I'll be the queen if you'll be the king." The proposition irritated Duke, but professionalism, decency, and self-interest outweighed prejudice. Harvey was too important a part of the film to risk offending. Duke awkwardly shrugged off the entreaty and walked away.[28]

The film was a challenge for cinematographer Clothier. He had signed on with Wayne-Fellows in 1952 and became known in Hollywood as John Wayne's cameraman. He certainly knew that "*The Alamo* was the biggest film of my career." He began shooting test footage at Shahan's ranch early in August 1959 and remained there until filming ended on December 20. "Duke knew the script backwards. He knew every line better than the actors did. In the morning we'd have our breakfast together and go out on location and discuss every shot we're gonna shoot that day and figure out which we should start with and when we should do such and such a shot for light." More than once Wayne ruined a Davy Crockett scene because "he had a bad habit of mouthing the other guy's lines to himself. I'd motion to him and he'd go, 'Awww . . .' and we'd cut the camera and start over again. I'll tell you, he was happy when it was over."[29]

Wayne had limits as a director, limits that challenged Clothier and the actors. Dean Smith, a stuntman, thought that Duke was a "very good director" but "at times didn't have a whole lot of patience as he should have, but of course that was his character. If you're a sensitive person you don't need to have somebody to be a little too hard on you." After starting out as a property man and then spending three decades in the business, Duke had a good eye for individual shots. He knew what backdrop would look best on the screen and how to create the desired mood. But he was less talented explaining to other actors how to move in front of a camera. Part of the problem was time. The combined demands of producing, directing, and acting were too much, all but overwhelming him. With the pressure of production costs, he was in a hurry, given to barking orders at cast members and crew rather than taking the time to explain methodically what he wanted. But lack of time was not the only problem. Ken Curtis, a member of his troupe over the years, claimed that "Duke was great at action. But directing actors, I was not that pleased with him. All he told you to do was his mannerisms." But Wayne's mannerisms—the squinting eyes and exaggerated body language—were unique to him, not easily transferred to others. When others acted like John Wayne, their movements appeared contrived.[30]

Wayne and Clothier at first considered filming the movie in a Cinerama format. Cinerama used three projectors, electronically synchronized, to put a film on screen in three sections, creating a magnificent semicircular panorama in theaters adapted to it. Especially useful for films emphasizing landscapes or aerials, it was less so for those with a great deal of dialogue and an emphasis on personal interactions. The first film using the Cinerama technique—*This Is Cinerama*—was released in 1952 and featured aerial acrobatics and roller-coaster sequences. A number of outdoor documentaries followed throughout the 1950s. The action scenes in *The Alamo* were perfect for Cinerama, but Duke worried about distribution problems. Cinerama required specially constructed theater screens. Memories of *The Big Trail* still haunted him. So instead he opted for the new 70 mm Todd-AO film process, which had been used so successfully in *Oklahoma* (1955), *Around the World in Eighty Days* (1956), and *South Pacific* (1958), and did not require expensive theater adaptations.[31]

They spent most of December shooting the final battle scene, which involved blowing up much of the set. Clothier set up five Todd-AO cameras, supervising the cameramen with radio walkie-talkies. Before each scene, he visited with each cameraman, reviewing assignments and blocking out the shot. Duke would often accompany him from camera to camera. Hank Worden remembered his own incredulity watching the synchronized movements of thousands of actors and horses. "I had never seen anything like it."[32]

The original budget of $7.5 million for *The Alamo* proved woefully inadequate. By the time the film was in the can, costs had escalated past $12 million, well over the initial $8 million he had raised from United Artists and the Texas investors. The Yale Foundation kicked in $1.5 million, bringing Duke's total to $9.5. It still was not enough. Duke had to come up with the rest himself. Convinced that it was the most important work he had ever done, and that his country needed the film, Duke put everything he had on the line, pledging his own Alamo salary, taking out a second mortgage on the family estate in Encino and the coop apartment at the Hampshire House in New York, selling property in Mexico, and borrowing against his automobiles and the *Nor'wester*, his yacht. He built so much debt that he could not see a penny of his money until *The Alamo*'s gross exceeded $17 million. He told an interviewer in August 1960: "I've gambled everything I own in this picture—all my money . . . and my soul."[33]

Despite the risk it was right that he put his career on the line, and his soul. After all, *The Alamo* had never been about money. It was too personal, too autobiographical, too cathartic, too much of a personal crusade. Aissa Wayne believed that the film had a great deal to do with her father's decision not to enlist in World War II. "I think making *The Alamo* became my father's own form of combat. More than an obsession, it was the most intensely personal project of his career." He used the film to explain himself—his Cold Warrior passions, lifestyle, failed marriages, and patriotism. *The Alamo* was Duke's confessional, an open letter to 150 million Americans. The film tells more about John Wayne than about Texas in 1836.[34]

While President Kennedy was instructing Americans to "ask not what your country can do for you; ask what you can do for your country," John Wayne, through Davy Crockett, was telling America that it was time "to separate the sheep from the goats," to decide "who's on the right side." The film opens with Dmitri Tiomkin's heroic score, a classic call to arms, and a background narrative: "Generalissimo Santa Anna was sweeping north across Mexico toward them, crushing all who opposed his tyrannical rule. They now faced the decision that all men in all times must face . . . the eternal choice of men . . .

to endure oppression or to resist." Later in the film, when Davy Crockett is talking to his men about staying in Texas and fighting, one of them is reluctant: "It ain't our ox that's gettin' gored." Davy Crockett almost literally evokes the Munich crisis with his reply: "Talk about whose ox is gettin' gored. Figure this. A fellow gets in the habit of gorin' oxes, it whets his appetite. He may come up north and gore yours." For Wayne the only cause that mattered was freedom. In the back room of a San Antonio cantina, William Travis talks to Davy Crockett about "the many unendurable hardships the people have been subjected to under the tyrannical government of this military dictator Santa Anna. We have no rights in the courts, no market for our produce. He has forbidden trade with the north." Crockett responds: "'Republic.' I like the sound of the word. . . . Some words give you a feeling. Republic is one of those words that makes me tight in the throat. Same tightness a man gets when his baby takes his first step, or his baby first shaves, makes his first sound like a man. Some words can give you a feeling that makes your heart warm. 'Republic' is one of those words." *The Alamo* is full of heroes, most of them fashioned in Wayne's image. They are an undisciplined group of rugged individuals from Tennessee and Texas who love freedom and resent authority. They are hard-drinking, fun-loving, hell-raising, carefree men who enjoy the warm bosoms of Hispanic women and hate political tyranny. Davy Crockett's Tennesseans ride hard, play hard, and fight hard.

A scene near the beginning of the movie captures Wayne's vision of manhood. The Tennesseans finally reach San Antonio after a long, hard ride. They are hungry, thirsty, and horny. With Davy's blessing they rush headlong into the nearest cantina and start drinking, dancing, and singing, with Davy right in the middle of it all. The straitlaced William Travis comes into the cantina and asks Crockett for a minute of his time. Davy agrees and hands over his big-busted Mexican dance hall queen to a teenage Tennessee boy named Smitty (Frankie Avalon), telling him: "Well, son, you better start growing up." As Crockett and Travis head for a back room, Davy picks up a full bottle of booze, laughing to Travis: "Talkin's dry business." They pass Smitty, who's dancing cheek-to-cheek, and Davy tells him, "You're learning fast." Finally, just before they reach the back room, Crockett comes upon his friend "Beekeeper" (Chill Wills), who has a Mexican woman sitting on his lap. Beekeeper says to Davy: "I'm resignin' from you. I'm goin' marry up with Conchita here and be the *man* of this house." He then looks Conchita in the eye and demands, "Besame a kiss, señorita." Turning to Davy, he says with a smile, "I toss around a mess of that proud Spanish too." Davy smiles back and says: "Most important part too." Looking back at his señorita, Beekeeper says, almost lustily: "Let's gig a little, mamacita."

Here were the men Wayne always admired—men who were totally, or at least psychologically, unattached. Such men had formed the core of the Young Men's Purity, Total Abstinence, Snooker and Pool Association. Davy Crockett describes the real meaning of American freedom: "People can live free, talk free, go and come, buy or sell, be drunk or sober, however they choose."

They could also marry whomever they chose. Wayne got more explicit in *The Alamo* about his feelings about women. His marriages to Josephine Saenz, Chata Baur, and Pilar Pallete were proof of his attraction to Hispanics, especially younger women, and he illustrated those attachments in the film through Davy Crockett's relationship with Graciela de López (Linda Crystal), a young, beautiful Mexican. Wayne had long worried about how May-December marriages appeared. He was forty-seven when he married Pilar in 1954. She was less than half his age. When Lopez is sexually harassed by an Anglo politician, Crockett comes to her defense, as any real man would, and eventually kills the man. Davy and Graciela fall in love, and when she expresses her affection for him, Crockett smiles and says: "Old buck, young doe. Each has something the other lacks." At the time, in 1960, Wayne's marriage to Pilar was six years old and stable, and he wanted the world to know that all was well.

Redemption for Wayne depended on America's reaction to the film, and he launched one of the most politically conscious advertising campaigns in history. Russell Birdwell orchestrated the production. A native of Del Rio, Texas, Birdwell grew up in San Angelo and Fort Worth and graduated from the University of Texas. He was known as "the P. T. Barnum of advertising" in Hollywood, making a name as the publicist for *Gone With the Wind* but earning real notoriety for *The Outlaw*. Back in March 1941, Joe Breen, head of the Production Code Administration, was tiring of producers' attempts to go beyond the code. In fact he had scheduled his retirement from the administration for June 15, 1941. He wrote Will Hays, head of the Motion Picture Distributors and Producers Association: "In my more than ten years of critical examination of motion pictures, I have never seen anything quite so unacceptable as the shots of the breasts of the character Rio [Jane Russell in *The Outlaw*, produced by the breast-obsessed Howard Hughes]. Throughout almost half the picture the girl's breasts, which are quite large and prominent, are very substantially uncovered."[35]

In front of whomever would listen, including the Board of Directors for the Production Code Administration, Birdwell argued that Hollywood was in love with the female breast, and every studio chief knew it and catered to it. He gathered an extensive collection of cheesecake shots from different studios to prove his point. The board agreed and, after some minor cuts, overruled Breen's decision not to give the film the Seal of the Production Code. Birdwell then turned his attention to selling *The Outlaw* to audiences. Ignoring the trite plot, weak script, and bad acting, he focused on Russell's figure. Distributing revealing photographs to *Life*, and *Look*, and to *Pic*, *Click*, and other picture magazines, he made Russell's breasts national monuments. She became a star even before the premiere of her first film.

For Wayne, Birdwell sold patriotism, not breasts, linking *The Alamo* with the Cold War. He asked Governor Daniel of Texas to declare March 6, 1960—the 124th anniversary of the fall of the Alamo—as "Alamo Day" in Texas, and hoped the governor "would agree to help advertise the film." He asked the Daughters of the Republic of Texas to give John Wayne a special award, perhaps declaring him an "Honorary Hero of the Alamo." He even asked Vice President Richard Nixon to help promote the film, and Nixon, anticipating Duke's support during the election of 1960, readily agreed. "These are perilous times," Duke told Louella Parsons. "The eyes of the world are on us. We must sell America to countries threatened with Communist domination. Our picture is also important to Americans who should appreciate the struggle our ancestors made for the precious freedom we enjoy."[36] If Hollywood was a bellwether for national politics, Duke detected a shift in mood. After Senator McCarthy self-destructed in 1954, the anti-Communist crusade in America started losing steam. HUAC faded into the Washington background. Fear of the Soviet Union and nuclear war actually escalated, especially after the launching of *Sputnik I* in 1956, but the paranoia about domestic subversion abated. Hollywood liberals came out of exile. In the fall of 1959, actor Robert Ryan and comedian Steve Allen became active in the National Committee for Sane Nuclear Policy (SANE) to protest the arms race and America's U-2 reconnaissance flights over the Soviet Union. Wayne did not appreciate the drift. Communism remained, in his mind, as evil and malignant as ever.[37]

When cracks began appearing in the blacklist, especially for unrepentant former Communists, Duke let everyone know how he felt. In May 1960, he publicly criticized Frank Sinatra's decision to hire Albert Maltz, one of the Hollywood Ten, to write a screenplay about Eddie Slovak, the one American executed for desertion during World War II. His meddling incensed Sinatra, especially after the negative press and public outcry forced him to fire Maltz.

Sinatra went into a slow burn over the incident, and he exploded in anger on May 13 at the Moulin Rouge. A number of Hollywood stars had gathered at the nightclub for a hundred-dollar-a-plate benefit for retarded children. The stars came in costume—Wayne in a checkered Western shirt, yellow necker-chief, and white cowboy hat, and Sinatra in an Indian outfit, complete with moccasins, beads, leather shirt and leggings, and a headband with a single feather. Wayne sang a verse of "Red River Valley," and Sinatra crooned "The Lady Is a Tramp," but they almost came to blows when Sinatra kept badger-ing Duke about "minding his own business." Friends had to get between the cowboy and the Indian to prevent a fistfight in front of the children. Publicity about the incident did not bother Wayne; it only advertised his conviction that Communists should not be working in the industry.[38]

At the time, Sinatra was a liberal Democrat backing John F. Kennedy for president. When the fracas occurred at the Moulin Rouge in May, Kennedy had the inside track on the Democratic nomination, and Duke suspected he would be a formidable challenge to Richard Nixon. Kennedy had been a reg-ular visitor to Hollywood since his sister Pat married actor Peter Lawford. Ac-cording to producer Milton Sperling, "Kennedy was a Hollywood figure before he became president. He used to come out here as a senator to meet girls; he was out here looking for ladies and Duke's agent, Charles Feldman was finding them for him. There was no big secret." Hoping to boost Nixon's chances and promote the film, Duke scheduled *The Alamo*'s premiere for San Antonio at the end of October, timing it to coincide with the final stage of the 1960 presidential election.

He was obsessed with the country's fortunes. In July 1960, on the *North to Alaska* set, after eating a thick steak and drinking a bottle of wine, he let sever-al crew members talk him into a poker game. Fueled by laughter and booze, the game lasted well into the next morning. But at 8:00 A.M., the fifty-three-year-old Wayne was on the set, fully costumed and already made up. Filming was delayed by red-eyed stragglers who had missed wake-up calls. When they finally made it to the set, Wayne loudly proclaimed: "Well, here come the kids. I had to tuck them in last night." Under his breath, he added: "The country's going soft."[39]

Much of America agreed with him, and the issue of toughness became a central theme in the presidential election. Wayne enthusiastically supported Nixon for his tough anticommunism. He positively despised the Kennedys for their "lace-curtain arrogance and unctuous liberalism." Liberated from the need to work by their "daddy's money," he believed they were self-serving snobs lusting after power and lacking any moral vision. He called Jack Kennedy a "snot-nosed kid who couldn't keep his dick in his pants." Wayne heard the rumors that Kennedy's Pulitzer Prize–winning *Profiles in Courage* had been ghostwritten by Theodore Sorenson, and he believed them. In July, a week before the Democratic and Republican conventions, he spent $152,000 on a three-page red-white-and blue ad in *Life* magazine, which appropriately appeared in the Fourth of July edition. The message was clear:

> Very soon the two great political parties of the United States will nominate their candidates for President. One of these men will be assigned the awesome duties of the White House. . . . In this moment when eternity could be closer than ever before, is there a statesman who for the sake of a vote is not all things to all men; a man who will put America back on the high road of security and accomplishment, without fear or favor or compromise; a man who wants to do the job that must be done and to hell with friend or foe who would have it otherwise; a man who knows that the American softness must be hardened; a man who knows that when our house is in order no man will ever dare to trespass. . . . There were no ghostwriters at the Alamo. Only Men.

Several times during the next few weeks reporters asked John Kennedy if he thought the ad was aimed at him. Kennedy dodged the question. Wayne later wrote: "I've been told by experts that our gate-fold ad has brought us more than five million dollars worth of editorial recognition—influential, selling space in newspapers, magazines as well as network television and radio shows."[40]

As the opening date approached the patriotic hype became even more exaggerated. "Nobody should come to see this movie unless he believes in heroes," Wayne announced. Then Nikita Khrushchev helped the film. In October 1960 the Soviet premier came to the U.N., took off his shoe and began pounding it rhythmically on the desk, sending the assembly into an uproar. The premier's aggressiveness made front-page headlines. Wayne forgot about his previous year's Christmas gift from Khrushchev, telling Hedda Hopper (who then told the world): "He is always trying to belittle this country, to downgrade it, to sneer and boast and toss out insults and to brawl and threaten. Why don't Kennedy and Nixon take this yelling braggart and boor apart? When Nixon was in Moscow he took him on in his own backyard and made him like it. . . . I'm proud the President of the United States is a gentleman; but I wouldn't care if he walked up and punched Khrushchev in the nose. I'd applaud and holler, 'Attaboy Ike'!"[41]

The San Antonio premiere came at the height of the election campaign and

Khrushchev's antics. It was a gala affair, full of stars and hype, but the reviews of the film disappointed Wayne. He had not expected much from the New York critics, who more and more panned his work. Nor was he worried about the liberal media, whom he was just as certain would be critical. In fact he welcomed their criticisms. The *Southern California Prompter* gave what Wayne considered to be the typical knee-jerk response: "If he is saying that what America needs is about 10 million men with the courage and determination of Davy Crockett, Jim Bowie, and Colonel Travis the point is well taken. It may also occur to some he is suggesting that the easy answer to today's complex problems is to pit this raw courage against Russia's 10 million Santa Annas, the result of which may well be a worldwide Alamo and instead of a shrine we may have only a cosmic incinerator full of ashes. If this is what Wayne is proposing, the defenders of the Alamo were not only brave but smarter than those who speak for them. Their fate was extinction but this was not their purpose." Other reviews, especially in the East Coast newspapers, offered similar warnings. *The New Yorker* accused him of having "turned a splendid chapter of our past into sentimental and preposterous flapdoodle. . . . Nothing in *The Alamo* is serious . . . nothing in it is true. . . . [It] is a model of distortion and vulgarization." *Newsweek* said that the film's "place in history will probably be that of the most lavish B picture ever made. . . . B for banal." *Time* announced: "*The Alamo* is the biggest Western ever made. Wayne & Co. have not quite managed to make it the worst." Unconcerned by such attacks, he and Birdwell planned on using them to stir up controversy and publicity.[42]

But he did worry about the trade papers, and their reviews were mixed. *Variety* claimed that his characterization of Davy Crockett seemed stiff, almost tense, that he acted "like a man with $12 million on his conscience." It *had* been stiff. Linda Crystal recalled Duke's preoccupation. During the love scenes "his eyes were open," she said, "but the shutters were down." A universal conclusion, among critics and the San Antonio audiences alike, was that at 206 minutes *The Alamo* was too long and too boring, especially the first half in which James Edward Grant's wordy script had William Travis expound at length on Jeffersonian values. The second half had a long birthday scene featuring four-year-old Aissa Wayne. *Variety* called the sequence "embarrassing . . . the film momentarily seems on the verge of dissolving into a family musical." At the San Antonio premiere, Ford said that *The Alamo* was "the most important motion picture ever made. It's timeless. It's the greatest picture I've ever seen. It will last forever—run forever—for all peoples, all families—everywhere." After previewing the film, critic John Cutts said:

"May I humbly suggest to Mr. Ford that the film *only* seems to last forever."[43]

Wayne was willing, even comfortable, with political shots, but the film could not be boring or embarrassing—not if he had any hope of getting his money back and establishing his credentials as a director. And he did not want to be the butt of any industry jokes, not as Otto Preminger had been for *Exodus*, the epic film about the founding of Israel. In the spring of 1960, Preminger invited a number of leading lights in the entertainment industry to a prerelease screening. At three hours fifteen minutes into the film, with the audience growing a bit restless, Mort Sahl, the political satirist, stood up from his seat, raised his arms to the heavens, turned to Preminger, and in his best Moses-like voice roared: "Otto, let my people go!" Hollywood was still laughing six months later. Not wanting to be a joke, Wayne flew out of San Antonio the day after the premiere, spent four long days slicing nearly thirty minutes from the film—including the Jeffersonian monologue and Aissa's birthday scene—and released the film to its thirteen scheduled theaters by the next weekend.[44]

Despite bad reviews it was not too soon to write speeches and prepare the publicity campaign for the April 1961 Oscars. *The Alamo* earned $2 million during its first three months, hardly a trifle by 1960 standards, but far from the $17 million Wayne needed to break even, so the Oscars became a crucial make-or-break point. The advertising campaign Birdwell had launched early in 1960 became even more hyperbolic. When *The Alamo* earned six nominations—Best Sound, Best Song, Best Cinematography, Best Score, Best Supporting Actor (Chill Wills), and Best Movie—Wayne approached the awards elections with all the enthusiasm of a reform politician crusading to eliminate graft and corruption.[45]

For Wayne the Academy Awards were a moral battleground. He was concerned about the "garbage" that Hollywood was producing. At a press conference in Hollywood on January 10, 1960, Duke—echoing Will Hays—bellowed: "I don't like to see the Hollywood bloodstream polluted with perversion, and immoral and amoral nuances. Filthy minds, filthy words and filthy thoughts have no place in films." He lashed out against *On the Beach*, an end-of-the-world movie set in Australia after nuclear holocaust, because "the growing defeatist attitude in the Cold War imposed on us by the Soviets is a disgrace, and it is disgraceful that a Hollywood film would reflect such an attitude." He condemned Gary Cooper's role in *They Came to Cordura* (1959) because the film "demeaned" the Congressional Medal of Honor. He decried *Suddenly Last Summer*, starring Katharine Hepburn, Montgomery Clift, and Elizabeth

Taylor, for what he claimed was its depiction of homosexuality, murder, and psychotherapy. *The Alamo*, on the other hand, "is a film made up of men and women who believed that in order to live decently one must be prepared to die decently."[46]

The other nominees for Best Picture dwelled on corruption, greed, and perversion. In *Elmer Gantry* Burt Lancaster played a philandering revival preacher of the 1920s. In *The Apartment*, Jack Lemmon portrayed a gray-flannel-suited organization man who pimped for his bosses. *Sons and Lovers* presented the film version of D. H. Lawrence's novel about a dysfunctional working-class family. In *The Sundowners* Robert Mitchum played a hard-drinking Australian sheep shearer. Elizabeth Taylor secured a Best Actress nomination for her role as a seductress in *Butterfield 8*, and Melina Mercouri won the same nomination for her role as a prostitute in *Never on Sunday*. Shirley Jones's prostitute role in *Elmer Gantry* won her a nomination for Best Supporting Actress.[47]

The sleaze factor was only part of Duke's strategy. *Spartacus,* whose story was untouchable, raised special problems that called for a different attack. Epic films like *The Robe* and *Ben Hur* in the mid-1950s had popularized the Jewish struggle for freedom in the Roman Empire, and *Spartacus*, the story of the slave uprising against their Roman masters, was more of the same. The film was based on a novel by Howard Fast, a Communist party member who had served time in prison. Furthermore, liberal Democrat Kirk Douglas bought the movie rights. As interested as Wayne in "political epics," Douglas detested the blacklist and wanted to make a statement against it with the freedom struggle of the movie's story. He decided to hire Dalton Trumbo, one of the Hollywood Ten, who was still blacklisted but ghostwriting scripts, to do the screenplay. Trumbo had been ghostwriting for ten years, using pseudonyms and the names of other writers to support himself. He wrote the *Spartacus* screenplay as "Sam Jackson." Not once in ten years had Trumbo set foot on a studio lot. Yet Douglas decided to break the blacklist by giving Trumbo screen credit. When he learned of Douglas's decision, Trumbo told him: "Thanks, Kirk, for giving me back my name."[48]

Douglas later wrote that *Spartacus* was about "thousands and thousands of slaves carrying rocks, beaten, starved, crushed, dying. I identify with them. As it says in the Torah: 'Slaves were we into Egypt.' I came from a race of slaves. That would have been *my* family, *me*." The film celebrated the dignity of poor people, the crass materialism of the rich and powerful, social rebellion, redistribution of property, yet, also, individual rights. Douglas premiered the film in New York late in October. Hedda Hopper was enraged, proclaiming that the "story was sold to Universal from a book written by a Commie and the screen script was written by a Commie, so don't go to see it." For similar reasons the American Legion organized a boycott against it, urging its millions of members: "Don't See *Spartacus*."[49]

The Alamo was just as much a political statement, but it was the WASP version of the liberation epic. If the slaves of *Spartacus* were, as some critics suggested, "Marxists in togas," the Alamo defenders were patriots in coonskin hats. Wayne knew that *Spartacus* would provide Academy Award competition for *The Alamo*. The July Fourth advertisement, "There Were No Ghostwriters at the Alamo," in *Life* was doing double duty for Wayne. He meant it as a sideswipe at John Kennedy but also at Dalton Trumbo and Kirk Douglas. He wanted Hollywood to know how he felt about using a Communist to write a movie about revolution.[50]

In March Wayne's plans went awry. Birdwell's advertising campaign spun out of control, triggering an embarrassing backlash. Nobody was really surprised. Just when the 2,300 members of the Motion Picture Academy were about to vote, Wayne and Birdwell spent a final $150,000. They placed huge ads in *Variety* and the *Hollywood Reporter*, asking: "What Will Oscar Say to the World This Year?" Just below the bold type was a portrait of the embattled Alamo fortress. When a reporter asked him how he felt about *The Alamo*'s chance for Best Picture, Duke replied, "This is not the first time 'The Alamo' has been the underdog. We need defenders today just as they did 125 years ago this month." But Hollywood insiders wondered how *The Alamo* could have secured a Best Picture nomination when it had not managed nominations for Best Director or Best Actor or Best Actress or Best Screenplay. They wondered if Wayne's efforts to tie Best Picture voting for *The Alamo* into good citizenship had intimidated the academy. Otto Preminger, disgusted with the Birdwell hyperbole, took out his own full-page ads for *Exodus*, urging Academy voters to "judge the picture, not the ads." When columnist Dick Williams of the *Los Angeles Mirror* criticized the blatant appeal to patriotism, claiming that "one [could] be the most ardent of American patriots and still think *The Alamo* was a mediocre movie," Birdwell took out four-page ads in *Variety* and the *Hollywood Reporter* lambasting him. Wayne, however, sensed that Birdwell's rejoinder had a petty, desperate look, and John Wayne was *never* petty. He complained to the *Los Angeles Times* that he was "sickened by all this belittling." Michael Wayne in 1992 described the Birdwell campaign as an example of "unbelievably poor taste."[51]

T hen Chill Wills managed to make *The Alamo* a laughingstock. At the age of fifty-seven, after a lifetime of B westerns, Wills knew the movie was his only chance for an Oscar. Short of money, he hired a publicist who was a newcomer to the business. W. S. "Bow-Wow" Wojeiechowicz had been a prison physical education teacher before marrying and divorcing Sheilah Graham, the Hollywood columnist. She introduced him to a few insiders, and in no time Bow-Wow went independent. Wills was one of his first clients. Bow-Wow placed a full two-page ad for Wills in the trade papers listing hundreds of members of the academy, and said: "Win, Lose or Draw, You're Still My Cousins, and I Love You All." Groucho Marx, whose name was on the list, could not resist taking out his own ad a few days later: "Dear Mr. Chill Wills: I Am Delighted to Be Your Cousin, but I Voted for Sal Mineo."[52]

Bow-Wow did not get the joke. On March 24, 1961, he bought another full page in the *Hollywood Reporter*. Against a backdrop of *The Alamo* cast, complete with an enlarged photo of Chill in buckskins and coonskin cap, was the message: "We of the Alamo cast are praying—harder than the real Texans prayed for their lives in the Alamo—for Chill Wills to win the Oscar as the Best Supporting Actor—Cousin Chill's acting was great." It was signed: "Your Alamo Cousins." Texas newspapers erupted with outraged letters to the editor condemning the comparison, and Duke placed his own disclaimer ads in *Variety* and the *Hollywood Reporter*: "I wish to state that the Chill Wills ad . . . is an untrue and reprehensible claim. No one in the Batjac organization or in the Russell Birdwell office has been a party to his trade paper advertising. I refrain from using stronger language because I am sure his intentions were not as bad as his taste." Groucho Marx had the last laugh, proclaiming that "for John Wayne to impugn Chill Wills's taste is tantamount to Jayne Mansfield criticizing Sabrina for too much exposure."[53]

Birdwell sensed disaster. He believed that the Wills ad had ruined everything. When Wayne returned to Hollywood from Africa, where he had been filming *Hatari*, he knew the film was doomed. "It was in horrible taste," Birdwell later told Maurice Zolotow, "like taking a bucket of fecal [matter] and throwing it over a beautiful rose. . . . From the morning the ad showed up, there was just a pall, like something had hit the town. . . . I guess some people enjoyed our discomfiture." In truth many people were amused. The Screen Writers Guild gave *The Apartment* its 1961 Best Picture Award, and in his acceptance speech, Billy Wilder told thirteen hundred people: "Keep praying, cousins. We hope Oscar will say the right thing this year." Wilder's prayers worked better than Chill Wills's. On Oscar night *The Apartment* won Best

Picture. Peter Ustinov beat out Chill Wills for Best Supporting Actor for his role in *Spartacus*, and the only Oscar for *The Alamo* went to Dmitri Tiomkin for Best Score. Despite all of Wayne's rhetoric, all his denunciations of "gutter movies," sleaze carried the day. Elizabeth Taylor and Shirley Jones won Oscars as prostitutes, and Burt Lancaster won Best Actor as the flawed preacher. Over drinks on Oscar night, Duke lamented to a friend: "Sonofabitch. After all this work I thought we'd win something." *The Alamo* died a slow death at the box office. A year later it had grossed only $14 million.[54]

United Artists was the only real winner. For several decades the studio had signed independent producers and distributed films. Since it had no studio overhead, profit margins were the healthiest in the industry. *The Alamo* was a perfect example of the studio's strategy. By 1970, after United Artists had rereleased it several times, the film had earned more than $16 million in foreign and domestic rentals, making it one of the more profitable films in Hollywood history—number 117 on a list of the 400 top-grossing movies. Duke was able to pay off the Murchisons, McCulloughs, and the Yale Foundation. *The Alamo* did as well at the box office as such other hits as *Exodus*, *Mr. Roberts*, *Battle Cry*, *Old Yeller*, and *Some Like It Hot*. But never, at least not during Wayne's lifetime, did *The Alamo* go past the $17 million he needed to make any money from it himself.[55]

Not only did the film not make Wayne money, it also did not help to elect Nixon. Nor was it the greatest movie ever made. It was, of course, a near superhuman effort. Duke had financed, produced, directed, and starred in a Hollywood epic, doing what few others could have done. But in spite of his best efforts, Hollywood still did not view him as a talented director; he was going to have to continue to be a cowboy-soldier-action star for as long as he could get roles. His financial troubles were doomed to continue. He also lost his best friend. A week after *The Alamo* premiered in San Antonio, Ward Bond suffered a massive heart attack in a Dallas hotel room. The bad years had begun.

18

In Harm's Way

The loss of his fortune and the public relations disaster at the 1961 Academy Awards were crises for Wayne. For weeks he was angry, embarrassed, and sleepless. Still, his professional anxiety was not an emotional disaster. He had never confused wealth with happiness. "Money never made an unhappy person happy," he told Mary St. John, "and I'll be damned if losing money is going to make me miserable. Hell, it's just money. I can make more." In fact he had already begun to do just that. After wrapping up the editing on *The Alamo* in the spring of 1960, he agreed to make *North to Alaska*, to be directed by Henry Hathaway, as part of the three-picture deal he had signed with Twentieth Century-Fox in 1958. The studio was paying him $200,000 a year, and he was in the third year of the contract.[1]

Wayne was still in the middle of editing *The Alamo* when the cast and crew went on location in May 1960. *North to Alaska* was shot at Point Mugu, California, a two-hour drive from Los Angeles. On days when Hathaway did not need him on the set, Duke worked at the Batjac offices in Beverly Hills, putting the finishing touches on *The Alamo*.

North to Alaska was not the easiest film to make. When Duke arrived in Point Mugu, he learned to his dismay that a script did not even exist, even though Charlie Feldman had assured him everything was ready. Feldman represented Buddy Adler, head of production at Fox, as well as John Lee Mahin and Martin Rackin, two of the three men responsible for the screenplay. He was also living with Capucine, the beautiful French actress whose career he was trying to promote. Feldman had promised her the part of Angel. He told Buddy Adler to hire Richard Fleischer, who had just finished making *Compulsion*, as the director. Fleischer was thrilled. "My heart gave a little jump. John Wayne! Doing a picture with John Wayne was important."

But when Fleischer asked for a copy of the screenplay, Adler said it was not ready. He asked for a draft. The first draft was not completely finished yet, Adler told him. Fleischer requested an outline. Again Adler apologized. Fleischer contacted Mahin and Rackin, and they were pleasantly optimistic, promising to iron out the wrinkles by the end of the week. But he came away from the meeting unnerved. Neither writer could even tell him the plot summary.

Feldman invited Fleischer to his Bel-Air home a week later to discuss the project over lunch. Capucine was there. "Her English, like her experience," Fleischer remembered, "was minimal. In fact, she hardly spoke at all. I felt that in her case still waters ran shallow. Although she was beautiful, there was no spark of personality to back it up. I wondered how this bland, rather shy beauty was going to portray a spirited prostitute in an Alaskan whorehouse opposite John Wayne. It worried me." When he mentioned reservations about directing the film, suggesting that "I haven't decided whether I want to do this picture," Feldman promised to get him a plot summary the next day.[2]

But the next day there was no plot summary, only Feldman's booming announcement: "You're all set with John Wayne. He's approved you, just like I said he would." Angry about being manipulated, Fleischer backed out of the film. "I told you not to set me with Wayne before I'd made up my mind. Well, I've made up my mind. Next time you speak to him you can tell him that I'm not doing the picture." Feldman visibly stiffened. "If he hears that you don't want to do it . . . that there isn't a screenplay . . . we're liable to lose him." Feldman leaned forward in his chair, puffed a cloud of cigar smoke into the air, and chilled Fleischer to the bone: "And I can tell you one thing, we're not going to lose him." Fleischer faced a painful dilemma—make a bad picture and hurt his career, or defy Feldman and ruin it. Feldman was powerful, one of the men who decided who worked in Hollywood and who did not. Fleischer did not want to offend him. He sought counsel from his friend Phil Gersh, an agent with Famous Artists. Gersh provided a way out. "You know how nuts Charlie is about Capucine?" he told Fleischer. "Of course," he replied. "All you have to do is call Buddy Adler," Gersh told him, "and tell him you don't think she's right for the part. You'll be off the picture in two minutes." Fleischer made the call. In two minutes he was off the picture. Feldman then told Duke that Fleischer did not want to make a John Wayne film. Instead he hired Henry Hathaway, another of his clients.

Hollywood writers went on strike early in 1960, before Hathaway had a completed script. Strikes by the various guilds were not uncommon. Writers commonly complained about credits and residuals, and always wanted more money. But the 1960 writers' strike was also another sign that the Hollywood left was coming out of its Red Scare closet. As the most left-wing of the industry's craft guilds, the Screen Writers Guild had taken the brunt of HUAC and the MPA's anti-Communist crusade in the 1950s, and for more than a decade, writers had assumed a very low political profile. Kirk Douglas's decision to give Dalton Trumbo screen credit for *Spartacus* spelled the end of the blacklist. After a decade of forced political exile, Hollywood liberals were ready to reassert themselves.

With the political battle lines forming, Duke proceeded to make *North to Alaska*. Buddy Adler promised Hathaway he would finish the script himself, but he took off for London before completing it. When shooting began, Hathaway had to improvise all the way. The filming went slowly. "Then the writers' strike came along," Wayne told a *New York Times* reporter, who spoke with him during one of the long delays. "I guess the studio thought the strike would be ended before we started the picture. All I know is, I'd go broke if I tried this in an independent production." Bedecked in sunglasses and swimming trunks, his skin bathed in tanning lotion and reclining on a beach lounge, Ernie Kovacs, a costar in the film, had a different perspective: "This is great. I've been here since 9 this morning and we're behind schedule, so I haven't even put on my costume. I didn't do anything during the actors' strike and now I'm back at work and I'm still not doing anything. It's a great way to make a living."3

Somehow Hathaway muddled through. He wrapped up the *North to Alaska* shooting in mid-August 1960, edited the film in September, and released it early in November. A lighthearted slapstick comedy, complete with several knock-down-drag-out brawl scenes, *North to Alaska* nonetheless manages to hold true to John Wayne's screen persona. The film tells the story of Sam Mc-Cord (John Wayne), George Pratt (Stewart Granger), and Pratt's little brother Billy (Fabian), three partners who strike it rich in the Alaska gold rush of 1900. Pratt had been postponing marriage, telling his fiancée in Seattle to be patient until he discovered the mother lode. McCord, an unattached man's man, cannot understand Pratt's obsession with a woman. "I've never met one yet," he tells McCord, "that was half as reliable as a horse." McCord later remarks: "My only politics is anti-wife." With Pratt protecting the gold mine from sleazy claim jumper Frankie Canon (Kovacs), McCord heads for Seattle to fetch Granger's fiancée and bring her to Nome. He arrives too late: She has married another man. Following an any-woman-will-do philosophy, McCord purchases some time in a Seattle brothel, meets Angel (Capucine), a high-class prostitute, and offers her the chance to set up housekeeping in Nome. Angel is skeptical, telling McCord: "I'm selling, not buying," but, under the impression that she will play house with McCord, who treats her decently, she agrees to go.

North to Alaska continues the redemption-of-a-prostitute theme Wayne started in *Stagecoach* (1939). Hating people who look down on others who are doing them no harm, he gave Claire Trevor respectability in *Stagecoach*, and she fell in love with him for it. In the *Sands of Iwo Jima* (1949), it was Wayne himself who had had to insist that his character not have sex with a prostitute. In *North to Alaska*, McCord and Angel have a few days to kill before the steamer sails for Nome, and they visit some of his old friends. At a picnic of Scandinavian families, several "proper" wives publicly humiliate Angel. She decides to leave. McCord accompanies her and, his voice dripping sarcasm, tells the other women: "I bid you good-bye and am sorry you don't find us worthy to sit on your lousy grass." Angel is enchanted with him. McCord fears marriage and commitment, but he eventually falls in love with her. The film ends predictably with claim jumpers punished, hard work rewarded, and love triumphant.[4]

Reviewers liked the film. *The Hollywood Reporter* said the film "plays for laughs, and in its purely male, boisterous way, it gets a good many of them. It is a thoroughly enjoyable film." *Variety,* too, was positive, though more reserved. "*North to Alaska* . . . is a sort of easy-going, slap-happy entertainment that doesn't come around often anymore in films, a product that wins friends without influencing people. . . . The Henry Hathaway production must be accepted in absolutely the right spirit to be fully appreciated." It was. The film grossed more than $10 million and turned a nice profit for Twentieth Century-Fox.[5]

North to Alaska helped put money in Duke's depleted accounts, but money was soon the least of his problems. In the strapped months of 1959 and 1960, Wayne had frequently told Mary St. John: "At least, I still have my family, my friends, and my health." But soon Wayne's friends and his health began to disappear. Grant Withers was the first to go. They had been close friends for thirty years and fellow members of the Young Men's Purity Total Abstinence and Snooker Pool Association. But while Duke had become a superstar,

Withers had turned into an incompetent drunk, chronically broke and out of work. After five failed marriages, he was a lonely alcoholic. On the evening of March 26, 1959, Withers wrote a note asking forgiveness "for letting my friends down. It's better this way." He swallowed a handful of barbiturates and washed them down with a bottle of vodka. Wayne wept when he learned of Withers's death, blaming himself for not being sensitive enough when it might have mattered.[6]

But it was Ward Bond's sudden death on November 5, 1960, that hit Wayne hardest. It seemed as if the two had grown up together. Their friendship went back to USC football days and their work on *Salute*. Both men were at the pinnacles of their careers. Duke was basking in the glow of *The Alamo*'s San Antonio premiere, and Bond was the star of television's top-rated *Wagon Train*.

Bond did not handle his long-awaited stardom very well. After a long dry spell in the 1950s, when his strident politics had cost him friends and jobs, *Wagon Train* gave him delusions of grandeur. He reveled in the attention, hobnobbing with conservative millionaires like Clint Murchison of Texas, supporting such superpatriotic groups as the John Birch Society, and, like a starving man confronted with a free buffet dinner, accepting every offer of a meal and every invitation to a party. He ignored doctors' warnings to slow down. He did not just star in *Wagon Train*, he managed every element of it, from casting to the final editing, all the while smoking, drinking, and eating too much. To control his ballooning weight and stay awake through long days, he popped "amphetamines as if they were candy."[7]

During the last days of his life, Bond was in Dallas to make a personal appearance at the half-time show of a Cowboys-Rams football game and discuss politics with Clint Murchison, owner of the Cowboys. They badmouthed John F. Kennedy, convinced one another of a deepening Communist conspiracy, and discussed ways of bringing America back to its senses. It was typical Bond, all pure talk. When he returned to his room at the Baker Hotel, he suffered a massive heart attack. Duke found out when Mary Lou Bond called from Dallas. He flew there immediately to accompany the body back home and delivered the eulogy at Bond's funeral, nostalgically remembering: "We were the closest of friends, from school days right on through. This is just the way Ward would have wanted it—to look out on the faces of good friends. He was a wonderful, generous, big-hearted man."[8]

Duke was on the boat that dumped Bond's ashes into the Catalina Channel. Bond's will stipulated a burial at sea because "I loved lobster all my life, and I want to return the favor." Duke chuckled at the probate settlement, under which Bond willed him the shotgun with which Wayne had accidentally wounded him years before. Later that evening, after coming home from the reading of the settlement, Wayne sat in the living room and watched that night's episode of *Wagon Train*. The program was especially poignant. Back in August, for "old times' sake," Bond got Wayne to appear in it as Gen. William Tecumseh Sherman. Ford had frequently ridiculed Bond for prostituting himself in a weekly television series, and when he heard that Duke had signed on for one episode, he quipped: "I taught him better than that. I've given up on Bond, the big, ugly, stupid gorilla, but I thought Duke had more intelligence." Within a few days, Bond had talked Ford into directing the segment, which was titled "The Colter Craven Story." On November 23, when the show ended and the credits appeared, Wayne turned to Pilar and said: "There will never be another Ward Bond. I remember telling him, a hell of a long time ago, that he was too damn ugly to be a movie star. But I was wrong, Pilar. He was beautiful where it counted—inside." Wayne wept uncontrollably, his body convulsing and shaking in huge sobs of grief. The funeral rituals were over, the raucous stories about Ward Bond had been told and retold, and life was supposed to return to normal. But Duke was slow to recover. Mary St. John remembered: "I had never seen him so preoccupied, so subdued, so quiet, so depressed. He lost fifteen pounds over the next two weeks because he didn't want to eat. It was as if someone had cut out his heart."[9]

Soon after the funeral, he left for Tanganyika in East Africa to shoot *Hatari!*, directed by Howard Hawks. Pilar and the children made the trip with him. When Hawks had approached him in the summer about doing the film, Duke readily accepted, even though Leigh Brackett's screenplay was pathetically short on plot. In fact, the story of African game hunters who capture wild animals for sale to major zoos around the world had no plot at all. Sean Mercer (John Wayne) leads a crew consisting of "Indian" (Bruce Cabot), "Pockets" (Red Buttons), and Kurt Mueller (Hardy Kruger). They spend half of their time, in fifteen-minute segments, chasing zebras, elephants, monkeys, giraffes, wildebeests, and white rhinos. When the crew is not capturing wild animals, they are back at the hunting lodge playing cards and flirting with Anna Maria D'Allesandro (Elsa Martinelli) and Brandi de la Corte (Michele Girardon). But Duke had trusted Howard Hawks since *Red River*.

It was not the best of times to be halfway around the world. He was depressed when he left Encino. Until Bond's death he had been carefully planning a prank. He wanted to get Bond over to Tanganyika for a cameo appearance. Wayne planned a scene in which Bond would chase and subdue a rhinoceros. Duke asked cameramen Russell Harlan and Joseph Brun to take as much film as they could, hoping to get at least one decent still of Bond's rear end alongside the backside of a rhino. Duke would then have the photograph enlarged to poster size and carry it around to Hollywood parties, taking bets on whether Bond or the rhino had the biggest butt. Bond was trying to schedule a week off from *Wagon Train* to make the trip when he died.[10]

Duke was also in the midst of worrying about Russell Birdwell and *The Alamo*'s Oscar campaign. He tried to perform some damage control from East Africa, but there was little anyone could do to stop Chill Wills. All Duke could do was apologize afterward.

In spite of everything, the months in East Africa lifted Wayne's spirits. The Serengeti Plain of the Great Rift Valley in Kenya and Tanganyika, with its vast flatlands surrounded by low, dry mountains, possessed an austere beauty not unlike southern Arizona, where Hawks had filmed *Red River*. But there was also a frontier quality to central Tanganyika. Wayne had played in a make-believe wilderness all of his life, but the Serengeti was the real thing. Noble Masai warriors, disdainful of the white intruders, herded their cattle as they had done for hundreds of years. The landscapes were vast, the colony's potential unlimited. A handful of British settlers living in East Africa were ready to do to the land what millions of their American cousins had done to the American West. Wayne felt young again. He was unsympathetic with the Tanganyikan nationalists' attempt to throw off British imperialism. When Julius Nyerere, the nationalist leader, took control of an independent Tanganyika in December 1961, Wayne was prophetic. He told Mary St. John that Nyerere's half-baked socialist schemes would ruin the country. "The whole damn place won't be worth a shit in ten years." A decade later, with Tanganyika (joined with Zanzibar since 1964 and known as Tanzania) in political and economic turmoil after Nyerere had imposed a dictatorship and nationalized major economic assets, Wayne told a reporter from *Life* magazine: "Your generation's frontier should have been Tanganyika. It's a land with eight million blacks and it could hold 60 million. We could feed India with the food we could produce in Tanganyika. It could have been a new frontier for any American or English or French kid with a little gumption! But the do-gooders had to give it back to the Indians!" Up until the middle of the twentieth century, most Americans would have endorsed Wayne's view—and indeed, Tanganyika could quite possibly have served as a breadbasket to the world. But in the 1960s and 1970s, such thoughts could hardly have been farther from acceptance.[11]

Hatari! premiered in May 1962. Even without a story line, the film did well. Hawks improvised many of the animal chase scenes, and Wayne refused doubles during the stunts, insisting on being strapped into a chair atop a Land Rover and lassoing wild animals himself. The chase scenes were real, as were the rhinos charging the hunters, ramming the jeeps and land rovers, and almost dumping Duke out of his mobile perch. David Bongard, film critic for the *Los Angeles Herald-Examiner*, praised what he called the "thrilling and un-believable bit of photography engineered by producer-director Howard Hawks and cameraman Russell Harlan." Audiences agreed. By the end of the year, *Hatari!* had grossed more than $14 million, almost exceeding *The Alamo*'s take and doubling investors' profits.[12]

But six weeks after Duke returned from Africa, he lost another friend. For years Bev Barnett had worked as Wayne's publicist and alter ego, advising him about Hollywood politics and the risks of the business. Soft-spoken, some-what frail, and hard of hearing, Barnett was the antithesis of his cohort of Hollywood publicists. He was given to understatement, and the Hollywood press corps knew his releases could be trusted. During the late 1940s and early 1950s, when Duke was active in the alliance, Barnett had helped him pro-mote his career in spite of his controversial politics. They were never drinking buddies—Barnett rarely touched the stuff—but Barnett was one of the few people whom Duke trusted implicitly and absolutely. Wayne later remarked: "God, I miss Bev. His death is so hard to take."[13]

Despite *Hatari!*'s success, Wayne's image and his future seemed in doubt. *The Alamo*, neither a box-office smash nor an artistic triumph, was not going to be a stepping-stone to a career as a director. The future worried him. Wayne's generation—Hollywood's leading men of the 1940s and 1950s—were passing from the scene. Humphrey Bogart died in 1957, and he was fol-lowed by Tyrone Power in 1958, Errol Flynn in 1959, Clark Gable in 1960, and Gary Cooper in 1961. Jimmy Cagney retired, and Cary Grant announced that 1962 would be his last year in films. Duke claimed that he could not af-ford to retire or to die. To make a living and recoup his fortune, he had to work. The problem was to reconcile his age with his image. At fifty-four, he was too old to play a romantic lead and a rugged cowboy-adventure hero. He needed roles that would preserve his image as a strong man who righted wrongs but at the same time soften that profile with wisdom and maturity.

The Comancheros, the last of his lucrative three-picture deal with Twentieth Century-Fox, was the first of those films. In June 1960 Duke took Pilar and the kids to Moab, Utah, for the location. It was like a reunion. Jimmy Grant wrote the screenplay, reducing Paul Wellman's complicated novel *The Co-mancheros* to a 107-minute film. Patrick Wayne, Aissa Wayne, Bruce Cabot, Bob Steele, Edgar Buchanan, and Jack Elam all had roles. Alfred Ybarra did the art direction, Cliff Lyons took care of the second-unit shooting, and Bill Clothier was behind the camera. Duke enjoyed the location—its orange and yellow hues, sculpted sandstone mountains, shallow river-cut canyons, and vast landscapes. Moab reminded him of Monument Valley, one hundred miles due south. Pleasant memories of better days comforted him.

Set in Texas during the early 1840s, the film tells the story of a Texas Ranger Jake Cutter (John Wayne) who teams up with an itinerant gambler, Paul Regret (Stuart Whitman), to foil a Comanchero gun-running operation. *The Comancheros* opens with Wayne arresting Whitman in Galveston, hand-cuffing him to a horse, and setting out for New Orleans, where Whitman is to stand trial for murder. Texas audiences guffawed at Grant's careless script, because it appears that Wayne and Whitman go from Galveston to New Orleans by way of West Texas. There is no sign of the 400 miles of lush, green timberland and swamps separating Galveston and New Orleans. When Cutter learns that Regret is not a murderer but had killed a man in a duel, he recruits him into the Texas Rangers. Together they set out to find the dreaded Comancheros—renegade whites supplying weapons to the Comanches. The Indians are on the warpath, burning farmhouses, killing livestock, and perpetrating heinous atrocities against innocent white settlers. Cutter and Regret go undercover as gun merchants themselves, infiltrate the Comanchero camp, and finally see to it that a combined force of cavalry and Texas Rangers wipes out the rogue operation, restoring peace to the frontier.

Duke's most formidable challenge during filming was director Michael Curtiz. Actor Eddie Albert once accused Curtiz of loving "horses better than actors. He would treat them likewise." But at the age of seventy-two, Curtiz had lost his ability to direct. *The Comancheros* would be his last film. On the set, he was very ill, frail, and forgetful. George Sherman, the producer, could see a financial disaster in the making. Curtiz did not have the energy to coordinate the script with individual scenes, remember actors' names, or express himself coherently. Sherman asked Wayne to take over many of the directing chores, but to do it discreetly, if only to preserve Curtiz's self-respect. He agreed. Although the film's credits did not acknowledge his contribution, he did most of the real work. Curtiz died a few months after the October 1961 premiere.[14]

The Comancheros did well at the box office. Duke believed it could be a model for other roles. He had no romantic interest in the film. Ina Balin, who played the female lead as the daughter of a Comanchero leader, falls in love with Regret and eventually betrays her father. Wayne's love interest with her was purely vicarious. With her long black hair, parted in the middle and tied up in the back, Balin looked like Pilar Wayne and exuded self-confidence and Latin beauty. Not coincidentally, her character was named Pilar. When they returned from location to Encino, the real Pilar was pregnant. She gave birth to a son—John Ethan Wayne, named after Ethan Edwards from *The Searchers*—on February 22, 1962. If Duke could be a mature father, why not a mature male lead?[15]

On the set of *The Comancheros*, a few weeks of dealing with Michael Curtiz's problems left Duke grateful for his own health. On a hot day in August 1961, he and Mary St. John were working on some Batjac correspondence during a break in *The Comancheros* shooting. "What the hell," he told Mary. "The sun's still going to come up tomorrow morning whether I'm pissed or depressed. I'm gonna get up with it and get on with my life." The fact that movie offers were coming from every direction helped his mood. Earlier in the summer, Duke had signed a ten-picture deal at Paramount, which included a $6 million advance. Most of his money problems evaporated. During the course of the next thirty months, he starred in *The Man Who Shot Liberty Valance*, *Donovan's Reef*, *McLintock!*, *Circus World*, and *In Harm's Way*.[16]

The most important of those films, at least to cinema historians, was also the most difficult for Wayne. John Ford directed *The Man Who Shot Liberty Valance*, filming most of it on a soundstage in the fall of 1961. It was not a typical Ford western. The great outdoor canvases of *She Wore a Yellow Ribbon* or *The Searchers* were replaced by black-and-white contrasts and interior sets. On the surface it follows the traditional Western formula of good versus evil. Liberty Valance (Lee Marvin) is a brutal gunman, self-indulgent and ruthless; Tom Doniphon (John Wayne) is a local rancher committed to integrity, honesty, and independence; and Ransom Stoddard (Jimmy Stewart) is an attorney determined to bring civilization and law and order to the town of Shinbone. The plot revolves around an archetypal struggle between Valance and Stoddard—between random brutality and social stability. In the end the mild-mannered but determined Stoddard finds himself facing a gunfight with Valance on a darkened Shinbone street. Doniphon, knowing Stoddard will lose, hides off a side street and, at the moment Valance and Stoddard draw, shoots Valance dead. Everyone in the town of Shinbone believes Stoddard did it. And on the basis of that mistake, Stoddard becomes a U.S. senator.

The film contains all the classic tensions central to American mythology—

East versus West, individual versus community, and wilderness versus civilization. The Western genre had always placed those moral contrasts in a static historical context, in which civilization and wilderness coexisted permanently and in which every man could choose between them. But in *The Man Who Shot Liberty Valance*, Ford used the closing of the frontier to try to resolve an unresolvable tension between the two. No longer idealizing the frontier, he wanted to portray the disappearance of the Old West and its integration into the larger society. But it was not simply a matter of the triumph of good over evil. Tom Doniphon, always ready to resort to violence and gunplay to resolve problems, albeit for good causes, is as much an anachronism as Liberty Valance. The triumph of Ranse Stoddard represents the destruction of the frontier villain as well as the frontier hero.[17]

Wayne was uncomfortable with the role. "Ford was a monster on the set," actor Ken Murray recalled. "He was an ogre; I was scared of him." He was particularly nasty to Wayne, making his life miserable. Historian Ronald Davis speculates that Ford was upset that Duke had not used him more on *The Alamo*. The old man was probably jealous of Duke's success as well. Between takes one afternoon, Duke casually suggested a scene change to the director. In front of most of the cast and crew, Ford lost his temper, screaming to Wayne: "Jesus Christ, here I take you out of eight-day Westerns, I put you in big movies, and you give me a stupid suggestion like that!" Ford also ridiculed his failure to enlist during World War II, reminding him again and again that Woody Strode, who played Doniphon's companion Pompey, had served his country. Wayne went into a slow burn. At one point, he almost came to blows with Strode. During the scene when Tom Doniphon and Pompey are racing back to the ranch house after learning that Doniphon's girlfriend Hallie (Vera Miles) has fallen in love with Ranse Stoddard, Wayne actually lost control of the horses. Strode recalled: "John was working the reins, but he couldn't get the horses to stop. I reached up to grab the reins to help him, and John swung and knocked me away. When the horses finally stopped, he fell out of the wagon. I jumped down and was ready to kick his ass." At this point Ford saw a disaster brewing. The last thing he needed was a fistfight between the two. Woody was forty-seven at the time and Duke fifty-five, but Strode still had the body of the UCLA football player he had been twenty-five years before. Wayne would lose the fight, and the delays in shooting would cost hundreds of thousands of dollars. "Woody, don't hit him!" Ford pleaded. "We need him!" Ford stopped shooting for a couple of hours so both men could cool off.[18]

Years later Duke complained to Dan Ford about how difficult the film had been for him. "He [John Ford] had Jimmy Stewart for the shitkicker hero, he had Edmund O'Brien for the quick-wit humor, and he had Andy Devine for the clumsy humor. Add Lee Marvin for a flamboyant heavy, and, shit, I've got to walk through the goddamn picture." He could not get a handle on Tom Doniphon. Lee Marvin's role as Liberty Valance was crystal clear, as was Jimmy Stewart's. But Doniphon seemed an enigma. Later in his career, in such films as *The Cowboys* and *The Shootist*, Wayne again would play anachronisms, but he was not ready for such a role in 1961. When Mary St. John said that the role was a complicated one, full of ambiguity, Duke replied: "Screw ambiguity. Perversion and corruption masquerade as ambiguity. I don't like ambiguity. I don't trust ambiguity."[19]

Most critics at the time had similar problems. The *Variety* reviewer felt that Liberty Valance "falls distinctly shy of its innate story potential, and this will bother the more discriminating screengoer." Hazel Flynn of the *Hollywood Citizen-News* clearly wanted to praise the film but struggled to say, "*Liberty Valance* is Ford if not perhaps at his greatest then at least at his middle best." The *Hollywood Reporter* liked the film but missed the point—"The story is a lusty one set in a raw frontier territory." But *Liberty Valance* grew in stature as the years passed. In 1986 Tag Gallagher hailed it as a "masterpiece" that represents "John Ford at the apex of his career." Critic William Pechter wrote in 1971: "The uniqueness of *The Man Who Shot Liberty Valance* consists in its bringing into explicitness what has for so long lain beneath the surface." Ford, the older man, was ahead of the *zeitgeist* in a way Wayne never could be.[20]

In November 1961 Wayne accepted a cameo in *How the West Was Won*. A saga filmed in three-lens Cinerama, it was an old-fashioned but expensive Hollywood blockbuster designed to lure audiences away from their television sets and back to movie theaters. It worked, earning more than $12 million in rental revenue from theaters, one of the best takes up to that point in Hollywood history. Ford directed a sequence of the film, and he asked Wayne to reprise the role of Gen. William T. Sherman, whom Duke had played on *Wagon Train*. He enjoyed the two days in Paducah, Kentucky, working and reminiscing with Ford.[21]

Duke then did another cameo, this one for Darryl F. Zanuck's *The Longest Day*, a black-and-white film depicting the Allied invasion of France on June 6, 1944. Accepting the role was a measure of revenge. During the furor over *The Alamo*, Zanuck, who opposed independent production, had remarked to the press, "I have great affection for Duke Wayne, but what right has he to write, direct, and produce a motion picture? Everyone is becoming a corporation. Look at poor Duke. He's never going to see a nickel for his film and he put all his money into finishing *The Alamo*." The comment infuriated Wayne, who exploded to Pilar: "It's s.o.b.'s like Zanuck that made me become a producer. Who the hell does he think he is, asking what right I have to make a picture? What right does he have to make one?" When, a year later, Zanuck offered $25,000 to play Lt. Col. Benjamin Vandervoort, a tiny role requiring only two days of shooting, he turned it down, claiming that he just did not "have the time." Zanuck called back four hours later, upping the offer to $50,000. He still did not have the time. Zanuck kept calling and Wayne kept declining. Suddenly, when Zanuck offered $250,000, he found the time. "What the hell," he chuckled to Pilar. "It may be highway robbery, but it serves the bastard right."[22]

On the set of *How the West Was Won*, Ford and Duke also finalized plans for *Donovan's Reef*, the last film they would make together. Thirty-six years had passed since they met at Fox in the summer of 1926. Hollywood now hailed Ford as its most talented director and Wayne its most popular star. But at age sixty-seven, time had caught up with Ford. Biographer Andrew Sinclair described *Donovan's Reef* as "not so much a film as a farewell to the *Araner* and a way of life that Ford could no longer support." Upkeep on the yacht was steep, and sailing was rigorous. For more than a quarter of a century, he used the yacht to escape Hollywood's politics and revel in the companionship of his closest friends. Now, in July 1962, he prepared for what perhaps would be one last voyage, and one last film with Duke.[23]

Ford wanted to make the most of the trip. *Donovan's Reef* was filmed in Hawaii, on the island of Kauai; Pappy invited Duke and Lee Marvin and their families to join him en route. Marvin remembered the trip as "summer fun, his [Ford's] last return to paradise." Ford had moored the *Araner* in Honolulu since 1954. With his admiral's flag hoisted on the mast, he enjoyed sailing it into Pearl Harbor and past every navy ship anchored along the way, since protocol demanded that each ship's commander pipe his crew and dip the colors. Ford loved every minute of the attention.

Ford had not been on the island twenty-four hours when he learned that Paramount had pulled the financing from *Donovan's Reef*, although they still agreed to distribute it. He decided to produce the film himself, even though a screenplay did not exist. Ford rejected Jimmy Grant's first draft and fired him. He then asked Frank Nugent to come up with something quickly. "The result is what you saw on screen," cameraman Bill Clothier said. "I suppose you've got to blame the Old Man for that. It was just plain bad judgment." Lee Marvin, at his boozy worst in 1962 and still years away from Alcoholics Anonymous, was often so hung over in the morning that shooting had to be rescheduled. Elizabeth Allen, the female lead in the picture, remembered one night when a smashed Lee Marvin removed every stitch of his clothing, climbed up on the bar at the Kawaii Hotel, and performed a hula. Shorter-tempered than usual, and no longer himself intellectually, Ford was more irritable than ever. Wayne, very protective of Ford and aware that the old man was slipping, again almost became assistant director. Ford took a particular dislike to actress Dorothy Lamour—until she had had enough. "Look, Mr. Ford," she reminded the director. "I didn't ask for this part. You asked for me. I've made a lot of money for this studio in years past, and I don't have to take this treatment from you or anyone." Later Ford came to her room to apologize. "That man could charm the apples right off of a tree," Lamour claimed.[24]

Donovan's Reef was released in June 1963. The setting is a South Pacific island—Haleokaloa—in the early 1960s. During World War II three navy men were shipwrecked on the island and finished the war fighting guerrilla skirmishes with the Japanese. Paradise bewitched two of the men—Michael Patrick "Guns" Donovan (John Wayne) and "Doc" William Dedham (Jack Warden)—who decided to live there after the war. "Guns" opened a bar known as Donovan's Reef and built a successful business shipping goods between the local islands. Dedham abandoned his family and a wealthy shipping business in Boston to stay on the island. He threw in his fortunes with French Catholic missionaries serving on Haleokaloa, built a hospital there, and married the local Polynesian princess. They had three children. Thomas "Boats" Gilhooley (Lee Marvin) stayed in the navy but returned to the island every December 7 for a fistfight with Donovan. Amelia Dedham (Elizabeth Allen) suddenly arrives at Haleokaloa hoping to find her long-lost father living in a state of moral depravity, which would allow her to seize control of the family shipping business. Instead, she discovers that he is a dedicated physician, revered by islanders and missionaries alike. In an attempt to conceal the fact that Dedham has three half-white, half-Polynesian children, "Guns" Donovan pretends to be their father. Eventually the truth comes out, but by that time Amelia has reconciled with her father and fallen in love with Haleokaloa, Donovan, and the three children. In a predictable ending Donovan and Amelia agree to marry, after which Guns takes Amelia over his knee, gives her a good spanking to establish his role as the one who "will wear the pants in the family," and then kisses her passionately.

The film was not Ford's best. It lacked the energy, tension, and creative genius of his earlier work. *Donovan's Reef* reflected his favorite themes—Catholicism, family, Irish culture, and the confrontation between white society and an indigenous people—but they seemed out of place in the South Pacific. The drunken brawls; broad masculine humor; and rejection of eastern values are transplanted artificially from the Old West to a tropical paradise, and much is lost along the way. The *Hollywood Reporter* considered it "trivial material for such weighty moviemakers as producer-director John Ford and star John Wayne." Philip Scheuer of the *Los Angeles Times* was more negative. Ford and Wayne had regressed to "the slambang hoakum of their western years, with the difference that they have simply picked up and transported their fighting men, along with process plates and color, to the South Seas. . . . the trick is to keep so much happening all the time that we won't notice that the screen—and a lot of other things—have gone fuzzy on us."[25]

Ford wrapped up the Hawaii shooting on *Donovan's Reef* in August 1962, and the Waynes returned to Encino. It was hardly a fitting end to a long and often glorious collaboration. Late in September the Waynes headed to Arizona to shoot Andy McLaglen's *McLintock!* for Batjac. It was almost a home movie. Michael was producing, Patrick had a lead role, Aissa had a bit part, and Pilar was on location. Chuck Roberson, Duke's favorite stuntman, played the town sheriff, and William Clothier, another old friend, worked the camera. Bruce Cabot had a small part as well. During his long friendship with actor Victor McLaglen, Duke had watched McLaglen's son Andy grow up, and seeing the "boy" as a director was a pleasure. Ford even showed up for a few days to direct when McLaglen became ill. Stephanie Powers, one of the female leads, remembered Ford's arrival on the set. "It was like a caricature. I promise you, he pushed Duke aside and pushed Maureen aside, pushed everybody aside, and walked over to Bill Clothier, put his hand on him and said, 'Let's go to work, Bill.' I will never forget that day, because it was so unbelievably dramatic. There was never anything about John Ford that was normal or human."[26]

But what Wayne enjoyed most about *McLintock!* was the chance to team up again with Maureen O'Hara. They had first worked together in *Rio Grande* in 1950. John Ford noted the chemistry between them, on- and offscreen, and two years later signed them for *The Quiet Man*. Ever since those months on location in Ireland in 1951, Duke had harbored a special fondness for O'Hara. Smart, gifted, beautiful, strong-willed, independent, with a developed, raucous sense of humor, she was Wayne's ideal, the only woman he had ever met who could more than hold her own in his world. She could laugh, drink, and curse with a beguiling Irish charm that Wayne found almost irresistible. Duke was especially fond of the mudhole scene in *McLintock!* The script called for a town brawl on the edge of a huge, fifty-foot hill with a mudhole at the bottom. Dozens of people were to slide down the hill and into the muck during the fighting. To get ready for the scene, the crew lined the hill and the pond with gunite, an epoxy used in swimming pools. They then covered the gunite with lubricated, oil-drilling-rig mud to make the hill especially slippery. But the first stuntman slipped, tumbled, and rolled down the hill, landing headfirst and putting a fifteen-stitch gash in his scalp. The other stuntmen began demanding hazard pay to complete the scene.[27]

With a disgusted smirk on his face, Wayne stood up at the top of the hill and shouted: "Well then, I guess that means I have to do it, you white-livered chicken shits! It's about as dangerous as diving into a swimming pool, and Maureen and I will prove it, won't we, Maureen?" Dressed in a green velvet gown with yellow feathers, O'Hara turned to stuntman Chuck Roberson and said, "That old bastard wants me to slide down the hill with him, but I won't do it, and I don't give a damn what he says until you say it's safe." He told her it was safe if she kept her head up and slid down on her backside. According to Roberson, O'Hara looked at the stuntmen and tongue-in-cheek scolded them: "That's good enough for me. A bunch of chicken bastards, aren't you." She then turned to Wayne and said: "Hell yes, I'll do it, and I'll beat you into the mud." Duke laughed uproariously, took her by the arm, and beamed. "That's my girl. You boys heard the lady, now get out of the way, and we'll show you how to earn your stunt pay." Down the hill they went.

O'Hara was one of the few women on earth with whom Wayne felt completely comfortable, and whose company he would go out of his way to keep. He had fallen in love with Hispanic women whose demeanors were passive and demure, and marital problems developed as soon as they acquired and expressed a more powerful sense of self. Maureen O'Hara's sense of self was as well developed as any woman around. Duke called her "Big Red" or "Herself." More than once, especially during bad times with Chata and Pilar, Duke mused with St. John about what married life might have been like with O'Hara. "It was a friendship that never, fortunately, turned into marriage," St. John said. "They are the strongest two people I have ever known. They would have been like oil and water as man and wife." But *McLintock!* oozes with the magic between John Wayne and Maureen O'Hara.[28]

Yvonne De Carlo, who played the handsome widow Louise Warren, was a late addition to the cast, and Jimmy Grant had to do some last minute scrambling to fill out her part. De Carlo, a veteran actress, was married to Bob Morgan, a stuntman Wayne had known and worked with for years. During filming of *How the West Was Won*, Morgan had accidentally fallen under a moving train, suffering multiple fractures and losing a leg. His days as a stuntman were over. When Duke found out about their financial straits, he insisted on giving De Carlo a well-paying role in *McLintock!* Chuck Roberson recalled in his autobiography: "If Bob had been able, right then, I was damn sure Duke would have found a part for a one-legged man. . . . Somehow he managed to lend a hand without damaging anyone's sense of dignity."[29]

Grant based his screenplay on William Shakespeare's *Taming of the Shrew* but changed the locale to late-nineteenth-century Texas. George Washington "G. W." McLintock (John Wayne), a land and cattle baron, rules the town of McLintock like a paternalistic feudal lord. Katie McLintock (Maureen O'Hara) is his estranged wife, a feisty, strong-willed woman who prefers the more urbane, sophisticated East to the dusty, uncivilized West. Their daughter, Becky (Stephanie Powers), returns from a private school education, and Katie hopes to find her thoroughly easternized. G. W. wants Katie back, but only on his terms; he has no intention of abandoning McLintock for city life and its noisy crowds and effete men. The film reflects Duke's and Grant's attitudes toward big government as well as, inadvertently, the contradictions inherent in the government's encouragement of frontier land-grabs and the antigovernment individualism that resulted. When a group of homesteaders tells McLintock that the government has given them land, G. W. booms back: "The government never *gave* anybody a thing." Later in the film, when the federal government promises to relocate a band of Comanches to a reservation and to provide them with all the necessities of life, G. W. nods approvingly when the Indian chief rejects the offer, insisting that "charity is for widows and children, not for men." G. W. hires Dev Warren (Patrick Wayne), one of the homesteaders, who promptly thanks him "for giving me a job." McLintock takes umbrage, thundering back: "I don't give away anything. I hire men! You will work hard, and I will pay you for it. You won't owe me a thing, and I won't owe you a thing!" Like *Donovan's Reef*, another Grant comedy, the film ends with Katie falling in love with her husband after he administers a spanking, and Becky McLintock falls in love with Dev Warren after he spanks her. They all decide to live in the West.

McLintock! was a Batjac production scheduled for distribution by United Artists, and it was Michael Wayne's debut as a producer. With a budget of $4 million—all of it Duke's money—Michael had to deal with a cast and crew of several hundred people, manage two thousand head of cattle, negotiate daily use of Southern Pacific Railroad lines; work with director Andrew McLaglen and such stars as Duke, Maureen O'Hara, Yvonne De Carlo, Stephanie Powers, and Chill Wills; and supervise set construction and location shooting in Tucson, Nogales, and Benson, Arizona. Each day on location ate up more than $50,000, and Michael demanded an account for every penny. At the end of one day's shooting in Nogales, Wayne went over to his friend Ralph Wingfield's ranch for dinner. Commenting on Michael's business acumen, Wayne told Wingfield: "Goddamnit, Ralph, that kid of mine runs a tight ship. He's all business and no nonsense. He's gonna pull this off. Shit, I should have let him invest all of my money instead of Bo Roos." Michael brought *McLintock!* in within budget projections. Most reviewers loved the film, and it won the National Screen Council's Boxoffice Blue Ribbon Award as the best new film in December 1963. Audiences agreed. *McLintock!* took in more than $10 million in domestic and foreign rentals, turning a nice profit for Batjac and establishing Michael Wayne's credentials as a producer.[30]

Wayne did not make any movies between January 1963, when Batjac finished filming *McLintock!*, and September, when the location shooting for *Circus World* began, except for a two-day cameo role in *The Greatest Story Ever Told*. Playing a Roman centurion witnessing the crucifixion of Christ, Duke received $25,000 for looking up at the cross and saying: "Truly, this man was the son of God." George Stevens, the director, shot the scene three times. Displeased with Duke's delivery on the first take, Stevens told him to "put a little more awe into the line." When the cameras rolled again, Duke grinned up at the cross and, his voice exaggerating a Western accent, drawled out: "Aawe, truly this man was the son of God," giving everyone on the set a good laugh. The third take worked.[31]

By summer it was time to return to full-time work. Duke had dreamed for years of sailing across the Atlantic, but his 75-foot yacht *Nor'wester* was too small for such a voyage. In 1962 he sold the *Nor'wester* and purchased the *Wild Goose*, a 135-foot converted U.S. navy minesweeper. Since Frank Capra's *Circus World*, his next film, would be shot on location in Spain, he had the perfect excuse. In September 1963, he sailed the *Goose* down the coast of Mexico, mooring at Acapulco for a week of fishing and relaxing. Merle Oberon hosted a party for the Waynes. They continued down the coast to Panama to visit the Arias brothers. Duke sailed the *Goose* through the Panama Canal and across the Caribbean to Bermuda, where he put Pilar, Aissa, and

John Ethan in a hotel. The Atlantic crossing was too risky. They stayed in a hotel until Duke called from the Azores, assuring them that the trip had been a success and telling them to come to Lisbon. Ralph and Marjorie Wingfield joined them on the *Goose*, as did Skip Hathaway, Henry's wife. Bill and Ardis Holden came aboard in Majorca. Together they sailed the north shore of the Mediterranean until he received a call from Madrid with the news that *Circus World* was ready to shoot.[32]

"I looked forward to making a . . . film with John Wayne," Capra wrote in his autobiography. "For years he [Ford] needled me about using Cooper, Gable, and Stewart, but never Wayne. I had kept him in mind, because I was sure that in that big chunk of solid man there was the depth and the humanity of another Mr. Deeds, a Mr. Smith, or a John Doe." But sadly Capra and Wayne never got the chance to work together.

Capra later came to think that Duke's loyalty to Jimmy Grant had pulled his career into an artistic rut. Samuel Bronston, the producer, signed Grant to do the screenplay, and Capra wanted to have it in hand when he left for Spain in the spring of 1963. When Grant had not even delivered a story line in time, Capra tried to pressure him. But Grant went to Spain, met with Capra, and insisted:

> there is no use writing anything until Wayne gets here. Duke makes his own pictures, now. So relax, fella. When he gets here, he and I will knock you out a screenplay in a week. All you gotta have in a John Wayne picture is a hoity-toity dame with big tits that Duke can throw over his knee and spank, and a collection of jerks he can smash in the face every five minutes. In between, you fill in with gags, flags, and chases. That's all you need. His fans eat it up.[33]

Capra wanted nothing to do with this rut. Grant's screenplay, he feared, would be "cheap, trashy burlesque." He started working on a script of his own, one emphasizing character development and plot consistency. The story revolved around a circus master in 1910 who loses everything when a ship carrying his combined circus and Wild West show sinks on its way to Europe. Capra wanted to portray John Wayne as a beleaguered but determined man who triumphed over a personal disaster. He finished writing on March 27 and showed a draft to Grant, who flew into a rage. "I have full authority to accept or reject any script material," he told Capra, "and your script is a piece of shit." Capra could see no way out of the impasse. "I cannot possibly make a picture up to Bronston's standards out of the Grant version," he wrote home to a friend. "I have very high hopes for the Capra version. But if Grant prevails, I will reluctantly step out of the picture and return to Bronston the $50,000 paid to Frank Capra Productions." Sure enough, Jimmy Grant prevailed. Wayne was not going to cross an old friend. When the *Wild Goose* docked in Lisbon in October 1963, Grant left Madrid, spent a few days with Duke, and produced a script in a week, just as he had promised. Rita Hayworth and Claudia Cardinale provided the "big tits," and the script had the requisite "jerks" for Duke to "smash." Samuel Bronston, an independent producer with his own studio in Madrid, faced a simple choice: John Wayne or Frank Capra. He picked Wayne and replaced Capra with Henry Hathaway. Capra later wrote, "What I didn't realize was that when one took on Duke Wayne, you took on a small empire . . . and part of that empire was James Edward Grant. . . . [He] was something new to me—a writer who attached himself to a male star and then functioned as that star's confidant, adviser, bosom playpal, babysitter, flatterer, string-puller, and personal Iago to incite mistrust between his meal ticket and film directors."[34]

Wayne had looked forward to working with Rita Hayworth, but he found her as insufferable as her character in the film. Hayworth played a has-been, guilt-ridden trapeze artist in *Circus World*, a woman whose role in the accidental death of her aerialist husband turned her into an alcoholic. Off the set she seemed just the same. Temperamental and egocentric, she was chronically late and frequently unsure of her lines. She may already have been suffering from the Alzheimer's disease that eventually killed her, but nobody on the cast and crew knew it. After a single glass of wine or mug of beer, her speech was slurred, her clothing disheveled, and she turned into a drunk whom Wayne detested. Far worse, at least as far as Duke was concerned, were her manners. Hayworth was rude and condescending to the crew and the locals. He went out to dinner with her only once. She was nasty and petulant with the waiters, embarrassing Duke, who tried to make up for it by smiling, tipping generously, and handing out autographed cards. On the way home from dinner, he told Pilar and his daughter Aissa: "Never think anyone is better than you, but never assume you're superior to anyone else. Try and be decent to everyone, until they give you reason not to."[35]

Duke had bigger problems with *Circus World* than Rita Hayworth. The film almost killed him. He played Matt Masters, a circus owner barnstorming across Europe, and the script called for a spectacular fire in which Masters risks his own life to save the circus animals. When Wayne found out how Hathaway was going to compose the scene, he cabled Chuck Roberson, his stunt double, and demanded: "Get your rear end over here." But Roberson was on location with John Ford, making *Cheyenne Autumn*, and the old man could not afford to let him go. Duke did the tent-fire scene himself. The shooting took five days. On the last day the fire got out of control, forcing the entire crew into a panicky retreat from the set. Duke was the only one who did not get away. In the commotion and the smoke, he did not see the evacuation, and he stayed with the scene, hacking his way through the fire with an ax. When he could smell his own hairpiece burning and could no longer breathe because of smoke inhalation, he finally fled. All through the night, he coughed violently, spitting up blood-specked phlegm. That night Pilar started hounding him to go see a doctor.[36]

Stardom carried other risks. By 1963 he owned the most recognizable face in the world. He attracted crowds everywhere. Usually fans were polite, satisfied with his engaging smile and one of the autographed cards Duke kept in his pocket. But occasionally groups of fans became unruly, unpredictable mobs. One morning during the *Circus World* shooting, Duke invited eight-year-old Aissa to join him for a morning stroll through a small village on the outskirts of Madrid. Three men recognized him immediately and started shouting "John Wayne! John Wayne! Duke! Duke!" attracting dozens, and then hundreds. The crowd closed in, grasping at their hair and clothes. Within a few seconds, they pressed between Duke and his daughter, and she was soon lost in the crowd. Terrified, Aissa began screaming for help, and Duke shouted at the top of his lungs: "Get off! Get off! Get the fuck off!" Only when he flung a handful of autographed cards into the air did the crowd scatter momentarily, and Duke then snatched Aissa into a store, whose owner quickly locked the door and called police. Aissa remembered: "I wished we had never set foot in Spain. I wished that my father was not so monstrously famous."[37]

Hathaway finished most of the location filming on *Circus World* before Christmas, and after the holidays the cast and crew spent six weeks in London shooting interiors. The *Wild Goose* sailed to Acapulco, and in March 1964, with the interiors done, the Waynes rejoined the boat there. Duke hoped for a peaceful, relaxing voyage up the Pacific Coast, but it was not to be. On March 21, the *Wild Goose* anchored near Cabo San Lucas at the tip of Baja California. Four crew members—Efrem Montez, Daly Davies, Eduardo Zamora, and Raoul Torres—wanted to go ashore for the San Lucas Fiesta. They asked Peter Stein, the *Goose's* captain, if they could take a twelve-foot skiff into town. The water was choppy, and he told them to take the little boat ashore and hire a taxi into town. Against Stein's orders, to save cab fare, they took the skiff over six miles of water to town.

They returned early Sunday morning after a night of drinking, and instead of hugging the shoreline and coming around a large peninsula, they headed as the crow flies, into deep water. On the way back Raoul tripped and fell overboard, and when the others tried to pull him back on board, the skiff capsized. One of the men drowned immediately, and two others died several hours later as they tried to swim to shore. Only Montez, who clung to the skiff until morning, was rescued. Duke spent the next several days with morticians, travel agents, and funeral directors. Even though alcohol and youthful hubris had been the culprits, he took the deaths personally.[38]

Not only the *Circus World* trip ended in disaster; the movie proved to be a failure as well. According to Martin Ritt: "Hathaway knew he had made a piece of shit." When it was released at the end of the year, critics noted gaps in the plot and incomplete characterizations, but they reserved their sharpest barbs for Paramount's decision to release *Circus World* in a Cinerama format. For its touted big-screen virtues, the process had never adapted well to nonepic movies. *How the West Was Won*, the first Cinerama film with a story line, had been a great box-office success, even though audiences complained about the blurred wobble of the film at the point where the three screens met. The three-projector technique was abandoned later in 1962 and replaced by a new single-lens Cinerama technique, but its definition and focus were still not sharp enough.

Circus World premiered at the new Warner Hollywood Cinerama Theater. Except for the tent-fire scene, most of the film's scenes focused on individual actions not requiring any panoramic sweep of a camera. Forcing it into the Cinerama mold gave it a stretched-out look, as if the audience were viewing it through a slightly distorted lens. One critic characterized *Circus World* as a film in which the director was like the "Prince attempting to fit the glass slipper on the foot of Cinderella's stepsister." The box office reflected the problems. The film barely recouped its costs.[39]

I n the 1960s Duke did not have the luxury of turning down bad roles. He made such weak films as *North to Alaska* and *Circus World* and accepted cameos to make up for Roos's financial disaster. He made it out of his financial straits, as someone with his phenomenal starpower certainly should. The professional rut, however, was more confining. How could he redefine the singular persona he had built for so long?

More deeply, why was it only now, after nearly thirty years in the business playing exactly the same character, that Capra and others talked of a "rut?"

Wayne's popularity with his traditional audience was not ebbing; except for *Circus World*, each of his recent films had done well at the box office. But the country was changing. John Kennedy in the White House and the rise of the civil rights movement added luster to Hollywood liberalism. The success of films like *The Apartment, Sons and Lovers, Never on Sunday*, and *Elmer Gantry* heralded a new era in Hollywood. Barry Goldwater was beaten handily by Lyndon B. Johnson, and cultural critics continued to rise.

Duke had little patience with them. In the fall of 1962, he appeared on a television talk show in Chicago, where *Sun-Times* columnist Irv Kupcinet hosted a discussion about America. Wayne was on the panel, as was Herman Finer, the distinguished sociologist at the University of Chicago. When Finer commented that "American heroes are really American legends," Wayne got irritated. When he complained that "my wife and daughter can't even walk the streets at night anymore," Duke edged to the front of his seat. And when Finer said: "I'm a college professor and I can barely make a living; if it weren't for Social Security, I don't know what I'd do," Duke had had enough. He leaned into Finer's face and shouted: "The people who developed Chicago didn't know whether they were going to be alive the next day, or whether their kids would be chopped up by Indians, or whether they could raise enough food and develop this place for you. And now you're whining, sitting in your easy chair over at the university and teaching kids this philosophy." If Duke had stopped there, the program might have survived without editing. But Mary St. John, who had accompanied Duke on the trip, remembered his scathing critique of academics: "You professors kiss ass for years to get a Ph.D. and tenure. Then you spend the rest of your life trying to change the values of eighteen-year-olds. How pathetic!" Finer later remarked: "Duke feels pretty strongly about these things."[40]

Beyond the problems of his age, temporary financial difficulties, changing Hollywood tastes, and the resurgence of American liberalism, a bigger threat loomed. In the age of Vietnam, when the moral superiority of anticommunism edged into the hell of a stalemated proxy war, how could America celebrate its cowboy hero? And what was John Wayne's place in the new era?

In the spring of 1964, just when his bank accounts were flush again, Duke faced more personal challenges—first the near deaths of his brother and son, and then the beginnings of his own ill health. Bobby and Michael were nearly killed in an automobile accident. Bobby had been barhopping in Burbank on May 26, 1964, and along the way he picked up Sonia Grant, a twenty-eight-year-old woman looking for a night on the town. Michael Wayne and his secretary, Jeanne Seech, had been working late at Batjac, and when they finished they decided to have a drink together. The two couples ran into each other, and Bobby convinced the others to visit a few waterholes around town. Speeding erratically, Bobby sideswiped an oncoming car; the collision totaled both vehicles and reversed their directions. Seech suffered a fractured pelvis and internal injuries; Grant ended up with a severe brain contusion and a collapsed lung; Bobby broke his leg and collarbone, had his chest crushed, went into shock, and had to undergo cardiac resuscitation to survive; and Michael spent weeks in the hospital recovering from a broken leg, a blood clot on his lung, and a bad case of pneumonia. Duke's relief that they survived soon gave way to anger. His screen persona was nothing if not wholesome, and he hated unseemly rumors about his family.[41]

Duke's own odyssey with hospitals began a few days later. In June 1964 he underwent a physical, not at Pilar's behest but because Paramount needed to insure him for *In Harm's Way*, a World War II film costarring Kirk Douglas and directed by Otto Preminger. He underwent routine tests at Scripps Institute in La Jolla, California, and received a clean bill of health and the insurance policy, in spite of a one-centimeter shadow on his left lung that the radiologists misdiagnosed, attributing it to a childhood case of double pneumonia. The report calmed Pilar's nerves, but it did not subdue his cough.

The summer after the physical, Duke made *In Harm's Way*. Based on a novel by James Bassett, the film begins on December 6, 1941, the eve of the Japanese attack on Pearl Harbor, and ends with the decisive naval battles in the Solomon Islands in 1942 and 1943. Preminger enjoyed the enthusiastic support of the U.S. Navy, which supplied him with the USS *St. Paul*, a cruiser, and sailed the entire cast and crew from Seattle to Hawaii. On the way Preminger shot a number of the onboard scenes, ordering the *St. Paul*'s captain and crew around as if they were employees. The naval base at Pearl Harbor became a Preminger set, as his heavily accented German voice boomed instructions to admirals and ordinary seamen alike. John Wayne plays Capt. and then Adm. Rock Torrey, a cruiser and then task force commander, while Kirk Douglas is his gifted but emotionally tormented executive officer, Cdr. Paul Eddington. Patricia Neal is navy nurse Lt. Maggie Haynes. Ens. Jeremiah Torrey, Rock Torrey's estranged son, is played by Brandon de Wilde. The supporting cast includes Henry Fonda as Adm. Chester Nimitz, Burgess Meredith as Cdr. Egan Powell, Dana Andrews as the supercautious Adm. "Blackjack" Broderick, and Patrick Neal as Rep. Neal Owynn.[42]

Wayne was his old self, even as a middle-aged, twentieth-century naval officer. Rock Torrey is aggressive, a man of action willing to break the rules to win a battle. One officer remembers him back at Annapolis as "All Navy and nothin' but Navy." But, Commander Eddington reminds him, "He's willing to throw away the book to win." Torrey trusts Eddington implicitly, in spite of the man's private demons, because he loves a good fight. On the day Pearl Harbor is attacked, Eddington grabs Torrey by the shoulders and shouts: "Oh, Rock of Ages. We got ourselves another war. A gut-bustin' mother-lovin' navy war." Together, they take an assignment from Admiral Nimitz, who is disappointed with the performance of Admiral Broderick. While Broderick is cautious to a fault— afraid to attack the Japanese without overwhelming superiority and in the process almost giving enemy troops an island foothold—Torrey launches a bold offensive, without consulting the senior officer, and wins the decisive engagement. In the end Eddington's demons consume him. After he rapes the fiancée of Jeremiah Torrey and causes her suicide, Eddington kills himself in a successful, single-handed suicide mission against the Japanese fleet.

For all his impetuous bravery, Rock Torrey possesses a few demons of his own. Like most of John Wayne's characters, Torrey is unattached and uncommitted, a man who left his family twenty years before because he did not want to be what his wife wanted him to be—a stuffy, moneygrubbing stockbroker. When Jeremiah and Rock meet for the first time in twenty years, they do not recognize each other. Jeremiah Torrey is a sycophant, an opportunistic yes-man ensign who badmouths "Roosevelt's trumped-up war," hopes to use his position as a stepping-stone for his own career, and loathes his father. When Rock and Paul meet Jeremiah, the young man is holding down a cushy job as an aide to Neal Owynn. Rock keeps his mouth shut, as the offscreen Wayne did when faced with his children's anger. "I can't start acting like a father now," he tells Maggie Haynes. "I threw that opportunity away eighteen years ago when I gave Jer' up to his mother. I wouldn't know how to talk to him." Eddington is not so shy. "I'm afraid I cannot accept you as Rock Torrey's son," he smirks to Jeremiah. "I think someone got in there ahead of him." Eventually the son comes to respect his father's strengths, and he requests a transfer to a combat post on a PT boat and is killed in action, redeeming himself and his father's faith in him.

Just a few years before—in *North to Alaska*, *Hatari!*, and *Donovan's Reef*— Wayne had portrayed middle-aged men in love with women young enough to be his daughters. He had been particularly displeased with the bedroom and kissing scenes with Elsa Martinelli in *Hatari!*; he was too old and she too young for such a relationship. It reminded him of how Gary Cooper appeared in the 1956 film *Love in the Afternoon* with Audrey Hepburn, at the time when Cooper was an old-looking fifty-five and Hepburn a young-looking twenty-six. Wayne thought Cooper appeared unseemly in the film, more pathetic than virile. He made a decision after *Donovan's Reef* that he would confine his romantic interests to mature women. *In Harm's Way* was the first. Patricia Neal was a thirty-eight-year-old actress recovering from a recent stroke. As Lt. Maggie Haynes, she is Rock Torrey's lover in the film. At the outset Torrey is uninterested. There is a war to fight and little time for women. When they meet at a party, he cannot even recognize Maggie as the nurse who removed the cast from his broken arm at the base hospital a few days before. But Rock falls in love with Maggie's strength and honesty. She makes the first move, and on the evening before they are both shipped out to the combat zone, they spend the night together at her apartment. Never again would John Wayne make love in a movie to a younger woman.

For many of the actors, the set of *In Harm's Way* was not a pleasant place to spend a summer. Otto Preminger was a tyrant. When Hollywood learned that John Wayne and Kirk Douglas had agreed to do the film, pundits predicted bruised egos and monumental temper tantrums. Preminger, bald as a bullet, strutted around the set repeating to anybody who would listen: "I'm the man with no hair who shoves around the people with hair." He was absolutely merciless with Tom Tryon, who played the young officer William McConnell. Whispered rumors that Tryon was gay might have inspired Preminger's venom. In his autobiography, Kirk Douglas remembered: "Otto would scream. He would come right up to Tom, saliva spitting out of his mouth, and he would just yell. I've never seen anyone treated that way. Tom was shattered." Douglas begged Tryon to stand up to the old man. "The next time Otto screams at you," Douglas counseled him, "just yell right back, 'Otto, Go fuck yourself!' and walk right off the set." Tom Tryon did not like confrontations and kept his peace, suffering through the abuse. Preminger tried to bully Douglas a few times, but the star would have none of it. "Once, he raised his voice in a nasty way toward me. I walked over to him, nose to nose. In a very low voice, I said, 'Are you talking to me?' That was the end of it. He never insulted me again." Only one person on the set escaped Preminger's wrath—John Wayne. "He never shouted at John Wayne," remembered one woman. "Perhaps he felt he could not."[43]

Preminger did not need to insult Wayne. Liberated from Grant's scripts, he delivered an extraordinary performance. Wendell Mayes, who wrote the screenplay, recalled: "John Wayne's a great pro. John Wayne never blows a line. The other actors will blow lines but he will stand there patiently, wait for them to get their lines, say his in his own way." Kirk Douglas agreed. "The perfect movie star is John Wayne . . . he brings so much authority to a role he can pronounce literally any line in a script and get away with it." But one line in the film was so corny, Douglas mused, that it might have tripped Wayne up. The script called for Rock Torrey to repeat Revolutionary War hero John Paul Jones's famous quote: "I wish to have no connection with any ship that does not sail fast, for I intend to go in harm's way." Douglas thought: "Oh shit, I've gotta hear him say this line. But you know what? He said it, and he got away with it. Now that's John Wayne." Reviewers hailed Wayne's performance as well. "This picture was tailored for John Wayne," *Variety* claimed. "He is in every way the big gun of 'In Harm's Way.' Without his commanding presence, chances are Preminger probably could not have built the head of steam this film generates and sustains for 2 hours, 45 minutes."[44]

The fact that Wayne was sick throughout the summer of 1964 was another testimonial to his acting skills. In the four months separating *Circus World* from *In Harm's Way*, he aged considerably. He turned fifty-seven just before boarding the USS *St. Paul* for the cruise to Hawaii, and he appeared every year of it. He was no longer middle-aged and fit. His eyes reflected a wet, cloudy luster, and the thick, heavy eyelids and jowly cheeks were those of an older man. At 260 pounds he was corpulent, and he battled a vicious cough all summer. Loud, hacking, and persistent, the cough often interrupted shooting, frustrating Wayne and worrying Pilar, who started up her "You've got to see a doctor" refrain again. He was exhausted by the time Preminger wrapped up the location shooting late in August.[45]

He had little time for rest. Duke was scheduled to begin shooting *The Sons of Katie Elder* in November. Needing a new insurance policy anyway, he made another appointment at Scripps. He asked Louis Johnson to meet him at the hospital and, after the physical, to spend the afternoon with him at the racetrack in Del Mar.[46]

They returned to the clinic the next morning for the test results. Wayne expected it to be routine, like all the previous physicals, and he promised Louis they would have plenty of time to get over to the track. But at the clinic station the receptionist routed Duke back down to radiology for more X rays. It was unusual, but he did not give it a second thought, laughing to Johnson that someone in the "developing room must have screwed up." This time the technician took numerous shots, placing Duke in a variety of positions and postures to get several angles. Wayne and Johnson had some coffee and doughnuts in the clinic cafeteria, but Duke returned to the X ray station to retrieve a book he had left. The technician, trying to be helpful, approached him, sat down with the films, and said: "Mr. Wayne . . . it certainly looks like it's there." Duke frowned a bit and, with a slight edge to his voice, asked: "What the hell's there?" The technician, puzzled, innocently replied: "Cancer. There's no doubt about it being there." Now, with more than a little edge to his voice, Wayne boomed: "What the hell are you talking about? Nobody said anything about cancer!" The blood drained out of the technician's face. "Mr. Wayne! I thought you knew!" The cardinal sin of technicians was thus committed against the hospital's premier patient, against one of the most famous men on the planet. He started apologizing profusely, wringing his hands in anguish, shaking his head, mumbling to himself how sorry he was and that he was going to get fired. "Jesus Christ," Wayne said. "What are you *talking* about?" The young man explained his predicament. Duke took a deep breath, calmed down, and softly reassured him: "Don't worry, kid. I won't tell anybody." Two hours later, when surgeon Thomas Lambert told him that he had lung cancer, Duke feigned surprise. It may have been the greatest acting performance of his life.

The horses ran without Duke and Louis. Wayne drove back to Los Angeles, and Johnson returned to Arizona. During that three-hour drive, Duke's thoughts returned several times to his old friend Pedro Armendariz. Over the years they made several movies and emptied scores of tequila bottles together. "I thought a lot about what Pete Armendariz did," Wayne later told a reporter from *Chicago's American Magazine.* "He had it [cancer], and he stuck that old .45 in his mouth and blew his head open." That was not exactly how it happened, but close enough. Late in May 1963, in London on the set of *From Russia with Love,* Armendariz became ill. X rays revealed several metastatic tumors in his neck, upper thorax, and lymph nodes, and the doctors told him he might have six months to live. Armendariz's wife insisted that they go to UCLA for another opinion. They stopped off in Mexico City on the way, where Pedro bought a .357 Magnum, far bigger than needed; he was determined not to die by inches. To make extra sure, he purchased a package of armor-piercing bullets. They checked into UCLA on June 12. President Adolfo López Mateos of Mexico personally called UCLA to make sure that Armendariz got the best treatment. But there was no treatment, nothing the physicians could do. On June 18 Armendariz complained about the hospital food and asked his wife to go get him a hamburger. He waited a few moments, placed the barrel of the gun to his chest, and pulled the trigger. The bullet exploded through his heart, pierced the mattress and box spring, rico-cheted off the floor, and embedded itself in the wall.[47]

Wayne did not give suicide serious consideration, but he feared becoming an invalid. Finding out about the cancer was "like somebody hit me across the belly with a baseball bat. It wasn't just the fear of death, although there's that too, when the doctor taps you on the shoulder and says, 'You have cancer.' The sun sure doesn't shine any brighter. But how to tell my wife, my mother, those kids who are the joy of my life and who'd never seen me sick? I'd always been big, healthy, somebody they could kind of depend on. It's . . . the help-lessness. I couldn't see myself lying on a bed, not able to do anything for my-self, no damn good to anybody. I felt like a jerk." Duke raised the possibility of doing nothing, wondering if perhaps the cancer would just "go away" on its own, but deep down he knew that was really not an option.[48]

The physicians at Scripps referred Duke to Dr. John E. Jones, a skilled tho-racic surgeon at Good Samaritan Hospital in Los Angeles. Wayne met with Jones on Saturday morning, September 3, 1964. Duke would rather have been sleeping in the cabin of the *Wild Goose*, somewhere off the coast of Baja California. After examining the X rays, Jones told Wayne, "The cancer is quite obvious. We have a fine surgical team here at Good Samaritan."

"Okay," Wayne replied. "When?"

"Wait a minute," Jones protested. "I think you should learn a little bit more about me before you . . ."

Wayne interrupted. "Dr. Jones, my friend and lawyer, Frank Belcher, had a cancer operation here. They left a sponge in him during the operation. They had to go back, open him up and get the sponge. Are you the fellow who left the sponge in Frank Belcher?"

"That's me," Jones said.

"Then, you'll do," Wayne laughed.

Wayne continued, asking Jones if he "could maybe send something down my throat and burn the tumor off without cutting me. That way I'll still be able to film *The Sons of Katie Elder* in November."

Jones had a simple answer: "No way, Duke. We'll have to open you up to get at it, and it's going to take a lot out of you. If we find out the lymph nodes are positive, that the disease has spread, you'll need to have six weeks of daily cobalt radiation therapy, and we can't start that until the surgical wound has healed. You'll have to reschedule the movie."[49]

Wayne immediately informed Hal Wallis, who was producing *The Sons of Katie Elder*, about the impending surgery, and Wallis went to work reschedul-

ing the location shooting. Wayne then told Henry Hathaway, who was directing the film. Hathaway, a colon cancer survivor, talked at length with Wayne
about the disease, asking intelligent, pointed questions, reassuring him that
he would recover, but warning him that major surgery "is no piece of cake.
We're not young men anymore; expect to be tired and expect the recovery to
take longer than you think. You're gonna be sore as hell."[50]

Wayne wondered about what to tell the press. There would have been no
debate if Bev Barnett were still alive. Bev always urged the truth. "Falsehoods
are difficult to sustain," he always said. But he was dead. Duke's agent, Charlie Feldman, took the opposite approach, arguing that Wayne's image—the
virile, tough man of action—might not survive revelations that he was a victim of lung cancer. The debate was still going when orderlies took Duke to
the operating room. By the time the anesthesiologist was putting him under,
Wayne's closest advisers had reached a consensus. Batjac released a statement
to the press explaining that John Wayne was in Good Samaritan to repair an
old ankle injury that he had incurred during the 1957 filming of *Legend of the
Lost* and reinjured on *Circus World*.[51]

Jones performed the surgery on September 17. His scalpel sliced into
Wayne's chest, beginning under the left breast and continuing twenty-eight
inches under the left arm and into the middle of the back. Muscles had to be
separated. To get the chest open, Jones cracked Duke's ribs and removed one
of them. He installed metal braces to spread the rib cage, exposing the left
lung. The doctor was used to seeing diseased lungs, but Wayne's was something else. An average of six packs a day for forty years—some 1,752,000 cigarettes—had taken their toll. Duke's lung had none of the pinkish, spongelike
texture of healthy tissue; it was dark gray and dense, more like an old, dried-
out sponge, badly pocked with black blotches of nicotine. There, in the upper
lobe, was a tumor the size of a large chicken egg. Jones guessed right away that
it was malignant, and pathologists quickly confirmed it. The tumor was large,
but it also seemed more self-contained than most, with a well-defined visual
border. There was a slim chance that it had not metastasized to surrounding
tissues. Jones lifted out the entire lobe, scooped up regional lymph nodes,
clipped and sutured the attached arteries and veins, and closed up Wayne's
chest. The operation took more than six hours.[52]

The next few days were hell. Wayne did not experience a textbook recovery. The hacking cough plaguing him since *Circus World* was worse than ever,
exploding through his bandaged chest, dislodging drainage tubes, bursting
the sutures of his incision, and rupturing lung tissue. The popped lung sacs

were so bad that air escaped into the chest cavity and out into the tissues of his head, neck, and torso, creating a condition known as subcutaneous emphysema. The visual reality was horrific. Large volumes of air filtered their way into the layers of his skin, swelling Duke's head and upper body, turning him into a pain-racked Humpty Dumpty who could barely open his eyes. On September 22 Jones went back into his chest to repair the damage in another six-hour operation. The spin doctors went to work again, telling the world that Duke had come down with a case of pneumonia and a "lung abscess," which had to be removed. The swelling soon disappeared. More good news arrived the next day. The pathologist reported that the lymph nodes were negative—there was no evidence, visually or microscopically, of metastasis, and no need for cobalt treatments.[53]

John Wayne left Good Samaritan on October 7. He did not want to put on his toupee, so he wore a cloth hat with the brim turned down. A sport coat and cotton shirt buttoned all the way to the top camouflaged some of his thirty-pound weight loss. He was hunchbacked because of the chest surgery, looking six feet tall instead of six feet four. Orderlies wheelchaired him down to the hospital lobby but let him walk out on his own to meet the assembled press. He did not have the telltale limp of somebody who had undergone ankle surgery, and he was not looking forward to seeing reporters because he knew they were going to ask about the surgery. He later recalled: "The statements [about the ankle injury and lung abscess] were given out while I was still under sedation. By the time I got on my feet, the damage was done." Gossip columnists were already questioning the old injury story, and the first questioner wanted to know if Wayne had suffered from a critical illness. John Wayne did not like to mislead people—ever—but he kept up the charade. "There's nothing wrong with me that getting out of the hospital won't cure," he answered. "I haven't had a heart attack, and I don't have cancer. I just want to go home."[54]

19

"I've Just Got My Second Wind"

Duke's health was a hot topic in Hollywood in the fall of 1964, and rumors circulated freely. The ankle injury story did not play well; on his way out of the hospital, Duke had appeared weak and fatigued, but the fact that he had walked out to the car on his own, without a limp, raised eyebrows and suspicions among the press corps. After several weeks in the hospital, he had lost a lot of weight. He looked like someone who had undergone a major operation, not the draining of a lung abscess or the repair of ankle tendons. Gossip columnists decided he was hiding behind a fiction of his own making. For his part he did not want to seem so disabled, but he did not want to be a liar either. The white lie seemed petty and small, especially for someone whose public image revolved so consistently around candor and honesty. Rumors also abounded about Nat King Cole in December, and in the middle of the month Duke learned that the velvet-voiced crooner was being treated for lung cancer. Reporters had been sneaking around Cole's room at St. John's Hospital in Santa Monica and finally bribed the truth out of a technician. Duke did not want America to discover the truth about his lung cancer that way, and besides, he was just tired of covering up. "Maintaining lies," he told Mary St. John, "consumes too much energy." It was time, Duke said, "to get 'The Wound' off my back."[1]

Wayne had to reveal the truth in a way that would enhance his professional career and relieve his own discomfort. He was scheduled to head down to Durango, Mexico, on January 3, 1965, to film *The Sons of Katie Elder*. The script called for several difficult stunts at more than six thousand feet of altitude, and he wanted to prove a point, to make a statement, by doing many of them himself. Producer Hal Wallis let Hollywood know that he had been able to purchase a million-dollar life insurance policy on Duke—standard procedure to protect motion picture companies in case of the death or illness of a star during filming. The real message was John Wayne was insurable. Actuaries, of course, were not fooled. Insurance companies were more than willing to bet that he would live another four months, long enough to finish the film. Whether he would survive for five years was not their problem.[2]

On December 29, 1964, Duke gave an exclusive interview to James Bacon, a friend and syndicated columnist. They sat down over drinks in the den of Wayne's home in Encino. Two months before, he had told Bacon privately about the lung cancer and had promised him the exclusive when the time came to go public. It was time. Duke told Bacon:

> I wanted to tell [the truth] right from the start but all the statements were given out while I was doped up under sedation. By the time I got on my feet, the damage was done. . . . My advisers all thought it would destroy my image, but there's a lot of good image in John Wayne licking cancer—and that's what my doctors tell me. . . . I had the Big C, but I've beaten the son of a bitch. Maybe I can give some poor bastard a little hope by being honest. I want people to know cancer can be licked. . . . I feel great now. On January 4, I'll go to Durango, Mexico, to start *The Sons of Katie Elder*. It's a typical John Wayne western, so you know I have to be in good health. I didn't get famous doing drawing room comedies.[3]

After Bacon left with the story, Duke got in his car and drove over to St. John's Hospital to see Nat King Cole. They visited amiably for about thirty minutes. Duke was full of "I licked the Big C, you can too" encouragement, and Cole was, as always, polite. Actually their conditions did not have a great deal in common. Wayne's tumor was relatively small and contained; the surgeons had achieved the elusive "margin" and all of his lymph nodes had been negative. Cole's tumor was so large it was inoperable. Physicians were giving him a large dose of cobalt therapy as a preoperative treatment, hoping to reduce the tumor enough to be able to remove it surgically. Surgeons took out the crooner's left lung three weeks later, but they could not get a margin of tumor-free tissue, and lab reports revealed that Cole's lymph nodes were loaded with the disease. He died on February 15, 1965.[4]

Cole's death caught Duke off guard. It seemed too sudden. With his own three-month check-up at Scripps Clinic in La Jolla just two months away, and in spite of his continuing public protests that he had "beaten the Big C," he started worrying. Among his closest friends and family members, Duke stopped referring to his cancer as "The Wound" and began calling it the "Red Witch" after *Wake of the Red Witch*. Duke equated the ship *Red Witch* with his cancer and hoped that he, like Captain Ralls, would survive many years before the Red Witch got him. When he left for his check-up in April 1965, Duke told Mary St. John: "Well, I'm going down to La Jolla to see if the Red Witch is waiting for me." When he returned, he said, "Well, the bitch wasn't there this time."[5]

Bacon's story in the *Los Angeles Herald-Examiner* made Duke the most famous cancer patient in the country. The public reaction to his announcement in December had been extraordinary. Dr. Charles Mayo, head of the Mayo Clinic, praised him for going public and encouraging people to get regular check-ups. "If I suggest that one have a check-up, the immediate reaction is that I'm looking for business," Mayo said. "People react differently to an announcement from a movie star." Duke received more than one hundred thousand letters from cancer patients and their families in 1965, and every cancer society in the country invited him to serve on its board of directors. He told Hedda Hopper: "Why, people have written me from all over the world. Their letters are different—warm, personal, like letters from old friends."[6]

The letters, hoopla, three-month check-ups, and the death of screenwriter Jimmy Grant kept the Red Witch in the forefront of Duke's mind in 1965 and 1966. Grant and Duke had been best of friends, drinking and working and carousing and cardplaying together ever since the 1940s. They both chain-smoked cigarettes, both came down with lung cancer within months of each other, and both had their chests cracked open to remove malignant tumors. But there, their destinies parted. Jimmy Grant's cancer came back in 1966, and he died the hard way, wasting away in a hospital and nursing home. Duke visited Grant regularly, wondering why the Red Witch had spared him and not Jimmy, and wondering when she would finally pay him a visit.[7]

The public adulation over his courage in describing his cancer, and his own private fears created an extraordinary tension. He kept doing interviews about his cancer in 1965 and 1966, kept reminding people to get their check-ups so they could benefit from early detection, to have hope if they got cancer because "I licked the Big C." He talked openly about the disease, calling on Americans to stop acting as if "cancer [were] leprosy." But like all cancer patients, he harbored constant, gut-wrenching fears about a recurrence, about pain and suffering and death. In March he remarked to a reporter that "the cancer societies want me on their campaigns. They're welcome to use my case, but I don't want to make a profession out of this. Before I know it I'll be 'The Man Who Had Cancer.' Thanks to the Man upstairs and my doctor I've got my life back and I want to go on living—that's the whole point."[8]

For John Wayne the only way to get the Red Witch out of his mind was to start work again. He did so with a vengeance. Henry Hathaway, who was looking forward to working with Wayne, took personal control of Duke's reentry into the world of the living. Hathaway was convinced that work was the key to a quick recovery. "Don't baby yourself," he advised Wayne just after the September operation, "or you'll become a psychological cripple. The way to get over what you've been through is to forget it ever happened and get on with your life." Coming from a trusted friend and cancer survivor, the counsel seemed good advice.[9]

Less than four months after his cancer operation in 1964, John Wayne went back to work. In early January, at the age of fifty-seven, he headed south to Durango. During the flight he had breathed through an oxygen mask, but when the plane landed Duke still could not catch his breath. Durango rested at 6,200 feet in the Mexican Sierras; the air was thin. Ten minutes after climbing down from the airplane, Duke knew it was too soon to make a physically demanding film. His body reminded him every time he moved. The twenty-eight-inch U-shaped scar running from his chest under his left arm to the middle of his back was still an ugly purple. Half of his left lung—a chunk the size of a "baby's fist"—and a rib had been removed, and his left arm and side ached. As a result of medication, inactivity, and overeating, he had also finally lost the ten-year battle with his waistline. But dozens of photographers—the Hollywood papparazzi—greeted him in Durango, snapping hundreds of photographs of resurrection.[10]

Sheer willpower got Duke through the film. Hathaway was a demanding taskmaster. Chuck Roberson remembered: "Hathaway was . . . himself a man who had undergone successful surgery for cancer of the colon. . . . I guess he figured that even if Duke turned blue in the effort, he was going to do the same work with one lung as he did before with two." At the high elevation Duke labored for breath, sucking constantly on an oxygen inhalator. His work was a gritty effort by a weak man. His makeup had never looked worse. His distinctive cadence took on an unusual breathy quality, as if he had run a race before each take. Duke remembered that he rode his horse—one of his few particular points of pride—"like a *cheechako* [tenderfoot]," grimacing and swaying with an awkward roll because every movement stretched those muscles and ribs on his left side.

Hathaway refused to go easy on him. He was hard on everyone. Hundreds of American expatriates lived in Durango, and Hathaway used many of them as extras. Earl Holliman, who played one of the Elder boys in the film, remembered a scene in which several men were riding into town. Hundreds of extras were watching the shooting. Suddenly Hathaway's enraged voice came booming over the street through a megaphone: "Tighten up! You're spread out like a widow woman's shit!" Holliman thought, "Oh, God, Henry, did you really say that in front of all these people?" But Hathaway was hardest on Wayne. One scene was especially taxing. It called for Wayne and one of his brothers, manacled at the ankle, to jump out of the right side of a wagon into the icy Rio Chico and then, joined by his other two brothers, fight a prolonged gunfight from under the bridge. It was a brutal scene. Chuck Roberson pleaded with Hathaway to double Wayne in the scene. Duke agreed, but Hathaway would have none of it. "You can't use a double for that scene. Do it yourself." Roberson tried again. "Couldn't he get pneumonia, Mr. Hathaway? That mud and water are like a deep freeze—damn cold stuff . . . there's nothing he's doing, I can't do. He could catch cold or something." Hathway stared Roberson down and ended the conversation with three words: "So could you." Wayne could not even cheat the cold by wearing a wet suit under his clothes—something his smaller costars did—because he was already too fat for his character. All he could do was suffer, and occasionally laugh.[11]

It took five days to shoot the entire scene. Wayne ruined a few takes; Dean Martin, Michael Anderson Jr., and Earl Holliman ruined a few others. As much as he loved his work and as pleased as he was to be alive, it was a cruel stretch. Wayne cursed his costars, director, and himself. But, as usual, he did not remain angry very long, and between takes he chewed tobacco—having temporarily given up cigarettes—and joked with reporters.

Cold and wet after one take, the now-health-conscious Wayne took several vitamin C tablets and washed them down with a warming mouthful of mescal. Observing himself being observed, he shook off the effect of the drink, smiled at the handful of reporters, and said: "Goddamn! I'm the stuff men are made of."[12]

It was personally important, and professionally critical, for Duke to reestablish his image as a man's man. He was convinced, as was his agent, Charles Feldman, that the future depended on it. When some of the locals in

Durango decided to re-create the Grauman's Chinese Theater motif on the porch of the Alamo Courts motel where the cast was staying, Wayne stood near the wet cement, waited until everybody was watching, made a fist, pointed it up in the air, and then jammed it down into the cement and wrote his name next to it, just as he had done back in 1950 at the real Grauman's Chinese Theater. But when Gene Sysco, a photographer for the *Globe,* took a picture of Wayne breathing air out of an oxygen tank after a difficult scene a few days later, Duke exploded in rage, throwing a can at him, and screaming: "You goddamned sonofabitch! Give me that fucking film!" The set became deadly silent as Sysco handed over the film. The reaction was a mistake, and Duke knew it. He must not appear petty or desperate either. Four hours later, in the motel dining room, he walked over to Sysco's table, raised his arms to quiet the crowd, and said loudly enough for everyone to hear: "I'm a grown man. I ought to be able to control myself better than I did today. I'm sorry." But he gave no film back with the apology. The last thing he wanted was to have America see him with his face in an oxygen mask.[13]

The crew worked overtime on *Katie Elder* to keep Duke going and looking fit. Dean Martin reassured a *Time* reporter: "Someone else would have laid around feeling sorry for himself for a year. But Duke, he just doesn't know how to be sick. . . . He's recuperating the hard way. He's two loud-speaking guys in one. Me, when people see me, they sometimes say, 'Oh, there goes Perry Como.' But there's only one John Wayne and nobody makes any mistakes about that." Hathaway reshot scenes that displayed too much of Duke's paunch. Web Overlander, Wayne's makeup man, kept redoing his eyes, restyling the hairpiece, and resmearing Nivea cream over the double chin. Ralph Volkie, Duke's trainer, rubbed Duke's aching muscles down with Absorbine Jr., stinking up the entire set. "Actors don't die," Overlander quipped. "They just smell that way." Hathaway wanted America to see the old Duke, and he wanted Wayne to act and feel like the old Duke.[14]

It worked. Wayne appeared his old self. He rode, shot, and fought like he always had. In *The Sons of Katie Elder*, three men return home to West Texas for Katie Elder's funeral and get reacquainted with their kid brother Bud Elder (Michael Anderson). The three older brothers left home years before and ignored their mother, even though she was a generous woman beloved by the townsfolk. John Wayne plays the oldest of the Elder boys, a gunslinger with a tarnished reputation. Tom Elder (Dean Martin) is a gambler, and Matt Elder (Earl Holliman) runs a store. After the funeral, as a tribute to their mother, the older boys decide to fulfill her last dream by seeing that Bud gets a college degree. In the process of wrapping up Katie Elder's affairs, however, they discover that the local tycoon, Morgan Hastings (James Gregory), murdered their father and seized the Elder ranch. Sheriff Billy Wilson (Paul Fix), more interested in peace and quiet than in justice, ignored the crimes. The Elder brothers expose the conspiracy, kill Hastings and his hired guns, and recover the family land.[15]

When the location work for *The Sons of Katie Elder* ended in March 1965, Duke spent some more time working on the interiors and on his health, trying to get back in shape. He started a weight lifting regimen and tried scuba diving again. But exercise frustrated him. On a trip to Catalina Island that summer, he tried to teach Bert Minshall how to scuba dive. Inner-ear pain kept Minshall close to the surface, and Duke did not get down very deep either. He could not inhale enough oxygen from the scuba tank to compensate for the exertion of diving. Forced to surface after a few minutes underwater, he ripped off his mask and screamed: "Goddamnit! I'll never have any more fun!" Later in the evening, he yelled at Minshall: "You white-toothed bastard! You wouldn't even go down. Why didn't you go deeper?" When Minshall explained his ear problems, Duke calmed down and apologized: "Ah, what the hell. I've had a lot of fun diving over the years. It's too bad your ears can't take it. You don't know what you're missing."[16]

Early that summer Duke also learned that CBS Television was planning a prime-time *Tribute to John Wayne,* complete with clips from his greatest films and reminiscences from his closest friends and Hollywood colleagues. At first he was flattered, liking the idea of having tens of millions of Americans focus on him. But the more he thought about it, the more nervous he became. The message Duke wanted America to hear was that he was feeling just fine, that he had survived cancer, and that life was back to normal. He worried that the television tribute might look like some kind of memorial or, worse yet, a premature eulogy. He told Hedda Hopper and Mary St. John: "What are they trying to do, bury me? Tell them to forget it. I've just got my second wind."[17]

By the time *The Sons of Katie Elder* premiered at the end of August 1965, many Americans yearned for the past. The nonviolent movement of Martin Luther King Jr. had been eclipsed by the Watts riots in Los Angeles, and antiwar protesters were taking President Lyndon B. Johnson to task for escalating Vietnam far beyond the limits imposed by Eisenhower and Kennedy. There was great fear that the old heroes had now become anachronisms. For those who longed for the old John Wayne, the one they were used to, the symbol of their traditional faith, the Hathaway charade was like water in the desert. John Wayne was back, king of a mountain where doubt and uncertainty had been conquered, where, as Joan Didion wrote, "a man could move free, could make his own code and live by it; a world in which, if a man did what he had to do, he could one day take the girl and go riding through the draw and find himself home free." Howard Thompson of the *New York Times* was more succinct: "Mr. Wayne is [a good actor] in a part that fits him like a bullet."[18]

Riding horses and performing stunts on the *Katie Elder* set were not the only signs that Duke was back. The newspapers were full of John Wayne family stories in 1965 and 1966. Michael and Gretchen Wayne had a baby girl— Josephine Michele Wayne—in September 1965, Duke's tenth grandchild, and Patrick Wayne married Peggy Hunt in December. In March 1966 Don and Toni LaCava presented him with his eleventh grandchild—Peter LaCava. Melinda had Duke's twelfth in July 1966. But the real story was Wayne's announcement to the press in October 1965 that Pilar was pregnant with his seventh child. She gave birth to Marisa Carmela on February 22, 1966, a few months shy of Duke's fifty-ninth birthday.[19]

There were other signs of change. On the evening of January 3, 1965, Duke was getting ready to head for Durango, where shooting on *Katie Elder* was about to begin. Aissa was not in bed yet, and the maid was in the kitchen cleaning up the dinner dishes. Pilar was packing some of Duke's personal items when they both heard a loud scream downstairs. Aissa bolted into their bedroom, wide-eyed and shrieking. The maid had encountered a burglar in the house. Dennis Lee Parker, a deranged, out-of-work carpenter, had spent his last dollar buying a tour guide to Hollywood homes. He took a cab out to the Wayne estate in Encino, jumped the high fence, came in the back door, and started prowling around. Duke picked up the loaded .45-caliber revolver he kept on the headboard above his bed. He chased him outside, but the cancer surgery had robbed him of his strength, and he lost the intruder in the dark. Several squad cars arrived on the scene, and the police began searching the estate, finding Parker cowering in the entrance to the basement. They handcuffed him and were leading him to the squad car, when Parker turned to Duke and said: "You know, I'm sorry about this whole thing and would like to ask a favor." Duke furrowed his brow, squinted an eye, and with just the slightest smile on his face replied: "What favor?" "Well," Parker said: "I'm broke and can't even pay the taxi bill." Duke told the cops to wait a moment, went into the house, found his wallet, took out a twenty dollar bill, went back outside, and gave it to Parker, who promptly paid the cabbie. On the flight down to Durango the next day, Duke related the story to Mary St. John. When she asked him why he handed twenty dollars over to a burglar who had terrorized his family, he shrugged and said, "Well, I felt sorry for the cabbie. The poor bastard's working the night shift and I thought he might have to cough up the fare himself. Anyway, maybe the whole thing's symbolic. We've decided to sell the house and get out of this shithole of a Los Angeles."[20]

The incident made Duke an even more inveterate opponent of gun control. He enjoyed firearms and kept a small arsenal on the *Wild Goose*, along with a good supply of ammunition and a spring-loaded catapult for trap-shooting. He used the shotguns for hunting along the Mexican coast, a .22-caliber rifle for shooting sharks from the deck of the yacht, handguns for protection, and a fully automatic M-1 carbine, and later an M-16, just for fun. He had little sympathy for liberals bent on disarming law-abiding Americans. "I'm sorry they feel that way," he told Bert Minshall. "But ya know, the first time they come across some bastard breakin' into their home or tryin' to take one of their kids, they'd be damn glad to have a gun around."[21]

The Waynes desperately needed a new beginning, a fresh start, after the battle with lung cancer. Both were weary of the artificial, fishbowl existence in the film colony. Most of Duke's closest friends in Hollywood were dead, and he had little in common with the new breed of stars, directors, and publicists who had taken their places. Pilar did not want to have to worry about which fanatical fan was coming over the fence next with a Hollywood street guide, and she was tired of attending the same old parties with the same people, all of whom could talk of nothing but movies, salaries, box-office receipts, and the latest gossip in the *Hollywood Reporter* and *Variety*. It was a life of endless chatter about who was sleeping with whom and who had gotten what part. And it was all so old.[22]

Pilar had been more than just weary of Hollywood. Throughout the country women were taking a second look at their lives, wondering how, in the midst of so much prosperity, they could be so miserable, so unfulfilled, until Betty Friedan focused their malaise in *The Feminine Mystique* in 1963. According to Friedan, American femininity was a terrible taskmaster, forcing women to equate their own happiness with that of their husbands and children. Friedan urged women to start over, first meeting their own professional and emotional needs. "When women do not need to live through their husbands and children," she wrote, "men will not fear the love and strength of women, nor need another's weakness to prove their own masculinity."[23]

If Betty Friedan had wanted to choose a single relationship to exemplify her critique, the Wayne marriage would have been perfect. Nothing made that clearer than the sale of the house in Encino. Duke and Pilar had talked in the most general terms about moving, but they had never discussed specifics about the time or place. Two days before Christmas in 1964, Duke came home one afternoon and informed Pilar that he had sold their house to Walt Disney's daughter. The sale caught Pilar off guard, reducing her in an instant to tears. She did not doubt Duke's legal right to sell the property without her signature; he had purchased it when he was married to Chata. What she could not understand was the abruptness of the decision—even if the Disneys had made an offer Duke "couldn't refuse"—and his willingness to do it without even consulting her.[24]

She exacted her own revenge. When Duke was in Durango, she bought a new home for the family in Newport Beach, without asking her husband's permission or even his opinion. She did it with fear and trembling, however. When he found out Duke reacted quite passively. He had always liked Newport Beach, and maybe, since Pilar had picked out the home on Bayshore Drive, she would be happy there. Her life and their relationship began to change. Aissa was ten years old and in the fifth grade and John Ethan was starting kindergarten. It had become increasingly difficult to take the children out of school and pack them off on location, and Pilar started staying home instead of going along. She made new friends among the Newport Beach elite, developed a passion for tennis, became active in a number of local charities, and started her own business—the Fernleaf Cafe. She also abandoned the Roman Catholic Church and converted to Christian Science. Gradually she was spinning out of her husband's orbit.[25]

The Waynes were not the only people moving to Orange County. Before the San Diego Freeway and the Santa Ana Freeway linked southern Orange County with Los Angeles in the late 1950s, the county was largely a sleepy land of orange groves, cattle ranches, and truck farms. During the 1960s and early 1970s, however, it became the fastest-growing region in the United States. Walt Disney had seen the change coming and built Disneyland in Anaheim in 1955. The Orange County population jumped from 219,390 in 1951 to 688,920 in 1960 and 1,110,210 in 1965, when Duke moved there. It reached 1,646,314 in 1974. During the 1960s bulldozers pushed down orange groves for the construction of more than two hundred thousand suburban tract homes. Shopping malls sprouted all along the freeways, and thousands of schools were built. Home prices began their spectacular ascent, and Orange County became the centerpiece of the "California dream"—fair weather, beaches, mountains, cars, malls, and lots of home equity.[26]

Newport Beach was at the heart of the county. At the outlet of the Santa Ana River, Newport Beach was long known as San Joaquín Bay because it was part of the Rancho San Joaquín. City fathers in the late 1800s renamed the town Newport and hoped to build a deepwater harbor there, but their plans fell through when San Pedro emerged as the major port for the Los Angeles Basin. Instead the city was destined to become the capital of a residential land empire. In 1864 Newport Beach real estate developer James Irvine had purchased the 47,000-acre Rancho San Joaquín, and in subsequent years he vastly enlarged the new "Irvine Ranch." When the exodus from Los Angeles to Orange County produced the boom in tract homes, Irvine Ranch was worth billions.[27]

The county had a throwback demographic profile. Orange County in the 1960s looked a lot like Glendale did in 1910—a community of midwestern transplants. In the late 1970s and 1980s, northern Orange County would become more "ethnic," with the immigration of hundreds of thousands of Hispanics and Vietnamese, but the south coast, from Newport Beach down to the San Diego County line, remained the province of middle- and upper-class whites. It was also one of the most conservative Republican counties in the country—and certainly the wealthiest conservative area anywhere. Orange County had more chapters and more members of the John Birch Society than the rest of the country combined, and in Newport Beach, Republicans outnumbered Democrats by three to one in the 1960s and early 1970s. Barry Goldwater maintained a home in Newport Beach, and President Richard Nixon's Casa Pacifica was a few miles down the coast in San Clemente. In 1966 Orange County voted overwhelmingly to send Ronald Reagan to the governor's mansion in Sacramento.[28]

It was perfect for John Wayne. He became the crown prince of Orange County, and Pilar was his princess. Being part of the upper crust was new; it took the smug new money of California's richest suburb to accept him. No matter how many millions of dollars he might have made and did make in Los Angeles he was never accepted as a blueblood. Orange County was different. The year after they bought the house on Bayshore Drive, the Waynes were listed in *The Orange Book*, the local social register. And they were not just celebrities. To his new neighbors Duke was a genuine American hero with gilt-edged Republican and anti-Communist credentials, a veteran of the Cold War who continued the good fight against powerful bureaucracies, government interference, high taxes, defeatism, liberalism, socialism, and communism.[29]

In his 1990 novel, *The Golden Orange*, Joseph Wambaugh noted Wayne's status in the community. "There's an annual softball event in a Southland beach city," he wrote,

> wherein dozens of teams enter a three-day elimination event, mainly just to drink and party. Entrants are encouraged to pick imaginative names for the teams, and crassness is not discouraged. For example, one team composed of police detectives called itself 'The Swinging Dicks.' And yet, the *only* caveat insofar as picking out a name is that no entrant can, in any way, denigrate the United States of America, or John Wayne. *That* is how profanity gets defined in *these* parts."[30]

Bill Kronberger Jr. of the Old Mission Bay Athletic Club in California once remarked: "He was a macho, sexist chauvinist. Anything that reflected on him would diminish what we stand for. Dishonor your mother if you want, but don't mess with the Duke."

While Pilar was remodeling the Newport Beach house before they moved in, Duke became involved in another man's dream. Screenwriter and director Melville Shavelson had worked in Hollywood since the late 1940s. His more successful films included *The Seven Little Foys* (1957) and *Houseboat* (1958). Shavelson became obsessed with Ted Berkman's book *Cast a Giant Shadow*, the true story of David "Mickey" Marcus, a West Point graduate and attorney who served as New York Commissioner of Corrections under Mayor Fiorello LaGuardia during the 1930s. In World War II Marcus rose to the rank of colonel and parachuted into Europe in advance of the D-day invasion. After the war Palestinian Jews helped him resurrect his own Jewish identity, and he, in return, whipped their ragtag army into an effective fighting force that helped secure independence for Israel in 1947. Shavelson wanted desperately, passionately, to make a movie about Marcus's life. He purchased the film rights to the book, wrote a screenplay, and planned to produce and direct the film, but he failed to secure financial backing.[31]

Shavelson had known Duke since the early 1950s when he had produced *Trouble Along the Way*. The two men had talked at length about Israel and the Alamo, comparing stories of courageous men and women fighting for freedom. Otherwise their politics were poles apart. But Shavelson remembered Wayne as an eminently fair man, so he tried a long shot. He took the project to him and asked for help.

Wayne was sympathetic. Shavelson's commitment to the project reminded him of his own passion for *The Alamo*. Mickey Marcus had similarities to Davy Crockett and Jim Bowie—fighting desperately for a new nation—despite the vast differences in the origins and results of their struggle. Shavelson needed money and Duke's name on the marquee. Shavelson remembered approaching him with the project. "Why can't you get it made?" he asked Shavelson. "Well," Shavelson replied, "they tell me everyplace, 'Who wants to see a movie about a Jewish general?'" "What do you want me to do?" Wayne queried. "Nobody will believe I ever went to *shul.*" Shavelson replied: "I just want to make the picture gentile by association. If your name is attached to the movie they can't say it's a Jewish movie anymore." Duke agreed to play Gen. Mike Randolph, an American officer who provides moral support to Colonel Marcus in his plan to assist Israel. "So once I had Duke," Shavelson said, "I had the picture. That's how the film got made."[32]

Shavelson also wanted financial backing from Batjac, and although Wayne thought the film had potential, he worried about putting his own money into the project. "Shavelson is a nice fellow," Duke told Mary St. John, "but the film is a passion to him, a baby, a labor of love, a crusade. I'll be damned if I'm going to give free rein to a Jewish true believer making the movie of his lifetime with my money." This was less anti-Semitism than simple recognition of the profligacy of passion; after all, he had nearly bankrupted himself on *The Alamo*, and he hadn't minded doing so. He agreed to make *Cast a Giant Shadow* as a Batjac production, but only if Michael was named coproducer. He trusted his son to keep an eye on the bottom line. Shavelson agreed.

Duke persuaded Kirk Douglas to play Col. Mickey Marcus and Yul Brynner to play Asher Gonen, the Israeli commander. Frank Sinatra, Angie Dickinson, Senta Berger, and Topol also accepted important parts. They shot the film in Italy and Israel during mid-1965. Duke spent months in both countries overseeing the project, while Pilar supervised the remodeling of the Bayshore Drive home. He appeared in only fifteen minutes of the movie, but one scene was especially memorable. Early in the movie Colonel Marcus, in a flashback, remembers the moment when he and General Randolph liberated a Nazi death camp in 1945. Shavelson wanted to portray the horror of the Holocaust, but out of respect he did not want to use any newsreels depicting the victims. Because he felt there was no way a makeup artist could make actors look anywhere near as tortured as the death-camp survivors had been when Allied troops liberated them, Shavelson eliminated all scenes portraying the liberation, except for one. He told the story through Wayne's eyes. The camera focuses close-up on the face of General Randolph as he walks through the gates of the concentration camp. When Randolph catches his first glimpse of Nazi genocide, disbelief gives way to outrage. Duke takes a slightly startled breath, pulls back his chin just a bit, clenches the muscles of his jaw, squints his eyes, breathes deeply and does not say a word. It was a monumental acting challenge. When Shavelson looked at the rushes later in the day, he was profoundly moved. "It depended for effect," Shavelson remembered, "on what John Wayne could convey to an audience with his eyes. It worked."

During the location shooting, Duke returned to Newport Beach for a two-day break with Pilar and the children. The couple enjoyed each other's company, examining the remodeling work, emptying a bottle of champagne, and making love. When he completed the film, he returned home to surprising, even startling news. "Duke," Pilar told him, "I'm pregnant." "Who the hell's the father?" he protested. "You are, Duke. Don't you remember the night you surprised me by flying home from Rome during the filming?" Marisa Carmela Wayne was born on February 22, 1966. Duke was fifty-eight.

After *Cast a Giant Shadow*, Duke moved into his newly remodeled nine-thousand-square-foot, seven-bedroom home in Newport Beach. He was tired and sore. On August 13 he had torn a back muscle jumping from a jeep. Italian doctors had put him in the hospital for the night, and though he had not been seriously hurt, stories filtered back to Hollywood that the cancer had returned. Mary St. John tried to stop the rumors with honest press releases, but reporters were not as ready to believe them as before.[33]

No sooner was he at home, however, than he became restless again. Pilar was pregnant, concerned about the possibility of a miscarriage, and not willing to serve as his constant companion. Aissa was nine and Ethan three, and Duke enjoyed spending time with his kids, but he missed his old friends and had yet to forge many Newport connections. He spent hours watching the overhaul of the *Wild Goose*, standing in the sawdust that covered the deck or sitting on a stack of lumber, joking with the carpenters and disagreeing loudly with the interior decorator. At one point the decorator described his "vision" for the main salon, which included cabinet doors with ornate gold handles and avocado-and-gold-foil wallpaper. Duke roared: "I don't want my boat turned into a goddamned French whorehouse."[34]

After a time he needed more activity, and in October he began another film, his third in 1965. Joining Howard Hawks and Robert Mitchum in Tucson, Arizona, he went to work on *El Dorado*, a film about male friendship, professionalism, and growing old. In the mid-1960s there were questions in

Hollywood about the futures of all three men. Duke's health, Mitchum's attitude, and Hawks's age were constant sources of rumors. Every month that
Wayne lived helped to dispel the notion that he was a dying man, and Hawks,
for one, believed that Mitchum's "I-don't-give-a-shit" persona was at least partially a pose. But Hawks was almost seventy, and the 1960s had not been kind
to him. *Hatari!* (1962), *Man's Favorite Sport?* (1964), and *Red Line 7000*
(1965) had raised serious doubts about his abilities. Perhaps the industry had
passed him by; perhaps like John Ford he had lost his ability to speak to the
times; perhaps he had just plain lost his ability.

He needed a hit, and he knew it. He had bought Harry Brown's novel *The
Stars in Their Courses*, and Leigh Brackett, his favorite screenwriter, had
worked it into a script that emphasized its elements of Greek tragedy. Still,
Hawks had gnawing doubts. "Hey, this is going to be the worst picture I've
ever made," he told Brackett. "I'm no good at the downbeat stuff." Together
they started from scratch and wrote another script. They kept a key early
scene in which Cole Thornton (John Wayne) shoots an innocent boy, who,
unable to stand the pain, commits suicide. "One of the reasons we did it,"
Hawks recalled, "was because we felt that would start the picture off as a
tragedy, and then we could turn it into fun." From that point Hawks returned
to comfortable ground. Dipping into his own past, he grafted scenes, sequences, gags, and stunts from *Only Angels Have Wings*, *To Have and Have
Not*, *Red River*, *The Big Sleep*, and especially *Rio Bravo* onto the screenplay.
The result, many critics believed, was an inferior product, a pleasant bag of
tricks from a great director's past but nothing new, nothing alive.[35]

The end result, however, is considerably more than the sum of its pieces,
and *El Dorado* is in its own way as important a Hawks film as *Red River* or
Only Angels Have Wings. The film's title comes from the legendary city of El
Dorado, a place that can be located on no map. As Robin Wood noted in his
study of the movies of Howard Hawks, "there is no El Dorado, the film suggests, either in life or in death; there is only the search."[36]

At first glance *El Dorado* seems a typical John Wayne Western. The action
revolves around a range war and Bart Jason's (Edward Asner) vision of a cattle
empire. Determined to destroy everything in his path, he hires a professional
gunman to get rid of Kevin MacDonald, a rival rancher, and his family. The
film moves toward a confrontation between two professionals: Nelse McLeod
(Christopher George), Jason's hired gun, and Thornton, who feels obligated
to the MacDonalds because he shot their son.

But *El Dorado* is only tangentially about the surface action. Though fighting for a brutal and dishonest man, McLeod is something of an idealistic young knight for whom the code of the gunman is everything. He believes in fair fights and high-noon shoot-outs, in "professional courtesy." For him El Dorado is a real place. Thornton, on the other hand, has ridden through enough valleys to know that there is no El Dorado, only pain and suffering and inevitable death. Life has robbed him of illusions. J. P. Harrah (Robert Mitchum), his best friend, is a pathetic drunk; Maudie (Charlene Holt), his best girl, has a tarnished reputation; and his life has been reduced to a series of painful moments, the result of a bullet lodged near the nerves of his spine. He clutches his side after any strenuous activity, and at key moments his gun hand is in a state of paralysis.

Hawks reinforces the themes of age and degeneration, as well as the loss of a vision of El Dorado, by shooting the climactic scenes at night. Darkness seems literally to be closing in on Thornton and Harrah. Outside the warm light of the sheriff's office are the dark streets of El Dorado, threatening, ominous, teeming with hired guns. Gunmen are in the saloon and the church; comfort can be found neither in the bottle nor in religion. Finally the sole option left to Thornton and Harrah is to draw on their only weapon: experience. They have been through it all before. They know how gunmen act and where they hide, and they survive not because they are faster but because they have lost their vision. Thornton, his gun hand crippled, asks McLeod to abstain from a gun battle out of "professional courtesy" but then shoots him from beneath a wagon. "You didn't give me a chance at all, did you?" the dying McLeod asks. "No, I didn't. You're too good to give a chance to," Thornton bluntly replies.

The film ends with Thornton and Harrah walking down the sunlit streets of El Dorado on crutches, both wounded but both alive. For Hawks—and Wayne—the goal was the same: getting the job done and staying alive.[37]

Hawks finished the interior work in February 1966, but he had a hard time letting editor John Woodcock do his job. Too much was at stake, and he tinkered with the film, editing and reediting it a dozen times. When Paramount released the movie in June 1967, Hawks was not disappointed with its reception. It quieted Hollywood's gossips. The *Hollywood Reporter* admitted as much in its review. "*El Dorado*, Howard Hawks' latest for Paramount, is his best since *Rio Bravo*. . . . [It] will appeal to all ages and attitudes, rake in profits in domestic and foreign release, and enhance Hawks' position in the directorial Pantheon of the auteur critics." Audiences lined up all over the country on the day of its general release. Within a year *El Dorado* had earned $12 million in box-office receipts.[38]

Pleased by Hawks's triumph, Duke was just as determined to silence his own critics and continue to make films with the same gusto as *The Sons of Katie Elder*. In September 1966 he flew to Durango, where Batjac and Marvin Schwartz were producing *The War Wagon* for Universal. Clair Huffaker wrote a screenplay based on his own novel *Badman*. Duke hired Dmitri Tiomkin to compose the score, Bill Clothier to head the camera crew, and Bruce Cabot to star as the evil Frank Pierce, a sleazy businessman who corrupts local lawmen and railroads Taw Jackson (John Wayne) into prison on trumped-up charges. During Jackson's three-year sentence in a New Mexico penitentiary, Pierce manages to steal his land and the gold mine on it. Using the "War Wagon," an armored stagecoach, and a hired posse of thirty gunmen, Pierce moves the gold from the mine to the railroad. On his release from prison, Taw Jackson returns home, teams up with Lomax (Kirk Douglas), a fancy gunslinger; and Levi Walking Bear (Howard Keel), a Kiowa Indian; and together they ambush the War Wagon, killing Pierce and recovering some of the gold.

Burt Kennedy directed the film, but everyone knew who was really in charge. Except in John Ford films, Duke was not the easiest person to direct. When Batjac money was on the line, he could be even more difficult. Burt Kennedy described him as "tough, you know. Especially when it was his own company, and I never worked with him except for his own company. He felt responsible for everything and he would get into everything; he'd make it tough." Kirk Douglas, who was always urging people to stand up for their rights, remembered: "Kennedy was having trouble with Wayne. Burt was a very talented director, but gentle. Wayne was a less talented director, and far from gentle. I tried to get Burt to stand up to him. It wasn't easy." Duke had an opinion about every element of the production. "He was always first on the set," Douglas recalled. "He was interested in everything. I used to get a kick out of him. He'd be down there arguing with the special effects man about how much dynamite to put in the charges." According to Bill Clothier, one day Howard Keel almost belted Duke on the set. Clothier recalled: "Duke started pushing him [Keel] around, grabbing him, showing him how to play the scene. . . . After the scene was over, I went over to Keel and said, 'I saw your reactions. . . .' Before I could finish, he [Keel] said: 'If he puts his hands on me again I'm gonna clobber that son of a bitch.' 'Duke doesn't mean anything by it. That's just the way he is,'" Clothier told Keel. Kennedy was more understanding than Keel. "You cannot change [Duke]," Kennedy argued in 1966. "He is obdurate and obstinate and he thinks one way. Now Duke has been a movie star . . . a long time. The great thing about Wayne is that despite this he is not a movie star. He acts and talks like a real person. He has held on to his humanity and not lost it. Sometimes he is rough and sometimes he is mean, but he is always himself and he is not phoney and bogus. And it comes across. . . . That's why the people love him."

The War Wagon was vintage John Wayne. Taw Jackson gets even with the men who have exploited and abused him, not by appealing to legislatures and courts but by resorting to six-guns and dynamite. He gets back his land and his gold; rough justice prevails. *Life* magazine's film reviewer noted that Wayne was a "kind of natural phenomenon, rather like a spectacular geological remnant of a vanished age, and if he is to be fully appreciated he must be viewed from a carefully selected vantage point. . . . this is what has been thoughtfully provided by *The War Wagon*."[39]

He may indeed have seemed a remnant of a vanished age to many in 1966. But he still had tens of millions of fans for whom his vision of America's past and present was not irrelevant. In his personal life, however, Duke occasionally made the same mistakes.

He needed someone to take over his business affairs. After Bo Roos, this time he wanted somebody close, geographically and personally, whom he could trust, preferably someone who was family. He finally decided on Don LaCava, his daughter Toni's husband. LaCava had been in law school when he married Toni, but he soon went to work at Batjac, and Duke had planned to move him into the production end of the business. Instead he put LaCava in charge of his money. LaCava had no training as an accountant or investment counselor, but Wayne did not have high expectatons. "Hell," he told Pilar. "I don't expect him to make a lot. I told him to be conservative and make damn sure he didn't lose any." LaCava eventually formed Markand Management Associates in April 1966—eerily complete with fancy offices and lavish expense accounts—and let the world know that John Wayne was his client.[40]

Rebuilding Wayne's "fortune" was a daunting task. He had lost much of it when he had divorced Josie back in the 1940s, some more with the split from Chata, and the rest with Bo Roos. *The Alamo*'s expense and disappointing box office had kept Duke in financial trouble for several more years, and his bout with cancer set him back again in 1964. But in 1965 he had completed *The Sons of Katie Elder* and now, through 1966, *Cast a Giant Shadow, War Wagon,* and *El Dorado*. On the last two films, he earned a salary of $1 million each and a percentage of the receipts, but he was in a 70 percent federal income tax bracket. He sold the Batjac building in West Hollywood in February 1965, then jettisoned several of Bo Roos's pink elephants, including the Culver City

Hotel, which he donated to the YMCA and wrote off as a two hundred thousand dollar loss. Batjac regained control of *The Alamo* from United Artists in February 1965 and quickly sold rerelease rights back to them. The company then invested several million dollars in a Malibu Beach condominium project and a Beverly Hills convalescent home.[41]

But he was still not secure. In October he and Pilar decided to do their Christmas shopping early. They settled into their jet for the ride from Los Angeles to Dallas, the latest Neiman-Marcus catalog resting on his lap. He especially enjoyed getting the Christmas catalog in the mail each year to see what the most expensive gifts were going to be, even though he could not afford to buy the his-and-hers Lear jets or the private island in the Caribbean or whatever Neiman-Marcus was hawking that year. The catalog often triggered his addiction to shopping, and the Waynes decided to go on a binge in Texas—spending thousands of dollars at pricey Dallas department stores and boutiques.[42]

The jet landed at Love Field, and a limousine met them at the tarmac. Duke felt flush and strong. He had completed filming on the *War Wagon* and *El Dorado*, Pilar had given birth to Marisa, he was a daddy again, and his latest physical at Scripps indicated that the Red Witch was still at bay. When John Wayne felt flush, he wanted to shop, really shop, either in stores or in mail order catalogs. Ever since he was a kid he had loved department store catalogs. He used to sit in that Mojave Desert outhouse and flip through the pages of the Sears catalog, always careful to wipe with a page advertising items of little interest, like farm machinery, tools, or clothes. He would even rip out a supply of the boring pages and leave them for Bobby and his parents, not wanting them absentmindedly to tear out the pages with toys, athletic equipment, and fishing and hunting gear. Bert Minshall remembered that he "would browse through catalogs by the hour, marking all the merchandise he wanted. Then he'd ask his secretary, Mary St. John, to write the appropriate checks and send away for the items."[43]

"I used to dream," he once told Pat Stacy, "that someday I'd have enough dollars to order everything in that damn catalogue. Catalogues became an obsession with me." He enjoyed wandering through stores, looking at Early American furniture, smelling perfumes, handling decorative accessories, and pulling garments off the racks and holding them up against Pilar to see if he liked them. And he was good at it, correctly sizing his friends and their wives and buying stylish ensembles that matched and fit perfectly. When women like Mary St. John or Alice Johnson would get surprise packages delivered by United Parcel from some corner of the world, they knew that Duke had been shopping and thinking about them. If he did not have time to get to the stores, he would methodically page through the catalogs marking items with a pencil so that his secretaries could order them and send them off as gifts.[44]

During the Christmas spree in Dallas, he and Pilar shopped with abandon, going from store to store, buying gifts for themselves, the kids, and their friends. They put more than thirty thousand dollars on charge cards in less than two days. A month later the bills started showing up at the offices of Markand Management Associates. More than a little irritated, and scared, La-Cava drove over to Batjac and said to Duke, "How could you spend so much money? You don't have this kind of money in the bank! How the hell am I supposed to pay these bills?" Duke cursed back: reminding LaCava that he had turned millions over to him in the last three years. "There goddamn well better be money in the bank to pay these bills!" Wayne was immediately suspicious, developing an instant, sickening, gut-wrenching sense of *déjà vu*. It had been the letter from Saks Fifth Avenue about a ninety-days-overdue bill that had marked his awareness of Roos's failure. This time the news was not that bad, but it was bad enough. Money to pay the bills was not there. LaCava had squandered Duke's liquid assets in a series of poorly timed, ill-conceived investments—dry oil wells, marginal real estate, broker fees, and overhead on Markand Management. He fired LaCava immediately, son-in-law or not.[45]

Actually because of his film salaries and the Arizona cotton farm, Duke's net worth was climbing steadily in spite of the LaCava affair. Under Louis Johnson's shrewd, scrupulously honest management, the Arizona property had ballooned in value. It did not help Wayne's cash flow because profits were plowed back into the operation, redeeming the land and the equipment from all the mortgages, but it put his net worth well into the black. The income from the farm increased even more in 1970, when the Department of Agriculture reduced acreage allotments and paid cotton farmers not to produce. The Arizona property received hundreds of thousands of dollars from the USDA each year. In 1980, a year after Wayne's death, Johnson sold the farm for $45 million.[46]

In 1966 one other challenge came into Duke's life, on the political front, one that blended Hollywood and politics. During the filming of *The War Wagon* in the fall of 1966, the fault lines of California politics shook in a great ideological earthquake. Voters enjoyed a choice between liberalism and conservatism as clear as the Johnson-Goldwater presidential election two years before. Much to Duke's disgust, Edmund "Pat" Brown, the Democratic incumbent, had constructed the Golden State's version of the Great Society.

Courtesy UPI/Bettmann

After two failed marriages Duke was anxious to bring his personal life more in line with his screen persona. He met Pilar Pallete, a young Peruvian actress, in a South American jungle and had dinner with her and her estranged husband, Richard Weldy *(above)*. Soon after his divorce to Chata became final, he married Pilar in Hawaii *(below left)*. For a time, his relations with his mother even seemed to improve *(below right)*.

Almost as a reaction to his personal life, Duke's favorite film roles emphasized men living apart from women. In *Hondo* (1953) *(above)*, made during the middle of his divorce, he plays the lean outsider; in *The Searchers* (1956) *(below left)*, which critics hail as his finest movie, he portrays the psychologically tormented outsider; and in *The Wings of Eagles* (1957), the story of Spig Wead (sitting), he captures the essence of a man who simply cannot exist outside the company of other men. In fact, his bookend friends Ward Bond and John Ford *(below right)* were the most permanent relationships in his life.

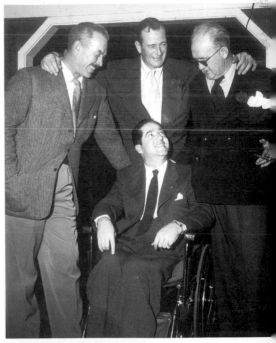

During the 1950s Wayne moved increasingly into politics, and his conservative beliefs showed in the films he produced. *The Alamo* (1960) *(above right)* was the fullest expression of his political beliefs. But producing, directing, and starring in the 192-minute epic exacted a toll. For almost a year he seemed to exist on steak and cigarettes. Yet the film brought him great satisfaction, if very little money. His daughter Aissa, *(right)*, one of his three children with Pilar, had a small part in the film. After *The Alamo* he turned to a series of Westerns to make money. *McLintock!* (1963), with Maureen O'Hara and a spectacular mud fight *(above left)*, was one of his most popular.

In the early 1960s Wayne's career began to sag. Ward Bond died (*below left*, with John Ford). John Ford's talent declined, as is apparent in *Donovan's Reef* (1963), in which Duke played opposite Elizabeth Allen (*above*). Finally, in 1964 Wayne was operated on for lung cancer. The effects of alcohol, cigarettes, and cancer were etched on his face (*below right*).

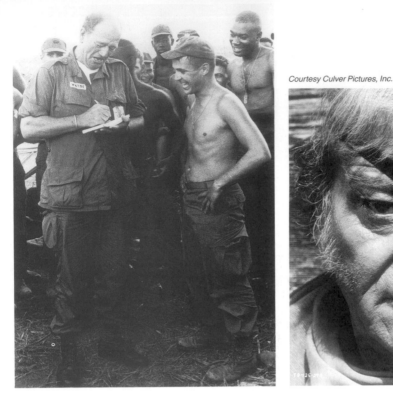

Though in the mid-1960s critics had pronounced the end of Duke's career, it blossomed again at the end of the decade. He made his position on the war in Vietnam clear in *The Green Berets* (1968) *(above left)* and confirmed his institutional status in *True Grit* (1969) *(above right)*. Barbra Streisand presented him with the Oscar for his portrayal of Rooster Cogburn *(below)*.

By the 1970s John Wayne was an American icon, the voice of Richard Nixon's silent majority. In 1972 he was inducted as a Master Mason *(below left)*. In 1974 he was given the Brass Balls Award by the staff of *The Harvard Lampoon;* he arrived at the event in an armored personnel carrier *(above)*. By then he had also left Pilar and formed a relationship with his personal secretary, Pat Stacy *(below right)*.

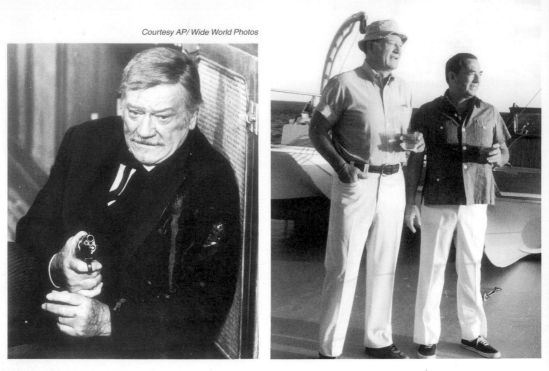

In Duke's last film, *The Shootist* (1976), he played an old gunfighter dying of cancer *(above left)*. By the time the film opened, his own health was beginning to fail. The good times aboard the *Wild Goose* with such close friends as Joe De Franco *(above right)* were getting fewer and the hospital visits more frequent. His last public appearance was at the 1979 Academy Awards ceremony *(below left)*. Thin, frail, and close to death, he put on his best John Wayne face and promised to be around for other Oscar nights. He wasn't. But nobody since has filled his boots. His son Ethan *(below right)* touches his spurs.

During his tenure social spending, taxes, and the size of the state bureaucracy increased dramatically as liberals tried to end poverty and guarantee civil rights for all Californians. Opposing Brown was Ronald Reagan, the actor and former president of the Screen Actors Guild, a right-wing Republican conservative like Wayne, and an unabashed supporter of Barry Goldwater, a man who had concluded at midlife that modern American liberalism was morally and politically bankrupt.

Debates about the California election reverberated through the set of *The War Wagon*. As usual Wayne and Douglas were on opposite sides of the political fence. "Our strange relationship of professional respect in spite of extreme personal and professional differences continued," Douglas recalled years later. "During the picture, I made political statements for Democratic candidates, Wayne made statements for Republicans." Douglas wanted more of the same in California—more programs for social justice, more government, more of the liberal agenda. Duke wanted Ronald Reagan to dismantle the monster Governor Pat Brown had constructed.

He had never minced words about his political opinions, and more than once he expressed them in gestures as well. In March, when he was leaving the house in Encino for the last time, Duke hurried back inside to retrieve one last memento. For years he had kept a framed portrait of Sen. Hubert Humphrey, the liberal Democrat from Minnesota—complete with the inscription: "Dear Duke, Thanks for your continued support"—taped to the toilet tank in the guest bathroom; it was easy to overlook but the joke meant too much to leave behind.[47]

Though lung cancer had cut short his work on behalf of Senator Goldwater in the 1964 election, in 1966 he stumped California for Ronald Reagan. He had been friends with the Reagans for years, and Nancy Reagan was a particular admirer of him. "Duke Wayne was," she told her husband, "the most gentle, tender person I ever knew." She had strong memories of Duke's early support. In 1960, when Reagan was president of the Screen Actors Guild, he took the Guild out on strike. The studios launched a media campaign against the walkout, and Reagan found himself the target of intense, and often vicious, criticism. Aware that such criticism would be particularly difficult for Nancy to accept, Duke called her daily, reassuring her that everything would be just fine and telling her to "not let those bastards get you down." She never forgot the courtesy. He was also convinced that Reagan would make an excellent governor. Reagan, he believed, possessed a charismatic personality and, best of all, was a convert to the cause, a man who had abandoned liberalism in favor of the conservative movement. Duke took great pleasure in Reagan's stunning victory, as well as in the general thrashing Republicans gave the Democrats in Congress that year.[48]

Life was sweet again. The devastating reversals of the early 1960s—a lost fortune, the deaths of so many friends, the ravages of the Red Witch—were behind him. Duke's apparent victory over cancer had added a new dimension to the John Wayne persona. With courage and aplomb, he had conquered a real enemy and given encouragement to millions of people fighting the dread disease. In Orange County he had formed new friendships and taken a more active interest in his family. There were no changes in his priorities, just a restoration of energy and passion. He still loved movies, money, and the Republican party, and he was bent on promoting all of them. His patriotism ran deeper than ever. Then the summer after Reagan's victory, Lyndon B. Johnson signed the orders to send two hundred thousand more American soldiers to Vietnam. John Wayne had another war to fight.

20

Working-Class Hero

In August 1965 Duke had just returned from Rome and Israel, in between *Cast a Giant Shadow* and *El Dorado*. He was in downtown Los Angeles for meetings at the Shriner Temple to discuss plans for a charity benefit on behalf of burn patients at the children's hospital. Taking a few minutes to relax, he walked across the street with Mary St. John and strolled about the USC campus. They talked about how the campus had changed in forty years. The day was blistering hot, with Santa Ana desert winds sandblasting the basin, and sweat made his shirt cling to his back. But the green lawns, eucalyptus trees, and reddish brown brick buildings improved his mood, reminding him of simpler times.[1]

They were standing in the grass facing the Doheny Library when a commotion erupted near the sidewalk to their right. A student group had set up tables and posters to protest the Vietnam War, and they were heckling a young marine who was walking toward his car. Dressed in crisply ironed khakis, his black shoes gleaming with a lacquerlike shine, his back ramrod stiff, his chin jutting forward, the man's chest displayed a good-conduct medal, a marksmanship medal, a Navy and Marine Corps Overseas Service Ribbon, a National Defense Service Medal, a Vietnam Service Medal, a Combat Action Ribbon, a Republic of Vietnam Campaign Medal, a Sea Service Deployment Medal, and a Purple Heart. Two stripes with crossed rifles identified him as a corporal. The soldier seemed unaware of the protesters. "My drill instructor taught me to ignore impolite slimy civilians," he later told Wayne. "Maintain tack and bearing. Don't give the scum the satisfaction of noticing them."

But when Duke looked a little closer at the marine, he lost what little composure he had. The right sleeve of the soldier's uniform, where an arm should have been, was neatly folded and pinned down to keep it from flapping. A booby trap had splattered the boy's arm all over some nameless village on the other side of the world. The soldier would soon be mustered out of the corps, and he had decided to go back to school on the GI Bill. Duke walked him to the car, gave him an autographed card, and thanked him for serving his country.

He waved as the car moved away and then jogged back across the street. He walked right by Mary without a word, heading back down the sidewalk by the library and up to the protesters' table, while she scurried after him. "I knew all hell was going to break loose," Mary remembered. He slammed both fists onto the students' table, leaned into their faces, his voice wavering in barely controlled rage, and exclaimed through his teeth: "You stupid bastards! Blame Johnson if you must; blame that sonofabitch Kennedy; blame Eisenhower or Truman or goddamnfuckingRoosevelt, but don't blame that kid. Not any of those kids. They served! Jesus, the kid's arm is gone!" Spent, he backed away from the table, lifted his arms only to let them fall to to his sides, sighing to no one in particular: "What the hell is happening to this country?"

The young soldier had been part of the Ninth Marine Expeditionary Brigade, a force of 3,500 combat troops Johnson deployed to Danang, South Vietnam, on March 8, 1965—the first American ground troops sent to Vietnam. Eleven years earlier the Vietnamese had finally triumphed over the colonial French in the Battle of Dien Bien Phu. By that time the United States was in the throes of the Cold War, and the Eisenhower administration viewed Ho Chi Minh and his agrarian communism with alarm. Eisenhower believed that if Vietnam fell to communism, it was only a matter of time before Laos, Cambodia, Thailand, Burma, the Philippines, and Japan suffered the same fate. He sought to shore up democratic forces in Vietnam. Duke accepted the domino theory. He had supported Sen. Robert Taft of Ohio at the 1952 Republican Convention, and during the 1950s he had been aware of the Communist guerrilla movements in British Malaya, French Indochina, Dutch Indonesia, and the Philippines. If Vietnam was the place to make a stand, to keep communism from American shores, then so be it.[2]

The decision to Americanize and militarize the conflict in Vietnam energized an antiwar movement. At the University of Michigan in Ann Arbor, several faculty members organized a "teach-in"—patterned after the 1960 civil rights sit-ins—for March 24, 1965. More than 3,500 students attended, listening to faculty members discuss the nature of the war and the "morality" of American involvement. Similar teach-ins mushroomed at campuses across the country in the spring of 1965, culminating with the "National Teach-In" at 122 colleges and universities on May 15.

Later that year producer Ken Hyman and MGM offered Duke the part of Major Reisman in *The Dirty Dozen*. He loved the part, except he did not like the beginning of the script, where Reisman is having an affair with an English-woman whose husband is a soldier fighting on the Continent. Wayne never wanted to portray an adulterer, let alone an unfeeling one, and the idea of sleeping with a soldier's wife was repulsive. He discussed his objections with Hyman and asked for a change in the script. MGM wrote the objectionable scene out of *The Dirty Dozen*, but he still turned down the part. He decided that he wanted to make a Vietnam war movie.[3]

Duke's views on Vietnam were carved in stone and remained so throughout the 1960s and 1970s. The war was in the best interests of the United States and the free world. Like many conservatives, John Wayne blamed Harry Tru-man for losing China to Mao Zedong and for not letting General Douglas MacArthur deal a death blow to the North Koreans. To those who argued that Vietnam was really an internal civil war, or that nationalism, not communism, was the force driving the Vietcong and North Vietnamese, Duke had one word: "Horseshit!" Late in 1967 he told a columnist from *Movie Life*, "I can't believe that people in the U.S. don't realize that we are at war with internation-al communism. I think somebody should take Senator Kennedy and Senator Fulbright to the forward areas of Vietnam to talk to the guys and see the kind of communist equipment they are getting wounded with."[4]

Wayne was convinced that the war was winnable, that the U.S. military ef-fort could stem the Communist tide in Indochina. He often cited the 1965 intervention in the Dominican Republic, when President Lyndon Johnson sent the marines to prevent a Communist takeover by Juan Bosch. "They [lib-erals] said," Duke remarked in 1967, "that if we went into the Dominican Re-public we'd ruin everything and bring down the world against us. We went in; they now have a republic that's probably as good as any in Latin America." He argued that the British had successfully defeated a Communist insurgency in Malaya in the 1950s, and that the Filipinos had similarly crushed the Huk Rebellion. "Indonesia," he claimed, "got enough guts to throw the Commu-nists out. . . . It's ridiculous—it's impractical—to think any other way."[5]

In the fall of 1966, he agreed to appear on a program with Bob Hope at the University of Southern California to raise money for the school's scholarship endowment. By that time the USC campus had been the scene of a number of antiwar sit-ins, teach-ins, bomb scares, boycotts, and protests. More than ten thousand people were in the audience, and Wayne was prepared to offer some brief introductory remarks before Hope's monologue. But the crowd was unruly. Small scuffles, catcalls, chants, and obscenities interrupted the rehearsal. Wayne decided to drop all pleasantries in favor of some tough talk. He showed the changes to Hope, who blanched, "You can't give a speech like that here, Duke, unless you intend to turn those kids out there into a lynch mob howling for your blood." Wayne calmly replied, "I don't give a shit. . . . It's about time someone talked turkey to those kids. Let 'em lynch me." He then walked on stage, stood behind the microphone until the catcalls subsided, and said: "A university should be a quiet place where you go to learn, not to destroy property belonging to someone else. Getting an education is a privilege, not a right. Your professors and administrators should be treated with courtesy and respect. While you're here you ought to be learning a sense of responsibility. We aren't going to sit by and let you destroy our schools and system. This is a great university. You owe it your best. Thank you very much." He exited the stage to a standing ovation.[6]

He could not understand the sources of student complaints. "What do they have to bitch about?" he asked Mary St. John. Practically all of them came from upper-middle-class and upper-class families whose fathers were paying their tuition, buying them expensive cars, dressing them in the latest fashions, and keeping their pockets filled with money. The protesters reminded him of the Hollywood liberals of the 1930s and 1940s—privileged people whose lifestyles reeked of capitalism and money and who, for reasons completely baffling to him, "wanted to shoot the golden goose."[7]

He took it all very personally. It went against the grain of every role he ever played, as well as the man he tried to be. He determined to rally Americans to the cause of anticommunism, and to the support of the boys going over to Vietnam to fight and die, in the best way he knew how—to make a pro-American, pro-soldier, guts-and-glory film, just as he had done so many times in the past. Deciding on a focus for the film was easy. John Wayne titled it *The Green Berets*.

The Green Berets was an elite, army counterinsurgency unit from Special Forces, which had been first authorized by John F. Kennedy to wear the distinctive beret. Kennedy once remarked: "The Green Beret is becoming a symbol of excellence, a badge of courage and a mark of distinction in the fight for freedom." Theoretically at least, men became Green Berets only if they were ranger- and airborne-qualified, fluent in at least one foreign language, and in peak physical condition. They studied the enemy by reading the books and speeches of Mao Zedong, Ho Chi Minh, and Vo Nguyen Giap. David Halberstam wrote of them: "They were all uncommon men, extraordinary physical specimens and intellectual Ph.D.'s, swinging through trees, speaking Russian and Chinese, eating snake meat and other fauna, springing counter-ambushes at night on unwary Asian ambushers."[8]

John Kennedy was not the only American infatuated with Green Berets. In 1963 Robin Moore asked the Pentagon for assistance in writing a novel about the Special Forces. Army officials gave Moore the necessary travel authorizations and the right to interview a number of Green Berets stationed in South Vietnam. Published in 1965, *The Green Berets* sold three million copies and rocketed to the top of the bestseller lists, earning the wrath of the Pentagon in the process. The novel's accuracy frightened army brass, who considered it a breach of security. Hanson Baldwin, a *New York Times* columnist, wrote that *The Green Berets* "has stirred up a fuss in Washington. The official objection to the book apparently is that it is too close to the facts." Taking advantage of the success of Moore's novel, songwriter Barry Sadler composed "Ballad of the Green Berets," which topped the music charts in 1966.[9]

By then, however, many liberals and radicals had turned against the war, and most Hollywood studio heads believed that the war was too controversial to be entertainment. Political films often spelled box-office disaster. David Wolper and Columbia Pictures took out an option on Robin Moore's novel in 1963, long before it was even published, and he asked the Department of Defense for assistance in making the movie. The Pentagon agreed on one condition: The Department of Defense's Public Affairs Office would have final say on the script. Columbia was not able to come up with a screenplay acceptable to the hypersensitive Pentagon. Army officials objected to Moore's description of Green Beret raids into North Vietnam, even if such raids had been reported in the press. Regular army brass were not too thrilled about glorifying the Special Forces anyway. They had long resented the elitism of the Special Forces and had laid plans in the late-1950s to phase out the unit, until Kennedy's interest and the unit's notoriety made that impossible.[10]

Columbia Pictures and the Pentagon mutually agreed to abandon the project, and Wayne bought the movie rights for fifty thousand dollars. In December 1965 he wrote President Johnson about his plans. The two had met several times in 1959 and 1960, when *The Alamo* was in production, and again in 1961 and 1962, when they were both in Austin and San Antonio. Though Duke campaigned for Barry Goldwater in 1964, he sent a congratulatory telegram to Johnson the day after the election. The president returned the courtesy: THANKS FOR THE THOUGHTFUL TELEGRAM. EVEN DURING THE CAMPAIGN I NEVER LOST MY ZEST FOR JOHN WAYNE MOVIES. YOU AND I HAVE BEEN IN OUR RESPECTIVE FIELDS—MOVIES AND PUBLIC SERVICE—FOR ABOUT THE SAME TIME. I CAN ONLY HOPE THAT NEITHER OF US TRIES TO SWAP PROFESSIONS. YOU ARE A GOOD AMERICAN AND I AM CHEERED BY YOUR WIRE."[11]

Duke's letter emphasized his personal support for the war effort as well as his conviction that the administration needed a vehicle for explaining that it was "extremely important that not only the people of the United States but those all over the world should know why it is necessary for us to be there. . . . The most effective way to accomplish this is through the motion picture medium." Duke then promised the president that his film would "inspire a patriotic attitude on the part of fellow-Americans—a feeling which we have always had in this country in the past during times of stress and trouble." The assistance of the Department of Defense, he explained, was critical to the success of the movie. Duke also cited similar films he had done—*The Longest Day*, *The Sands of Iwo Jima*, and *The Fighting Seabees*—as evidence of successful collaborations in the past. To presidential press secretary Bill Moyers, Duke wrote: "We don't want people like Kosygin, Mao Tse-Tung, or the like 'gorin' our oxes.'"[12]

President Johnson was intrigued with the letter, and he asked Jack Valenti, a domestic adviser soon to become president of the Motion Picture Association of America, for his opinion. Valenti wrote to Johnson that "Wayne's politics are wrong, but insofar as Vietnam is concerned, his views are right. If he made the picture he would be saying the things we want said. . . ." He recommended that the government support Duke's efforts. Johnson agreed, and on January 18, 1966, Bill Moyers wrote Wayne suggesting that he send a script to Arthur Sylvester, assistant secretary of defense.[13]

Wayne wrote Moyers several weeks later outlining his vision for the film, reassuring him that the final script would please the administration. The film would show "such scenes as the little village that erected its own statue of liberty to the American people. We want to bring out that if we abandon these people, there will be a blood bath of over two million souls." He promised that *The Green Berets* would portray the professional "soldier carrying out his duty of death, but, also, his extra-curricular duties—diplomats in dungarees—helping small communities, giving them medical attention, toys for their children, and little things like soap, which can be so all important."[14]

With the government behind him, Wayne began to recruit a production unit in February 1966. He had Michael Wayne produce the film; there was nobody in the business he trusted more to protect his own image and the family's resources. Duke was confident that Hollywood wisdom was wrong, that the public interest in a good war movie was as strong as ever, but in case there was a problem with the market, he still wanted the film brought in at a low $6.1 million production cost.[15]

Next the Waynes needed a screenwriter. Jimmy Grant, Duke's favorite, was unavailable because his lung cancer was already well advanced, and Duke vetoed Robin Moore. The novelist had been doing too many interviews critical of the Defense Department. Since Batjac needed official approval of the script before filming could begin, he did not want any unnecessary provocation of the Pentagon. He decided to hire James Lee Barrett, a former marine who had written the screenplay for *The D.I.*, a popular film starring Jack Webb, in 1957, and an outspoken supporter of the American effort in Vietnam. Wayne assured Bill Moyers that Barrett was an "extremely competent writer" and that he would produce an original screenplay, with little similarity to Moore's novel.[16]

In April 1966, at the suggestion of the Pentagon, Duke visited Fort Bragg, North Carolina, to tour the John F. Kennedy Special Warfare Center, where Green Berets were trained. Base officials gave him the red carpet treatment, and he came away convinced that with army support, which appeared certain, he could make a great movie. He wrote to Moyers praising the soldiers at Fort Bragg and attaching a letter he had written to every member of the U.S. Senate, arguing that a defeat of the United States in Vietnam would damage American credibility throughout the world and inspire Communist rebellions closer to home.[17]

With the basic arrangements complete, Duke flew to South Vietnam in June 1966 to get a firsthand look at the war. He went as part of a three-week USO tour and to narrate a Department of Defense film. Wayne stayed in Saigon the first few days of the tour, and he was astonished at how quickly the Vietnamese recognized him. He could hardly step out of the Rex Hotel before brakes screeched, horns blared, traffic jams materialized, and Vietnamese started to shout: "Ah, John Wayne, Numbah One Cowboy, Numbah One Cowboy!" While he was signing autographs for the 3rd Battalion of the 7th Marine Regiment near Chu Lai, Vietcong snipers fired several AK-47 rifle rounds that kicked up dust within a few yards from Duke's feet and sent the marines scrambling for cover. "Hell," he later remarked, "I didn't even know we were being fired at until I saw the marines running for cover."[18]

At Pleiku in the Central Highlands, he sat through a screening of *Fort Apache* with some Green Berets. Standing by watching the film were several dozen Montagnard tribesmen, most of whom did not speak English, but whom the Green Berets considered completely loyal to the American cause. They could not understand any of the dialogue in the film, but whenever Indians attacked the U.S. Cavalry, the Montagnards instinctively cheered. "They knew nothing about United States history," Wayne recalled with glee, "but they knew what they liked: brown people killing white people." For the rest of his life, Duke treasured, and wore on his left wrist, a gold bracelet the Montagnards gave him that night.[19]

While Duke toured South Vietnam, Michael continued to work with Barrett on the script and arranged for distribution of *The Green Berets* once Batjac finished production. It was a tough sell. Antiwar protests were escalating, and the studios were running scared. Barrett wrote out a story line, and Michael took it to Universal, along with the endorsement from Duke and his promise to star in the movie, and studio executives agreed to provide help financing and distributing it, as long as they had script approval in advance. Barrett now faced the daunting challenge of writing a screenplay that would please John Wayne, the Pentagon, *and* Universal.[20]

Barrett submitted a first draft to the Pentagon in August 1966, but the army rejected it out of hand. His plot had a Special Forces team carrying out a covert raid in North Vietnam, which involved the kidnapping of a North Vietnamese general and the destruction of several bridges. The Green Berets' mission in South Vietnam was reconnaissance and training, not aggression against North Vietnam. "The development of the plot," a Pentagon official told Michael Wayne, "is not acceptable in that the type of mission evolved is not one which Special Forces would be involved in under present policy." Green Berets would not invade North Vietnam.[21]

Michael did not tell Duke that the army had rejected the script. "I was actually afraid to because he would have said, 'You dumb son of a bitch!'" Michael recounted to historian Lawrence Suid. Also, Hollywood was well aware that Batjac was producing the film, and Michael did not need any negative publicity. News that the script was bad would spread across Hollywood like a prairie fire. It was better, Michael reasoned, simply to have Barrett rewrite the script. Instead of a covert mission into North Vietnam to kidnap a North Vietnamese general, the Green Berets would remain in South Vietnam and kidnap a Vietcong general on the wrong side of the line. He also added material on the Green Berets working with South Vietnamese military officials in the defense of a base camp. A Vietcong assault on the camp became the focus for the movie's primary battle scenes. This revision had a better reception, but the Pentagon eventually suggested hundreds of changes, from plot line to dialogue to the smallest details of military operations. Barrett repeatedly had to rewrite the script, and each new rewrite forced Michael to revise the production schedule. After several more readings, the Pentagon gave final approval to Batjac on March 30, 1967, telling Duke that the film "promises to be a most worthwhile and, we trust, successful production."[22]

Finding a location for the exterior filming was the next challenge. Duke flirted with the idea of shooting the movie in Vietnam, but the security problems were too great. "If you start shooting blanks over there," he told codirector Ray Kellogg, "they [the Vietcong] might start shooting back." Fort Bragg was out of the question because base officials could not provide a reliable schedule for use of aircraft and helicopters. The same problem ruled out army facilities on Okinawa. Location filming was too expensive to risk forced postponement.[23]

The Pentagon suggested Fort Benning, Georgia. In May 1967 the Waynes visited the base. It was perfect, or at least almost perfect. Set in the pine forests of western Georgia, Fort Benning was the center for army infantry training. Huge banners bearing the words INFANTRY—QUEEN OF BATTLE graced several brick buildings on the base, and Duke was impressed with the army's confident efficiency. They guaranteed him the necessary complement of military hardware, including Huey helicopters, when the shooting schedule required them, as well as safe locations for explosive special effects, facilities for housing and feeding the Batjac crew, and all the extra personnel needed to complete the film. Wayne promised in return to build a permanent $150,000 replica of a rural village in South Vietnam that the army could use for training when the filming was finished.[24]

Two weeks after the trip and just two months before shooting was scheduled to begin, Universal backed out. On April 15 more than 125,000 antiwar protesters had clogged midtown Manhattan, and similar demonstrations occurred in most other major American cities. One month later Sen. Frank Church of Idaho wrote a letter to President Johnson, bearing the signatures of sixteen other senators, calling for an end to the war. Universal got cold feet. One studio executive said that the Pentagon-approved script "was the worst screenplay I have ever read," that it "makes anti-war protestors look like pinko creeps. . . . Nobody wants to see a guy getting killed in the Vietnam War when guys are actually getting killed in the Vietnam War." Duke approached Paramount, but studio executives wanted nothing to do with the film. He finally went to Jack Warner and talked him into having Warner Bros. distribute *The Green Berets*. Like other studio heads, Warner too was skeptical, but Duke, appealing to their long-term relationship, asked Warner to trust him. Batjac and Warners signed the necessary agreement on June 21, 1967.[25]

Batjac began shooting at Fort Benning early in August. Duke, Pilar, and Ethan, along with the rest of the cast, took over the Camellia Motel in Columbus, Georgia, and the company worked at a furious pace, shooting day and night, six days a week. As usual when he directed, Duke was preoccupied and short-tempered. Years later Burt Kennedy, a Hollywood director, remembered a friend asking him: "Are you going to direct *The Green Berets*? I said, 'I'd rather join the Green Berets.'" The army cooperated with Wayne, even if the weather did not. Duke had all the soldiers, jeeps, helicopters, M-16s, mortars, and explosives he needed. On August 9 a Special Forces team from Fort Bragg parachuted onto Eubanks Field at Fort Benning and put on a demonstration of unconventional warfare weapons and tactics, which Duke filmed in front of an audience sitting in the bleachers. Combat footage was shot at a "C Camp" near Kelley Hill. Duke used the briefing rooms at Infantry Hall for inside scenes, Todd Field for barracks shots, Warner Range for M-60 machine-gun firings, and Watson Field for bayonet drills. The Danang landing scene was shot at Lawson Air Field, with a cast of one hundred men from Company A, 1st Battalion, of the 197th Infantry Brigade. When John Wayne needed wind for scenes, the army provided huge CH-53 Sikorsky helicopters to hover over the set. With the exception of documentaries, it was one of the most extensive cooperations of the armed services and Hollywood in history.[26]

Unfortunately, the weather turned cold—very cold—sooner than they expected, and Duke had to race against autumn. He could not have the jungles of Indochina turning brown; the trees, even if a few too many were pines, had to be green. Before he started filming, Duke had worried about the scrub pines' authenticity. When the cold weather arrived, he was only too happy to have so many evergreens nearby. Health problems added to his concerns. An eye infection complicated matters. Duke had to take several days off, and Warner Bros. panicked, dispatching veteran director Mervyn LeRoy to assist Wayne. "If it had been anyone else but Mervyn," Duke told a reporter, "I would have walked off the picture. But he has been very helpful." The filming was done early in November, except for a few final scenes shot at Warner Bros. studio in Burbank. Batjac had the movie in the can by mid-November 1967. To celebrate, and to express his appreciation to the cast, crew, and military police, who had provided his personal security, Duke staged a barbecue and a football game for everybody, complete with new uniforms. He coached the cast and crew, who defeated the military police 35–28.[27]

By that time the nation was in an uproar. Late in October the "March on the Pentagon" brought more than one hundred thousand protesters to Washington. Approximately fifty thousand of them actually marched on the Pentagon, where U.S. Army troops had to be called out to keep them from entering the building. It was a media circus. Folksinging troubadours performed antiwar ballads, smiling hippies placed flower stems down the barrels of army M-16s, earnest professors lectured on the terrible price of war, peace activists preached jeremiads, and photographers and film crews recorded the event for the world and for history. Norman Mailer wrote that these people had found "their temple in that junction where LSD crosses the throb of an electric guitar at full volume in the ear, solar plexus, belly, and loins." It was, for Mailer, an "oceanic stew of drugs, nipples, arms, phalluses, mouths, wombs, armpits, short-hairs, navels, breasts and cheeks, incense of odor, flower and funk." Duke's reaction was somewhat less fulsome. "I think they oughta shoot 'em if they're carrying the Vietcong flag," he told a reporter. "A lot of our boys are getting shot lookin' at that flag. As far as I'm concerned, it wouldn't bother me one bit to pull the trigger on one of them myself."[28]

Duke left Fort Benning just after the demonstration and a few days before Gen. William Westmoreland's speech to the National Press Club on November 21, 1967. The general proclaimed: "We are making progress. We know that you want an honorable and early transition to the last phase. . . . So do your sons and so do I. It lies within our grasp—the enemy's hopes are bankrupt. . . . We have reached an important point when the end begins to come into view." Interviewed for *Meet the Press* on national television, he assured Americans that "within two years or less the enemy will be so weakened that . . . we will be able to phase down the level of our military effort and withdraw some troops . . . an attitude of confidence and growing optimism . . . prevails all over [South Vietnam], and to me this is the most significant evidence I can give you that constant, real progress is being made."[29]

Wayne exulted in Westmoreland's announcement, praying for his country's sake that victory was at hand, and hoping for his own sake that it might just coincide with the scheduled spring 1968 release of *The Green Berets*. He saw nothing inconsistent, or unseemly, in combining patriotism, politics, and profit. As he once told a friend in Arizona: "I love America because it's the only place in the world where a man can do what he wants, say what he wants, and make a buck doing it." In 1960, when *The Alamo* was released, he hoped that the film would become a patriotic symbol, help elect Richard Nixon as president, and make a lot of money. Though it failed on all three counts, it was now eight years later, and Duke was an eternal optimist. He did not love Democrats, but LBJ deserved his support against such a domestic siege. "I think our picture will help re-elect LBJ," Wayne told *Variety*, "because it shows that the war in Vietnam is necessary."[30]

What John Wayne and the rest of America did not anticipate was the Tet Offensive. While he was shooting *The Green Berets*, North Vietnam and the Vietcong were planning a massive, nationwide assault that would bring South Vietnam to its knees and eventually drive American troops back across the Pacific. While Duke was editing the film, on January 31, 1968, the carefully planned attack began throughout South Vietnam, including the United States embassy in Saigon. During the next several weeks, the American military responded brilliantly, killing nearly seventy thousand Vietcong soldiers and wiping them out as a fighting force. But the Tet Offensive, although a tactical defeat, proved to be an overwhelming strategic victory for the Communists. It was the political watershed of the war. Westmoreland's promise just a few months before that the enemy was "bankrupt" now appeared hopelessly naive, as did his conviction that the end of the war was in sight.

Walter Cronkite, the beloved anchor of CBS News, was personally stunned by Tet, and after a visit to South Vietnam during the last two weeks of February 1968, he reported that "the bloody experience of Vietnam is to end in stalemate." Johnson told an adviser: "If I have lost Walter Cronkite, I have lost Mr. Average American Citizen."

In the United States it was the season of change. Eugene McCarthy made a surprisingly good showing against Johnson in the New Hampshire primary; Bobby Kennedy broke a promise to Johnson and announced his own candidacy; and soon thereafter Johnson was out. Vietnam had destroyed his presidency. In April, Martin Luther King Jr. was assassinated. Outraged blacks rioted. In June, Kennedy was shot. In July, Hubert Humphrey was nominated for the Democrats while protests erupted in the streets of Chicago.

In late June *The Green Berets* opened. Barrett's script was indeed weak in plot and characterization. The movie tells two completely unrelated stories. The first part features "Dodge City," a base camp near the Cambodian and Laotian borders, where Green Beret advisers teach the South Vietnamese how to defend themselves. Eventually a huge battle ensues in which the Vietcong, using human-wave assaults, attack and overrun the camp. The battle scenes are part–*Alamo*, part–*Fort Apache*, part–*The Fighting Seabees*. Vietcong troops hoist ladders against the base-camp walls like Mexican soldiers did at the Alamo, and Patrick Wayne, playing a navy engineer, drives a bulldozer against the Vietcong, just as Duke had done to the Japanese in *The Fighting Seabees*. American air power eventually saves the day, with C-47 gunships cutting the Vietcong to pieces and allowing the Green Berets to retake the base camp, but not before the Vietcong have systematically murdered all the Vietnamese civilians there.[31]

The second section begins with a shift into a *Dirty Dozen* mode. A team of Green Berets parachutes into Vietcong country to capture an enemy general. A beautiful young Vietnamese woman, who hates the Vietcong and secretly spies for the Americans, seduces the general, luring him into her boudoir at a secluded villa. As he is making love to her, the Green Berets kill his bodyguards and capture him. They then make their way back through the jungle to friendly territory. Along the way Sergeant Peterson, a beloved scrounger who has befriended a Vietnamese orphan, steps into a Vietcong booby trap and is impaled on dozens of punji stakes. The film ends with Col. Mike Kirby (John Wayne) comforting Hamchunk, the Vietnamese orphan, and reassuring him that all will be well because "you're what this war is all about."

The unifying focus of the movie is the awakening of George Beckwith (David Janssen), a liberal journalist, to the real nature of American involvement. At first Beckwith is skeptical; he doubts the domino theory, the threat of communism, and the viability of the government of South Vietnam. But after observing a series of heinous Vietcong atrocities and following the activities of Green Beret Colonel Kirby, he reverses his earlier opinions. Beckwith abandons civilian clothes for army fatigues and picks up the slack during battle scenes, readily helping the Americans fight off the Vietcong. The journalist realizes that it will be difficult to tell the true story of the war in Vietnam because of the liberal bias of the American press. "If I say what I feel," he informs Kirby, "I may be out of a job."

Like *The Alamo* the film defiantly and blatantly opposed the liberal consensus, and Wayne knew it was going to be attacked in New York and Los Angeles. "*The Green Berets* is a film so unspeakable, so stupid, so rotten and false . . . that it passes through being fun, through being funny, through being camp, through everything and becomes an invitation to grieve, not for our soldiers in Vietnam or for Vietnam (the film could not be more false or do a greater disservice to either of them) but for what has happened to the fantasy-making apparatus. . . . Simplicities of the right, simplicities of the left, but this one is beyond the possible. It is vile and insane. On top of that, it is dull," wrote Renata Adler in the *New York Times*. Michael Korda, reviewing the film for *Glamour* magazine, described it as "immoral, in the deepest sense. It is a simple-minded tract in praise of killing, brutality, and American superiority over Asians. . . . [it] is racist in the hallowed tradition of Rudyard Kipling. . . . [It] is an insult to every man in uniform on *both* sides of the war." Frank Martarella of *Cinema Magazine* was even more severe: "*The Green Berets* is so wretched and so childishly sleazy that it is embarrassing to criticize its pretentiousness and banality." But this time, even trade journals took on the film. The *Hollywood Reporter* called it "a cliché-ridden throw-back to the battlefield potboilers of World War II, its artifice readily exposed by the nightly actuality of TV news coverage." And in *Life* magazine, Wayne was laughed at by Richard Schickel: "Mr. Wayne's code name in the movie is 'Bulldog,' and it is highly appropriate, for this movie is surely a canine. And an old one at that, incapable of learning new tricks. Peaceniks may safely leave their picket signs at home. *The Green Berets* is its own worst enemy."[32]

Even on his own terms, Duke made some mistakes. Green Beret advisers howled with laughter when the film portrayed a Vietcong general moving through the jungle in a chauffeur-driven limousine and living in a villa complete with champagne, caviar, and female companions dressed for an evening at the opera. The film's closing scene has the sun setting on the South China Sea, a body of water east of Vietnam. Most of the actors portraying Vietnamese were of Hawaiian, Chinese, or Japanese extraction, not Vietnamese. And Fort Benning had its scrub pines. But for all its faults, reviewers attacked the film as if it was the primary cause of the war.

Duke premiered *The Green Berets* in Atlanta on June 25, to coincide with the city's sixth annual "Salute to America" celebration. He served as grand marshal in the parade that attracted more than three hundred thousand spectators. But in New York City, Los Angeles, and university towns throughout the country, protesters picketed the opening. Demonstrations also greeted the premieres in London, Paris, and Rome. At the Warner Theater on Times Square in New York City, angry protesters scuffled with policemen and with ticket buyers. Representatives of Veterans and Reservists to End the War in Vietnam carried posters reading GREEN BERETS, SS, UP AGAINST THE WALL JOHN WAYNE, and GREEN BERETS—SAGA OF FASCIST TERROR.[33]

To Wayne the political backlash signaled millions of dollars of free advertising. It seemed a producer's dream. The controversy spilled into the Capitol. Rep. Benjamin S. Rosenthal, an antiwar Democrat, held a press conference at the end of June 1969 accusing the Pentagon of supplying more than $1 million in services—the use of "Huey" helicopters, M-16 rifles, M-60 machine guns, mortars, bulldozers, cranes, trucks, and personnel from the 10th Aviation Group and the 197th Infantry Brigade—to Batjac for production of *The Green Berets*, and receiving only an eighteen-thousand dollar fee in return. Actually the eighteen-thousand dollars Batjac paid the Pentagon covered the cost of fuel for military equipment used in the movie. Wayne told Mary St. John that Rosenthal was just another "asshole liberal politician trying to make news." He told the *Hollywood Reporter* that Rosenthal was an "irresponsible, publicity seeking idiot. . . . I wish this were the 1800s. I'd horsewhip him."[34]

Duke felt the criticism was unjustified. Pentagon regulations specifically prohibited the military from actually staging exercises for film crews. Film companies had to make do by filming regularly scheduled exercises. Nor could film companies use military personnel while they were on duty. Even John Wayne could not get, nor did he ask for, an exception to these rules. "All we did was use the real estate and we paid for all the Army personnel used." Duke argued:

> We installed $171,000 worth of permanent improvements [the replica of a Vietnamese village] at Fort Benning. We used equipment as it was available. If it used gasoline, we paid for it. We never used military personnel if they were on duty. We paid $305,000 for extras for 70 days of shooting, and 80 percent was for off-duty military personnel and their families. We also paid our room and board expenses.

Nothing came of the controversy except more free publicity for Representative Rosenthal and *The Green Berets*.[35]

Duke reacted gleefully to all of it, knowing that the liberal media could not help but hate the movie. He accused Renata Adler of the *New York Times* of "foaming at the mouth" and "going into convulsions. She and other critics wouldn't believe that the Viet Cong are treacherous—that the dirty sons of bitches are raping, torturing guerillas." Duke refused to give an inch. "I've been to Vietnam, and I've talked to the men there, and I don't have the slightest doubt about the correctness of what we are doing." And besides, patriotism came before correctness. "It's my country, right or wrong, and pure as the driven snow. Americans will be the heroes of *The Green Berets*." Tongue deep in his cheek, he denied having any political agenda in making the movie. "This picture is naturally from the hawk's point of view . . . [but] is made strictly for entertainment."[36]

For all of Universal and Paramount's concerns, for all the problems and the reviews, the film *was* a box-office success. For the rest of his life Wayne remained convinced that the liberal media and vocal left wings on both coasts had co-opted the Vietnam debate, and that there really was a "silent majority," as Richard Nixon would soon describe it, in middle America who were true patriots and who embraced his film. Against a $6.1 million production budget, the film generated more than $16 million in ticket sales during its first six months, returning more than $8 million to Batjac and Warner Brothers. It was among the top ten box office hits of 1968.

Within eighteen months, its domestic ticket sales approached $20 million. Foreign rentals brought in millions more. For John Wayne, it was dollars-and-cents proof that millions of Americans and Europeans loved the soldiers and supported the war. "Luckily for me," he told the *Los Angeles Times* in 1977, "the critics overkilled it." Gloating about how much money the film made, he remarked to Will Tusher of the *Hollywood Reporter*: "All I know is that it gave me great pleasure to pass that [profit information] on to Universal. . . . I let them off the hook, but they wouldn't let it go at that. They kept telling everybody that the picture couldn't make money, that it wouldn't go foreign, that it was an unpopular war. What the hell war isn't unpopular?"[37]

The film's popularity was deeply rooted in both John Wayne's persona and in the pain his traditional audiences felt in 1968. The antiwar movement had triggered a clash of cultures in the United States. At its roots the controversy was based on class distinctions. Many antiwar protesters were middle- and upper-class college students who had managed to avoid the draft. As historian Christian G. Appy has written, Vietnam was a "working-class war." The men who fought and died in South Vietnam during the years of the war came overwhelmingly from the bottom half of the country's economic structure. Young men from working-class or poverty-level families were four times more likely than middle-class men to die in Vietnam. Economic class proved to be far more important than race or ethnicity in determining the social composition of the military. The system was hopelessly biased in favor of the privileged and against the poor and the working classes.[38]

Such discrimination against their own sons left many working-class Americans with painfully ambivalent feelings. They loved their country, hated the war, loved their boys, and despised the antiwar movement. Their visceral anger exploded into the "hardhat demonstrations" of May 1970, when more than one hundred thousand construction workers in New York City gathered to express love for the United States. They waved flags, sang the national anthem, and praised the young men in the military who were putting their lives on the line. Many of them carried portraits of John Wayne. *Time* magazine described the event: "For three hours, 100,000 members of New York's brawniest unions marched and shouted . . . in a massive display of gleeful patriotism and muscular pride. [It was] a kind of workers' Woodstock."[39]

The Green Berets tapped into the smoldering resentments of the working classes, the people who had been watching John Wayne movies since the 1930s, and he became even more popular among them. He was equally popular among conservative Republicans. The reception of *The Green Berets* and Lyndon Johnson's withdrawal from the presidential race convinced Duke that the country needed a change, and he believed Richard M. Nixon was the man of the moment. The bond between Wayne and Nixon was a result of similar experiences more than personal friendship. Both of their political identities were rooted in 1940s and 1950s anticommunism. Both had been targeted by the intellectual Left for their roles in the Red Scare. Wayne believed that Nixon was a man of courage and commitment; he had supported Nixon's presidential campaign in 1960, and in 1968 he hoped the Republicans could do something about Vietnam and what he regarded as the bloated welfare state. What was going on in Vietnam stupefied him. By the fall of 1968 nearly thirty thousand Americans had died there, and he believed that their deaths were a blot on the conscience of their fellow Americans who did not support them at home. Lyndon Johnson, he remarked, "was a man of indecision. He was interested in what everybody had to say about the war. Always had his ear to the ground. Johnson thought the butcher's opinion was as important as a general's. . . . Instead of everybody sticking their nose in, why didn't [he] let the military run the war? If you're going to war and you send kids over there to get shot at, for Christ's sake, you'd better go in all the way!" Believing that Nixon would go all the way, he campaigned enthusiastically for him and was delighted with his victory over Hubert Humphrey in the election.[40]

In the spring of 1968, while stumping for Nixon and putting the finishing touches on *The Green Berets*, Wayne made a movie for Universal about hardhats. *Hellfighters* was a film based on the life of oil-well firefighter Red Adair of Houston. Adair was a legend in oil patches around the world for his ability to put out oil-well fires, even the "sour" blowouts exuding poisonous burning clouds of high-content hydrogen sulphide. Adair first became a national personality in 1963, when he managed to quell "the Devil's Cigarette Lighter," a huge blowout consuming 500 million cubic feet of natural gas a day in the Sahara Desert. The fire reached a thousand feet into the sky, and astronaut John Glenn could see it from his Mercury spacecraft as he orbited the earth. Duke and Red spent hours together on the set of *Hellfighters*, though they looked like the odd couple. Adair had a full head of red hair sitting on top of a five-foot six-inch body. Duke was bald and towered over him. But they shared a get-the-job-done-no-matter-what attitude. During the filming in Houston and Baytown, Texas, they spent some weekends in Adair's speedboat, plying the cantinas and bars of the Gulf Coast, drinking and laughing. One Sunday afternoon they took Adair's boat and a few bottles of Mexico's finest out for a cruise. While the boat was idling its way across Gulf waters, both men fell asleep, only to wake up several hours later, twenty miles from Galveston and out of gas. They had to be towed in.[41]

Vietnam was still on Duke's mind, and he was intrigued when Adair told him the fires were not always the greatest threat to his crew. In Asia, Africa, and South America, they had to worry about Communist guerrilla snipers occasionally trying to shoot them. Duke made sure that Clair Huffaker, the screenwriter, wrote that danger into the script. In the film Chance Buckman (John Wayne) is called down to Venezuela to put out a fire in a remote jungle. Communist guerrillas are just as intent on letting the fire burn, and with it the profits of the capitalist oil company. When Mary St. John read the script, it seemed unrealistic to her. "Why would Communist guerrillas want an oil well to keep burning?" she complained to Duke. "How the hell do I know," Duke replied, "but Red's had to dodge bullets more than once. I guess Communists just don't like people making money."

He and Adair developed a lasting friendship. Duke mentioned more than once that he would like to watch Adair put out a fire. He got his chance in 1974, when Adair brought a crew to the foothills near Burbank, California, to fight a canyon oil-well fire. Wayne was limping a bit; he had injured his knee filming *Rooster Cogburn* with Katharine Hepburn. Suddenly the wind changed, pushing the flames in their direction. Red told Duke: "We better get outta here." Wayne started limping along, yelling good-naturedly at Adair, "You got me up here and you're gonna have to get me out." Adair led him through the smoke to safety, laughing most of the way.

By the time Wayne had finished *Hellfighters*, Nixon was in the White House, implementing a phased withdrawal from Vietnam. He pulled the 9th Infantry Division out of Vietnam in August 1969, the 3rd Division in November, and the Third Brigade of the 82nd Airborne in December. The withdrawals continued throughout 1970. At the end of the year, there were 334,600 American soldiers left, down from 548,000 early in 1969. When Nixon announced the invasion of Cambodia on April 1, 1970, to eliminate the Communist sanctuaries, Duke roared exultantly: "It's about time someone went after those bastards." As far as he was concerned, Richard Nixon was doing what Lyndon B. Johnson would not do: punish the enemy and then bring the boys home. By that time Duke, too, was relieved to see the war winding down. He agreed with Sen. Barry Goldwater, who had concluded: "If we're not going to even try to win the damn thing, then let's get the hell out. Good men are dying for nothing."[42]

With the war winding down, he became even more impatient with protesters. "What do they want us to do," he said to friend Danko Gurovich. "Just get the hell up and leave? Jesus, we've got commitments!" In January 1971 he was in Sacramento, California, celebrating the beginning of Ronald Reagan's second term as governor, performing at an inaugural gala with Frank Sinatra, Sammy Davis Jr., and Dean Martin. During the course of the evening, more than three hundred antiwar protesters gathered outside the Memorial Auditorium hoping to confront the governor and his more famous supporters. When it was time for Reagan and the performers to leave, police tried to hustle them out a side exit to avoid the crowd, which was growing more hostile. "The hell with that," Wayne said. "I'm 63 years old, too damn old to run away from a bunch of kids." Reagan, Martin, Sinatra, and Davis went out the side exit, but Duke waded into the crowd. Four young men, led by twenty-two-year-old Gregory Kirkwood, came up shouting and waving Vietcong flags in his face. At first Duke calmly, though testily, replied: "Please don't do that, fellows. I've seen too many kids your age wounded or dead because of that flag—so I don't take too kindly to it." Kirkwood and the others persisted, getting close enough with one of the flags to nick Duke's nose. Wayne grimaced, and said: "Why, you no good little shits," and lunged at them. They backed up quickly, and he lunged again, pulling his arm abruptly from a security guard trying to restrain him. The protesters jumped, turned, and fled. Even at sixty-three, he was every bit the fighter that he had acted for so long.[43]

Of all whom he opposed, Jane Fonda seemed to characterize the antiwar movement. He had known Henry Fonda since the 1930s, when the two had taken cruises together with John Ford, and he had played Friday-night card games with him. And he admired Jane's work as an actress, commenting that her performance in *Klute* showed she was the best actress in the industry. But he *hated* her politics. She had married Roger Vadim, the French film producer, in 1964, and during her years in Paris she had followed the war closely. When her marriage failed in 1967, she returned to the United States and became active in the antiwar movement. "The war in Vietnam," she said, "is being fought by a new kind of soldier. . . . They're not John Wayne freaks over there. No order goes unchallenged. When they're sent out on a patrol, they just go out a little way, lie down on a little knoll, and blow grass and stargaze." Duke found the comment offensive, not just because of what she was saying about him, but because of what it implied about American soldiers. "How could she say something like that," Duke told Mary St. John. "God! More than three hundred thousand boys were killed or wounded over there in combat. That doesn't happen hiding in the bushes and smoking dope!"[44]

In the summer of 1972 Fonda visited Hanoi, speaking with selected American POWs in person and addressing all American soldiers in Indochina via Hanoi radio, earning her the nickname "Hanoi Jane" (after "Tokyo Rose" of World War II). When he saw the news reports of Fonda's visit to Hanoi, Duke remarked, "God, would you look at that! How must her father feel? Can't she see she's being used by those Commies? That shit may play well in New York and Los Angeles, but in between she's going to be infamous. What a fool!"

But in time he forgave her. In 1978 the Hollywood Women's Press Club had asked Duke to present Fonda with their Golden Apple Award as female star of the year. He readily agreed. At the ceremony, when he handed the trophy to Fonda, Duke good-naturedly said to the crowd: "I have known her father for forty years, and therefore I had a special reason to watch her grow from childhood. Evidently I didn't make too much of an impression on her. I'm certainly surprised to find her standing to the right of me." Later in the year, when the American Film Institute paid a special tribute to Henry Fonda, Jane's children scurried over to Duke's table to get his autograph. Wayne looked over at her, smiled, and winked.[45]

The war was over by then. In April 1975 Wayne watched the final act of the war on television. Panic-stricken South Vietnamese pounded on the gate of the U.S. Embassy in Saigon, crowded helicopters lifted the last Americans off the roof, Russian tanks and North Vietnamese army troops rolled through the city. He called Mary St. John about a business item and asked her if the television was on. Mary was watching Walter Cronkite describe the debacle. Duke disgustedly remarked over the telephone: "Fifty thousand of our best boys dead and another quarter of a million who left their arms or eyes or legs or faces or dicks behind in that godforsaken jungle. All for nothing, absolutely nothing. Mark my words, Mary. They're going to start killing their own people now. They'll slaughter millions and turn the whole country into a stinking cesspool."[46]

John Wayne did not know much about people like Le Duan or Pham Van Dong or Pol Pot, or about the Pathet Lao or the Khmer Rouge or the Vietcong, but he suspected something about Communists. Mary did mark his words, and ten years later, long after Duke was dead, when news of the holocaust came out of Cambodia, when all of Vietnam had been reduced to abject, numbing poverty, she remembered his warning.[47]

The Green Berets was and remains the only prowar Vietnam movie to come out of Hollywood. It was also, of course, the only Vietnam war film produced before the Tet Offensive. Hollywood released a series of antiwar films in the 1970s and 1980s. In 1968, when the Tet Offensive was just grinding down, Sam Peckinpah directed *The Wild Bunch*, a graphically violent Western set in early-twentieth-century New Mexico and northern Mexico, where American bandits, Mexican soldiers, and pro–Pancho Villa insurgents fight one another for money, prostitutes, and ideals. During the orgy of violence, the ideals become hopelessly confused, and hundreds of innocent Mexicans and Americans are slaughtered. *The Wild Bunch* premiered in 1969, just when Dustin Hoffmann was making *Little Big Man*, the fictional story of Jack Crabb, a man who had survived Custer's Last Stand. In the film the U.S. Cavalry appear as violent, bloodthirsty racists whose raison d'être is the slaughter of Sioux women and children. Released in 1970, *Little Big Man* was, like *The Wild Bunch*, an anti-Vietnam film masquerading as a Western.

The Green Berets, despite the Pentagon's guidance, was a Western masquerading as a prowar film. Michael Wayne echoed his father's feelings when to a reporter: "I'm not making a picture about Vietnam, I'm making a picture about good against bad." *The Green Berets* had little to do with the actual war in Vietnam, and much more with stock mythology, like *The Alamo*'s heroism or the high moral character of Wayne's hundred previous roles.[48]

In February 1965 Lyndon B. Johnson and his advisers received a CIA briefing on the nature of the war in South Vietnam. At the time the president was trying to make a decision about whether to send in American ground troops. To prove that the insurgency movement was inspired by external Communists, the CIA presented a wealth of evidence that the Vietcong were fighting with Russian, Chinese, and Czech weapons. The Pentagon supplied James Lee Barrett, *The Green Berets* screenwriter, with transcripts of the briefing, which he then used to construct the opening scene of the film.[49]

The Green Berets begins with a detachment of Special Forces troops at Fort Bragg briefing the press about the war. When George Beckwith argues that Vietnam is a civil war and the United States should "let them handle it," Sergeant Muldoon (Aldo Ray), somewhat miffed, retorts: "Their war, Mr. Beckwith?" He points to a weapons display and takes down an automatic weapon. "Captured weaponry from Red China. Chi-Com 57. Chinese Communists." Muldoon ceremoniously places the weapon in front of Beckwith, and takes another. "SKS Soviet-made carbine. Russian Communists." He dumps the weapon on top of the Chinese rifle. Picking up an ammunition box, Muldoon claims: "Czechoslovakian-made. Czech Communists." He pours them into Beckwith's lap. "No sir, Mr. Beckwith. It doesn't take a lead weight to fall on me or a hit from one of those weapons to reveal that what's involved here is Communist domination of the entire world." When another reporter inquires about the Vietcong, Sergeant McGee (Raymond St. Jacques) launches into a lecture of his own:

> We can understand the killing of the military, but the extermination of the civilian leadership, the intentional murder and torture of women and children. . . . If this same thing happened here in the United States, every mayor in every city would be murdered, every teacher you have ever known would be tortured and killed, every professor you have ever heard of, every governor, every senator, every member of the House of Representatives and their combined families would be tortured and killed and a like number kidnapped. But in spite of this, there's always some little fellow out there willing to stand up and take the place of those who've been decimated.

The irony was that the February 1965 briefing on which Barrett constructed the opening scene of *The Green Berets* was a fabrication. The CIA had intentionally misled President Johnson in order to make the case for ground intervention more compelling. The president had then escalated the war. James Lee Barrett had only written a screenplay.[50]

Ever since the late 1920s, John Wayne had portrayed scouts, cowboys, and soldiers in his films—men who earned genuine reputations for courage in protecting American values and institutions from those who would destroy them. By the early 1960s, Duke's screen persona had assumed mythical proportions, transforming him from a Hollywood celebrity into a powerful cultural icon, and his movies were merely struggling to keep up. In 1966, after a visit to Cam Ranh Bay, LBJ told Hugh Sidey, a columnist for *Life* magazine, that "he had gone into Vietnam because, as at the Alamo, somebody had to get behind the logs with those threatened people."[51]

Americans in Vietnam employed the frontier analogy throughout the war to justify their presence there. In the lexicon of battle, Vietnam became widely known as "Indian country," and the United States "the world." Search-and-destroy missions became "playing cowboys and Indians." When the Vietcong bloodied a company of troops from the army's 7th Cavalry at the Ia Drang Valley in 1965, the comparisons to Custer's Last Stand were inevitable. Even Maxwell Taylor, the U.S. ambassador to South Vietnam during the Kennedy administration, called for escalation of the war so that the "Indians can be driven from the fort and the settlers can plant corn." Ex-Vietcongs now working for the Americans were nicknamed "Kit Carson Scouts." Hunting Vietcong was dubbed "Native Sport." Soldiers in the 1st Cavalry were known as "Pony Soldiers." The names theater commanders selected for Allied military operations were often like those of Duke's B Westerns: "Apache Snow," "Badger Tooth," "Buffalo," "Crazy Horse," "Davy Crockett," "Dewey Canyon," "Double Eagle," "El Paso," "Klamath Falls," "Montana Mauler," "Montana Raider," "Nevada Eagle," "Prairie," "Sam Houston," "Texas," "Texas Star," "Utah," and "Yellowstone."[52]

When Duke visited Vietnam in June 1966, the commander of the 5th Special Forces compared the Green Berets to the "tough, self-reliant, combat-tested soldier who fought on the Indian frontier of our country during the 1870s." Wayne agreed: "It sounds crazy but, in one way, it's like the old cowboy and Indian wars on the frontier. You maintain patrols and outpost forts. If they are attacked, men stand up on the ramparts and shoot at the enemy like in the old days. And if they are in trouble, they have to call for help. And the cavalry still comes to the rescue." Michael Wayne described *The Green Berets* as a "cowboys and Indians" film. "In a motion picture you cannot confuse the audience. The Americans are the good guys and the Viet Cong are the bad guys. It's as simple as that. . . . When you are making a picture, the Indians are the bad guys."[53]

The Green Berets could have been set in the Pacific during World War II or in the West during the Indian wars. If it is all white hats and black hats, the former were badly outnumbered by the latter. Despite every material disadvantage, however, good triumphs. The Vietnamese in the film even speak the pidgin English of the Indians in Wayne's Westerns. At one point a South Vietnamese tells Kirby: "We build many camps, clobber many V.C." The

American-Vietnamese base camp is named "Dodge City," and when Sergeant Muldoon heads out on a search-and-destroy mission, he asks a platoon leader: "Are you ready to go hunting?" The stagecoaches and horses are replaced with helicopters and the skin color of the enemy is different. But the good war remains. The Vietcong are portrayed as evil incarnate—indiscriminately violent soldiers whose favorite blood sport is gang-raping South Vietnamese women, including little girls. Captain Nim (George Takei), the South Vietnamese commander of Dodge City, hates the Vietcong. He tells Kirby: "My home is Hanoi. Someday I will go home. Kill the stinking Cong. Then I will go home." His torture and killing of one Vietcong prisoner of war outrages Beckwith, who protests to Kirby: "There's such a thing as due process." Kirby offers the same answer Ethan Edwards would have given in *The Searchers*: "Out here, due process is a bullet."

With the cult of the frontier embedded in their memories and images of John Wayne on their minds, many young Americans joined the army and Marine Corps in the mid-1960s. David Halberstam, in *The Best and the Brightest*, wrote of the John Wayne persona in Vietnam: "It influenced the officers and the men, everyone. The Wayne image of the guy cleaning up the town, the good guy standing alone was there . . . the swagger, the tough guy walk . . . there were a lot of guys out there playing John Wayne." In his book *A Rumor of War* (1977), Philip Caputo remembered joining the Marine Corps because of John Kennedy's stirring inaugural address in 1961 and because he saw himself "charging up some distant beachhead, like John Wayne in *Sands of Iwo Jima*, and then coming home a suntanned warrior with medals on my chest. The recruiters started giving me the usual sales pitch, but I hardly needed to be persuaded." Such was the world before Tet and My Lai that he forgot that Duke's character died in *Sands of Iwo Jima*.[54]

Other voices sounded as well. The John Wayne persona had survived, but Vietnam robbed it of some of its innocence. Just before the nationwide release of *The Green Berets*, Richard Schickel of *Life* magazine wrote:

> For some of us who have grown up in his shadow, measuring our changing personalities against his towering constancy, Wayne has become one of life's bedrock necessities. He reminds us of a time when right was right, wrong was wrong, and the differences between them could be set right by the simplest of means.
>
> . . . Most men of his paunch have given up righteous violence in favor of guileful acquiescence in the world's wickedness; the Duke is still banking away at it . . . an unconscious existential hero.[55]

Ron Kovic, a Long Island teenager who joined the Marine Corps in 1965, had a different point of view. As a junior-high-schooler, he had watched *Sands of Iwo Jima* on a double bill at the local theater. "The Marine Corps hymn was playing in the background," he recalled in *Born on the Fourth of July*, "as we sat glued to our seats . . . watching Sergeant Stryker . . . charge up the hill and get killed just before he reached the top. And then they showed the men raising the flag on Iwo Jima with the marines' hymn still playing. . . . I loved the song so much, and every time I heard it I would think of them and cry. . . . John Wayne in *Sands of Iwo Jima* became one of my heroes." A few years later, in 1964, Kovic was in high school. At an assembly Marine Corps recruiters stoked the fires of patriotism in several hundred young men. "As I shook their hands and stared up into their eyes, I couldn't help but feel I was shaking hands with John Wayne and Audie Murphy."

Ron Kovic joined the Marine Corps and went off to war. But Vietnam was not Bataan or Guadalcanal or Iwo Jima. It all seemed a waste, a great lie. He came home—without his innocence and paralyzed from the chest down—to a country that did not value his sacrifice. He lamented his impotence. "It is over with," he wrote. "Gone. And it is gone for America. I have given it for democracy . . . I have given my dead swinging dick for America. I have given my numb young dick for democracy. . . . Oh god! Oh God I want it back! I gave it for the whole country, I gave it for every one of them. Yes, I gave my dead dick for John Wayne. . . . Nobody ever told me I was going to come back from this war without a penis. But I am back and my head is screaming now and I don't know what to do."[56]

During the course of his lifetime, Duke toured dozens of military bases, and hundreds of servicemen announced that they had joined up because of him. According to Mary St. John, such admissions over the years, especially if they took place in military hospitals, moved Duke and reminded him of his own decision not to serve. World War II and Korean War veterans understood the value of their service, which they had offered in a defense of freedom. Vietnam was different. Soldiers often searched in vain for the meaning of their sacrifices, and Kovic's pain would no doubt have made Wayne wince.[57]

But it was because of pain like Kovic's, and the frustrations of those Americans who had offered up themselves or their sons in sacrifice, that Duke became so outspoken in their behalf. Ralph Coles, a firefighter who lost his son in Vietnam, recalled: "You bet your goddamn dollar I'm bitter. It's people like us who give up our sons for the country. The business people, they run the country and make money from it. The college types, the professors, they go to

Washington and tell the government what to do. . . . But their sons, they don't end up in the swamps over there, in Vietnam. Let's face it: if you have a lot of money, or if you have the right connections, you don't end up on a firing line in the jungle." Coles's wife felt the same way: "I'm against this war, too—the way a mother is, whose sons are in the army, who has lost a son fighting in it. The world doesn't hear me, and it doesn't hear a single person I know."[58]

John Wayne heard her. Paul Keyes, a writer for *Photoplay* who covered Wayne's 1966 trip to Vietnam, later told Maurice Zolotow that he saw Duke walk up "to men in the field." The soldiers "felt this giant hand on their shoulder and a voice saying: 'Hello, soldier. I'm John Wayne and I just want you to know a hell of a lot of folks back home appreciate what you're doing.' These kids would turn around and break into tears. For fourteen days from six o'clock in the morning to ten at night, Wayne would walk around and introduce himself to GIs." His prosoldier, pro-Vietnam point of view enraged critics in the cultural elite but endeared him to those who had sacrificed the most. "This so-called intellectual group aren't in touch with the American people," Wayne argued, "regardless of Fulbright's blatting, and Eugene McCarthy and McGovern and Kennedy. In spite of them the American people do not feel that way. Instead of taking a census, they ought to count the tickets that were sold to that picture." Until the Vietnam War, and until the release of *The Green Berets*, John Wayne was a popular icon known throughout the world for his screen exploits as a cowboy and a soldier. But the Vietnam War, and its aftermath, pushed his persona past mere iconography. He threw down the gauntlet over Vietnam, setting himself up for a bitter attack from liberals. They behaved predictably, and so did he, refusing to back down. By war's end John Wayne the man was as popular as John Wayne the personality among the working classes of the United States.[59]

21

Crown Prince of the Silent Majority

For years the *New York Times* had been critical of most of his movies. The Wayne persona played well in the theaters of the South and West, but east of the Mississippi and north of the Mason-Dixon line, audiences and reviewers had been more hostile. After the Red Scare, something in the East had changed, and Duke's withering attitude toward the media elite had developed. Vincent Canby, who ascended to the film desk at the *New York Times* in the mid-1960s, readily admitted "I have never really been particularly partial to Westerns." Duke believed the critics were unduly harsh on his films because of his politics. "A little clique back in the East has taken great satisfaction in reviewing my politics instead of my pictures," he told Roger Ebert for a *New York Times* interview. "And they've drawn up a caricature of me." Caricature or not, it took Vietnam to bring the confrontation to a head. Renata Adler's review of *The Green Berets* oozed with venom. "After *The Green Berets*," wrote Canby, "I never thought I'd be able to take John Wayne seriously again."[1]

A year later, painful as it must have been, Vincent Canby *had* to take him seriously. *True Grit* opened nationwide on July 3, 1969, just a year after the controversial *The Green Berets*. For decades John Wayne and a few other controversial stars had generated love and hate around the world, but no star in Hollywood history had ever released back-to-back films that inspired such loathing on the one hand and such reverence on the other. With *True Grit* Duke got his due in every possible way. Even from the *New York Times*.

Charles Portis wrote the novel *True Grit*, and before it was published, his agent distributed galleys to several major studios. He intended to auction the film rights, and if the offers reached three hundred thousand dollars from more than one bidder, Portis would make the final selection personally, using artistic considerations, not money, as the final criterion. At Paramount, Hal Wallis loved the book and entered a bid of three hundred thousand dollars the next day. Several other studios matched Wallis's offer, and Portis took a vacation to Central America for several weeks to think about it, keeping everyone waiting anxiously. Duke got a copy of the manuscript from Henry Hathaway, but only after the bidding had been closed. He saw the novel's film potential immediately and told Michael to put in a Batjac bid and not to be too stingy: Wayne wanted the property. Batjac offered four hundred thousand dollars. Portis decided to stick with the rules. When he sold the rights to Hal Wallis, Duke was badly disappointed, calling Wallis himself to say so. Wallis chuckled knowingly over the phone. Only one man on earth could play Rooster Cogburn, and that was John Wayne. He offered Duke the part on the spot. Wayne roared his approval and accepted immediately.[2]

Casting the part of Mattie Ross, the female lead, proved far more difficult. The role called for a fourteen-year-old young woman with innocence, vulnerability, and plucky determination. Wallis offered the part to Mia Farrow, who had recently achieved stardom giving birth to Satan's child in Roman Polanski's *Rosemary's Baby*. She loved the script, and over a bottle of wine in Wallis's office, Farrow accepted. Filming would begin in September 1968 after she had finished making *Secret Ceremony* with Robert Mitchum. During the filming, however, Mitchum convinced Farrow that Hathaway was dictatorial, someone she would find exceedingly difficult. She called Wallis and asked him to replace Hathaway with Roman Polanski. It was a silly idea. Hathaway had proved himself again and again over the years making Westerns, and Duke loathed *Rosemary's Baby*, calling it a "sick, perverted film." Wallis told Farrow that Hathaway was going to direct the film, and she backed out. Years later Farrow confessed to Wallis, "It was the biggest personal and professional mistake of my life."[3]

Farrow's decision, coming six weeks before shooting was to start, left Wallis in a bind—preproduction work was well advanced and he had no leading lady. For several days he thought about various actresses, but none of them seemed quite right for the part. One evening early in August 1968, he saw

Kim Darby on a television show and decided immediately that she should play the part of Mattie Ross. Darby was, Wallis felt, perfect for the role— "clean-scrubbed, keen-eyed, strong-boned, full of spunk and determination. . . ." She was also independent, strong-willed, and contrary. She had recently had a baby and decided to retire and become a full-time mother, hoping to live off the income of James Stacy, her actor husband. When Wallis made the offer at Darby's home, the scene had a surrealistic quality, reminding him of how much Hollywood had changed. Here he was, the biggest producer in the industry, "begging an obscure actress to accept the leading role in a $300,000-property starring John Wayne, the world's greatest leading box-office star, to be directed by the great Henry Hathaway. It would be one of the biggest pictures of the year, and she was reluctant to do it." After pondering Wallis's offer for two days, Darby agreed, extracting "a very large sum of money" from him. Stacy even insisted, Wallis remembered, on a fee of his own for "allowing" Kim to take the part.[4]

Charles Portis then objected to making the picture in Colorado and casting John Wayne as the lead. The novel's setting was Arkansas, and Portis told Hathaway that Arkansas looked nothing like Colorado. "Look," Hathaway replied. "In Arkansas nobody's been ten miles from their house in their whole fucking lives. And when they see the picture they'll be happy to know that some part of Arkansas looks like that." Hathaway was even less tolerant of Portis's objections to Duke. He told Hal Wallis, "I don't know what you think, but if we've got a motion picture, he's got a book. I like the picture the way it is. So you'll have to settle it with him." Wallis returned later with Portis's approval.[5]

In September 1968 the cast gathered in Montrose, Colorado. Duke was ready for a respite from *The Green Berets* wars. The controversy generated huge volumes of free publicity, but the constant interviews, demonstrations, and criticism tired him. Quiet, isolated, and gorgeous, Montrose was the ideal refuge from Duke's struggle with liberals. Located on the western slopes of the Rockies, at about seven thousand feet, with the Dallas Divide and Blue Mesa Reservoir in the background, it was extraordinarily beautiful that fall, its hills studded with evergreens, golden birches, and aspens. Dean Smith, a stuntman with a small speaking part in the film, remembered: "We watched the changing of the aspen trees; they went from green to yellow to red, or whichever way, and then they started dropping off." Wallis wanted to finish filming in December, before really cold weather descended on the valley, and nature cooperated, delivering enough snow to give several scenes a wintery realism, but not enough to delay shooting. The snow was powdery and dry and the humidity low enough to make work comfortable.[6]

With more than forty years in the business and more than 160 films in the can, Duke knew as much about making movies as anybody in Hollywood, and in recent years he had become accustomed to giving unsolicited—and not always welcomed—advice to directors and producers, which he expected them to take. But Hal Wallis wanted none of it. A few days after their telephone conversation, at a meeting over lunch, Wallis mentioned that Rooster Cogburn would have a moustache and eye patch. Duke protested immediately, "Hell: the fans pay to see me—not some sonofabitch who looks like a pirate in an Errol Flynn movie." Wallis stood firm. "The eye patch stays, but I'll compromise. You can forget the mustache." But Wallis was worried. Only two men in Hollywood could defy John Wayne on a movie set, and he needed one of them. John Ford's health was failing, as were his skills, and he had not made a film since *Cheyenne Autumn* in 1964. Wallis had decided to use Henry Hathaway, a man who had first directed Wayne in *Shepherd of the Hills* (1941), and in recent years in *North To Alaska* (1960), *Circus World* (1964), and *The Sons of Katie Elder* (1965).[7]

Hathaway took charge immediately. When Wayne again objected to wearing the eye patch, Hathaway insisted: "Listen, Duke, I'm in charge of the picture and you're going to have to do what I say. Cogburn can win you the Oscar if you'll play him true. So quit bitching about it. Anyway, you won't have to go on a diet. I want you big-bellied at 260 pounds." It was Hathaway's picture, and Wayne learned to live with it. Even appreciate it. "It's sure as hell my first decent role in twenty years," he told Roger Ebert. "And my first chance to play a character role instead of John Wayne. Ordinarily they just stand me there and run everybody up against me."[8]

Duke was not the only uppity actor Hathaway had to control. The director bullied and screamed at everyone else. Hathaway confined his criticisms of Wayne to the motel room or set trailer, but the rest were fair game. Robert Duvall (Lucky Ned Pepper) could barely stomach Hathaway, and more than once they got into a shouting match. After one outburst Wayne amusedly remarked: "I do believe Henry's got the boy's dander up." Kim Darby seemed difficult and petulant, distant and isolated most of the time. There were reasons for her mood: She was caring for her new baby on location and having marital problems as well. Mary St. John remembered James Stacy showing up in Montrose on several occasions and the two of them getting into loud arguments. Wayne had little sympathy. Actors should be professionals, leaving their personal problems at home. As far as he was concerned, Darby was nothing more than a "spoiled brat."[9]

For Wayne, Hathaway was the ideal director and *True Grit* the perfect movie. Over the years critics had accused Wayne of being too formulaic, playing the same character repeatedly, and Wayne had fueled their disdain, saying ad nauseam: "I don't act, I react," and feeding the belief among those who have never acted that his talent was extremely limited. But insiders in Hollywood—directors, actors, and cameramen—knew that Wayne was a fine actor, and *True Grit* gave him a chance to prove it. On the surface his character had the familiar implacability, the committed inflexibility that marked his best film roles and actual life. Rooster Cogburn is a federal marshal in Arkansas tracking desperadoes who murdered Mattie Ross's father. It is set in 1880, and he has to cross Choctaw land in search of them. Although Cogburn represents the law, he does not trust the system, preferring to shoot criminals rather than bring them back to courts and judges that, at best, only rarely mete out true justice. Like other John Wayne characters, Rooster Cogburn restores order, sometimes harshly but always fairly. In one scene Cogburn notices a rat in the house. "Mr. Rat," he says. "I have a writ here says you have to stop eating Mr. Chin Lee's food." The rodent does not move. "See?" Cogburn says to Ross. "Doesn't pay any attention." Cogburn pulls out a six-gun and dispatches the rat. "I'm serving some papers," Cogburn tells Ross. "Can't serve paper on a rat. You got to kill him or let him be."

The scene made a broader political point. Duke had little sympathy for criminals. "This new thing of genuflecting to the downtrodden," he told Roger Ebert of the *New York Times*. "I don't go along with that. We ought to go back to praising the kids who get good grades, instead of making excuses for the ones who shoot the neighborhood groceryman." In a *Playboy* interview Duke criticized "these people who carry placards to save the life of some criminal, yet have no thought for the innocent victim." "In *True Grit* . . . ," he recalled, "there's that scene where Rooster shoots the rat. That was a kind of reference to today's problems. Oh, not that *True Grit* has a message or anything. But that scene was about less accommodation, and more justice."[10]

Rooster Cogburn is a classic frontier hero, an autonomous man unencumbered by women and family. He lives alone, except for a Chinese cook and a house cat, and spends his time hunting criminals. During a long evening with Mattie, he delivers a soliloquy on how his wife and baby left him years ago, how he missed her some but would gladly rather lose a wife than his own independence. Wayne's favorite scene in the film was the climactic confrontation between Rooster Cogburn and Ned Pepper's murderous desperadoes. The men are all on horseback, facing one another across a grassy meadow. When Cogburn announces his intention to bring the men to justice, Pepper taunts: "Bold talk for a one-eyed fat-man." An outraged Cogburn does a one-eyed doubletake and retorts: "Fill your hands, you son of a bitch!" He then spurs his horse forward in a frontier joust, holding the reins in his teeth, shooting a carbine with his right hand and a pistol with his left, dispatching evil with old-fashioned efficiency.[11]

But unlike the cliché Western lead, there is also an undeniable warmth and vulnerability to Cogburn. Over the decades Wayne had embodied men who were somehow free of the usual laws of physiology. They could eat, drink, and smoke as they pleased without physical consequences. But nature's laws have exacted justice on Rooster Cogburn. He is an old, bloated, profane, one-eyed lawman who can no longer hold his liquor or get up on time in the morning. In one scene, Cogburn falls off his horse, dead drunk after a long day's ride, and, failing several times to get on his feet, announces to Mattie Ross and La Boeuf (Glenn Campbell): "We'll camp here for the night." Unlike other John Wayne characters who are free of women and families, Cogburn falls under the virtuous spell of fourteen-year-old Ross, whose determination more than matches his own. He worries about Mattie, taking her to the doctor to make sure that a snake-bit hand heals, and talking her out of her precocious cynicism. In playing Rooster Cogburn, Wayne conveyed strength, subtle emotions, and a beguiling humor, flirting at times with a camp caricature of himself but always managing to preserve credibility. *True Grit* is a deeply felt statement about the honor and decency of the traditional Wayne character, melded with the mournful recognition that the country had changed, that the cowboy as dispenser of rough justice was an aging institution. In the closing scene, he bids Ross farewell, inviting her to "come see a fat old man sometime." Then he jumps his horse over a four-foot fence and rides off into the sunset. For film critic Vincent Canby: "The last scene in the movie is so fine it will probably become Wayne's cinematic epitaph."[12]

While riding horses in Montrose in the fall of 1968, Duke kept close track of the presidential election campaign—and even had to face the defining question of entering it. He had delivered a rousing patriotic speech at the Republican National Convention in Miami in August, telling everyone who asked that he supported Richard M. Nixon for president. Once Nixon secured the nomination, Duke recorded a few radio spots for his campaign and then went to work in Montrose. But late in September, on the *True Grit* set,

Wayne received a telephone call from Gov. George Wallace of Alabama, who was running on the segregationist American party ticket. Wallace launched his third-party campaign late in the summer of 1968. By the end of September he was scrambling for a running mate. J. Edgar Hoover, head of the FBI, turned him down flat, and when Wallace offered the post to Happy Chandler, former governor of Kentucky, a number of Wallace supporters in Kentucky howled in protest, claiming that Chandler was too liberal on racial matters. Wallace unceremoniously withdrew the offer. He was calling to offer it to Duke. On the phone he claimed: "You and I think the same way about what's happening to this country." Wayne politely declined, telling the governor: "I am working for the other Wallis—Hal Wallis—the producer of *True Grit*, and I'm a Nixon man." On October 4, 1968, Wallace announced that retired Air Force general Curtis LeMay was his running mate.[13]

Mary St. John had taken the call, and when Wayne hung up the phone, he told her about the conversation. Part of what Wallace had said was true. Wayne did not like the Civil Rights Act of 1964 because he could not agree with its provisions concerning public facilities. In his mind private property was private property, and people who owned stores, restaurants, and hotels should be free to refuse service to anyone. But he blamed George Wallace and white southern Democrats for the civil rights movement as much as he blamed Martin Luther King Jr. and Chief Justice Earl Warren. The Fifteenth Amendment, he believed, gave everybody the right to vote. "If blacks had been allowed to vote all along," he told Mary St. John, "we wouldn't have all this horseshit [civil rights movement] going on. George Wallace is part of the goddamn problem, not the solution." Several months later, when rumors reached the press that Wayne had contributed thirty thousand dollars to the Wallace campaign, Duke vehemently, angrily, even self-righteously denied the allegation.[14]

He resented being characterized as an extremist. He considered himself a mainstream conservative Republican. In 1964 he vigorously backed Barry Goldwater for president. Their friendship had begun in the 1920s, when they met at a Sigma Chi convention, and in the early 1960s Wayne touted Goldwater's presidential candidacy. During the primary campaigns in 1964, Duke became especially critical of Gov. Nelson Rockefeller of New York and Gov. William Scranton of Pennsylvania, two liberal Republican candidates who badly distorted Goldwater's conservatism. He knew Goldwater to be an honest, thoughtful, reasonable man, not at all the trigger-happy menace of liberal editorials and political cartoons. "The Democrats didn't make Goldwater lose," he later told an interviewer from *Motion Picture* magazine. "The Republicans of that ilk did. I don't forgive fellows very easily when I realize that they are that unprincipled." He labored to offset the damage to Goldwater's campaign, even filming a campaign television spot just three weeks after cancer surgery.[15]

John Wayne was not at all the fanatic reactionary that the press—and sometimes his own off-the-cuff statements—made him appear. He was, rather, a principled antigovernment classical liberal, someone who would perhaps have seemed a bit too socially tolerant but otherwise perfectly understandable in the days of both Herbert Hoover and FDR; someone who fitted easily into the Eisenhower era; and someone whom Ronald Reagan and the era he helped usher in would easily appreciate. Only in the context of the 1960s and 1970s was he misunderstood, caricatured, and dismissed by so many.

His membership in the John Birch Society was a case in point. Established in 1959 by Robert Welch, a candy manufacturer, the organization was named after Capt. John Morrison Birch, a Baptist missionary killed by Chinese guerrillas in 1945 while serving with Chennault in China. The group found it relatively easy to recruit new members in the upper-middle-class suburbs of the San Fernando Valley and Ventura and Orange Counties in California. Wayne was initially attracted to the organization because of its opposition to high taxes, welfare payments, diplomatic recognition of Red China, United States membership in the United Nations, and the decisions of the Supreme Court under Earl Warren, as well as its passionate conviction that communism was the single greatest threat to the world. In 1960 he joined the organization and was pleased when the group threw its support behind Goldwater in 1964.[16]

But Wayne broke ranks after the election. The society's conviction that the public-health campaign to fluoridate public water supplies was a secret Communist plot to weaken America seemed utterly silly to him, and he laughed at Robert Welch's charge that Communists had dictated the outcome of every presidential nominating convention—Republican as well as Democratic—since 1920. When Welch's book *The Politician* accused former President Dwight D. Eisenhower of being a "dedicated conscientious agent of the Communist conspiracy," Wayne was aghast. "What a bunch of horseshit," he told a friend. "Ike was not my favorite politician, but he sure as hell wasn't a Commie." Duke's alienation deepened after his lung cancer operation in 1964. During the 1960s the John Birch Society led the right-wing assault on the American medical establishment, claiming that American physicians, hospitals, universities, pharmaceutical companies, insurance companies, and the federal government were engaged in a secret, Communist-inspired cover-up to keep cancer cures off the market. When one of his Bircher friends warned him that the Scripps Institute and Good Samaritan hospital were part of the sinister plot, a frustrated Wayne responded: "Jesus Christ, you people are getting scary."[17]

Despite his renunciation of it, Wayne's association with the John Birch Society magnified his reactionary public image. It was a symbol that people on both sides of the spectrum took to mean "nutty conspiracy monger." In 1966 ABC Television and QM Productions wanted Wayne to do the weekly narration for the *FBI* series, starring Efrem Zimbalist Jr. J. Edgar Hoover, head of the FBI, enjoyed complete control over scripts for the show, and he was delighted with the suggestion. Wayne and Hoover had been friends since the late 1940s. The director placed Duke on his special correspondence list and kept in touch with him over the years. Always on guard to protect the agency, however, Hoover assigned agents to look into Duke's background. When he learned that Wayne had once been a member of the John Birch Society, Hoover vetoed his participation in the television series, "in order to prevent any possible criticism of the Bureau by using someone with known John Birch Society connections." By that time, of course, Wayne wanted nothing to do with the Birchers. "I'm part of the Republican mainstream," he chuckled to Mary St. John in 1968, "although I guess I stick to the right bank."[18]

Nixon's victory encouraged Duke. The margin had been razor thin—43.4 percent of the popular vote for Nixon; 42.7 percent for Humphrey, and 13.5 percent for Wallace. When the networks called the election on the morning after Duke raised a glass of tequila with a few friends in Montrose and toasted the Republican triumph. Along with the rest of America's Republicans, Duke spent most of January celebrating Nixon's victory. Nixon made sure that Duke and Pilar had special invitations to all the inaugural festivities.[19]

D uke took a month off after finishing *True Grit*. The cast and crew had returned from Montrose just before Christmas, and he enjoyed the holidays at home, eating too much and watching football games. A week after New Year's Day in January 1969, Hal Wallis drove down to Newport Beach, ecstatic over the *True Grit* rushes. "I knew we had a winner. Duke was extraordinary. . . . Familiar as I was with the script, I often laughed out loud viewing the film." They talked of Academy Awards, and Wallis planted in Duke's mind the possibility that maybe, just maybe, his time had come.[20]

Early in February Duke flew down to Durango, Mexico, to make *The Un-*

defeated, the story of officers from the Confederate and Union armies who join together to fight their way into and out of Mexico after the Civil War. For Hollywood studios he was money in the bank in 1969, as he had been for the previous twenty-five years. Twentieth Century-Fox wanted to team up John Wayne and Rock Hudson for the first time, and to get Duke to sign, they gave him a lucrative contract and complete control of the film. Duke selected Andy McLaglen to direct and Bill Clothier to film it. James Lee Barrett, who had written the screenplay for *The Green Berets,* was hired to adapt Stanley L. Hough's story for the screen. Most of Duke's friends got parts in the movie, including Ben Johnson, Harry Carey Jr., John Agar, Chuck Roberson, Bruce Cabot, and Paul Fix.[21]

McLaglen wasted no time filming, and Duke kept up, even though he sustained a painful injury when a horse he was riding stumbled, throwing him into the dirt and breaking two ribs on the side where physicians had removed one in 1964. He took several days off, and McLaglen shot around him. Wayne returned to the set taped up and in pain, but he worked anyway. McLaglen finished in Durango at the end of February, and Duke returned to Newport Beach for a few weeks to recover. Near the end of March, the cast and crew reassembled in Baton Rouge, Louisiana, to shoot plantation scenes in the old sugar homes along the Mississippi. Duke's run of bad luck continued. The script called for him to ride a horse at breakneck speed, leading a cavalry column of Union troops into a Confederate position. During one of the takes, a stirrup on his saddle came loose. "I twisted around in the saddle," he recalled, "and the damn stirrup was completely loose. I fell right under that god-damned horse; I'm lucky I didn't kill myself." The fall dislocated his right shoulder. X rays revealed no broken bones, and again he returned to work, keeping his right arm tucked against his torso as much as possible to reduce the pain. The shooting continued, and McLaglen finished under budget at the end of the month.

Duke and Hudson developed a friendly relationship on location. Hudson was nervous about working with Wayne because, as his biographer wrote, Wayne "symbolized America's ideal of masculine strength" and Hudson feared homophobia. He first met Duke on the set. Wayne was standing in front of a small mirror applying some natural lipstick. He turned to Hudson, narrowed his eyes, and drawled: "Well, I hear you're a good bridge player." On the first day's shooting, he started making suggestions to Hudson about how to talk, move, and shoot his gun. "They sounded like good ideas," Hudson remembered, "so I tried them, but that night I started thinking, am I going to be directed by this guy? Is he trying to establish dominance or something? So the next day, I said to him, 'Why don't you turn your head this way . . . ?' Wayne pointed his finger at him. 'I like you,' he said. And we became great friends."

Everybody in Hollywood knew that Hudson was gay, and same-sex images repulsed Duke, who did not like being around gay men. Don Collier, one of the actors in *The Undefeated*, years later remembered: "Duke didn't like that faggot stuff." One afternoon on location, watching Hudson perform a scene, Duke said to Aissa, who was fourteen years old: "Look at that face. What a waste of a face on a queer. You know what I could have done with that face?" But he did not let his feelings get in the way of business, and he was a true laissez-faire Republican, despite his likes and dislikes. One Sunday afternoon at the motel in Baton Rouge, Hudson was sitting at a table near the pool playing cards with Don Collier and several other cast members. Duke was in the motel room taking a nap. A pleasant couple from Nebraska approached Hudson for an autograph. He politely declined, telling them that it was his policy not to sign autographs on Sundays, but directed them to Wayne's room. "John Wayne's in that room over there, and he loves signing autographs. He's not doing anything right now and would probably like to sit down and visit with you. He'll probably invite you in." The couple jogged quickly over to the room and woke Duke up. He opened the door snarling, but immediately calmed down when he saw the couple. As he made small talk and handed out autographed cards, Duke noticed Hudson laughing uproariously, and he good-naturedly cursed him.

In the evenings they frequently played bridge. Both men were excellent at the game, and it was as strong a bond as their acting. In her autobiography, Pilar Wayne asked Duke what he thought of Hudson's homosexuality. Duke's reply was straightforward: "What Rock Hudson does—in the privacy of his own room—is his own business. He's a professional on the set and a real gentleman—and he plays a hell of a hand of bridge."

Duke worked the rest of the spring in Hollywood shooting interiors for *The Undefeated*, preparing to film *Chisum* for Batjac in the fall, and awaiting the release of *True Grit*. Released nationally in July, *True Grit* received rave reviews and did excellent business. Oscar talk echoed in the trades and major newspapers, even among eastern critics, who seemed to have a very difficult time praising Wayne. Roger Ebert, writing for the *New York Times*, admiringly wondered: "Can that fat old man be John Wayne?" Vincent Canby felt that the "curious thing about *True Grit* is that although he is still playing a variation on the self-assured serviceman he has played so many times in the past, the character that seemed grotesque in Vietnam fits into this frontier land-scape, emotionally—and perhaps politically too. . . . Hathaway obtains from Wayne the richest performance of his long career. Wayne is the Western movie hero approaching his last years with almost heroic vitality and humor." *Newsweek* described his performance as "a tour de force of self-parody." Even the *New Republic* was generous. Praise from the *Village Voice* particularly pleased Duke. "If that left-wing ragsheet liked the film," he told Mary St. John, "it must be good."[22]

Duke was pleased by the attention, but he had bigger problems on his mind in July and August. His five-year cancer check-up, the statistical point at which disease-free cancer survivors can claim a cure, was coming up in September. He would find out if he really was "cured," if all the rhetoric and bluster about beating the "Big C" were true. Not knowing whether he had cancer again was its own exquisite torture. In the mid-1960s, when he went for a check-up every three months and then every six months, after examining his X rays, his physicians would talk about the "progress of the disease," about remission or recurrence, about the length of his future. The reports had always been good, though couched in the cautious jargon of radiologists: "The chest appears to be free of active disease."[23]

Duke had worried about the tests for several weeks. It was almost as if he were expecting bad news, confirmation that the cancer was back again. Sometimes life has a nasty way of humbling people, of injecting a dose of reality into the sweetest moments. *Box Office Magazine* had just named him Hollywood's top attraction for 1969. The word was out that Wayne was going to get a Best Actor nomination for *True Grit,* and that he had an inside track for the Oscar. The possible irony of winning an Oscar and sucking in Hollywood's most rarefied air while a lung tumor slowly suffocated him was not lost on Duke.

At the Scripps Institute, finally, technicians X-rayed him. A white-frocked physician then entered the room—with a smile on his face. The news was good. John Wayne's chest still "appeared to be free of active disease." And this time, given the length of the remission, he was considered clinically cured. The physicians wanted him back once a year for a routine check-up, but they assured him that, statistically at least, his chances of dying of lung cancer were now just the same as those of the general public. Maybe the Red Witch would stay buried.

Several weeks after the check-up, Duke and Mary flew to Durango for *Chisum,* a Batjac production. Pilar did not come along. She hated Durango, and so did the kids. Aissa remembered it from her stay during *The Sons of*

Katie Elder. It was a town of "dirt streets with no names, one horseshoe-shaped motel, and one hole in the wall that everyone called a diner. . . . I took one look at my new home for the week and began counting the days." Pilar later remembered: "Comfortable motels or hotels, modern plumbing, television, sophisticated shops, grocery stores—all the things urban men and women take for granted were unheard of luxuries in that community. . . . The city seemed to have been caught in a time warp."[24]

Which, of course, was exactly why Duke loved it. Good locations were more important than ever because audiences had become much more sophisticated. Durango was attractive because it was so isolated. Relatively free of modern noises, surrounded by Sonora Desert landscapes, it was inexpensive and, also, outside the control of Hollywood's craft unions. Duke believed that Mexicans worked harder than their American counterparts, at half the wages, and were not bound by tight union rules. Making movies there was dirt cheap compared to the United States. As producer Michael Wayne could make a movie well within the $4.4 million targets Batjac often set in the late 1960s. In the next several years, he would produce *Big Jake*, *The Train Robbers*, and *Cahill* there.[25]

Cancer-free and surrounded by his stock company, Duke felt good on the set of *Chisum*. He felt even better when, just before wrapping up *Chisum*, he learned of the Oscar nomination. Pilar was visiting for a few days when the news reached them. At first he brushed it off. "Hell, I'm honored," he replied to her question about how he felt. "Who wouldn't be? But you can't eat awards, and you sure as hell can't drink 'em." Actually, of course, he *could* eat an Oscar. *Chisum* was scheduled for release in May 1970, a month after the awards, and an Oscar would virtually guarantee that it would make money. In the meantime, though, the brush-off was warranted, for there was always work to do. *The Undefeated* opened in November 1969, and Duke worked hard promoting it for Twentieth Century-Fox. He spent much of January and February reading the script for *Rio Lobo* and talking about the upcoming film with Howard Hawks, whom Twentieth Century-Fox had hired to direct it. Wayne was scheduled to go on location at Old Tucson in March. But Hal Wallis and Paramount kept their eye on the Oscar, putting on a media blitz touting *True Grit* to academy members, and Duke acquiesced to most interview requests.[26]

The nomination revived interest in him in Hollywood, where many experts, like the New York critics, believed that he was out of step with the industry. Aptly enough, the other nominees comprised both the best British stage actors and some new Hollywood talents. Dustin Hoffman and Jon Voight both had nominations for *Midnight Cowboy*. Peter O'Toole secured another for *The Lion in Winter*, and Richard Burton got the last for playing Henry VIII in *Anne of the Thousand Days*. Wayne privately screened all three films in Newport Beach and thought that O'Toole and Burton were brilliant and that both films were quality productions. He had a more difficult time with *Midnight Cowboy*. The film carried an X rating, and Wayne thought the assessment was well deserved. The movie made him wince, forcing him to close his eyes occasionally. As the film ended and lights came on, he told a group of friends: "Damn, Hoffman and Voight were good. Both of them. More than good—great. That is acting. But if I had to choose between the two of them, I'd pick Hoffman. He had the better role." A few days later, at the office, he told Mary St. John: "Whoever thought I'd say good things about a movie featuring a gigolo, a homeless Italian dwarf, and gang rape."[27]

But on Duke's side was a lifetime of never-yet-rewarded efforts. By April 7, 1970, the night of the awards, the columnists were predicting he would win. The reasoning went roughly as follows: Jon Voight did not have a chance because he was a newcomer. Hoffman had been great in *The Graduate* in 1967, and better in *Midnight Cowboy*, but he too was too young—he would have a career full of Oscar-caliber performances and future opportunities for Academy Awards. Burton and O'Toole were gifted actors, world-class talents, but they were English, and insiders assumed that academy members, given a choice between two Brits and a sentimental American favorite, would finally come round to the sentimentality they had been dismissing over the last decades. Still, Wayne's politics were an issue. The controversy surrounding *The Green Berets* and his stand on the Vietnam War reverberated throughout the country, and Hollywood liberals still resented his leadership of the Motion Picture Alliance. But most of those critics realized that Wayne had become a Hollywood institution and a popular culture icon. Even for liberals he had become something like Hollywood's politically and socially outrageous-but-beloved grandfather.[28]

By the day of the ceremony, Wayne had decided that Richard Burton would win. He talked about it with Pilar during the drive from Newport Beach to Los Angeles, and for several hours at the Beverly Hills Hotel before the ceremonies at the Dorothy Chandler Pavilion. The more he talked about Burton's performance, the more emotionally prepared he became for disappointment. Burton and his wife, Elizabeth Taylor, were also at the Beverly Hills, staying in an adjoining bungalow. The two couples spent an hour together before the rehearsal and agreed, win or lose, to have a private party after the ceremony. The two men regaled each other with stories, hoping bravado would shroud their anxieties. Both wanted to win. Both thought they should win. Elizabeth Taylor, after a ten-year absence from the Oscar ceremony, agreed to present the Best Picture Award, hoping that her cooperation might sway a few votes Burton's way. Duke's only nomination had been for *Sands of Iwo Jima*, and Burton had been nominated for *Becket* in 1964, *The Spy Who Came in from the Cold* in 1965, and *Who's Afraid of Virginia Woolf?* in 1966, so the "it's about time" argument could have gone either way. But the Oscars—their Oscars—had gone to other actors.[29]

Anxious to secure Oscars and boost the box office, the studios unashamedly hyped their own films. *Anne of the Thousand Days*, a richly textured but ponderous historical costume drama, had been a box-office disaster. Hoping to recoup its investment, Universal implemented a subtle political strategy. During a series of private screenings late in 1969 and early in 1970, the studio hailed the film's virtues in between servings of imported champagne, three-inch prime ribs, and beef Stroganoff. In the words of Universal's public relations spokesman: "We cultivated the hell out of the artistic branches. And, boy, did it work." *Anne of the Thousand Days* surprised everyone by garnering ten nominations, including Best Picture, Richard Burton for Best Actor, and Genevieve Bujold for Best Actress.

Twentieth Century-Fox took notes and put on a similar spread for *Hello, Dolly!*, an overrated $25 million film starring Barbra Streisand. One of Fox's publicity men remembered: "We decided that lavish advertising would do no good for this one; the whole town was already gossiping about how bad it was. We decided to blow the budget on prime ribs from Kansas City and imported champagne. Then we had the showings. The branch voters saw the movie through champagne-colored glasses." *Hello, Dolly!* secured ten nominations, including Best Picture.

Countercultural films enjoyed a high profile in 1970. *Midnight Cowboy* was the most prominent, with a nomination as Best Picture, two nominations for Best Actor, and a Best Supporting Actress nomination for Sylvia Miles. *They Shoot Horses, Don't They?*, the story of desperate, poverty-stricken marathon dancers during the Great Depression, also won a slate of nominations, including Best Director for Sydney Pollack, Best Actress for Jane Fonda, and Best Supporting Actor for Gig Young. Jack Nicholson received a Best Supporting Actor nomination for *Easy Rider* and Arthur Penn was nominated Best Director for *Alice's Restaurant*. *Butch Cassidy and the Sundance Kid*, which elevated bandits into heroes, won a Best Picture nomination.

No film, however, totally awed the voters. Prime rib and imported champagne did not help *Anne of the Thousand Days* or *Hello, Dolly! Midnight Cowboy* won Best Picture, becoming the first and only X-rated film to achieve such a distinction, and John Schlesinger received an Oscar for directing it. But Maggie Smith surprised everyone with her Best Actress Oscar for *The Prime of Miss Jean Brodie*. So did Goldie Hawn with her Best Supporting Actress award in *Cactus Flower*. Gig Young took the statue for Best Supporting Actor.

Finally Barbra Streisand presented the Best Actor award. The pavilion was quiet. When she opened the envelope, her face stretched into a huge, classic Streisand smile, and she bellowed: "And the winner is—John Wayne for *True Grit*." He had waited for years, and yet he was still surprised. He strode up to the stage, hunched over to embrace Streisand, and whispered in her ear: "Beginner's luck." Leaning into the microphone, Duke faced the audience and said: "Wow. If I'd known that, I'd have put on that eye patch thirty-five years ago." His voice breaking, and, wiping a tear from his eyes, he went on: "Ladies and gentlemen, I'm no stranger to this podium. I've come up here and picked up these beautiful golden men before—but always for a friend. One night I picked up two; one for Admiral John Ford and one for our beloved Gary Cooper. I was very clever and witty that night—the envy of Bob Hope. But tonight I don't feel very clever, very witty. I feel grateful, very humble, and I owe thanks to many, many people. I want to thank the members of the academy. To all you people who are watching on television, thank you for taking such a warm interest in our glorious industry." The last line was the most fitting—his fans had never abandoned him, despite his politics, despite the critics, despite the academy.

After the ceremony Richard Burton and Elizabeth Taylor returned to their bungalow at the Beverly Hilton, and Duke held forth for the Hollywood paparazzi, spending two hours posing for pictures and politely answering questions. He did not get back to the hotel until well after midnight. While Duke celebrated, Burton had sat in his room complaining that "thirty years from now, Peter O'Toole and I will still be appearing on talk shows plugging for our first Oscar." At that point Duke kicked in the door to his bungalow, walked up to him, and placed the statuette in his hands, saying: "You should have this, not me." It was heartfelt, from one professional to another. The two men stayed up the rest of the night telling stories and drinking.

Two days later Duke flew from Los Angeles to Tucson, where he was filming *Rio Lobo*. Howard Hawks, who was directing the film, had had the choice of making *Rio Lobo* with John Wayne or *Monte Walsh* with Lee Marvin. After

Red River, *Rio Bravo*, *Hatari!*, and *El Dorado*, he understood Duke completely and considered him a fine actor, one of Hollywood's best. He was not so sure about Lee Marvin, but he had enjoyed the actor's work in *Raintree County*, *The Man Who Shot Liberty Valance*, and *The Dirty Dozen*. In 1969 Hawks invited Marvin to meet with him to discuss *Monte Walsh*. Hawks remembered that Marvin came to the meeting drunk. After a few moments Marvin told him: "I just want to make sure that it's a Lee Marvin western, not a John Wayne western." Hawks, said, "That ought to be pretty easy." "Why?" Marvin queried. Because, Hawks responded, "you're about 1/4 as good as John Wayne and I don't think you could do a John Wayne western." Hawks quickly decided that he wanted nothing to do with a Lee Marvin Western and accepted *Rio Lobo* instead. Wayne was still on an Oscar high when he flew into Tucson. Finally, after scores of films and a career that had made him the first global pop culture icon in the history of the world, he owned an Academy Award. A car picked him up at the airport and drove him down to the set in Old Tucson. The entire cast and crew were assembled in front of the adobe church, waiting for him to arrive. The car moved through the dirt streets of the imaginary town and up to the plaza. Wayne stepped out, laughed uproariously at first, and then settled down into a teary-eyed smile. Everybody, horses included, was sporting an eye patch, and the crowd was clapping and whistling congratulations to the best actor in the world.[30]

Chisum opened in June 1970, just two months after the Oscars. *The Hollywood Reporter* predicted success. "*Chisum*—-is John Wayne's return from Oscar, large on panoramic viewing and enjoyable, G-rated and will be, with Wayne's resident following plus the pickup of the curious who will turn out to see what follows Rooster Cogburn, a summer box-office success." *Variety* agreed, even though the "film is a rehash at times of the time-honored western formula of the heavy out to move in and take over all the hero has suffered and fought for." Paramount rereleased *True Grit* to take advantage of the Oscar publicity. Both films did well. *True Grit's* domestic gross by the end of the year had reached $29 million, and *Chisum's* had gone past $12 million.[31]

Armed with an Oscar and a liberating sense of good health, Duke fought more battles in the culture wars. The spring of 1970 had been good to Wayne, but the rest of the country appeared to be in turmoil. Everywhere there were signs of division. Four days before the Academy Awards, hundreds of thousands of antiwar protesters gathered in Washington, D.C., to demand an end to the Vietnam conflict. When President Nixon sent American troops to invade Cambodia at the end of the month, a storm of protest thundered across the country. Several days later National Guardsmen killed four students at Kent State University. Lt. William Calley was about to go on trial. A Black Panther spokesman in May urged black men to strike out against their white "oppressors like panthers—smiling, cunning, scientific, striking back by night and sparing no one!" Cesar Chavez launched a nationwide boycott of California grapes. On August 26, 1970, the fiftieth anniversary of ratification of the Nineteenth Amendment, feminist groups from around the country mounted a nationwide Strike for Equality. Ti-Grace Atkinson excoriated marriage as "slavery and rape." On Thanksgiving Day, American Indians convened a National Day of Mourning, protesting the white genocide of native peoples.

The noisy protesters, Duke believed, did not represent what President Richard Nixon had called "the great silent majority of Americans." Award or not, Duke had long been the crown prince of that silent majority, even if the media portrayed him as a right-wing reactionary. Much of that image came from his unabashed love for the United States. "I am," he readily admitted, "an old-fashioned, honest-to-goodness, flag-waving patriot." But now, when traditional values and traditional institutions had fallen into disrepute, his patriotism seemed old-fashioned to some, anachronistic to others. "It's kind of a sad thing," he lamented in 1974, "when a normal love of country makes you a superpatriot."[32]

Wayne's brutal, outspoken honesty did not help allay that image. He could not abide people who lived well in America and yet criticized, often savagely, the country and the system that made it all possible. In the 1940s and 1950s, he harbored a special disdain for Hollywood's "country club Communists," who made five thousand dollars or more a week and joined Communist cells dedicated to preaching the Stalinist gospel. At a dinner party back in 1962, he expressed his bewilderment to Eddy Dmytryk, who had directed him in *Back to Bataan*. Dmytryk, a confessed Communist, had spent a year in prison during the Red Scare for contempt of Congress. Putting his arm around the director, Duke asked, "Jesus Christ, Eddy, why did you do it? Weren't you making a good living? Weren't you happy with your life? What's the bitch about America?"[33]

Wayne's explanation for liberalism in the 1960s and 1970s was the same as his explanation of Hollywood communism in the 1930s and 1940s. Guilt. "They're Beverly Hills–Bel–Air liberals, feeling guilty about living in million-dollar homes, driving Rolls-Royces and Mercedes, and making obscene amounts of money," he told an old friend. Liberalism, he claimed, was cheaper than a psychiatrist. Somehow, by finding themselves a cause—some downtrodden individual or group—and throwing money after it, they could live with the fact that they were the capitalists, the elite, the filthy rich, the most privileged people in the history of the world. "I am too," Wayne said. "The difference between me and them is that I don't feel the least bit guilty about having worked my ass off and made a good living."[34]

It was that refusal—as well as the Oscar—that brought a telephone call from *Playboy* in August. Hugh Hefner invited him to sit for an interview. Centerfolds really sold *Playboy* each month, but interviews with controversial, influential Americans generated front-page newspaper coverage and bolstered the magazine's claim to respectability. Hefner wanted quotable quotes. With an Oscar on his mantle and more than forty years on the silver screen, Duke's star had never shone brighter. His name would sell magazines. So would his answers to *Playboy* questions. Wayne's barbed conservatism made for good contrarian copy. He was highly opinionated and brutally honest. The interview would be a guaranteed winner. Duke agreed to talk if the magazine could wait until the end of the year, when he had finished making *Big Jake*.[35]

Just after Christmas, interviewer Richard Warren Lewis arrived at Duke's Newport Beach home at midmorning. They chatted for several hours over a brunch of Dungeness crabs and hot black coffee, and at 1:00 P.M. the two men drove over to Newport Harbor and boarded the *Wild Goose*, where charbroiled steaks, lettuce, and cottage cheese greeted them. Two hours later a steward produced a bottle of Conmemorativo tequila, complete with glasses, fresh lemon juice, coarse salt, and a bucket of Alaskan glacier ice shards. The two men sipped icy, burning tequila into the early evening. They resumed the interview a week later at the Batjac offices.

Lewis acted at first as if he were approaching a wary politician, gently easing Duke into the interview with questions about the movie industry. Lewis quickly learned, however, that there was little need for caution. Dan Ford once remarked of Wayne: "Half the people who went to his movies were Democrats, but he was not afraid of alienating them." He had nothing to hide and did not give a damn what people thought of his opinions. They discussed his childhood and favorite films, and Lewis then steered him into politics, soliciting his opinions about the state of America. He weighed in, readily blaming liberals who perverted "the natural loyalties and ideals of our kids, filling them with fear and doubt and hate and downgrading patriotism and all our heroes of the past." Lewis asked Duke what he thought about Angela Davis, the black radical philosopher at UCLA. Duke responded: "I don't want Angela Davis inculcating an enemy doctrine in my kids' heads."

Delighted with his candor, and certain that a few questions about liberalism would evoke his wrath and produce the sought-after quotes, Lewis jumped into the question of welfare. Somewhat hesitant, Wayne responded: "I'm not gonna give you one of those I-was-a-poor-boy-and-I-pulled-myself-up-by-my-bootstraps stories, but I've gone without a meal or two in my life. . . . Hard times aren't something I can blame my fellow citizens for." Critics who later charged that Wayne did not understand the impersonal forces that pulled people into poverty and kept them there—often generaton after generation—were unfair, or at least forgetful, of Clyde and Molly Morrison's troubles, the lost USC scholarship, the failure of *The Big Trail,* Fox and Columbia canceling his contracts, Mascot dropping his name from first billing to second and then third, Universal losing confidence in his adventure series. For the first thirty years of his life, he had experienced failures large and small. "You can't whine and bellyache," he told Lewis, "because somebody else got a good break and you didn't."

Lewis then eased into the issue of racial discrimination and affirmative action. Wayne had little patience for people who complained loudly, blamed other people for their problems, and wanted something for nothing. Eschewing responsibility for the American past, Duke delivered the first of several memorable comments. "I don't feel guilty," he told Warren, "about the fact that five or ten generations ago these people were slaves. Now, I'm not condoning slavery. It's just a fact of life, like the kid who gets infantile paralysis and has to wear braces so he can't play football with the rest of us." The most quotable quote came next: "With a lot of blacks there's quite a bit of resentment along with their dissent, and possibly rightfully so. But we can't all of a sudden get down on our knees and turn everything over to the leadership of blacks. I believe in white supremacy until the blacks are educated to a point of responsibility. . . . I think any black man who can compete with a white today can get a better break than a white man. I wish they'd tell me where in the world they have it better than right here in America." When asked how blacks could address the problems of the past, Duke's answer was straightforward: "By going to school. I don't know why people insist that blacks have been forbidden to go to school. They were allowed in public schools wherever I've been."

Lewis then pushed another button, asking Duke about the suffering of American Indians. "I don't feel we did wrong in taking this great country away from them, if that's what you're asking. Our so-called stealing of this country from them was just a matter of survival. There were great numbers of people who needed new land, and the Indians were selfishly trying to keep it for themselves." (At this point, Lewis was probably losing count of the quotes.) He then posed a question about the contemporary plight of American Indians. "This may come as a surprise to you," Duke responded, "but I wasn't alive when the reservations were created . . . what happened 100 years ago in our country can't be blamed on us today. . . . What happened between their forefathers and our forefathers is so far back—right, wrong, or indifferent—that I don't see why we owe them anything."

Lewis kept bushing buttons, and Duke kept responding, expounding on William Kuntsler's defense of the Black Panthers ("why is that dirty, no-good son of a bitch allowed to practice law?"), on William Calley and the My Lai massacre ("I could show you pictures of what the Viet Cong are doing to our people over there"), on the Vietnam War generally ("If we're even going to send one man to die, we ought to be in an all-out confict"), and on a host of other topics. Lewis concluded the interview with a question about the American future. "Had [the United States] lost its dignity," and was it "headed for destruction. Are you gloomy about the future of America?"

But here Duke surprised Lewis. Despite his opinions, he was no hellfire-and-damnation preacher waiting for the apocalypse. Although liberal critics of every stripe were assaulting the American ideal, John Wayne remained a true believer. "Absolutely not," he replied. "I think that the loud roar of irresponsible liberalism . . . is being quieted down by a reasoning public. I think the pendulum is swinging back. We're remembering that the past can't be so bad. We built a nation on it. We have to look to tomorrow."

The interview appeared in the May 1971 issue, and distributors had a difficult time keeping it on the shelves. Batjac phones rang off the wall for several days, the callers heaping either praise or abuse on Duke. The reaction did not surprise him. Back in November, a month before the interview, he told Morton Moss of the *Los Angeles Herald-Examiner*, "Very few of the so-called liberals are open-minded. . . . They shout you down and won't let you speak if you disagree with them. . . . Some people tell me everything isn't black and white. But I say why the hell not?" Mary St. John remembered that the reaction to the interview pleased him. "I must have said some things a lot of people have been thinking but were afraid to express," he told her.[36]

22

"Only a Fool Would Think That Anything Is Forever"

The Oscar put some extra money in the bank, but it did not boost Duke's box-office take on other Batjac productions. After finishing *Rio Lobo* in June 1970, he made four Westerns in quick succession. Batjac produced *Big Jake*, shooting it between October and December of 1970, and National General Cinema distributed it in mid-1971. Duke starred in *The Cowboys* for Warner Bros. It was filmed in northwestern New Mexico in the spring of 1971. Michael Wayne produced *The Train Robbers* in the spring of 1972 for Batjac and Warner Bros., and he followed it with *Cahill, U.S. Marshal* at the end of the year. *The Train Robbers* premiered in February 1973, as did *Cahill* in July.

Rio Lobo netted only $4.25 million, just enough to exceed costs. *Big Jake*, with $7.5 million in rentals, turned a nice profit for Batjac, and *The Cowboys* took in $7.4 million for Warner Bros. *The Train Robbers* did not crack *Variety*'s $4 million minimum as an "All-Time Film Rental Champ." *Cahill, U.S. Marshal*, another disappointment, came in with just $4 million in rentals. The real movie hits of the early 1970s were not Westerns at all. *The Godfather* (1972) earned $86 million from theater owners. In 1973 *The Exorcist*'s take in rentals totaled $82 million, and *The Sting* came close with $78 million. John Wayne was losing some of his punch.[1]

Demographics provided at least a partial explanation. The baby boomers, and the youth culture they generated, came of age in the 1960s. By that time they constituted more than 20 percent of the American population. Raised in affluent suburbs, they did not connect with the image of the frontier in the same way their parents and grandparents had, at least not in its traditional guise of sagebrush, dust, horses, cows, rifles, six-shooters, cowboys, and Indians. As children in the 1950s and early 1960s, they had overdosed on television Westerns, watching thousands of hours of *Wagon Train, Gunsmoke, Have Gun, Will Travel, Rawhide, Tales of the Century, Bonanza, Cheyenne, Lawman, The Life and Legend of Wyatt Earp, Lone Ranger, Rifleman, Sugarfoot,* and *Wanted, Dead or Alive.*

But in the 1960s many baby boomers traded in their toy pistols, chaps, spurs, cowboy hats, and coonskin caps for long hair, bell-bottoms, beads, and protest placards. The moral clarity of a shoot-out at high noon became a victim of the times. In the chaotic atmosphere of the civil rights crusade, youth rebellion, drug culture, and the antiwar movement, the traditional Western appeared increasingly irrelevant, an anachronism more suited to the nineteenth than to the twentieth century.

To survive the Western had to adapt. If the folk heroes of the past no longer inspired reverence, perhaps a new generation of antiheroes would. Hollywood began producing countercultural Westerns.[2]

Sam Peckinpah's *The Wild Bunch* premiered the same week as *True Grit* in 1969. Starring William Holden, Ernest Borgnine, Robert Ryan, and Ben Johnson, the film's settings were frontier towns and open spaces on both sides of the Mexico–New Mexico border early in the twentieth century. Railroad agents have cornered several aging train robbers, whose livelihood is threatened by civilization. The opening scene, according to historian Richard Slotkin, "violates the most fundamental taboo of the Western"—the slaughter of innocent women and children. A temperance parade marches its way down Main Street in a small New Mexico border town, the crusaders singing while a band plays "Shall We Gather at the River." The agents ambush the bandits, but caught in the crossfire of two hardened groups, dozens of innocent women and children fall. The train robbers flee across the border, pursued by the agents, and stumble into the middle of the Mexican Revolution. During the scenes of Peckinpah's exquisitely choreographed violence, it becomes impossible to differentiate good from evil, right from wrong, terrorism from revolution. The film is a savage, if indirect, critique of the Vietnam War, when the fine line between right and wrong blurs and innocent people die. For Slotkin *The Wild Bunch* testifies "to the failure of American values and beliefs and the rising tide of insane violence here and abroad."[3]

Even more pointed than *The Wild Bunch* were *Little Big Man* and *Soldier Blue*, both released in 1970. In November 1969, *Life* magazine had published grisly photographs of the My Lai massacre. The images of twisted bodies, bloodied black pajamas, and naked, mutilated babies—all victims of the American war machine—galvanized the antiwar movement and all but muted the voices of those still supporting the war. *Little Big Man* and *Soldier Blue* were post–My Lai, anti-Vietnam Westerns. Arthur Penn, who directed *Bonnie and Clyde* (1967) and *Alice's Restaurant* (1968), described his objective in *Little Big Man* (1970): "What we're saying is, here is another body of fable, which at least is counterpoint to the fable we've all been fed, which is that Custer was this great heroic man and that the white press westward was against this vast quantity of red savages who were hostile. . . . History has been a little less than honest about it." *Little Big Man* and *Soldier Blue* posited a brutal honesty about U.S. Cavalry treatment of the Cheyenne. *Soldier Blue* features the infamous Sand Creek massacre of 1864, while *Little Big Man* portrays the Washita Massacre of 1869. In both instances U.S. soldiers are malignant murderers, guilty of wanton violence, torture, rape, and mayhem.[4]

The Wild Bunch, *Little Big Man*, and *Soldier Blue* were not the only countercultural Westerns. Copying success with a cookie cutter, producers rapidly stamped out *A Man Called Horse* (1970), *Two Mules for Sister Sara* (1971), *Billy Jack* (1971), *Butch Cassidy and the Sundance Kid* (1971), *The Great Northfield Minnesota Raid* (1971), *Buck and the Preacher* (1971), *McCabe and Mrs. Miller* (1971), *Jeremiah Johnson* (1972), and *Pat Garrett and Billy the Kid* (1973). A number of them were box-office smashes. The rentals from *Butch Cassidy and the Sundance Kid* totaled $46 million, and low-budgeted *Billy Jack* pulled in $32.5 million. The sequel to *Billy Jack—The Trial of Billy Jack* (1974)—earned $28.5 million. *Jeremiah Johnson's* rental take was $21 million. Except for *Butch Cassidy*, which he found charming and well done, Duke hated them all, and not just because of the competition for his market. Peckinpah's violence was too graphic. "Pictures go too far, he told *Playboy* in 1971, "when they use that kind of realism [and] have shots of blood sputting out and teeth flying, and when they throw liver out to make it look like people's insides." Worse, of course, counterculture Westerns smacked of an anti-American cynicism that Wayne had not really seen on film since *High Noon*. Mary St. John remembered him in the Batjac offices on mornings after screening a few of them: "He was disgusted with the films and the industry and wondered why Hollywood was pandering to the country's worst instincts." Howard Hawks felt the same way. Interviewed on the set of *Rio Lobo* on April 29, 1970, he described *The Wild Bunch* as "a very bad picture. I never made a message picture, and I hope I never do."[5]

Ironically, traditional Western themes, and the John Wayne persona, survived in the 1970s in urban landscapes. Many Americans despised the anti-hero and still revered the lone, uncompromising, hard man who punished evil, but they wanted to see justice enforced in cities, not on the deserts and prairies of yesteryear. The city had become the wilderness—the domain of outlaws and predators, the place where doors were locked at night and decent citizens stayed inside. Saul Pett, a writer for the Associated Press, captured the fears of many Americans in 1970:

> We walk safely among the craters of the moon but not in the parks of New York or Chicago or Los Angeles. Technology and change run berserk, headlights hide by day and moral values shred overnight. The unthinkable multiplies until it seems "things fall apart—the center cannot hold. . . ." The young mock our past, robbing us of the comfort of our victories in depression and war . . . America is no longer immune to history. . . . America, we seem suddenly to have discovered, is no longer infinite in space or resources or hope. There is no next valley of quiet or virgin forest to tread.

Urban crime was the new enemy and cities the place where savages abused the innocent. Handcuffed by a liberal angst more concerned with criminals than with their victims, the police and judges seemed incapable of meting out justice on this new frontier where brute power held sway. Downtown needed Ethan Edwards and the Ringo Kid.[6]

Gene Hackman tried to fill the role in *The French Connection* (1971), a film about a New York City detective willing to use every weapon at his disposal—legal and illegal—to break an international drug cartel. So did Charles Bronson as an urban vigilante in *Death Wish* (1974), ruthlessly seeking out and executing muggers and rapists. Duke had a chance to try his hand at cityscapes in 1970 when Paramount offered him the part of Harry Callahan in *Dirty Harry*, a film Don Siegel was going to direct about a San Francisco cop who does not play by the rules. But too busy with *Rio Lobo*, *The Cowboys*, and *Big Jake*, Duke turned them down. The part, of course, went to Clint Eastwood, who had already played a similar role in *Coogan's Bluff* (1968).[7]

Eastwood first surfaced in American popular culture in the mid-1960s, starring in a string of Italian-produced "spaghetti westerns"—*A Fistful of Dollars* (1964), *For a Few Dollars More* (1965), *The Good the Bad and the Ugly* (1966), and *Hang 'em High* (1968). Just like the Ringo Kid or Ethan Edwards,

Eastwood's characters are hard-boiled, steely-eyed, cynical loners, willing at the drop of hat to draw a six-gun and kill predators. Duke enjoyed the Eastwood films, and recognized elements of his own work at every turn. But he also noticed the differences. Eastwood exaggerated the persona. In *A Fistful of Dollars* and *For a Few Dollars More*, Eastwood's character does not even have a name. He's just "the stranger." In *The Good the Bad and the Ugly*, he had acquired a first name—Joe. Not until *Hang'em High* does the gunslinger have a complete name—Jed Cooper. Jed Cooper seems liberated from any semblance of vulnerability; he is almost too hard. There is a mean streak to him that even Ethan Edwards did not possess. "If it had been Jed Cooper instead of Ethan Edwards finding Natalie Wood in *The Searchers*," Duke told an associate in 1968, "he probably would have shot her."[8]

Dirty Harry changed all that. When he saw the movie, Duke realized his mistake. Harry Callahan *was* John Wayne, equipped with an unmarked police car, a .357 magnum, and an unfailing sense for sniffing out criminals. Equally unintimidated by bloodthirsty murderers, avaricious drug dealers, conniving politicians, and gutless bureaucrats, Harry Callahan gave millions of Americans the vicarious satisfaction of ruthlessly gunning down the perpetrators of evil, regardless of the dictates of municipal codes, police rules of engagement, or the U.S. Constitution. "How did I ever let that one slip through my fingers?" Duke lamented to Mary.[9]

Batjac tried to capitalize on the success of *Dirty Harry* with *McQ*, which was released in February 1974. Wayne plays Lon McQ, a Seattle cop who goes after drug dealers and exposes a case of police corruption. A year later Duke appeared in *Brannigan*, the story of a Chicago cop who travels to London to extradite a big-time gang leader who has fled Illinois jurisdiction. In both films Brannigan and McQ are Harry Callahan–types willing to shoot at anybody—police or criminals—who gets in their way, breaking every rule and any law to implement justice. But McQ and Brannigan are poor clones of Dirty Harry. Duke weighed 260 pounds and was sixty-seven years old. In both films a heavy toupee of dark hair topped a wrinkled, thick-skinned face. In the real world, cops as old as McQ or Brannigan are jockeying desks or enjoying retirement. Gunning down criminals on the streets of Seattle or London is the work of the young. The urban resurrection of Wayne's persona worked for a lean, hard Clint Eastwood, but not for a paunchy John Wayne.[10]

Both films failed. Critics took note of Duke's hapless attempts to transplant himself to urban jungles. Reviewing *McQ* for *The New Yorker*, Pauline Kael wrote: "In *McQ*, [Wayne] imitates his juniors; he lifts his name from

Steve McQueen and his tough police officer character from Clint Eastwood's Dirty Harry Callahan. Incompetence like this prostrates me; I got so stoned by the boringness I forgot to get up and go home." *Brannigan* fared no better. "It has been a long time since *True Grit*," a reviewer for *Time* magazine intoned. "Maybe one of our Bicentennial projects ought to be a search for a movie worthy of a national treasure like John Wayne. It is maddening to see him caught up in incompetencies like *Brannigan*." Duke's fans agreed. Both films failed. *McQ* earned $4.1 million in rentals, barely covering Batjac's costs, and *Brannigan* did not crack the $4 million mark. *Dirty Harry*, on the other hand, had earned $18 million in rentals.[11]

Although his film career was flagging, Duke's popularity with the "silent majority" had never been higher. Ivor Davis, a columnist for *Los Angeles Magazine*, in 1975 overheard one of his more liberal colleagues say, "I disagree with almost everything he says, but you've just got to admire him. He's more like a monument than a man. He believes in himself and his country in a way that other men don't any more." In a world in which the media appeared to be promoting doubt and discord, he epitomized confidence and stability. He said what millions of Americans felt. He reacted the way they did.[12]

Academy Award ceremony politics were a case in point. Marlon Brando earned Duke's wrath in 1973 when he received the Best Actor award for his role as Vito Corleone in *The Godfather*. Liv Ullman and Roger Moore opened the Best Actor envelope and announced Brando the winner to a thunderous ovation. The applause sputtered into hushed murmurs as a young woman in a white buckskin dress and a leather thong headdress moved down the aisle to accept Brando's award. Unctuously, with all the trappings of subdued outrage, she said:

> Hello. My name is Sacheen Littlefeather. I'm Apache, and I am president of the National Native American Affirmative Image Committee. I'm representing Marlon Brando this evening, and he has asked me to tell you . . . that he very regretfully cannot accept this very generous award. And the reasons for this are the treatment of American Indians today by the film industry and on television in movie reruns. . . . I beg at this time that I have not intruded upon this evening and that we will, in the future, in our hearts and our understanding meet with love and generosity. Thank you on behalf of Marlon Brando.

Looking the part of a downtrodden Apache, "Sacheen Littlefeather" then slowly exited the stage to a waiting throng of reporters and read a very long statement from Brando.[13]

Within a few days, enterprising reporters exposed Littlefeather as Maria

Louise Cruz, an Arizona native raised in Salinas, California, by white grandparents. When reporters asked Duke for a comment, he said: "If he had something to say, he should have appeared that night and stated his views instead of taking some little unknown girl and dressing her up in an Indian outfit." Privately Duke found the incident uproariously funny, not the fact that Brando had used the Academy Awards ceremony as a bully pulpit, but his extraordinarily bad judgment in employing a fake Indian to protest Hollywood's portrayal of Indians. "My God," he told Mary St. John. "The big beef of the Indians has always been the use of white actors to portray them. So Brando gets a pretend Indian to protest. How dumb can you get!" Actually Littlefeather was half white and one-quarter Yaqui and Apache, a woman who had adopted the name Sacheen Littlefeather after joining the Alcatraz occupation of 1969 with the group known as Indians of All Tribes. She was an aspiring actress who had worked in the radio business and had been named Miss American Vampire of 1970.

The next year, 1974, Duke had to be physically restrained at the Academy Awards ceremony. He was casually chatting backstage with Bob Hope and Frank Sinatra, waiting for his turn as a presenter, when the award for Best Documentary Feature was announced. The Oscar went to *Hearts and Minds*, a brilliant collage of interviews and war footage and a scathing indictment of the Vietnam War. Peter Davis and Bert Schneider, the coproducers, both came to the podium to accept their award. Both felt the need to comment on the war. Davis told the audience at the Dorothy Chandler Pavilion: "It's ironic to get a prize for a war movie while the suffering in Vietnam continues. [I hope] my children grow up in a better atmosphere and a better country." Davis took his Oscar and gave way to Schneider, who proceeded to read a telegram he had solicited from the Vietcong delegation at the Paris Peace talks. Backstage Duke became apoplectic, his face draining into a ghostly white and then flushing into an enraged red, as Schneider read: PLEASE TRANSMIT TO ALL OUR FRIENDS IN AMERICA OUR RECOGNITION OF ALL THEY HAVE DONE ON BEHALF OF PEACE AND FOR THEIR APPLICATION OF THE PARIS ACCORDS ON VIETNAM. THESE ACTIONS SERVE THE LEGITIMATE INTERESTS OF THE AMERICAN PEOPLE AND THE VIETNAMESE PEOPLE. GREETINGS OF FRIENDSHIP TO ALL AMERICAN PEOPLE. Schneider, he bellowed, "is a pain in the ass and way out of line." Wayne, Hope, and Sinatra insisted that Howard Koch, the producer of the awards ceremony, read a disclaimer, or Duke was going to go to the microphone himself, taking a shot at Schneider along the way. Shirley MacLaine, who was waiting to give an honorary Oscar to Jean Renoir, shouted: "Don't you dare!" The three men scribbled out a statement, got

Koch to endorse it, and Sinatra went back onstage and announced, to a chorus of boos and cheers: "We are not responsible for any political references made on the program, and we are sorry they had to take place this evening."[14]

Although the media and the cultural elite portrayed Duke as a right-wing fanatic, the rest of the country loved him. Recognition awards came steadily in the 1970s. *Photoplay* magazine gave him its Gold Medal commendation. Other prizes soon followed, including one from the Mexican government for his contribution to their film industry, the Golden Saddleman award from the Western Writers of America, the Iron Mike award from the U.S. Marine Corps League, the Americanism Gold Medal award from the Veterans of Foreign Wars, the opening of the John Wayne Theater at Knotts Berry Farm, the Call Achievement Award from the University of Southern California, a special Kindness to Animals award from the American Humane Association, the George Washington Award from the Freedom Foundation, the Scopus Award from the Friends of Hebrew University, the American Patriot Award of the Americanism Educational League, and dozens of others. A patron saint of the American Right, John Wayne was one of the most highly recognized, and respected, men in the world.[15]

But as Duke mentioned many times, awards "don't pay the bills." He needed money. Again. Happy Shahan, who owned the 22,000-acre ranch and movie set near Brackettsville, Texas, where *The Alamo* had been filmed in 1959, fondly remarked that "Duke would think nothing of dropping a million bucks into some marginal scheme but wouldn't invest ten dollars for a guaranteed twenty-dollar return." He was also a soft touch for every hard-luck story that came his way. Celebrities get letters all the time, hundreds and thousands of them, from hucksters as well as from genuinely desperate people, requesting financial assistance. Wayne was no exception. But unlike most celebrities, he often read the letters, tried to discern which people were really in dire straits, and wrote checks for one hundred dollars to buy children school clothes or enable somebody to visit his or her sick mother. Checkbooks littered every room of the office, the house, and the *Wild Goose,* so that writing checks would always be convenient, but he never made a recording in the register. Balancing the checkbook was usually a nightmare for his secretaries and business manager.[16]

He kept making movies in the 1970s because he felt he had no choice. In 1976 Joseph Bell, a reporter for the Hearst newspapers, asked him why he kept working when he did not have to, and Wayne, with a real edge to his voice, retorted: "What makes you think I don't have to work? Have you checked my financial statements? If you did, you'd know that if I'm going to continue to live this way, I do have to work. Maybe I should be in a position where I don't have to work, but I'm not." At a time when contemporaries like Bob Hope, Gene Autry, and Fred MacMurray owned financial empires worth hundreds of millions of dollars, Duke was a comparative pauper. His net worth at the end of his life would be less than $30 million, after making more than two hundred films, with salaries in the 1960s exceeding $600,000 each. The divorce from Josie back in 1944 had been a financial setback, as was the divorce from Chata in 1953. Bo Roos's shenanigans in the 1950s wiped him out completely, as did some of his own mistakes, like the shrimp-boat deal in Panama and a whiskey-importing business with Bruce Cabot. The Don La-Cava incident in 1967 was another financial drain.[17]

The nearly $30 million estate he possessed when he died had few income-producing assets. Probably 98 percent of it consisted of the Newport Beach home, proceeds from the sale of the *Wild Goose,* the cotton farm and feed lot in Stansfield, Arizona, and the cattle ranch in Springerville, Arizona. The ranch drained him for several years until Louis Johnson took it over and stopped its hemorrhaging, prompting Wayne to extend his ultimate accolade to Johnson: "Louis's no bullshit artist." But both men had agreed to plow all of the profits back into the businesses. None of Duke's assets produced an income Duke could use to support his family and his lifestyle. He suffered from constant cash-flow problems.[18]

Wayne worked with a vengeance, but even then he had a hard time. Given the fact that his salaries often reached into the highest income tax brackets, Duke paid Uncle Sam anywhere from $200,000 to $500,000 a year, and even then he was subject to tax audits that often tapped him for even more. In 1971 the IRS charged him with underpaying his 1965 taxes by $237,000. Upkeep on the *Wild Goose,* the private jet *Commando,* and the helicopter, and salaries for their crews, cost Wayne another quarter of a million a year. It cost him more than $200,000 a year to support Pilar, Aissa, Ethan, and Marisa in the style to which they had become accustomed. He often complained about Pilar's extravagance. His affection for Josie and his guilt about the demise of their marriage were still alive in the 1970s, and he continued to help support her financially, doling out nearly $50,000 a year. Even in his will Duke made sure to establish a trust fund that would supply Josie with $36,000 a year for the remainder of her life. Agents received 10 percent of Wayne's film salaries.[19]

During the 1970s he pumped a significant amount of money into several risky business enterprises, ranging from a snake-oil treatment for baldness called "Hair Trigger Formula 6" to attempts to take advantage of the Arab oil boycott of 1973 and the rocketing price of crude oil. Most of the enterprises were joint ventures with friends, who promised to manage the businesses if Duke would invest in them. He helped finance Separation and Recovery Systems, Inc., a company managed by his friend Joe De Franco, that marketed a process for getting the oil out of bilgewater in ships. Bill Chambers, another friend, convinced him to invest in the Duke Engineering Company (DECO) to extract petroleum from shale, coal, and worn-out tires. Wayne spent considerable time and money trying to coax money out of the Japanese or American coal companies or Navajo reservation officials. Although De Franco's Separation and Recovery Systems proved viable, Duke could never, much to his frustration, get DECO off the ground. It lost money. He dumped $300,000 into another friend's cockeyed plan to extract methane gas from cow manure. Duke wasted time hawking a half-baked scheme known as "Product 76"—a rhyolite gimmick that could supposedly cure skin ailments like psoriasis as well as insulate buildings. He sank hundreds of thousands of dollars into the Statesman Mining Corporation, which had a concession of over 45,000 square miles of supposedly rich mineral properties in Nigeria. He also lent his name to Apollo Motor Homes and owned part of the Executive Air Service, an aircraft rental business operating out of the Orange County Airport. And Batjac's annual payroll totaled several hundred thousand dollars. Finally, he also had three secretaries, a business manager, chauffeur, and house servants to pay. Not counting his own living expenses, he needed $1.5 million a year in the 1970s just to break even. He made more than that in the early part of the decade, but not much more.[20]

Cash-flow troubles forced Duke to accept offers for television commercials. Early in 1977 he signed a $200,000-a-year contract with Bristol-Myers to advertise Datril 500, the company's new headache remedy. Filming the commercials was a nightmare, and when he saw the finished product on tape he was terribly disappointed. The idea of John Wayne selling headache pills was unseemly, and appearing unseemly was something he had avoided all his life. His own personality had long since been subsumed by his screen persona, and he abhorred appearing weak. Marlene Dietrich summed it up best: "You can't be King Lear and selling some kind of product a minute later. John Wayne . . . dressed as a cowboy from head to foot. . . . I think it's the most ludicrous thing I've ever seen . . . a 'he-man of the great outdoors' on horseback with his hat and all the other trappings of a real cowboy on, praising the effect of a headache tablet. Too funny for words." Duke agreed and voided the contract with Bristol-Myers, making himself a solemn promise never to do a commercial again.[21]

Never is a long time, especially when you need money. Later in the year Great Western Savings, a large California savings-and-loan, approached him with an offer of $350,000 a year to praise the virtues of the company. He was skeptical at first, but once they assured him of editorial control of the final product, he agreed. The commercials were filmed in Grants Pass, Oregon, and Duke got to talk about the great outdoors, the frontier West, and Great Western Savings. When the commercials were aired, he was pleased. He looked as rugged and strong as the countryside, and Great Western reaped tens of millions of new deposits and then promptly picked up the option for several more years of commercials, at a salary of $400,000 a year.[22]

More than just financial problems, however, fueled Wayne's obsession with working hard. He had never really learned to relax, had no interest in tennis or golf or jogging, and could not stand to be alone. When he was alone he was immediately on the phone trying to talk a friend into playing cards or getting in the car and going somewhere. If friends were not available, Duke would pester Aissa or Marisa or John Ethan to go somewhere with him. When he woke up in the morning, he wanted everybody else in the house to get up as well. But as he got older and filming dates became fewer and fewer, he had more time on his hands and was often bored and irritable. The kids were older as well, and they wanted to spend time with Newport Beach friends, not with their sixty-eight-year-old father. The business ventures of the 1970s often made little economic sense, but they helped fill an emotional void. Duke flew from town to town, drumming up support, visiting with old friends, making new ones, and filling his time. He loved it all, even if it cost him money.[23]

Wayne's favorite business pursuit—the one that was the most profitable and the most fun—was his partnership with Louis Johnson. Their personal and professional relationship had always been close. Johnson once remarked: "We have never had a disagreement. Not one. He's one of the greatest people in the world. When he gives you his word, that's it." Early in the 1970s, the Department of Agriculture began reducing cotton acreage nationwide, and in return for substantial subsidy payments, Wayne and Johnson put the land into alfalfa and pasture. They had already gone into the cattle business, purchasing the three-thousand-acre 26 Bar Ranch near Springerville, and raising Hereford cattle. Every Thanksgiving weekend during the 1970s, Wayne headed over to Stanfield to spend the holiday with the Johnsons and participate in the annual cattle sale. On Thanksgiving Day in 1974, the Johnsons had a party for their cattlemen friends, and Wayne mixed with them. That afternoon, with a drink in his hand, Duke lost his balance at the edge of an indoor pool and fell in. The house shook with laughter and someone yelled: "Sheee-it. He can't walk on water after all." Duke bellowed louder than the rest. He loved cattlemen because they seemed to have few pretensions and treated him as they would anybody else.[24]

Throughout his life Duke had enjoyed the company of men, with their talk, jokes, pranks, and fun. Fans worshiped him, but he needed close friends who did not take him too seriously, which the cattlemen never did. A no-holds-barred one-upmanship governed the relationships. One was with Danko Gurovich, who owned several Arizona motels. In 1966 Wayne got Gurovich and Johnson drunk and convinced them to invest $2,500 each into a fictitious enterprise he called the Danko Cattle Company. He then took the $5,000 and gave it to Chick Iverson, a mutual friend who was going on his honeymoon to Hawaii.

It took them three years to get even. Johnson purchased a young Palomino colt for $1,500 and named the horse Snicker Bar Dan. Gurovich and Johnson placed fictitious bets on fictitious horse races and bragged about their winnings until Wayne asked if he could buy a piece of the animal. Johnson sold him a half interest for $12,500. Later in the year, at the annual Thanksgiving cattle sale, Wayne bragged about Snicker Bar Dan, the great quarter horse. Nobody had heard of him. Duke started getting suspicious, and just about that time Johnson started letting everyone in on the joke. Wayne was out $12,500, but the real joke was his public embarrassment in front of the cattlemen. He was mad enough for Johnson and Gurovich to go into hiding for a few hours.

Wayne often described the Arizona properties as a hobby, but they were actually the backbone of his assets. He did not know just how valuable it was. In 1975, when he was especially strapped for cash, Wayne hatched a scheme to subdivide the cotton acreage and sell it to Vietnamese immigrants just arriving in the United States. Former South Vietnamese vice president Nguyen Cao Ky endorsed the idea and suggested that he manage the enterprise, establishing Israeli-like cooperatives in the desert and bringing in tens of thousands of Vietnamese to live there. It seemed a perfect way to help them, partially resolve a difficult national problem, and make some money for Louis and himself. But Gov. Raul Castro of Arizona, anticipating a nativist reaction of major proportions, immediately scuttled the plan, citing the state's already high unemployment problem as the reason. It turned out to be a financial godsend, for in 1980, several months after Wayne's death, Johnson sold the properties for $45 million; of that, $22.5 million went to Duke's estate. Everything else he owned at the time of his death was worth only $6.8 million.[25]

Another reason for Duke's obsession with work in his later years was a self-imposed obligation to build up an adequate trust fund for each of his children. Since he was a small child, family life had been tempestuous—full of doubt, misunderstanding, uncertainty, neglect, fear, and denial—and the 1970s were no different. His feelings about not serving his country during World War II were matched only by the guilt he felt about the kind of father he had been. Over and over again, to close friends like Mary St. John or Louis Johnson, Wayne had lamented: "The greatest mistake I ever made was leaving Josie and those kids." He felt that his older children had paid a heavy emotional price for his absence.[26]

He did not want to make the same mistakes with Aissa, John Ethan, and Marisa. Maureen O'Hara explained in 1973 how hard he was trying: "Have you ever been on the set of any of his pictures? Not only are his own children around . . . but any number of his grandchildren. For God's sake, there's never been a time that one, two, or three of them aren't crawling all over him, even when he's playing cards with the guys. They are on his lap, his shoulders, around his legs, and he's a great picker-upper, a hugger and a kisser." He did not want to neglect them, and when he was home, he tried to spend time with them.

Sometimes he tried too hard, however. When Aissa, John Ethan, and Marisa were little, they enjoyed his attention. But in 1970, after returning from the *Big Jake* location, Wayne wanted the kids to spend the weekend with him on the *Wild Goose*. John Ethan and Marisa were thrilled at the prospect, but Aissa, who was fifteen, wanted to stay in Newport Beach with her friends. He begged and cajoled and then got angry: "Oh, okay. You'd rather be at your friend's house than be with me. I'm home from making a movie and you'd rather be there. You don't care that I'm here, do you? You just don't care."[27]

In her 1991 autobiography, Aissa accused her father of imposing excessive emotional demands that erected a painful barrier between himself and his younger children, bringing about exactly what he had hoped to avoid. At times he was short-tempered, demanding, and difficult. Like most concerned fathers, he worried about who Aissa was with, what she wore, where she went, and when she was coming home at night. Duke missed the little girl who had once worshiped him. Teenagers frustrated and bewildered him. There were other times, however, when he epitomized patience and understanding. On the day he learned that Aissa and several friends had been caught smoking marijuana in a neighbor's house, he simply said: "We need to talk." They sat down at the kitchen table, and in a calm, kind, measured voice, he told her, "Aissa, I love you very much. The people that gave you that stuff, they don't love you the way that I do. You can take their word that his stuff is good, or you can listen to me when I tell you it's bad." "My father had called me no names," Aissa remembered. "He had not used rage or self-righteousness." He reacted similarly in December 1972, after giving Aissa her first car—a new yellow Porsche 914. A few weeks later she stayed out all night drinking beer and listening to Rolling Stones tapes. Aissa let a friend get behind the wheel, and he wrecked the Porsche. On top of it all, she had lost track of the time and had not told her parents where she was. Duke paced the driveway most of the night until she came stumbling in at dawn. He ordered her to her room, stating grimly: "We've been looking for you all night." The next day, after learning about the car, he told Aissa: "If I gave you what you deserved, I'd have to ground you forever. So let's just forget it."[28]

Guilt about family life found its way into many of Wayne's later films. The characters were always having trouble of some kind with the women they loved. In *Hellfighters* (1969) "Chance" Buckman's wife Madelyn (Vera Miles) and daughter (Katharine Ross) are alienated from him because of his work, which is dangerous and takes him away from home for extended periods. Although Chance and Madelyn loved each other, they could not live together and had been separated for twenty years. *Big Jake* (1971) was set in a different century and a different place, but it carried the same domestic message. Jake McCandles (John Wayne) is an aging man who has been separated from his family for twenty years. His wife Martha (Maureen O'Hara) calls on his assistance only when the ranch has been ravaged and a grandchild kidnapped by desperadoes. Jake comes to the rescue, proving his love for them, his willingness to sacrifice for them, and his commitment to die for them. But in the end, as always, what he cannot do is live with them.[29]

He found it easier to express some of these emotions on film than in real life. Onscreen, if not in person, John Wayne expressed his deepest feelings—his loves, fears, and inadequacies—and he hoped that Michael, Patrick, Toni, Melinda, Aissa, John Ethan, and Marisa were watching and listening. Onscreen he would ask for their forgiveness. It was the only apology, and explanation, they were ever going to get. *Cahill, U.S. Marshall* (1973), for example, is very close to autobiographical. Andrew McLaglen, who directed the film, said it was "not the usual John Wayne movie. It's a very deep, personal story about children neglected by a father who is just trying to do his job." Wayne plays the role of Marshal J. D. Cahill, an aging widower whose two children are in trouble because of his lack of attention. At one point midway through the film, J.D. says to his seventeen-year-old son Daniel, "Things seem to happen to you two when I'm not around." "Pa," Danny replies, "You ain't never around." J.D. then responds, "You're dead right, Daniel. I can't argue that. I've been gone a lot of times when you kids really needed me. And I've missed a lot too. Missed watching you two grow up. I think about it a lot. On every job. And when it's over I'll come home and the three of us will get to know each other. But even before that job was finished another one seemed to crop up. . . . I don't want what I'm saying to sound like excuses. There is no excuse for negligence."[30]

He sought understanding as well as forgiveness. At one point in *Hellfighters*, an uncle explains to Chance Buckman's daughter what went wrong with her parents' marriage, why her father let his career destroy his family: "You're father is the very best at what he does. No man can walk away from that." Even in *Cahill*, when the marshal says to his boys, "There is no excuse for negligence," he quickly adds: "But there's no excuse for a man ignoring his duty either." Most of all Wayne tried to be a good father. For all his faults, he worked hard to give his children what he had spent a lifetime achieving: financial security and self-respect.

Wives were a different matter. He was not willing to apologize and ask forgiveness for the demands of his career. He firmly believed that his mother's unhappiness stemmed from those hard years scraping out an existence with Clyde. Molly hated their poverty and complained roundly about it. No wife of John Wayne's could ever express a similar complaint. Duke was far less tolerant of his wives' concerns than he was of the kids'. At the end of *Hellfighters*, when a reconciliation between Chance Buckman and his estranged wife, Madelyn, begins to develop, he warns her that his return to fighting fires "was bound to happen. It will happen again. And each time I'll go." The marriage is saved only when Madelyn overcomes her fears and submits to her husband's sense of duty. She returns to him on his terms. The message was the same in *Cahill*. Talking to his sons about their mother and his wife, Cahill describes her last words: "Your mother, God bless her, when she was dying, the last thing she said on earth was, 'Go get 'em, J.D.' And I've been going and gettin' ever since 'till it's no longer just my job. It's part of my life. And that's what I want you to try and understand. Your old man's life."[31]

Wayne's wives were hardly as understanding as J. D. Cahill's. As the movie was being made, Wayne's marriage to Pilar was dying. They announced their separation to the press in November 1973.[32]

He had always found women unfathomable. He was always careful and cautious around them, anxious to please if he could but unwilling to make sacrifices to do so. In 1973 he looked astonished when May Mann, a reporter from *Photoplay* magazine, asked him if Pilar was his best friend. Duke made it quite clear: "My wife is not my best friend." He was convinced that it was impossible for a man and woman to be best friends. Men were supposed to have other men as their best friends, and women were supposed to have other women as their confidantes. Any other social relationship seemed ludicrous, since, in his view, men and women were so fundamentally different and so completely out of touch with one another's feelings. His films had always celebrated the rites of male kinship, and his personal philosophy mirrored those images.[33]

His image of women was thoroughly stylized and domestic. Women were not best friends for men; they were wives, mothers, lovers, occasional companions, employees, and associates. Whenever he was on location, he wanted Pilar and the kids to come with him. If they could not, he preferred renting a house and having a woman hired to cook homemade meals and take care of the place. Living in hotels and eating catered or restaurant meals three times a day had no attraction for him. Above all else, he believed that the ideal woman stayed at home and took care of her husband and children. He did not believe that every woman should be forced to stay at home; he was just convinced that true happiness for women was inside the home, not outside. Two of his daughters—Toni and Aissa—wanted to become actresses, but he discouraged those ambitions, although he had no problems with his son Patrick entering the profession. Wayne knew that sexual biases ran deep in American culture, that the vast majority of actresses, unless they were extraordinarily gifted, did not have careers after they were thirty because audiences would no longer consider them sexually attractive. Toni and Aissa, although both were beautiful women, had inherited his frame—big-boned and physically strong. With contemporary films gratuitously revealing more and more female flesh on screen, Duke realized that neither of them had the bodies to make it in pictures, and that both would probably suffer rejection and disappointment if they tried to become actresses. He wanted to protect them from that pain, so he encouraged them to get a good education, marry, and raise a family. Refusing to give Aissa a role in *True Grit*, Wayne told her: "There's some awful people in this business. I didn't want to see Toni get hurt. You know what I told her? I told her she should get married, and have a whole bunch of children. And that's what Toni did."[34]

He thought all women should be like Josephine Saenz, his first wife, and Margot Fonteyn, the famous ballerina. He had enormous respect for both of them because of their loyalties. Josie had been a devout Roman Catholic all her life, and a devoted mother. If Wayne had not destroyed their marriage, she would have remained a devoted wife as well. In spite of the pain of the divorce, she diligently raised the children and spoke well of their father in front of them. Because of her, Wayne was convinced, their children had turned out to be fine human beings. Margot Fonteyn had similar qualities. She was a beautiful, talented, internationally renowned ballerina who had married Duke's Panamanian friend, Roberto Arias. When an assassination attempt left Roberto a paraplegic in 1965, Fonteyn remained completely devoted to him until his death in 1989. For John Wayne, Margot Fonteyn was "the most beautiful person I've known in my whole life."[35]

Wayne found those same qualities in Louis Johnson's wife, Alice. She maintained a lovely home in Stanfield and enjoyed being around Louie and his friends, as well as going with her husband to the cattle sales and conventions. In 1972 Duke agreed to accompany the Johnsons to Nashville, where Alice's brother was promoting a record deal. One evening during the trip Duke, Louis, and Alice went out to a restaurant, and over the course of several hours the two men became drunk and mellow. Wayne looked at Alice, then looked right into Louis's eyes, and said, "God, Louis, you're a lucky man."[36]

Pilar would not and could not fulfill his expectations, not if she was going to have any sense of herself. In 1965, when they sold the Encino house and moved to Newport Beach, she constructed a new life. Aissa was ten years old and in the fifth grade, John Ethan was starting kindergarten, and she was pregnant with Marisa. It had become increasingly difficult to have the children out of school and pack them off to some exotic location, and she started staying home instead of going along. Her Newport Beach friends and Christian Science church activities filled her days.[37]

Pilar's changes disrupted the rhythms of Duke's life. She was no longer on location catering to him, and more often than not, when he was at home, she was off with her friends enjoying activities in which he played no part. She saw the children off to school and greeted them when they came home in the afternoons, and she enjoyed evening meals with the family, but during the day she played tennis, visited her friends, and watched over her restaurant. On Sundays she went to church. Duke resented her time at the tennis club, and he had absolutely no patience with "oddball" religions and their irrational demands on members. God, he reasoned, wanted his children to be strong and to take care of almost all of their problems by themselves, and he gave them the tools to do it. It bothered him when Pilar became a Christian Scientist and began talking about faith healing and avoiding physicians and drugs. As far as he was concerned, modern medical science was progress, a gift of God to the modern world, and he was living proof of it. He respected the comfort Pilar found in Christian Science, but he hated the thought that Aissa, Marisa, and Ethan might grow up believing in such nonsense. In 1970, during the filming of *Rio Lobo*, Aissa got sick with diarrhea and asked Mary St. John what she should do. Mary told her to go see a physician and get some medication. Aissa asked her father, and he agreed, insisting, however, that she not tell Pilar, and that if Pilar did find out, to make sure she knew that it was Mary's advice, not his. Otherwise there "would be hell to pay." Duke complained that he wanted the "old Pilar back." He was sick and tired of "all that damn bullshit about women's lib."[38]

I n 1967, two years after the move to Newport Beach, Duke and Pilar took separate bedrooms on Bayshore Drive. The children noticed right away, but both parents blamed the move on Wayne's snoring. The truth, however, was not that simple. Pilar confided to a few friends that they were having sexual problems, intimating that Duke was impotent. He had confessed to Pilar: "I'm old, tired. I don't feel well, and I'm taking a lot of medication. I just can't be a real husband to you anymore." But there was more to it than that. At the age of sixty-one, his testosterone levels and libido were hardly what they used to be, but he was also angry with Pilar. Either one of those would have been enough to damage their sexual relationship. Both combined were fatal.[39]

Jealous of her new interests and feeling neglected, he became bitter, accusing Pilar of enjoying the role of "Mrs. John Wayne" more than being a "real wife." Pilar later commented that he "wanted his own idea of a wife, not some female who was struggling to develop a life and an identity of her own. He wanted children who jumped when he said jump. . . . I wanted to be able to play tennis, to see my friends, to stay home while Duke was on location without feeling guilty." Their marriage reached a critical stage in the spring of 1972, when Duke wanted to take the *Wild Goose* up the Pacific Coast to Alaska for several weeks. She loathed such trips. All day long, for weeks on end, she would have to cook and clean for Wayne and his buddies, and play bridge, and she refused to go. Enraged, he insisted that she come with him. He even flew her mother up from Lima, Peru, to give Pilar a lecture on how a "proper wife" should obey her husband. Pilar still refused, and the fragile marriage shattered.[40]

The moving force behind the separation was Duke, not Pilar. He could understand part of their problem, but only part. Wayne admitted to a *Photoplay* reporter that "the going has been pretty rough because of my picture schedule, and the fact that I'm all wrapped up in my career. Sometimes I'm gone three or four months at a stretch when I make a picture on a foreign location. Pilar and I can't seem to get an understanding between us anymore." He wanted her to be like Marshal Cahill's or Chance Buckman's wives, letting him do whatever he wanted. She wanted him to consider retirement or at least a less frenetic schedule, maybe cutting back to one picture a year. He insisted that they needed the money. There was no ground for compromise.[41]

Even if Wayne had cut back, it would hardly have mattered. John Wayne did not have the foggiest notion of what was bothering Pilar, and his semiretirement would only have made their relationship worse. He would have been home all the time wanting to know what she was doing or where she was going. In 1972, when the marriage was bottoming out, he wondered to Louis Johnson: "Louis, I can get along with everybody. Why the hell can't I get along with women?" Pilar managed to get him to a session of marriage counseling, but it was a failure. Duke had a hard enough time expressing his feelings to the people he loved; the idea of talking about them to strangers was out of the question. Also, he hated the whole notion of psychotherapy and the rise of a narcissistic culture in America. California in general, and Newport Beach in particular, was a spawning ground for the "feel-good" movement, and Wayne thought it was self-indulgent, telling Pilar: "I don't believe in all that mumbo jumbo. We're grown people and we ought to be able to settle our problems ourselves." He added that "I stay away from psychoanalysts' scenes. Couches are only good for one thing." So much for marriage counseling.[42]

His answer to problems with a wife was replacement. He had replaced Josie with Chata and then Chata with Pilar. By 1973 it was time for Pilar to go, and Duke had already found the replacement. Mary St. John had worked as Duke's personal secretary since 1946, but early in the 1970s she decided to retire. Her mother-in-law, who had lived with the St. Johns for more than twenty years and taken care of the St. John household when Mary was working, had died, and Mary felt the need to be at home. Also, she had increasingly found herself serving as a mediator between Duke and Pilar, and she was uncomfortable with the role. Wayne did not want her to retire; he could not understand why anyone would want to retire and not work anymore. But eventually he agreed, as long as Mary would interview, select, and train her replacement. In 1972 Mary offered the job to thirty-year-old Patricia Stacy. Gradually, over the next year, Mary St. John withdrew from the job while Stacy assumed her responsibilities.[43]

Pat Stacy was bright, attractive, and absolutely enchanted with John Wayne. A graduate of Northeastern Louisiana State University, she moved to California in 1968 and went to work in the Los Angeles office of Arthur Andersen & Company, which handled Duke's tax affairs. About the time Stacy's boss was transferred to Chicago, Mary St. John called William Neuhauser, head of the tax division, and told him she was going to retire. Mary asked Neuhauser if he could suggest someone to replace her, and he mentioned Stacy. Neuhauser helped arrange the interview with Mary, and Stacy got the job. Duke seemed larger than life to her and, at the same time, friendly and unassuming. Before long Wayne noted that Pat had a crush on him. She stared, she fawned, she catered to his slightest suggestion. In June 1973 Duke had his crew take the *Wild Goose* to Seattle, where he was going to film *McQ*. Mary St. John had broken her shoulder in a fall and she had to beg off the trip, sending Pat instead. Pat was thrilled. Soon Duke was paying as much attention to her as she was to him. He was a sixty-five-year-old man whom a thirty-year-old woman found overwhelmingly attractive. It was an irresistible situation. Three weeks into the location they were lovers. They remained together until Duke's death in 1979.[44]

But Wayne's relationship with Stacy was full of ambiguities. According to Mary St. John, Pat Stacy was a "man's woman" who enjoyed the company of men, felt comfortable serving as a hostess to Duke's buddies, loved locations and the trips on the *Wild Goose*, and all but worshiped Wayne. She was everything he wanted in a companion. But he had no intention of marrying her. Even after Pilar learned of their relationship and offered a divorce, Wayne declined, preferring the permanent separation. He did not want his younger children to know about the affair and would not let Pat stay overnight at the house. When the press inquired about their relationship, Duke brushed off the questions, suggesting that it was no more than a casual friendship and professional association. In 1975 he told Will Tusher of *Photoplay* magazine, when asked about Stacy: "I've taken her out a couple of times. But I have no particular romance. . . . I'm past the age of romance. I'm getting smart enough to know."[45]

As always, he was extremely concerned about his public image. The affair with Pat was absolute proof of his continuing virility, but at the same time, he feared being perceived as a dirty old man. It was the sort of affair he had shied away from in his films. The original script of *The Train Robbers* called for a romantic relationship between Duke and Ann-Margret. Wayne had the script rewritten. In the closing scene, when Ann-Margret lets him know she's available, he begs off going to bed with her, instead saying: "No. I've got a saddle older than you."[46]

Duke had spent decades trying to figure women out, and at the end of his life he was no closer to understanding them than at the beginning. He felt the same way about politicians. One of the saddest coincidences of Wayne's last years was the betrayal of Watergate, just as he was winding down his films and calling it quits on his marriage. Though he had often remarked: "I hate politicians," he genuinely felt that President Richard Nixon and Vice President Spiro Agnew were different. Nixon accomplished, as far as Wayne was concerned, what Johnson had failed to do. "The only way to get 520,000 men home . . . was to make the decision to mine Haiphong harbor. President Nixon had the courage to make that decision, and when the other side started using prisoners of war as pawns, he had to make the awesome decision to bomb Hanoi. Which he did, and then he brought our prisoners of war home." Wayne's chronology was a bit confused when he made those remarks in 1976; most of the 520,000 troops were home long before the mining of Haiphong or the bombing of Hanoi, but that was hardly the point. He believed that Nixon honorably ended the war. And Nixon appreciated Wayne's support, inviting him, along with Bob Hope and several other politically conservative celebrities, to the White House in May 1973 to celebrate with the POWs and their long-suffering families. Wayne considered them, and Nixon, real heroes.[47]

Nixon was not as successful in dismantling the welfare state, mostly because, in Wayne's opinion, he was too worried about the opinions of liberal Republicans like Nelson Rockefeller of New York, William Scranton of Pennsylvania, and Mark Hatfield of Oregon. Duke's opposition to the welfare state had philosophical and personal roots. In a 1962 *Saturday Evening Post* interview, he said: "I don't want any handouts from a benevolent government. I think government is naturally the enemy of the individual, but it's a necessary evil. . . . I do not want the government to take away my human dignity and insure me anything more than a normal security. I don't want handouts." In his 1971 *Playboy* interview, Wayne offered a simple opinion about government welfare programs: "I don't think a fella should be able to sit on his backside and receive welfare. I'd like to know why well-educated idiots keep apologizing for lazy and complaining people who think the world owes them a living." Government welfare robbed people of their dignity and any sense of incentive. A generation of people on the public dole would only produce a new generation of welfare recipients who had never had to work—or ever had seen anyone working—for a living. Closer to his heart and pocketbook, he also resented paying the bills. "Hell. I'm in the 90 percent bracket. Why should I have to pay all these taxes for nonsense? If I could just get a fair break on taxes, I'd be a millionaire many times over!" Even though Nixon had failed to ease his tax problems, Duke believed that the president had done a much better job than Kennedy or Johnson, and he actively supported him for reelection in 1972, describing Nixon as "the right man in the right office at the right time."[48]

He was even more vociferous in his support of Vice President Spiro Agnew, who he felt was the only politician in America honest enough to speak frankly about crime and political unrest. He blamed the liberal media for trying to "humiliate Agnew . . . and [trying] to laugh him out of political value to his party." When some Republicans began speculating about dumping Agnew from the ticket in 1972, Wayne became the official spokesman of Americans for Agnew, a group of conservative Republicans. "It will be awfully hard for the liberal media," he wrote, "to twist the facts around when we give them regular, solid proof that a substantial mass of voters wants Agnew as our spokesman, and want him on the Nixon ticket next fall."[49]

Duke also became involved in the local California election. His independent streak enraged many conservatives. He was increasingly disturbed about the trend toward more explicit sex and violence, but he was also a realist—about human nature and economics. "If people want to see nude pictures," he told the *Hollywood Reporter*, producers are "going to make nude pictures. If they want to see dirty pictures, they're going to make dirty pictures." He had a clear focus on the type of movies and movie roles he would accept. "I want to play a real man in all my films," he told critics, "and I define manhood simply: men should be tough, fair, and courageous, never petty, never looking for a fight, but never backing down from one either." But, he added on another occasion, "I don't want ever to appear in a film that would embarrass a viewer. A man can take his wife, mother, and his daughter to one of my movies and never be ashamed or embarrassed for going."[50]

What he definitely did *not* want, however, was to have the government censoring films. Such proposals had been introduced a number of times in the California legislature but had never moved out of committee. But in 1972, a referendum to that effect got on the statewide election ballot. Backed by a number of conservative political and religious groups, the measure provided for a state film commission to set rigidly defined "codes of decency" and greatly broaden existing definitions of pornography. The proposal was similar to the censorship boards established in the first three decades of the century. A united film industry condemned the proposal and enlisted Wayne's help. He, too, opposed the measure, arguing in several radio commercials that "you don't get rid of a bad situation with a badly written law or cut off a foot to cure a sore toe." On election day the proposal was soundly defeated, and he was roundly criticized by disappointed California conservatives.[51]

When the Watergate scandals began making news in 1973, Duke's appetite for politics soon soured. At first he was convinced that a secret cabal of liberal, eastern journalists was bent on destroying the Nixon administration. He watched television news the same way Lyndon B. Johnson had, switching back and forth from network to network or even having more than one set on at a time. When Walter Cronkite of CBS, John Chancellor of NBC, or Howard K. Smith of ABC went after Nixon or Agnew, Wayne would often go into paroxysms of rage, shouting epithets at the television set and occasionally throwing things at the screen. They were, he thought, petty and unfair. "Those bastards!" he shouted at a reporter in Durango, Mexico, in 1973, "They don't give anybody a chance to do anything. They have to be cute and know ahead of time what the President is doing. They should make them rerun their old newscasts, make them listen to what they said!"

Agnew's resignation from office in October 1973, under the cloud of bribery charges and accusations of receiving kickbacks when he was governor of Maryland, was a profound disappointment. The vice president had turned out to be just what Wayne hated—a small-time hack politician using public office to fleece his constituents. A few months after Agnew left office, Wayne remarked to a reporter: "I endorsed Spiro Agnew's attitudes, but I knew nothing of his private affairs. I was sadly disappointed to discover his feet of clay." Duke had, of course, a healthy appreciation for the weaknesses and foibles of human nature. At a press conference eighteen months after the resignation, a journalist asked Wayne about Agnew, and he said: "I loved Agnew. I enjoyed Agnew. Down here we had a great deal of feeling for the man. I guess he did something wrong. I don't know." When some journalists began to laugh, Wayne angrily reacted: "Let's have none of that half-assed laughter." For John Wayne the resignation of the vice president of the United States was no laughing matter. It was a political tragedy for the country.[52]

Spiro Agnew's resignation had been quite unsettling, especially after all the rhetoric, the self-righteous denials of wrongdoing, the public relations posturing, and the "damage control." With the congressional and press investigations of President Nixon and the Watergate scandal gaining momentum, the same denials surfaced again. This time Duke wanted to be sure before he put himself on the line. Late in 1973, during a visit to Nixon's home in San Clemente, the president assured Duke that he was not involved in the Watergate incident.[53]

A few weeks later, in January 1974, Duke was in Cambridge, Massachusetts, holding a tongue-in-cheek press conference for some Harvard students. Only one question interrupted the revelry momentarily. A student asked Duke if Nixon should be impeached. Wayne stopped talking, his eyes riveted in a steely blue glaze, and replied with an absolutely frozen smile, carefully enunciating each word: "We're getting a little too serious, don't you think? We'll make a serious day some other time and talk about that." As raucous as they were that afternoon, the Harvard students knew that Wayne had established a boundary he did not want them to cross. None of them tried.[54]

As the Watergate plot unfolded during the spring and summer of 1974, Wayne stood by Nixon. He remained convinced that the press, especially people like Dan Rather of CBS, were out to get the president at any cost. Wayne felt Rather had no respect for Nixon or the office of the presidency. Still, Duke knew that the Watergate break-in was wrong. There was no question about that, and he condemned the political fanatics responsible, arguing in March 1974 that "Watergate is a sad and tragic incident in our history. They're wrong, dead wrong, those men at Watergate. Men abused power, but the system still works. . . . Men lied and perjured themselves, but the system still works."[55]

But six months later, Nixon resigned in disgrace when the tapes revealed that he had indeed covered up the investigation of the Watergate incident and then lied about it, repeatedly, to the American people. Wayne had to admit that only then, with impeachment proceedings under way, did the system *really* work. He was shocked by the entire scandal, but nothing bothered him more than the fact that Nixon had lied to him personally. Wayne was in Arizona at Louis Johnson's home during the first week of August 1974, when the recently released Watergate tapes made it abundantly clear that the president had participated in the cover-up and was guilty of obstruction of justice. Wayne listened to the news broadcast on television, looked over at Louie Johnson, and said, "Damn. He lied to me." Richard Nixon had committed the ultimate sin: He had lied, face to face and man to man, to a friend.[56]

Despite this terrible blow, Duke campaigned actively against Jimmy Carter and for President Gerald Ford in the fall of 1976, and he was disappointed when the Democrats won. But he was delighted—and more than a little surprised—when President-elect Jimmy Carter invited him to the preinaugural festivities in Washington, D.C., on January 19, 1977, and asked him to speak at the Kennedy Center Gala. It turned out that Carter had long been an enthusiastic fan of John Wayne movies. Duke's remarks were fitting. He congratulated Carter and said: "I'm privileged to be present and accounted for in this capital of freedom, to watch a common man take on uncommon responsibilities that he has won fair and square by stating his case to the American people. . . . I'm considered a member of the opposition, the loyal opposition. Accent on the 'loyal.' I'd have it no other way." At a banquet later that evening, Carter broke out of a receiving line, almost like a starstruck teenager, when Wayne came into the room. They enjoyed a friendly and relaxed conversation. Carter was struck by Wayne's intelligence, and Duke was impressed by the president's sincerity, quiet grace, and good humor.[57]

But mutual respect did not erase their political differences. On January 21, 1977, the day after his inauguration, President Carter, in a good-faith effort to close a painful chapter in American history, extended a unilateral pardon to all those who had fled the United States during the Vietnam War to avoid the draft and to all servicemen who had deserted the armed forces. The decision ignited bitter controversy, and Wayne burned with outrage. For him such a pardon was unpardonable, an insult to the more than 58,000 men and women who had died in Vietnam, the more than 250,000 who had been seriously wounded there, and all their families and friends. Many of them, he argued, had opposed the war but had still supported their country. Wayne also protested to the president that the pardon would undermine military morale and make it more difficult for future presidents to send Americans into combat. Carter politely disagreed.[58]

When he communicated with Carter a year later, the pardon issue was still on his mind. Patricia Hearst, the heir to William Randolph Hearst's publishing empire, had been kidnapped and held for ransom by a radical group known as the Symbionese Liberation Army (SLA) in 1973. In the course of her captivity Hearst converted to her kidnappers' ideology and willingly participated in several of their robberies. She was captured in 1977, tried and convicted of robbery, and sentenced to prison, all the time protesting that she was an innocent victim of the SLA brainwashing. Tongue in cheek, Wayne wrote to President Carter in December 1978 pleading that the president also pardon the "brainwashed Miss Patricia Hearst." Once again Carter politely declined to do so.⁵⁹

Wayne and Carter kept up their correspondence during the next several years. Whenever Duke was upset by a Carter policy, he wrote him. He called Carter to protest reductions in the defense budget and in military retirement pay. The retired soldiers deserved every penny they got, and the defense budget needed to be maintained in order to keep the Russians at bay and to guarantee national security. He called for Carter to crack down on international terrorists, and he criticized U.S. policy toward Africa, wondering why the Carter administration insisted on getting behind people like guerrilla leader Robert Mugabe of Rhodesia while good anti-Communists like Ian Smith needed American support. Carter politely responded to each letter from Wayne, at the same time acknowledging each recognition award Duke received. All the while he and Rosalynn kept ordering up John Wayne movies for White House screenings.⁶⁰

Had Wayne been a doctrinaire conservative, he and Carter would never have discovered common ground. But Duke was not doctrinaire, and he sided with Carter on the Panama Canal Treaty. The United States first assumed control of what became the Panama Canal Zone in 1903, when President Theodore Roosevelt signed the "quickie" Hay-Bunau-Varilla Treaty. When Colombia refused to allow the United States to build the canal, Roosevelt supported a Panamanian revolt against Colombia and immediately recognized the independence of Panama. Roosevelt later remarked; "I stole the canal." In return the United States received "in perpetuity the use, occupation and control of a zone of land and land under water" needed to build and maintain a canal across the Isthmus of Panama. The width of the zone was set at ten miles and extended from the Caribbean Sea to the Pacific Ocean. The cities of Panama City and Colón were excluded from the zone. Finally the United States agreed to pay to Panama $10 million in gold and an annual payment of $250,000. Over the years it became perhaps the most valuable piece of real estate controlled by the United States.⁶¹

As the years passed, however, the Canal Zone became a *cause célèbre* for most Panamanians, an insult to their growing sense of nationalism. It cut their country in half and was under the absolute control of the U.S. Army. The army would not lease back any of the territory to Panama to help absorb the young country's growing population, and the prosperity of forty thousand American "Zonians" stood in sharp contrast to the lifestyles of most Panamanians. Resentment about the 1903 treaty gradually escalated among left-wing

Communists and Socialists as well as among the right-wing, conservative Panamanian elite. The zone was an affront to their sovereignty. In 1964 the resentment exploded into what became known as the "flag riots." When some Panamanian students tried to raise the Panamanian flag over their high school, which was located inside the zone, several American students resisted them. In the ensuing riot twenty-one Panamanians and three Americans were killed.

After the flag riots, President Johnson began exploring the possibility of settling the issue diplomatically, but the pressures of the Vietnam War distracted him, and the negotiations stalled. President Richard Nixon took a hard line on the issue, insisting that American treaty rights be upheld, but by the early 1970s the canal was losing some of its strategic significance. Constructed in an earlier day, when ships were small and the United States had only one navy with global responsibilities, the Panama Canal had been a geopolitical lifeline. But since then ships had grown larger. American aircraft carriers could not use the canal, nor could the increasingly large oil tankers that were being constructed. Also, the United States had separate fleets operating in the Pacific and Atlantic Oceans. The need to move one fleet around the world rapidly had virtually disappeared. Finally, the United States was anxious, especially after the fiasco in Vietnam, to improve its image in the Third World, particularly in Latin America. The Canal Zone smacked of colonialism, and Fidel Castro made the most of it in his hemispheric rhetoric. Father Marcos McGrath, the Roman Catholic archbishop of Panama, campaigned actively in the U.S. for return of the Canal Zone to Panamanian sovereignty, and the United States Catholic Conference endorsed his point of view.[62]

During the Ford administration, some American policymakers began to worry that the Canal Zone issue might eventually destabilize the government of strongman Omar Torrijos. He was dealing militarily, and successfully, with Communist-backed guerrilla movements in Panama, but they were more than ready to exploit the Canal Zone issue in order to build political support. The last thing the United States wanted, especially with Vietnam in the so recent past, was another jungle war. The negotiations accelerated during the Ford administration, but Republican conservatives, led by Sen. Strom Thurmond of South Carolina, apoplectic about surrendering the canal, sabotaged any final settlement. President Jimmy Carter picked up the negotiations after his inauguration in 1977.[63]

The negotiations moved quickly forward, and on September 5, 1977, the treaties were signed by Panamanian and American officials. Collectively the treaties provided for the United States to hand over control of the Panama Canal and the Panama Canal Zone to Panama in the year 2000. To answer conservative critics that loss of the canal would compromise American national security, Panama agreed to allow the United States to keep military forces stationed there until the change in sovereignty. Panama also agreed to allow the United States to intervene unilaterally with military forces until the year 2023, in order to protect American security interests. Left-wing groups in Panama complained loudly about those provisions, but Omar Torrijos knew that they were necessary in order to get ratification in the United States. In return the United States agreed to pay Panama a $50 million annual fee for use of the canal and to design a hefty foreign aid package. By a 2–1 margin, Panamanians supported the treaty in an October referendum.[64]

John Wayne entered the controversy inadvertently. When the negotiations concluded and the treaty was signed in September, he made a simple telephone call to Torrijos, a man whom he greatly admired and with whom he had established a friendship after Torrijos's successful military coup in Panama in 1968. He offered his congratulations on the signing of the treaty. Two weeks later Torrijos told a *New York Times* reporter about Wayne's telephone call, catapulting Duke into the middle of a political firestorm. At that point Wayne made a careful study of the treaty, visited with such Panamanian friends as Archbishop McGrath and members of the Arias family, and concluded that the treaties "modernize an outmoded relationship with a friendly and hospitable country. They also solve an international question with our Latin American neighbors. Finally, the treaties protect and legitimize the fundamental interests of our country."[65]

Deserting his conservative friends, he vocally supported ratification. More hate mail than he had ever received poured into his home and office, more even than during the controversial years of the late 1940s and early 1950s. Writers called him a "traitor," "Commie bastard," "pinko liberal," and "Marxist stooge." He found his role as the target of right-wing fanatics annoying, but he was surprised at the depth of their anger and their irrationality. Still, he was not about to back down, even when conservative Republicans, smelling an issue with which to crucify President Jimmy Carter, began attacking the treaty as anti-American, a sellout of the country's birthright.[66]

As the debate over ratification of the treaty became more intense, Duke found himself at odds with an old friend and political ally—Ronald Reagan. The former California governor was positioning himself for a presidential run in 1980, and he used the canal treaty as a weapon for attacking Carter. Wayne had always felt Reagan was different from most politicians, but he found the governor's arguments on the treaty to be self-serving political drivel. Wayne had Archbishop McGrath's brother Arturo visit with Reagan and explain his position on the treaty, but to no avail. On November 11, 1977, Duke wrote a scathing letter to Reagan, accusing him of political posturing and innuendo: "Now I have taken your [statement], and I'll show you point by goddamn point in the treaty where you are misinforming people. If you continue to make these erroneous remarks, someone will publicize your letter to prove that you are not as thorough in your reviewing of this treaty as you say or are damned obtuse when it comes to reading the English language." By that time, of course, Wayne knew it was too late. "Even if he [Reagan] wanted to change his mind," Duke told Pat Stacy, "he has gone so far in the other direction that it's too late."[67]

During the winter of 1977–1978, Wayne worked tirelessly for ratification. Republicans said he sounded like a born-again Democrat. He wrote hundreds of letters to influential Republicans, often using Republican National Committee stationery, arguing that the treaty would restore a sense of nationhood to Panama, protect American national security interests, and by eliminating a painful vestige of colonialism improve United States relations with Latin America. Emphasizing a simple fairness, he also argued that Panama had always been a loyal friend to the U.S. and deserved fair treatment. He personally wrote a seven-page position paper on the treaty and sent it to every United States senator. When the treaty was ratified on April 18, 1978, by a 68–32 vote—only a one-vote margin—President Jimmy Carter again thanked Wayne for his support in bringing it about.[68]

In October 1975 Quigley Publications released its annual list of the top ten male and female box-office movie stars, and for the first time since the late 1940s, John Wayne did not make the list. It was a sign of the times for Wayne, more proof, as he said to Pat Stacy, that "everything has to end . . . nothing is permanent." Robert Redford was number one, and the list included Paul Newman, Al Pacino, Gene Hackman, Woody Allen, Burt Reynolds, Charles Bronson, and Steve McQueen. Duke's declining status in Hollywood became painfully clear to him in 1976. William Friedkin was producing the Academy Awards show for ABC Television. Wayne called him up and asked him if he could give out the Best Picture Award. Friedkin had already asked Jack Nicholson to do it, and Wayne said, "Well, take it away." Friedkin refused. After *Easy Rider*, *Five Easy Pieces*, and *One Flew over the Cuckoo's Nest*, Nicholson was a certifiable superstar, especially with younger audiences. Friedkin would not risk crossing Nicholson, not even for Duke. Wayne was hoping that his upcoming film *The Shootist* would help him regain the old status, but it was not to be. "Everything has to end . . . only a goddamned fool would think that anything is forever," he said. And the Red Witch was coming out of hiding.[69]

23

"You Just Can't Give In To It"

Pappy looked awful. Wayne knew that John Ford was sick, but he had no idea just how bad it was until he drove out to Palm Desert, California, for a visit on August 30, 1973. Ford wanted to see his old friend. Wayne found Pappy propped up in bed—thin, even gaunt, and unkempt. The bedroom had a distinct peculiar odor, dank and almost offensive. Wayne did not recognize what it was, but the smell of death was in the air. Ford was drunk, or at least high, managing to get down a few hits of Guinness Stout every few hours even though the stomach cancer was gnawing at his insides. He was irritable and frustrated, only a shell of himself, but he enjoyed the visit. When Duke walked in, Ford asked him if he had come "down for the deathwatch," and Wayne jokingly retorted, "Hell no, you'll bury us all." They spoke of times past, of friends and places and events, but they avoided what lay ahead. They shared some brandy and laughed about Ward Bond and the Young Men's Purity Total Abstinence and Yachting Association. Wayne left an hour later. He never saw Pappy again. Ford died the next day, surrounded by priests and clutching his rosary. Duke returned to Palm Desert immediately and sat around with the Ford family, regaling them with stories of the old days.[1]

Inside Wayne was not laughing. He hated cancer. It had become a personal nemesis, a plague, the killer of his family and friends. The disease took his brother and mother in 1970. Molly died with her abdomen full of tumors, and three months later Bobby went as well. He had throat cancer and died coughing, wheezing, and gasping for breath, even with an oxygen tent bathing him in pure air. Right up to the end he was yelling at his wife, screaming for cigarettes. Wayne remembered Jimmy Grant's death in 1966. He had visited Grant almost every day toward the end, and he had seen what lung cancer did to him. Jimmy wasted away to only ninety pounds. Back in 1963 Pedro Armendariz got throat cancer after surviving a battle with lymphoma. He committed suicide rather than go through it again. For John Wayne, cancer was horrible, a "real bitch."[2]

In the weeks after Ford's death, Wayne slipped into a deep, though not clinical, depression. Since 1964 and the first bout with cancer, reporters had referred to him as the "invincible John Wayne." But he knew better, and Ford's death reinforced that point with vivid certainty. He called Ford his mentor and ideal, saying: "John Ford was like a father to me, like a big brother." Most people do not think about their own death until they lose a father or mother, until the last generation standing between them and oblivion is in the ground. When John Ford died, Wayne realized that he would not be able to cheat death much longer.[3]

It was no wonder he got so excited about Glendon Swarthout's novel *The Shootist* in 1974. After decades of using films to explain his most intimate feelings, he had now found a vehicle to talk about cancer and death. *The Shootist* is the story of John Bernard Books, an aging gunfighter who has outlived the Old West. He finds himself in Carson City, Nevada, in 1901. The killer of more than thirty men, Books has become a celebrity, famous to some and infamous to others, but a celebrity nonetheless. He is also full of prostate and rectal cancer, facing a horrible death, and hoping to die in privacy. After reading the novel, Wayne tried to buy the movie rights, but Paramount bought them first. The studio hired Swarthout's son Miles to write the screenplay, Don Siegel to direct, and John Wayne to star. Duke found the screenplay a bit too graphic and too much of a "downer." He wanted Books to have cancer, but not specifically rectal and prostate cancer, and he wanted the film to end on an upbeat note, with Gillom Rogers (Ron Howard) eschewing rather than embracing violence. Siegel went along with his changes.[4]

The Shootist is John Wayne's dialogue with death, spoken by J. B. Books. When he was making the film, he told writer Wayne Warga, "Sometimes the irony of this film gets to me." When Dr. Hostetler (Jimmy Stewart) tells Books: "You have a cancer—advanced," the gunfighter wonders whether the physician can "cut it out." Shaking his head, Hostetler pessimistically replies: "I'd have to gut you like a fish." When Books protests: "You once told me I was strong as an ox," Hostetler quietly responds: "Even an ox dies." The gunfighter wants to know what his death will be like, but the reluctant Hostetler says: "Unless you insist, I'd rather not talk about it." Books does insist, something John Wayne would never do in real life, and the doctor tells him: "There will be an increase in the severity of the pain . . . the pain will become unbearable. No drugs will moderate it. If you're lucky you'll lose consciousness and until then, you'll scream. . . . One more thing I'd say. This isn't advice, just a suggestion, . . . I would not die a death like I just described if I had your courage."[5]

Books rents a room in a local boarding house run by Bond Rogers (Lauren Bacall). He wants privacy and a quiet death, but news of the famous gunfighter's presence in town, and his looming demise, spreads quickly. Books is reduced to pleading for privacy. He resents a newspaperman writing articles about him and a former girlfriend approaching him with a book contract about his life, which will make her rich. To Marshal Walter Thibodeaux of Carson City, Books says: "You can do me a favor. My being here, maybe that's news. But dying's my own business. Keep it under your hat." Later, when Mrs. Rogers tries to get him to see a preacher, Books declines: "No. A man's death is the most private thing in his life. It's mine."

What John Bernard Books, and John Wayne, did not want was to waste away into an emaciated wretch of a human being screaming in agony for death, with the world aware of every pain and every scream down to the last gasp. There had to be a better way to go, and in *The Shootist* J. B. Books does it his way. During those eight days in Carson City, he melts the heart of the widow Rogers, saves her son, Gillom, from a life of delinquency, and goes down in a blaze of gunfire, shooting and being shot, killing three bad guys in a barroom before dying himself. Books's death was heroic, befitting his life and his image.[6]

Unfortunately for Wayne there was no real way to die of cancer in a blaze of glory. There wasn't even a way to do it neatly. "There's no such thing as growing old gracefully," he told Pat Stacy. "It's all deterioration, decay." Stacy remembered that he sometimes seemed jealous of her youth, and that of his children. But he also said of old age: "You just can't give in to it."[7]

Wayne had always been emotionally resilient, bouncing back from lung cancer, financial reversals, media criticism, and family problems. What he could not come back from in the 1970s, however, were the ravages of old age.

Few people had ever gotten away with so much abuse of their own bodies for so long. As late as 1976, he bragged:

> You know I was never sick in my life. I had the flu back in the First World War, when I was about eight. I had an appendicitis operation and a six month bout with ulcers when I was in my early thirties. . . . The doctors said to do what I was told and I'd be over it in six months. So I did everything they said—drank cream, ate baby food, brown-bagged it to work and finally, on the last day of the six months, I bought a couple of bottles of tequila and drank 'em. Then I knew I was cured.

Like a lot of people, Duke had gout, an excess of uric acid in his body. When he was younger he had suffered the pain of having uric acid crystals collect in the joints of his big toes. The development of allopurinol, a drug that blocks uric acid production, was a godsend, and he took a three-hundred-milligram tablet every day. Aside from these minor irritants, he had remained illogically healthy in the face of a lifetime of smoking six packs of cigarettes a day, regularly washing his insides with prodigious amounts of whiskey, tequila, and wine, and consuming a diet filthy with animal fats. He worked too hard, slept too little, and raised too much hell. That huge, beautiful body stood up to it all for sixty-seven years, but by 1974 it had had enough.[8]

The trouble began at Harvard University, of all places, on a cold New England day in 1974. Wayne stopped there on his way to London where he was to appear in a Glen Campbell television special. Late in 1973 the editors of the *Harvard Lampoon* playfully wrote Duke and told him: "You think you're tough. You're not so tough. You've never dared to set foot in the wilderness of Cambridge territory. We dare you to have it out, head-on, with the young whelps here who would call the supposedly unbeatable John Wayne the biggest fraud in history." James M. Downey, president of the *Lampoon*, dared him to come to Cambridge, "the most traditionally radical, the most hostile territory on earth." Wayne had just finished *McQ*, and he thought going to Harvard might generate some free publicity. He wrote back, accepting "with pleasure your challenge to bring my new motion picture, *McQ*, into the pseudo intellectual swamps of Harvard Square. I was most happy to find that my age and balding head and gray hair had not made cowards out of the purported gentlemen of the mother college. May the Good Lord keep you well until I get there." At the appointed time of "high noon" on January 15, 1974, he rode into Harvard Square atop an armored personnel carrier borrowed from a local National Guard outfit.[9]

McQ was previewed at the local theater, and Duke then did an impromptu press conference, which turned into one of the best performances of his career. He ad-libbed right through it. To the question: "Where did you get that phony toupee?" he said: "It's not phony. It's real hair. Of course, it's not mine, but it's real." When another student irreverently asked: "Why do you refuse to allow midgets in your major films?" he smirkingly replied: "It's too hard to find their mouths to punch." When an undergraduate asked him if he had ever received any suggestions about filmmaking from President Nixon, Wayne retorted: "No, they've all been successful." Or "Is it true that since you've lost weight, your horse's hernia has cleared up?" He said: "No, he died and we canned him, which is what you are eating at the Harvard Club." There were dozens of similar exchanges, and the students loved it. The *Lampoon* staff later sent him their Brass Balls sculpture in recognition of "outstanding machismo and a penchant for punching people in the mouth."[10]

He was delighted with the appearance. As soon as he got back to the hotel, he called Stacy:

> Pat, I had the best damn time of my life. I want to tell you that after it was over, they gave me a dinner at the *Lampoon*, these young guys, and they were such refreshing young men, goddammit, and they appreciated the fact that I had accepted their humor, and they really gave me a thoroughly enjoyable evening.

By the time he got to London, however, he felt miserable. He developed a fever and a bad cough, a really deep cough with blood coming up with the phlegm. He cursed the blood, wondering if the cancer was back. For lung cancer survivors, hacking, bloody coughs are terrifying. Nick Sevano, the executive producer of the Glen Campbell special, remembered: "Boy, would he cough up phlegm! And, I tell you, I felt it down to my toes each time he would cough!" A London physician listened to Wayne's lung sounds, decided it was probably pneumonia, and put him on antibiotics. The doctor said he was crazy to keep smoking, and inhaling, cigars. Once again he solemnly promised to quit smoking. They finished filming the special and Wayne returned to California.[11]

The promise, like the ones before, was empty. He was smoking cigars a few weeks after returning to Newport Beach. "It's a foolish weakness," he told a reporter, "but not smoking is the hardest thing in the world for me. I guess because I've been smoking since I was a kid." Soon the breathing problems returned, and the cough, the hacking, painful cough came back. Concerned, he checked into the Scripps Clinic in La Jolla, California, to have his cancer team look him over, and after a run of tests they told him he was allergic to perfume, cosmetics, and tobacco. The cigars would have to go. This time, he told himself, he really would quit. Still the cough lingered, though not nearly as bad as before.[12]

He was back in the hospital at the end of the year, after finishing *Rooster Cogburn*. The film had been a throughly delightful experience, giving Duke his first opportunity to work with Katharine Hepburn. Hal Wallis, who produced it, asked Richard Fleischer to direct it. Fourteen years before, Fleischer had backed out of *North to Alaska* because he thought the script was terrible, but Charles Feldman had told Duke that Fleischer did not want to do the movie with him. Duke stored the incident in his memory, waiting for an opportunity to get even. He enjoyed absolute director approval on his films, and he vetoed Fleischer for *Rooster Cogburn*. Wallis tried to get him to reconsider, but he would not budge. Fleischer did not get the job. In his memoirs he recalled the incident:

> John Wayne's revenge. It had taken fourteen years, but he got it. I had broken an unwritten law: No varmint turns down a John Wayne picture. When you do that, pard, you're hurtin' his feelin's and woundin' his pride. And there's no forgivin' that. Ever.
>
> I was the victim of a massive case of pique. It was petty. It was small. It was mean. It was Duke Wayne. Once again my life and my career had been influenced by this man I'd rarely seen and hardly knew. My instincts about him [on the set of *Back to Bataan* in 1944] had been right, though.
>
> This was not someone you wanted to offend.

Wallis gave the director's job to Stuart Miller.[13]

*R*ooster Cogburn* was part *True Grit*, part *African Queen*. In *The African Queen*, Rose Sayer (Katharine Hepburn) is a British missionary working in German East Africa. When World War I breaks out, German soldiers attack the mission and murder her missionary brother. She joins forces with Charles Allnut (Humphrey Bogart) and chugs downriver in his boat, the *African Queen*, to attack German forces on Lake Victoria. In *Rooster Cogburn*, Eula Goodnight (Katharine Hepburn) is an American missionary working among the Indians. Gunslingers murder her missionary father, and she teams up with Rooster Cogburn, a federal marshal, to bring the murderers to justice. They float down the Rogue River on a raft to outsmart the criminals. Rooster Cogburn is another Charles Allnut, a hard-drinking, profane man who charms the prim Miss Goodnight and is charmed in return.

Skeptics predicted fireworks on the set, sparked by Duke's conservatism rubbing against Hepburn's legendary liberalism. But the two stars got along famously. A love of movies and life, of laughter and camaraderie, brought them together. She found him polite, sensitive, talented, and considerate, a real gentleman. "He's a very, very good actor, in the highbrow sense of the word." At lunch one day, she remarked to producer Hal Wallis: "I love working with Duke, but he tells everyone what to do, bosses everyone around, and I'm the one who usually gets to do that. Now I don't get to." Wallis replied: "The next time he acts as if he knows everything, remind him of *The Alamo* and *The Green Berets.*" Duke admired her determination, particularly her willingness to ride horses and rafts, neither of which were much to her liking. "She's so feminine—she's a man's woman. Imagine how she must have been at age 25 or 30 . . . how lucky a man would have been to have found her," Duke confessed. When the last scene was shot, he pushed his eye patch up on his forehead, gathered up Hepburn in his arms, and planted a big kiss on her lips. She was speechless, but he thundered: "Damn! There's a woman!" A few moments later, her thoughts collected, Hepburn returned the compliment: "What a wonderful experience. He's one hell of an actor."

During one of the raft scenes, Duke slipped on some gun-shell casings and injured his right knee, which had suffered some damage during his football days at USC. "I kept having to kneel down on a raft, and I was shooting a Gatling gun," he recalled to *Photoplay* reporter Will Tusher. "Well, you know those big brass shells that come out of the gun. Every time I'd get down on that knee, I'd hit one of those brass shells. Well, I had that knee raw and open. I got it so sore that after the picture I just couldn't bear it." He managed to finish shooting the film without causing any delays, but even with rest the knee did not heal. A few days after finishing the film, he had it X-rayed. He needed surgery and checked into Hoag Hospital in Newport Beach, where an orthopedic surgeon repaired the damage. Wayne hated hospitals, hated being around sick people, and immobility made him nervous and restless. He slept too much in the hospital during the day and then lay awake during the long, boring nights. More than anything he needed a cigarette; he settled for a thin cigar and started to smoke again. He checked out of Hoag four days before Christmas.[14]

More troublesome was the cough, which became chronic during the location shooting for *Rooster Cogburn.* Because of the altitude at Grants Pass, Oregon, Duke needed an oxygen tank, and he attributed the cough to the thin, dry air. Katharine Hepburn harbored different suspicions, telling him to get to a doctor because "that's no ordinary cough." The moister air and lower altitude of Newport Beach seemed to help around the holidays, but the cough came back a month later. This time he blamed "allergies," but a visit to an allergist didn't help. He was back at Hoag in March 1975 with a case of "walking pneumonia." The doctors pumped him full of antibiotics and then let him go home. "A lot of people have the stuff down there," he remarked to a reporter. "A friend of mine was in bed with it for a month. I thought if I had to lie in that frigging bed up there [Hoag] for a month, I'd go crazy." The cough cleared up for a while but returned in June. Frustrated and irritated, Duke went back into Hoag in mid-August, received another load of antibiotics but then picked up a staph infection. He stayed in the hospital until the end of the month, claiming that the only silver lining was a decline in weight from 265 to 250 pounds.[15]

He lost another ten pounds before the filming of *The Shootist* started (in 1975), but the weeks on location in Carson City, Nevada, were a physical nightmare, the worst ever. Not since making *The Sons of Katie Elder* in 1965 had he felt so bad on a set, and then he had a good excuse—doctors had cut out a lung and a rib just a few months before. Still, he had performed many of the stunts and wrapped the film up on schedule. Not this time. After any scene requiring even the least exertion, he hustled into his trailer and inhaled pure oxygen from a tank that had to be refilled several times during the six weeks. Making matters worse, he came down with an inner ear infection and the flu. The pain from the earache was constant, and the infection affected his sense of equilibrium. He returned to the hospital for two weeks until it cleared up. They were able to shoot scenes around him during his absence, but he hated causing so much inconvenience. "It's so damn irritating to feel bad when you haven't felt bad all your life," he told a reporter. "I have been abnormally healthy. Even when they told me I had cancer, I hadn't had any pain . . . *nothing.* . . . But this last year it's been one thing after another . . . that's the worst thing about getting old . . . having to use your will power to drive yourself instead of natural physical energy. Before, it all came so easy. Now I have to push it."[16]

He could tolerate an earache or the flu, even if he did not like the inactivity they caused. The cough stopped filming and demanded retakes. It made him angry and made him feel unprofessional. Over the years he had been almost obsessive about being on time and finishing on schedule. He had no patience with weaklings or prima donnas who delayed pictures and cost people money.[17]

But no matter how hard he tried, he just could not shake the cough. It was guttural and hacking, rumbling up from deep in his chest, doubling him over, reddening his face, causing his eyes to water, and burning his throat in repetitive spasms. *Los Angeles Herald-Examiner* columnist Jim Bishop remembered seeing Wayne coughing and "punching trees" in frustration. Subtly, almost imperceptibly, thoughts of the "Big C" returned. Maybe the tumor had only been hiding for the last twelve years, or maybe inhaling those cigars had jump-started a new cancer. Maybe that was why he needed so much oxygen from the damn tank—the tumor was crowding his lung and keeping air out. Maybe it was only bronchitis. The accumulated maybes haunted his nights, when his cough awoke him and kept him up. As soon as they finished the location shooting, he hurried back to Hoag for chest X rays. John Rumsfield, the lung specialist, told him there were no tumors in his chest.[18]

The assurance still did not help the cough much, and he was feeling more and more short of breath, even in sea-level Newport Beach. Ever since the loss of the left lung in 1964 he had been short of breath during exercise, but now he felt that way even sitting in a chair. His voice had a gravelly, strained quality to it, as if he were forcing air through the larynx to make sounds. If the heart was not pumping enough blood into his arteries, there was no way, without the other lung, he was going to have much energy. In addition, his weight was getting out of hand. Now back to 265 pounds, he was too big, not so much around the waist as in the face. His barrel chest let him get away with a growing midsection, but he had a jowly, thick look that even made his nose seem somehow outsize. Ever since the early 1960s, several months before he started each new film, Wayne had gone on a fifteen-hundred-calorie-per-day diet and a regimen of physician-prescribed amphetamines.[19]

Now the diets did not work as well, and he was bloated. The puffiness around his eyes and neck robbed him of the healthy ruggedness he so prized. Doctors listening to his heart detected congestive heart failure, which explained the shortness of breath. Actually his mitral valve, which connects the upper and lower left chambers, was defective and was not closing properly. Blood and fluids backed up from his heart to his lungs and then to the rest of his body, causing the water retention and puffiness.[20]

Heart specialists at Hoag prescribed digitalis and digoxin to help Duke's heart pump more efficiently. To get rid of all the water, they put him on Lasix, a diuretic that flushed excess fluids out through his kidneys. But a dangerous side effect of the powerful diuretic was a loss of potassium. Older people with low potassium levels, especially those who also have gout, are candidates for cardiac arrest and sudden death, so the doctors also prescribed potassium. Digitalis, digoxin, Lasix, potassium, allopurinol—his medicine cabinet looked like a pharmacy, and he hated the physical weakness that it symbol-ized. He took the medicines but bitched and moaned about them, wondered whether he would ever be healthy again.[21]

He was also having some plumbing problems. He first noticed it in the spring of 1976. More often than not he had to get up several times at night to urinate, and even though the urge was strong, he had a hard time of it, never feeling that he emptied himself. At first he gave it little thought, attributing the problem to old age, not unlike the liver spots on his hands or the little broken blood vessels in his skin. But the condition deteriorated all summer. All day long he felt he had to go to the bathroom, but there never seemed to be any relief. He even had to lean into the urinal or over the toilet to keep from dribbling on his shoes. It was not normal, even for an old man. Something was wrong.[22]

The cancer ghost arose yet again. He worried about prostate cancer and all the possibilities—facing surgery and becoming impotent or incontinent. If prostate cancer spread, there was the chance—a pretty good one—of castra-tion, the last step doctors take to starve testosterone-devouring tumor cells. He distracted himself with promotional tours for *The Shootist* and with the rubber-chicken circuit in support of Ronald Reagan's and then Gerald Ford's 1976 presidential campaigns. He procrastinated for a few more days, waiting to finish ABC television's salute to his fiftieth year of moviemaking in early November. But when the election and special were over, Wayne knew he had to do something. Urinating was a real chore.

He went to Hoag in mid-November for an examination. Sure enough, the urologist found what he expected to find, an enlarged prostate gland squeez-ing the ureter and restricting urine flow from the bladder. The doctor was concerned but not alarmed. The gland was much bigger than it should have been, but he could not feel any really hard, knotty bumps. Wayne went on antibiotics to clear up any prostate infection and was scheduled for surgery for early December. He checked into Hoag on December 2, 1976. The surgery, a transurethral resection, was simpler and more routine than its fancy name, consisting of boring out and suctioning the insides of Wayne's prostate. He was in the hospital for a couple of days, but the only real physical discomfort came when the nurse tugged the catheter back out. The psychological ten-sion, however, was something else. A pathologist got the tissues, and Wayne waited for the lab results. He was tense and preoccupied until the doctor walked in and told him that everything was just fine, that he had been suffer-ing from "benign prostatic hypertrophy"—a somewhat swollen prostate gland just like millions of other elderly men.

In January 1977 Andy Devine died of leukemia. Wayne had first met Devine in the early 1930s, but they became close friends in 1938 during the filming of *Stagecoach*, and like everybody else who knew Devine, he had an immediate fondness for the portly actor with the high-pitched, whining voice. Over the years Devine managed to support himself in the business, even if the parts had become more mundane than those he had once received from John Ford. Younger audiences remembered Devine as "Jingles," the jovial, hapless sidekick to Guy Madison in the 1950s television series *Wild Bill Hickok*. He was hardly jovial at the end. Chemotherapy robbed Devine of his hair and girth but did nothing for the leukemia. Devine was buried at Pacific View Memorial Park in Newport Beach, and Duke decided during the funeral that he wanted to be buried there as well.[23]

Throughout 1977 and early 1978 Wayne continued to deteriorate physically. Early in 1978 President Carter invited him to attend the formal ceremony exchanging the signed and ratified Panama Canal treaties, but by that time he was sick again, this time seriously.

The cough, hoarseness, shortness of breath, and water retention grew steadily worse. He could barely get around, and after St. Patrick's Day in March 1978, he checked back into Hoag, with Michael telling the press it was bronchial pneumonia. Dr. Joel Manchester, Hoag's cardiac specialist, performed an angiogram, pumping an iodine solution into Wayne's bloodstream and then X-raying the heart as it pumped. The verdict was swift. The mitral valve had to be replaced or the heart would fail. Manchester told Wayne that the surgery was risky but that Massachusetts General Hospital in Boston was the best in the world at mitral valve replacement. Michael Wayne flew to Boston to make the arrangements, placing a premium on secrecy and privacy. Fluor Corporation, the huge Orange County engineering and construction firm, agreed to fly Wayne and his family to Boston in the corporate jet on March 29. Massachusetts General put him into the VIP room of the eighth floor, listing him on their charts as Marion Morrison. Nonetheless, within a day the news was out that John Wayne was a patient, and the hospital had to hire additional security to keep strangers out of his room.[24]

The physicians soon became reluctant about performing the operation. Open-heart surgery on a weak seventy-one-year-old man with one lung and chronic bronchitis was risky, with as much as a 10 percent failure rate. Massachusetts General did not want its name broadcast around the world as the place where John Wayne died. Dr. Roman DeSanctis, a lung specialist, stalled for a few days until Wayne insisted on the operation. He considered the prospect of being an invalid worse than death. When DeSanctis speculated that his problems might be lung-related rather than heart-related, Duke cut him short, ordering the doctor to "open that window. You're going to operate on me or I'm gonna jump out that window." DeSanctis relented, but when he started to describe the surgery, Wayne cut him off again: "Don't tell me. I don't want to know. If you want to talk to the kids, go ahead, but don't tell me." As always, Duke simply would not talk about pain.[25]

On the evening before the operation, Duke left Massachusetts General for dinner with a large company of family and friends. All his children were there. One of his physicians arranged a private dining room at Maison Robert, an exclusive restaurant at Boston's old City Hall. Pat Stacy remembered that the dining room, with its stained-glass windows and heavy wood tables, had an "almost ecclesiastical atmosphere." The mood in the room was subdued, with everyone thinking the same thought but refusing to voice it. Duke's physicians gave him permission to have one drink, and he "ordered the largest martini your bartender can concoct." A waiter filled a large glass with the martini and handed it to Duke. He stood and, catching the mood, raised his glass in a first toast: "To the last supper." Speechless, everyone groaned and refused to drink until Joe De Franco broke the ice with an amendment to the toast: "Last supper until Newport." The party continued until 10:30 P.M., when Duke returned to the hospital.

On April 3 they wheeled Wayne into surgery, put him under the anesthetic, and a medical team headed by Dr. Mortimer J. Buckley cracked open his chest, cutting through the skin and splitting the sternum to expose Duke's heart. They placed him on a heart-lung machine to keep his body and brain oxygenated, chemically chilled the heart into dormancy, sliced into the left side of his heart, and replaced his own faulty mitral valve with one from a pig's heart. The three-hour surgery was "uneventful"—exactly what Massachusetts General hoped for. Duke's recovery was uneventful as well, and he returned to Newport Beach on the Fluor jet at the end of April. He felt and looked, at 229 pounds, better than he had in years.[26]

A nasty case of hepatitis then complicated his recovery. Within a few weeks of returning home, he developed a low-grade fever, some pain in his right side, nausea, and fatigue. He put up with the illness until the end of May, when he went back to Hoag. Blood tests showed that he was suffering from hepatitis, probably picked up from the blood transfusions at Massachusetts General. The doctors ordered him back to bed for six weeks. He was not in much shape to do anything else. Physicians checked him every day and took blood samples each week. Slowly they flushed out the hepatitis, and his strength returned. Wayne got out on the *Wild Goose* several times during the summer, and in August he resumed the boisterous card games at the Big Canyon Country Club, even though he had an allergy to alcohol. He complained to Roderick Mann of the *Los Angeles Times*: "I can't drink. We had a little party here a couple a nights ago and, Jeez, I wanted a drink so bad. . . . Grape juice. Can you believe it? I've had more damn grape juice and root beer and coffee these past few weeks."[27]

He interrupted his convalescence once that summer, even though he did not feel much like going to a party. But Crown Prince Hussein of Jordan wanted to meet him, and the State Department had asked Duke to oblige. He drove over to the trendy Cellar restaurant at the Newporter Inn on July 24. He was sick and tired and, as he told a friend, "just too damn old for this shit." To make matters worse, he was kept waiting, and—a rigorously prompt man himself—he really hated that. As he complained to a group of friends he nervously tugged at his collar and pulled up his pants and coughed. It was past 7:00 P.M., past the scheduled dinner hour. Why wait? Why wait for a man he had never met, for a formal dinner he probably would not enjoy, when his head and body ached and he was still trying to kick the aftereffects of his bout with hepatitis? It was all the price he paid for being an institution, as big a part of Southern California, of the United States of America, as Hollywood and Disneyland. Joe De Franco, whom Duke had invited to the dinner, recalled that Wayne was not allowed to drink, a development that did not improve his mood. As the members of the Wayne party waited, periodically checked their watches, and engaged in small talk, Duke complained that he was cold and that he felt lousy.

Finally Crown Prince Hussein arrived, with his wife, Arafat, his children, and an assortment of nannies, servants, bodyguards, security agents, and friends. After everyone was formally introduced and the children sent off to their rooms, the guests and the bodyguards sat down for dinner. There were only two tables in the restaurant, a large one for the twenty-five FBI agents, Secret Service agents, Treasury agents, local police, state police, and private bodyguards, and a smaller one for the prince, John Wayne, and their friends. Conversation around the main table was stilted. Though everyone tried to make the best of an awkward gathering, the efforts only served to underscore the total absence of chemistry.

Dinners were ordered. A sommelier appeared with several bottles of expensive wine and offered a taste to Wayne. Duke took a small sip. His face reddened and he began to cough. While the other guests looked on, frozen in horror, and the sommelier stood by helplessly, Duke continued to cough, loud and hard. The jag lasted thirty seconds, maybe longer. Then as abruptly as it began, it ended. Duke took a breath, looked at the crown prince, and said: "It's all right with me." For a moment everyone was silent. Then Prince Hussein began to laugh. He laughed harder and louder and longer than Wayne had coughed. Tears filled his eyes and ran down his face. The room was filled with his laughter as everyone at both tables shared the prince's moment of pure merriment. When he was finally able to stop laughing, the prince looked across the table at Hollywood's greatest box-office star and said: "I'll drink to the Duke." "And I'll drink to the prince," Wayne replied. The chemistry in the room was suddenly perfect. Members of the royal family of Jordan and friends of John Wayne discovered that they had all sorts of things in common that demanded immediate, spirited conversation. Once again John Wayne had played a part perfectly. "I don't act, I react," he had said hundreds of times during his career. Once again his reactions had created a memorable scene.

Throughout the evening he continued to play his role. After dinner the party was transported to his Newport home. It was Princess Arafat's birthday, and Duke had ordered a cake for the occasion. He cut it himself, but not in any pedestrian manner. Grabbing his cavalry saber and taking it out of its sheath, he sliced the cake into sections. "Okay, now help yourselves," he said. More laughter. Another perfect performance.[28]

He did not have many perfect performances left. In September he began to experience some abdominal discomfort, a sense of being full all the time, and then constant heartburn. Food tasted bad, and when he swallowed there was a mild, rising nausea, as if the food could not settle in place. The discomfort was especially acute after a heavy meal. Meat did not sit well. It filled him up too much and left him with the sensation that even after he had swallowed, the meat was still sitting up near his throat. John Wayne had always loved to eat—hot Mexican dishes and char-broiled steaks, the food then washed down with wine or tequila. Maureen O'Hara recalled Wayne's 1977 trip to the Virgin Islands to visit her: "I would say, what do you want for dinner? Steak. I would say, what do you want for lunch? Steak. . . . And one day he went down into the supermarket in the town of Christiansted, because he decided he should go shopping and buy some food for the house . . . he started filling his market basket with all the steaks that he could find." Now he could not eat or drink what he wanted. He could barely stand the smell of booze, let alone tolerate the pain it generated in his stomach.[29]

The heartburn and nausea became acute in October. He told Pat Stacy that his stomach "feels like I've swallowed broken glass." He was unable to finish his meals and pushed food away in disgust. He had a hard time sleeping at night, and his weight began to slip. By the end of October, he weighed 225 pounds, falsely fit and trim enough to get into shirts and pants he had not worn in years. Meals became pudding or watermelon or crushed apples, the only foods that seemed to soothe his stomach. Like J. B. Books in *The Shootist*, he was wincing in pain now, unconsciously reaching to his belly when the shooting sensations, the grinding of "broken glass," swept through. Only at Pat Stacy's insistence did he finally see gastrointestinal specialists at Hoag, and they told him it sounded like gallbladder trouble. It was not at all uncommon, they told him, for older people to have gallbladders that were infected or even gangrenous, and that only surgical removal of the organ would bring them any relief.[30]

Duke roared at the idea of more surgery, especially during Christmas, but privately he was a bit relieved when the doctors mentioned the gallbladder. Pappy Ford's cancer symptoms had begun with terrible stomach pain, and for several weeks his old fears returned, even though he refused to discuss them. If it was just a gallbladder, he could postpone doing anything about it until after Christmas. For that matter, even the doctors at Hoag were not thinking stomach cancer. Stomach cancer was primarily a Japanese disease; its incidence in the United States had become a rarity, dropping from thirty cases per one hundred thousand people in 1930 to less than eight cases per one hundred thousand in the mid-1970s. It was even less likely to strike older white males. The odds against two close friends—Pappy and Duke—dying from stomach cancer were practically astronomical.[31]

There were other distractions that Christmas, although none of them was worse than the pain. The FBI told Wayne to beef up security around his house and at the Batjac offices in Beverly Hills. For several months they had been watching an obviously disturbed individual who complained publicly that certain celebrities—including John Wayne, Bob Hope, and Johnny Carson—were not cooperating with his plans to rid America of crime, drugs, and dissidents. He blamed the Trilateral Commission, David Rockefeller, and Chase Manhattan Bank for leading the conspiracy that put Jimmy Carter in the White House. He also wrote threatening letters describing his private arsenal, and how uncooperative superstars "would be taken care of." The FBI warned Wayne to be prepared for the possibility of extortion attempts, which implied the kidnapping of his children or grandchildren. Such threats were hardly new to Wayne, but they had to be taken seriously.[32]

Christmas was an endurance contest. The grinding stomach pains were constant, and Wayne's weight was down to 210 pounds. His clothes were hanging loosely, and he looked pale, his skin was thinner, and the liver spots on his hands more pronounced. He was moody and short-tempered, barking in frustration at everyone, then apologizing, only to bark and get angry again when the pain came back. Like J. B. Books, he was "living on the raw edge." Pat, Marisa, and Aissa put together his favorite Christmas dinner—champagne, wine, brandy, turkey, dressing, mashed potatoes, rolls, green salad, and fruit salad, but he only toyed with the food, pushing it back and forth across the plate, taking a taste now and then before excusing himself and going to bed, where he spent all of Christmas Day.[33]

This was no life. He went back to Hoag after New Year's, and his doctors scheduled him for surgery on January 12. But they urged him to go to UCLA for the operation. That was a bad sign. Gallbladder removal is a routine procedure, but the physicians at Hoag now suspected worse. The pain and weight loss were more than they would have expected with a gallbladder problem. They made him drink a couple of glasses of thick, barium-laced mush and then X-rayed his upper gastrointestinal tract. The radiologist noticed a disturbing mass in the stomach. Knowing Duke's dread of cancer and his unwillingness to discuss it, they kept talking about the gallbladder, but his fear of cancer was thoroughly aroused. A few days before he checked into UCLA, Wayne stopped off at Pilar's restaurant in Newport Beach. It was the last time she would ever see him, and he told her: "I'm sick again. The doc is talking like I've got a bad gallbladder, but I know better. I can't eat anymore. Hell, I can't even drink."[34] He postponed the surgery one more time in order to do an interview for Barbara Walters and ABC News. It was their first meeting, but Walters was already inclined to like Wayne. Two years earlier, after leaving NBC for ABC and a $5 million contract, she had been pilloried in the press and become the object of Gilda Radner's savage parody "Baba Wawa" on *Saturday Night Live*. In the midst of it all, when she was particularly depressed about the criticism, she had received a telegram from Wayne. It was one sentence: "Don't let the bastards get you down." He wanted the interview as much as Walters did, and they agreed to do it at the house and aboard the *Wild Goose* the day before he went into UCLA.

Walters did not learn about the impending surgery until she arrived at

Bayshore Drive. The interview at first addressed typical concerns about acting and filmmaking. Then it took an unusual philosophical turn, when she asked him about the meaning of life. "I have deep faith that there is a Supreme Being. There has to be . . . The fact that He's let me stick around a little longer, or She's let me stick around a little longer, certainly goes great with me, and I want to hang around as long as I'm healthy and not in anybody's way." Has it been a good life? "Great for me," he replied. Do you fear death? "I don't look forward to it, because, maybe He won't be as nice to me as I think He will, but I think He will." Do you watch your old movies on television? "Occasionally, when there's a real oldie. Like, they had *Wake of the Red Witch* on the other night. I looked at it."[35]

Wayne checked in to UCLA on January 10. There was no doubt about who was in charge. In order to protect his father's privacy, Michael Wayne carefully orchestrated the flow of information. The physicians spoke only to him, and he then relayed the news to the other six children, who then passed on whatever they heard to Josie and Pilar. Aissa, Marisa, and John Ethan often resented their dependence on half-brother Michael, but they had no choice. Duke had put him in charge. Only Michael and Pat Stacy had unrestricted access. The press received a simple message: John Wayne was in excellent health but needed routine gallbladder surgery. The hospital put him in Suite 948 on the ninth floor of the Wilson Pavilion—VIP accommodations at $345 a day—not just because Wayne could afford it but because all the major medical centers in the United States go out of their way to give special treatment to the rich and famous, people who may someday endow new research facilities. People who were rich but not famous, however, had their charts coded so that nurses and physicians would be able to recognize immediately just how important they were. But Duke did not need this "1a" description; everybody knew him on sight.[36]

Suite 948 in the Wilson Pavilion was a tastefully appointed private room complete with extra beds and a kitchenette. It was also a long way from the cancer treatment facilities downstairs. The UCLA Medical Center contrasts sharply with the Spanish stucco architecture of the rest of the campus. Red brick and contemporary, lean and efficient, its lines are simple and clean-cut, lacking individuality and perhaps even humanity, but also symbolizing confidence, power, and scientific detachment, visible proof that its hordes of experts are gaining ground in the fight against disease. The patients inside, except for celebrities, receive assembly-line treatment, becoming, whether they survive or succumb, the statistical averages that shape future research.

A peculiar fragrance sweetened the air in UCLA's cancer treatment stations, subtle but forever familiar to the initiated—a pungent mix of floor wax, antiseptic, body odor, and anticancer chemicals. The aroma was not really overpowering, just distinctive, and people stopped noticing it until the next time they visited. The UCLA cancer stations are for people in trouble, when their family physicians or local doctors can no longer treat them. The hospital clinics are full of the walking wounded—limping amputees and people with artificial limbs; sorrowful men and women with head and neck tumors and unreconstructed surgical wounds; bald women in babushkas, wigs, scarves, and turbans, and bald men in baseball caps, knit hats or bareheaded; and those whose tumors are invisible. John Wayne received state-of-the-art cancer medicine and the best oncology available anywhere. But it would not be good enough. UCLA put Duke through a series of blood tests, urine tests, chest X rays, and electrocardiograms on January 11 as part of the presurgical routine. The next day at 7:45 A.M., Dr. William Longmire, one of the country's preeminent gastrointestinal surgeons, and a team of seven other physicians, operated on him, ostensibly to go after a bad gallbladder but actually to get a closer look at that mass in his stomach. When he opened him up, Longmire knew right away that Wayne was a dying man. Stomach cancer has a wretched prognosis, an overall survival rate of less than 15 percent. If the disease had not spread elsewhere—to other organs or to nearby lymph nodes— Wayne's chances were better, but the tumor was a large one and the likelihood of metastasis was high.[37]

Although the tumor had not perforated the stomach lining or visibly spread to other regional tissues, it was too large to leave Duke with a stomach. Longmire excised a tissue sample for a waiting team of pathologists, who quickly made a frozen section and declared it a malignant carcinoma. In *The Shootist*, Dr. Hostetler couldn't operate on J. B. Books because "I'd have to gut you like a fish." But this was not a family-practice office in Carson City in 1901, it was UCLA in 1979, and they *could* gut Duke like a fish. They did—a total gastrectomy. Longmire lifted the stomach and its tumor out *en masse* and cut out the gallbladder. Blood vessels, arteries, and nerves had to be severed and reconnected. The bottom of Duke's esophagus was prepared for suturing to the end of the small intestine. Longmire built two small pouches out of a portion of Duke's small intestine to serve as a pseudostomach. Then he scooped out the regional lymph nodes that drained the stomach, and sent them to pathologists for detailed studies. Hospital aides wheeled Wayne into the recovery room at 4:30 in the afternoon. The operation took more than nine hours.[38]

Michael Wayne released a carefully engineered document to the press, and Bernard Strohm, an assistant administrator at UCLA, answered their questions. They called it a "low-grade tumor" with no "clinical evidence" that the disease had spread, declaring his prognosis "excellent." What the double-talk actually meant was that the tumor was extremely dangerous. Surgeons had not been able to actually see, with the naked eye, any tumor tissue outside the stomach, although it was probably microscopically present. Duke's chances of recovering from the surgery were quite good, but not from the disease. During the next several days, Strohm continued to tell the press that Wayne was doing just fine. Reporters cornered Dr. Carmack Holmes, a member of the surgical team, and he also told them there was no clinical evidence that the disease had spread. When a reporter asked Holmes if he was sure the cancer had not spread, he very carefully replied: "I did not categorically state that it hasn't spread. I said there is no evidence." To a question about survival odds, Holmes backpedaled again, giving the standard reply that statistics "really aren't pertinent to individual cases because so many variables are involved." Back in the recovery room, Wayne regained consciousness and uttered one word: "Cancer?"[39]

The next day, after Wayne was taken into surgical intensive care, Dr. Longmire told him about the cancer, the surgery, and the possibility of metastasis. Because his stomach was gone and his digestive system lacked many acids needed for digestion, Wayne would be on a diet for the rest of his life. When he asked Longmire if he had "gotten it all," Longmire said he could not see any more tumor anywhere else, but that the lymph-node reports, which were several days away, would tell the rest of the story. If they were positive, he would probably need radiotherapy as well as chemotherapy. Duke was up and walking around on January 17, when the pathologists reported to Longmire that the gastric lymph nodes were full of microscopic tumor cells. Wayne displayed no outward reaction when Longmire gave him the news. It was almost as if he were not listening, or not hearing the feared fact that the disease was spreading. Bernard Strohm quickly released a news report to the press: "The final pathological report of the tissue removed at operation has disclosed evidence of microscopic metastasis in the gastric lymph nodes that were removed with the stomach. Such microscopic involvement was not detected at the time of the operation or upon the initial gross pathological examination . . . there is a probability that it has spread. I am not prepared to say any more." Although the press reports over the next several days described the positive lymph nodes as "noncritical," Longmire knew that Wayne's survival chances were much bleaker. This time it would not be like 1964, when they really did "get it all."[40]

The rest of Wayne's stay in the hospital was uneventful, except for a nasty infection in the surgical incision, which kept him there longer than expected. On February 10, under elaborate security precautions and secrecy, he left UCLA by a back entrance and went to Newport Beach in a motor home. He was relieved to get out of the hospital, but he lashed out at Pat Stacy when she asked him how soon the radiation treatments at Hoag would begin. Suddenly he denied ever hearing about radiation treatments from Longmire, claiming that the surgeon had told him that all of the tumor had been removed in the operation and that he was going to be just fine. Everyone else in the family, including Stacy, knew about the radiation, but he insisted emphatically and angrily that he had not been told, that he did not want any more surprises, that he was sick of hospitals and doctors and nurses and medicine and cancer.[41]

He eventually agreed to undergo the treatments, although he insisted on absolute secrecy. As J. B. Books had said: "Dying's my own business." UCLA radiotherapists designed the regimen, but they waited six weeks before starting because the incision had to be fully healed. They decided to give Duke between 4,500 and 5000 rads in daily doses of 170 rads each. The idea behind radiotherapy is simple: Cancer cells, in spite of their capacity to kill, are actually weaker than normal cells. They divide at abnormally high rates, but while dividing they are vulnerable. Enough radiation will kill any cancer, of course, but the science of radiotherapy is to give cancer patients just enough radiation to destroy every last tumor cell without ruining normal tissue in the process. Using a purple Magic Marker, specialists at Hoag drew the radiation target over Wayne's stomach. The target covered the central part of his abdomen from the navel up to the sternum, and then broadened out to include the left side of his chest up to the level of his armpits. Each day, Monday through Friday, he drove or was driven to Hoag, waited in a private alcove for his turn, lay down under the huge machine, and received the radiation "buzz." The setup—to make sure that each "buzz" hit exactly the same spot—took longer than the actual delivery of radiation. The treatments themselves were painless.[42]

Their cumulative effect, however, was not painless. Radiation treatments kill rapidly dividing cells, but cancer cells are not the only rapidly dividing cells in the body. The lining of the digestive tract, as well as hair follicles, also consists of rapidly dividing cells, which is why cancer patients undergoing radiation or chemotherapy often lose their hair and experience nausea. As Duke received the radiation at Hoag day after day and week after week, the targeted area on his chest developed a bright red "radiation sunburn," and what little was left of his appetite fled. He did not want to eat or drink, and his weight continued to fall, going below 190 pounds at the end of March. He had not been that light since his second year in high school. His mood was no better than his appetite. For a man accustomed to an active life, one greedily grasped and devoured, this was not living. And he bitterly resented having a disease dictate his every action.[43]

Everyone around him felt his wrath. Wayne's temper had always been somewhat unpredictable, but it was mitigated by his willingness to forgive and his omnipresent love for life. He hated pettiness, but with his body crumbling and his life slipping away, he found himself becoming just that—angry, frustrated, irritable, and petty. At the end of March, for example, he was desperate for food, for the taste of something he liked. Suddenly he wanted a bowl of Grape Nuts cereal and told Pat Stacy to get some from the store. When she returned with a bowl of Grape Nuts Flakes, he screamed: "This is not what I wanted. . . . Don't you know anything. . . ? Go get the box! . . . remove this crap, because I'm not going to eat it!"[44]

While the wire services carried stories of his recovery, fierce will to live, indomitable spirit, weight gain, and future plans, Wayne was barely holding his own. Hundreds of requests for personal appearances made their way to Batjac, and all but one were politely refused. That one would be his last time to strut out for a thundering ovation, his last set of lines to memorize and deliver as if they were impromptu, his last time to be John Wayne. He wanted to go to the Academy Awards ceremony and make a presentation. And he was invited to present the Oscar for Best Picture.

Fittingly for the last decade of his life and the 1970s in America, it would be an ironic evening. *The Deer Hunter*, a film Wayne despised because of its negative portrayal of the Vietnam War, won the award. And Jon Voight and Jane Fonda won Best Actor and Best Actress for their performances in *Coming Home*, another antiwar film. But those were the least of his problems. If anyone ever epitomized "true grit," he did on April 9, 1979, at the Dorothy Chandler Pavilion. He spent most of the morning at Hoag getting a radiation treatment, then drove into Los Angeles for the rehearsals. The grinding pains were back where his stomach once had been. He could not eat. He looked weak and thin, but he made sure that Dave Grayson, his makeup man, used only a light powder. "I'd rather not look as if I'd just been embalmed," he said.[45]

But when he walked out onstage at the Dorothy Chandler Pavilion in Los Angeles to present the Oscar, there was an audible gasp from the crowd. The forty pounds he had lost since Christmas had taken their toll. Although he did not look embalmed, there was no hiding the fact that he was dying. The jowls were gone and the skin around his face and neck was loose and flabby. Even the toupee seemed too big. He fooled nobody. Everybody knew he had cancer. Tom Kane, an editor with Batjac Productions, commented in 1973: "No one looks better than Duke in a tux, white tie, and tails. He has the height, broad shoulders, and build to look superb." But Duke did not look good. Several weeks before the Oscars he discovered that his own tuxedo was too big, beyond the skills of the best tailor. He had purchased a new, smaller tux, only to find that by Oscar night he was already too thin for it, too. He fetched a wet suit from the *Wild Goose* to wear under his shirt. It was a reversal of 1965 when, on the set of *The Sons of Katie Elder*, he had been too fat to wear a wet suit as others did to keep them warm during the frigid scenes in the river. He spoke with great bravado that night, basking in the genuinely sincere ovation, telling academy members, and a billion television watchers, that "Oscar and I have something in common. Oscar first came to the Hollywood scene in 1928. So did I. We're both a little weather-beaten, but we're still here and plan to be around a whole lot longer."[46]

But John Wayne was more than a little weather-beaten. His days were numbered. Why had he insisted on a rewrite of the cancer descriptions in *The Shootist*? At the time they seemed too harsh, almost unreal in their graphic description of pain. But now reality was much, much worse than even the original script. There would be no more outdoors locations or chess games or movies or steaks or Tootsie Rolls or french fries or tequila. No more poker, bridge, Klabberjass, or backgammon at Big Canyon Country Club. *Beau James*, a film he had hoped to make after *The Shootist*, would never be. There would be no more public appearances, no more ovations, no more Academy Awards or Academy Award ceremonies, no more trips down the Mexican coast in the *Wild Goose*, no more long shopping trips or catalog orders. The cancer was spreading throughout his abdomen, reaching up into the esophagus, and strangling the intestine. Cachexia—the literal starvation caused by cancer—had set in, and his body was feeding on itself. Duke was anorexic, robbed of his appetite and his taste, and the tumors were metabolically hyperactive. They devoured the few calories he managed to get down, trimmed away every ounce of his fat, and finally turned on muscle tissue, eating into what was left of him.[47] The weekend after the Oscar presentation, Wayne wanted to get out of the house and do something fun, maybe go out on the water for the weekend. He called Ralph and Marjorie Wingfield, his longtime friends from Nogales, Arizona, to fly out to Los Angeles and sail with him to Catalina Island on the *Wild Goose*. Marjorie was fighting her own battle against cancer. Still, he would not talk about his except to mention several times that he figured the doctors had gotten it all this time, just like they had back in 1964. They nodded their heads but knew better. They all played gin rummy, talked about the old days, and walked a little in Avalon. He was short-tempered with the *Goose* crew but quickly apologized. The medicines he was taking, he told Bert Minshall, would "turn a Sunday school teacher into a sonofabitch." He even talked about selling the *Goose* to cut expenses. On Sunday he said a last good-bye to the Wingfields and then asked them to wait a minute. He left, returning in a few moments with his favorite John B. Stetson. He put it on Wingfield's head, saying it looked better there than on his own head. Both men knew what it meant. It was a cowboy good-bye.[48]

A couple of days later the hacking cough returned. By April 17 it was so violent that Duke was unable to sleep at night. Worse yet, blood was coming up with the phlegm. He had to keep a towel handy to catch the discharge every few minutes. Pat Stacy called Dr. Rumsfield, telling him to meet them at Hoag, and Wayne went through another round of tests, including the chest X ray to find out if the cancer was back in his lungs. It was not, but pneumonia was, so Rumsfield put Wayne back on a heavy regimen of antibiotics. The good news about the absence of cancer in his chest, however, brought Wayne little relief. He hated being in the hospital again, hated the tapioca pudding that was the only thing he could keep down, hated the pain in his gut, hated the fact that his life was slipping painfully away. He was under 180 pounds, and he hated the sight of himself in the mirror.[49]

Death was preferable to life. In *The Shootist* Doc Hostetler told J. B. Books "not to die a death like I just described," and Marshal Thibodeaux told him, "Just don't take too long to die. Be a gent and convenience everybody and do it soon." Maybe Pedro Armendariz had done the right thing back in 1963, firing that armor-coated bullet from his .357 Magnum through his chest. Duke asked his son Patrick to go home to Newport Beach and bring back the Smith & Wesson .38 he kept on the bedside table. When Patrick refused, he asked Pat Stacy to get it. "I want," he told her, "to blow my brains out." When she, too, refused, he exploded in frustration, screaming at her: "Then get the hell out of here, and don't bother to come back! You're no fucking use to me anymore!" Then, less abrasively, he shouted: "Don't you understand. I want to kill myself, get it over with! You'll all be better off. I'll be better off." Wayne left Hoag a few days later and he had the Smith & Wesson at his disposal. But he couldn't do it. He was still hoping against hope for some kind of Hollywood miracle. He also had an image to maintain, and suicide was an unseemly way for him to die. He was John Wayne, not Pedro Armendariz. Suicide and true grit did not go together. For John Wayne courage in 1979 meant dying the miserable death Doc Hostetler had warned against.[50]

When he left Hoag on April 25, he was particularly upset with the media. He looked so weak and feeble—so unlike himself—that he was paranoid about reporters and cameramen sneaking into the hospital and getting a picture of him. Like J. B. Books, he considered them all to be "prying, pipsqueaking asses," and he believed that "a man's death is the most private thing in his life. It's mine." The idea of having his emaciated body pictured on the front page of the *Star* or the *National Enquirer* made him apoplectic. When news that he was undergoing radiation treatments reached the press the week before, he had a fit at home, accusing everybody in the family of talking to the press and then blaming the staff at Hoag for letting the news out. He did not want the public to know that John Wayne was getting radiation, getting skinny, and getting scared. So, in a bitter rage against the media, he released a petty, nasty statement:

> The bronchial pneumonia irritation cleared up eight hours after the antibiotics, but they decided to keep me over there for a couple of days and check my condition before releasing me, which they did. I haven't lied to the press about anything but they will not take our reports as truthful. They sneak around trying to bribe people to say something that won't coincide with the official reports. I don't know why it is necessary but I guess that is modern-day news methods. It used to be considered yellow journalism. Anyway, have a happy day.[51]

There were few happy days left. Instead of a quick exit, he was doomed to die slowly. At the end of the month Maureen O'Hara came for a visit, and like everyone else who had not seen him in a while, she drew in a sharp breath when he greeted her at the house in Newport Beach. Claire Trevor and her husband, Michael Breen, came by a few days later. Breen was dying of brain cancer. The two men shared hospital stories, joked about their emaciated appearances, compared radiation marks, and wished each other well, not saying what they both already knew. The parade of close friends continued during the week after his release from Hoag. Most of them quickly realized he was dying.[52]

The world heard the news early in May. A few days after Maureen O'Hara returned to her home on St. Croix, Wayne wrenched up in a screaming pain and insisted on getting over to Hoag immediately. It was not like him. Over the years he had avoided hospitals like the plague, waiting until the last minute to address a medical problem. Hoag radiologists X-rayed him, noticed masses of strange tissue obstructing the small intestine, and sent him straight back to Suite 948 in the Wilson Pavilion at UCLA. On May 1 Dr. Longmire operated on Wayne again, going back into his abdomen to see what was happening, but this time there was no hope, no chance of getting the "surgical margin" between tumor cells and normal tissue. He was suffering from "diffuse carcinomatosis"—cancer everywhere the eye could see—and, no doubt, wherever it could not. Bernard Strohm was blunter than he had been back in January. "The tissues removed on Wednesday," he said, "did have cancer all through them. The probability that cancer has spread throughout his body is now greatly increased. . . . I suspect he feels like he just fell off a horse." Strohm went on to tell the reporters that Wayne "has volunteered to remain in our in-patient program for treatment." In other words, Duke would not leave UCLA alive.[53]

There were no more standard therapies to try. The radiation treatments had failed to shrink the tumor, and the cancer was now so diffuse that surgery was useless. Still, John Wayne expected more treatment; he wanted to live. He was not ready to accept reality. Nor were his doctors. Just as a test pilot who is about to crash is willing to try anything to stop the spin, even though he knows there is really no hope, so the modern physician keeps trying in even the most hopeless situations. The oncologists at UCLA considered putting him on chemotherapy. They knew it was a long shot at best. Chemotherapy worked in stomach cancer only when surgeons had removed all visible tumor. When the tumors were advanced, the clinical evidence for chemotherapy remissions was dismal. The drugs themselves—with ominous-sounding names like Adriamycin, 5-Fluorouracil, Mitomycin-C, chlorambucil, or cytosine arabinoside—were highly toxic, with vicious side effects. Patients need to be prepared for the irony of it. All their lives they have taken pills and shots to relieve pain and restore health, but chemo makes them very sick before making them better. It was like the frontier days or earlier, when barbers and physicians adminstered bleedings, scourgings, leeches, enemas, purgatives, and untried elixirs, insisting over patients' screams that the treatment was necessary. Fortunately the UCLA oncologists decided that Wayne's general health was just too poor, his strength too depleted, and that chemotherapy would probably kill him.[54]

Instead they asked him if he was interested in an experimental program designed to stimulate his own immunological system. At the time there was a good deal of optimism among cancer specialists about the possibilities of a drug named interferon. First discovered in 1957, interferons are natural chemicals produced by the body. Scientists knew that interferons made it difficult for viruses inside human cells to reproduce, and they seemed to have antitumor properties, especially for diseases like leukemia and lymphoma. Whether or not interferon had any effect on solid tumors in general and stomach tumors in particular was the issue at hand, but Wayne agreed to become part of the program. It gave him some hope and, at the same time, made for a nice press release: "John Wayne agrees to undergo experimental treatment." Nobody even whispered to him that he was dying or how long he had to live because he still could not talk about it. On the day Duke began the interferon program, Bernard Strohm said: "There has been no mention in any way to Mr. Wayne of how long he might have to live. . . . It is strictly experimental medicine that we have come to . . . The treatment was suggested to him and he said: 'Yes.'"[55]

Experimental medicine is just that—experimental—and Wayne's cancer was growing too fast for the interferon to have any chance. Cancer cells divide rapidly and tumors grow geometrically, doubling in size within a certain period of time. Sooner or later, when they have doubled enough times, the tumors simply overwhelm the body's systems. By the time Wayne started on the interferon it was already too late. The doctors at UCLA knew it, but they were human beings, too. They had a famous patient on their hands who was still denying his own imminent death, refusing to talk about it, and willing to try something—anything—to preserve his life. To keep his hopes up and to maintain their own images as healers and scientists, they went ahead with the treatments, and Wayne dutifully submitted to the needles, tests, and examinations. Ollie Carey called Duke several days after the surgery. Uncharacteristically, he was feeling sorry for himself, explaining how the doctors had gutted him. "They didn't leave me anything," he complained. She coaxed a laugh out of him with her reply: "Well, you've still got your balls and your brain, don't you?"[56]

The only possible comfort now could be religious. There was no doubt among any of his friends that he believed in God. When he was a child the Morrisons attended Protestant churches—usually Methodist or Presbyterian—regularly, and Molly was a prayerful woman. But Wayne never developed a denominational loyalty. Over the years, in the same breath, he had described himself as a "Presby-goddamn-terian" and a "cardiac Catholic."

Like his father, Clyde, Duke had also been an active member of the Masonic Lodge. As a kid in Glendale, he had joined DeMolay, the Masonic auxiliary for boys, at his father's insistence. He was initiated into the Malaikah Temple of the Shrine of North America in Los Angeles in 1970, and in 1972 he became a Master Mason at the Marion McDaniel Lodge in Tucson, Arizona. From 1970 to 1976 he served as ambassador-at-large for the Malaikah Temple. For centuries, in Europe and the United States, Catholics and Masons had been at odds, accusing each other of persecution, intolerance, moral deviance, and political conspiracies to take over the world. By the 1970s both groups had become more tolerant of each other, but nothing better illustrates John Wayne's ecumenical personality than the fact that he was simultaneously a loyal Mason and a "cardiac Catholic."[57]

In fact, he had no appreciation for sectarian bickerings and doctrinal debates or, for that matter, the tendency of Protestant ministers and do-gooders to interfere with a man's private life. They condemned sex, drinking, and gambling—activities he thoroughly enjoyed. Michael Wayne described his father as a "deeply religious man" but with no "formal religion." In *The Shootist*, when Bond Rogers asked him, "Do you want to see the reverend?" J. B. Books replied, "No. My soul is what I've already made it." In addition, he could hardly sit still long enough to listen to a preacher's sermon. He was bored in church. God, for Duke, was simply the "Big Man Upstairs" to whom you turned for problems you could not solve yourself.[58]

Faith did not imply a belief in miracles. He "knew the Lord," in the words of Happy Shahan, but he did not think that God, in all his power, made a habit of interfering in the daily affairs of every human being. He had never seen or heard God and he was extremely skeptical of those making claims that they had. His faith was more inductive than deductive: "There must be some higher power," he told a reporter in May 1979, "or how does all this stuff work?" Like J. B. Books, Duke's "church has been the mountains and the solitude," and he felt close to something divine near the orange and rusty hues of Monument Valley, not in pulpits and cathedrals.[59]

Nor was he much of a believer in miracles. For Wayne, such notions were just silly. Russell Birdwell told Maurice Zolotow that in 1960, when he and Wayne were in Europe promoting *The Alamo*, they got an invitation to an audience with Pope John XXIII. Excited about the invitation, Birdwell purchased a host of medals to Saints Genesius, Christopher, and Hubert. Wayne asked him why he was carrying such a load into the Vatican, and Birdwell replied that if the pope would bless them, they would become special gifts and blessings for his family. Wayne simply shook his head, smiled, and said: "I don't believe in that superstition." He also laughed uproariously when they got inside the Vatican and saw that the "audience" included ten thousand other people.[60]

In the end the "cardiac Catholic" side to Wayne's faith prevailed. He always appreciated the fact that the Catholic Church had nothing to say about drinking or gambling or cardplaying, that the priests were less likely than Protestant ministers to get nosy about private affairs. Josie had been a devout Roman Catholic, and Duke had a tremendous respect for her fidelity to the church. Michael, Patrick, Toni, and Melinda all attended parochial schools, including Loyola University, and Wayne had paid tuition to Catholic schools most of his adult life. And he thought that the church schools had done well by his children: They had all grown up to be good people. Not one of them had "ever caused him a minute of trouble." For a while Patrick even considered becoming a priest. Duke was also aware, and had been for years, that his older children all wanted him to be a Catholic. For nearly four decades he had felt acutely guilty about what kind of father he had been to them when they were little, and turning to the Catholic Church was one way of making amends. Over the years all of Wayne's Panamanian friends were Catholics. But most important of all, John Ford had been a Catholic, and during his last days he found great peace in the church.[61]

Now, just like Ford, Duke was eaten up with stomach cancer, and, as he said through the lips of J. B. Books: "I'm a dying man afraid of the dark." He was not more or less afraid than any other normal person. He said that much in his interview with Barbara Walters, when she asked him if he feared death. Three months after the January 1979 interview, when he turned to the Catholic Church, he was not having any apparitions of the Virgin Mary or going through deathbed repentance or trying, with one foot in the grave, to get the other foot into heaven. He had not decided that the Catholic Church was the only true church or that he needed a priest to open up for him the gates of heaven. He was just getting ready to meet his maker, as a man should, and the Catholic Church—the church of his family and of his closest friends—was as good a way as he knew to do it.[62]

On the night of May 13, Duke hurt, in the words of J. B. Books, "like sin." The pain was constant, not quite the "screaming pain" Doc Hostetler described, but certainly bad enough. He was also throwing up bilious fluids from down in his small intestine every few minutes, and he could not sleep. Life was quickly boiling down to mere survival, just hanging on until it got even tougher. The next day Archbishop Marcos McGrath arrived at UCLA, and Michael Wayne asked his father if McGrath could visit with him. Duke agreed. He sat down at a chair in the hospital room and spent part of the afternoon with the priest. They talked about many things—Panama, the treaty fight during which they had first met, life, death, and meeting their Maker—and he agreed to have a priest give him the last rites before his death.[63]

The deathwatch inspired a nation. Beginning early in 1979, just after Duke's stomach surgery, the White House began receiving suggestions from the around the country that something be done, and quickly, to acknowledge John Wayne's contribution to America. The president enthusiastically endorsed the proposal that a special gold medal be struck on Duke's behalf, and Congressman Barry Goldwater of Arizona put it in the form of congressional legislation. Congress convened hearings on the measure on May 21, 1979. Maureen O'Hara testified before a House subcommittee, pleading with them to give Duke the recognition. "John Wayne is not just an actor. John Wayne *is* the United States of America," she tearfully told the committee. "Please let us show him our appreciation and love. He is a hero and there are so few left." O'Hara then suggested a title for the medal: "John Wayne, American." Congress approved the measure, and Jimmy Carter signed it. On Duke's seventy-second birthday the White House sent him a special letter explaining the medal.[64]

The letter provided a special touch to the birthday celebrations at UCLA. But Duke had always said that "awards won't put food on the table." They would not stave off death either. The end was rapidly approaching. After the first week of May he did not want any more visitors except his family. Frank Sinatra, Jimmy Carter, Jimmy Stewart, and Arturo McGowan had stopped in, but Wayne noticed their reactions to his appearance. He was also too tired to put up with the obligatory small talk. Doc Hostetler told J. B. Books that "one morning you're just gonna wake up and say, I'm in this bed and here I'm gonna stay." By the third week of May, Duke had stopped taking his daily walks down the hospital corridors. He was too weak. He needed help getting out of bed to go to the bathroom, and he occasionally cried in frustration at what had happened to him. His esophagus closed up at the end of the month, and although physicians tried to reopen it mechanically, it was hopeless. His insides were completely blocked. On May 29 the doctors began administering a permanent morphine intravenous drip lest the pain reach the screaming level. A few days later they removed the high-protein nutrient solution they had been feeding him. The smell of death was in the air, just as it had been in Ford's room back in 1973. Cancer cells not only divide rapidly, they also die rapidly, and when a patient has a body full of tumors, the body is full of an increasing volume of necrotic tissue. When those tumors are in the digestive tract, the odors escape more readily from the body and fill the room.[65]

Nurses took the scale from the room so that he would not try to weigh himself. That huge, leathery, tough body that had served him so well was shrinking. Just two years before Katharine Hepburn had written an ode to the Duke's body: "From head to toe he is all of a piece. Big head. Wide blue eyes. Sandy hair. Rugged skin—lined by living and fun and character. Not by just rotting away. A nose not too big, not too small. Good teeth. A face alive with humor. . . . His shoulders are broad—very. His chest is massive—very. . . . His hands so big. . . . Good legs. No seat. A man's body . . . And the base of this incredible creation. A pair of small sensitive feet." So it seemed to Hepburn in 1977. But now Duke was only 160 pounds, his skin just hanging on those large bones, the fat gone. Those wonderful blue eyes had a watery look and his face was deeply etched now, more by pain than old age. His complexion was pale, almost translucent. He was bald and completely gray. His hands and thick fingers now seemed even larger, especially compared with the rest of his body. And he was scarred by the futile attempts of modern medicine to save him. The twenty-eight-inch scar from the 1964 lung surgery was still there. It was especially thick because of the edema and the fact that the doctors had been forced to open him up again through the same incision. The 1978 scar from heart surgery went from just below his neck down the center of his chest, intersecting with the lung scar. There was a fresh, deep purple scar from January's stomach surgery, and another from the May operation to relieve the intestinal obstruction. The radiation target field still had a sunburned, reddish hue. And there were bruises on his arms and legs where IVs, blood tests, and interferon and morphine injections punctured him.[66]

Within the Wayne family, and throughout the nation at large, the death-watch began. Newspaper stories described his "losing battle with cancer" or his "true grit" in the face of the "Big C." Pilar drove in from Newport Beach and got a hotel room at the Westwood Marquis to be as close as she could to the hospital. She was not allowed to visit Duke, mostly because, as Wayne told Mary St. John: "I don't want her to see me this way." Michael and Patrick made their way back and forth from the Batjac offices in Beverly Hills to the Medical Center in Westwood. Pat Stacy, Aissa, and Marisa got a room at the Holiday Inn on Wilshire. Ethan stayed there when he took time off from school in Newport Beach. Every day the family went up to the hospital, and when they returned to the hotel rooms, Aissa called Pilar to keep her up-to-date. Michael, Patrick, Melinda, and Toni passed similar news on to their mother, Josie.[67]

Wayne refused to talk with anyone about his imminent death, but he symbolically acknowledged it by selling the *Wild Goose* early in June. Although the boat had been expensive over the years, he had loved it dearly, especially the memories of going out to sea with his children and cronies. He had often talked about selling it in order to get rid of the upkeep bills or to generate some badly needed cash, but he could never bring himself to do it, at least not until he was on his deathbed and realized he would never see the *Goose* again. A Santa Monica attorney, Lynn Hutchins, paid $750,000 for the *Wild Goose*, receiving a certificate that it was in excellent condition. After the sale, when Duke learned that the *Goose's* engines needed a $40,000 overhaul, he decided to pay for it himself. "I gave him my word. I'm not selling anyone a turkey."[68]

So it was at the end. During the first week of June, Duke slipped in and out of consciousness; the morphine doses had to be increased to at least blunt the pain, but at the same time they sent him into a coma. He would have the medication reduced when the children wanted to visit, but doing so made him extremely uncomfortable. Five days before Wayne's death, Michael placed a call to Louis and Alice Johnson in Arizona, telling them that if they wanted to see "J.W.," they had better get to Los Angeles as soon as possible. They arrived at UCLA and were astonished at how quickly he had "turned to nothing but skin and bones." Mary St. John visited with him three days before he died. Duke was in a bathrobe and a Los Angeles Dodgers baseball cap, hooked up to IVs and a catheter. He was searching for peace and asked Mary what she thought of death. She quoted a passage from *The Rubáiyát of Omar Khayyám*:

> Strange, is it not? that of the myriads who
> Before us pass'd the door of Darkness through,
> Not one returns to tell us of the Road,
> Which to discover we must travel too.

Wayne looked at her quizzically and asked her to repeat the passage, which Mary did. He quietly remarked: "You know, I never thought of it that way."

She took his hand and kissed it. "Well, Mary," he then said, "I guess the Red Witch finally got me."[69]

Two days before his death, he was suffering terribly, and Patrick asked him if maybe it was time for him to see the priest. "Yeah," he answered, "I think that's a good idea." Patrick called Father Robert Curtis, the Roman Catholic chaplain of the UCLA Medical Center, who came up to the room, baptized John Wayne, and then pronounced the last rites. Michael Wayne later remarked: "I don't know the technicalities of the church or what constitutes a conversion. But Dad did die in the church. I guess you could say he died a Catholic. . . . Naturally, all of us are very happy that Dad joined the church." Later that evening Duke slipped into a deep coma. "If you're lucky, you'll lose consciousness," Doc Hostetler told J. B. Books. Duke did. On Monday, June 11, his blood pressure began falling and his breathing became more shallow. He took his last gasping breath at 5:23 P.M. on June 11, 1979.

When the family realized he was gone, several of them lapsed into tearful good-byes. Michael then told them all, including himself, to wipe away the tears, bite their lips, leave the room, and calmly tell the press nothing. When the family was out of the hospital, Bernard Strohm told the assembled press that John Wayne was dead. Within minutes the news was spreading around the world. KFWB Radio in Los Angeles began playing the theme song from *The High and the Mighty* continuously.[70]

Even in his contemporary films John Wayne seemed like a man from another century, so it is fitting that a 19th century man [Francis Parkman], wrote what can be taken as the perfect epitaph for him: "Civilization must eventually sweep from before it a class of men, its own precursors and pioneers, so remarkable both in their virtues and their faults, that few see their extinction without regret." (Writer David Sutton, 1976)

He is the very last cowboy saint. Up on the screen he is a living anachronism, but seeing him in that scruffy cowboy suit is like eating Christmas dinner with the folks. Year after year, nothing changes. Duke, like the Christmas tree, always comes out looking the same. (Writer Richard Goldstein, 1967)

I would like to be remembered—well, the Mexicans have an expression, Feo Fuerte y formal. Which means: he was ugly, was strong, and had dignity. (John Wayne, 1970)

Even though UCLA's daily press releases had prepared the world for John Wayne's death, his passing seemed to catch the country by surprise, inspiring a momentary disbelief, almost as if he was supposed to be immortal. When comedian Richard Pryor learned of Wayne's passing, he told a reporter, "Really? I thought he was going to kick Death's ass one more time!"

He was a simple, complex man, both more and less than he seemed. He loved the poetry of Walt Whitman and the prose of Zane Grey, the stillness of a game of chess and the jocularity of a game of cards, the sea and the desert. But most of all, he loved the movies. Hollywood was his home, film his identity. Because over time it became impossible to separate the man and the image, he seemed a mass of contradictions—a soldier who never served, a cowboy who lived on the beach, a man of violence who longed for peace. No wonder one of his favorite passages from Whitman was: "I contradict myself? Very well . . . I contradict myself. I am large; I contain multitudes." It was those very contradictions that film critic Michael Wilmington believed made Duke into an American icon: "John Wayne does—phony as it might sound, maudlin as it might sound—stand for America. He embodies its contradictions. . . . The cracks and fissures of America—its charms, its flaws, its strengths, weaknesses, grossness, and beauty. Its insipidity and its grandeur."

If John Wayne the man embodied America's contradictions, his image reflected his country's strengths, even though critics rarely acknowledged them. On horseback, framed against a sparse landscape with buttes or mountains in the deep background, he was as eloquent as a Whitman poem, the solitary, in-

Epilogue
Our Heroes Have
Always Been Cowboys

Oh, hell: the last century had its Iron Duke, Wellington; this century has its Granite Duke, Wayne. Every era gets the leader it deserves; John Wayne is ours. (Theater critic John Simon, 1975)

If every other Western movie were put to the torch, and only Wayne films survived, the whole genre would still be encapsulated and preserved perfectly. He was the complete Westerner. To the inch, he measures up to D. H. Lawrence's definition of the type: "harsh, isolate, stoic, and a killer. . . . He brought something back to the Western—something William S. Hart had recognized, and Tom Mix had banished—controlled viciousness, a sense of survival, ruthless tactics when the odds demanded them." (Film critic Michael Wilmington, 1979)

It is Wayne as the gentle patriarch, the last and best of what I hope is a dying breed, that I love. (Film historian Molly Haskell, 1975)

John Wayne is not one of us, if by us, we stipulate the kind of people who read and contribute to *The New Republic*. John Wayne was the Other. He had graduated by 1939 from the trivial pulp Westerns and adventure romances in which cardboard heroes wrestled with stock villains. In the grown-up Westerns of subsequent decades villainy was supplanted by evil, and Wayne confronted evil directly with ruthless, unblinking violence. (Film critic Andrew Sarris, 1979) dependent hero who seems always to be riding across the pages and screens of American epics. "He was something special," Harry Carey Jr. recalled. "Directors needed a Western canvas to keep him from filling the entire screen." Just before Wayne's death, Maureen O'Hara testified before Congress: "To the people of the world, John Wayne is not just an actor and a very fine actor. John Wayne is the United States of America. He is what they believe it to be. He is what they hope it to be. And he is what they hope it will always be." No other actor cast such a long cultural shadow.

Those who hope to understand America must understand John Wayne's appeal. No other country could have produced him. The fact that he never really was a cowboy hero or soldier is cause not for scorn but for reflection. He was an American original, entering the world as Marion Robert Morrison, the first child of a troubled, Iowa couple. Five years later, his mother renamed him Marion Mitchell Morrison, bestowing Robert on a new baby boy. More name changes followed. When he was in junior high, local firemen dubbed him "Duke" after a tagalong Airedale. The nickname stuck, and to close friends, he was "Duke" for the rest of his life. Billions of moviegoers knew him as John Wayne after Raoul Walsh renamed him for *The Big Trail*. Marion Mitchell Morrison remained his legal name for income tax forms, selective service records, deeds, mortgages, and wills, but the name never suited him. So he changed it. Early in the 1930s, when studio biographies at Fox and Columbia mistakenly identified him as Marion Michael Morrison, he decided to go along. Whenever interviewers asked him his real name, he told them it was Marion Michael Morrison. "I really liked the name Michael," he told Mary St. John. "Michael was our own firstborn. What the hell. It was as good a middle name as any. So I took it."

That's how he lived his life, doing what he wanted to do when he wanted to do it. Like his country, he possessed the energy and determination to shape a destiny, to reinvent himself, to become what he wanted to be. He did, constructing a screen persona and a private personality that reinforced one another in a continual, symbiotic dance. In the process he became a permanent fixture of American popular culture, an icon. During much of the twentieth century, for millions of Americans, watching a John Wayne movie was like peering, over and over again, into a great cultural mirror; we saw ourselves, what we thought was our past, and what we believed was a birthright of freedom, opportunity, security, and justice.

During the last years of his life, when his country flirted temporarily with liberalism, John Wayne appeared out of step. The change was sudden and caught him off-guard, momentarily at least. After all, he hadn't changed. Wayne insisted, no doubt correctly, that most of America hadn't changed either, and that a conservative "silent majority" still occupied the heartland. To be a conservative in the late 1960s and 1970s was to be a reactionary. His patriotism seemed maudlin, his faith simpleminded, his hopes naive. He preached individuality in an age of bureaucracy and *laissez-faire* in an era of social engineering. When others called for détente and pacifism, he insisted that evil exists in the world and must be crushed with righteous violence. John Wayne's feet were firmly planted in American bedrock. When the liberal interlude ended in the 1980s, and faith, individualism, and love of country were no longer suspect, John Wayne was home again.

They buried him in an unmarked grave on a hill overlooking the Newport Harbor. For years he had talked about being cremated, but he made no provisions in his will, and his family opted for burial. But the location, the view toward the Pacific Ocean and Catalina Island, would have pleased him. He had spent most of his life close to that ocean, he had fished its waters with John Ford and Ward Bond, and he had gotten drunk and played cards and cursed and laughed away hundreds of nights with friends aboard the *Araner* and the *Wild Goose*. Often he had escaped from Hollywood producers and his own fans to a small, intimate world of family and friends.

The exact location of his grave is unknown to everyone except a small group of people. There was talk about erecting a memorial to Duke, but as of 1995 it had not been done. "It's not right," Mary St. John said shortly before she died. "It's not right that nothing marks where Duke rests."

But in the end there was no need for another monument to a man who left two hundred or so films that say more about him than any monument could ever say. Somewhere, every day, he strides across a television screen, seemingly too large for the medium. With a western landscape filling the background, he looks snake-eyed at a villain, goes for his gun, and restores order. He speaks American. He walks American. He is remembered. As the protagonist in Walker Percy's novel *The Moviegoer* says, "Other . . . people treasure memorable moments in their lives: the time one climbed the Parthenon at sunrise, the summer night one met a lonely girl in Central Park and achieved with her a sweet and natural relationship. . . . What I remember is the time John Wayne killed three men with a carbine as he was falling to the dusty street in *Stagecoach*."

Notes

Chapter 1. God, Lincoln, and the Golden Gate

1. Mary St. John interview.
2. John Wayne, "It Happened Like This," *American Weekly* (November 7, 1954), 5.
3. Madison County, Iowa, Register of Births, book 2, page 329, and book 3, page 165, Madison County Historical Society; Pilar Wayne with Alex Thorliefson, *John Wayne: My Life with the Duke* (1987), 9; Rose Mitchell interview; Mary St. John interview.
4. John Dubourdieu, *Statistical Survey of the County of Antrim* (1812), 497–498; Leonard A. Morrison, *The History of the Morison or Morrison Family* (1880), 19–20.
5. Canon Hugh Forde, *Round the Coast of Northern Ireland* (1928), 14–15; Lillian Colletta and Leslie E. Puckett, *Tombstone Inscriptions of Cherry Fork Cemetery, Adams County, Ohio and Genealogical Gleanings* (1964), 79–80.
6. Henry J. Ford, *The Scotch-Irish in America* (1915); James Leyburn, *The Scotch-Irish: A Social History* (1962).
7. Colletta and Puckett, *Tombstone Inscriptions of Cherry Fork Cemetery,* 79–80; *Place Names, Past and Present, in Adams County, Ohio* (1980), 2–3; *Adams County, Ohio* (1988), 17, 183; Lindsay M. Brien, *Abstracts From History of Adams County, Ohio* (1966), 32. To trace Robert Morrison, see the Chester County, South Carolina, listing in *Index to the 1800 United States Census for South Carolina,* 85–86, and the Wayne Township, Adams County, Ohio, listings in *Index to the 1820 United States Census for Ohio,* 74; *Index to the 1840 United States Census for Ohio,* 45–46; and *Index for the 1850 United States Census for Ohio,* 181; *Biographical Directory of the General Assembly of Ohio, 1929–1950* (1931), 332.
8. Elsie Ewing Rayburn, *Early Marriage Records of Adams County, Ohio,* Film #0317308, Family History Library, Church of Jesus Christ of Latter-day Saints, Salt Lake City, Utah;

Brien, *Abstracts,* 32; Elwilda Osborn and Ethel Trego, *Warren County, Illinois, Death Records, 1876–1915* (1985), 106; *The Past and Present of Warren County, Illinois* (1877), 157, 217.

9. *Index to Certificates of Birth, Warren County, Illinois,* 251, film #1377923, Family History Library, Church of Jesus Christ of Latter-day Saints, Salt Lake City, Utah; W. C. Martin, *Warren County, Iowa* (1908), 129; 1895 Iowa State Census, White Oak Township, Warren County, 891, film #1022190, Family History Library, Church of Jesus Christ of Latter-day Saints, Salt Lake City, Utah; Nancy Marshall interview.

10. See *Zenith: Simpson College Yearbook, 1902–1903,* 136, and the Clyde Morrison File, Office of Alumni Relations, Simpson College, Indianola, Iowa; *Earlham Echo,* July 2, 1970; Dean Nelson, Office of the Registrar, Iowa State University, Ames, Iowa; *Des Moines Register,* December 4, 1973.

11. Hoag Christensen to Priscilla Steenhoek, April 19, 1990, Madison County Historical Society; *Iowa Registered Pharmacists,* 106, State Office of Pharmacy Examiners, 1209 East Court, Des Moines, Iowa. For a history of the College of Pharmacy at Drake University, see *Drake University Catalog, 1989–1990* (1990), 118.

12. 1910 United States Census, Madison County, Iowa, Madison Township, Earlham Town, 88, film #1374425, and *Marriage Records of Marion County, Iowa,* License No. 1550, film #1019717, Family History Library, Church of Jesus Christ of Latter-day Saints, Salt Lake City, Utah; Mary Isabelle Plum to Priscilla Steenhoek, November 5, 1990, Madison County Historical Society; Rose Mitchell interview; Mary St. John interview; *United States Census, 1920,* vol. 61, enumeration district 66, sheet 8, line 18, film #1240453, Family History Library, Church of Jesus Christ of Latter-day Saints, Salt Lake City, Utah.

13. Rose Mitchell interview; *Marriage Records of Marion County, Iowa,* film #1019717, Family History Library, Church of Jesus Christ of Latter-day Saints, Salt Lake City, Utah.

14. Frank Hoyt interview; Paul Barrus interview; Rose Mitchell interview; Nancy (Morrison) Marshall interview; Wayne, "It Happened Like This," 4.

15. Rose Mitchell interview; Mary St. John interview; Barbara Boyd interview; William Harris interview; Paul Barrus interview; Mary St. John interview; Alice Miller interview; Pilar Wayne, *John Wayne,* 8–12.

16. *Winterset Madisonian,* June 13, 1973; *Los Angeles Times,* November 6, 1983; *Antique Week,* March 20, 1989.

17. Herman A. Mueller, ed., *History of Madison County, Iowa, and Its People* (1915), 12–14, 29–33, 248–49.

18. Charles Champlin, *The Flicks: Or Whatever Became of Andy Hardy?* (1977), 3–4.

19. Paul Barrus Recollections, Madison County Historical Society; Joe Graham interview, Madison County Historical Society; Paul Barrus interview.

20. Ibid.

21. *The History of Madison County, Iowa, Containing a History of the County, its Cities, Towns,* etc. (1879); Joe Graham interview, and Paul Barrus Recollections, Madison County Historical Society.

22. *The Past and Present of Warren County, Illinois* (1877), 183, 195; Lisa Ray Clever, *John Wayne's Roots: An American Drama* (1972), 6–8.

23. Richard Scammon, *America at the Polls. A Handbook of American Presidential Election Statistics, 1920–1964* (1965); Richard Burnham, *Presidential Ballots 1836–1892* (1932); Edgar Robinson, *The Presidential Vote 1896–1932* (1955); Mueller, *History of Madison County,* 74–76.

24. 1910 *United States Census, Madison County, Iowa, City of Winterset,* film #1374425, Family History Library, Church of Jesus Christ of Latter-day Saints, Salt Lake City, Utah.

25. See the section on Madison County churches in Blair Young, *Madison County, Iowa* (1984); *The History of Madison County, Iowa, Containing a History of the County, its Cities, Towns, etc.,* 356–74; Paul Barrus to David E. Trask, June 15, 1988, Madison County Historical Society; Paul Barrus interview; Mueller, *History of Madison County,* 94–95; *Journal of the Iowa State Medical Society* (December 1916), 536.

26. James S. Olson, *Catholic Immigrants in America* (1987), 232; Mueller, *History of Madison County,* 183–184.

27. Paul Barrus to David E. Trask, June 15, 1988, Madison County Historical Society; Rose Mitchell interview; William Harris interview; Will C. Johnson interview, Madison County Historical Society; Mary St. John interview; Avery Rennick interview.

28. *Brooklyn* (Iowa) *Chronicle,* May 22, 1975; John Wayne to Harold J. Nevenhoven, January 29, 1975, Madison County Historical Society; *The History of Poweskiek County, Iowa* (1880), 558–64; Joyce Morgan interview.

29. *Des Moines Tribune,* May 5, 1976; "Bill of Sale of Personal Property, W. A. Bickford and R. W. Orris to Clyde L. Morrison, February 22, 1910, Madison County Historical Society.

30. Paul Barrus interview; Mueller, *History of Madison County,* 248–249; Clyde L. Morrison to C. C. Couch, Chattel Mortgage Record No. 45-255, Madison County Historical Society; Wayne; "It Happened Like This," 4; Rose Mitchell interview.

31. General Register of the George Washington School, Keokuk Public Schools, 1912, Madison County Historical Society; Paul Barrus interview; *Des Moines Tribune,* May 5, 1976; Rose Mitchell interview; *The Earlham Echo,* July 2, 1970; Maurice Zolotow, *Shooting Star: A Biography of John Wayne* (1974), 8.

32. *Los Angeles City Directory 1915* (1915), 1484; Nancy Marshall interview; see the budget signed by Marion M. Morrison, "Final Proof," No. 021610, Los Angeles Office, Bureau of Land Management, RG 48, National Archives, Pacific Southwest Division; "Notice of Intention to Make Proof," No. 021610, Los Angeles Office, Bureau of Land Management, RG 48, National Archives, Pacific Southwest Division.

33. For discussions of Owen Wister and the origins of the Western novel, see Jane Tompkins, *West of Everything: The Inner Life of Westerns* (1992), 131–156; Richard Slotkin, *Gunfighter Nation: The Myth of the Frontier in Twentieth-Century America* (1993), 169–183.

34. James S. Olson, *Dictionary of United States Economic History* (1992), 155–56.

35. "Favorable Report Document" and "Final Report," No. 021610, Los Angeles Office, Bureau of Land Management, and O. W. Gauss to T. J. True, January 4, 1915, No. 021610, RG 48, Bureau of Land Management, National Archives, Pacific Southwest Division.

36. Wayne, "It Happened like This," 5; "Favorable Report Document" and "Final Report," No. 021610, Los Angeles Office, Bureau of Land Management, and O. W. Gauss to T. J. True, January 4, 1915, No. 021610, RG 48, Bureau of Land Management, National Archives, Pacific Southwest Division.

37. Clyde Morrison Affidavit, "Final Proof," Desert Land Entry, No. 021610, Los Angeles Office, Bureau of Land Management, RG 48, National Archives, Pacific Southwest Division; Mary St. John interview.

38. *Los Angeles City Directory 1917* (1917), 445; "John Wayne's Boyhood Memories," *Photoplay* 82 (November 1972), 38, 69–70; Frank Hoyt interview.

39. Glen Allen Settle, *The Antelopes Left and the Settlers Came* (1986), 4–6; *Antelope Valley*

Press, April 22, 1990; Centennial Committee of the City of Lancaster, *Lancaster Celebrates a Century* (1984), 1–15; Mary St. John interview.

40. Centennial Committee of the City of Lancaster, *Lancaster Celebrates a Century,* 27–28; J. Shelton Gordon, "Incredible Tales," September 1, 1973, 108, unpublished manuscript, Palmdale Public Library, Palmdale, California.

41. "John Wayne's Boyhood Memories," 38, 69–70; Mary St. John interview; Maurice Zolotow, "John Wayne: The Boy, the Man, the Star—the Duke," *Extra* (July 1979), 22.

42. "Final Proof, Testimony of Witness," No. 021610 and "Township Tract Book, 1870–1972," 82–83, Box 3a, Box 347; "Desert Land Entry," No. 027452, Los Angeles Office; Records Group 48, Bureau of Land Management, National Archives, Pacific Southwest Region.

43. Glen A. Settle, *Along the Rails from Lancaster to Mojave* (1982), 26.

44. Bill Kelly, "John Wayne," *South Bay* (July 1961), 70.

45. James Gregory, "John Wayne: The Man Behind the Flag," *Movie Digest* (January 1972), 131–132; Settle, *Along the Rails,* 26; Lawrence Christian, "This Is John Wayne—Fer Chrissake," *Orange County Illustrated* (January 1977), 41.

46. J. Shelton Gordon, "Incredible Tales," September 1, 1973, 39, unpublished manuscript, Palmdale Public Library, Palmdale, California.

47. *Los Angeles City Directory 1917* (1917), 445.

48. John Wayne to Glen A. Settle, February 5, 1975, Reference Department, Palmdale Public Library, Palmdale, California; James Gregory, "John Wayne's Memories of the Beloved Brother He Lost," *Motion Picture* (November 1970), 22–23; Mary St. John interview.

49. John Wayne to Glen A. Settle, February 5, 1975, Reference Department, Palmdale City Library, Palmdale, California.

50. Centennial Committee of the City of Lancaster, *Lancaster Celebrates a Century,* 28; Settle, *Along the Rails,* 43–46.

51. Tompkins, *West of Everything,* 157–177; Slotkin, *Gunfighter Nation,* 211–217.

52. Slotkin, *Gunfighter Nation,* 230–247; George N. Fenin and William K. Everson, *The Western: From Silents to Cinerama* (1962), 48–68.

53. "Declaration of Applicant," No. 027452, Los Angeles Office, Bureau of Land Management, RG 48, National Archives, Pacific Southwest Region.

54. Wayne, "It Happened Like This," 5; Mary St. John interview.

55. See the manuscript on Marion M. Morrison, Archives, Glendale Public Library; "John Wayne's Boyhood Memories," 38, 69–70.

56. *Palmdale Post,* June 12, 1915; "John Wayne's Boyhood Memories," 38, 69–70.

57. *Glendale City Directory, 1915/1916* (1916), 112.

Chapter 2. "He's Just Been Playing Himself All These Years"

1. Frank Hoyt interview.

2. E. Caswell Perry and Carroll W. Parcher, *Glendale Area History* (1974), 29.

3. Perry and Parcher, *Glendale Area History,* 1–22.

4. For the best study of the loss of Hispanic land in California, see Leonard Pitt, *The Decline of the Californios: A Social History of Spanish-Speaking Californians, 1848–1890* (1966).

5. See the extensive section on Otis and the *Los Angeles Times* in David Halberstam, *The Powers That Be* (1984).

6. "Los Angeles Becomes the Largest City in Area in the United States," *American City* 15 (July 1916), 65–66; B. C. Forbes, "Cities in the Making," *Overland Monthly* 88 (October 1930), 305–18.

7. Perry and Parcher, *Glendale Area History,* 23.

8. Perry and Parcher, *Glendale Area History,* 30; John Steven McGroarty, ed., *History of Los Angeles County* (1923), 447–50.

9. McGroarty, *History of Los Angeles County,* 447.

10. *U.S. Census for 1910, Los Angeles County, Burbank Township, Glendale City,* film #1374092, Family History Center, Church of Jesus Christ of Latter-day Saints, Salt Lake City, Utah.

11. John Calvin Sherer, *History of Glendale and Vicinity* (1922), 237–64.

12. *Glendale City Directory, 1915/16* (1916); Frank Hoyt interview; *Glendale Evening Press,* June 11, 1979; Perry and Parcher, *Glendale Area History,* 463; *U. S. Census, 1920,* vol. 52, enumeration district 26, sheet 11, line 15.

13. Frank Hoyt interview; Carroll Parcher interview; *Glendale News-Press,* February 9, 1973.

14. *Glendale Evening News,* March 10, 1920. To trace the moves of the Morrison family, see the 1915/16 to 1921 issues of the *Glendale City Directory;* Jeannette Mazurki interview.

15. Frank Hoyt interview; *Glendale News-Press,* February 9, 1973; John Wayne, "It Happened Like This," *American Weekly* (November 7, 1954), 7.

16. Frank Hoyt interview.

17. Ibid., Gregory, "John Wayne: The Man Behind the Flag," 132–33; James Gregory, "John Wayne's Boyhood Memories," *Photoplay* 82 (November 1972), 69–70.

18. Wayne, "It Happened Like This," 7.

19. For the best look at the early years of the Boy Scouts and the YMCA, see David I. Macleod, *Building Character in the American Boy. The Boy Scouts, YMCA, and Their Fore-runners, 1870–1920* (1983); *Glendale Evening News,* March 9 and 11, 1920; *Glendale News-Press,* March 3, 1923.

20. *Glendale Daily Press,* March 23, 1923; *Glendale Evening News,* July 12, 1922.

21. *Glendale Daily Press,* July 21, 1922; *Glendale Evening Press,* June 11, 1979.

22. *Glendale News-Press,* February 9, 1973; Brendan Elliott, "The Duke—America's Royalty," *Photoplay* (July 1979), 35.

23. E. Caswell Perry, Shirley Catherine Berger, and Terri E. Jonisch, *Glendale: A Pictorial History* (1990), 84, 104; Gregory, "John Wayne's Boyhood Memories," 69.

24. Wayne, "It Happened Like This," 7; George N. Fenin and William K. Everson, *The Western: From Silents to Cinerama* (1962), 109–42.

25. *Glendale Evening Press,* June 11, 1979; Elliott, "The Duke—America's Royalty," 35; Perry, Berger, and Jonisch, *Glendale,* 51; Wayne, "It Happened Like This," 7; *Glendale News-Press,* February 9, 1973.

26. Nancy Marshall interview; Mary St. John interview.

27. *Glendale News-Press,* October 22, 1968, and June 13, 1979; Nancy Marshall interview.

28. *Glendale News-Press,* June 13, 1979; *Glendale Ledger,* May 30, 1979; Wayne, "It Happened Like This," 70.

29. *Glendale Evening News,* June 13, 1979; *Glendale News-Press,* June 11, 1979.

30. *Glendale Ledger,* May 30, 1979; Frank Hoyt interview.

31. *Glendale News-Press,* June 15, 1939, and June 13, 1979; *Glendale Evening News,* January 29, 1921; Glendale Union High School Senior Class, *Stylus 1924–1925* (1925), 65.

32. Gene Schoor, *Red Grange: Football's Greatest Halfback* (1952); *Glendale News-Press,* June

11, 1979; *Glendale Evening News,* December 7 and 10, 1923; *Glendale Daily Press,* November 7, 1922; Glendale Union High School *Stylus 1924–1925,* 115–30.

33. *Los Angeles Times,* December 19, 1976.
34. Glendale Union High School, *Stylus 1921* (1921), 64; Glendale Union High School, *Stylus 1924* (1924), 31, 47, 50, 59, 75, 121, and 137; Glendale Union High School, *Stylus 1924–1925,* 29, 31, 33, 40, 107, 120, and 165.
35. Gregory, "John Wayne: The Man Behind the Flag," 141.
36. Kevin Starr, *Material Dream: Southern California Through the 1920s* (1990), 151–55.

Chapter 3. Scholarship Boy

1. Mary St. John interview.
2. "USC Friends Remember Duke," *USC Family* (August/September 1979), 1–3; Associated Students of the University of Southern California, *El Rodeo 1926* (1926), 476.
3. Manuel P. Servin and Iris Higbie Wilson, *Southern California and Its University* (1969), 1–54.
4. Kevin Starr, *Material Dreams: Southern California Through the 1920s* (1990), 151–53; Woody Strode and Sam Young, *Goal Dust* (1990), 27–28.
5. Starr, *Material Dreams,* 154–55; Jerry Brondfield, *Rockne: Football's Greatest Coach* (1976).
6. Associated Students of the University of Southern California, *El Rodeo 1927* (1927), 376; Strode and Young, *Goal Dust,* 27–28.
7. Associated Students of the University of Southern California, *El Rodeo 1926* (1926), 380; University of Southern California, *Footballetter,* (June-July-August 1973), 4.
8. Servin and Wilson, *Southern California and Its University,* 117–18.
9. Barry Goldwater to James S. Olson, March 24, 1992; Egar Yuhl interview.
10. Mary St. John interview; Wayne, "It Happened Like This," 19; Joe Morella, *Loretta Young: An Extraordinary Life* (1986), 12, 22.
11. Ralph Wingfield interview; *Los Angeles Times,* June 19 and 25, 1933; Henry Dobyns, *Spanish Colonial Tucson: A Demographic Study* (1976); James E. Officer, *Hispanic Arizona, 1536–1856* (1987), 241–42, 253–54, 263–66, 320.
12. Louis Johnson interview; James S. Olson, *The Ethnic Dimension in American History* (1979), 316.
13. James S. Olson, *Catholic Immigrants in America* (1987), 155–56; *Los Angeles Times,* June 19, 1933; Mary St. John interview.
14. Pilar Wayne, *John Wayne, My Life with the Duke* (1987), 21; Mary St. John interview.
15. Starr, *Material Dreams,* 161–65.
16. John Wayne interview, CU.
17. Robert Sklar, *Movie-Made America* (1975); Ted Sennett, *Warner Brothers Presents* (1971); Bosley Crowther, *The Lion's Share* (1957).
18. Lary May, *Screening Out the Past: The Birth of Mass Culture and the Motion Picture Industry* (1980).
19. James Robert Parish, *The Fox Girls* (1971); Marjorie Rosen, *Popcorn Venus* (1973); David Yallop, *The Day the Laughter Stopped: The True Story of Fatty Arbuckle* (1976); Noel Botram and Peter Donnelley, *Valentino: The Love God* (1976).
20. David Stenn, *Clara Bow: Runnin' Wild* (1988), 112–14; Kenneth Anger, *Hollywood Babylon* (1975), 137–38.
21. Tim Lilley, "First Footsteps: The Duke's Film Work Before the Big Trail," *The Big Trail* (June 1989), 2; "The Duke's Family Album," *Photoplay* (December 1976), 3.

22. Upton Sinclair, *Upton Sinclair Presents William Fox* (1933).

23. Miriam Hughes, "Oh, For a Haircut," *Photoplay* (December 1930), 42–43; John Wayne interview, CU; *The Big Trail* (December 1989).

24. Hughes, "Oh, For a Haircut," 42–43.

25. Frank Hoyt interview; *Glendale Ledger,* May 30, 1979; *Glendale City Directory* (1926).

26. See the 1926–1930 editions of the *Glendale City Directory.* See also William L. O'Neill, *Divorce in the Progressive Era* (1967).

27. See the 1930, 1931, and 1932 issues of the *Glendale City Directory.*

28. Nancy Marshall interview.

29. *Trojan Family* 9 (April 17, 1977), 1; *Arizona Daily Star,* April 15, 1979.

30. "USC Friends Remember Duke," *USC Family* (August/September 1979), 1–3; *Arizona Daily Star,* April 15, 1979; University of Southern California, *Pigskin Preview* (October 9, 1926), 6, 15; University of Southern California, *Pigskin Preview* (December 4, 1926), 30.

31. "USC Friends Remember Duke," 1–3; *Arizona Daily Star,* April 15, 1979; Wayne, "It Happened Like This," 17–18.

32. Mary St. John interview; Nancy Marshall interview; *Arizona Daily Star,* April 15, 1979.

33. Nancy Marshall interview.

34. James Reid, "Mustangs to Marlene," *Silver Screen* (November 1940), 76.

35. Mary St. John interview; Nancy Marshall interview; *Arizona Daily Star,* April 15, 1979; Wayne, "It Happened Like This," 17–18.

36. James Gregory, "John Wayne's Memories of the Beloved Brother He Lost," *Motion Picture* (November 1970), 36–37, 80; Mary St. John interview.

37. Pilar Wayne, *John Wayne,* 21.

Chapter 4. Driven by a Ford

1. Ford's life and art have been well documented in Dan Ford, *Pappy: The Life of John Ford* (1979); Andrew Sinclair, *John Ford* (1979); Tag Gallagher, *John Ford: The Man and His Films* (1986); Andrew Sarris, *The John Ford Mystery Movie* (1975); and Ronald L. Davis, *John Ford: Hollywood's Old Master* (1995). Although the present interpretation of Ford is our own, we benefited from the careful work of these authors.

2. Gallagher, *John Ford,* 4.

3. Ford, *Pappy,* 2–10.

4. Quoted in Gallagher, *John Ford,* 6–17.

5. Ibid., 23.

6. Ibid., 6–25; Ephraim Katz, *The Film Encyclopedia* (1979), 206.

7. Frank Capra, autobiography manuscript, vol. 3, notes, 6; Cinema Archives, Wesleyan University; *Variety,* March 30, 1973; Sinclair, *John Ford* (1979), 49.

8. Gallagher, *John Ford,* 39, 380; Ford, *Pappy,* 126; Harry Carey Jr. interview confirmed this view of Ford.

9. *New York Times,* September 2, 1973; Ford, *Pappy,* 26–34; Gallagher, *John Ford,* 498.

10. John Wayne interview, JFP.

11. Maurice Zolotow, *Shooting Star: A Biography of John Wayne* (1979), 65–75; Nancy Marshall interview.

12. Donald Shepherd and Robert Slatzer, *Duke: The Life and Times of John Wayne* (1985), 94–97; Zolotow, *Shooting Star,* 65–75; Mary St. John interview; Alice Johnson interview.

13. Peter Bogdanovich, "The Duke's Gone West," *New York,* June 25, 1979, 68. Ford remembers the story but gives a slightly different account in Peter Bogdanovich, *John Ford* (1978), 49–50. Ford, however, had a much more creative memory than did Wayne.

14. John Wayne interview, MZP.

15. Ibid., quoted in Davis, *John Ford,* 64.

16. For the details on *Salute* see John Wayne interview, JFP; Ford, *Pappy,* 47–51; Davis, *John Ford,* 63–64; Avery Rennick interview; "Contract for Duke Morrison," Fox Film Corporation, Department of Special Collections, UCLA.

17. *Variety,* August 21, 1929; Gallagher, *John Ford,* 498.

18. Bogdanovich, "The Duke's Gone West," 69.

19. John Wayne interview, JFP.

20. Shepherd and Slatzer, *Duke,* 102–3.

21. Raoul Walsh, *Each Man in His Time: The Life Story of a Director* (1974), 238–39; Pressbook, Raoul Walsh, "The Log of The Big Trail," *The Big Trail* file, MHL.

22. Pressbook, Walsh, "The Log of The Big Trail," *The Big Trail* file, MHL.

23. Douglas Gomery, "The Coming of the Talkies: Invention, Innovation, and Diffusion," in Tino Balio, ed., *The American Film Industry* (1976), 189–205; Douglas Gomery, *Shared Pleasures: A History of Movie Presentation in the United States* (1992), 217–21; Stephen M. Silverman, *The Fox That Got Away: The Last Days of the Zanuck Dynasty at Twentieth Century-Fox* (1988), 44–53; *New York Times,* August 15, 1926.

24. Michael Freedland, *The Warner Brothers* (1983), 36–51.

25. Ibid., 43–44.

26. Gomery, "The Coming of Talkies," 193–206.

27. Ibid., 205–10; *New York Times,* November 4, 1929; Neal Gabler, *An Empire of Their Own: How the Jews Invented Hollywood* (1988), 64–72, 112–14; Silverman, *The Fox That Got Away,* 54–56; Ronald Brownstein, *The Power and the Glitter: The Hollywood-Washington Connection* (1990), 36–37.

28. Brownstein, *The Power and the Glitter,* 19–37.

29. *New York Times,* July 19, 1929; ibid., September 18, 1929; Richard Koszarski, *An Evening's Entertainment: The Age of the Silent Feature Picture, 1915–1928* (1990), 85.

30. Walsh, *Each Man in His Time,* 237–38; *Variety,* January 7, 1981; Paul F. Boller Jr. and Ronald L. Davis, *Hollywood Anecdote* (1987), 91.

31. Raoul Walsh interview, MZP; *Los Angeles Herald-Examiner,* October 18, 1960.

32. Mary St. John interview; Mike Tomkies, *Duke: The Story of John Wayne* (1971), 37–38.

33. Walsh, *Each Man in His Time,* 239.

34. Raoul Walsh interview, MZP.

35. Ibid.

36. "'I Come Ready': An Interview with John Wayne," *Film Heritage* (Summer 1975), 11.

37. Ibid.; Walsh, *Each Man in His Time,* 241.

38. Shepherd and Slatzer, *Duke,* 113–14, quoted in Peter Hay, *MGM: When the Lion Roars* (1991), 69.

39. Mike Tomkies, *Duke,* 36–37; Zolotow, *Shooting Star,* 82–83; Shepherd and Slatzer, *Duke,* 113–14.

40. Harry Carey Jr. interview.

41. Pressbook, Walsh, "The Log of The Big Trail," *The Big Trail* file, Academy of Motion Picture Arts and Sciences, MHL.

42. Ibid.

43. Walsh, *Each Man in His Time,* 241.

44. Raoul Walsh interview, MZP.

45. Walsh, *Each Man in His Time,* 241.

46. Pressbook, Walsh, "The Log of The Big Trail," *The Big Trail* file, MHL; Walsh, *Each Man in His Time,* 242–43.

47. Pressbook, Walsh, "The Log of The Big Trail," *The Big Trail* file, MHL; Walsh interview, MZP.

48. Walsh, *Each Man in His Time,* 243–44.

49. For a discussion of Breck Coleman as a romantic hero see Richard D. McGhee, *John Wayne: Actor, Artist, Hero* (1990), 144–52.

50. For an insightful exploration of the frontier legend see especially Richard Slotkin, *Gunfighter Nation: The Myth of the Frontier in Twentieth-Century America* (1992).

51. Miriam Hughes, "Oh, For a Hair Cut," *Photoplay Magazine* (December 1930), 45, 128; Jane Tompkins, *West of Everything: The Inner Life of the Western* (1992), 65.

52. *New York Times,* November 4 and 28, 1929; December 7, 1929; January 18, 1930; April 8, 1930.

53. Unless otherwise noted, the premiere of *The Big Trail* is from the *New York Times,* April 8, 1930; Zolotow, *Shooting Star,* 87; Mary St. John interview; Nancy Marshall interview; David Karnes, "The Glamorous Crowd: Hollywood Movie Premieres Between the Wars," *American Quarterly* 38 (Fall 1986), 553–72; *Los Angeles Times,* October 25, 1930.

54. *Film Daily,* October 12, 1930; *New York Times,* October 25, 1930; *Variety,* October 28, 1930.

55. Dorothy Cummins, "A Football Hero Scores Again," *Screen Play* (February 1931); Miriam Hughes, "Oh, For a Hair Cut!," 45; Elizabeth Goldbeck, "Samson of Hollywood," *Motion Picture* (February 1931), 76, 112.

56. Zolotow, *Shooting Star,* 88; John Wayne interview, MZP.

57. Ibid., 89–91.

58. Ibid.; *Boston Post,* November 4, 1930.

59. Marguerite Churchill, color biography, Publicity Department, William Fox West Coast Studios, Marguerite Churchill file, MHL.

60. "I Come Ready," 10; *Variety,* February 11, 1991.

61. Shepherd and Slatzer, *Duke,* 129; Zolotow, *Shooting Star,* 93.

Chapter 5. Poverty Row

1. Tino Balio, *United Artists: The Company Built by the Stars* (1976), 96–97; Robert Sklar, *Movie-Made America: A Cultural History of American Movies* (1975), 161–62.

2. Mary St. John interview; Peter Bogdanovich, "The Duke's Gone West," 69.

3. Bernard F. Dick, ed., *Columbia Pictures: Portrait of a Studio* (1992), 2–10; Bernard F. Dick, *The Merchant Prince of Poverty Row: Harry Cohn of Columbia Pictures* (1993), 73–76; Charles Starrett interview, SMU. For a somewhat more favorable portrait of Cohn, see Gail Gifford interview, SMU.

4. Dick, *Columbia Pictures,* 2; Dick, *The Merchant Prince of Poverty Row,* 7–13; Frank Capra, *The Name Above the Title* (1971), 84; Gabler, *An Empire of Their Own,* 151–83.

5. Gabler, *An Empire of Their Own,* 179; Dick, *The Merchant Prince of Poverty Row,* 73.

6. Gabler, *An Empire of Their Own,* 151–83.

7. Charles Maland, "Frank Capra at Columbia: Necessity and Invention," in Dick, *Columbia Pictures,* 71–88.

8. *New York Times,* August 17, 1931.

9. Jon Tuska, *The Filming of the West* (1976), 371; Bob Thomas, *King Cohn: The Life and Times of Harry Cohn* (1967), xix, 109–10; "Looking Back: John Wayne Talking to Scott Eyman," *Focus on Film* (Spring 1978), 18.

10. Tuska, *The Filming of the West*, 371; "Range Feud," *The Big Trail* (August 1986); "Texas Cyclone," *The Big Trail* (February 1989); "Two Fisted Law," *The Big Trail* (August 1991). *Texas Cyclone* and *Two Fisted Law* were not released until 1932, the year after Duke departed Columbia.

11. Dick, *The Merchant Prince of Poverty Row*, 11; *New York Times*, December 19, 1931; Mary St. John interview.

12. Zolotow, *Shooting Star*, 96–97; Shepherd and Slatzer, *Duke*, 138–40.

13. Jon Tuska, *The Vanishing Legion: A History of Mascot Pictures, 1927-1935* (1982).

14. Ibid., 8–9.

15. Ibid., 10–17.

16. Ibid., 16–19; Bob Thomas, "Hollywood's General of the Armies," *True* (July 1966), 48; "Yakima Canutt," *The Big Trail* (February, 1989); Yakima Canutt, *Stunt Man: The Autobiography of Yakima Canutt* (1979).

17. Quoted in Tuska, *The Vanishing Legion*, 19.

18. Quoted in ibid., 25–26, 47.

19. Ibid., 25–26, 46–47; Tuska, *The Filming of the West*, 209–14.

20. Tuska, *The Vanishing Legion*, 41–43; Zolotow, *Shooting Star*, 98–99; George E. Turner and Michael H. Price, *Forgotten Horrors: Early Talkie Chillers from Poverty Row* (1979), 47.

21. Quoted in Shepherd and Slatzer, *Duke*, 143.

22. Tuska, *The Vanishing Legion*, 54.

23. Canutt, *Stunt Man*, 88–89.

24. Ibid., 89; Tuska, *The Vanishing Legion*, 56, 73; John Wayne interview, CU.

25. John Wayne interview, CU.

26. Tuska, *The Vanishing Legion*, 83.

27. "The Hurricane Express," *The Big Trail* (June 1988).

28. Andrew Bergman, *We're in the Money: Depression America and Its Films* (1971), 3–61.

29. Yakima Canutt interview, "A Directors' Guild of America Oral History" (1977), MHL.

30. Thomas, "Hollywood's General of the Armies," 86.

31. Ibid., 48.

32. Tuska, *The Vanishing Legion*, 92–94; Zolotow, *Shooting Star*, 102.

33. Tuska, *The Vanishing Legion*, 94.

34. Tuska, *The Filming of the West*, 159–67; Zolotow, *Shooting Star*, 105–6; "Ride Him, Cowboy," *The Big Trail* (February 1991).

35. Shepherd and Slatzer, *Duke*, 147–51; "Ride Him, Cowboy," *The Big Trail* (February 1991); "The Big Stampede," *The Big Trail* (August 1985); "Haunted Gold," *The Big Trail* (December 1987); "The Telegraph Trail," *The Big Trail* (December 1993).

36. *New York Times*, June 24, 1933; "40 Productions Made Since Last Shutdown," April 6, 1933, Warner Bros. Collection, 1933, USC.

37. "His Private Secretary," *The Big Trail* (August 1984).

Chapter 6. "Suppose You Could Tell Her You Like Her Biscuits?"

1. *New York Times*, December 27, 1932.

2. Morella, *Loretta Young*, 9–10, 22, 60, 63.

3. *Los Angeles Times,* June 25, 1933; Nancy Marshall interview.

4. Mary St. John interview.

5. Ibid.

6. John Wayne interview, MZP; Nancy Marshall interview.

7. Ibid.; Bogdanovich, "The Duke's Gone West," 69.

8. Ford, *Pappy,* 74–77.

9. Ibid., 74–77, 115–16; John Wayne interview, JFP; Henry Fonda and Howard Teichmann, *Fonda: My Life* (1981), 132–33.

10. John Wayne interview, JFP.

11. *Log Book for the Araner,* JFP. Except where noted the tale for the trip is based on the log.

12. Ibid.; Ford, *Pappy,* 118.

13. John Wayne interview, JFP; Henry Fonda interview, ibid.; Ford, *Pappy,* 117–19.

14. Ford, *Pappy,* 118; John Wayne interview, JFP.

15. John Wayne interview, JFP; Mark Armistead interview, ibid.; Ford, *Pappy,* 118–19.

16. On Ford's political beliefs see Ford, *Pappy,* 71–74.

17. Ibid., 112.

18. "Rabbi" Harry Wurtzel to Y.M.P.T.A.S.P.A., January 23, 1937, JFP; C. E. Wingate Smith to Dudley [Nichols], January 22, 1937, ibid.; Nichols to Smith, January 22, 1937, ibid.; Gene Fowler to Y.M.P.T.A.S.P.A., January 28, 1937, ibid.; Nichols to Smith, February 1, 1937, ibid.

19. [Memo] To All Members, [n.d.], ibid.

20. [Memo] To All Members, [n.d.], ibid.; Liam O'Flaherty to [John] Ford [n.d.], ibid.

21. [Memo on change of name], [n.d.], ibid.; [Memo on admission to Southern California Yachting Association], [n.d.], ibid.; [Memo] to All Members, December 7, 1938, ibid.; Art LaShelle to John Ford, April 26, 1940, ibid.; Ford, *Pappy,* 113–15.

22. Robert Sklar, *Movie-Made America: A Social History of American Movies* (1975), 167–70.

23. Charles Flynn and Todd McCarthy, "The Economic Imperative: Why was the B Movie Necessary?" in Todd McCarthy and Charles Flynn, eds., *King of the Bs: Working Within the Hollywood System* (1975), 13–43.

24. Ibid., 17.

25. *New York Times,* December 30, 1934.

26. Ted Okuda, *The Monogram Checklist: The Films of the Monogram Pictures Corporation, 1931–1952* (1987), 1–6; Paul Malvern interview, *The Big Trail* (February 1989).

27. Flynn and McCarthy, "The Economic Imperative," 13, 22–23.

28. Steve Broidy interview, *King of the Bs,* 269–71.

29. John Wayne interview, MZP; Edward Buscombe, ed., *The BFI Companion to the Western* (1988), 98–99. Malvern said that Bill Bradbury sang in the picture, although Shepherd and Slatzer suggested that it was Jack Kirk, and Gene Autry thought it was Smith Ballew. See Paul Malvern interview, *The Big Trail* (February 1989); Shepherd and Slatzer, *Duke,* 423–24; and Gene Autry, *Back in the Saddle Again* (1978), 36; George E. Turner and Michael H. Price, *Forgotten Horrors: Early Talkies from Poverty Row* (1979), 127.

30. Autry, *Back in the Saddle Again,* 35–36.

31. Paul Malvern interview, *The Big Trail.*

32. Ibid.

33. Release dates are from Okuda, *The Monogram Checklist.* Richard D. McGhee, *John Wayne: Actor, Artist, Hero* (1990) lists slightly different dates for several of the films, which is understandable because it is not unusual to find multiple running times and release dates in the trade papers.

34. *Motion Picture Herald*, December 23, 1933; *Variety*, February 13, 1934; *Motion Picture Herald*, July, 27, 1934; ibid., May 12, 1934; ibid., review quoted in "'*Neath the Arizona Skies*," *The Big Trail* (October 1986).

35. Jon Tuska, *The Filming of the West* (1976), 373.

36. "How Four Generations of Waynes Spend Christmas Together," *Modern Screen*, (January 1969), 30.

37. Bert Minshall, *On Board with the Duke: John Wayne and the Wild Goose* (1992), 105.

38. Canutt, *Stunt Man*, 90; "West of the Divide," *The Big Trail* (October 1984).

39. Ibid., 3; Canutt, *Stunt Man*, 91.

40. "Sagebrush Trail," *The Big Trail* (February 1990); "Randy Rides Alone," ibid. (February 1994).

41. Canutt, *Stunt Man*, 90.

42. McGhee, *John Wayne*, 6.

43. Quoted in *The Young Duke: The Making of a Film Star* (Republic, 1992). A documentary hosted by Leonard Maltin.

44. Tuska, *The Vanishing Legion*, 73; *Los Angeles Times*, February 21, 1981; ibid., October 17, 1983; Mary St. John interview; Harry Carey Jr. interview; *The Young Duke;* Harry Carey Jr., *Company of Heroes: My Life in the John Ford Stock Company* (1994), 73.

45. Zolotow, *Shooting Star*, 119.

46. Quoted in "The Man from Utah," *The Big Trail* (December 1991).

47. As quoted in *Out West* from the series Hollywood: A Celebration of the American Silent Film (1980).

48. John Wayne to Dr. Cory SerVaas, April 27, 1979, reprinted in the *Saturday Evening Post* (July–August 1979), 4.

49. Tuska, *The Vanishing Legion*, 183–84; Okuda, *The Monogram Checklist*, 3; Richard Maurice Hurst, *Republic Studios: Between Poverty Row and the Majors* (1979), 1–3; Gene Autry Interview, CU. When Monogram merged to form Republic, Duke was under contract with Trem Carr, and Republic only paid Carr $1,750 a picture for Duke's services.

50. *New York Times*, April 13, 1935; Gertrude Walker and David Johnson, "Hacking Out the Bs—A Republic Writer Remembers," *Los Angeles Times*, July 9, 1978.

51. Walker and Johnson, "Hacking Out the Bs."

52. John Wayne interview, MZP.

53. George N. Fenin and William K. Everson, *The Western: From Silents to Cinerama* (1962), 213–15; Gene Autry Interview, CU; Richard Maurice Hurst, *Republic Studios: Between Poverty Row and the Majors* (1979), 135–46.

54. *New York Times*, June 29, 1936; *Film Daily*, November 3, 1936.

55. Tuska, *The Vanishing Legion*, 184; Hurst, *Republic Studios*, 2–3.

56. Arthur Lubin Interview, *King of the Bs*, 364–365; David Bordwell, Janet Staiger, and Kristin Thompson, *The Classical Hollywood Cinema: Film Style and Mode of Production to 1960* (1985), 327.

57. John Wayne interview, MZP.

58. *New York Times*, January 18, 1937; ibid., August 2, 1937; ibid., December 4, 1937; ibid., December 20, 1937; *Motion Picture Herald*, November 13, 1937.

59. John Wayne interview, MZP.

60. Nancy Marshall interview.

ayne interview, JFP; "Burt Kennedy Interviews John Ford," *Directors in Action,* Bob
nomas, ed. (1971), 133–37.

dy Devine interview, *Directors in Action,* 166; John Carradine interview, ibid., 168.

ne descriptions of Ford's treatment of Wayne in *Stagecoach* come from John Wayne inter-
ew, JFP; Mary St. John interview; Harry Carey Jr. interview; John Wayne interview, *Di-
ctors in Action,* 159–60; Claire Trevor interview, ibid., 160–61.

rry Carey Jr. interview.

rd, *Pappy,* 84–86.

d., 86.

ry St. John interview; Walter Reynolds interview, *Directors in Action,* 166.

ter Bogdanovich, *John Ford* (1978), 69–70; John Ford interview, *Directors in Action,*
4–35; Todd McCarthy, "John Ford and Monument Valley," *American Film* (May
78), 10–16; Bogdanovich, "The Duke's Gone West," 70.

he Goulding Story," produced by David Bowyer (1990); McCarthy, "John Ford and
onument Valley," 10–16; Ronald L. Davis, *John Ford: Hollywood's Old Master* (1995),
–96.

scombe, *Stagecoach,* 38–46.

in Wayne interview, CU.

e Buscombe, *Stagecoach,* 64–69; Canutt, *Stunt Man,* 106–15.

scombe, *Stagecoach,* 55–58; Behlmer, *Behind the Scenes,* 114–15; Tag Gallagher, *John
rd: The Man and His Films* (1986), 145–62.

eph I. Breen to Walter Wanger, October 28, 1938, Box 1, JFP; Joseph I. Breen to Wal-
Wanger, November 9, 1938, ibid.; Joseph I. Breen to Walter Wanger, November 14,
38, ibid.

gdanovich, "The Duke's Gone West," 70.

noted in Davis, *John Ford,* 98–99; Zolotow, *Shooting Star,* 113.

aire Trevor interview, *Directors in Action,* 161; Dorothy Spencer interview, ibid., 166;
nlmer, *Behind the Scenes,* 116.

ry St. John interview; Wayne, "I Come Ready," *Film Heritage,* 19.

scombe, *Stagecoach,* 9.

yne, "I Come Ready," 19.

d.; John Wayne interview, *Directors in Action,* 160.

iety, February 3, 1939; *Hollywood Reporter,* February 3, 1939; *New York Times,* March
939; ibid., March 12, 1939.

ayed and Earned: *Stagecoach,*" Box 93, Walter Wanger Papers; "*Stagecoach:* Producer's
Shares of Distribution Receipts," January 29, 1949, JFP; *Variety,* February 3, 1939;
n Ford interview, *Directors in Action,* 147.

ry St. John interview.

ncy (Morrison) Marshall interview; *Glendale News-Press,* June 19, 1939.

8. Foreign Affairs

details of the trip, see John Ford to Captain Elias Zacharias [December 1939], JFP,
Dan Ford, *Pappy: The Life of John Ford* (1979), 148–50.

d, *Pappy,* 150; *New York Times,* January 29, 1939.

ry St. John interview; Sam Adams, "Re-discovered: John Wayne," *Screenland* (October
9), 63; Jerry Asher, "Devil-may-care!" *Movie Mirror* (June 1939), 45.

Chapter 7. Stagecoach

1. The *Variety* review is reprinted in "Born to the West," *The I*
   Pappy, 117.
2. "Young Duke: The Making of John Wayne" (1992).
3. Memo on contracts of John Wayne, 1948, File 1919, Charle
   John interview.
4. Mary St. John interview; Hurst, *Republic Studios,* 128–35; 1
   335–39; "Overland Stage Raiders," *The Big Trail* (April 199
   ing B films, see Lloyd Nolan interview, SMU; Peggy Stewart
5. Hurst, *Republic Studios,* 122–35.
6. Reviews quoted in "Pals of the Saddle," *The Big Trail* (Octo
   view, MZP.
7. Bill Kelly, "The South Bay Interview: John Wayne," *South B*
8. Mary St. John interview.
9. The story of Wayne getting the role of the Ringo Kid is i
   Shooting Star, 140–42; and Donald Shepherd and Rober
   Duke: The Life and Times of John Wayne (1985), 177–78 pre
   with different dates. Our date is based on what Wayne rem
   tion of the preproduction details in the John Ford Papers; M
10. William K. Everson, *A Pictorial History of the Western Film* (
11. Mary St. John interview.
12. John Wayne interview, JFP; Mary St. John interview; Bog
    West," 69.
13. Thomas, *King Cohn,* 142.
14. Edward Buscombe, ed., *The BFI Companion to the Western*
15. Ethan Mordden, *The Hollywood Studios: House Styles Du*
    (1988); Gabler, *An Empire of Their Own,* 187–236.
16. David Thomson, *Showman: The Life of David O. Selznick* (
17. Rudy Behlmer, *Behind the Scenes* (1989), 107–8; Rudy Beh
    Selznick (1972), 120–21; Edward Buscombe, *Stagecoach* (1!
18. Tino Balio, *United Artists: The Company Built by the Stars*
    Bernstein, "Defiant Cooperation: Walter Wanger and Ind
    wood, 1934–1949 (Ph.D. dissertation, University of Wiscc
19. Balio, *United Artists,* 174.
20. Behlmer, *Behind the Scenes,* 108; "Negative Cost Report,"
    Wisconsin Center for Film and Theater Research, State H
    Madison, Wisconsin.
21. Ford, *Pappy,* 123; "Tentative Budget" for "Stage Coach,
    coach,'" Walter Wanger Papers, Box 93; "'Stage Coach':
    Outline," JFP.
22. Ford, *Pappy,* 123–24; John Wayne interview, JFP.
23. Wayne, "'I Come Ready': An Interview with John Wayne,'
    18–19; John Wayne interview, JFP; Jack Mathis, *Republic*
    (1989), 112.
24. Details of the Ford set from Mary St. John interview; H

25.
26.

27.
28.
29.
30.
31.

32. "

33. I
34. J
35. S
36. I

37. J

38. P
39. C
40. C

41. M
42. B
43. W
44. It
45. V

46. "I

47. M
48. N

Chapt

1. Fo
   an
2. Fo
3. M
   19

4. Mary St. John interview.

5. John Wayne interview, MZP; "Playboy Interview: John Wayne," *Playboy* (May 1971).

6. Donald Hough, "I Can't Act," *Los Angeles Times This Week* magazine (June 29, 1941); *New York Times,* November 10, 1939.

7. "Allegheny Uprising," *The Big Trail* (December 1986).

8. Quoted in Richard Maurice Hurst, *Republic Studios: Between Poverty Row and the Majors* (1979), 15.

9. Mary St. John interview; Frank R. Reid, "A Guide to the Discussion of the Photoplay Based on W. R. Burnett's Novel The Dark Command," *The Dark Command* file, Herrick Library (MHL).

10. *Hollywood Reporter,* April 5, 1940; *Variety,* April 5, 1940; *New York Times,* April 11, 1940; *Motion Picture Herald,* April 13, 1940.

11. *New York Times,* April 11, 1940; *Hollywood Reporter,* April 5, 1940; *Variety,* April 5, 1940.

12. Bill Kelly, "The South Bay Interview: John Wayne," *South Bay* (July 1981), 34–35; Mary St. John interview.

13. Mary St. John interview; Larry Ceplair and Steven Englund, *The Inquisition in Hollywood: Politics in the Film Community, 1930–60* (1983), 94–98.

14. Ceplair and Englund, *The Inquisition in Hollywood,* 47–128, is an indispensable source for politics in Hollywood during the 1930s. Also see Ronald Brownstein, *The Power and the Glitter: The Hollywood-Washington Connection* (1990), 48–103.

15. Quoted in Ceplair and Englund, *The Inquisition in Hollywood,* 84.

16. Ibid., 124.

17. Ibid., 124–28.

18. Ibid., 129–134; quoted in Brownstein, *The Power and the Glitter,* 70.

19. Ford, *Pappy,* 77–79, 150–51; quoted in ibid., 79.

20. Henry Fonda and Howard Teichmann, *Fonda: My Life* (1981), 190; *Playboy* (May 1971); Wayne, "'I Come Ready': An Interview with John Wayne," *Film Heritage* (Summer 1975), 6–7.

21. David F. Prindle, *The Politics of Glamour: Ideology and Democracy in the Screen Actors Guild* (1988), 16–62; John Wayne interview, MZP.

22. *New York Times,* August 19, 1940.

23. Ibid.; Bernard F. Dick, *Radical Innocence: A Critical Study of the Hollywood Ten* (1989), 23–25.

24. Wayne, "'I Come Ready,'" 18.

25. Ibid.; James Reid, "Foreign Mustangs to Marlene," *Screenland Magazine* (November 1940), 26; Zolotow, *Shooting Star,* 166, suggests that Charles Feldman set Duke up with Massen.

26. *New York Times,* May 26, 1940.

27. Aissa Wayne with Steve Delsohn, *John Wayne: My Father* (1991), 134; Mary St. John interview.

28. *New York Times,* August 14, 1940; ibid., August 18, 1940.

29. *Variety,* October 8, 1940; *Hollywood Reporter,* October 8, 1940; *New York Times,* October 9, 1940.

30. *Variety,* October 8, 1940; *Hollywood Reporter,* October 8, 1940; *New York Times,* October 9, 1940; *Variety* (weekly), October 9, 1940.

31. Quoted in Clayton R. Koppes and Gregory D. Black, *Hollywood Goes to War: How Politics, Profits, and Propaganda Shaped World War II Movies* (1987), 25; ibid., 17–36.

32. Mason Wiley and Damien Bona, *Inside Oscar: The Unofficial History of the Academy Awards* (1993), 109–10.

33. Mary St. John interview; Reid, "From Mustangs to Marlene," 27.

34. Quoted in Steven Bach, *Marlene Dietrich: Life and Legend* (1992), 257–58; also see Charles Higham, *Marlene: The Life of Marlene Dietrich* (1977), 196–97.

35. Mary St. John interview; Leo C. Rosten, *Hollywood: The Movie Colony the Movie Makers* (1941), 93–94.

36. Donald Shepherd and Robert Slatzer, *Duke: The Life and Times of John Wayne* (1985), 193–95; Bach, *Marlene Dietrich,* 258; David Thomson, *Showman: The Life of David O. Selznick* (1992), 458.

37. Bach, *Marlene Dietrich,* 258; Shepherd and Slatzer, *Duke,* 194–95. Shepherd and Slatzer suggest that by the spring of 1939 Duke had acquired the services of Charles K. Feldman and formally renegotiated his contract with Republic. An examination of the Feldman papers, however, gives no indication of this. Duke did not renegotiate his contract until 1943, and it is doubtful if he had acquired the services of Feldman as early as 1939.

38. Ibid., 127.

39. Quoted in ibid., 161.

40. Ibid., 144–62.

41. Ibid., 230–47.

42. Anna Lee interview; *New York Times,* November 18, 1940; *Hollywood Reporter,* October 29, 1940; *Variety,* October 29, 1940; *Harrison's Reports,* November 9, 1940; *The New Yorker,* November 30, 1940; *Time* (November 1940), *Seven Sinners* file, MHL.

43. Sally Reid, "'Mother' Wayne," *Photoplay* (October 1940), 26, 97.

44. John Wayne interview, MZP; Mary St. John interview.

45. John Wayne interview, MZP; Pilar Wayne with Axel Thorleifson, *John Wayne: My Life with the Duke* (1987), 30–31, 37–38.

46. John Wayne interview, MZP; Zolotow, *Shooting Star,* 163–66; Mary St. John interview.

47. Mary St. John interview; Harry Carey Jr., interview; Bert Minshall, *On Board with the Duke: John Wayne and the Wild Goose* (1992), 81.

48. Bach, *Marlene Dietrich,* 253–65.

49. Mary St. John interview; Anna Lee interview; Pilar Wayne, *John Wayne,* 39–41; friend's name withheld on request; Barbara Walters's John Wayne interview, ABC Television, 1979; Anna Lee interview.

50. Higham, *Marlene,* 201–2.

51. Henry Hathaway interview, SMU; Harry Carey Jr. interview; Marlene Dietrich, *Marlene* (1987), 183–84. The loss of Duke was a blow to the Leo Morrison Agency, and they put up a fight. They accused Feldman of unethical conduct and Dietrich of luring Wayne away from them. In February 1941 Leo Morrison demanded that the Artists-Managers Guild launch an investigation. Feldman denied enticing Duke away from Morrison. So did Dietrich. Duke told lawyers that he had long been dissatisfied with the Morrison agency, and that his decision to switch agents had been completely aboveboard. The legal proceedings consumed several years during World War II, and Duke found himself being billed by two agents—Feldman and Morrison. He stopped paying Morrison and got Feldman to agree that if an eventual court settlement found in favor of Morrison, Feldman would reimburse the rival agency for all of Duke's fees. See John Wayne to Leo Morrison, August 10, 1941; Leo Morrison to Artists-Managers Guild, February 14, 1941; Charles Feldman to Artists-Managers Guild, September 2, 1941; John Wayne deposition, Septem-

ber 2, 1941; John Wayne to Screen Actors Guild, October 9, 1941; Marlene Dietrich to Screen Actors Guild, October 10, 1941; Frank Belcher to Charles Feldman, September 11, 1944; all in CFP.

52. "Biography of John Wayne," *Paramount* (November 1940), John Wayne file, MHL; quoted in Hurst, *Republic Studios,* 15.

53. Quoted in Roderick Nash, *The Nervous Generation: American Thought, 1917–1930* (1970), 139–40.

54. John Wayne interview, JFP; Harry Carey Jr. interview; "The Shepherd of the Hill," *The Big Trail* (December 1988)

55. Donald Hough, "I Can't Act," *Los Angeles Times* (July 6, 1941); John Wayne interview, JFP.

56. *New York Times,* March 27, 1941.

57. Ibid., May 15, 1941.

58. Ibid., March 27, 1941; ibid., May 15, 1941; Mary St. John interview.

59. Kelly, "The South Bay Interview: John Wayne," *South Bay,* 36.

60. Ibid.; John Wayne interview, Columbia University Oral History Project.

61. Kelly, "The South Bay Interview: John Wayne," *South Bay,* 44; John Wayne interview, Columbia University Oral History Project.

62. Koppes and Black, *Hollywood Goes to War,* 37–39.

63. Ibid., 40; Gerald P. Nye, "War Propaganda: Our Madness Increases as Our Emergency Shrinks," *Vital Speeches* (September 15, 1941), 720–23.

64. Koppes and Black, *Hollywood Goes to War,* 42–47; Ceplair and Englund, *The Inquisition in Hollywood,* 159–61.

Chapter 9. John Wayne and Hollywood Go to War

1. *Los Angeles Times,* December 7, 1941; ibid., December 8, 1941; Editors of *Look, Movie Lot to Beachhead: The Motion Picture Goes to War and Prepares for the Future* (1945), 5.

2. *Los Angeles Times,* December 8, 1941; *Movie Lot to Beachhead,* 5; *Variety,* December 10, 1941.

3. *Los Angeles Times,* December 8, 1941; ibid., December 9, 1941; Allan M. Winkler, *Home Front U.S.A.: America During World War II* (1986), 26.

4. Garth Jowett, *Film: The Democratic Art* (1976), 293; Richard R. Lingeman, *Don't You Know There's a War On? The American Home Front, 1941–1945* (1970), 168, 210; *Variety,* December 10, 1941; ibid., December 17, 1941.

5. *Variety,* December 17, 1941; Rosten, *Hollywood,* 35.

6. *Variety,* December 17, 1941; ibid., December 10, 1941.

7. Shepherd and Slatzer, *Duke: The Life and Times of John Wayne* (1985), 195–96.

8. *Variety,* December 31, 1941.

9. Ibid.; Gabler, *An Empire of Their Own,* 187–236.

10. *Variety,* December 31, 1941.

11. Pilar Wayne, *John Wayne,* 43.

12. Fonda and Howard Teichmann, *Fonda,* 144–47.

13. Ford, *Pappy,* 150–62.

14. Ibid., 163–65.

15. *Movie Lot to Beachhead,* 70–71.

16. Gene Autry interview, Columbia University Oral History Project; Otto Friedrich, *City of*

Nets: A Portrait of Hollywood in the 1940's (1986), 105–7; Leo C. Rosten, "Hollywood Goes to War," *Woman's Home Companion* (December 1942), 14–15, 60–64; Donald Curtis interview, SMU.

17. Lingeman, *Don't You Know There's a War On?*, 111–13.

18. Allan R. Millett and Peter Maslowski, *For the Common Defense: A Military History of the United States of America* (1984), 408.

19. *New York Times*, January 4 and February 9, 1942; Lingeman, *Don't You Know There's a War On?*, 170; "Hollywood in Uniform," *Fortune* (April 1942), 132; Koppes and Black, *Hollywood Goes to War*, 57–58.

20. Lingeman, *Don't You Know There's a War On?*, 175–80.

21. *New York Times*, September 5, 1943; George Montgomery interview, SMU.

22. Pilar Wayne, *John Wayne*, 43–47; Mary St. John interview; Aissa Wayne, *John Wayne, My Father*, 46; Catalina Lawrence interview.

23. John Ford to Mary Ford, October 2, 1941, JFP; John Ford to Mary Ford, March 1942, ibid.

24. John Wayne to John Ford, May 1942, ibid.; Fredrick Spencer to John Wayne, May 27, 1943, ibid.; John Wayne to John Ford, August 1, 1943, ibid.

25. John Wayne interview, JFP.

26. Catalina Lawrence interview.

27. Marion Mitchell Morrison (John Wayne) Classification History. Selective Service Serial No. 2815, Order No. 1619. Selective Service System, Washington, D.C.; Paula Sweeney interview.

28. Cecil B. De Mille Speech to the Associated Motion Picture Advertisers, CBDP; *Photoplay* (June 1942), 25.

29. Koppes and Black, *Hollywood Goes to War*, 48–65; Lingeman, *Don't You Know There's a War On?*, 183; *New York Times*, December 19, 1942.

30. Koppes and Black, *Hollywood Goes to War*, 65–70; Lingeman, *Don't You Know There's a War On?*, 183–93; *Government Information Manual for the Motion Picture Industry*, Record Group 208, OWI files, National Records Center, Suitland, Maryland.

31. Lingeman, *Don't You Know There's a War On?*, 183–92; Koppes and Black, *Hollywood Goes to War*, 82–112, 142–247.

32. For Hollywood as America's "last frontier" see Rosten, *Hollywood*, 3–31.

33. *New York Times*, May 22, 1942.

34. "In Old California," *The Big Trail* (August 1991).

35. *New York Times*, June 18, 1942; ibid., May 22, 1942; *Variety*, April 10, 1942; *Chicago Tribune*, April 5, 1942.

36. "The Spoilers," *The Big Trail* (August 1986), 6; Pilar Wayne, *John Wayne*, 39–42; Marlene Dietrich, *Marlene* (1989), 183–84; Higham, *Marlene*, 201–2.

37. *New York Times*, March 27, 1942.

38. Robert B. Ray, *A Certain Tendency of the Hollywood Cinema, 1930–1980* (1985), 111–21.

39. Ibid.

40. Ibid., 120.

41. Harry B. Price to Earl Minderman, September 22, 1942, Box 3516, Record Group 208, OWI files, National Record Center, Suitland, Maryland (hereafter cited as RG 208, OWI files, NRCS); Marjorie Thorson review of *Flying Tigers*, September 23, 1942, Box 3516, RG 208, OWI files, NRCS.

42. Harvey Greenlaw to Nelson Poynter, November 4, 1942, Box 3516, RG208, OWI

Records, NRCS; Ronald H. Spector, *Eagle Against the Sun: The American War with Japan* (1985), 324–27.

43. *Hollywood Reporter,* September 21, 1942; *Variety,* September 23, 1942; ibid., January 6, 1943.

44. *Hollywood Reporter,* September 21, 1942; *Variety,* September 23, 1942; *New York Times,* October 23, 1942.

45. Mary St. John interview, January 25, 1982; Tichi Wilkerson and Marcia Borie, *The Hollywood Reporter: The Golden Years* (1984), 130; Pilar Wayne, *John Wayne,* 43.

46. Ibid., Aissa Wayne, *John Wayne: My Father,* 30.

47. Gabler, *An Empire of Their Own,* 189, 211–18.

48. Rosten, "Hollywood Goes to War," 14.

49. Marjorie Thorson review of *Reunion in France,* November 24, 1942, Box 3529, RG 208, NRCS.

50. Ibid., "The People Don't Stop Fighting," *The War and Films,* United Nations Information Office, May 15, 1943, Box 3524, RG 208, NRCS; "Weekly Summary and Analysis of Feature Motion Pictures," Report no. 11, Office of War Information, Bureau of Intelligence, Media Division, February 26, 1943, Papers of Philleo Nash, Box 4, Harry S Truman Presidential Library. For an overview of the Bureau of Intelligence see Gregory D. Black and Clayton R. Koppes, "OWI Goes to the Movies: The Bureau of Intelligence's Criticism of Hollywood, 1942–1943," *Prologue* (Spring 1974), 44–59.

51. "The People Don't Stop Fighting," *The War and Films,* United Nations Information Office, May 15, 1943, Box 3524, RG 208, NRCS; *New York Times,* May 5, 1943; *Variety,* January 5, 1944.

52. Lillian Bergquist review of *Pittsburgh,* November 30, 1942, Box 3524, RG 208, NRCS.

53. Nelson Poynter to Cliff Work, December 2, 1942, Box 3524, RG 208, NRCS; Cliff Work to Nelson Poynter, December 4, 1942, ibid.; Robert Fellows to Nelson Poynter, December 4, 1942, ibid.; Nelson Poynter to Lowell Mellett, December 2, 1942, ibid.; Koppes and Black, *Hollywood Goes to War,* 97–98.

54. Koppes and Black, *Hollywood Goes to War,* 98; *Motion Picture Herald,* December 5, 1942; *Variety,* November 30, 1942; *New York Times,* February 25, 1943.

55. Koppes and Black, *Hollywood Goes to War,* 48–141. Of course the reaction of the film industry did not hinge on the failure of *Pittsburgh,* but the film did indicate the existence of larger problems between Hollywood and Washington.

56. Koppes and Black, "OWI Goes to the Movies," 56–57; Koppes and Black, *Hollywood Goes to War,* 287–96.

57. *New York Times,* January 22, 1943.

Chapter 10. In the Catbird Seat

1. Lingeman, *Don't You Know There's a War On?,* 234–70.

2. Tino Balio, ed., *The American Film Industry* (1976), 225–26; Balio, *United Artists,* 170; Robert Sklar, *Movie-Made America: A Cultural History of American Movies* (1975), 250; "Hollywood in Uniform," *Fortune* (April 1942), 93; Gregory D. Black and Clayton R. Koppes, "OWI Goes to the Movies: The Bureau of Intelligence's Criticism of Hollywood, 1942–43," *Prologue* (Spring 1974), 48–49.

3. *Movie Lot to Beachhead* 228–43.

4. Ibid., 229, 240–41; Friedrich, *City of Nets,* 108–10.

5. Mary Ford to John Ford, November 4, 1943, JFP; Mary Ford to John Ford, November 22, 1943, ibid.; Mary Ford to John Ford, November 30, 1943, ibid.

6. Rosten, "Hollywood Goes to War," 14; Lingeman, *Don't You Know There's a War On?*, 169.

7. Frank S. Nugent, "Hollywood Counts the Pennies," *New York Times Magazine* (August 30, 1942), 15.

8. Ibid., 14–15, 28; Lingeman, *Don't You Know There's a War On?*, 176–77.

9. Nugent, "Hollywood Counts the Pennies," 14; Lingeman, *Don't You Know There's a War On?*, 176–77; Garth Jowett, *Film: The Democratic Art* (1976), 309–10.

10. "Hollywood in Uniform," 95.

11. Ibid., 95; Ford, *Pappy*, 181; Rosten, *Hollywood*, 212–28.

12. Kyle Crichton, "Hollywood Holocaust," *Collier's* (February 13, 1943), 16, 23.

13. Ibid.

14. Ford, *Pappy*, 181.

15. Lillian R. Bergquist review of *A Lady Takes a Chance*, July 15, 1943, Box 3520, RG 208, OWI files, NRCS.

16. *New York Times*, September 16, 1943; *Variety*, January 5, 1944; James Agee, *Agee on Film: Essays and Reviews by James Agee*, vol. 1 (1958), 53–54.

17. Koppes and Black, *Hollywood Goes to War*, Clayton G. Koppes and Gregory D. Black., "What to Show the World: The Office of War Information and Hollywood, 1942–1945," *Journal of American History* 64 (1977), 101.

18. Tichi Wilkerson and Marcia Borie, *The Hollywood Reporter: The Golden Years* (1984), 144–46; William Manchester, *The Glory and the Dream: A Narrative of American History, 1932–1972* (1974), 307–9.

19. Lingeman, *Don't You Know There's a War On?*, 267–70.

20. Leonard J. Leff and Jerold L. Simmons, *The Dame in the Kimono: Hollywood, Censorship, and the Production Code from the 1920s to the 1960s* (1990), 125–26.

21. Mary St. John interview; Richard English, "The Man Who Worries for the Stars," *Saturday Evening Post* (February 24, 1951), 32–33.

22. English, "The Man Who Worries for the Stars," 75.

23. Ibid., 32–33, 67, 70–75; *Variety*, August 13, 1973.

24. Art LaShells to John Ford, April 26, 1940, JFP; Zolotow, *Shooting Star*, 173–74.

25. Zolotow, *Shooting Star*, 173–74; English, "The Man Who Worries for the Stars," 71.

26. Mary St. John interview.

27. Ibid., Catalina Lawrence interview.

28. Mary St. John interview; Catalina Lawrence interview; Pilar Wayne, *John Wayne*, 45; Zolotow, *Shooting Star*, 176; Ruth Waterbury, "Sunrise Serenade," *Photoplay*, Constance McCormick Collection, USC.

29. Waterbury, "Sunrise Serenade"; Pilar Wayne, *John Wayne*, 45; Mary St. John interview; Catalina Lawrence interview.

30. Mary St. John interview.

31. Louella O. Parsons, "John Wayne," *Los Angeles Times*, Constance McCormick Collection, USC.

32. Shepherd and Slatzer, *Duke*, 202–6, 425; Morella, *Loretta Young*, 171.

33. Shepherd and Slatzer, *Duke*, 202–6.

34. Mary St. John interview; Zolotow, *Shooting Star*, 180–81; John Wayne to John Ford, August 1, 1943, JFP; Jack Mathis, *Republic Confidential*, vol. 2 *The Players* (1992), 2.

35. Mary St. John interview; Ford, *Pappy*, 98–99, 103.

36. Catalina Lawrence interview; Ford, *Pappy,* 22, 181.

37. Mary Ford to John Ford, June 1, 1943, JFP.

38. John Ford to John Wayne, July 9, 1943, ibid.; John Wayne to John Ford, August 1, 1943, ibid.

39. Morella, *Loretta Young,* 40–48; Grant Withers Clipping File, Academy of Motion Picture Arts and Sciences, MHL.

40. Leff and Simmons, *The Dame in the Kimono,* 5.

41. Samuel Marx and Joyce Vanderveen, *Deadly Illusions: Jean Harlow and the Murder of Paul Bern* (1990), 171–72.

42. Memo on John Wayne contracts, File 1919, CFP.

43. Zolotow, *Shooting Star,* 186–87.

44. Fredrick Spencer to John Wayne, May 27, 1943, JFP; John Wayne to John Ford, August 1, 1943, ibid.

45. Friedrich, *City of Nets,* 169–75, 185–92; Leff and Simmons, *The Dame in the Kimono,* 109–40; *New York Times,* February 7, 1943; ibid., June 11, 1943; ibid., June 17, 1943.

46. Peg Fenwick review of *War of the Wildcats,* March 15, 1943, Box 3519, RG 208, OWI files, NRCS (*War of the Wildcats* was the working title for the movie that was released as *In Old Oklahoma*). In addition to a general review of the script, the review contains separate reports evaluating the domestic and foreign impact the project was likely to have.

47. Ibid.

48. Sidney Harmon to Walter Goetz, October 29, 1943, Box 3519, RG 208, OWI files, NRCS; Sandy Roth review of *In Old Oklahoma,* October 27, 1943, ibid.; *Variety,* January 5, 1944; *New York Times,* December 6, 1943; *Hollywood Reporter,* October 20, 1943.

49. *Hollywood Reporter,* October 20, 1943.

50. John Wayne to John Ford, August 1, 1943, JFP; Marion Mitchell Morrison (John Wayne) Classification History, Selective Service Serial No. 2815, Order No. 1619, Selective Service System, Washington, D.C.

51. Koppes and Black, *Hollywood Goes to War,* 113–41; "What to Show the World," 87–105.

52. Koppes and Black, *Hollywood Goes to War,* 113, 140–41; "What to Show the World," 103–5.

53. Koppes and Black, "What to Show the World," 100–101; *Hollywood Goes to War,* 127–28; "OWI Goes to the Movies," 50.

54. Eleanor Berneis review of the script for *The Fighting Seabees,* September 3, 1943, Box 3516, RG 208, OWI files, NRCS; William S. Cunningham to Walter Goetz, September 11, 1943, ibid.; Eleanor Berneis review of the revised script of *The Fighting Seabees,* October 8, 1943, ibid.; Sidney Harmon to Walter Goetz, October 12, 1943, ibid.; Ulric Bell to M. J. Siegel, October 21, 1943, ibid.; Albert J. Cohen to Ulric Bell, October 22, 1943, ibid.

55. Marion Michelle review of *The Fighting Seabees,* January 18, 1944, Box 3516, RG 208, OWI files, NRCS; William Roberts to Walter Goetz, January 24, 1944, ibid.; *New York Times,* March 26, 1944; *Variety,* October 29, 1942; Hurst, *Republic Studios,* 67–68; *Variety, The Fighting Seabees* clipping file, MHL.

56. *Los Angeles Times,* January 28, 1944; *Los Angeles Examiner,* January 18, 1944.

57. *Los Angeles Examiner,* March 12, 1944; *Los Angeles Herald,* July 7, 1944; *Los Angeles Times,* October 7, 1944; *Los Angeles Examiner,* October 8, 1944.

58. Mary Ford to John Ford, October 20, 1943, JFP; Mary Ford to John Ford, November 18, 1943, ibid.

59. Mary Ford to John Ford, November 22, 1943, JFP; Mary Ford to John Ford, November 30, 1943, ibid.; Mary Ford to John Ford, Christmas 1943, ibid.; Ford, *Pappy*, 181–82.

60. Mary St. John interview.

61. Ford, *Pappy*, 182.

62. Quoted in Tuska, *The Vanishing Legion*, 94; Mary St. John interview.

63. *Movie Lot to Beachhead*, 82–83.

64. Ibid.

65. Travel Orders for Marion Mitchell Morrison, December 6, 1943, War Department, Records of the Adjutant General's Office 230.42, Operations Branch, National Archives, Washington, D.C.; John Wayne interview, JFP; Ford, *Pappy*, 182; certificate from William J. Donovan to John Wayne, October 1, 1945, JFP.

66. *Los Angeles Herald*, March 22, 1944; *Los Angeles Times*, March 22, 1944, JFP; John Wayne to Mary Ford, January 19, 1944; Sears Tower News, John Wayne file, Academy of Motion Picture Arts and Sciences, MHL.

67. *Los Angeles Times*, March 22, 1944; *Los Angeles Herald*, March 22, 1944.

68. "John Wayne Comes Home," *Screen Guide* (1944), Constance McCormick Collections, USC.

69. Marion Mitchell Morrison (John Wayne) Classification History, Selective Service Serial No. 2815, Order No. 1619, Selective Service System, Washington, D.C.

70. Sandy B. Jones review of the script for *Tall in the Saddle*, March 28, 1944, Box 3527, RG 208, OWI files, NRCS; Gene Kern to William Gordon, March 31, 1944, ibid.; Virginia Richardson review of *Tall in the Saddle*, September 16, 1944, ibid.; Arnold M. Picker to Vladimir Lissim, May 5, 1945, ibid.; Motion Picture Clearance, Far East, *Tall in the Saddle*, August 22, 1945, ibid.; Marion Michelle review of the script of *Flame of the Barbary Coast*, June 14, 1944, Box 3516, RG 208, OWI files, NRCS; William Roberts to Steve Goodman, June 15, 1944, ibid.; Marion Michelle review of *Flame of the Barbary Coast*, August 24, 1944, ibid.

71. Memo on John Wayne's contracts, 1946, File 1919, CFP; "Tall in the Saddle," *The Big Trail* (April 1992).

72. *New York Times*, December 15, 1944; ibid., May 28, 1945.

73. Ray Kellogg to John Ford, July 29, 1944, JFP; "The Man with The Trigger-Happy Tongue," *TV Guide* (June 14, 1958), 23.

74. Marion Mitchell Morrison (John Wayne) Classification History, Selective Service Serial No. 2815, Order No. 1619, Selective Service System, Washington, D.C.

75. *Los Angeles Times*, June 5, 1943; ibid., October 31, 1943; ibid., November 1, 1944; *Los Angeles Examiner*, November 1, 1944; *Hollywood Citizen News*, October 31, 1944; *Los Angeles Times*, November 30, 1944. The judge issued an interlocutory decree, which became official a year later.

76. *Los Angeles Times*, November 1, 1944; Helen Itria, "Big John," *Look* (August 11, 1953), 67–71.

77. Mary St. John interview; Louis Johnson interview; Joe De Franco interview; Pilar Wayne, *John Wayne*, 139; Aissa Wayne, *John Wayne*, 58.

78. Ronald H. Spector, *Eagle Against the Sun: The American War with Japan* (1985), 427–28.

79. Ben Barzman, "The Duke & Me," *Los Angeles Magazine* (January 1989), John Wayne clippings file, MHL.

80. William Cunningham to Claude Buss, July 25, 1944, Box 3511, RG 208, OWI files, NRCS; William Cunningham to Claude Buss, July 28, 1944, ibid.; Claude Buss to William Cunningham, July 26, 1944, ibid.; Barzman, "The Duke & Me."

81. Barzman, "The Duke & Me"; Ceplair and Englund, *The Inquisition in Hollywood,* 314–15, 400–402; Victor S. Navasky, *Naming Names* (1980), 283; Edward Dmytryk interview, CU.

82. Barzman, "The Duke & Me"; Edward Dmytryk interview, SMU.

83. Ibid.

84. Interview with John Wayne, *Playboy* (May 1971), 88.

85. John W. Dower, *War Without Mercy: Race and Power in the Pacific War* (1986), 77–93; Koppes and Black, *Hollywood Goes to War,* 248–77.

86. "Speaking of Pictures," *Life* (November 12, 1942), 12–15; Koppes and Black, *Hollywood Goes to War,* 253–54, 271–75.

87. Eleanor Berneis review of the script of *The Invisible Army*—Part I (later renamed *Back to Bataan*), September 21, 1944, Box 3511, RG 208, OWI files, NRCS; Eleanor Berneis review of *The Invisible Army*—Part II, September 28, 1944, ibid.; Claude A. Buss to William Cunningham, October 4, 1944, ibid.; Gene Kern to William Gordon, October 9, 1944, ibid.; Eleanor Berneis review of the script of *The Invisible Army* (Second Version), December 7, 1944, ibid.; Gene Kern review of *Back to Bataan,* May 4, 1945, ibid.; Claude A. Buss to William S. Cunningham, June 4, 1945, ibid.; Kramer to Peter Picker, July 26, 1945, ibid.

88. *Hollywood Reporter,* May 19, 1949; *Liberty,* July 14, 1945; *Hollywood Citizen-News,* July 17, 1945; *Los Angeles Examiner,* July 19, 1945; *Los Angeles Times,* July 19, 1945; *New York Herald Tribune,* September 13, 1945; *New York Times,* September 13, 1945.

Chapter 11. New Beginnings and Dead Ends

1. Richard Fleischer, *Just Tell Me When to Cry: A Memoir* (1993), 9–12.

2. Ibid., 12–13.

3. Ford, *Pappy,* 162–90.

4. James Forrestal to Charles Cheston, September 12, 1944, JFP; quoted in Ford, *Pappy,* 192; John Ford to James McGuinness, August 5, 1943, JFP; John Ford to Spig Wead, February 11, 1944, ibid; John Ford to Dudley Nichols, March 22, 1943, ibid.

5. James McGuinness to John Ford [March 1944], JFP.

6. Ford, *Pappy,* 193–97.

7. Ibid., 197–98; *They Were Expendable* Pressbook, *They Were Expendable* file, MHL.

8. In 1995, the Smithsonian's Air and Space Museum sponsored a special exhibit—including a display of the *Enola Gay*'s fuselage—on the fiftieth anniversary of the atomic bombing of Hiroshima and Nagasaki. The exhibition ignited a firestorm of political controversy. Conventional wisdom had long held that President Harry Truman's decision to employ nuclear weapons brought about a quick surrender in August 1945, preventing a bloody American invasion of Japan and the loss of hundreds of thousands, and perhaps millions, of Japanese and American lives. Some revisionist historians, such as Barton Bernstein of Stanford University, argue that Truman knew that an invasion of Japan would entail only minimal American casualties and dropped the atomic bombs for other reasons. In an attempt to walk a politically correct line, the Smithsonian Institution tried to give equal weight to both points of view. American veterans' groups, such as the American Legion and the Veterans of Foreign Wars, were outraged and launched bitter protests against the exhibition. Politicians ran for cover and the Smithsonian eventually cancelled the exhibit.

9. W. L. White, *They Were Expendable* (1942), 3–4.

10. Peggy Gould review of script of *They Were Expendable,* November 21, 1944, Box 3516, RG 208, OWI files, NRCS; William S. Cunningham to Captain Louis S. Chappelear Jr., November 22, 1944, ibid.

11. Quoted in Gallagher, *John Ford,* 221; John Ford to Mary Ford, February 19, 1945, JFP; John Ford to Mary Ford, February 28, 1945, ibid.

12. John Wayne interview, JFP; Harry Carey Jr. interview.

13. Ford, *Pappy,* 190–201.

14. Harry Carey Jr. interview.

15. Quoted in Ford, *Pappy,* 200.

16. Naval Command to Charles Chester, May 22, 1945, JFP; John C. Wilson, M.D., To Whom It May Concern, July 9, 1945, ibid.; John Wayne interview, ibid.; Marion Mitchell Morrison (John Wayne) Classification History, Selective Service Serial No. 2815, Order No. 1619, Selective Service System, Washington, D.C.

17. Quoted in Ed Lowry, "Program Notes: *They Were Expendable,*" *Cinema Texas* (March 25, 1976), *They Were Expendable* file, MHL.

18. James McGuinness to John Ford, September 24, 1945, JFP; *New York Times,* December 17, 1945; *New York Herald Tribune,* December 17, 1945; *New York Morning Telegraph,* December 21, 1945; *PM Reviews,* December 21, 1945.

19. John Wayne interview, JFP; Gallagher, *John Ford,* 499; *Variety,* January 8, 1947.

20. Allen Eyles, *John Wayne and the Movies* (1976), 94; Mary St. John interview; Harry Carey Jr. interview.

21. David Wallechinsky, *The Complete Book of the Olympics* (1984), 582; Hurst, *Republic Studios,* 20–21; Joseph Kane interview in Todd McCarthy and Charles Flynn, eds., *King of the B's: Working Within the Hollywood System* (1975), 321.

22. Joseph Kane interview, *King of the B's,* 322.

23. Peggy Shepherd review of script of *Dakota,* June 20, 1945, Records Group 208, OWI files, NRCS; William Roberts to Steve Goodman, June 30, 1945, ibid.; Virginia Richardson review of *Dakota,* October 11, 1945, ibid.; *Hollywood Review,* November 5, 1945; *New York Times,* December 17, 1945.

24. Charles Flynn and Todd McCarthy, "The Economic Imperative: Why Was the B Movie Necessary?" in Flynn and McCarthy, *King of the B's,* 25–31.

25. Memo on the contracts of John Wayne, 1948, CFP.

26. Ibid.

27. *New York Times,* June 8, 1946.

28. *Variety,* January 8, 1947.

29. Mary St. John interview; "Without Reservations," *The Big Trail* (October 1988); Mervyn LeRoy, *Mervyn LeRoy: Take One* (1974), 164.

30. *Hollywood Review,* November 5, 1945.

31. *Los Angeles Examiner,* January 1946, Constance McCormick Collection, University of Southern California; ibid., January 18, 1946; *Los Angeles Times,* January 17, 1946.

32. Hedda Hopper newspaper article, January 1946, John Wayne file, MHL; *Los Angeles Examiner,* January 1946, Constance McCormick Collection, USC; *Los Angeles Times,* January 17, 1946.

33. Except when noted, details of Wayne's relationship with Chata and her mother come from Mary St. John interview and Catalina Lawrence interview; Harry Carey Jr. interview was also helpful.

34. Mary St. John interview; Shepherd and Slatzer, *Duke,* 216.

35. Catalina Lawrence interview.

36. Mary St. John interview.

37. T. F. James, "The Man Who Talks Back to John Wayne," *Cosmopolitan* (August 1960), 60–65; "Biography of James Edward Grant," James Edward Grant file, MHL.

38. *Los Angeles Examiner,* September 8, 1946.

39. "The Wages of Virtue," *Time* (March 3, 1952), 66; Harry Carey Jr. interview; Bill Kelly, "The South Bay Interview: John Wayne," *South Bay* (July 1981), 69.

40. Catalina Lawrence interview; "Hedda Hopper's Hollywood," January 29, 1956, Gail Russell file, MHL; "Gail Russell Death Autopsy Scheduled" [undated], ibid.; Andrew J. Fenady, "Gail Russell by Candlelight," *Variety* (October 26, 1982); Mary St. John interview.

41. *Chicago Tribune,* May 11, 1947.

42. *New York Times,* March 3, 1947; "Angel and the Badman," *Focus on Film* (Autumn 1972), John Wayne file, MHL; *Hollywood Reporter,* February 6, 1947.

43. *Los Angeles Examiner,* October 21, 1953; Mary St. John interview.

44. *Los Angeles Examiner,* October 21, 1953; ibid., October 29, 1953; Mary St. John interview.

45. Except when noted, the conflict over Gail Russell is based on *Los Angeles Herald Express,* October 20, 1953; ibid., October 28, 1953; *Los Angeles Daily News,* October 21, 1953; *Los Angeles Times,* October 21, 1953; ibid., October 29, 1953; *Los Angeles Examiner,* October 21, 1953; ibid., October 29, 1953.

46. Mary St. John interview; Catalina Lawrence interview; Pilar Wayne, *John Wayne,* 49–50; Aissa Wayne, *John Wayne, My Father,* 11.

47. *Los Angeles Examiner,* October 21, 1953; ibid., October 29, 1953; *Los Angeles Times,* October 29, 1953; Catalina Lawrence interview.

48. *New York Times,* January 22, 1947; Catalina Lawrence interview.

49. Gerald Eskenazi, *The Lip: A Biography of Leo Durocher* (1993), 203–5; Catalina Lawrence interview.

50. *New York Times,* December 26, 1947; Agee, *Agee on Film,* vol. 1, 296.

51. *Variety,* January 5, 1947; "Tycoon," *The Big Trail* (October 1989); Mary St. John interview.

Chapter 12. *"All I Can See Is the Flags"*

1. Anna Lee interview; Anna Lee interview in Tim Lilley, ed., *Campfires Rekindled* (1994), 86.

2. Anna Lee interview; Anna Lee interview, SMU.

3. James Warner Bellah, "Massacre," *Saturday Evening Post* (February 22, 1947), 18–19, 140–46.

4. Carey Jr., *Company of Heroes,* 7.

5. Joseph McBride, *Hawks on Hawks* (1982), 116.

6. Mary St. John interview; Anna Lee interview.

7. Ford, *Pappy,* 216–17.

8. John Agar interview; Ronald L. Davis, *John Ford: Hollywood's Old Master* (1995), 210–11.

9. Quoted in Ford, *Pappy,* 217; John Agar interview.

10. Quoted in Davis, *John Ford,* 209.

11. Ibid., 208–9.

12. *Fort Apache* production files, JFP.

13. Fonda and Teichmann, *Fonda: My Life,* 189–90.

14. Dan Ford interview.

15. Bogdanovich, *John Ford,* 86.

16. *New York Times*, June 25, 1948; *Motion Picture Herald*, March 13, 1948; *Hollywood Reporter*, March 10, 1948; *Los Angeles Times*, May 28, 1948; *Variety*, January 5, 1949.

17. Gerald Mast, *Howard Hawks, Storyteller* (1982), 297; Robert Sklar, "Empire of the West: *Red River*," in John E. O'Connor and Martin A. Jackson, eds., *American History/American Film: Interpreting the Hollywood Image* (1988), 170–71.

18. John Wayne interview, MZP; Wayne, "'I Come Ready,'" 14–15; Zolotow, *Shooting Star*, 230–31.

19. "John Wayne Asks for $100,000 Damages," April 10, 1948, unidentified clipping in the John Wayne file, MHL; Joseph McBride, *Hawks on Hawks* (1982), 116; Mary St. John interview.

20. Patricia Bosworth, *Montgomery Clift: A Biography* (1978), 118–19.

21. Mary St. John interview; Ralph Wingfield interview.

22. Mary St. John interview; McBride, *Hawks on Hawks*, 123; Robert LaGuardia, *Monte: A Biography of Montgomery Clift* (1977), 53.

23. LaGuardia, *Monte*, 55–56; McBride, *Hawks on Hawks*, 123.

24. McBride, *Hawks on Hawks*, 123.

25. Howard Hawks interview, Howard Hawks Papers, BYU.

26. Naomi Goodwin and Michael Wise, "An Interview with Howard Hawks," *Take One* (November-December 1971), 21.

27. Bosworth, *Montgomery Clift*, 120–21.

28. John Wayne interview, JFP; Mary St. John interview.

29. Bosworth, *Montgomery Clift*, 120–21.

30. Sklar, "Empire of the West," 170–72; Mast, *Howard Hawks*, 297–99.

31. Mast, *Howard Hawks*, 343–45.

32. Ibid., 333–37.

33. Ibid. "'I Come Ready,'" 14.

34. Mast, *Howard Hawks*, 299–300.

35. Kyle Crichton, *Collier's* (October 9, 1948), 64; *New York Times*, October 1, 1948; *Variety* (Daily), July 12, 1948; *Hollywood Reporter*, July 12, 1948; *Film Daily*, July 14, 1948; see also reviews from *Variety*, *Showmen's Trade Review*, *Motion Picture Daily*, and *Motion Picture Herald* in the file on *Red River* in the United Artists Collection, Wisconsin Center for Film and Theater Research, Wisconsin State Historical Society.

36. *Variety*, July 12, 1948; *Showmen's Trade Review*, *Red River* file, Wisconsin State Historical Society; quoted in Mast, *Howard Hawks*, 329.

37. Mast, *Howard Hawks*, 51–52, 302–3, 329; Jeanine Basinger, "John Wayne: An Appreciation," *American Film* (June 1976), 53.

38. Harry E. Soholar to Frank Belcher, July 13, 1951, Howard Hawks Papers, Brigham Young University; *Variety*, January 5, 1949.

39. Zolotow, *Shooting Star*, 247; *New York Times*, November 7, 1948.

40. Ibid.

41. Carey, *Company of Heroes* (1994), 2–4; Harry Carey Jr. interview.

42. Bogdanovich, *John Ford*, 43; Carey, *Company of Heroes*, 4–5; Harry Carey Jr. interview.

43. Harry Carey Jr. interview; Carey, *Company of Heroes*, 15–17.

44. Ibid., 12–43.

45. Harry Carey Jr. interview.

46. Quoted in Ford, *Pappy*, 228; Carey, *Company of Heroes*, 22–23.

47. Carey, *Company of Heroes*, 22–23.

48. Ibid., 26.

49. Details on the domino games come from John Wayne interview, JFP; Harry Carey Jr. interview; and Carey, *Company of Heroes,* 27–30.

50. Mildred Natwick interview, SMU.

51. Carey, *Company of Heroes,* 41–43.

52. Gallagher, *John Ford,* 261.

53. Quoted in "The Wake of the Red Witch," *The Big Trail* (February 1987); *Variety,* January 4, 1950; Mary St. John interview.

54. Quoted in Ford, *Pappy,* 228; James Warner Bellah notes for *She Wore a Yellow Ribbon,* JFP; Mary St. John interview.

55. Ford, *Pappy,* 228–9; Bogdanovich, *John Ford,* 87.

56. Ford, *Pappy,* 229; Davis, *John Ford,* 225–26.

57. Daily life on the set is from Carey, *Company of Heroes,* 55–71; Harry Carey Jr. interview; Harry Carey Jr. interview, SMU; Ben Johnson interview, SMU; Ben Johnson interview, JFP.

58. Carey, *Company of Heroes,* 63–65.

59. *Hollywood Reporter,* July 27, 1949; *Variety,* July 27, 1949; *Los Angeles Times,* October 27, 1949; *Variety,* January 4, 1950.

60. Wayne, "'I Come Ready,'" 31; Mary St. John interview; Harry Carey Jr. interview.

61. *Los Angeles Times,* c. 1948–49, Constance McCormick Collection, USC; *Motion Picture Herald,* September 10, 1949.

62. John Boswell and Jay David, *Duke: The John Wayne Album* (1979), 76.

63. Marie Windsor interview in Tim Lilley, ed., *Campfires Rekindled* (1994), 158; *Variety,* January 4, 1950.

64. Lawrence Suid, *Guts and Glory: Great American War Movies* (1978), 94.

65. Ibid., 92; *New York Times,* August 7, 1949.

66. "The Making of *Sands of Iwo Jima*" (1994); quoted in Suid, *Guts and Glory,* 96–97.

67. *New York Times,* August 7, 1949.

68. Ibid.

69. Mary St. John interview; John Agar interview; John Agar interview, Tim Lilley, ed., *Campfire Conversations* (1992), 8; "The Making of *Sands of Iwo Jima.*"

70. Hurst, *Republic Studios,* 190–91; Mason Wiley and Damien Bona, *Inside Oscar: The Unofficial History of the Academy Awards* (1993), 194; "The Making of *Sands of Iwo Jima.*"

71. *New York Times,* December 31, 1949; Mary St. John interview.

72. *Variety,* January 3, 1951; Boswell and David, *Duke,* 76.

73. Suid, *Guts and Glory,* 92.

74. Ford, *Pappy,* 232–33.

75. Carey, *Company of Heroes,* 117–18; Harry Carey Jr. interview; Ford, *Pappy,* 233.

76. Davis, *John Ford,* 240; "Bad Chuck" Roberson with Bodie Thoene, *The Fall Guy: 30 Years as Duke's Double* (1980), 69; Carey, *Company of Heroes,* 118–19.

77. The details of the Johnson-Ford incident come from Carey, *Company of Heroes,* 120–22; Harry Carey Jr. interview; Ben Johnson interview, SMU. Johnson later recalled that either Wayne or Bond made the comment, but since Wayne was sitting next to Ford and Bond was not in *Rio Grande* his version was probably, as Dobe Carey said, "mis-remembered."

78. Quoted in Davis, *John Ford,* 238.

79. Quoted in ibid., 204; Ford, *Pappy,* 113–14; John H. Lenihan, *Showdown: Confronting Modern America in the Western Film* (1980), 27–31.

80. *Daily Mail,* January 18, 1974, quoted in Tony Crawley, ed., *Chambers Film Quotes* (1991), 224.

Chapter 13. A Different War

1. John Wayne to Famous Artists [Charles K. Feldman's agency], October 21, 1948, CFP; Mary St. John interview.
2. Charles K. Feldman to John Wayne, October 22, 1948, CFP.
3. Except where mentioned, the emergence of the Motion Picture Alliance for the Preservation of American Ideals is from *Variety* (February 9, 1944); "The Battle of Hollywood," *Time* (February 14, 1944), 23; Matthew Bernstein, *Walter Wanger: Hollywood Independent* (1994), 193; R. B. Hood to J. Edgar Hoover (February 9, 1944), Motion Picture Alliance for the Preservation of American Ideals file (hereafter referred to as Alliance file), FBI; Ronald Brownstein, *The Power and the Glitter: The Hollywood-Washington Connection* (1992), 88–92.
4. Quoted in Ceplair and Englund, *The Inquisition in Hollywood,* 209.
5. Ibid., 210.
6. Gabler, *An Empire of Their Own,* 79–119, 209–36.
7. R. B. Hood to J. Edgar Hoover, March 22, 1944, Alliance file, FBI; quoted in Ceplair and Englund, *The Inquisition in Hollywood,* 157.
8. Brownstein, *The Power and the Glitter,* 77–78, 88; Mary St. John interview.
9. "Our Own First," *Congressional Record,* appendix (March 7, 1944), Alliance file, FBI; R. B. Hood to J. Edgar Hoover, March 22, 1944, ibid.; R. B. Hood to J. Edgar Hoover, May 10, 1944, ibid; "Repudiation of a Smear," ibid; "Time to Name Names," *Variety,* March 15, 1944, ibid; R. B. Hood to J. Edgar Hoover, June 8, 1944, ibid; D. M. Ladd to J. Edgar Hoover, July 20, 1944, ibid.
10. Quoted in the *Los Angeles Examiner,* April 29, 1944, and contained in R. B. Hood to J. Edgar Hoover, May 10, 1944, Alliance file, FBI.
11. John Wayne interview, JFP.
12. R. B. Hood to J. Edgar Hoover, February 5, 1945, Alliance file, FBI.
13. Recruitment pamphlet, Motion Picture Alliance for the Preservation of American Ideals, Alliance file, FBI; Ceplair and Englund, *The Inquisition in Hollywood,* 262.
14. Ceplair and Englund, *The Inquisition in Hollywood,* 254–98; Brownstein, *The Power and the Glitter,* 113.
15. *Los Angeles Examiner,* March 24, 1949; *Hollywood Citizen-News,* March 25, 1949; Zolotow, *Shooting Star,* 256–57.
16. John Wayne interview, MZP.
17. *Playboy* (May 1971), 82; Wayne, "'I Come Ready,'" 32.
18. Harold M. Groves, *Postwar Taxation and Economic Progress* (1946), 176; Mary St. John interview; Joe De Franco interview; John Ford to John Wayne, January 10, 1957, JFP.
19. Lawrence Christon, "This Is John Wayne—Fer Chrissake," *Orange County Illustrated* (January 1977), 46; "John Wayne as the Last Hero," *Time,* (August 8, 1969), 55; Avery Rennick interview; Joe De Franco interview; Danko Gurovich interview.
20. Mary St. John interview.
21. Several sources, including one interview with Wayne, say that he only served three terms as president, but in June 1953, when Roy Brewer became president of the alliance, he succeeded John Wayne. See *Hollywood Reporter,* June 6, 1953; ibid., June 4, 1953; *Los Angeles Times,* June 6, 1953; Rob Bryant, "The Duke," *Orange County Newport Life Magazine* (December 1976), 9.
22. Pilar Wayne, *John Wayne,* 154; Zolotow, *Shooting Star,* 116, 118, 170–71, 259; Mary St. John interview.

23. Ceplair and Englund, *The Inquisition in Hollywood,* 65–66, 328–31, 455.

24. John Wayne interview, JFP; Brownstein, *The Power and the Glitter,* 115; *Hollywood Reporter,* December 11, 1950.

25. Bryant, "The Duke," *Orange County Newport Life Magazine,* 8.

26. Mary St. John interview; Zolotow, *Shooting Star,* 256.

27. Zolotow, *Shooting Star,* 256, *Daily Variety,* July 20, 1950; *Los Angeles Times,* July 20, 1950; *Hollywood Reporter,* July 20, 1950.

28. *Los Angeles Evening Herald & Express,* May 15, 1950; *Hollywood Citizen-News,* May 15, 1950.

29. Lester Cole, *Hollywood Red* (1981), 320; Ceplair and Englund, *The Inquisition in Hollywood,* 361–71.

30. Ceplair and Englund, *The Inquisition in Hollywood,* 371–79, Victor Navasky, *Naming Names* (1980), 342.

31. Quoted in Navasky, *Naming Names,* 199–222.

32. Ibid., 268–73, 249–52.

33. Quoted in Max M. Kampelman, *The Communist Party vs. the CIO: A Study in Power Politics* (1957), 110; *CIO News,* November 20, 1950.

34. Frank J. Donner, *The Age of Surveillance: The Aims and Methods of America's Political Intelligence System* (1981), 144–47; also see David Caute, *The Great Fear: The Anti-Communist Purge Under Truman and Eisenhower* (1978); and Ellen W. Schrecker, *No Ivy Tower: McCarthyism and the Universities* (1986).

35. Quoted in Ceplair and Englund, *The Inquisition in Hollywood,* 376.

36. Ibid., 386–397; Navasky, *Naming Names,* 97–143.

37. Quoted in Gallagher, *John Ford,* 339; quoted in Tom Stempel, *Screenwriter: The Life and Times of Nunnally Johnson* (1980), 123–24; Elizabeth Allen interview, JFP.

38. *New York Times,* March 22, 1951; Navasky, *Naming Names,* vii–x; "John Wayne as the Last Hero," *Time,* 55.

39. *New York Times,* March 23, 1951.

40. John Wayne interview, MZP; John Wayne interview, JFP; Mary St. John interview.

41. John Wayne interview, JFP; George Eells, *Hedda and Louella* (1972), 292–293; *Los Angeles Times,* March 23, 1951; ibid., March 30, 1951; *Los Angeles Daily News,* March 30, 1952.

42. Eells, *Hedda and Louella,* 285; *Los Angeles Times,* March 23, 1951; Mary St. John interview.

43. Geraldine Page interview, CU.

44. *Playboy* (May 1971), 82; Anthony Holden, *Behind the Oscar: The Secret History of the Academy Awards* (1991), 200–202.

45. Tony Thomas, *Howard Hughes in Hollywood* (1985), 103–04; Charles Higham, *Howard Hughes: The Secret Life* (1993), 133–35; Ephraim Katz, *The Film Encyclopedia* (1979), 584–85; Fleischer, *Just Tell Me When to Cry,* 50.

46. *New York Times,* September 26, 1948; Thomas, *Howard Hughes in Hollywood,* 104; Fleischer, *Just Tell Me When to Cry,* 41.

47. Thomas, *Hughes in Hollywood,* 106.

48. Ceplair and Englund, *The Inquisition in Hollywood,* 389.

49. Allen Eyles, *John Wayne and the Movies* (1976), 160.

50. Higham, *Howard Hughes,* 144–45.

51. Ibid., 145–46; Janet Leigh, *There Really Was a Hollywood* (1984), 110.

52. *New York Times,* October 5, 1957.

53. For an outstanding discussion of the revival of World War II films, see Lawrence H. Suid, *Guts and Glory: Great American War Movies* (1978), 71–139.

54. *New York Times,* January 10, 1951; ibid., February 3, 1951; *Los Angeles Times,* January 9. 1951; *Los Angeles Examiner,* January 10, 1951; *Hollywood Reporter,* January 9, 1951.

55. *New York Times,* September 20, 1951; *Hollywood Reporter,* June 18, 1951.

56. *Los Angeles Examiner,* February 9, 1951; *Variety,* January 2, 1952; *Motion Picture Herald,* January 13, 1951.

57. Mary St. John interview.

Chapter 14. The Unquiet Man

1. Gerry McNee, *In the Footsteps of the Quiet Man* (1990), 16–21; Ford, *Pappy,* 210; Maurice Walsh, *The Quiet Man and Other Stories* (1992), 125–49.

2. McNee, *In the Footsteps of the Quiet Man,* 24.

3. John Ford to Lord Killanin, July 11, 1946, reprinted in McNee, *In the Footsteps of the Quiet Man,* 26; John Ford to Lord Killanin, August 9, 1946, ibid., 26–27; John Ford to Lord Killanin, January 30, 1947, ibid., 29; John Ford to Lord Killanin, December 8, 1947, ibid., 29–30.

4. Quoted in Gallagher, *John Ford,* 234; quoted in Ford, *Pappy,* 210.

5. Gallagher, *John Ford,* 234–43; Ford, *Pappy,* 212–13.

6. Quoted in McNee, *In the Footsteps of the Quiet Man,* 30.

7. Quoted in Ford, *Pappy,* 232.

8. Ibid.

9. Ibid., 232–34; McNee, *In the Footsteps of the Quiet Man,* 32; *Variety,* January 3, 1951.

10. Ford, *Pappy,* 234–37; Gallagher, *John Ford,* 275–77.

11. Wingate Smith interview, JFP.

12. John Ford to John Wayne, June 1, 1950, JFP; Ford, *Pappy,* 240–42; McNee, *In the Footsteps of the Quiet Man,* 63–64.

13. Ford, *Pappy,* 241.

14. *New York Times,* August 5, 1951; McNee, *In the Footsteps of the Quiet Man,* 77, 114; Winton Hoch interview, JFP; Ford, *Pappy,* 243.

15. Joe Mellotte interview, JFP.

16. Ibid.; Mary Farragher interview; quoted in McNee, *In the Footsteps of the Quiet Man,* 86, 96–98.

17. Joe Mellotte interview; quoted in McNee, *In the Footsteps of the Quiet Man,* 103–4.

18. Quoted in Gallagher, *John Ford,* 278; McNee, *In the Footsteps of the Quiet Man,* 69–84.

19. For the story of Ford's illness see Ford, *Pappy,* 243–44; John Wayne interview, JFP; Joe Mellotte interview.

20. John Wayne interview, JFP.

21. Ford, *Pappy,* 244.

22. Quoted in McNee, *In the Footsteps of the Quiet Man,* 126.

23. Joe Mellotte interview.

24. Quoted in McNee, *In the Footsteps of the Quiet Man,* 118.

25. Quoted in ibid., 119; Andrew McLaglen interview in Leonard Maltin, "The Making of the Quiet Man" (1992).

26. Ibid., 67, 125; quoted in Ford, *Pappy,* 245.

27. Sinclair, *John Ford,* 168.

28. Gallagher, *John Ford,* 283; Joe McInerney, "John Wayne Talks Tough," *Film Comment* (September 1972), 53; Maureen O'Hara interview.

29. Mary St. John interview; Ford, *Pappy,* 245.

30. Quoted in Ford, *Pappy,* 146.
31. *New York Times,* August 22, 1952; ibid., August 31, 1952; *Variety,* May 12, 1952; *Los Angeles Times,* October 3, 1952; *Newsweek,* September 8, 1952; *Los Angeles Examiner,* October 3, 1952.
32. Quoted in McNee, *In the Footsteps of the Quiet Man,* 129.
33. Mary St. John interview; Anthony Holden, *Behind the Oscar: The Secret History of the Academy Awards* (1993), 199–203.
34. *Variety,* January 7, 1953; Ford, *Pappy,* 250–56; McNee, *In the Footsteps of the Quiet Man,* 132–36.
35. Mary St. John interview.
36. The details of the Wayne-Yates breakup come from the Mary St. John interview.
37. Hurst, *Republic Studios,* 22–29.
38. Memo of contracts of John Wayne, 1948, CFP; John Boswell and Jay David, *Duke: The John Wayne Album* (1979), 76.
39. *New York Times,* April 27, 1951; Mary St. John interview.
40. Balio, *The American Film Industry,* 315–31; Edward Buscombe, ed., *The BFI Companion to the Western* (1988), 427; Sklar, *Movie-Made America,* 269–85; Janet Staiger, "Individualism versus Collectivism," *Screen* (July-October 1983), 68–73.
41. Staiger, "Individualism versus Collectivism," 71–72; Michael Conant, "The Impact of the *Paramount* Decrees," in Balio, *The American Film Industry,* 349; John Izod, *Hollywood and the Box Office, 1895–1986* (1988), 126.
42. Izod, *Hollywood and the Box Office,* 126; Conant, "The Impact of the *Paramount* Decrees," 349–50.
43. Helen Itria, "Big John," *Look* (August 11, 1953), 70.
44. *Hollywood Citizen-News,* August 31, 1953; "Biography of Robert M. Fellows," Warner Bros. Studios, Fellows file, MHL; *Variety,* May 13, 1969.
45. *Los Angeles Daily News,* September 1, 1952.
46. Staiger, "Individualism versus Collectivism," 76–79.
47. Mary St. John interview.
48. Carl Foreman, *Punch,* August 14, 1974.
49. For a discussion of the election of 1952 see: James T. Patterson, *Mr. Republican: A Biography of Robert A. Taft* (1972), 373, 535–65; Brownstein, *The Power and the Glitter,* 123–32.
50. Mary St. John interview.
51. Nora Sayre, *Running Time: Films of the Cold War* (1982), 80.
52. Ibid., 79–83; Russell E. Shain, "Hollywood's Cold War," *Journal of Popular Culture* (Fall 1974), 335–50.
53. Quoted in Sayre, *Running Time,* 94–97; Stephen J. Whitfield, *The Culture of the Cold War* (1991), 136–41.
54. Carl Milliken to Finlay McDermit, March 18, 1952, Wayne-Fellows 1952 file, Warner Bros., USC.
55. Lee Pfeiffer, *The John Wayne Scrapbook* (1989), 163–64.
56. SAC, Honolulu to Director, FBI, May 12, 1952; John Wayne file, FBI; *Honolulu Advertiser,* May 5, 1952; Richard Gid Powers, *Secrecy and Power: The Life of J. Edgar Hoover* (1987), 435–36.
57. *New York Times,* September 18, 1952.
58. *Hollywood Reporter,* August 25, 1952; *Variety,* August 25, 1952; *Los Angeles Examiner,* August 30, 1952.

59. *Variety,* January 7, 1953; Robert Fellows to Jack Warner, March 2, 1954, Wayne-Fellows 1954 file, Warner Bros., USC.

60. Mary St. John interview.

61. Ibid.; *Los Angeles Examiner,* October 29, 1953.

62. *Los Angeles Times,* October 21, 1953.

63. "John Wayne," circa 1952, John Wayne file, Academy of Motion Picture Arts and Sciences, MHL. This undated and unsigned typewritten document details Wayne's marital troubles with Chata. Obviously written by someone close to Wayne, probably in Beverly Barnett's press agency office, it was not intended for public release. No article or interview has such precise details. Other helpful details come from Mary St. John interview; Catalina Lawrence interview; Harry Carey Jr. interview; George Armstrong, "The Story John Wayne Has Never Told," *Photoplay Magazine* (October 1953), 38, 78–79.

64. "John Wayne," MHL; Mary St. John interview.

65. "John Wayne," MHL.

66. Mary St. John interview.

67. "John Wayne," MHL.

68. Pilar Wayne, *John Wayne,* 59; Mary St. John interview.

69. *Los Angeles Times,* October 21, 1953; *Los Angeles Tribune,* January 18, 1952; *Time* (January 28, 1952).

70. "The Wages of Virtue," *Time,* (March 3, 1952); *Los Angeles Times,* February 20, 1952; *Los Angeles Examiner,* February 20, 1952.

71. *Los Angeles Examiner,* October 29, 1952; Mary St. John interview.

72. *Los Angeles Examiner,* June 18, 1952; *Hollywood Citizen-News,* June 18, 1952; *Los Angeles Times,* June 18, 1952.

73. Pilar Wayne, *John Wayne,* 59–67. Except where noted, the early relationship of Pilar and Wayne is based on this account.

74. Laraine Day interview, SMU; Mary St. John interview.

75. Pilar Wayne, *John Wayne,* 71–74; Shepherd and Slatzer, *Duke: The Life and Times of John Wayne,* 251; Radio Scripts, March 31, 1953, Louella Parsons Papers, USC.

76. Pilar Wayne, *John Wayne,* 76.

77. Ibid., 80–82; Mary St. John interview.

78. *Los Angeles Times,* September 11, 1952; ibid., September 13, 1952; *Los Angeles Examiner,* September 3, 1952.

79. *Los Angeles Times,* March 26, 1953; ibid., April 30, 1953; ibid., May 1, 1953; *Los Angeles Herald Express,* April 29, 1953; *Hollywood Citizen-News,* April 30, 1953; *Los Angeles Mirror,* April 30, 1953; ibid., May 1, 1953; *Los Angeles Examiner,* April 30, 1953; ibid., May 1, 1953.

80. John Wayne to John Ford, June 6, 1953, JFP.

81. Melville Shavelson interview, SMU.

82. Pilar Wayne, *John Wayne,* 90–93.

83. Mary St. John interview; Geraldine Page interview, CU.

84. Pilar Wayne, *John Wayne,* 97–98.

85. *Los Angeles Examiner,* May 9, 1953; *Los Angeles Herald-Express,* May 15, 1953; ibid., May 18, 1953; ibid., May 19, 1953; *Hollywood Citizen-News,* May 16, 1953; ibid., May 19, 1953; *Variety,* May 19, 1953; *Los Angeles Mirror,* May 29, 1953.

86. *Los Angeles Herald Express,* May 19, 1953; ibid., May 20, 1953; *Los Angeles Times,* May 19, 1953; *Los Angeles Daily News,* May 19, 1953; ibid., May 20, 1953; *Los Angeles Examiner,* May 29, 1953.

87. *Los Angeles Times,* May 20, 1953; ibid., May 21, 1953; ibid., May 22, 1953; *Hollywood Citizen-News,* May 20, 1953; *Los Angeles Herald Express,* May 21, 1953; ibid., May 22, 1953; *Los Angeles Examiner,* May 22, 1953.

88. *Los Angeles Examiner,* May 23, 1953.

89. Pilar Wayne, *John Wayne,* 97; *Los Angeles Examiner,* May 23, 1953; *Los Angeles Daily News,* May 23, 1953; *Los Angeles Times,* May 23, 1953.

90. *Los Angeles Times,* June 2, 1953; Mary St. John interview.

91. *Hollywood Citizen-News,* June 6, 1953; *Los Angeles Examiner,* June 5, 1953; *Los Angeles Times,* June 5, 1953; ibid., June 6, 1953.

92. *Los Angeles Daily News,* June 2, 1953; *Los Angeles Herald Express,* June 23, 1953; *Los Angeles Times,* June 23, 1953; ibid., June 21, 1953; ibid., June 31, 1953; *Los Angeles Examiner,* June 31, 1953.

93. *Los Angeles Times,* August 1, 1953; ibid., August 19, 1953; *Los Angeles Herald Express,* August 17, 1953; ibid., August 18, 1953; ibid., August 21, 1953.

94. *Los Angeles Times,* October 17, 1953; *Los Angeles Examiner,* October 17, 1953; *Los Angeles Mirror,* October 19, 1953.

95. Unless noted the details of the divorce are from *Los Angeles Times,* October 20–29, 1953; *Los Angeles Examiner,* October 20–29, 1953; *Los Angeles Mirror,* October 20–29, 1953; *Hollywood Citizen-News,* October 20–29, 1953; *Los Angeles Daily News,* October 20–29, 1953; *Los Angeles Herald Express,* October 20–29, 1953. The fullest coverage is in the *Examiner* and the *Times.*

96. Mary St. John interview; Pilar Wayne, *John Wayne,* 99.

97. Mary St. John interview.

98. *News Life,* October 23, 1953.

99. Pilar Wayne, *John Wayne,* 99; Harry Carey Jr. interview.

Chapter 15. "That'll Be the Day"

1. "The Wages of Virtue," *Time,* March 3, 1952, 64–69.

2. John Wayne to Florence Morrison, November 14, 1952, NMP.

3. Unless otherwise mentioned the material on *Hondo* is taken from Pilar Wayne, *John Wayne,* 94–98; *Houston Chronicle,* June 23, 1993; Mary St. John interview; Geraldine Page interview, CU; John Wayne to Steve Trilling, July 7, 1953, Wayne-Fellows File, Warner Bros., USC; Andrew McLaglen interview, SMU.

4. Shepherd and Slatzer, *Duke,* 238–39; *Los Angeles Times,* July 7, 1953.

5. "The Wages of Virtue," 65.

6. Pilar Wayne, *John Wayne,* 97; Mary St. John interview.

7. Andrew McLaglen interview, SMU.

8. John Wayne to John Ford, June 17, 1953, JFP.

9. Jane Tompkins, *West of Everything: The Inner Life of the Western* (1992), 4.

10. Quoted in ibid., 71.

11. Ibid., 71.

12. *Variety,* November 25, 1953; *Hollywood Reporter,* November 25, 1953; *Cue,* December 5, 1953; *Houston Chronicle,* June 23, 1993.

13. *Time,* April 13, 1960, 104–6; Mary St. John interview; *Newsweek,* December 14, 1953, 88.

14. Unless otherwise mentioned the material on *The High and the Mighty* comes from "The High and the Mighty," *The Big Trail* (April 1992); *Los Angeles Daily News,* July 7, 1954;

Los Angeles Times, December 6, 1953; Robert Stack, *Straight Shooting* (1980), 156; "*The High and the Mighty,*" Los Angeles County Museum of Art, August 22, 1980; Burt Kennedy interview, SMU; Robert Stack interview, SMU; Ted Taylor interview, BYU.

15. Andrew McLaglen interview, SMU.

16. *Hollywood Reporter,* May 26–27, 1954; *Variety,* May 26, 1954

17. Mary St. John interview.

18. Ibid., *Hollywood Citizen-News,* May 26, 1954; *Los Angeles Times,* April 26, 1955.

19. Unless otherwise mentioned the material on *The Conqueror* is based on *Los Angeles Times,* June 28, 1981; Pilar Wayne, *John Wayne,* 102–3; Mary St. John interview; Beverly Linet, *Susan Hayward: Portrait of a Survivor* (1980), 178–79; *Los Angeles Daily News,* March 12, 1954; "John Whitcomb Watches the Filming of the Fabulous Life of Genghis Khan," *Cosmopolitan,* November 1954, 74–77; "The Conqueror," Vital Statistics, RKO Radio Studio, MHL; Grayce Pike interview, BYU, Howard Koch interview, BYU.

20. *Los Angeles Herald-Examiner,* November 3, 1980.

21. *People,* October 1, 1979, 26–29; ibid., November 11, 1980, 42–45; *Variety,* April 21, 1980, 33.

22. *Los Angeles Herald-Express,* August 24, 1954; *Los Angeles Examiner,* October 29, 1954.

23. John Wayne to Steve Trilling, September 15, 1954, Wayne-Fellows 1954 File, Warner Bros. Papers, USC.

24. Mary St. John interview; Lana Turner, *Lana: The Lady, the Legend, the Truth* (1982), 182–86; *The New Yorker,* June 18, 1955, 54; *Cue,* June 11, 1955, 20; *New York Herald Tribune,* January 2, 1955.

25. Avery Rennick interview.

26. *Los Angeles Examiner,* August 3, 1954; *Hollywood Citizen-News,* February 11, 1958; Mary St. John interview.

27. *Honolulu Star-Telegram,* November 1, 1954; *Los Angeles Herald-Express,* November 1, 1954; *Los Angeles Times,* November 2, 1954; *Los Angeles Examiner,* November 2, 1954; Mary St. John interview.

28. Pilar Wayne, *John Wayne,* 109.

29. Robert Fellows to Jack Warner, March 2, 1954, Warner Bros. Papers, USC; David F. Prindle, *Risky Business: The Political Economy of Hollywood* (1993), 29–31.

30. *Los Angeles Times,* January 17, 1955; ibid., January 26, 1965; ibid., February 27, 1955; *Hollywood Citizen-News,* February 11, 1955; *Los Angeles Examiner,* February 12, 1955; Pilar Wayne, *John Wayne,* 109–11; Mary St. John interview.

31. *Newsweek* 46 (October 10, 1955), 117; *Time* 66 (October 17, 1955), 112.

32. Unless otherwise mentioned, the material on *The Searchers* is taken from Carey, *Company of Heroes,* 171–77; Ford, *Pappy,* 271–74; Ronald Davis, *John Ford: Hollywood's Old Master* (1995), 270–79; Andrew Sinclair, *John Ford* (1983), 177–89; Mary St. John interview; Harry Carey Jr. interview; Ollie Carey interview, JFP; "The Searchers," Los Angeles County Museum of Art, 1980, MHL.

33. Davis, *John Ford,* 271. Nugent was a *New York Times* film critic until 1940.

34. Quoted in ibid., 273.

35. Ibid., 272.

36. Ibid., 273; Brian Huberman interview.

37. Ollie Carey interview, JFP; Carey, *Company of Heroes,* 173–74.

38. Quoted in Stuart Byron, "The Searchers: Cult Movie of the New Hollywood," *New York* March 5, 1979, 2.

39. The analysis of *The Searchers* is based on Jane Tompkins's brilliant *West of Everything*.
40. Ibid., 48.
41. Frank Nugent, "The Searchers," screenplay manuscript, JFP.
42. Byron, "The Searchers," 2.
43. *Hollywood Reporter,* March 13, 1956; "The Searchers," *Look,* June 12, 1956, 90; *Los Angeles Times,* May 31, 1956; *Variety,* March 13, 1956; *New York Times,* May 31, 1956.
44. Quoted in Byron, "The Searchers," 2; Howard Hawks interview, BYU.
45. Pilar Wayne, *John Wayne,* 117–18.

Chapter 16. Second-guessing

1. Pilar Wayne, *John Wayne,* 119–20.
2. Mary St. John interview; *Los Angeles Times,* October 18, 1955; ibid., December 31, 1955; Los Angeles *Examiner,* October 18, 1955.
3. Pilar Wayne, *John Wayne,* 120.
4. *Hollywood Reporter,* June 25, 1956; ibid., June 26, 1956; *Los Angeles Times,* July 13, 1956; *Hollywood Citizen-News,* July 2, 1956; ibid., October 6, 1956.
5. *Motion Picture Daily,* January 29, 1957; "Wings of Eagles," *Cinema Texas Program Notes,* 19 (November 19, 1980), 1–7; *Hollywood Reporter,* January 19, 1957; *New York Journal-American,* February 1, 1957; Ernest Lee Sullivan to John Wayne, February 25, 1956, JFP.
6. John Ford Memo, File 24, JFP.
7. John Wayne interview, JFP; Katherine Clifton interview, JFP.
8. John Ford to John Wayne, December 26, 1957, JFP; Davis, *John Ford,* 283.
9. *Hollywood Reporter,* February 7, 1957; *Los Angeles Times,* April 1 and 7, 1957, and February 25, 1957; *Los Angeles Examiner,* June 9, 1957.
10. John Ford to John Wayne, February 11, 1957, JFP; Pilar Wayne, *John Wayne,* 125.
11. Ibid., 124–26; Henry Hathaway interview, SMU.
12. Henry Hathaway interview, SMU.
13. Unless otherwise mentioned the material on *The Barbarian and the Geisha* is taken from John Huston, *An Open Book* (1980), 265–67; Lawrence Grobel, *The Hustons* (1989), 448–52; Mary St. John interview; Louella O. Parsons, "John Wayne: Christmas in Japan," *Pictorial TView* (December 22, 1957), 3; Sam Jaffe interview, SMU; *Los Angeles Times,* December 27, 1957; Pilar Wayne, *John Wayne,* 127–30; *Los Angeles Herald-Examiner,* December 11, 1957; John Wayne to John Ford, November 27, 1957, JFP.
14. *Los Angeles Mirror,* November 18, 1957; *Los Angeles Times,* November 20, 1957; Pilar Wayne, *John Wayne,* 128.
15. *Los Angeles Times,* May 25, 1958.
16. *Variety,* September 30, 1958; Mary St. John interview; John Wayne interview, JFP; Pilar Wayne, *John Wayne,* 128.
17. *Los Angeles Mirror,* January 14, 1958; *Los Angeles Herald Express,* January 14, 1958; Pilar Wayne, *John Wayne,* 129–30.
18. Quoted in Robin Wood, *Howard Hawks* (1983), 163; Joseph McBride, *Hawks on Hawks* (1982), 60.
19. Quoted in McBride, *Hawks on Hawks,* 130.
20. Ibid., 40; Nick Tosches, *Dino: Living High in the Dirty Business of Dreams* (1992), 319.
21. Tosches, *Dino,* 320; McBride, *Hawks on Hawks,* 41–42; *Los Angeles Mirror-News,* May 24, 1958.

22. Tosches, *Dino*, 320–21.

23. McBride, *Hawks on Hawks,* 116.

24. Ibid., 117–18.

25. Wood, *Howard Hawks,* 35.

26. *New York Times,* March 19, 1959; *Film Daily,* February 17, 1959; *Variety,* February 17, 1959; *Los Angeles Times,* March 14, 1959.

27. *New York Herald Tribune,* November 21, 1958.

28. Aissa Wayne, *John Wayne,* 34–35; Pilar Wayne, *John Wayne,* 127.

29. *Los Angeles Times,* September 7–8, 1958; *Los Angeles Examiner,* September 7, 1958; Mary St. John interview.

30. Unless otherwise mentioned, the material on *The Horse Soldiers* is from Bob Thomas, *Golden Boy: The Untold Story of William Holden* (1983), 123–25; *Variety,* December 10, 1958; Davis, *John Ford,* 290–95; Ford, *Pappy,* 275–76; Gallagher, *John Ford,* 348–54; John Lee Mahin interview, JFP.

31. Pilar Wayne, *John Wayne,* 133–34; Aissa Wayne, *John Wayne,* 35–36.

32. Pilar Wayne, *John Wayne,* 133–35; *Los Angeles Examiner,* January 11, 1959; *Los Angeles Times,* December 17, 1958.

33. Louis Johnson interview; Alice Johnson interview; Mary St. John interview; John Chohlis, "John Wayne, Cattleman," *Persimmon Hill* 7 (1977), 38–39.

34. *Parade,* April 7, 1991, 3; *New York Herald Tribune,* April 24, 1959.

35. *Los Angeles Times,* April 22, 1959; *New York Post,* April 23, 1959; *New York Mirror,* April 24, 1959; *New York Daily News,* April 24, 1959; John Wayne File, Federal Bureau of Investigation, Washington, D.C.

36. *Motion Picture Herald,* June 13, 1959; *Variety,* June 12, 1959.

Chapter 17. *"The Country's Going Soft"*

1. The following material on Wayne's financial problems comes from Arthur Marx, *Red Skelton* (1979), 234–43, and the Mary St. John Interview.

2. Mary St. John interview; Louis Johnson interview; Avery Rennick interview; Pilar Wayne, *John Wayne,* 137–38; *New York Morning Telegraph,* July 25, 1958; *Los Angeles Herald-Examiner,* June 12, 1960.

3. Linda Crystal interview, Brian Huberman, "John Wayne's *The Alamo,*" MGM, 1992.

4. *Austin-American Statesman,* November 27, 1977; Harvey Fergusson, *Footloose McGarnigal* (1930), 50–51; Don Graham, "Remembering the Alamo: The Story of the Texas Revolution in Popular Culture," *Southwestern Historical Quarterly,* 89 (July 1985), 35–66.

5. Pilar Wayne, *John Wayne,* 31, 136; John Wayne interview, CU; Patrick Ford, "Alamo," in Patrick Ford Papers, BYU.

6. *San Antonio Express,* July 18, 1951; *Austin-American Statesman,* November 15, 1959; Orin Kirkpatrick to Herbert Yates, June 21, 1951, Daughters of the Republic of Texas Library, San Antonio; Mary St. John interview; Happy Shahan interview.

7. Don Graham, "Remembering the Alamo," 54; John Wayne interview, CU, 21–22; Hedda Hopper, "Hedda Hopper's Hollywood," press release, October 23, 1960, MHL.

8. *Cinema Texas Program* Notes (December 4, 1978), 88–90; Frank Thompson, *Alamo Movies* (1991), 67.

9. Happy Shahan interview; Mary St. John interview; Louis Johnson interview.

10. Happy Shahan interview.

11. Happy Shahan interview; *San Antonio Light,* July 18, 1958; *Los Angeles Times,* November 1, 1959; *Hollywood Reporter,* July 29, 1959; *Los Angeles Mirror,* September 20, 1961; *Variety,* October 23, 1960; *New York Times,* October 4, 1959; Thompson, *Alamo Movies,* 68, 71–72; Happy Shahan interview, "John Wayne's *The Alamo.*"

12. *New York Times,* October 4, 1959; *Pictorial TView* (October 23, 1960), 3; Russell Birdwell, "The Alamo," unpublished press release, MZP; Michael Wayne interview, "John Wayne's *The Alamo.*"

13. *Beverly Hills Citizen,* September 9, 1959; *Hollywood Reporter,* September 1, 1959; Mary St. John interview; *Motion Picture Herald,* January 16, 1960; *San Antonio Light,* September 21, 1960.

14. Mary St. John interview.

15. Ibid.; *San Antonio Express and News,* October 31, 1959.

16. *Variety,* September 23, 1959.

17. *San Antonio Light,* September 11, 1959; ibid., December 24, 1959; *Los Angeles Mirror News,* October 20, 1959; ibid., October 22, 1959; *Los Angeles Times,* December 16, 1959; Ronald L. Davis, *John Ford: Hollywood's Old Master* (1995), 301.

18. Pilar Wayne, *John Wayne,* 140; Happy Shahan interview; Mary St. John interview.

19. Pilar Wayne, *John Wayne,* 145; Happy Shahan interview; Mary St. John interview.

20. *New York Daily News,* October 12, 1959; ibid., October 16, 1959; *Wilmington* (Delaware) *Morning News,* October 16, 1959.

21. Frankie Avalon interview, "John Wayne's *The Alamo*"; Hank Worden interview; Hank Worden interview, SMU.

22. Mary St. John interview; Happy Shahan interview, "John Wayne's *The Alamo.*"

23. *New York Herald Tribune,* January 28, 1950; *Los Angeles Mirror,* November 4, 1960; William Clothier interview, JFP.

24. Mary St. John interview; Ford, *Pappy,* 286–88.

25. Ibid.

26. Ibid.; William Clothier Interview, "John Wayne's *The Alamo*"; John Wayne to John Ford, October 1, 1960, JFP; Davis, *John Ford,* 300–301.

27. *Variety,* October 23, 1960; Mary St. John interview; Russell Birdwell interview, MZP.

28. William Clothier interview, "John Wayne's *The Alamo*"; Mary St. John interview; Joe De Franco interview; Happy Shahan interview.

29. Thompson, *Alamo Movies,* 75–77.

30. Ken Curtis interview, "John Wayne's *The Alamo*"; Harry Carey Jr. interview; Linda Crystal interview, SMU; Dean Smith interview, SMU.

31. Thompson, *Alamo Movies,* 74; Leslie Halliwell, *The Filmgoer's Companion* (1977), 148.

32. Thompson, *Alamo Movies,* 77; Hank Worden interview, "John Wayne's *The Alamo.*"

33. *Los Angeles Mirror,* September 20, 1961; Jack Hamilton, "John Wayne: The Big Man of the Westerns," *Look,* August 2, 1960, 86; Russell Birdwell interview, MZP; *Variety,* October 23, 1960; *New York Times,* July 29, 1959.

34. Aissa Wayne, *John Wayne,* 46.

35. Leonard J. Leff and Jerold L. Simmons, *The Dame in the Kimono: Hollywood, Censorship, and the Production Code from the 1920s to the 1960s* (1990), 112–113, 118, 123–24.

36. *San Antonio Light,* October 23, 1960; Russell Birdwell to Gov. Price Daniel, January 18, 1960, and January 25, 1960; Daughters of the Republic of Texas Library, San Antonio, Texas; Mary St. John interview; Russell Birdwell to Marg-Riette Montgomery, January 12, 1960; and Marg-Riette Montgomery to Russell Birdwell, January 19, 1960; Daughters of

the Republic of Texas Library, San Antonio, Texas; Milton Weiss to Richard Nixon, September 15, 1959, and Richard Nixon to John Wayne, September 23, 1959, John Wayne File, Pacific Southwest Region, National Archives.

37. Brownstein, *The Power and the Glitter,* 145–46.

38. *New York Daily News,* May 15, 1960; *Los Angeles Times,* May 16, 1960; Jack Hamilton, "John Wayne: The Big Man of the Westerns," *Look,* August 2, 1960, 84–85; Mary St. John interview.

39. Mary St. John interview; *Newsweek,* July 25, 1960, 107; Brownstein, *The Power and the Glitter,* 147.

40. Richard Nixon to John Wayne, June 10, 1959, John Wayne File, Richard Nixon Papers, Pacific Southwest Region, National Archives; ibid., July 7, 1959; ibid., January 19, 1961; ibid., November 8, 1961; *Variety,* July 5, 1960; ibid., October 26, 1960; Lyndon B. Johnson Chronology, January 30, 1960, Lyndon Baines Johnson Presidential Library, Austin, Texas; *Boxoffice,* July 11, 1960; *Life,* July 4, 1960, 1; John Wayne to Russell Birdwell, November 23, 1960, *Alamo* File, Daughters of the Republic of Texas Library, San Antonio, Texas.

41. William Manchester, *The Glory and the Dream* (1974), 1113; "Hedda Hopper's Hollywood," October 21, 1960, MHL.

42. *Southern California Prompter* (October 1960), 26; *The New Yorker,* November 5, 1960; Marg-Riette Montgomery to *Time,* November 10, 1960, Daughters of the Republic of Texas Library, San Antonio, Texas; *Los Angeles Times,* September 17, 1960; *Time,* November 7, 1960; *Newsweek,* October 31, 1960.

43. *New York Times,* October 27, 1960; Pilar Wayne, *John Wayne,* 148–49; Brian Huberman interview.

44. *Variety,* October 26, 1960; *Hollywood Reporter,* October 26, 1960; *Limelight,* October 27, 1960; *Los Angeles Times,* October 26–27, 1960; *Hollywood Citizen-News,* October 27, 1960; *Cinema Texas Program Notes,* (December 4, 1978), 88; *Houston Chronicle,* June 23, 1991; Los Angeles *Mirror News,* October 21, 1959; *New York Times,* November 3, 1960.

45. Aissa Wayne, *John Wayne,* 43–45; *Cinema Texas Program Notes* (December 4, 1978), 88–90.

46. *Hollywood Reporter,* January 11, 1960; *Beverly Hills Citizen,* January 12, 1960; John Wayne Memo on *Suddenly Last Summer* Box 14, Folder 6, Bosley Crowther Papers, BYU.

47. *Hollywood Citizen-News,* May 30, 1960; *Newark Evening News,* May 30, 1960; *New York Times,* April 2, 16, 17, 18, and June 2, 1961.

48. Kirk Douglas, *The Ragman's Son: An Autobiography* (1988), 303–10, 323.

49. Ibid., 304, 331–32.

50. Mary St. John interview.

51. *Variety,* March 21, 1961; *Los Angeles Mirror,* March 1, 7, and 15, 1961; *New York Times,* April 2, 1961; Russell Birdwell press release, Daughters of the Republic of Texas Library, *Alamo* File, San Antonio, Texas.

52. *New York Times,* April 2, 1961; *Atlanta Constitution,* April 2, 1961; *Los Angeles Times,* March 27, 1977; *Hollywood Reporter,* March 17–28, 1961; *San Antonio Light,* April 4, 1961.

53. *Hollywood Reporter,* March 24, 1961; ibid., March 27, 1961; *Los Angeles Mirror,* March 30, 1961; *Variety,* March 27, 1961; Emanuel Levy, *And the Winner Is* (1990), 299.

54. *Hollywood Reporter,* April 18, 1961; *Variety,* April 18, 1961; *Los Angeles Mirror,* September 20, 1961; *Newark Evening News,* November 1, 1961; "John Wayne's *The Alamo;*" Russell Birdwell interview, MZP.

55. Balio, *United Artists,* 91–94; *Variety,* January 7, 1970, 25, 27, 32.

Chapter 18. *In Harm's Way*

1. *New York Times,* June 19, 1960; Fleischer, *Just Tell Me When to Cry,* 15–24.
2. Fleischer, *Just Tell Me When to Cry,* 15–24.
3. *New York Times,* June 6, 1960.
4. Harry Brand, "Vital Statistics on *North to Alaska,*" unpublished manuscript, Publicity Department, Twentieth Century-Fox Studios, MHL.
5. *Variety,* November 7, 1960; *Hollywood Reporter,* November 7, 1960.
6. Mary St. John interview; Los Angeles *Herald-Examiner,* March 29, 1959; Pilar Wayne, *John Wayne,* 152–53.
7. Ford, *Pappy,* 288; Harry Carey Jr. interview.
8. Aissa Wayne, *John Wayne,* 58.
9. Harry Carey Jr. interview; Mary St. John interview; Avery Rennick interview; Dean Jennings, "The Woes of Box-Office King John Wayne," *Saturday Evening Post,* October 27, 1962, 29–33; *Los Angeles Times,* November 6, 23, and 24, 1960; Pilar Wayne, *John Wayne,* 153–54, Davis, *John Ford,* 301–02.
10. Mary St. John interview.
11. Mary St. John interview; John Wayne interview, CU; *Variety,* September 2, 1960; *New York Times,* January 22, 1961; Eric Bentley, "The Political Theater of John Wayne," *Film Society Review* (March/May 1972), 1; *Life,* January 1972, 46.
12. *Los Angeles Herald-Examiner,* June 29, 1962; *Variety,* May 17, 1962; Red Buttons interview, SMU.
13. Mary St. John interview; Jennings, "The Woes of Box-Office King John Wayne," 29–33; Pilar Wayne, *John Wayne,* 154.
14. Pilar Wayne, *John Wayne,* 154–56; Mary St. John interview; Eddie Albert interview, SMU; Olivia De Havilland interview, BYU.
15. *Variety,* October 30, 1961; Pilar Wayne, *John Wayne,* 151–54; Aissa Wayne, *John Wayne,* 54–58.
16. Mary St. John interview; Ford, *Pappy,* 292.
17. "The Man Who Shot Liberty Valance," *Cinema Texas Program Notes,* 11 (November 4, 1976), 60–64; Tag Gallagher, *John Ford,* 413; Robert B. Ray, *A Certain Tendency of the Hollywood Cinema, 1930-1980* (1985), 243–44.
18. Woody Strode and Sam Young, *Goal Dust* (1990), 211–12; Davis, *John Ford,* 308–10.
19. John Wayne interview, JFP; Mary St. John interview.
20. *Hollywood Citizen-News,* April 18, 1962; *Variety,* April 11, 1962; *Hollywood Reporter,* April 11, 1962; Gallagher, *John Ford,* 384; William S. Pechter, *Twenty-four Times a Second: Films and Film-Makers* (1971), 226, 231.
21. Pilar Wayne, *John Wayne,* 159; *Variety,* January 5, 1979.
22. Pilar Wayne, *John Wayne,* 149–50, 159; Mary St. John interview; Leonard Mosley, *Zanuck: The Rise and Fall of Hollywood's Last Tycoon* (1984), 327.
23. The following discussion of *Donovan's Reef* is taken from Sinclair, *John Ford* (1979), 205–6; Gallagher, *John Ford,* 379–80, 413–29; Davis, *John Ford,* 318–19; and J. A. Place, *The Non-Western Films of John Ford* (1982), 274–77.
24. Quoted in Davis, *John Ford,* 318–19; Pilar Wayne, *John Wayne,* 184–85; Elizabeth Allen interview, JFP.
25. *Hollywood Reporter,* June 20, 1963; *Los Angeles Times,* July 18, 1963.
26. Quoted in Davis, *John Ford,* 319.

27. Chuck Roberson, *The Fall Guy: 30 Years As the Duke's Double* (1980), 259–61.

28. Mary St. John interview, Maureen O'Hara interview.

29. Roberson, *The Fall Guy,* 255–58.

30. *Los Angeles Times,* November 25, 1963; *Variety,* November 13, 1963, and January 5, 1967; *Boxoffice,* January 13, 1964; Ralph Wingfield interview.

31. Pilar Wayne, *John Wayne,* 160.

32. Pilar Wayne, *John Wayne,* 168–73; Bert Minshall, *On Board with the Duke: John Wayne and the Wild Goose* (1992), 26–27.

33. Frank Capra, *The Name Above the Title: An Autobiography* (1971), 489–90.

34. Ibid; *Hollywood Citizen-News,* December 23, 1964; Frank Capra to Phil Youdan, April 2, 1963; Frank Capra to Phil Youdan, n.d.; Frank Capra to Tambi Larsen, n.d., Frank Capra Sr. to Frank Capra Jr., Correspondence File, Frank Capra Papers, Wesleyan University; William A. Wellman, *A Short Time for Insanity. An Autobiography* (1974), 96–97.

35. Aissa Wayne, *John Wayne,* 91–92.

36. Pilar Wayne, *John Wayne,* 174–75; Roberson, *The Fall Guy,* 279.

37. Aissa Wayne, *John Wayne,* 64–66.

38. *Los Angeles Times,* March 23, 1964; Bert Minshall interview; Bert Minshall, *On Board with the Duke,* 22–23.

39. *Hollywood Citizen-News,* December 23, 1964; *Variety,* January 5, 1967; Martin Ritt interview, SMU.

40. Mary St. John interview; Jennings, "The Woes of Box-Office King John Wayne," 30.

41. *Hollywood Citizen-News,* May 27 and June 16, 1964; Los Angeles *Herald-Examiner,* May 27, 1964; Pilar Wayne, *John Wayne,* 139; Mary St. John interview.

42. Unless otherwise mentioned the material on *In Harm's Way* comes from Mary St. John interview; Kirk Douglas, *The Ragman's Son: An Autobiography* (1988), 379–81; Otto Preminger, *Preminger: An Autobiography* (1977), 161; Willi Frischauer, *Behind the Scenes of Otto Preminger* (1974), 214–15; Pilar Wayne, *John Wayne,* 169, 176; Aissa Wayne, *John Wayne,* 97–98.

43. Douglas, *Ragman's Son,* 379–81.

44. Ibid.; *Hollywood Reporter,* March 31, 1965; *Variety,* March 31, 1965.

45. Pilar Wayne, *John Wayne,* 176.

46. Unless otherwise mentioned the material on the discovery of Wayne's lung cancer is based on the Louis Johnson interview, Mary St. John interview, and Roy Newquist, "John Wayne Wins His Toughest Battle," *Chicago's American Magazine,* June 25, 1967, 12; Pilar Wayne, *John Wayne,* 178–80; Aissa Wayne, *John Wayne,* 100–102; Bert Minshall interview; Jane Ardmore, "Cancer Doesn't Fight Fair," *Family Health,* September 1976, 30.

47. *Hollywood Reporter,* June 19, 1963; *Los Angeles Herald-Examiner,* June 19, 1963; *Los Angeles Times,* June 19, 1963; Mary St. John interview.

48. Newquist, "John Wayne Wins His Toughest Battle," 12.

49. The Jones's conversation is based on a Jane Ardmore interview with Wayne that appeared as "Cancer Doesn't Fight Fair," 32–33, and *Chicago's American Magazine,* June 25, 1967, 12.

50. Mary St. John interview; *Chicago's American Magazine,* June 25, 1967, 12; Pilar Wayne, *John Wayne,* 178–79; Ardmore, "Cancer Doesn't Fight Fair," 32–33; Hal Wallis, *Starmaker: The Autobiography of Hal Wallis* (1980), 157–58.

51. *Los Angeles Herald-Examiner,* September 23, 1964.

52. Mary St. John interview; Pilar Wayne, *John Wayne,* 180–82; Ardmore, "Cancer Doesn't Fight Fair," 30.

53. Louis Johnson interview; Mary St. John interview; Aissa Wayne, *John Wayne*, 103–5; *Los Angeles Herald-Examiner*, September 23, 1964; *Los Angeles Times*, September 24, 1964; *New York Post*, October 6, 1964.

54. *Los Angeles Herald-Examiner*, October 8, 1964; *Los Angeles Times*, October 8, 1964; Ardmore, "Cancer Doesn't Fight Fair," 33; *Los Angeles Times*, July 1, 1973.

Chapter 19. *"I've Just Got My Second Wind"*

1. *Milwaukee Journal*, January 31, 1965; Phyllis Feinstein, "Some Guys Just Never Learn," *Movie Life*, February 1968, 58–59; Mary St. John interview.

2. *Hollywood Reporter*, June 25, 1965; Mary St. John interview.

3. *Los Angeles Times*, December 30, 1964; *New York Times*, December 31, 1964; Pilar Wayne, *John Wayne*, 189–90.

4. Louis Johnson interview; *New York Times*, December 17, 1964, and February 16, 1965; Mary St. John interview; Paul Henry, "You Can Beat It—I Did," *Photoplay*, February 1965, 2, 64–65.

5. Mary St. John interview; *Los Angeles Times*, May 7, 1965; John Wayne interview, CU.

6. *Los Angeles Times*, March 2, 1965; *New York Daily News*, March 7, 1965.

7. Mary St. John interview; Pilar Wayne, *John Wayne*, 209.

8. *Los Angeles Times*, March 2, 1965.

9. Pilar Wayne, *John Wayne*, 196.

10. Ibid., 196–97.

11. Roberson, *The Fall Guy*, 264–65; Earl Holliman interview, SMU.

12. Earl Holliman interview; Louis Johnson interview; Mary St. John interview; *Newsweek*, March 1, 1965, 86; Phylis Feinstein, "Some Guys Just Never Learn," *Movie Life* (February 1968), 28, 59–60.

13. Earl Holliman interview; Mary St. John interview; Ted Bonnet press release, Paramount Studio, "The Sons of Katie Elder" File, John Wayne File, MHL; Martha Hyer interview, SMU.

14. *Time*, March 1, 1965; Tosches, *Dino*, 378.

15. *Hollywood Reporter*, June 25, 1966; *Time*, March 1, 1965.

16. Bert Minshall, *On Board With the Duke: John Wayne and the Wild Goose* (1992), 37–38, 42–43.

17. *Los Angeles Times*, March 2, 1965; Mary St. John interview.

18. *Hollywood Reporter*, June 25, 1966, and May 23, 1967; *New York Journal-American*, February 21, 1965; *Hollywood Reporter*, June 12, 1967; *Los Angeles Times*, October 9, 1966; *Variety*, May 23, 1967; John Didion, "John Wayne: A Love Song," *Saturday Evening Post*, August 14, 1965, 77; *New York Times*, August 26, 1965.

19. *Hollywood Reporter*, February 23 and March 8, 1966; *Los Angeles Times*, October 6 and December 12, 1965, and February 23 and March 17, 1966; *Newsweek*, December 6, 1965; *Los Angeles Citizen-News*, September 16 and November 23, 1965; *Variety*, March 17, 1966.

20. *Los Angeles Times*, January 4 and 6, 1965; *Los Angeles Herald-Examiner*, January 4, 1965; Mary St. John interview.

21. Minshall, *On Board with the Duke*, 84–86.

22. Pilar Wayne, *John Wayne*, 202–3.

23. Betty Friedan, *The Feminine Mystique* (1970), 364; Pilar Wayne, *John Wayne*, 127, 132–33; Mary St. John interview.

24. Pilar Wayne, *John Wayne,* 192–93.

25. Pilar Wayne, *John Wayne,* 133–34, 202–6, 211–12; Aissa Wayne, *John Wayne,* 32–36, 115–17, 123–24.

26. John Clements, *California Facts* (1989), 169–70; C. E. Parker and Marilyn Parker, *Orange County: Indians* (1963), 17–27; Louis Reichman and Gary Cardinale, *The Orange County Experience* (1975), 80; *Orange County Progress Report* 11 (October 1974), 17–23.

27. Reichman and Cardinale, *The Orange County Experience,* 50–80.

28. *Orange County Progress Report,* 11 (October 1974), 17–23.

29. Marian Ginang, *The Orange Book* (1967), 114.

30. Joseph Wambaugh, *The Golden Orange* (1990), 35; Paul Dickson, *The Worth Book of Softball* (1993), 147.

31. The material on *Cast a Giant Shadow* comes from *The Big Trail;* Pilar Wayne, *John Wayne,* 205–8; Douglas, *The Ragman's Son,* 381–83; Melville Shavelson interview, SMU.

32. Melville Shavelson interview, SMU.

33. *Los Angeles Times,* August 14–15, 1965; *Los Angeles Herald-Examiner,* August 14, 1965.

34. Minshall, *On Board with the Duke,* 29–31.

35. McBride, *Hawks on Hawks* (1982), 137.

36. Wood, *Howard Hawks,* 152–68.

37. See the *El Dorado* script in Box 5, Folder 10, HHP; William R. Meyer, *The Making of the Great Westerns* (1979), 367–79.

38. *Hollywood Reporter,* June 12, 1967; *Variety,* January 6, 1969.

39. Burt Kennedy interview, SMU; *The Big Trail,* (October 1988); Douglas, *The Ragman's Son,* 398–99; *Los Angeles Times,* October 9, 1966; *Variety,* May 23, 1967.

40. Pilar Wayne, *John Wayne,* 224; Louis Johnson interview; *Hollywood Reporter,* April 6, 1966.

41. *Variety,* February 10 and June 6, 1965, and November 14, 1967; *Hollywood Citizen-News,* November 14, 1967; *Los Angeles Times,* November 6, 1967; *Hollywood Reporter,* April 6, 1966; Douglas, *The Ragman's Son,* 399–400.

42. Pilar Wayne, *John Wayne,* 226–28.

43. Mary St. John interview; Nancy Marshall interview; Frank Hoyt interview; Minshall, *On Board with the Duke,* 101.

44. Aljean Harmetz, "I'm Married to John Wayne," *Pageant,* August 1970, 95; Mary St. John interview; Alice Johnson interview; Pat Stacy, *Duke: A Love Story* (1983), 3–4.

45. Pilar Wayne, *John Wayne,* pp. 226–27; Louis Johnson interview; Mary St. John interview.

46. Louis Johnson interview; Alice Johnson interview; Mary St. John interview; John Chohlis, "John Wayne, Cattleman," *Persimmon Hill* 7 (1977), 38–35.

47. Pilar Wayne, *John Wayne,* 164. In the summer of 1965 Duke became a trustee of the conservative Americans for Constitutional Action. The left wing, except for a few liberal supporters of Gov. Nelson Rockefeller of New York, was moribund in Orange County.

48. Ronald Reagan, "Unforgettable John Wayne," *Reader's Digest,* October 1979, 115; Stacy, *Duke,* 119–120; *Variety,* October 19, 1966; *New York Times,* October 13, 1964; Harry Carey Jr. interview; Mary St. John interview; *Hollywood Reporter,* July 8, 1965.

Chapter 20. Working-Class Hero

1. Mary St. John interview.

2. For the Vietnam War history described in this chapter, see James S. Olson and Randy Roberts, *Where the Domino Fell: America and Vietnam 1945 to 1990* (1991).

3. Mary St. John interview; Edwin T. Arnold and Eugene L. Miller, *The Films and Career of Robert Aldrich* (1986), 188; Charles Higham and Joel Greenberg, *The Celluloid Muse: Hollywood's Directors Speak* (1969), 38.

4. Phylis Feinstein, "Some Guys Just Never Learn," *Movie Life* (February 1968), 27–28.

5. *New York Times,* December 24, 1967.

6. Pilar Wayne, *John Wayne,* 215–16; Mary St. John interview.

7. Mary St. John interview; Edward Dmytryk interview, CU.

8. Alasdair Spark, "The Soldier at the Heart of the War: The Myth of the Green Beret in the Popular Culture of the Vietnam Era," *Journal of American Studies* 18 (1984), 29–48; *Los Angeles Times,* January 28, 1968.

9. *New York Times,* May 29, 1965.

10. Much of the narrative on making *The Green Berets* comes from Lawrence H. Suid, *Guts and Glory: Great American War Movies* (1978), 221–30.

11. Lyndon B. Johnson to John Wayne, November 12, 1964, White House Central File—Name File—John Wayne, Johnson Library.

12. The quotations are taken from Lawrence H. Suid, *Guts and Glory,* 222. The original letter from Wayne to Johnson, written on December 28, 1965, can be found in the White House Central File—Name File—John Wayne, Johnson Library. For the quote on oxen getting gored, see John Wayne to Bill Moyers, February 18, 1966, ibid.

13. Bill Moyers to John Wayne, January 17, 1966; ibid., January 18, 1966; ibid., February 22, 1966.

14. The quotations from Wayne are taken from Suid, *Guts and Glory,* 223. Also see Jack Valenti to Lyndon B. Johnson, January 6, 1966, ibid.; Hal Pachios to Adam Yarmolinsky, January 4, 1966, ibid.

15. Suid, *Guts and Glory,* 234.

16. *Hollywood Reporter,* October 18, 1989; *Film Daily,* January 8, 1968; John Wayne to Bill Moyers, February 18, 1966, White House Central File—Name File—John Wayne, Johnson Library.

17. John Wayne to J. W. Fulbright, April 15, 1966, ibid.; John Wayne to Bill Moyers, April 18, 1966, ibid.; Bill Moyers to John Wayne, April 21, 1966, ibid.

18. *Variety,* June 13, 1966; ibid., June 29, 1966; *Los Angeles Times,* June 21, 1966; ibid., July 6, 1966; *New York Daily News,* June 21, 1966; *Hollywood Citizen-News,* July 6, 1966; Richard Goldstein, "The Last Cowboy Saint," *Lively Arts* (New York *World Journal Tribune*), December 18, 1966, 22–24; Kal Vorgang interview.

19. Mary St. John interview.

20. Suid, *Guts and Glory,* 224.

21. Ibid.

22. Quoted in ibid., 226.

23. Ibid., 229; *Time,* June 9, 1967, 67.

24. Mary St. John interview; Suid, *Guts and Glory,* 229–30.

25. Lawrence Suid, "The Making of *The Green Berets,*" *Journal of Popular Film* 6 (February 1977), 106–25; Pilar Wayne, *John Wayne,* 220–22; *Variety,* June 22, 1967; *New York Times,* September 27, 1967; James R. Jones to Arthur B. Krim, June 22, 1967, White House Central File—Name File—John Wayne, Johnson Library.

26. *The Bayonet* (Fort Benning), July 14, 1967; August 4, 11, 18, and 25, 1967; September 1 and 8, 1967; October 6 and 27, 1967; and November 3 and 17, 1967; Burt Kennedy interview, SMU.

27. *Los Angeles Times,* September 22, 1967; Robert Solomon interview.

28. *New York Times,* December 24, 1967; Norman Mailer, *Miami and the Siege of Chicago* (1969), 139.

29. *New York Times,* November 22, 1967.

30. Mary St. John interview; Danko Gurovich interview; *Variety,* November 13, 1967.

31. *The Green Berets,* Batjac/Warner Bros., 1968.

32. *New York Times,* June 30, 1968; ibid., July 14, 1968; *Hollywood Reporter,* June 17, 1968; *Glamour,* October 1968, 62; *The New Yorker,* July 6, 1968, 44; *Life,* July 19, 1968, 8.

33. *Variety,* June 26, 1968; *New York Times,* June 20, 1968; ibid., August 16, 1968; ibid., October 6, 1968.

34. *The Hollywood Reporter,* June 26–27, 1969.

35. *Variety,* July 2, 1969; *Hollywood Citizen-News,* June 26, 1969; *Los Angeles Times,* June 27, 1969; *Hollywood Reporter,* June 30, 1969.

36. *New York Times,* September 27, 1967; *The Big Trail* (June 1993); *Playboy,* May 1971, 89.

37. *Wall Street Journal,* July 3, 1968; *Variety,* June 26, 1968; ibid., July 2, 1969; *Los Angeles Herald-Examiner,* August 9, 1968; *Hollywood Reporter,* February 5, 1975; *Los Angeles Times,* October 23, 1977.

38. Christian G. Appy, *Working-Class War: American Combat Soldiers & Vietnam* (1993), 12–14.

39. Ibid., 39–40.

40. *Los Angeles Herald-Examiner,* July 21, 1972; *New York Daily News,* August 21, 1972; *Los Angeles Times,* October 5, 1971; *New York Post,* May 8, 1973; Mary St. John interview; Danko Gurovich interview; *Paterson* [New Jersey] *Morning Call,* December 1, 1966.

41. Folmar Blangsted, "Hellfighters, From Texas to Hollywood," *Cinemaeditor* 19 (1969), 12–26; *Variety,* November 24, 1968; Mary St. John interview; Red Adair interview.

42. Mary St. John interview; Goldwater quoted in Olson and Roberts, *Where the Domino Fell,* 217.

43. Pilar Wayne, *John Wayne,* 218–19; *Los Angeles Herald-Examiner,* January 7, 1971; *Los Angeles Times,* January 7, 1971; Mary St. John interview.

44. Christopher Anderson, *Citizen Jane: The Turbulent Life of Jane Fonda* (1990), 236; Mary St. John interview.

45. Mary St. John interview; Pat Stacy, *Duke: A Love Story* (1983), 127; *Hollywood Reporter,* December 22, 1977.

46. Mary St. John interview.

47. Ibid.

48. Quoted in "The Spokesman," *Esquire,* May 1968, 133.

49. Slotkin, *Gunfighter Nation,* 520–33.

50. George Kahin, *Intervention: How America Became Involved in Vietnam* (1987), 290.

51. Quoted in Olson and Roberts, *Where the Domino Fell,* 168; Hugh Sidey, "The Presidency," *Life,* October 10, 1969, 4.

52. Shelby L. Stanton, *The Rise and Fall of an American Army: U.S. Ground Forces in Vietnam, 1965–1973* (1985).

53. *Los Angeles Times,* September 22, 1967; Michael Wayne quoted in Suid, *Guts and Glory,* 233.

54. Quoted in Suid, *Guts and Glory,* 104–8.

55. *Life,* August 4, 1967, 8.

56. Ron Kovic, *Born on the Fourth of July* (1976), 43, 61, 98.

57. Mary St. John interview; *Variety,* June 15, 1966.

58. Quoted in Appy, *Working-Class War,* 41–42.

59. "John Wayne as the Last Hero," *Time,* August 8, 1969, 56; Paul Keyes interview, MZP.

Chapter 21. Crown Prince of the Silent Majority

1. *New York Times,* June 20 and 30, 1968, and July 4 and 6, 1969; Aissa Wayne, *John Wayne, My Father,* 134.

2. Wallis, *Starmaker,* 158–62.

3. Ibid.

4. Ibid.

5. Henry Hathaway interview, SMU.

6. Dean Smith interview, SMU.

7. Pilar Wayne, *John Wayne,* 231.

8. *Los Angeles Times,* October 8, 1968, and June 21, 1970.

9. Judith Slawson, *Robert Duvall, Hollywood Maverick* (1985), 48; Mary St. John interview; Pilar Wayne, *John Wayne,* 230–32.

10. *Hollywood Reporter,* May 19, 1969; *New York Times,* June 29, 1969; *Playboy,* May 1971, 82; Mary St. John interview; Avery Rennick interview.

11. *New York Times,* June 29, 1969.

12. *New York Times,* July 4 and 6, 1969; Barbara Bernstein, "Not Likely: John Wayne & *True Grit,*" *Focus* (September 1970), 1–2.

13. Lloyd Shearer, "Heart Repairs and All, at 71, the Duke Is King," *Parade,* October 22, 1978, 10; Jody Carlson, *George C. Wallace and the Politics of the Powerlessness* (1981), 82–83; *Playboy,* May 1971, 86; Mary St. John interview.

14. *Los Angeles Times,* May 8, 1969; Mary St. John interview.

15. Barry Goldwater to James S. Olson, March 24 and June 17, 1992; *Los Angeles Herald-Examiner,* January 12 and 22, 1976; David Sutton, "Image vs. Man," *Saturday Evening Post,* March 1976, 120; Molly Haskell, "What Makes John Wayne Larger than Life?," *Village Voice,* August 16, 1976; Will Tusher, "John Wayne Uncensored," *Motion Picture,* August 1976, 17–19.

16. Harry Overstreet and Bonaro Overstreet, *Strange Tactics of Extremism* (1964); Mary St. John interview; Danko Gurovich interview.

17. Avery Rennick interview; James Harvey Young, "Laetrile in Historical Perspective," in Gerald E. Markle and James C. Petersen, *Politics, Science, and Cancer: The Laetrile Phenomenon* (1980), 11–60.

18. See Mary St. John interview; Avery Rennick interview; "Memorandum," June 9, 1966, John Wayne File, FBI, Department of Justice, Washington, D.C.; J. Edgar Hoover to John Wayne, March 19, 1970, ibid.; J. Edgar Hoover to John Wayne, April 8, 1970, ibid.; John Wayne to J. Edgar Hoover, April 20, 1970, ibid.; John Wayne to J. Edgar Hoover, April 24, 1970, ibid.

19. *New York Times,* November 7, 1968; *Washington Post,* January 20–21, 1969; Mary St. John interview.

20. Wallis, *Starmaker,* 157–62.

21. The following material about *The Undefeated* is taken from Pilar Wayne, *John Wayne,* 244–45; *New York Times,* June 29, 1969; Don Collier interview; Aissa Wayne, *John Wayne,* 161; Mary St. John interview; Rock Hudson and Sara Davidson, *Rock Hudson: His Story* (1986), 154–55; Andrew McLaglen interview, SMU.

22. *New York Times,* June 29, July 4 and 6, 1969; *Newsweek,* 73 (June 23, 1969), 95–96; *New Republic,* July 26, 1969, 26; Aissa Wayne, *John Wayne,* 135; Mary St. John interview.

23. Mary St. John interview; Louis Johnson interview; *Los Angeles Herald-Examiner,* December 10, 1969; *Los Angeles Times,* December 23, 1969; *New York Post,* January 17, 1970.

24. Aissa Wayne, *John Wayne,* 110; Pilar Wayne, *John Wayne,* 194.

25. John Wayne interview, MZP; Michael Wayne interview, MZP.

26. Pilar Wayne, *John Wayne,* 234.

27. *Louisville Courier-Journal,* January 25, 1970; Danko Gurovich interview; Mary St. John interview; Pilar Wayne, *John Wayne,* 234–35.

28. *Los Angeles Times,* April 8, 1970; *New York Times,* July 6, 1969, and April 8, 1970.

29. The material on the 1970 Academy Awards ceremony is taken from Pilar Wayne, *John Wayne,* 236–38; Anthony Holden, *Behind the Oscar,* 274–75; *Los Angeles Herald-Examiner,* April 8, 1970; Aissa Wayne, *John Wayne,* 136–38; Mary St. John interview; Brown and Pinkston, *Oscar Dearest* (1987), 62–63; and Riese, *Her Name Is Barbra* (1993), 313.

30. Howard Hawks interview, BYU.

31. *Variety,* June 22, 1970; *Hollywood Reporter,* June 22, 1970.

32. Joseph N. Bell, "John Wayne's Very Private World," *Good Housekeeping,* February 1973, 131; quoted in Alan G. Barbour, *John Wayne* (1974), 15.

33. Mary St. John interview.

34. Avery Rennick interview.

35. *Playboy,* May 1971, 82–90.

36. Mary St. John interview.

Chapter 22. *"Only a Fool Would Think That Anything Is Forever"*

1. *Variety,* January 5, 1979.

2. Les Adams and Buck Rainey, *Shoot-Em-Ups: The Complete Reference Guide to Westerns of the Sound Era* (1985), 533.

3. Richard Slotkin, *Gunfighter Nation: The Myth of the Frontier in Twentieth-Century America* (1993), 596, 613.

4. "An Interview with Arthur Penn," *Cinema* 5 (1969), 36.

5. *Los Angeles Times,* January 20, 1975; Mary St. John interview; Howard Hawks interview, BYU; William Galperin, "History into Allegory: *The Wild Bunch* as Vietnam Movie," *Western Humanities Review* 35 (Summer 1981), 165–72; *Playboy,* May 1971, 79.

6. Associated Press, *The World in 1970* (1971), 127–28.

7. Robert B. Ray, *A Certain Tendency of the Hollywood Cinema* (1985), 309; Pat Stacy, *Duke: A Love Story* (1983), 38.

8. Mary St. John interview.

9. Ibid., Ray, *A Certain Tendency,* 309; Stacy, *Duke,* 38.

10. Stacy, *Duke,* 30–32, 45–55.

11. *The New Yorker,* February 11, 1975, 96–97; *Time,* May 5, 1975, 76; *Variety,* January 5, 1979.

12. Ivor Davis, "A Boozing, Brawling Evening with the Duke," *Los Angeles Magazine,* May 1975, 107.

13. Holden, *Behind the Oscar,* 290–91; Mary St. John interview; Peter Manso, *Brando: A Biography* (1994), 568–74.

14. Holden, *Behind the Oscar,* 300.

15. *Los Angeles Times,* September 2, 1970, February 19, 1974, and November 7, 1977; *Los Angeles Herald-Examiner,* August 17, 1971, and January 17 and August 29, 1972; *Boxoffice,* July 19 and August 23, 1971; *Variety,* April 14, 1977; *Hollywood Reporter,* February 2, 1975; *Tucson Daily Citizen,* April 18, 1970.

16. Happy Shahan interview; Stacy, *Duke,* 57.

17. Joseph N. Bell, "John Wayne," *Arizona Daily Star,* April 17, 1979. See also Wayne's last will and testament, Madison County Historical Society, Winterset, Iowa; *Los Angeles Herald-Examiner,* June 20, 1979; *Hollywood Reporter,* June 21, 1979; Dean Jennings, "The Woes of Box-Office King John Wayne," *Saturday Evening Post,* October 27, 1962, 32.

18. Pilar Wayne, *John Wayne,* 224–27; *Los Angeles Times,* November 16, 1979; *New York Times,* June 21, 1979.

19. John Wayne's last will and testament, Madison County Historical Society, Winterset, Iowa; Pat Stacy, *Duke,* 51–53; Pilar Wayne, *John Wayne,* 228, 250; Todd McCarthy, "Back Talk," *Film Comment* (March 1979), 78–79.

20. *Variety,* May 15, 1974; ibid., July 17, 1974; Wayne Warga, "Hollywood's Last Hero," *West,* January 25, 1970, 3; *Los Angeles Herald-Examiner,* January 9, 1976; *Los Angeles Times,* October 11, 1971; David Sutton, "Image vs. Man," *Saturday Evening Post,* March 1976, 120; Tom Alexander, "The Great Fox Powell, John Wayne, Magic-Dirt Medicine Show," *Fortune,* March 27, 1978, 64–67; "Three Generations of John Wayne's Family Star Together in 'Big Jake,'" Cinema Center Films Press Release, March 22, 1971, MHL; *Time,* January 28, 1974; Joe De Franco interview.

21. Dietrich, *Marlene* (1987), 117; *The Star,* August 29, 1978.

22. *Variety,* November 1, 1978; *Los Angeles Times,* December 1, 1977, and March 5, 1978.

23. Aissa Wayne, *John Wayne, My Father,* 154–55; Mary St. John interview; Danko Gurovich interview; Louis Johnson interview.

24. Alice Johnson interview; Louis Johnson interview; Danko Gurovich interview; John Chohlis, "John Wayne, Cattleman," *Persimmon Hill* 7 (1977), 28–35.

25. Louis Johnson interview; *New York Times,* May 27, 1975.

26. Louis Johnson interview; Mary St. John interview; Aissa Wayne, *John Wayne,* 24–25; Pilar Wayne, *John Wayne,* 83–84.

27. Dorothy Treloar, "What Makes John Wayne Hollywood's Favorite Lover?" *Photoplay,* October 1973, 66; Aissa Wayne, *John Wayne,* 148; Mary St. John interview.

28. Aissa Wayne, *John Wayne,* 158–59, 165–66.

29. "Big Jake," Cinema Center Films News Release, MHL; *Variety,* May 26, 1971.

30. *Variety,* December 29, 1972.

31. Ibid., June 15, 1973.

32. Mary St. John interview; Danko Gurovich interview; Louis Johnson interview; Alice Johnson interview; *Variety,* November 9, 1973.

33. "The John Waynes," *Photoplay* (an undated essay in the Constance McCormick Collection, USC).

34. Mary St. John interview; Danko Gurovich interview; Aissa Wayne, *John Wayne,* 130–33; Louis Johnson interview.

35. Ivor Davis, "A Boozing, Brawling Evening with the Duke," *Los Angeles Magazine,* May 1975, 3; *Parade,* April 7, 1991, 2.

36. Alice Johnson interview.

37. Pilar Wayne, *John Wayne,* 133–34, 202–6, 211–12; Aissa Wayne, *John Wayne,* 32–36, 115–17, 123–24.

38. Mary St. John interview; Jim Gregory, "The Calm Years Are Wild," *Photoplay*, March 1972, 7; Pilar Wayne, *John Wayne*, 211; Aissa Wayne, *John Wayne*, 124–25.

39. Aissa Wayne, *John Wayne*, 122; Pilar Wayne, *John Wayne*, 210–12, 255.

40. Mary St. John interview; Pilar Wayne, *John Wayne*, 247; Robert Shelton interview; Ralph Wingfield interview; Mary St. John interview; Louis Johnson interview.

41. Pilar Wayne, *John Wayne*, 242–43; Paxton, "John Wayne's Screaming Battles," 54.

42. Pilar Wayne, *John Wayne*, 252; Stacy, *Duke*, 25; Mary St. John interview; Louis Johnson interview; Jane Ardmore, "John Wayne's Wife Tells Why They've Split," *Photoplay*, February 1974, 53–54, 114–15; John Reddy, "John Wayne Rides Again, and Again, and Again," *Reader's Digest*, September 1970, 139.

43. Mary St. John interview; Stacy, *Duke*, 21–23.

44. Alice Johnson interview; Mary St. John interview; Stacy, *Duke*, 21–23, 27, 33.

45. Louis Johnson interview; Alice Johnson interview; Mary St. John interview; Will Tusher, "John Wayne Talks About Women," *Photoplay*, June 1975, 17.

46. *Hollywood Reporter*, January 30, 1973; Nancy Anderson, "John Wayne," *Photoplay*, August 1972, 97; Mary St. John interview; Tom Kane interview, MZP.

47. Guy Flatley, "Duke," 9; *Los Angeles Herald-Examiner*, July 21, 1972; *New York Daily News*, August 21, 1972; *Los Angeles Times*, October 5, 1971; *New York Post*, May 8, 1973.

48. *Orange County Chronicle*, September 29, 1976; "What John Wayne Tells His Children About Drugs . . . Hippies . . . the War . . . Sex . . .," *Photoplay*, July 1971, 46–47, 124–26; Jennings, "The Woes of Box-Office King John Wayne," 30.

49. *Playboy*, May 1971, 82.

50. *Hollywood Reporter*, February 5, 1975; *Los Angeles Times*, January 20, 1975; Mary St. John interview; *Los Angeles Herald-Examiner*, October 23, 1960; Richard Braff, "John Wayne," *Sound Stage*, December 1964, 35–39.

51. "What John Wayne Thinks of Today's Movies," *Hollywood Studio*, March 1973, 16; *Hollywood Reporter*, February 6, 1975; "Actor," *California Living*, May 13, 1973, 32; *Christian Science Monitor*, March 10, 1973.

52. Davis, "A Boozing, Brawling Evening," *Los Angeles Magazine*, May 1975, 104–5; Flatley, "Duke," 9; Lorraine Gauguin, "Duke in Durango," *National Review*, 25 (April 27, 1973), 472.

53. Louis Johnson interview; Alice Johnson interview.

54. *Los Angeles Times*, November 26, 1976; Fred Barron, "The Duke Takes Harvard," *Progressive*, 38 (March 1974), 52; Louis Johnson interview.

55. Bell, "John Wayne's *Very* Private World," February 1973, 131; "What John Wayne Tells His Children," 126.

56. Louis Johnson interview; Alice Johnson interview.

57. Jimmy Carter to John Wayne, January 24, 1977, Executive File, Jimmy Carter Presidential Library; *Washington Post*, January 20–21, 1977; *Los Angeles Herald-Examiner*, January 21, 1977; Stacy, *Duke*, 117–18; *Variety*, December 31, 1976; *Newsweek*, November 21, 1977, 62.

58. John Wayne to Jimmy Carter, January 23, 1977, and Jimmy Carter to John Wayne, January 31, 1977, Executive File, Jimmy Carter Presidential Library; *New York Times*, January 22, 1977; Olson and Roberts, *Where the Domino Fell*, 276.

59. John Wayne to Jimmy Carter, December 6, 1978, Executive File, Jimmy Carter Presidential Library.

60. Jimmy Carter to John Wayne, February 15, 1977, Executive File, Jimmy Carter Presidential Library; John Wayne to Jimmy Carter, February 28, 1977, ibid.; John Wayne to

Jimmy Carter, September 8, 1977, ibid.; Jimmy Carter to John Wayne, May 15, 1978, ibid.; John Wayne to Jimmy Carter, June 12, 1978, ibid.

61. The best treatment of the U.S. acquisition of the Canal Zone is David McCullough's *The Path Between the Seas: The Creation of the Panama Canal, 1870-1914* (1977).

62. Marcos G. McGrath, "Ariel or Caliban?" *Foreign Affairs* 52 (October 1973), 75–95.

63. Stephen S. Rosenfeld, "The Panama Negotiations—A Close-Run Thing," *Foreign Affairs* 54 (October 1975), 1–13.

64. *New York Times,* September 6, 1977.

65. *Los Angeles Herald-Examiner,* October 26, 1977; *New York Post,* March 14, 1978; *New York Times,* September 21, 1977; ibid., October 29, 1977; *Hollywood Citizen-News,* January 9, 1970; Joe De Franco interview.

66. *Los Angeles Herald-Examiner,* January 31, 1978; Joe De Franco interview.

67. This quote of the letter from Wayne to Reagan is taken from the *New York Times,* March 16, 1987. The letter itself—John Wayne to Ronald Reagan, November 11, 1977—can be found in the Executive File, Jimmy Carter Presidential Library. Also see Jimmy Carter to John Wayne, October 17, 1977, ibid.; *Atlanta Constitution,* March 4, 1987; Jimmy Carter to James S. Olson, December 11, 1991; *Atlanta Constitution,* March 14, 1977; *Los Angeles Times,* March 15, 1977; Ronald Reagan, "Unforgettable John Wayne," *Reader's Digest,* October 1979, 115; Stacy, *Duke,* 119–20.

68. Jimmy Carter to John Wayne, June 22, 1978, Executive File, Jimmy Carter Presidential Library; "Exchange of Instruments of Ratification of Panama Canal Treaties," *Department of State Bulletin,* 78 (July 1978), 52–57. For an example of one of those letters, see John Wayne to Senator John Sparkman, October 11, 1977, National Archives, Records Group 46, Records of the U.S. Senate, 95th Congress, Treaty Files, ExecN (95–1), Box 29; Joe De Franco interview.

69. Nat Segaloff, *Hurricane Billy: The Stormy Life and Times of William Friedkin* (1990), 167.

Chapter 23. *"You Just Can't Give In To It"*

1. John Wayne interview, JFP; Flatley, "Duke, 18.

2. Stacy, *Duke,* 36–37; Ford, *Pappy,* 316; Gallagher, *John Ford,* 452–53; "John Wayne's Agony," *Modern Screen,* (November 1970), 55, 68–69.

3. Stacy, *Duke,* 38; John Wayne interview, JFP; Flatley, "Duke," 18.

4. Stephen Farber, "Epitaph for a Dying Breed," *New West,* August 30, 1976, 79–81; *Variety,* January 29, 1976; ibid., July 23, 1976; *New York Daily News,* May 9, 1976; Molly Haskell, "What Makes John Wayne Bigger Than Life."

5. Bert Minshall, *On Board with the Duke: John Wayne and the Wild Goose* (1992), 156.

6. Stacy, *Duke,* 91.

7. Ibid., 104.

8. Will Tusher, "How Much Can a Human Body Endure?" *Photoplay,* (September 1975), 60, 78–79; *Los Angeles Times,* December 21, 1974.

9. *Los Angeles Times,* January 10, 1974; ibid., February 1, 1974; *New York Post,* January 16, 1974; *Los Angeles Herald-Examiner,* January 18, 1974; Charles Petersen, "John Wayne at Harvard," *Parade,* February 24, 1974, 20–21; Fred Barron, "The Duke Takes Harvard," *Progressive* 38 (March 1974), 52.

10. Pauline Kael, "*McQ,*" *The New Yorker,* February 11, 1974; *Motion Picture Product Digest,* February 13, 1974; *Variety,* January 23, 1974; David Sutton, "John Wayne is *McQ,*" *Motor Trend,* March 1974, 54–55; Warner Bros. Pressbook, "*McQ,*" MHL.

11. Jean Ardmore, "Cancer Doesn't Fight Fair," *Family Health*, September 1976, 30; *Los Angeles Times*, December 21, 1974; Stacy, *Duke*, 42.

12. Ardmore, "Cancer Doesn't Fight Fair," 58.

13. The material on *Rooster Cogburn* is taken from Anne Edwards, *A Remarkable Woman: A Biography of Katharine Hepburn* (1985), 386–87; Wallis, *Starmaker*, 178–83; Fleischer, *Just Tell Me When to Cry*, 24.

14. Tusher, "Wayne," *Photoplay*, August 1974, 46–47, 70, 74.

15. *Los Angeles Times*, August 30, 1975; *Hollywood Reporter*, August 25, 1975; ibid., October 25, 1975; *Variety*, March 8, 1975; ibid., October 25, 1975; Tusher, "How Much Can a Human Body Endure?" 79; Anne Edwards, *A Remarkable Woman*, 282–83; Michael Freedland, *Katharine Hepburn* (1984), 214–16.

16. Stacy, *Duke*, 100; *Variety*, January 29, 1976; Joan Dow, "John Wayne: Riding into the Sunset?" *Coronet*, August 1976, 33.

17. *Variety*, April 21, 1969.

18. *Los Angeles Herald-Examiner*, February 13, 1976; Pilar Wayne, *John Wayne*, 264.

19. Stacy, *Duke*, 85; Tusher, "Wayne," *Photoplay*, 78.

20. Jane Ardmore, "Duke: His Greatest Battle," *Sunday Woman*, March 4, 1979, 2–3; *Los Angeles Times*, August 6, 1978.

21. Stacy, *Duke*, 121, 127.

22. *Hollywood Reporter*, December 6, 1976; Stacy, *Duke*, 108; Harry S. Shelley, "The Enlarged Prostate: A Brief History of Its Treatment," *Journal of the History of Medicine and Allied Sciences* 24 (October 1969), 452–73; *Los Angeles Herald-Examiner*, November 9, 1976; Variety, November 10, 1976.

23. Stacy, *Duke*, 121; *Variety*, January 24, 1977.

24. Ralph Wingfield interview, May 21, 1991; Stacy, *Duke*, 128–29; *Los Angeles Times*, March 31, 1978; *Hollywood Reporter*, March 31, 1978; *Variety*, March 29, 1978.

25. John Wayne–Rona Barrett interview, quoted in the *Star*, August 29, 1978; *Los Angeles Herald-Examiner*, March 30, 1978; Joe De Franco interview; Stacy, *Duke*, 136–37; Aissa Wayne, *John Wayne*, 180–82.

26. *Los Angeles Herald-Examiner*, April 4, 1978; ibid., and April 16, 1978; *Hollywood Reporter*, April 4, 27–28, 1978.

27. See Jimmy Stewart's comments on Wayne's fatigue, *Village Voice*, August 14, 1978; *Los Angeles Times*, August 6, 1978.

28. Joe De Franco interview.

29. Stacy, *Duke*, 163–64; U. S. Congress, House of Representatives, Committee on Banking, Finance and Urban Affairs, *Hearings on H.R. 3767, A Bill to Authorize the President of the United States to Present on Behalf of the Congress a Specially Struck Gold Medal to John Wayne*, 96th Congress, 1st Session, 1979, 13.

30. Stacy, *Duke*, 165–167.

31. Vincent T. DeVita, Jr., Samuel Hellman, and Steven A. Rosenberg, *Cancer. Principles & Practices of Oncology*, 534–62; E. T. Silverberg, "Cancer Statistics 1980," *CA-A Journal for Clinicians* 30 (1980), 23.

32. See the telegrams from the Los Angeles Office of the Federal Bureau of Investigation to FBI Director, December 14, 1978, and Brooklyn-Queens Office of the Federal Bureau of Investigation to FBI Director, December 19, 1978.

33. Stacy, *Duke*, 169.

34. Pilar Wayne, *John Wayne*, 268–69; R. N. Cooley, "The Diagnostic Accuracy of Upper Gastrointestinal Radiologic Studies," *American Journal of Medical Science* 242 (1961), 628.

35. *People,* July 18, 1988; Stacy, *Duke*, 170–76.

36. Stacy, *Duke*, 182; *Los Angeles Times,* January 12, 1979; *New York Post,* January 12, 1979.

37. J. B. Dupont and I. J. Cohn, Jr., "Gastric Adenocarcinoma," *Current Problems of Cancer* 4 (1980), 25; J. B. DuPont, J. R. Lee, and G. R. Burton, "Adenocarcinoma of the Stomach: Review of 1497 Cases," *Cancer* 41 (1978), 941.

38. K. T. Okajima, "Surgical Treatment of Gastric Cancer with Special Reference to Lymph Node Removal," *Acta Medica Okayama* 31 (1977), 369; A. M. Desmond, "Radical Surgery in Treatment of Carcinoma of the Stomach," *Proceedings of the Royal Society of Medicine* 69 (1976), 867;

39. *Los Angeles Herald-Examiner,* January 13, 1979; *New York Post,* January 13, 1979; *Los Angeles Times,* January 13, 1979; ibid., January 20, 1979.

40. *Hollywood Reporter,* January 18, 1979; *Los Angeles Herald-Examiner,* January 18, 1979; Stacy, *Duke*, 186–87; *Variety,* January 18, 1979; *Los Angeles Times,* January 18, 1979.

41. *Hollywood Reporter,* February 9, 1979; ibid., February 12, 1979; *Los Angeles Herald-Examiner,* February 9, 1979; *Variety,* February 9, 1979; ibid., February 14, 1979; Stacy, *Duke*, 187–88; W. V. Lawrence, "Nutritional Consequences of Surgical Resection of Gastrointestinal Tract for Cancer," *Cancer Research* 37 (1977), 2379.

42. C. C. Nordman, "The Value of Megavolt Therapy in Carcinoma of the Stomach," *Strahlentherapie* 144 (1972), 635; H. T. Asakawa, "High Energy X-Ray Therapy of Gastric Carcinoma," *Journal of the Japanese Society for Cancer Therapy* 8 (1973), 362.

43. Stacy, *Duke*, 192–200; R. B. Roswit et al., "Radiation Tolerance of the Gastrointestinal Tract," in J. Vaeth Front, ed., *Radiation Therapy and Oncology* (1979), 160–81.

44. Stacy, *Duke*, 199.

45. Ibid., 15.

46. Tom Kane, "John Wayne Saved My Life," *Photoplay,* March 1973, 36; Pilar Wayne, *John Wayne*, 270; Stacy, *Duke*, 200; *New York Times,* April 11, 1979; Michael Freedland, *Jane Fonda: A Biography* (1988), 207–8.

47. DeVita, Jr., Hellman, and Rosenberg, *Cancer,* 534–62; James Brachman and David Wilson, "John Wayne," *Orange County Chronicle,* September 29, 1976, 1–2.

48. Ralph Wingfield interview; Minshall, *On Board with the Duke,* 158.

49. Stacy, *Duke*, 209–211; *Los Angeles Times,* April 24, 1979.

50. Stacy, *Duke*, 210–11; *The Hollywood Reporter,* June 19, 1963; *Los Angeles Times,* June 19, 1963; *Los Angeles Herald-Examiner,* April 26, 1979.

51. *Los Angeles Times,* April 26, 1979.

52. Stacy, *Duke*, 217–19.

53. *Los Angeles Herald-Examiner,* May 2–4, 1979; *Variety,* May 2–4, 1979; *New York Daily News,* May 5, 1979.

54. C. G. Moertel, "Chemotherapy of Gastrointestinal Cancer," *Clinical Gastroenterology* 5 (1976), 777.

55. E. C. Borden, "Interferons: Rationale for Clinical Trials in Neoplastic Disease," *Annals of Internal Medicine* 91 (1979), 472–79; *New York Daily News,* May 5, 1979.

56. Harry Carey Jr. interview.

57. *Glendale News Press,* December 7, 1970; *Los Angeles Times,* June 14, 1979; Douglas B. MacMullen and H. C. Pinky Meredith, *A Sentimental Journey—The First Hundred Years.*

The Malaikah Temple, 1888–1988 (1988), 126. Also see the photograph #55956 of Wayne being raised to the rank of Master Mason, July 11, 1972, at Tucson, Arizona, Arizona Historical Society, Tucson, Arizona; Kenneth H. Boucher to Kent C. Storer, September 7, 1988, Papers of the Al Malaikah Temple, Los Angeles, California; *Arizona Daily Star,* July 11, 1970.

58. May Mann, "John Wayne," *Photoplay,* May 1973, 98.

59. Happy Shahan interview; Diane Bibbee, "John Wayne: Profile of a Winner," *Orange Coast,* May 1979, 41.

60. Russell Birdwell interview, MZP.

61. Pilar Wayne, *John Wayne,* 46; May Mann, "John Wayne," *Photoplay,* May 1973, 98; Ford, *Pappy,* 316; Gallagher, *John Ford,* 452–53.

62. Barbara Walters–John Wayne interview, ABC News, March 13, 1979; Stacy, *Duke,* 171–77.

63. *Los Angeles Times,* June 14, 1979; *Irvine Daily Pilot,* June 15, 1979; *Los Angeles Herald-Examiner,* June 16, 1979.

64. *New York Times,* May 22–26, 1979; Maureen O'Hara interview.

65. *New York Times,* May 6, 1979; Stacy, *Duke,* 232–39.

66. Katharine Hepburn, "Hooked on John Wayne," *TV Guide,* September 17, 1977, 63.

67. *New York Daily News,* June 8, 1979; *Los Angeles Times,* June 9, 1979; Stacy, *Duke,* 223–24; Pilar Wayne, *John Wayne,* 270–71.

68. *Los Angeles Times,* June 9, 1979.

69. Mary St. John interview; Louis Johnson interview; Alice Johnson interview; *The Rubáiyát of Omar Khayyám* (1949), 90.

70. *Los Angeles Times,* June 12, 1979; ibid., June 14, 1979; *Irvine Daily Pilot,* June 15, 1979; *Los Angeles Herald-Examiner,* June 16, 1979; Stacy, *Duke,* 242.

John Wayne Filmography

Brown of Harvard (MGM, 1926). Director: Jack Conway. Cast: William Haines, Jack Pickford, Francis X. Bushman Jr., Mary Brian.

*Bardelys the Magnificent (MGM, 1926). Director: King Vidor. Cast: John Gilbert, Eleanor
Boardman, Roy D'Arcy, Lionel Belmore.

*The Great K & A Train Robbery (William Fox Studio, 1926). Director: Louis Sieler. Cast:
Tom Mix, Dorothy Duan, William Walling, Harry Grippe.

The Drop Kick (First National, 1927). Director: Millard Webb, Cast: Hedda Hopper, Richard
Barthelmess, Barbara Kent, Dorothy Revier, Eugene Strong.

*Annie Laurie (MGM, 1927). Director: John S. Robertson. Cast: Norman Kerry, Lillian
Gish, Creighton Hale, Joseph Striker, Hobart Bosworth.

*Noah's Ark (Warner Bros., First National, 1928). Director: Michael Curtiz. Cast: Dolores
Costello, George O'Brien, Noah Beery Sr., Louise Fazenda.

Mother Machree (William Fox Studios, 1928). Director: John Ford. Cast: Belle Bennett, Neil
Hamilton, Philippe De Lacy, Victor McLaglen, Pat Somerset.

Four Sons (William Fox Studios, 1928). Director: John Ford. Cast: Margaret Mann, James
Hall, Charles Morton, George Meeker, Francis X. Bushman Jr.

Hangman's House (William Fox Studios, 1928). Director: John Ford. Cast: Victor McLaglen,
June Collyer, Hobart Bosworth, Larry Kent.

*Speakeasy (William Fox Studio, 1929). Director: Benjamin Stoloff. Cast: Paul Page, Lola
Lane, Henry Walthall.

*The Black Watch (William Fox Studio, 1929). Director: John Ford. Cast: Victor McLaglen,
Myrna Loy, David Rollins, Lumsden Hare.

*Films with the asterisk indicate that, although Wayne was not billed nor readily visible on-
screen, he did play an extra in them.

Words and Music (William Fox Studios, 1929). Director: James Tinling. Cast: Lois Moran, David Percy, Helen Twelvetrees, William Orlamond, Duke Morrison.

Salute (William Fox Studios, 1929). Director: John Ford. Cast: George O'Brien, Helen Chandler, Stepin Fetchit, Joyce Compton, Duke Morrison.

The Forward Pass (First National, 1929). Director: E. Cline. Cast: Douglas Fairbanks Jr., Loretta Young, Phyllis Crane, Guinn Williams.

Men Without Women (William Fox Studios, 1930). Director: John Ford. Cast: Kenneth MacKenna, Paul Page, Frank Albertson, Duke Morrison.

Born Reckless (William Fox Studio, 1930). Director: John Ford. Cast: Edmund Love, Catherine Owen, Lee Tracy, Marguerite Churchill.

Rough Romance (William Fox Studio, 1930). Director: A. F. Erickson. Cast: George O'Brien, Helen Chandler, Antonio Moreno, Eddie Borden, Duke Morrison.

Cheer Up and Smile (William Fox Studio, 1930). Director: Sidney Lanfield. Cast: Arthur Lake, Dixie Lee, Whispering Jack Smith, Duke Morrison.

The Big Trail (William Fox Studio, 1930). Director: Raoul Walsh. Cast: John Wayne, Marguerite Churchill, El Brendel, Tully Marshall, Tyrone Power Sr.

Girls Demand Excitement (William Fox Studio, 1931). Director: Seymour Felix. Cast: Virginia Cherrill, John Wayne, Marguerite Churchill, Helen Jerome Eddy.

Three Girls Lost (William Fox Studio, 1931). Director: Sidney Lanfield. Cast: Loretta Young, John Wayne, Lew Cody, Joyce Compton.

Men Are Like That (Columbia, 1931), released earlier under the title *Arizona* (Columbia, 1931). Director: George B. Seitz. Cast: Laura La Plante, John Wayne, June Clyde, Forrest Stanley.

The Deceiver (Columbia, 1931). Director: Louis King. Cast: Lloyd Hughes, Dorothy Sebastian, Ian Keith.

Range Feud (Columbia, 1931). Director: D. Ross Lederman. Cast: Buck Jones, John Wayne, Susan Fleming, Ed LeSaint.

Maker of Men (Columbia, 1931). Director: Edward Sedgwick. Cast: Jack Holt, Richard Cromwell, Joan Marsh, John Wayne.

The Voice of Hollywood (Tiffany, 1932). Director: Mark D'Agostino. Cast: John Wayne, George Bancroft, El Brendel, Jackie Cooper, Gary Cooper, Lupe Velez.

The Shadow of the Eagle (Mascot, 1932). Director: Ford Beebe. Cast: John Wayne, Dorothy Gulliver, Yakima Canutt. (Twelve-chapter serial.)

Texas Cyclone (Columbia, 1932). Director: D. Ross Lederman. Cast: Tim McCoy, Shirley Grey, Wheeler Oakman, John Wayne.

That's My Boy (Columbia, 1932). Director: Roy William Neill. Cast: Richard Cromwell, Dorothy Jordan, May Marsh, Arthur Stone, Douglas Dumbrill.

Two-Fisted Law (Columbia, 1932). Director: D. Ross Lederman. Cast: Tim McCoy, Alice Day, Tully Marshall, John Wayne.

Lady and Gent (Paramount, 1932). Director: Stephen Roberts. Cast: George Bancroft, Wynne Gibson, Charles Starrett, James Gleason, John Wayne.

The Hurricane Express (Mascot, 1932). Directors: Armand Schaefer and J. P. McGowan. Cast: John Wayne, Shirley Grey, Tully Marshall, Conway Tearle. (Twelve-chapter serial.)

The Hollywood Handicap (The Thalians Club–Universal, 1932). Director: Charles Lamount. Cast: John Wayne, Anita Stewart, Bert Wheeler, Tully Marshall, Dickie Moore.

Ride Him Cowboy (Warner Bros., 1932). Director: Fred Allen. Cast: John Wayne, Ruth Hall, Harry Gribbon, Henry B. Walthall.

The Big Stampede (Warner Bros., 1932). Director: Tenny Wright. Cast: John Wayne, Noah Beery, Mae Madison, Luis Alberni.

Haunted Gold (Warner Bros., 1932). Director: Mack V. Wright. Cast: John Wayne, Sheila Terry, Erville Alderson, Harry Woods.

The Telegraph Trail (Warner Bros., 1933). Director: Tenny Wright. Cast: John Wayne, Marceline Day, Frank McHugh, Yakima Canutt.

The Three Musketeers (Mascot, 1933). Directors: Armand Schaefer and Colbert Clark. Cast: John Wayne, Ruth Hall, Jack Mulhall, Francis X. Bushman Jr. (Twelve-chapter serial.) In 1946 the footage was edited and released by Favorite Films as a feature called *Desert Command.*

Central Airport (Warner Bros., 1933). Director: William A. Wellman. Cast: Richard Barthelmess, Sally Eilers, Tom Brown, John Wayne.

Somewhere in Sonora (Warner Bros., 1933). Director: Mack V. Wright. Cast: John Wayne, Henry B. Walthall, Shirley Palmer, J. P. McGowan.

His Private Secretary (Showmen's Pictures, 1933). Director: Philip H. Whitman. Cast: John Wayne, Evalyn Knapp, Alec B. Francis, Reginald Barlow.

The Life of Jimmy Dolan (Warner Bros., 1933). Director: Archie Mayo. Cast: Douglas Fairbanks Jr., Loretta Young, Fifi D'Orsay, Mickey Rooney, John Wayne.

Baby Face (Warner Bros., 1933). Director: Alfred E. Green. Cast: Barbara Stanwyck, George Brent, Donald Cook, John Wayne.

The Man From Monterey (Warner Bros., 1933). Director: Mack V. Wright. Cast: John Wayne, Ruth Hall, Luis Alberni, Francis Ford.

Riders of Destiny (Lone Star–Monogram, 1933). Director R. N. Bradbury. Cast: John Wayne, Cecelia Parker, George Hayes, Forrest Taylor.

College Coach (Warner Bros., 1933). Director: William A. Wellman. Cast: Pat O'Brien, Ann Dvorak, Dick Powell, Hugh Herbert, John Wayne.

Sagebrush Trail (Lone Star–Monogram, 1933). Directors: Armand Schaefer. Cast: John Wayne, Nancy Shubert, Lane Chandler, Yakima Canutt.

The Lucky Texan (Lone Star–Monogram, 1934). Director: R. N. Bradbury. Cast: John Wayne, Barbara Sheldon, George Hayes, Yakima Canutt.

West of the Divide (Lone Star–Monogram, 1934). Director: R. N. Bradbury. Cast: John Wayne, Virginia Browne Faire, Lloyd Whitlock, George Hayes.

Blue Steel (Lone Star–Monogram, 1934). Director: R. N. Bradbury. Cast: John Wayne, Eleanor Hunt, George Hayes, Yakima Canutt.

The Man from Utah (Lone Star Monogram, 1934). Director: R. N. Bradbury. Cast: John Wayne, Polly Ann Young, George Hayes, Yakima Canutt.

Randy Rides Alone (Lone Star–Monogram, 1934). Director: Harry Fraser. Cast: John Wayne, Alberta Vaughn, George Hayes, Earl Dwire.

The Star Packer (Lone Star–Monogram, 1934). Director: R. N. Bradbury. Cast: John Wayne, Verna Hillie, George Hayes, Earl Dwire.

The Trail Beyond (Lone Star–Monogram, 1934). Director: R. N. Bradbury. Cast: John Wayne, Verna Hillie, Noah Beery Sr., Noah Beery Jr.

The Lawless Frontier (Lone Star–Monogram, 1934). Director: R. N. Bradbury. Cast: John Wayne, Sheila Terry, George Hayes, Earl Dwire.

'Neath the Arizona Skies (Lone Star–Monogram, 1934). Director: Harry Fraser. Cast: John Wayne, Sheila Terry, Jay Wilsey (Buffalo Bill Jr.), Shirley Rickert.

Texas Terror (Lone Star–Monogram, 1935). Director: R. N. Bradbury. Cast: John Wayne, Lucille Brown, LeRoy Mason, George Hayes.

✓ *Rainbow Valley* (Lone Star–Monogram, 1935). Director: R. N. Bradbury. Cast: John Wayne, Lucille Brown, LeRoy Mason, George Hayes.

✓ *The Desert Trail* (Lone Star–Republic, 1935). Director: Cullen Lewis. Cast: John Wayne, Lucille Brown, LeRoy Mason, George Hayes.

✓ *The Dawn Rider* (Monogram-Republic, 1935). Director: R. N. Bradbury. Cast: John Wayne, Marion Burns, Reed Howes, Yakima Canutt.

✓ *Paradise Canyon* (Monogram, 1935). Director: Carl Pierson. Cast: John Wayne, Marion Burns, Reed Howes, Yakima Canutt.

✓ *Westward Ho* (Republic, 1935). Director: R. N. Bradbury. Cast: John Wayne, Sheila Mannors (later Sheila Bromley), Frank McGlynn Jr., Jack Curtis.

✓ *The New Frontier* (Republic, 1935). Director: Carl Pierson. Cast: John Wayne, Muriel Evans, Murdoch MacQuarrie, Alan Cavan.

✓ *The Lawless Range* (Republic, 1935). Director: R. N. Bradbury. Cast: John Wayne, Sheila Mannors, Earl Dwire, Frank McGlynn Jr.

✓ *The Oregon Trail* (Republic, 1936). Director: Scott Pembroke. Cast: John Wayne, Ann Rutherford, E. H. Calvert, Yakima Canutt.

✓ *The Lawless Nineties* (Republic, 1936). Director: Joseph Kane. Cast: John Wayne, Ann Rutherford, Harry Woods, George Hayes.

✓ *King of the Pecos* (Republic, 1936). Director: Joseph Kane. Cast: John Wayne, Muriel Evans, Cy Kendall, Jack Clifford.

✓ *The Lonely Trail* (Republic, 1936). Director: Joseph Kane. Cast: John Wayne, Ann Rutherford, Cy Kendall, Bob Kortman.

✓ *Winds of the Wasteland* (Republic, 1936). Director: Mack V. Wright. Cast: John Wayne, Phyllis Fraser, Douglas Cosgrove, Yakima Canutt.

✓ *The Sea Spoilers* (Universal, 1936). Director: Frank Strayer. Cast: John Wayne, Nan Grey, William Bakewell, Fuzzy Knight.

✓ *Conflict* (Universal, 1936). Director: David Howard. Cast: John Wayne, Jean Rogers, Tommy Bupp, Eddie Borden, Ward Bond.

✓ *California Straight Ahead* (Universal, 1937). Director: Arthur Lubin. Cast: John Wayne, Louise Latimer, Robert McWade, Tully Marshall.

✓ *I Cover the War* (Universal, 1937). Director: Arthur Lubin. Cast: John Wayne, Gwen Gaze, Don Barclay, Pat Somerset.

✓ *Idol of the Crowds* (Universal, 1937). Director: Arthur Lubin. Cast: John Wayne, Sheila Bromley, Charles Brokaw.

✓ *Adventure's End* (Universal, 1937). Director: Arthur Lubin. Cast: John Wayne, Diana Gibson, Montagu Love, Maurice Black.

✓ *Born to the West* (Paramount, 1937). Director: Charles Barton. Cast: John Wayne, Marsha Hunt, Johnny Mack Brown.

✓ *Pals of the Saddle* (Republic, 1938). Director: George Sherman. Cast: John Wayne, Ray Corrigan, Max Terhune, Doreen McKay.

✓ *Overland Stage Raiders* (Republic, 1938). Director: George Sherman. Cast: John Wayne, Ray Corrigan, Max Terhune, Louise Brooks.

✓ *Santa Fe Stampede* (Republic, 1938). Director: George Sherman. Cast: John Wayne, Ray Corrigan, Max Terhune, William Farnum.

✓ *Red River Range* (Republic, 1938). Director: George Sherman. Cast: John Wayne, Ray Corrigan, Max Terhune, Polly Moran.

Stagecoach (Walter Wanger Productions/United Artists, 1939). Director: John Ford. Cast: Claire Trevor, John Wayne, John Carradine, Thomas Mitchell.

The Night Riders (Republic, 1939). Director: George Sherman. Cast: John Wayne, Ray Corrigan, Max Terhune, Doreen McKay.

Three Texas Steers (Republic, 1939). Director: George Sherman. Cast: John Wayne, Ray Corrigan, Max Terhune, Carole Landis.

Wyoming Outlaw (Republic, 1939). Director: George Sherman. Cast: John Wayne, Ray Corrigan, Raymond Hatton, Donald Barry.

New Frontier (Republic, 1939). Director: George Sherman. Cast: John Wayne, Ray Corrigan, Raymond Hatton, Phylis Isley (later Jennifer Jones).

Allegheny Uprising (RKO Radio, 1939). Director: William Seiter. Cast: Claire Trevor, John Wayne, George Sanders, Brian Donlevy.

The Dark Command (Republic, 1940). Director: Raoul Walsh. Cast: Claire Trevor, John Wayne, Walter Pidgeon, Roy Rogers.

Three Faces West (Republic, 1940). Director: Bernard Vorhaus. Cast: John Wayne, Charles Coburn, Sigrid Gurie, Spencer Charters.

The Long Voyage Home (Walter Wanger Productions/United Artists, 1940). Director: John Ford. Cast: John Wayne, Thomas Mitchell, Ian Hunter, Barry Fitzgerald.

Seven Sinners (Universal, 1940). Director: Tay Garnett. Cast: Marlene Dietrich, John Wayne, Albert Dekker, Broderick Crawford.

A Man Betrayed (Republic, 1941). Director: John H. Auer. Cast: John Wayne, Frances Dee, Edward Ellis, Ward Bond.

Lady from Louisiana (Republic, 1941). Director: Bernard Vorhaus. Cast: John Wayne, Ona Munson, Ray Middleton, Dorothy Dandridge.

The Shepherd of the Hills (Paramount, 1941). Director: Henry Harhaway. Cast: John Wayne, Betty Field, Harry Carey, Marjorie Main.

Stars Past and Present (Republic one-reel short, 1941), handled by Harriet Parsons. John Wayne appeared in two scenes with Ann Miller.

Lady for a Night (Republic, 1942). Director: Leigh Jason. Cast: Joan Blondell, John Wayne, Ray Middleton, Philip Merivale.

Reap the Wild Wind (Paramount, 1942). Director: Cecil B. DeMille. Cast: Ray Milland, John Wayne, Paulette Goddard, Raymond Massey.

The Spoilers (Charles K. Feldman Group/Universal, 1942). Director: Ray Enright. Cast: Marlene Dietrich, Randolph Scott, John Wayne, Margaret Lindsay.

In Old California (Republic, 1942). Director: William McGann. Cast: John Wayne, Binnie Barnes, Albert Dekker, Helen Parrish.

Flying Tigers (Republic, 1942). Director: David Miller. Cast: John Wayne, John Carroll, Anna Lee, Paul Kelly.

Reunion in France (MGM, 1942). Director: Jules Dassin. Cast: Joan Crawford, John Wayne, Reginald Owen, John Carradine.

Pittsburgh (Charles K. Feldman Group/Universal, 1942). Director: Lewis Seiler. Cast: Marlene Dietrich, Randolph Scott, John Wayne, Frank Craven.

A Lady Takes a Chance (RKO Radio, 1943). Director: William A. Seiter. Cast: Jean Arthur, John Wayne, Charles Winninger, Phil Silvers.

In Old Oklahoma (Republic, 1943). Director: Albert S. Rogell. Cast: John Wayne, Martha Scott, Albert Dekker, George Hayes.

The Fighting Seabees (Republic, 1944). Director: Edward Ludwig. Cast: John Wayne, Dennis O'Keefe, Susan Hayward, William Frawley.

Tall in the Saddle (RKO Radio, 1944). Director: Edwin L. Marin. Cast: John Wayne, Ella Raines, Ward Bond, Audrey Long.

Flame of Barbary Coast (Republic, 1945). Director: Joseph Kane. Cast: John Wayne, Ann Dvorak, Joseph Schildkraut, William Frawley.

Back to Bataan (RKO Radio, 1945). Director: Edward Dmytryk. Cast: John Wayne, Anthony Quinn, Beulah Bondi, Richard Loo.

They Were Expendable (MGM, 1945). Director: John Ford. Cast: Robert Montgomery, John Wayne, Donna Reed, Jack Holt, Ward Bond.

Dakota (Republic, 1945). Director: Joseph Kane. Cast: John Wayne, Vera Hruba Ralston, Walter Brennan, Ward Bond.

Without Reservations (RKO Radio, 1946). Director: Mervyn LeRoy. Cast: Claudette Colbert, John Wayne, Don DeFore, Anne Triola.

Angel and the Badman (Republic, 1947). Director: James Edward Grant. Cast: John Wayne, Gail Russell, Harry Carey, Bruce Cabot.

Tycoon (RKO Radio, 1947). Director: Richard Wallace. Cast: John Wayne, Laraine Day, Sir Cedric Hardwicke, Judith Anderson.

Fort Apache (RKO Radio, 1948). Director: John Ford. Cast: John Wayne, Henry Fonda, Shirley Temple, John Agar.

Red River (Monterey/United Artists, 1948). Director: Howard Hawks. Cast: John Wayne, Montgomery Clift, Joanne Dru, Walter Brennan.

Three Godfathers (Argosy Pictures/MGM, 1949). Director: John Ford. Cast: John Wayne, Pedro Armandariz, Harry Carey Jr., Ward Bond.

Wake of the Red Witch (Republic, 1949). Director: Edward Ludwig. Cast: John Wayne, Gail Russell, Gig Young, Adele Mara.

The Fighting Kentuckian (Republic, 1949). Director: George Waggner. Cast: John Wayne, Vera Hruba Ralston, Philip Dorn, Oliver Hardy.

She Wore a Yellow Ribbon (Argosy Pictures/RKO Radio, 1949). Director: John Ford. Cast: John Wayne, Joanne Dru, John Agar, Ben Johnson.

Sands of Iwo Jima (Republic, 1949). Director: Allan Dwan. Cast: John Wayne, John Agar, Adele Mara, Forrest Tucker.

Rio Grande (Argosy Pictures/Republic, 1950). Director: John Ford. Cast: John Wayne, Maureen O'Hara, Ben Johnson, J. Carrol Naish.

Operation Pacific (Warner Bros., 1951). Director: George Waggner. Cast: John Wayne, Patricia Neal, Ward Bond, Scott Forbes.

Flying Leathernecks (RKO Radio, 1951). Director: Nicholas Ray. Cast: John Wayne, Robert Ryan. Don Taylor, Janis Cater.

The Quiet Man (Argosy Pictures/Republic, 1952). Director: John Ford. Cast: John Wayne, Maureen O'Hara, Barry Fitzgerald, Ward Bond.

Big Jim McLain (Wayne-Fellows/Warner Bros., 1952). Director: Edward Ludwig. Cast: John Wayne, Nancy Olson, James Arness, Alan Napier.

Trouble Along the Way (Warner Bros., 1953). Director: Michael Curtiz. Cast: John Wayne, Donna Reed, Charles Coburn, Tom Tully.

Island in the Sky (Wayne-Fellows/Warner Bros., 1953). Director: William A. Wellman. Cast: John Wayne, Lloyd Nolan, James Arness, Andy Devine.

Hondo (Wayne-Fellows/Warner Bros., 1953). Director: John Farrow. Cast: John Wayne, Geraldine Page, Ward Bond, James Arness.

The High and the Mighty (Wayne-Fellows/Warner Bros., 1954). Director: William A. Wellman. Cast: John Wayne, Claire Trevor, Robert Stack, Laraine Day.

The Sea Chase (Warner Bros., 1955). Director: John Farrow. Cast: John Wayne, Lana Turner, David Farrar, Tab Hunter.

Blood Alley (Batjac/Warner Bros., 1955). Director: William A. Wellman. Cast: John Wayne, Lauren Bacall, Paul Fix, Joy Kim.

Rookie of the Year (Television: *Screen Directors Playhouse,* 1955). Director: John Ford. Cast: John Wayne, Vera Miles, James Gleason, Ward Bond.

A Challenge of Ideas (Documentary: U.S.A. Information Films, 1955). Cast: John Wayne, Helen Hayes, David Brinkley.

The Conqueror (RKO Radio, 1956). Director: Dick Powell. Cast: John Wayne, Susan Hayward, Pedro Armendariz, Agnes Moorehead.

The Searchers (C. V. Whitney Pictures/Warner Bros., 1956). Director: John Ford. Cast: John Wayne, Vera Miles, Natalie Wood, Harry Carey Jr., Ward Bond.

The Wings of Eagles (MGM, 1957). Director: John Ford. Cast: John Wayne, Maureen O'Hara, Dan Dailey, Ward Bond.

Jet Pilot (Howard Hughes–RKO Radio/Universal International, 1957). Director: Josef von Sternberg. Cast: John Wayne, Janet Leigh, Jay C. Flippen, Paul Fix.

Legend of the Lost (Batjac/Robert Haggiag/Dear Film Productions/United Artists, 1957). Director: Henry Hathaway. Cast: John Wayne, Sophia Loren, Rossano Brazzi.

I Married a Woman (Universal International for RKO Radio, 1958). Director: Hal Kanter. Cast: George Gobel, Diana Dors, Adolphe Menjou, John Wayne.

The Barbarian and the Geisha (Twentieth Century-Fox, 1958). Director: John Huston. Cast: John Wayne, Eiko Ando, Sam Jaffe.

Rio Bravo (Armada/Warner Bros., 1959). Director: Howard Hawks. Cast: John Wayne, Dean Martin, Angie Dickinson, Walter Brennan.

The Horse Soldiers (Mahin-Rackin/Mirisch Productions/United Artists, 1959). Director: John Ford. Cast: John Wayne, William Holden, Constance Towers, Hoot Gibson.

The Alamo (Batjac/United Artists, 1960). Director: John Wayne. Cast: John Wayne, Richard Widmark, Laurence Harvey, Richard Boone.

North to Alaska (Twentieth Century-Fox, 1960). Director: Henry Hathaway. Cast: John Wayne, Stewart Granger, Ernie Kovacs, Fabian.

The Colter Craven Story (Television: *Wagon Train* television episode, aired November 23, 1960). Director: John Ford. Cast: John Wayne, Ward Bond, John Carradine, Carleton Young, Hank Worden.

The Comancheros (Twentieth Century-Fox, 1961). Director: Michael Curtiz. Cast: John Wayne, Stuart Whitman, Lee Marvin, Ina Balin.

The Man Who Shot Liberty Valance (John Ford Productions/Paramount, 1962). Director: John Ford. Cast: James Stewart, John Wayne, Lee Marvin, Vera Miles.

Hatari! (Malabar/Paramount, 1962). Director: Howard Hawks. Cast: John Wayne, Elsa Martinelli, Hardy Kruger, Red Buttons.

How the West Was Won (Cinerama/MGM, 1962). Directors: John Ford, Henry Hathaway, George Marshall, and Richard Thorpe. Cast: John Wayne, Henry Fonda, Karl Malden, Robert Preston.

Flashing Spikes (Television: *Alcoa Premiere,* aired October 4, 1962). Director: John Ford. Cast: James Stewart, Jack Warden, Patrick Wayne, Harry Carey Jr., Edward Buchanan, John Wayne.

The Longest Day (Twentieth Century-Fox, 1963). Directors: Ken Annakin, Andrew Marton, Bernhard Wicki, Darryl F. Zanuck, Gerd Oswald. Cast: Eddie Albert, Richard Burton, Robert Mitchum, John Wayne.

Donovan's Reef (John Ford Productions/Paramount, 1963). Director: John Ford. Cast: John Wayne, Lee Marvin, Elizabeth Allen, Jack Warden.

McLintock! (Batjac/United Artists, 1963). Director: Andrew V. McLaglen. Cast: John Wayne, Patrick Wayne, Yvonne De Carlo, Maureen O'Hara.

Circus World (Bronston-Midway/Paramount, 1964). Director: Henry Hathaway. Cast: John Wayne, Claudia Cardinale, Rita Hayworth, Lloyd Nolan.

The Greatest Story Ever Told (George Stevens Production Company/United Artists, 1965). Director: George Stevens. Cast: Max von Sydow, Carroll Baker, Pat Boone, Victor Buno, John Wayne.

In Harm's Way (Sigma/Paramount, 1965). Director: Otto Preminger. Cast: John Wayne, Kirk Douglas, Patricia Neal, Paula Prentiss.

The Sons of Katie Elder (Hal Wallis Production/Paramount, 1965). Director: Henry Hathaway. Cast: John Wayne, Dean Martin, Martha Hyer, Michael Anderson Jr.

Cast a Giant Shadow (Mirisch–Llenroc–Batjac/United Artists, 1966). Director: Melville Shavelson. Cast: Kirk Douglas, Yul Brynner, Senta Berger, Frank Sinatra, John Wayne.

The War Wagon (Marvin Schwartz/Batjac/Universal, 1967). Director: Burt Kennedy. Cast: John Wayne, Kirk Douglas, Howard Keel, Keenan Wynn.

El Dorado (Lauren/Paramount, 1967). Director: Howard Hawks. Cast: John Wayne, Robert Mitchum, James Caan, Charlene Holt.

The Green Berets (Batjac/Warner Bros./Seven Arts, 1968). Director: John Wayne. Cast: John Wayne, David Janssen, Jim Hutton, Aldo Ray.

Hellfighters (Universal, 1969). Director: Andrew V. McLaglen. Cast: John Wayne, Katharine Ross, Jim Hutton, Vera Miles.

True Grit (Hal Wallis Production/Paramount, 1969). Director: Henry Hathaway. Cast: John Wayne, Glen Campbell, Kim Darby, Robert Duvall.

The Undefeated (Twentieth Century-Fox, 1969). Director: Andrew V. McLaglen. Cast: John Wayne, Rock Hudson, Tony Aguilar, Lee Merriwether.

Chisum (Batjac/Warner Bros., 1970). Director: Andrew V. McLaglen. Cast: John Wayne, Forrest Tucker, Christopher George, Pamela McMyler.

Rio Lobo (Malabar/Cinema Center/Twentieth Century-Fox, 1970). Director: Howard Hawks. Cast: John Wayne, Jorge Rivero, Jennifer O'Neill, Jack Elam.

No Substitute for Victory (Documentary: Alaska Pictures Corp., 1970). Director: Robert F. Slatzer. Cast: Gen. William Westmoreland, Gen. Mark Clark, Mayor Sam Yorty, John Wayne.

Chesty (Documentary: John Ford Productions, 1970). Director: John Ford. Cast: John Wayne (on-camera narrator).

Big Jake (Batjac, National General for Cinema Center, 1971). Director: George Sherman. Cast: John Wayne, Richard Boone, Maureen O'Hara, Patrick Wayne.

Directed by John Ford (Television: American Film Institute Productions, 1971). Director: Peter Bogdanovich.

The Cowboys (Sanford/Warner Bros., 1972). Director: Mark Rydell. Cast: John Wayne, Roscoe Lee Browne, Bruce Dern, Colleen Dewhurst.

Cancel My Reservation (Naho/Warner Bros., 1972). Director: Paul Bogart. Cast: Bob Hope, Eva Marie Saint, Ralph Bellamy, John Wayne.

The Train Robbers (Batjac/Warner Bros., 1973). Director: Burt Kennedy. Cast: John Wayne, Ann-Margret, Rod Taylor, Ben Johnson.

Cahill, United States Marshal (Batjac/Warner Bros., 1973). Director: Andrew V. McLaglen. Cast: John Wayne, George Kennedy, Gary Grimes, Neville Brand.

McQ (Batjac/Levy-Gardner/Warner Bros., 1974). Director: John Sturges. Cast: John Wayne, Eddie Albert, Diana Muldaur, Colleen Dewhurst.

Brannigan (Wellborn/United Artists, 1975). Director: Douglas Hickox. Cast: John Wayne, Richard Attenborough, Mel Ferrer, Judy Geeson.

Rooster Cogburn (Hal Wallis Production/Universal, 1975). Director: Stuart Millar. Cast: John Wayne, Katharine Hepburn, Richard Jordan, Strother Martin.

The Shootist (Dino D. Laurentis/Paramount, 1976). Director: Don Siegel. Cast: John Wayne, Lauren Bacall, Ron Howard, James Stewart.

Bibliography

From his starring role in *The Big Trail* in 1930 to his final appearance at the 1979 Academy Awards ceremony, John Wayne often occupied center stage in American popular culture. He evolved into a global icon, the most recognizable American of the twentieth century, and tens of thousands of articles have been written about him around the world. With the assistance of the Margaret Herrick Library of the Motion Picture Academy of Arts and Sciences (MHL) and the New York Public Library, we were able to read most of them, but we obviously cannot list all of them here. *John Wayne: American* is based on those articles as well as a wealth of manuscript collections, oral histories, and personal interviews. Our major sources are listed below. The following abbreviations have been used throughout the notes and bibliography:

BYU   Brigham Young University
CFP   Charles Feldman Papers
CU   Oral History Collection of Columbia University
FCP   Frank Capra Papers
JFP   John Ford Papers
MHL   Margaret Herrick Library, Motion Picture Academy of Arts and Sciences
MZP   Maurice Zolotow Papers, University of Texas, Austin
NMP   Nancy Marshall Papers, Private Collection
NRCS   National Records Center, Suitland, Maryland
SMU   Southern Methodist University Oral History Project
UCLA   University of California at Los Angeles
USC   University of Southern California

MANUSCRIPT COLLECTIONS

John Agar File, MHL
The Alamo File, Daughters of the Republic of Texas Library, San Antonio, Texas
Al Malaikah Temple Papers, Shriners, Los Angeles, California
Pedro Armendariz File, MHL
James Arness File, MHL
Russell Birdwell Papers, UCLA
Ward Bond File, MHL
R. N. Bradbury File, MHL
Walter Brennan File, MHL
Bruce Cabot File, MHL
Yakima Canutt File, MHL
Frank Capra Papers (FCP), Wesleyan University
Harry Carey File, MHL
Harry Carey Papers, BYU
Harry Carey Jr. File, MHL
Harry Carey Jr. Papers, BYU
Olive Carey File, MHL
Marguerite Churchill File, MHL
Montgomery Clift File, MHL
Merian C. Cooper File, MHL
Bosley Crowther Papers, BYU
Laraine Day File, MHL
Cecil B. De Mille Papers, BYU
Andy Devine File, MHL
Andy Devine Papers, BYU
Marlene Dietrich File, MHL
Kirk Douglas File, MHL
Joanne Dru File, MHL
Andrew Durkus Papers, BYU
Jack Elam File, MHL
Family History Library, Church of Jesus Christ of Latter-Day Saints, Salt Lake City,
    Utah
Charles Feldman Papers, American Film Institute
Robert Fellows File, MHL
Paul Fix File, MHL
John Ford File, MHL
Paul Fix File, MHL
John Ford Papers (JFP), Indiana University
Patrick Ford Papers, BYU
Fox Papers, UCLA
Kenneth Gamet Papers, UCLA
Tay Garnett Papers, UCLA
James Edward Grant File, MHL
Henry Hathaway File, MHL
Henry Hathaway Papers, American Film Institute

Howard Hawks File, MHL

Howard Hawks Papers (HHP), BYU

George Hayes File, MHL

Susan Hayward File, MHL

Rita Hayworth File, Federal Bureau of Investigation, Washington, D.C.

Hedda Hopper File, Federal Bureau of Investigation, Washington, D.C.

Ben Johnson File, MHL

Alan Le May Papers, UCLA

Albert Lewin Papers, USC

Cliff Lyon File, MHL

May Mann Papers, BYU

Dean Martin File, MHL

Lee Marvin File, MHL

Constance McCormick Collection, USC

Andrew McLaglen File, MHL

Victor McLaglen File, MHL

MGM Papers, UCLA

MGM Papers, University of Wisconsin–State Historical Society of Wisconsin Film Archives, Madison

Vera Miles File, MHL

Ray Milland File, MHL

Thomas Mitchell File, MHL

Robert Mitchum File, MHL

Robert Montgomery File, MHL

Clyde Morrison File, Los Angeles Office, Bureau of Land Management, Records Group 48, National Archives, Pacific Southwest Region

Marion Mitchell Morrison File, Selective Service System, Washington, D.C.

Motion Picture Alliance for the Preservation of American Ideals File, Federal Bureau of Investigation, Washington, D.C.

Nancy (Morrison) Marshall Papers, Private Collection

National Association of Theater Owners Papers, BYU

Dudley Nichols Papers, UCLA

Office of War Information Papers, Records Group 208, National Records Center, Suitland, Maryland (NCRS)

Phileo Nash Papers, Harry S. Truman Presidential Library

Patricia Neal File, MHL

Maureen O'Hara File, MHL

Geraldine Page File, MHL

Louella Parsons Papers, USC

Ella Raines File, MHL

Records of the Adjutant General's Office 230.42, Operations Branch, National Archives, Washington, D.C.

RKO Radio Papers, Glendale (California) Public Library

Bo Roos File, MHL

Gail Russell File, MHL

Max Steiner Papers, BYU

James Stewart File, MHL

Claire Trevor File, MHL

Twentieth Century-Fox Papers, UCLA

United Artists Papers, University of Wisconsin–State Historical Society of Wisconsin Film
    Archives, Madison

Universal Papers, USC

Universal Papers, University of Wisconsin–State Historical Society of Wisconsin Film
    Archives, Madison

Walter Wanger File, MHL

Walter Wanger Papers, State Historical Society of Wisconsin

Raoul Walsh File, MHL

Raoul Walsh Papers, Wesleyan University

Warner Bros. Papers, USC

Warner Bros. Papers, University of Wisconsin–State Historical Society of Wisconsin Film
    Archives, Madison

Warner Bros. Papers, Burbank (California) Public Library

John Wayne Exhibit, National Cowboy Hall of Fame and Western
    Heritage Center, Oklahoma City

John Wayne File, Arizona Historical Society

John Wayne File, Federal Bureau of Investigation, Washington, D.C.

John Wayne File, Glendale (California) Public Library

John Wayne File, Jimmy Carter Presidential Library

John Wayne File, Lyndon B. Johnson Presidential Library

John Wayne File, Madison County (Iowa) Historical Society

John Wayne File, MHL

John Wayne File, Richard Nixon Papers, Pacific Southwest Region, National Archives

John Wayne File, Palmdale (California) Public Library

William Wellman File, MHL

Chill Wills File, MHL

Grant Withers File, MHL

Loretta Young File, MHL

Maurice Zolotow Papers, University of Texas at Austin

UNPUBLISHED INTERVIEWS AND ORAL HISTORIES

All interviews without an institutional affiliation were conducted by the authors.
Red Adair
John Agar
John Agar, MZP
Eddie Albert, SMU
Elizabeth Allen, JFP
Mark Armistead, JFP
Gene Autry, CU
Gene Autry, SMU
Frankie Avalon, Alamo Project, Brian Huberman, Rice University
Paul Barrus
Paul Barrus, Madison County Historical Society
Richard Barthelmess, CU

James Warner Bellah, JFP
Bea Benjamin, JFP
Charles Bell
Charles Bennett, SMU
Russell Birdwell, MZP
Richard Boone, CU
Barbara Boyd
Walter Brennan, CU
Red Buttons, SMU
Bruce Cabot, Arizona Historical Society
Yakima Canutt, Arizona Historical Society
Frank Capra, CU
Frank Capra, BYU
Harry Carey Jr.
Harry Carey Jr., JFP
Harry Carey Jr., SMU
Marilyn Fix Carey
Olive Carey, JFP
Jimmy Carter (Personal Correspondence)
Katherine Clifton Interview, JFP
William Clothier, Arizona Historical Society
William Clothier, JFP
William Clothier, MZP
George Coleman, MZP
Jerry W. Coon
Bosley Crowther, CU
Linda Crystal, Alamo Project, Brian Huberman, Rice University
Linda Crystal, SMU
Donald Curtis, SMU
Ken Curtis, JFP
Dan Dailey, SMU
Laraine Day, SMU
Joseph De Franco
Olivia De Havilland, BYU
Ann del Valle, BYU
Cecil B. De Mille, CU
Cecele De Prita, JFP
Colleen Dewhurst
Barry Diller, MZP
Edward Dmytryk, CU
Edward Dmytryk, SMU
Joanne Dru, JFP
Joanne Dru, SMU
Philip Dunne, JFP
Allan Dwan, American Film Institute
Allan Dwan, JFP
Jack Elam, Arizona Historical Society

Harry Essex, SMU
Mary Farragher
Josephine Feeney, JFP
Charles Fitzsimmons, SMU
Henry Fonda, American Film Institute
Henry Fonda, CU
Henry Fonda, JFP
Zona Forbes
Barbara Ford, JFP
Dan Ford
John Ford, American Film Institute
John Ford, JFP
Mary Ford, JFP
Patrick Ford, BYU
Patrick Ford, JFP
Phil Ford, JFP
Carl Foreman, CU
Gail Gifford, SMU
Ben Goetz, JFP
Barry Goldwater (Personal Correspondence)
Joe Graham, Madison County Historical Society
Danko Gurovich
John Hagner
Earl Haley, Arizona Historical Society
William Harris
Henry Hathaway, BYU
Henry Hathaway, CU
Henry Hathaway, SMU
George Francis Hayes, CU
Howard Hawks, American Film Institute
Howard Hawks, Arizona Historical Society
Howard Hawks, BYU
Howard Hawks, CU
Chuck Hayward, JFP
Ben Hecht, CU
Tom Hennesy
Katharine Hepburn, JFP
Selma Herbert, BYU
Winton Hoch, JFP
William Holden, Arizona Historical Society
Lillian Holiday
Earl Holliman
Earl Holliman, SMU
Ace Holmes, JFP
Frank Hotaling, JFP
Lefty Hough, JFP
Frank Hoyt

Brian Huberman
Martha Hyer, SMU
Sam Jaffe, SMU
Wesley Jefferies, BYU
William Jews, CU
Alice Johnson
Ben Johnson, Arizona Historical Society
Ben Johnson, JFP
Ben Johnson, SMU
Louis Johnson
Nunnally Johnson, CU
Nunnally Johnson, JFP
Seth Johnson
Will C. Johnson, Madison County Historical Society
Thomas Kane, MZP
Burt Kennedy, MZP
Burt Kennedy, SMU
Paul Keyes, MZP
Michael Lord Killanin, JFP
Jerry Kobrin
Howard Koch, BYU
Catalina Lawrence
Anna Lee (Nathan)
Anna Lee (Nathan), JFP
Tim Lilley
Ann Little, Arizona Historical Society
John Lee Mahin, JFP
Adele Mara, SMU
Ann-Margret, MZP
John Marshall
Nancy (Morrison) Marshall
Lee Marvin, JFP
Jeanette Mazurki
Michael McCourt
Joel McCrea, CU
Roddy McDowell, CU
Roddy McDowell, JFP
Andrew McLaglen
Andrew McLaglen, SMU
Joseph Mellotte
Lester Midgeley, CU
Alice Miller
Bert Minshall
Walter Mirisch, SMU
Rose Mitchell
George Montgomery, SMU
Joyce Morgan

Ray Moyer, MZP
Richard Muno
Mildred Natwick, SMU
Dean Nelson
Lloyd Nolan, SMU
Henry Noerdlinger, BYU
Darcy O'Brien, SMU
George O'Brien, JFP
Maureen O'Hara
Geraldine Page, CU
Carroll Parcher
Louella Parsons, CU
Robert Parrish, JFP
Robert Parrish, SMU
Joseph Pasternak, CU
Jan Pergoli
Gil Perkins, SMU
Grayce Pike, BYU
Jean Porter, SMU
Otto Preminger, CU
Denver Pyle, Alamo Project, Brian Huberman, Rice University
Ella Raines, SMU
Francis Rich, JFP
Martin Ritt, SMU
Chuck Roberson, Arizona Historical Society
Chuck Roberson, MZP
Mary St. John
Stanley Scheuer, MZP
David O. Selznick, CU
Happy Shahan
Melville Shavelson, SMU
Skirball Sheba, CU
Robert Shelton
Vincent Sherman, CU
Vincent Sherman, SMU
Willard Simmons
Dean Smith, SMU
Wingate Smith Interview, JFP
Robert Solomon
Robert Stack, SMU
Charles Starrett, SMU
Priscilla Steenhook
Rod Steiger, CU
James Stewart, JFP
James Stewart, SMU
Peggy Stewart, SMU
Woody Strode

Lawrence H. Suid
Paula Sweeney
Hal Taliaferro, Arizona Historical Society
Ted Taylor, BYU
David Trask
Bobby Vinton, MZP
Kal Vorgang
Hal B. Wallis, CU
Hal B. Wallis, SMU
Raoul Walsh, MZP
John Wayne, Arizona Historical Society
John Wayne, CU
John Wayne, JFP
John Wayne, MZP
Michael Wayne, Alamo Project, Brian Huberman, Rice University
Michael Wayne, MZP
Albert Wedemeyer, JFP
Jack Williams, Arizona Historical Society
Terri Wilson, JFP
Ralph Wingfield
Hank Worden
Hank Worden, SMU
Jane Wyatt, SMU
Susie Yazzi
Edgar Yuhl

BOOKS

In addition to the primary sources listed above, we made use of a number of secondary sources in constructing the biography. Michael Tomkies's *Duke: The Story of John Wayne* (1971) was published in the wake of Wayne's 1970 Oscar for *True Grit*, but the book was superficial at best, offering little more than highlights of his career and descriptions of his most memorable roles. The most widely read biography—*Shooting Star: A Biography of John Wayne*—appeared in 1974. During the mid-1950s and again in the early 1970s, Maurice Zolotow conducted a series of interviews with Wayne, as well as with many of his associates, and the book is based on them. Wayne loathed it, accusing Zolotow of sloppy research and slander, but in spite of its flaws, *Shooting Star* became the standard work. George Carpozi's unfootnoted journalistic biography—*The John Wayne Story*—appeared soon after Wayne's death in 1979. The best of the Wayne biographies—lightly footnoted but addressing serious cultural and political issues—was Donald Shepherd and Robert Slatzer, with Dave Grayson, *Duke: The Life and Times of John Wayne* (1985).

In writing *John Wayne: American*, we used the Zolotow and Shepherd and Slatzer biographies more frequently than any others. Zolotow's papers are housed at the University of Texas at Austin, and we were able to compare the written biography with his own research notes, early drafts, and personal interviews. In writing *Duke: The Life and Times of John Wayne*, Shepherd and Slatzer relied heavily on the recollections and diaries of Dave Grayson, one of Wayne's makeup artists. Grayson supplied much of the first-person dialogue they employed.

Several other books about John Wayne have been extremely useful. Judith M. Riggin's *John Wayne: A Bio-Bibliography* (1992) contains the fullest bibliography of printed sources of John Wayne, including biographies, critical studies, filmographies, interviews, and articles in mass circulation and trade magazines. Emanuel Levy's *John Wayne: Prophet of the American Way of Life* (1988) analyzes the significance of Wayne's film career and political values, as does Richard D. McGhee's *John Wayne: Actor, Artist, Hero* (1990). See also Sam Shaw, *John Wayne in the Camera Eye* (1980); Don Nardo, *John Wayne* (1994); John Boswell and J. David, *Duke: The John Wayne Album* (1979); Charles John Kiest, *The Official John Wayne Reference Book* (1985); Lee Pfeiffer, *The John Wayne Scrapbook* (1989); George Bishop, *John Wayne: The Actor—The Man* (1979). The two best John Wayne filmographies are Allen Eyles, *John Wayne* (1976) and Mark Ricci, Boris Zmijewsky, and Steve Zmijewsky, *The Films of John Wayne* (1970).

Several of Wayne's family members and close friends have written their own memoirs, which we found helpful. Bert Minshall, who captained Wayne's yacht *Wild Goose*, wrote *On Board with the Duke: John Wayne and the Wild Goose* (1992). Wayne's close friend and fellow actor Yakima Canutt's autobiography—*Stunt Man: The Autobiography of Yakima Canutt* (1979)—was particularly revealing about the early years of the actor's career. Stunt man Chuck Roberson, known affectionately as "Bad Chuck," wrote *The Fall Guy: 30 Years As the Duke's Double* (1980). Harry Carey Jr.'s autobiography, published in 1994 as *Company of Heroes: My Life in the John Ford Stock Company*, is a first-rate memoir. Especially useful for the Wayne biographer are the recollections of Pilar Wayne, his third wife. Her book *John Wayne: My Life with the Duke* (1987) is a rich source for Wayne's career between 1950 and 1970. Aissa Wayne, Wayne's first child by his third marriage, wrote *John Wayne: My Father* (1991). Although based largely on her mother's book, it illuminates Wayne's relationship with several of his children. During his last years, Wayne's lover, companion, and secretary was Pat Stacy, and her book *Duke: A Love Story* (1983) is a rich source for his life in the 1970s.

We also relied on several of John Ford's biographers. By far the most useful was Dan Ford's *Pappy: The Life of John Ford* (1979). Dan Ford, a grandson of the famous director, conducted dozens of interviews with friends and associates of his grandfather, organized Ford's papers, and then constructed his biography based on those sources. The interviews and papers are housed today in the Lilly Library of Indiana University. Though lacking footnotes, the best scholarly biography of John Ford is Ronald L. Davis's *John Ford: Hollywood's Old Master* (1995), which is based on the rich oral history collection Davis has compiled at Southern Methodist University. Other Ford biographies and critical studies include Andrew Sinclair, *John Ford* (1979); Andrew Sarris, *The John Ford Movie Mystery* (1975); Tag Gallagher, *John Ford: The Man and His Films* (1986); and Joseph McBride and Michael Wilmington, *John Ford* (1975).

Wayne's career in Hollywood spanned a half century, during which he worked with many major producers, directors, and actors. Several of their autobiographies have been very revealing, including Gene Autry, *Back in the Saddle Again* (1978); Frank Capra, *The Name Above the Title: An Autobiography* (1971); Henry Fonda and

Howard Teichmann, *Fonda: My Life* (1981); Marlene Dietrich, *Marlene* (1989); Richard Fleischer, *Just Tell Me When to Cry: A Memoir* (1993); Raoul Walsh, *Each Man in His Time: The Life Story of a Director* (1974); Lana Turner, *Lana: The Lady, the Legend, the Truth* (1982); John Huston, *An Open Book* (1980); Kirk Douglas, *The Ragman's Son: An Autobiography* (1988); Hal Wallis, *Starmaker: The Autobiography of Hal Wallis* (1980); Woody Strode and Sam Young, *Goal Dust: An Autobiography* (1990); William A. Wellman, *A Short Time for Insanity: An Autobiography* (1974); and Rock Hudson and Sara Davidson, *Rock Hudson: His Story* (1986).

We made use of a number of Hollywood biographies. Wayne's career intersected with nearly every figure in the industry during the twentieth century, and the following biographies were particularly revealing: Peter Bogdanovich, *Allen Dwan: The Last Pioneer* (1971); Bob Thomas, *King Cohn: The Life and Times of Harry Cohn* (1967); Bernard F. Dick, *The Merchant Prince of Poverty Row: Harry Cohn of Columbia Pictures* (1993); Joe Morella and Edward Z. Epstein, *Loretta Young: An Extraordinary Life* (1986); David Thomson, *Showman: The Life of David O. Selznick* (1992); Steven Bach, *Marlene Dietrich: Life and Legend* (1992); Charles Higham, *Marlene: The Life of Marlene Dietrich* (1977); Maria Riva, *Marlene Dietrich, By Her Daughter Maria Riva* (1993); Matthew Bernstein, *Walter Wanger: Hollywood Independent* (1994); Tom Stempel, *Screenwriter: The Life and Times of Nunnally Johnson* (1980); Tony Thomas, *Howard Hughes in Hollywood* (1985); Charles Higham, *Howard Hughes: The Secret Life* (1993); George Eells, *Hedda and Louella* (1972); Beverly Linet, *Susan Hayward: Portrait of a Survivor* (1980); Lawrence Grobel, *The Hustons* (1989); Robin Wood, *Howard Hawks* (1983); Joseph McBride, *Hawks on Hawks* (1982); Nick Tosches, *Dino: Living High in the Dirty Business of Dreams* (1992); Bob Thomas, *Golden Boy: The Untold Story of William Holden* (1983); Leonard Mosley, *Zanuck: The Rise and Fall of Hollywood's Last Tycoon* (1984); Edwin T. Arnold and Eugene L. Miller, *The Films and Career of Robert Aldrich* (1986); Christopher Andersen, *Citizen Jane: The Turbulent Life of Jane Fonda* (1990); Randall Riese, *Her Name Is Barbra* (1993); Tay Garnett with Freda D. Balling, *Light Your Torches and Pull Up Your Tights* (1973); Melville Shavelson, *How to Make a Jewish Movie* (1971); Robert Stack, *Straight Shooting* (1980); Anne Edwards, *A Remarkable Woman: A Biography of Katharine Hepburn* (1985); Michael Freedland, *Jane Fonda: A Biography* (1988).

Studio histories and surveys of the movie industry were helpful in constructing *John Wayne: American*. Among the most useful were Tino Balio, ed., *The American Film Industry* (1976); Tichi Wilkerson and Marcia Borie, *The Hollywood Reporter: The Golden Years* (1984); Leonard J. Leff and Jerold L. Simmons, *The Dame in the Kimono: Hollywood, Censorship, and the Production Code from the 1920s to the 1960s* (1990); Ethan Mordden, *The Hollywood Studios: House Style in the Golden Age of the Movies* (1988); Jack Mathis, *Republic Confidential: The Players,* vol. 2 (1989); Douglas Gomery, *Shared Pleasures: A History of Movie Presentation in the United States* (1992); Stephen M. Silverman, *The Fox That Got Away: The Last Days of the Zanuck Dynasty at Twentieth Century-Fox* (1988); Michael Freedland, *The Warner Brothers* (1983); Neal Gabler, *An Empire of Their Own: How the Jews Invented Hollywood* (1988); Richard Koszarski, *An Evening's Entertainment: The Age of the Silent Feature Picture, 1915–1928* (1990); Peter Hay, *MGM: When the Lion Roars* (1991); Tino Balio, *United Artists: The Company Built by the Stars* (1976); Robert Sklar, *Movie-Made America: A Cultural History of American Movies* (1975); Bernard F. Dick, ed.,

Columbia Pictures: Portrait of a Studio (1992); Jon Tuska, *The Vanishing Legion: A History of Mascot Pictures, 1927–1935* (1982); Robert B. Ray, *A Certain Tendency of the Hollywood Cinema, 1930–1980* (1985); Richard Maurice Hurst, *Republic Studios: Between Povery Row and the Majors* (1979); and Ted Okuda, *The Monogram Checklist: The Films of the Monogram Pictures Corporation, 1931–1952* (1987).

From the late 1940s to the end of his life, Wayne was an outspoken conservative Republican, and a number of excellent histories describe how national politics played out in Hollywood. Ronald Brownstein, *The Power and the Glitter: The Hollywood-Washington Connection* (1990) and Larry Ceplair and Steven Englund, *The Inquisition in Hollywood: Politics in the Film Community, 1930–60* (1980) are particularly good overviews. Also see David F. Prindle, *The Politics of Glamour: Ideology and Democracy in the Screen Actors Guild* (1988). For revealing looks at the Red Scare in Hollywood, see Bernard F. Dick, *Radical Innocence: A Critical Study of the Hollywood Ten* (1989); Victor Navasky, *Naming Names* (1980); and Nora Sayre, *Running Time: Films of the Cold War* (1982).

Finally, a number of fine histories look at the significance of the Western and of war movies in American popular culture and Wayne's central role in both. On war films, we found helpful Clayton R. Koppes and Gregory D. Black, *Hollywood Goes to War: How Politics, Profits, and Propaganda Shaped World War II Movies* (1987); Bernard Dick, *The Star-Spangled Screen: The American World War II Film* (1985); and Lawrence Suid, *Guts & Glory: Great American War Movies* (1978). Among the best books on the Western are Richard Slotkin's *Gunfighter Nation: The Myth of the Frontier in Twentieth-Century America* (1992) and Jane Tompkins's *West of Everything: The Inner Life of the Western* (1992). See also Jon Tuska, *The Filming of the West* (1976); Will Wright, *Six-Guns and Society: A Structural Study of the Western* (1975); Christine Bold, *Selling the Wild West: Popular Western Fiction, 1860–1960* (1987); George N. Fenin and William K. Everson, *The Western: From Silents to Cinerama* (1962); John H. Lenihan, *Showdown: Confronting Modern America in the Western Film* (1980); and Les Adams and Buck Rainey, *Shoot-Em-Ups: The Complete Reference Guide to Westerns of the Sound Era* (1985).

Index